# Global
# Environment
# Outlook 3

# Global Environment Outlook 3

**Past, present and future perspectives**

Earthscan Publications Ltd
London • Sterling, VA

First published in the United Kingdom and the United States in 2002 by Earthscan
Publications Ltd for and on behalf of the United Nations Environment Programme

Copyright © 2002, United Nations Environment Programme

ISBN: 92-807-2087-2 (UNEP paperback)
     92-807-2088-0 (UNEP hardback)
     1 85383 845 4 (Earthscan paperback)
     1 85383 844 6 (Earthscan hardback)
ISSN: 1366-8080

United Nations Environment Programme
PO Box 30552, Nairobi, Kenya
Tel: +254 2 621234
Fax: +254 2 623943/44
E-mail: geo@unep.org
Web: **www.unep.org**
     **www.unep.net**

**DISCLAIMER**

Printed and bound in the UK by CPI

Earthscan Publications Ltd
120 Pentonville Road
London N1 9JN, United Kingdom
Tel: +44 (0)20 7278 0433
Fax: +44 (0)20 7278 1142
E-mail: earthinfo@earthscan.co.uk
Web: **www.earthscan.co.uk**

22883 Quicksilver Drive, Sterling, VA 20166-2012, USA

Earthscan is an editorially independent subsidiary of Kogan Page Ltd and publishes in association
with WWF-UK and the International Institute for Environment and Development.

This book is printed on 100 per cent recycled, chlorine free paper.

# GEO-3

## *Past, present and future perspectives*

### UNEP

in collaboration with

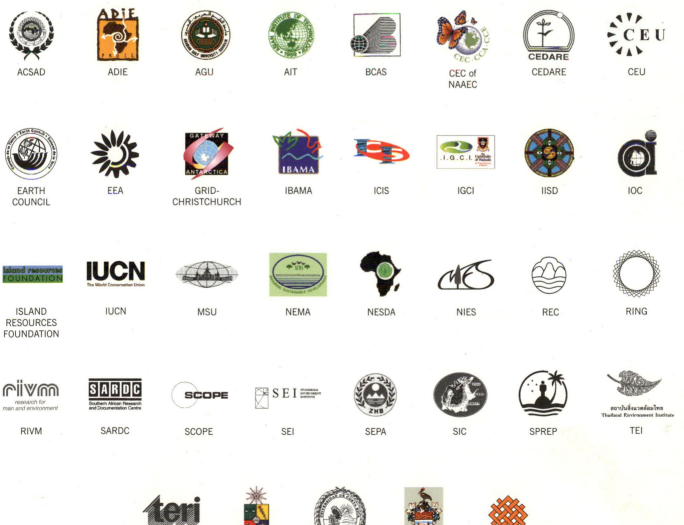

| | | | | | | | |
|---|---|---|---|---|---|---|---|
| ACSAD | ADIE | AGU | AIT | BCAS | CEC of NAAEC | CEDARE | CEU |
| EARTH COUNCIL | EEA | GRID-CHRISTCHURCH | IBAMA | ICIS | IGCI | IISD | IOC |
| ISLAND RESOURCES FOUNDATION | IUCN | MSU | NEMA | NESDA | NIES | REC | RING |
| RIVM | SARDC | SCOPE | SEI | SEPA | SIC | SPREP | TEI |

| | | | | |
|---|---|---|---|---|
| TERI | UNIVERSITY OF CHILE | UNIVERSITY OF COSTA RICA | UWICED | WRI |

# Acknowledgements

UNEP acknowledges the contributions made by the many individuals and institutions to the preparation and publication of *Global Environment Outlook 3*. A full list of names is included on page 416. Special thanks are extended to:

## GEO-3 Collaborating Centres

Arab Centre for the Studies of Arid Zones and Drylands (ACSAD), Syria

Arabian Gulf University (AGU), Bahrain

Asian Institute of Technology (AIT), Thailand

Association pour le Developpement de l'Information Environnementale (ADIE), Gabon

Bangladesh Centre for Advanced Studies (BCAS), Bangladesh

Brazilian Institute of the Environment and Natural Renewable Resources (IBAMA), Brazil

Central European University (CEU), Hungary

Centre for Environment and Development for the Arab Region & Europe (CEDARE), Egypt

Commission for Environmental Cooperation of the North American Agreement on Environmental Cooperation (CEC of NAAEC), Canada

Earth Council, Costa Rica

European Environment Agency (EEA), Denmark

GRID-Christchurch/Gateway Antarctica, New Zealand

Indian Ocean Commission (IOC), Mauritius

International Centre for Integrative Studies (ICIS), The Netherlands

International Global Change Institute (IGCI), New Zealand

International Institute for Sustainable Development (IISD), Canada

Island Resources Foundation, US Virgin Islands

Moscow State University (MSU), Russia

Musokotwane Environment Resource Centre for Southern Africa (IMERCSA) of the Southern African Research and Documentation Centre (SARDC), Zimbabwe

National Environmental Management Authority (NEMA), Uganda

National Institute for Environmental Studies (NIES), Japan

National Institute for Public Health and the Environment (RIVM), The Netherlands

Network for Environment and Sustainable Development in Africa (NESDA), Côte d'Ivoire

Regional Environmental Centre for Central and Eastern Europe (REC), Hungary

RING Alliance of Policy Research Organizations, United Kingdom

Scientific Committee on Problems of the Environment (SCOPE), France

Scientific Information Centre (SIC), Turkmenistan

South Pacific Regional Environmental Programme (SPREP), Samoa

State Environmental Protection Administration (SEPA), China

Stockholm Environment Institute (SEI), Sweden and United States

Tata Energy Research Institute (TERI), India

Thailand Environment Institute (TEI), Thailand

University of Chile, Centre for Public Policy Analysis (CAPP), Chile

University of Costa Rica, Development Observatory (OdD), Costa Rica

University of West Indies, Centre for Environment and Development (UWICED), Jamaica

World Conservation Union (IUCN), Switzerland

World Resources Institute (WRI), United States

## Funding

The United Nations Fund for International Partnerships (UNFIP) provided funding to support capacity building and involvement of Collaborating Centres in developing countries and development of the GEO Data Portal.

## *Global Environment Outlook 3*: the production team

### GEO Nairobi Coordinating Team
Marion Cheatle
Munyaradzi Chenje
Volodymyr Demkine
Norberto Fernandez
Tessa Goverse
Anna Stabrawa

### GEO Regional Coordinating Team
Habib El-Habr
Bob Kakuyo
Lars Kullerud
Choudhury Rudra Charan Mohanty
Surendra Shrestha
Ashbindu Singh
Ron Witt
Kaveh Zahedi

### GEO Support Team
Susanne Bech, Jeremy Casterson, Dan Claasen, Julia Crause, Arthur Dahl, Harsha Dave, Rob de Jong, Salif Diop, Sheila Edwards, Tim Foresman, Sherry Heilemann, Shova Khatry, Dave MacDevette, Timo Maukonen, Kakuko Nagatani-Yoshida, Adrian Newton, Everlyn Ochola, Samantha Payne, Mark Schreiner, Tilly Shames, Josephine Wambua, Mick Wilson and Jinhua Zhang, Brian Ochieng, Nick Nuttal

### Data
Jaap van Woerden
Stefan Schwarzer

### Editors
Robin Clarke
Robert Lamb
Dilys Roe Ward

### Graphics
Bounford.com

### Cover and page design
Paul Sands

### Web editing and graphics
Brian Lucas
Lawrence Hislop

# Contents

# List of illustrations

## List of satellite images: Our Changing Environment

# List of boxes

## List of tables

# Foreword

Thirty years ago, the international community gathered in Stockholm for the United Nations Conference on the Human Environment to sound an alarm about the perilous state of the Earth and its resources. That landmark event is widely credited with having put environmental issues on the international agenda, leading in turn to the establishment of environment ministries at the national level and increased awareness of the impact that even very local decisions can have on the global environment. But the conference also identified a knowledge gap: the lack of accurate, up-to-date information with which policy makers could chart a clearer path towards a better-managed environment. The conference therefore asked the United Nations Secretary-General to fill that gap — by reporting regularly on the state of the global environment and related issues, by helping countries to monitor the environment at the national level, and by carrying out educational programmes on environmental issues.

With this report — *Global Environment Outlook 3 (GEO-3): Past, Present and Future Perspectives* — the United Nations Environment Programme, itself a legacy of the Stockholm Conference, has once again fulfilled its cardinal responsibility to present, in clear, accessible terms, the challenges we face in safeguarding the environment and moving towards a more sustainable future.

Since the conference in 1972, the natural environment has borne the stresses imposed by a fourfold increase in human numbers and an 18-fold growth in world economic output. Despite the wealth of technologies, human resources, policy options, and technical and scientific information at our disposal, humankind has yet to break decisively with unsustainable and environmentally unsound policies and practices. What emerges from the data, analysis and forecasts contained in this report is the compelling need to go beyond taking stock to taking action.

The publication of *GEO-3* is timed to contribute to the World Summit on Sustainable Development in Johannesburg. Much was achieved at the 'Earth Summit' in Rio de Janeiro in 1992. But over the past decade, as our attention has been focused on conflict, globalization and terrorism, there is a sense of lost momentum. One important task at Johannesburg is to show that sustainable development is an exceptional opportunity for humankind — economically, to build markets and create jobs; socially, to bring people in from the margins; politically, to reduce tensions over resources, that could lead to violence; and of course, environmentally, to protect the ecosystems and resources on which all life depends — and thereby merits more urgent attention and high-level commitment.

*GEO-3* is a vital contribution to international debate on the environment. I hope it reaches the widest possible audience and inspires new and determined action that will help the human community to meet the social, economic and environmental needs of the present without compromising the ability of the planet to provide for the needs of future generations.

Kofi Annan
Secretary-General of the United Nations
United Nations Headquarters, New York, February 2002

# Preface

The third UNEP Global Environment Outlook report (*GEO-3*) provides an opportune brief for the 2002 World Summit on Sustainable Development (WSSD), to be held later this year in Johannesburg, South Africa.

It is a feat of collaboration between UNEP and some 1 000 individuals and 40 institutions from around the world. It picks up and weaves together the strands of debate and action on the environment that lead forward from that linchpin of modern environment and development thinking, the 1972 Stockholm Conference on the Human Environment, and through the 1992 United Nations Conference on Environment and Development (UNCED) to where we stand today. *GEO-3* sets out to provide global and regional perspectives on the past, present and future environment, linked together with telling examples from within the regions to form a comprehensive and integrated assessment.

An important aspect of the GEO process is capacity building for the collaborating centres directly involved in this initiative and for a wider range of individuals and institutions whose work forms the foundation of environmental assessment — from national through global levels. For example, UNEP has, through a comprehensive Internet-based data portal, made relevant data more accessible to collaborating centres to strengthen analysis and reporting. Capacity building has also involved formal and practical training in integrated environmental

assessment, and such training will be expanded in the coming years.

In terms of the *GEO-3* report itself, an overview of major developments between 1972 and 2002 highlights significant milestones and integrates environmental, economic and social factors within a unified world view. The retrospective chapter explores many of these developments in greater depth from global and regional standpoints. The report presents a global overview and also directs a spotlight onto two or three key issues that are considered paramount in each of the seven regional arenas under each of eight environmental themes in turn: land, forests, biodiversity, freshwater, coastal and marine areas, atmosphere, urban areas and disasters.

Analysing the most up-to-date and reliable information on these issues reveals the critical trends during the 30-year period — critical trends about the environment, and about the impacts that environmental change have had on people. Perhaps even more importantly, it highlights the evolution of environmental policy responses that society has (or sometimes has not) put in place to ensure environmental security and sustainability.

Sustainable development rests on three pillars — society, economy and environment. The environmental pillar provides the physical resources and ecosystem services on which humankind depends. Growing evidence that many aspects of the environment are still degrading leads us to the conclusion that people are becoming increasingly vulnerable to environmental change. Some countries can cope but many others remain at risk and when that risk becomes a reality their dreams of sustainable development are set back by decades. The notion of human vulnerability to environmental change has been incorporated specifically into this GEO assessment to demonstrate UNEP concern in an area which has a strong bearing on the success of sustainable development. UNEP places the concept of human vulnerability to environmental change high on its future programme of work.

*GEO-3* also breaks new ground by using scenario analysis to explore the environmental outlook, fast-forwarding the reader into an array of alternative futures that provide insight on where events could lead us at various stages between 2002 and 2032. While some of the possible developments may seem far removed from current circumstances, others have been predetermined by the decisions and actions we have already taken. We know that some of the policy approaches followed in the past have not lived up to

expectations and that institutional weaknesses have played an inevitable part in such slippages. At the Rio +5 event in 1997, it became clear that progress had fallen short of the goals set in 1992. Five years later the challenges remain no less exacting. Yet we at UNEP remain convinced that it lies well within the scope of human determination and ingenuity to come up with appropriate policy packages and use them to ensure that fundamental environmental conditions can and will get steadily better, not stealthily worse.

This report abounds with information that can serve as a firm foundation for the WSSD review of policies for sustainable development. I hope many will find it useful as an aid to prepare for the Summit, during the event itself and well beyond. It is being published in all the official UN languages so that people and communities round the world can make use of its insights to form their own position on what is at stake and what needs to be done. On a personal note, I hope that it will inspire you, the reader, to raise your commitment to environmental care to a summit of its own.

Klaus Töpfer
United Nations Under-Secretary General
and Executive Director, United Nations Environment Programme

# The GEO Project

The UNEP Global Environment Outlook (GEO) project was initiated in response to the environmental reporting requirements of *Agenda 21* and to a UNEP Governing Council decision of May 1995 which requested the production of a comprehensive global state of the environment report. The GEO project has two components:

- A global environmental assessment process that is cross-sectoral, participatory and consultative. It incorporates regional views and builds consensus on priority issues and actions through dialogue among policy makers and scientists at regional and global levels. It also aims to strengthen environmental assessment capacity in the regions through training and 'learning-by-doing'.
- GEO outputs, in printed and electronic formats, including the GEO report series. This series presents periodic reviews of the state of the world's environment, and provides guidance for decision-making processes such as the formulation of environmental policies, action planning and resource allocation. Other outputs include regional, sub-regional and national environmental assessments, technical and other background reports, a Web site, products for young people (GEO for Youth) and a core database — the GEO Data Portal.

The GEO Data Portal provides report producers with easy access — via the Internet — to a common and consistent set of datasets from primary sources (UN and others), while covering a broad range of environmental and socio-economic themes. The Portal addresses one of the major concerns expressed ever since the start of the GEO project — the need for reliable, harmonized data for global and regional level environmental assessment and reporting. As of March 2002, the Portal gives access to some 300 statistical and geographical datasets at national, sub-regional, regional and global levels. State-of-the-art functionality for on-line data visualization and exploration are available for creating graphs, tables and maps.

## The GEO process

The coordinated global network of collaborating centres (CCs) is at the core of the GEO process. These centres have played an increasingly active role in preparing GEO reports. Regional centres are now responsible for almost all the regional inputs, combining top-down integrated assessment with bottom-up environmental reporting. Other institutions provide specialized expertise on cross-cutting or thematic issues.

Working groups provide advice and support to the GEO process, particularly on integrated assessment methodologies and process planning.

Other United Nations agencies contribute to the GEO process, mainly by providing substantive data and information on the many environmental and related issues that fall under their individual mandates. They also participate in the review process.

## GEO report series

The GEO reports are produced using a regional and participatory approach. Input is solicited from a wide range of sources throughout the world, including the collaborating centre network, United Nations organizations and independent experts.

Working together with the GEO Coordinating Team in Nairobi and the regions, the CCs research, write and review major parts of the report. During the preparation of the report, UNEP organizes consultations inviting policy makers and other stakeholders to review and comment on draft materials. Drafts also undergo extensive peer review. This iterative process is designed to ensure that the

---

### Internet references in *GEO-3*

*GEO-3* has developed a special system for preserving the Internet references quoted in the bibliographies on the pages that follow. Each such reference is followed by a *GEO-3* tag of the form [Geo-x-yyy]. This electronic reference scheme — a unique feature of *GEO-3* — can be used both on the *GEO-3* website at www.unep.org/geo3 and on the CD-ROM available with the English version of this report. Search can be by author, title of document or *GEO-3* tag. Clicking on the tag brings up the full reference and text, even though the original Web page may have since disappeared from the Internet.

contents are scientifically accurate and policy relevant to users in different parts of the world and with different environmental information needs.

Previous reports published are *GEO-1* in 1997 and *GEO-2000* in 1999. The third in the series, *GEO-3*, places major emphasis on providing an integrated assessment of environmental trends over the 30 years since the 1972 Stockholm Conference.

The analysis of environmental trends takes into consideration the widest possible range of social, economic, political and cultural drivers and root causes — demographics, production and consumption, poverty, urbanization, industrialization, governance, conflict, globalization of trade, finance, information and others. It also investigates the relationships between policy and environment, showing how policy can impact the environment and how the environment can drive policy.

For structural and presentational clarity, sectoral areas are used as the entry points for assessment. However, the cross-cutting nature of environmental issues is also emphasized, with integrated analysis of themes and policy impacts where appropriate, and emphasis on geographical and sectoral interlinkages.

Description and analysis are primarily targeted at global and regional levels but include sub-regional differentiation where appropriate. The analysis focuses on priority issues, with assessment of vulnerability, hot spots and emerging issues.

The report analyses the increasing human vulnerability to environmental change to determine extent and impacts on people. The report breaks with the tradition of most environmental assessments which are organized around environmental resources rather than around human concerns.

Using a 2002–32 time frame, *GEO-3* also contains a forward-looking and integrated analysis, which is based on four scenarios and linked to the major issues of current concern. The global-level analysis is extended to regions and sub-regions, identifying

### GEO supports the principle of access to environmental information for decision making

The GEO report series addresses one of the important objectives of *Agenda 21* which emphasizes the role of information in sustainable development. One of the *Agenda 21* activities involves the strengthening or establishment of mechanisms to transform scientific and socio-economic assessments into information suitable for both planning and public information. It also calls for the use of both electronic and non-electronic formats.

This objective has been further reaffirmed by the Malmö Ministerial Declaration of May 2000, which among other issues states that:

- To confront the underlying causes of environmental degradation and poverty, we must integrate environmental considerations in the mainstream of decision-making. We must also intensify our efforts in developing preventive action and a concerted response, including national environmental governance and the international rule of law, awareness-raising and education, and harness the power of information technology to this end. All actors involved must work together in the interest of a sustainable future.
- The role of civil society at all levels should be strengthened through freedom of access to environmental information to all, broad participation in environmental decision-making, as well as access to justice on environmental issues.
- Science provides the basis for environmental decision-making. There is a need for intensified research, fuller engagement of the scientific community and increased scientific cooperation on emerging environmental issues, as well as improved avenues for communication between the scientific community, decision makers and other stakeholders.

*Note: the Declaration was adopted by ministers of environment in Malmö, Sweden, at the First Global Ministerial Environment Forum*

potential areas of vulnerability and hot spots of the future, and drawing attention to policy implications. Contrasting visions of the future are developed for the next 30 years using narrative and quantitative approaches.

The final chapter of *GEO-3* presents positive policy and action items, linked to the overall conclusions of the assessment and targeted at different categories and levels of decision makers and actors. It elaborates the conditions and capacities required for successful application of policies and actions.

# Synthesis

The year 1972 stands as a watershed in modern environmentalism. The first international conference on the environment — the United Nations Conference on the Human Environment — was convened in Stockholm in that year, bringing together 113 nations and other stakeholders to discuss issues of common concern. In the 30 years since then, the world has made great strides in placing the environment on the agenda at various levels — from international to local. Phrases such as 'think global and act local' have galvanized action at many different levels. The result has been a proliferation of environmental policies, new legislative regimes and institutions, perhaps an unspoken acknowledgement that the environment is too complex for humanity to address adequately in every sense.

Decisions made since Stockholm now influence governance, business and economic activity at different levels, define international environmental law and its application in different countries, determine international and bilateral relations among different countries and regions, and influence individual and society lifestyle choices.

But there are problems: some things have not progressed, for example, the environment is still at the periphery of socio-economic development. Poverty and excessive consumption — the twin evils of humankind that were highlighted in the previous two

GEO reports — continue to put enormous pressure on the environment. The unfortunate result is that sustainable development remains largely theoretical for the majority of the world's population of more than 6 000 million people. The level of awareness and action has not been commensurate with the state of the global environment today; it continues to deteriorate.

*GEO-3* provides an overview of the main environmental developments over the past three decades, and how social, economic and other factors have contributed to the changes that have occurred.

## State of the environment and policy responses

### Land

Since 1972, the main driving force leading to pressure on land resources has been increasing food production. In 2002, food is needed for some 2 220 million more people than in 1972. The trend during the decade 1985–95 showed population growth racing ahead of food production in many parts of the world. While irrigation has made an important contribution to agricultural production, inefficient irrigation schemes can cause waterlogging, salinization and alkalization of soils. In the 1980s, it was estimated that about 10 million ha of irrigated land were being abandoned annually. Human activities contributing to land degradation include unsuitable agricultural land use, poor soil and water management practices, deforestation, removal of natural vegetation, frequent use of heavy machinery, overgrazing, improper crop rotation and poor irrigation practices. The 1992 Earth Summit took a step forward in focusing attention on problems associated with land resources. National needs at times linked with *Agenda 21* have provided a basis for land resources policy, and the importance of land issues was reiterated in the review prepared for the UN Millennium Summit. This review identifies the threats to future global food security arising from problems of land resources.

### Forests

Deforestation over the past 30 years has been the continuation of a process with a long history. By the

## Regional highlights: Africa

The increasing numbers of African countries facing water stress and scarcity, and land degradation, are major environmental issues in the region. The rising costs of water treatment, food imports, medical treatment and soil conservation measures are not only increasing human vulnerability and health insecurity but are also draining African countries of their economic resources. The expansion of agriculture into marginal areas and clearance of natural habitats such as forests and wetlands has been a major driving force behind land degradation. The loss of biological resources translates into loss of economic potential and options for commercial development in the future. These negative changes, however, have been tempered by Africa's impressive wildlife conservation record, including a well-established network of protected areas and the region's commitment to multilateral environmental agreements. African countries also participate in many regional and sub-regional initiatives and programmes. Notable achievements include the 1968 African Convention on the Conservation of Nature and Natural Resources (currently being updated) and the 1991 Bamako Convention on the Ban of the Import into Africa and the Control of Transboundary Movement and Management of Hazardous Waste within Africa.

time of the Stockholm Conference, much forest cover had already been removed. Major direct causes of forest clearance and degradation include expansion of agricultural land, overharvesting of industrial wood, fuelwood and other forest products, and overgrazing. Underlying drivers include poverty, population growth, markets and trade in forest products, as well as macroeconomic policies. Forests are also damaged by natural factors such as insect pests, diseases, fire and extreme climatic events.

The net loss in global forest area during the 1990s was about 94 million ha (equivalent to 2.4 per cent of total forests). This was the combined effect of a deforestation rate of 14.6 million ha annually and a rate of reforestation of 5.2 million ha annually. Deforestation of tropical forests is almost 1 per cent annually. In the 1990s, almost 70 per cent of deforested areas were changed to agricultural land, predominantly under permanent rather than shifting systems. A recent study using globally comprehensive and consistent satellite data estimated that the extent of the world's remaining closed natural forests (where crown cover is more than 40 per cent) in 1995 was 2 870 million ha, about 21.4 per cent of the land area of the world.

The Stockholm Conference recognized forests as the largest, most complex and self-perpetuating of all ecosystems, and emphasized the need for sound land and forest use policies, ongoing monitoring of the state of the world's forests and the introduction of forest management planning. Today, the Stockholm Conference recommendations relating to forests remain valid and unfulfilled, in many ways, because of conflicting interests in managing forests for environmental conservation and economic development.

## Biodiversity

Global biodiversity is being lost at a rate many times higher than that of natural extinction due to land conversion, climate change, pollution, unsustainable harvesting of natural resources and the introduction of exotic species. Land conversion is most intensive in tropical forests and less intensive in temperate, boreal and arctic regions; atmospheric nitrogen deposition is largest in northern temperate areas close to cities; introduction of exotic species is related to patterns of human activity. Human population growth together with unsustainable

### Regional highlights: Asia and the Pacific

Overpopulation, poverty and lack of enforcement of policy measures have compounded environmental problems in many parts of the region. Biological resources have long been of subsistence importance, and have been increasingly exploited for trade. About three-quarters of known or suspected species extinctions have occurred on isolated islands in the region. Protected areas constitute only 5 per cent of the total area, compared to the IUCN benchmark of 10 per cent. Discharge of sewage and other wastes has heavily polluted freshwater. Sedimentation in rivers and reservoirs caused by large-scale deforestation has also resulted in big economic losses. Urbanization, industrialization and tourism, coupled with a growing coastal population, have degraded many coastal areas. More than 60 per cent of Asia's mangroves have been converted to aquaculture farms. Air pollution levels in some cities are among the highest in the world. While most environmental trends have been negative, positive changes have included improvement in governance by public authorities, growing environmental awareness and public participation, and increasing environmental awareness in industry.

patterns of consumption, increasing production of waste and pollutants, urban development and international conflict are further contributory factors to biodiversity loss. Over the past three decades, decline and extinction of species have emerged as major environmental issues. Although insufficient information is available to determine precisely how many species have become extinct in the past three decades, about 24 per cent (1 130) of mammals and 12 per cent (1 183) of bird species are currently regarded as globally threatened.

The past three decades have been marked by the emergence of a concerted response to the biodiversity crisis. Civil society, including a hugely diverse and increasingly sophisticated NGO network, has been a major driving force behind this. Increased stakeholder participation relating to conservation action has seen

### Regional highlights: Europe

The environmental situation is mixed: there have been some noticeable improvements over the past 30 years (for example, emissions to air); the state of biodiversity and forests has not changed greatly; and other situations have undergone marked degradation (freshwater, and some coastal and marine areas). By the 1990s, the European atmosphere had generally improved significantly. Increasing efforts to safeguard natural areas and biodiversity may signal a turn-around in species protection. Freshwater stocks are unevenly distributed, with parts of southern, western and southeastern Europe being noticeably water stressed. The health of coastal and marine areas has noticeably worsened, particularly in southern and western Europe and the Mediterranean coastline. Geographically, there has been an amelioration of some environmental problems in Western Europe, and a common (but far from universal) deterioration in Central and Eastern Europe, with recent signs of a broad recovery in many countries. The development of strong environmental policies in the European Union promises continuing progress in the area.

the emergence of partnerships between NGOs, governments and the private sector. A number of international conventions have been developed that deal specifically with conservation of threatened species. These include the 1973 Convention on International Trade in Endangered Species of Wild Fauna and Flora (CITES) and the 1979 Convention on the Conservation of Migratory Species of Wild Animals (CMS). A major policy response of the 1990s is the adoption, ratification and implementation of the Convention on Biological Diversity (CBD).

## Freshwater

About one-third of the world's population lives in countries suffering from moderate-to-high water stress — where water consumption is more than 10 per cent of renewable freshwater resources. Some 80 countries, constituting 40 per cent of the world's population, were suffering from serious water shortages by the mid-1990s. Increasing water demand has been caused by population growth, industrial development and the expansion of irrigated agriculture. For many of the world's poorer populations, one of the greatest environmental threats to health remains the continued use of untreated water. While the percentage of people served with improved water supplies increased from 79 per cent (4.1 billion) in 1990 to 82 per cent (4.9 billion) in 2000, 1.1 billion people still lack access to safe drinking water and 2.4 billion lack access to adequate sanitation. Most of these people are in Africa and Asia. Lack of access to safe water supply and sanitation results in hundreds of millions of cases of water-related diseases, and more than 5 million deaths, every year. Large, but poorly quantified adverse impacts on economic productivity have been noted in many developing countries. Emphasis on water supply, coupled with weak enforcement of regulations, has limited the effectiveness of water resource management, particularly in developing regions. Policy makers have now shifted from supply to demand management, highlighting the importance of using a combination of measures to ensure adequate supplies of water for different sectors. Measures

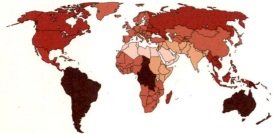

□ <1.0
catastrophically low

□ 1.0 to 2.0
very low

■ >2.0 to 5.0
low

■ >5.0 to 10.0
medium

■ >10.0 to 20.0
high

■ >20.0
very high

**Map shows water availability measured in terms of 1 000 m³ per capita/ year — see page 152**

include improving water use efficiency, pricing policies and privatization. There is also a new emphasis on integrated water resources management (IWRM), which takes into account all the different stakeholders in water resource planning, development and management.

## Coastal and marine areas

Marine and coastal degradation is caused by increasing pressure on both terrestrial and marine natural resources, and on the use of the oceans to deposit wastes. Population growth and increasing urbanization, industrialization and tourism in coastal areas are root causes of this increased pressure. In 1994, an estimated 37 per cent of the global population lived within 60 km of the coast — more people than inhabited the planet in 1950. The effects of population are multiplied by both poverty and human consumption patterns. Globally, sewage remains the largest source of contamination, by volume, of the marine and coastal environment, and coastal sewage discharges have increased dramatically in the past three decades.

Marine and coastal eutrophication from elevated nitrogen inputs has emerged as a worrying trend not foreseen three decades ago. There is increasing evidence that blooms of toxic or otherwise undesirable phytoplankton are increasing in frequency, intensity

### Regional highlights:
### Latin America and the Caribbean

Environmental degradation in Latin America and the Caribbean has increased over the past 30 years. The main pressures on the environment and natural resources are the rising population, increasing inequality of incomes, limited planning, especially in urban areas, and the high dependence of many economies on natural resources exploitation. More than 300 million ha of land have been degraded and almost 30 per cent of the reefs in the Caribbean are considered to be at risk. Of the more than 400 million ha of natural forest lost worldwide over the past 30 years, more than 40 per cent was in the region. Urban environmental problems, especially air pollution, water contamination and inadequate waste disposal, are having severe health impacts on people living in cities, currently 75 per cent of the population. The increasing frequency and intensity of natural disasters, possibly linked to climate change, is having a high human and financial cost. The poorest populations, especially urban ones, are the most vulnerable to such disasters.

and geographic distribution. Severe eutrophication has occurred in several enclosed or semi-enclosed seas, including the Black Sea. Human-induced changes in the natural flow of sediment have emerged since the Stockholm Conference as a major threat to coastal habitats. Urban and industrial development drives the construction of residential and industrial infrastructure which, depending on its nature, can alter sediment flow.

There is particular concern about the possible effects of global warming on coral reefs. During the intense El Niño of 1997-98, extensive coral bleaching occurred on coral reefs worldwide. While some reefs quickly recovered, others, particularly in the Indian Ocean, Southeast Asia, the far western Pacific and the Caribbean, suffered significant mortality, in some cases more than 90 per cent.

Progress in protecting the marine and coastal environment over the past 30 years has generally been confined to relatively few, mostly developed countries, and to a relatively few environmental issues. Overall, coastal and marine environmental degradation not only continues but has intensified.

## Atmosphere

Acid precipitation has been one of the most prominent environmental concerns over the past decades, especially in Europe and North America, and more recently also in China. Thousands of lakes in Scandinavia lost fish populations due to acidification from the 1950s to the 1980s. Significant damage to forests in Europe became a high priority environmental issue around 1980. Air pollutant

### Regional highlights: West Asia

Conservation and protection of freshwater resources is a top priority, particularly on the Arabian Peninsula where water deficits are being met mainly through exploitation of groundwater resources. Countries are developing water policies to manage water scarcity by increasing both water supply and conservation, and introducing more efficient irrigation. Land degradation and food security continue to be key environmental issues. The region's seas include some of the busiest shipping areas of the world, making the marine environment susceptible to pollution events such as oil spills. Per capita hazardous waste production is among the highest in the world due to the types of industry in the region. Air emissions from power stations, desalination plants and industrial installations are also of concern.

### Regional highlights: North America

North America is a major consumer of the world's natural resources and producer of its wastes, and its per capita impact on the global environment is larger than that of any other region. Resource conservation in North America has been less successful than pollution abatement, and per capita consumption has increased steadily since 1972. There has been significant progress in controlling some forms of air and water pollution and in continuing a trend to set aside protected areas. During the 1990s, North American free trade strengthened the economic ties between Canada and the United States. At the same time, regional environmental degradation led to an increased recognition of the interdependent nature of cross-border ecosystems. The two countries strengthened cooperative measures to address transboundary pollution, agreeing to more aggressive $NO_x$ emission controls, for example. They also undertook to conserve the continent's wetland habitats to protect waterfowl and other migratory species. The impact of introduced exotic species on biological diversity became of increasing environmental concern with the liberalization of trade.

emissions have declined or stabilized in most industrialized countries, largely as a result of abatement policies developed and implemented since the 1970s. Initially, governments tried to apply direct control instruments but these were not always cost-effective. In the 1980s, policies were directed more towards pollution abatement mechanisms that relied on a compromise between the cost of environmental protection measures and economic growth. Stricter environmental regulation in industrialized countries has triggered the introduction of cleaner technology and technological improvements, especially in the power generation and transport sectors.

Since the industrial revolution, the concentration of $CO_2$, one of the major greenhouse gases, in the atmosphere has increased significantly, contributing to the greenhouse effect known as 'global warming'. The increase is largely due to anthropogenic emissions of $CO_2$ from fossil fuel combustion and to a lesser extent land-use change, cement production and biomass combustion. Greenhouse gas emissions are unevenly distributed between countries and regions. Organization for Economic Cooperation and Development (OECD) countries contributed more than half of $CO_2$ emissions in 1998, with a per capita emission of about three times the world average. However, the OECD's share of global $CO_2$ emissions has decreased by 11 per cent since 1973. Climate change represents an important additional stress on those ecosystems already affected by increasing resource demands, unsustainable management practices and pollution. The United Nations Framework Convention on Climate Change and the

## Regional highlights: the Polar Regions

The major environmental issues in the polar regions include the depletion of the stratospheric ozone layer, the long-range transport of air pollutants, warming associated with global climate change, the decline of several bird, mammal and fish species, and pollution of major rivers. In the Arctic, average yearly ozone levels in the 1990s had declined by 10 per cent from the late 1970s, increasing the risk of snow blindness and sunburn. Climate change is expected to be more extreme in the polar regions than anywhere else. Human activities are major threats to biodiversity in the Arctic. The warming trend is reducing the ice habitat for species such as the polar bear and walrus. In the Antarctic, sealing and whaling have reduced populations in the Southern Ocean. Eutrophication is a recent problem in several lakes in Scandinavia. One of the major developments in the Arctic is public opposition to dam construction, particularly in the Nordic countries. For example, in 2001 Iceland's National Planning Agency rejected plans for a hydroelectric power project that would have dammed two of the three main rivers flowing from Europe's largest glacier and destroyed an extensive wilderness.

Kyoto Protocol are the key policy instruments adopted by the international community to try to address the problem of greenhouse gases emissions.

The protection of the ozone layer has presented one of the major challenges over the past 30 years, spanning the fields of environment, trade, industry, international cooperation and sustainable development. The depletion of the ozone layer has now reached record levels, especially in the Antarctic and recently also in the Arctic. In September 2000, the Antarctic ozone hole covered more than 28 million $km^3$. Continuous efforts by the international community have resulted in a marked decrease in the consumption of ozone-depleting substances. The ozone layer is predicted to start recovering in the next one or two decades and to return to pre-1980 levels by the middle of the 21st century— if the control measures of the protocols to the Vienna Convention are adhered to by all countries.

## Urban areas

About half of the world's population (47 per cent) now lives in urban areas, compared to little more than one-third in 1972. The accumulation of people, their consumption patterns, travel behaviour and their urban economic activities impact the environment in terms of resource consumption and waste discharges. Some 70 per cent of the world's urban population live in Africa, Asia or Latin America. The urban population is expected to grow by 2 per cent per year during 2000–15, and to reach an overall 65 per cent by 2050.

The implications of rapid urban growth include increasing unemployment and poverty, inadequate urban services, overburdening of existing infrastructure, lack of access to land, finance and adequate shelter, and environmental degradation. Managing the urban environment sustainably will therefore become one of the major challenges for the future.

Poverty is among the major drivers of urban environmental degradation. The urban poor, who are unable to compete for scarce resources or protect themselves from harmful environmental conditions, are most affected by the negative impacts of urbanization. It is estimated that one-quarter of the urban population lives below the poverty line and that female-headed households are disproportionately affected.

Inadequate waste collection and waste management systems are the cause of serious urban pollution and health hazards, especially in cities in developing countries. Cities in industrialized countries also face the consequences of past environmentally damaging production techniques and inadequate waste disposal. Well-planned, densely populated settlements can reduce the need for land conversion, provide opportunities for energy savings and make recycling more cost-effective.

## Disasters

People and the environment are suffering increasingly from the effects of natural disasters due to high

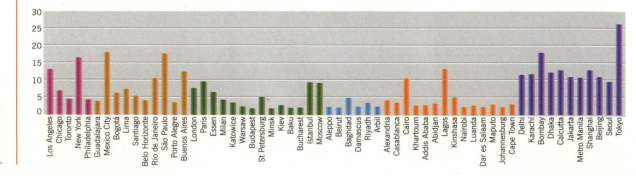

Population (in millions) of some of the largest cities in the world, by region — see page 244

population growth and density, migration and unplanned urbanization, environmental degradation and possibly global climate change. The number of people affected by disasters rose from an average of 147 million a year in the 1980s to 211 million a year in the 1990s. While the number of geophysical disasters has remained fairly steady, the number of hydrometeorological disasters (such as droughts, windstorms and floods) has increased. In the 1990s, more than 90 per cent of those killed in natural disasters lost their lives in hydrometeorological events. While floods accounted for more than two-thirds of people affected by natural disasters, they are less deadly than many other types of disaster, accounting for only 15 per cent of deaths. The most expensive disasters in purely economic terms are floods, earthquakes and windstorms but events such as drought and famine can be more devastating in human terms. While earthquakes accounted for 30 per cent of estimated damage, they caused just 9 per cent of all fatalities due to natural disasters. In contrast, famine killed 42 per cent but accounted for just 4 per cent of economic damage over the past decade. Among the least developed countries, 24 of the 49 face high levels of disaster risk; at least six of them have been affected by between two and eight major disasters per year in the past 15 years, with long-term consequences for human development. Since 1991, more than half of all the disasters reported occurred in countries with medium levels of human development. However, two-thirds of those killed came from countries with low levels of human development, while just 2 per cent came from highly developed countries.

Some experts link the recent trend in extreme weather events to an increase of the global mean temperature. Many parts of the world have suffered major heat waves, floods, droughts and other extreme weather events. A number of major accidents involving chemicals and radioactive materials have drawn attention worldwide to the dangers of mismanagement, particularly in the transport, chemical and nuclear power sectors. These events often have impacts that transcend national boundaries; they also emphasize the fact that issues of technological safety concern more than just the developed countries.

## Human vulnerability to environmental change

### Vulnerable groups

Everyone is vulnerable to environmental impacts of some kind but the ability of people and societies to adapt to and cope with change is very varied. People in developing countries, particularly the least developed, have less capacity to adapt to change and are more vulnerable to environmental threats and global change, just as they are more vulnerable to other stresses. Poverty is generally recognized as one of the most important causes of vulnerability to environmental threats, on the basis that the poor tend to have much lower coping capacities, and therefore they bear a disproportionate burden of the impact of disasters, conflict, drought, desertification and pollution. But poverty is not the only reason.

### Vulnerable places

Human exposure to environmental threats is unevenly distributed. Some locations, such as high latitudes, floodplains, river banks, small islands and coastal areas, pose more risk than others. Of the projected 1 billion new urban dwellers by 2010, most will probably be absorbed by cities in developing countries that already face multiple problems such as shortages of adequate housing, infrastructure, potable water supplies, adequate sanitation and transportation systems as well as environmental pollution.

Satellite image shows extensive smoke haze over Indonesia and neighbouring areas on 20 October 1997 — see page 307

### Environmental change

Degradation of natural resources such as land, fresh and marine waters, forests and biodiversity threatens the livelihood of many people but especially the poor. The 'sink' function of the environment operates through such processes as nutrient recycling, decomposition, and the natural purification and filtering of air and water. When these functions are impaired or overburdened, health can be jeopardized by contaminated water supplies including groundwater, and by urban air pollution and agrochemical pollution. Human health is increasingly determined by environmental conditions. For example:

- Deteriorating environmental conditions are a major contributory factor to poor health and a reduced quality of life.
- Poor environmental quality is directly responsible for some 25 per cent of all preventable ill-health, with diarrhoeal diseases and acute respiratory infections heading the list.
- Air pollution is a major contributor to a number of diseases.
- Globally, 7 per cent of all deaths and diseases are due to inadequate or unsafe water, sanitation and hygiene. Approximately 5 per cent are attributable to air pollution.

## Responding to human vulnerability

The cumulative evidence for increasing human vulnerability to environmental change calls for a significant policy response and action on several fronts. Governments need to assess and map national threats due to environmental change, particularly those that may be growing, and to institute early warning, mitigation and response measures to reduce the human and economic costs of disasters that are in part avoidable.

### Reducing vulnerability

There is a large and widening vulnerability gap between well-off people, with better all-round coping capacity, who are becoming gradually less vulnerable, and the poor who grow increasingly so. It is vital to the sustainable development effort that this gap is addressed, as well as vulnerability itself. For the most significant improvements, priority should go to policies that reduce the vulnerability of the poor as part of general strategies for poverty reduction.

### Adapting to threat

Where a threat cannot be reduced or eliminated, adapting to it can be an effective response. Adaptation refers both to physical adjustments or technical measures (such as constructing a higher sea wall) and to changing behaviour, economic activities and social organization to be more compatible with existing or emerging conditions or threats. The latter requires adaptive capacity, including the ability to develop new options and to deliver them to vulnerable populations.

### Early warning

One of the most effective responses to human vulnerability to environmental change is to strengthen mechanisms for early warning. Many actions can be taken to protect life and property if warning is received in time. While some threats are inherently unpredictable, many of those arising from environmental degradation and mismanagement, and from human activities, can now be anticipated with some precision.

## Assessing and measuring vulnerability

Vulnerability assessment measures the seriousness of potential threats on the basis of known hazards and the level of vulnerability of societies and individuals. It can be used to translate early warning information into preventive action and is a necessary element in early warning and emergency preparedness. Assessments of vulnerability can be made for both people and the environmental systems that provide goods and services. They should identify the location of vulnerable populations, the threats to their well-being and the extent of their vulnerability, the risks to the environmental capacity to provide goods and services, and the preventive steps that can be taken to improve environmental conditions and reduce the negative impacts of human action on the environment.

## Outlook 2002–32

GEO-3 emphasizes that the next 30 years will be as crucial as the past 30 for shaping the future of the environment. Old troubles will persist and fresh challenges will emerge as increasingly heavy demands are placed upon resources that, in many cases, are already in a fragile state. The increasing pace of change and degree of interaction between regions and issues has made it more difficult than ever to look into the future with confidence. GEO-3 uses four scenarios to explore what the future could be, depending on different policy approaches. The scenarios, which span developments in many overlapping areas, including population, economics, technology and governance, are described in the boxes that follow. They are:

- *Markets First*
- *Policy First*
- *Security First*
- *Sustainability First*.

## Markets First

Most of the world adopts the values and expectations prevailing in today's industrialized countries. The wealth of nations and the optimal play of market forces dominate social and political agendas. Trust is placed in further globalization and liberalization to enhance corporate wealth, create new enterprises and livelihoods, and so help people and communities to afford to insure against — or pay to fix — social and environmental problems. Ethical investors, together with citizen and consumer groups, try to exercise growing corrective influence but are undermined by economic imperatives. The powers of state officials, planners and lawmakers to regulate society, economy and the environment continue to be overwhelmed by expanding demands.

Some of the global and regional environmental implications arising out of the four scenarios are highlighted below.

The absence of effective policies to reduce emissions of carbon dioxide and other greenhouse gases in the *Markets First* and *Security First* scenarios leads to significant increases over the next 30 years. However, the policy actions taken under a *Policy First* scenario, notably carbon taxes and investments in non-fossil-fuel energy sources, effectively curb growth in global emissions and lead to actual reductions starting around 2030. The behavioural shifts under *Sustainability First,* together with improved production and conversion efficiencies, result in a rapid levelling off of emissions and a decline by the middle of the 2020s.

Biodiversity will continue under threat if there is no strenuous policy action to curb human activity. Continued urban and infrastructure expansion, plus the increased impacts of climate change, severely deplete biodiversity in most regions in all scenarios. Pressures will also increase on coastal ecosystems in most regions and scenarios.

The scenarios carry important implications for the provision of basic human needs. Growing populations and increased economic activity, particularly in agriculture, will lead to increased demand for freshwater in most scenarios. Similarly, the demands for food and the ability to meet them in the different scenarios reflect a combination of shifts in supply and demand, influenced by social, economic and environmental policies. In *Markets First,* even with a decrease in the percentage of the population facing hunger, the total number affected changes relatively little and even increases in some regions as populations grow. Under *Policy First* and *Sustainability First* the targeting of hunger reduction as a key goal, and the emphasis on more balanced development between regions, help to achieve dramatic reductions in the percentages and total numbers of people affected. The sharp increases in most regions in *Security First* points to the unsustainability of such a scenario in terms of social acceptability.

In Africa, there is increasing risk of land degradation. In *Policy First* and *Sustainability First,* easier access to support services helps farmers to manage soils better and policies based on integrated land management become commonplace in the region. At the other end of the spectrum, in a *Security First* scenario, while reasonable conditions are maintained in the protected areas serving the land-owning elite, the high concentration of people elsewhere contribute to severe land degradation and soil erosion. Similar problems arise in *Markets First* as better quality agricultural land is taken over for commodity and cash crop production.

Under the *Markets First* scenario in Asia and the Pacific, water withdrawals are expected to increase in all sectors, leading to an expansion of areas with severe water stress in South and Southeast Asia. Slower economic growth under *Security First* tempers growth in demand. With effective policies and lifestyle changes under the *Policy First* and *Sustainability First* scenarios, water withdrawals remain at current levels or even decrease in most of the region.

Infrastructure affects 72 per cent of the world's land area (black and red areas are the worst affected) by the year 2032 under a *Markets First* scenario — see page 354

## Policy First

Decisive initiatives are taken by governments in an attempt to reach specific social and environmental goals. A coordinated pro-environment and anti-poverty drive balances the momentum for economic development at any cost. Environmental and social costs and gains are factored into policy measures, regulatory frameworks and planning processes. All these are reinforced by fiscal levers or incentives such as carbon taxes and tax breaks. International 'soft law' treaties and binding instruments affecting environment and development are integrated into unified blueprints and their status in law is upgraded, though fresh provision is made for open consultation processes to allow for regional and local variants.

## 🔒 Security First

This scenario assumes a world of striking disparities where inequality and conflict prevail. Socio-economic and environmental stresses give rise to waves of protest and counteraction. As such troubles become increasingly prevalent, the more powerful and wealthy groups focus on self-protection, creating enclaves akin to the present day 'gated communities'. Such islands of advantage provide a degree of enhanced security and economic benefits for dependent communities in their immediate surroundings but they exclude the disadvantaged mass of outsiders. Welfare and regulatory services fall into disuse but market forces continue to operate outside the walls.

**Markets First**

**Policy First**

**Security First**

**Sustainability First**

The ability of Europe to address the issues of large-scale air pollution and greenhouse gas emissions will depend heavily upon developments in the areas of energy use and transportation. Extremely active policies to improve public transportation and energy efficiency can be expected in *Policy First* and *Sustainability First* worlds, but not in *Security First* or even *Markets First* circumstances.

Land and forest degradation as well as forest fragmentation remain among the most relevant environmental issues in Latin America and the Caribbean in all scenarios. Significant loss of forest area occurs in a *Markets First* scenario. In a *Security First* world, the control over forest resources by transnational companies that create cartels in association with the national groups in power, promotes the growth of some forest areas, but this is not enough to stop net deforestation. More effective management ameliorates some of these problems in *Policy First*. Unsound deforestation stops almost completely in a world of *Sustainability First*.

As the world's biggest emitter of greenhouse gases, North America plays a major role in determining the future climate of the planet. In *Markets First*, the region's refusal to participate significantly hampers international efforts to control the emissions of these gases, and per capita and absolute emissions remain high. The collapse of parts of the transport infrastructure and restrictions on fossil-fuel vehicle ownership in *Security First* result in even greater increases in emissions in this scenario. Under *Policy First*, emissions are reduced through increased fuel efficiency and greater use of public transport but most spectacular results are achieved in *Sustainability First*.

West Asia is one of the most water-stressed regions of the world, with more than 70 million people living in areas under severe water stress. Under the *Markets First* and *Security First* scenarios, population and economic growth lead to strong increases in withdrawals for households and industry, resulting in an increase in areas with severe water stress and affecting over 200 million people by 2032. A range of policy initiatives help to counteract additional demands related to economic growth in both *Policy First* and *Sustainability First*. Although total withdrawals drop in both scenarios, water scarcity persists and demand continues to exceed available water resources.

Fish and other marine stocks are a key area of concern in the polar regions. Under *Markets First*, massive increase in commercial harvesting and abandonment of targeted fisheries leads to some fish populations crashing. Illegal, unregulated and unreported fishing activities cease in *Security First* under direct pressure from powerful regulatory interests, but controlled exploitation rises to very high levels. Total collapse of any single fishery is averted under *Policy First* by enforcement of stringent harvesting quotas and other regulatory systems. In *Sustainability First*, fish and marine mammals are rigorously defended against overexploitation.

The environmental implications of the various scenarios illustrate the legacy of past decades and the level of effort that will be needed to reverse powerful trends. One of the major policy lessons from the scenarios is that there can be significant delays

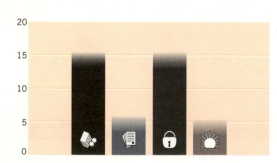

Percentage of 2002 cropland that becomes so degraded by 2032 that it is of little value for production for each of the four scenarios — see page 356

## ☀ Sustainability First

A new environment and development paradigm emerges in response to the challenge of sustainability, supported by new, more equitable values and institutions. A more visionary state of affairs prevails, where radical shifts in the way people interact with one another and with the world around them stimulate and support sustainable policy measures and accountable corporate behaviour. There is much fuller collaboration between governments, citizens and other stakeholder groups in decision-making on issues of close common concern. A consensus is reached on what needs to be done to satisfy basic needs and realize personal goals without beggaring others or spoiling the outlook for posterity.

between changes in human behaviour, including policy choices, and their environmental impacts, specifically:

- Much of the environmental change that will occur over the next 30 years has already been set in motion by past and current actions.
- Many of the effects of environmentally relevant policies put into place over the next 30 years will not be apparent until long afterwards.

## Options for action

The world is currently plagued by increasing poverty and continually widening divisions between the haves and the have-nots. These divisions — the environmental divide, the policy divide, the vulnerability gap and the lifestyle divide — all threaten sustainable development. They must be addressed urgently, and with greater success than has often been the case in the past. Certain key areas of attention have been identified for global action at all levels to ensure the success of sustainable development. Prime among them are alleviating poverty for the world's have-nots, reducing excessive consumption among the more affluent, reducing the debt burden of developing countries, and ensuring adequate governance structures and funding for the environment.

Underlying this action, however, must be the greater provision of and access to information in all its forms as the fundamental basis of successful planning and decision-making. The information revolution holds the possibility of providing cheap and reliable information in appropriate forms to all stakeholders in the environment — decision makers, local communities, the general public — thus enabling them to participate more meaningfully in decisions and actions that determine the courses of their daily lives and of those of succeeding generations.

The final section of *GEO-3* presents possible policy options for the future based on UNEP experience, the *GEO-3* assessment and wide consultations at different levels. The suggestions are intended as a check-list from which to make appropriate selections for action. The overriding need in policy development is for a balanced approach towards sustainable development. From the environment perspective, this means bringing the environment in from the margins to the heart of development. The fields where action is suggested cover the need to:

- Rethink environmental institutions because they need to adapt to new roles and partnerships to fulfil present obligations and confront emerging environmental challenges.
- Strengthen the policy cycle so that it becomes more rigorous, systematic, integrated and able to develop policies that are better attuned to specific localities and situations.
- Provide an enhanced international policy framework to overcome the fragmentation and duplication inherent in the present system.
- Use trade more effectively for the benefit of sustainable development to capitalize on the new opportunities provided by trade liberalization.
- Harness technology for the environment and manage the associated risks to maximize the potential of new technologies to deliver substantial environmental and social gains.
- Adjust and coordinate policy instruments, including various legal frameworks, and measures such as valuing environmental goods and services, ensuring that markets work for sustainable development and promoting voluntary initiatives, to develop appropriate packages that work more effectively for the environment.
- Monitor policy performance with the aim of improving levels of implementation, enforcement and compliance.
- Re-define and share roles and responsibilities between local, regional and global levels to provide efficient solutions to managing complex and varied situations at a variety of scales.

# The GEO-3 Regions

There are seven GEO-3 regions, divided into sub-regions:

**Africa;**
**Asia and the Pacific;**
**Europe;**
**Latin America and the Caribbean;**
**North America;**
**West Asia; and**
**the Polar Regions**

**The Arctic**
The eight Arctic countries are:
Canada, Greenland (Denmark), Finland, Iceland, Norway, Russia, Sweden, Alaska (United States)

**The Antarctic**

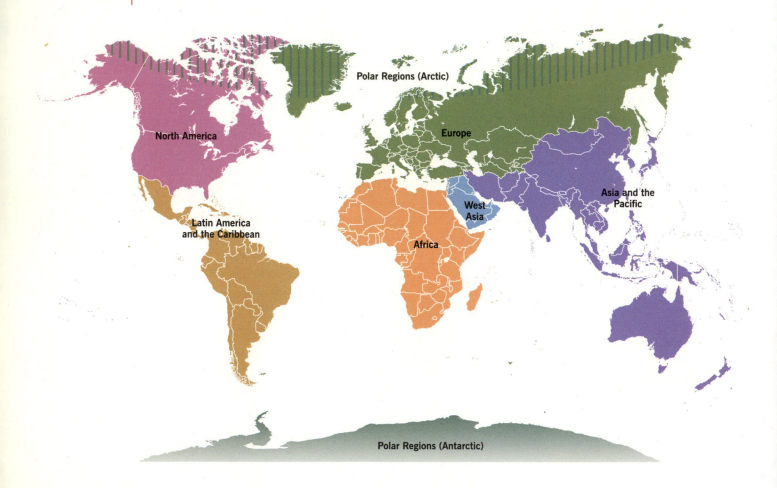

# Africa

**Northern Africa:**
Algeria, Egypt, Libyan Arab Jamahiriya, Morocco, Sudan, Tunisia

**Western Africa:**
Benin, Burkina Faso, Cape Verde, Côte d'Ivoire, Gambia, Ghana, Guinea, Guinea-Bissau, Liberia, Mali, Mauritania, Niger, Nigeria, Senegal, Sierra Leone, Togo

**Central Africa:**
Cameroon, Central Africa Republic, Chad, Congo, Democratic Republic of Congo, Equatorial Guinea, Gabon, São Tomé and Príncipe

**Eastern Africa:**
Burundi, Djibouti, Eritrea, Ethiopia, Kenya, Rwanda, Somalia, Uganda

**Western Indian Ocean:**
Comoros, Madagascar, Mauritius, Réunion (France), Seychelles

**Southern Africa:**
Angola, Botswana, Lesotho, Malawi, Mozambique, Namibia, South Africa, Swaziland, United Republic of Tanzania, Zambia, Zimbabwe

# Asia and the Pacific

**South Asia:**
Afghanistan, Bangladesh, Bhutan, India, Islamic Republic of Iran, Maldives, Nepal, Pakistan, Sri Lanka

**Southeast Asia:**
Brunei Darussalam, Cambodia, Indonesia, Lao People's Democratic Republic, Malaysia, Myanmar, Philippines, Singapore, Thailand, Viet Nam

**Northwest Pacific and East Asia:**
China, Democratic People's Republic of Korea, Japan, Republic of Korea, Mongolia

**Central Asia:**
Kazakhstan, Kyrgyzstan, Tajikistan, Turkmenistan, Uzbekistan

**Australia and New Zealand:**
Australia, New Zealand

**South Pacific:**
American Samoa (United States), Cook Islands, Fiji, French Polynesia (France), Guam (United States), Kiribati, Micronesia, Marshall Islands, Nauru, New Caledonia (France), Northern Mariana Islands (United States), Niue, Papua New Guinea, Pitcairn Islands (United Kingdom), Republic of Palau, Samoa, Solomon Islands, Tokelau (New Zealand), Tonga, Tuvalu, Vanuatu, Wallis and Futuna (France)

Eastern Europe

Western Europe

Central Europe

## Europe

### Western Europe:
Andorra, Austria, Belgium, Denmark, Finland, France, Germany, Greece, Holy See, Iceland, Ireland, Israel, Italy, Liechtenstein, Luxembourg, Malta, Monaco, Netherlands, Norway, Portugal, San Marino, Spain, Sweden, Switzerland, United Kingdom

### Central Europe:
Albania, Bosnia and Herzegovina, Bulgaria, Croatia, Cyprus, Czech Republic, Estonia, Hungary, Latvia, Lithuania, Poland, Romania, Slovakia, Slovenia, The Former Yugoslav Republic of Macedonia, Turkey, Yugoslavia

### Eastern Europe:
Armenia, Azerbaijan, Belarus, Russian Federation, Georgia, Republic of Moldova, Ukraine

## West Asia

### Arabian Peninsula:
Bahrain, Kuwait, Oman, Qatar, Saudi Arabia, United Arab Emirates, Yemen

### Mashriq:
Iraq, Jordan, Lebanon, Syrian Arab Republic, Occupied Palestinian Territories

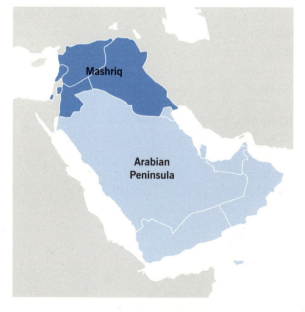

## North America

Canada
United States

Canada

United States

## Latin America and the Caribbean

Meso-America    Caribbean

South America

**Caribbean:**
Anguilla (United Kingdom), Antigua and Barbuda, Aruba (Netherlands),
Bahamas, Barbados, British Virgin Islands (United Kingdom),
Cayman Islands (United Kingdom), Cuba, Dominica,
Dominican Republic, Grenada, Guadeloupe (France), Haiti, Jamaica,
Martinique (France), Montserrat (United Kingdom),
Netherlands Antilles (Netherlands), Puerto Rico (United States),
St Kitts and Nevis, St Lucia, St Vincent and the Grenadines,
Trinidad and Tobago, Turks and Caicos (United Kingdom),
Virgin Islands (United States)

**Meso-America:**
Belize, Costa Rica, El Salvador, Guatemala, Honduras, Mexico, Nicaragua, Panama

**South America:**
Argentina, Bolivia, Brazil, Chile, Colombia, Ecuador, French Guyana (France), Guyana,
Paraguay, Peru, Suriname, Uruguay, Venezuela

# 1

# Integrating Environment and Development: 1972–2002

## Time line symbols

meeting

convention

disaster

publication

discovery

legal action

international event

new departure

new institution

The environment has always been critical to life but concerns over the balance between human life and the environment assumed international dimensions only during the 1950s. In the years that followed, supposedly unconnected pieces of a global jigsaw puzzle began to fit together to reveal a picture of a world with an uncertain future.

Paradigm-breaking books and articles such as Rachel Carson's *Silent Spring* (Carson 1962) and Garrett Hardin's 'The Tragedy of the Commons' (Hardin 1968) galvanized individual countries and the international community into action. A series of catastrophes added fuel to the environmental fire: thalidomide caused congenital deformations in babies, the *Torrey Canyon* spilled oil along France's picturesque northern coast, and Swedish scientists charged that the death of fish and other organisms in thousands of the country's lakes resulted from the long-range transport of air pollution from Western Europe.

At the end of the 1960s, the voice of environmental concern was heard almost uniquely in the West. In the communist world, the relentless destruction of the environment in the name of industrialization continued unabated. In developing countries, environmental concerns were regarded as Western luxuries. 'Poverty is the worst form of pollution,' held India's Prime Minister, Indira Ghandi, who played a key role in orienting the agenda of the UN Conference on the Human Environment, held in Stockholm in 1972, towards the concerns of the developing countries (Strong 1999). 'We hold that of all things in the world, people are the most precious,' said Tang Ke, leader of the Chinese delegation to the Stockholm conference (Clarke and Timberlake 1982).

### The tragedy of the commons

'The tragedy of the commons as a food basket is averted by private property, or something formally like it. But the air and waters surrounding us cannot readily be fenced, and so the tragedy of the commons as a cesspool must be prevented by different means, by coercive laws or taxing devices that make it cheaper for the polluter to treat his pollutants than to discharge them untreated.'

*Source: Hardin 1968*

In the early 1970s, attention was focused first on the biophysical environment, for example, on issues of wildlife management, soil conservation, water pollution, land degradation and desertification — and people were considered as the root cause of such problems. In the West, there were (and, to some extent, still are) two principal schools of thought about the causes of environmental degradation: one school blamed greed and the relentless pursuit of economic growth; the other blamed population growth. As one commentator put it, 'Unabated pollution and unstabilized population are real threats to our way of life and to life itself' (Stanley Foundation 1971).

These views were encapsulated in the most famous study of the time, the Club of Rome's computer model of the global future which attracted worldwide attention. The Club of Rome was a group of some 50 self-appointed 'wise men' (and women) who met regularly to try to put the world to rights, much as did the Pugwash group of scientists in relation to the Cold War. Published as *The Limits to Growth*, the Club of Rome model analysed five variables — technology, population, nutrition, natural resources and environment. Its main conclusion was that, if current trends continued, the global system would

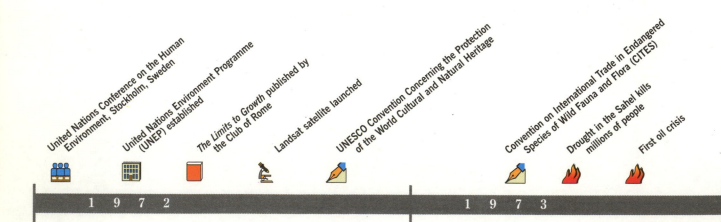

United Nations Conference on the Human Environment, Stockholm, Sweden

United Nations Environment Programme (UNEP) established

*The Limits to Growth* published by the Club of Rome

Landsat satellite launched

UNESCO Convention Concerning the Protection of the World Cultural and Natural Heritage

Convention on International Trade in Endangered Species of Wild Fauna and Flora (CITES)

Drought in the Sahel kills millions of people

First oil crisis

1 9 7 2          1 9 7 3

'overshoot' and collapse by the year 2000. If that were not to happen, both population and economic growth would have to cease (Meadows and Meadows 1972). Although *The Limits to Growth* has been heavily criticized, it publicized for the first time the concept of outer limits — the idea that development could be limited by the finite size of the Earth's resources.

## The 1970s: the foundation of modern environmentalism

The world of 1972 was very different from that of today. The Cold War still divided many of the world's most industrialized nations, the period of colonization had not yet ended and, although e-mail had just been invented (Campbell 1998), it was to be more than two decades before its use became widespread. The personal computer did not exist, global warming had only just been mentioned for the first time (SCEP 1970), and the threat to the ozone layer was seen as coming mainly from a large fleet of supersonic airliners that was never to materialize. Although transnational corporations existed and were becoming increasingly powerful, the concept of globalization was still 20 years away. In South Africa, apartheid still held sway and in Europe the Berlin Wall stood firm.

The world of the early 1970s was thus fiercely polarized, and in many different ways. Against this backdrop, it was surprising that the idea of an international conference on the environment should even be broached (by Sweden, in 1968); it was even more surprising that one should actually take place (in Stockholm, in 1972); and it was astonishing that such a conference could give rise to what later became known as the 'Stockholm spirit of compromise' in which

### Principles of the Stockholm Declaration

1. Human rights must be asserted, apartheid and colonialism condemned
2. Natural resources must be safeguarded
3. The Earth's capacity to produce renewable resources must be maintained
4. Wildlife must be safeguarded
5. Non-renewable resources must be shared and not exhausted
6. Pollution must not exceed the environment's capacity to clean itself
7. Damaging oceanic pollution must be prevented
8. Development is needed to improve the environment
9. Developing countries therefore need assistance
10. Developing countries need reasonable prices for exports to carry out environmental management
11. Environment policy must not hamper development
12. Developing countries need money to develop environmental safeguards
13. Integrated development planning is needed
14. Rational planning should resolve conflicts between environment and development
15. Human settlements must be planned to eliminate environmental problems
16. Governments should plan their own appropriate population policies
17. National institutions must plan development of states' natural resources
18. Science and technology must be used to improve the environment
19. Environmental education is essential
20. Environmental research must be promoted, particularly in developing countries
21. States may exploit their resources as they wish but must not endanger others
22. Compensation is due to states thus endangered
23. Each nation must establish its own standards
24. There must be cooperation on international issues
25. International organizations should help to improve the environment
26. Weapons of mass destruction must be eliminated

*Source: Clarke and Timberlake 1982*

'One of our prominent responsibilities in this conference is to issue an international declaration on the human environment; a document with no binding legislative imperatives, but — we hope — with moral authority, that will inspire in the hearts of men the desire to live in harmony with each other, and with their environment.' — *Professor Mostafa K. Tolba, Head of the Egyptian delegation to the Stockholm Conference, UNEP Executive Director 1975–93*

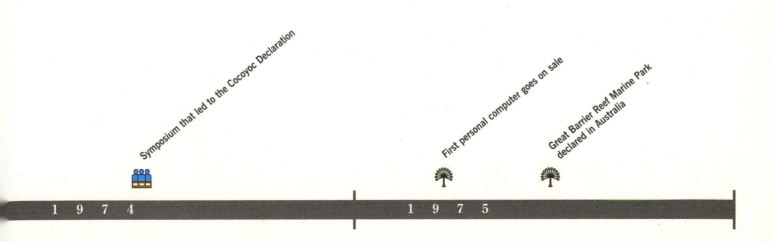

Symposium that led to the Cocoyoc Declaration

First personal computer goes on sale

Great Barrier Reef Marine Park declared in Australia

1 9 7 4          1 9 7 5

representatives of developed and developing countries found ways of accommodating each other's strongly divergent views. The conference was hosted by Sweden following severe damage to thousands of Sweden's lakes from acid rain falling as a result of severe air pollution in Western Europe.

## The United Nations Conference on the Human Environment

The United Nations Conference on the Human Environment, held in June 1972, was the event that turned the environment into a major issue at the international level. The conference drew together both developed and developing countries, but the former Soviet Union and most of its allies did not attend.

### The birth of the United Nations Environment Programme

The Stockholm Conference recommended the creation of a small secretariat in the United Nations as a focal point for environmental action and coordination within the UN system. This was established later in 1972 under the name of the United Nations Environment Programme (UNEP), and was headed by an executive director whose responsibilities included:

- providing support to UNEP's Governing Council;
- coordinating environmental programmes within the United Nations system;
- advising on the formulation and implementation of environmental programmes;
- securing the cooperation of scientific and other professional communities from all parts of the world;
- advising on international cooperation in the field of the environment; and
- submitting proposals on medium and long-range planning for United Nations programmes in the environment field.

UNEP's mission today is to 'Provide leadership and encourage partnership in caring for the environment by inspiring, informing, and enabling nations and peoples to improve their quality of life without compromising that of future generations'.

The Stockholm Conference produced a Declaration of 26 Principles and an Action Plan of 109 recommendations. A few specific targets were set — a 10-year moratorium on commercial whaling, prevention of deliberate oil discharges at sea by 1975 and a report by 1975 on energy uses. The Stockholm Declaration on the Human Environment and Principles constituted the first body of 'soft law' in international environmental affairs (Long 2000). The principles are loosely paraphrased in the box on page 3.

The conference also established the United Nations Environment Programme (UNEP, see box left) as 'the environmental conscience of the UN system'.

It is easy to claim that many of the major environmental milestones of the 1970s followed directly from Stockholm. It is important to remember, however, that Stockholm was itself a reflection of the mood of the times, or at least of the views of many in the West. That said, it is still instructive to itemize some of the major changes that followed Stockholm.

- Stockholm articulated the right of people to live 'in an environment of a quality that permits a life of dignity and well-being'. Since then, a number of organizations, including the Organization of African Unity (OAU), and about 50 governments worldwide, have adopted instruments or national constitutions that recognize the environment as a fundamental human right (Chenje, Mohamed-Katerere and Ncube 1996).
- Much national legislation on the environment followed Stockholm. During 1971-75, 31 major national environmental laws were passed in countries of the Organization for Economic Cooperation and Development (OECD), compared

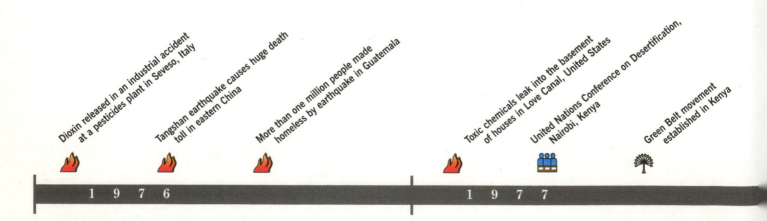

Dioxin released in an industrial accident at a pesticides plant in Seveso, Italy

Tangshan earthquake causes huge death toll in eastern China

More than one million people made homeless by earthquake in Guatemala

Toxic chemicals leak into the basement of houses in Love Canal, United States

United Nations Conference on Desertification, Nairobi, Kenya

Green Belt movement established in Kenya

1 9 7 6    1 9 7 7

to just 4 during 1956-60, 10 during 1960-65 and 18 during 1966-70 (Long 2000).

- The environment entered or was brought much nearer the top of many regional and national agendas. For example, before Stockholm there were only about 10 ministries of environment; by 1982 some 110 countries had such ministries or departments (Clarke and Timberlake 1982).

## Multilateral environmental agreements

One area in which governments and other stakeholders recorded qualified successes in the 1970s was wildlife conservation. This was achieved through a combination of legal actions at the global level which were (and still are) enforced at the national level with variable effectiveness. The foundation for some of these successes was laid by multilateral environmental agreements such as the:

- 1971 Convention on Wetlands of International Importance Especially as Waterfowl Habitat (Ramsar);
- 1972 Convention Concerning the Protection of the World Cultural and Natural Heritage (World Heritage);
- 1973 Convention on International Trade in Endangered Species of Wild Fauna and Flora (CITES); and
- 1979 Convention on the Conservation of Migratory Species of Wild Animals (CMS).

### The Ramsar Convention

The Ramsar Convention predates the Stockholm Conference, having been opened for signature in 1971. The convention, which became effective two years

> **'All peoples shall have the right to a general satisfactory environment favourable to their development.'** — *African Charter on Human and People's Rights, 27 June 1981*

after Stockholm, had 130 parties as of December 2001. It was developed largely out of NGO-led activities in the 1960s concerned with bird life and habitat. While its main focus was initially the conservation of waterfowl and their habitats, it now also deals with water quality, food production, general biodiversity and all wetland areas, including saltwater coasts.

Parties are obliged to list at least one wetlands site of importance, establish nature reserves, make wise use of those sites, encourage the increase of waterfowl populations on appropriate wetlands, and supply information on implementation of policies related to the sites. More than 1 100 areas, covering 87.7 million ha, are currently designated Ramsar sites, enhancing wildlife conservation in different regions (Ramsar Convention Bureau 2001).

### The World Heritage Convention

The World Heritage Convention, negotiated in 1972, is administered by the United Nations Educational, Scientific and Cultural Organization (UNESCO). It had 161 parties in mid-2001. Since 1972 when the Galapagos Islands were put under the aegis of UNESCO as 'a natural university of unique species', a total of 144 sites in different regions were designated as natural heritage sites as of December 2001. An additional 23 sites were of both natural and cultural significance (UNESCO 2001). The impact has been greater awareness of the importance of these sites for both present and future generations. However, the

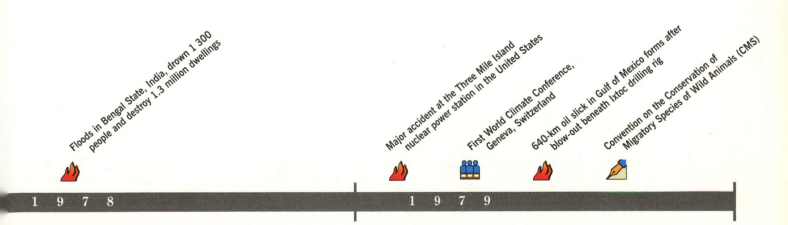

Floods in Bengal State, India, drown 1 300 people and destroy 1.3 million dwellings

Major accident at the Three Mile Island nuclear power station in the United States

First World Climate Conference, Geneva, Switzerland

640-km oil slick in Gulf of Mexico forms after blow-out beneath Ixtoc drilling rig

Convention on the Conservation of Migratory Species of Wild Animals (CMS)

1 9 7 8          1 9 7 9

early 2001 oil spill adjacent to the Galapagos Islands, which threatened species and habitats, underlines the fact that environmental management systems may never be foolproof.

---

**'People are no longer satisfied only with declarations. They demand firm action and concrete results. They expect that the nations of the world, having identified a problem, will have the vitality to act.'** — *Swedish Prime Minister Olof Palme, whose country hosted the Stockholm Conference, 1972*

---

## CITES

At the time of Stockholm, it was reported that 150 species of birds and animals had already been 'exterminated' and about 1 000 more were threatened with extinction (Commission to Study the Organization of Peace 1972). A UN Commission recommended the identification of endangered species without further delay, the conclusion of appropriate agreements and establishment of institutions to spearhead wildlife conservation, and the regulation of the international trade in threatened species.

The Commission's recommendation virtually endorsed a 1963 resolution by members of the World Conservation Union (IUCN) which catalysed the drafting of the CITES convention. The convention was eventually adopted in 1973 and became effective two years later. The convention controls and/or bans international trade in endangered species, including about 5 000 animal and 25 000 plant species (CITES Secretariat 2001). Controversy over charismatic species such the African elephant and the whale have often overshadowed the attention that has been placed on other species.

## Other achievements

In terms of demonstrable action, Stockholm apparently achieved much. While many of its 109 recommendations remain unfulfilled, they serve — now as then — as important targets. Equally important, however, were the Conference's achievements in repairing rifts, and in narrowing the gap between the views of the developed and the developing nations. The first attempt at this had been made at a conference in Founex, Switzerland, in 1969, and the Founex Report of June 1971 identified development and environment as 'two sides of the same coin' (UNEP 1981). The Drafting and Planning Committee for the Stockholm conference noted in its report in April 1972 that 'environmental protection must not be an excuse for slowing down the economic progress of emerging countries'.

Further progress had to wait until 1974 when a symposium of experts chaired by the late Barbara Ward, was held in Cocoyoc, Mexico. Organized by UNEP and the United Nations Commission on Trade and Development (UNCTAD), the symposium identified the economic and social factors which lead to environmental deterioration (UNEP/UNCTAD 1974). The Cocoyoc Declaration — the formal statement issued by the symposium — was influential in changing the attitudes of leading environmental thinkers. What was said at Cocoyoc foreshadowed the first paragraph of the *World Conservation Strategy* published in 1980 (see page 9) and was re-stated in *GEO-2000* in 1999: 'The combined destructive impacts of a poor majority struggling to stay alive and an affluent minority consuming most of the world's resources are undermining the very means by which all people can survive and flourish' (UNEP/UNCTAD 1974).

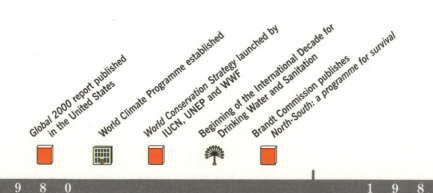

Global 2000 report published in the United States

World Climate Programme established

World Conservation Strategy launched by IUCN, UNEP and WWF

Beginning of the International Decade for Drinking Water and Sanitation

Brandt Commission publishes North-South: a programme for survival

Other statements in the Cocoyoc Declaration illustrate awareness of the difficulty of meeting human needs sustainably from an environment under pressure:

- 'The problem today is not one primarily of absolute physical shortage but of economic and social maldistribution and usage.'
- 'The task of statesmanship is to guide the nations towards a new system more capable of meeting the inner limits of basic human needs for all the world's people and of doing so without violating the outer limits of the planet's resources and environment.'
- 'Human beings have basic needs: food, shelter, clothing, health, education. Any process of growth that does not lead to their fulfilment — or, even worse, disrupts them — is a travesty of the idea of development.'
- 'We are all in need of a redefinition of our goals, or new development strategies, or new lifestyles, including more modest patterns of consumption among the rich.'

The Cocoyoc Declaration ends:

*'The road forward does not lie through the despair of doomwatching or through the easy optimism of successive technological fixes. It lies through a careful and dispassionate assessment of the 'outer limits', through cooperative search for ways to achieve the 'inner limits' of fundamental human rights, through the building of social structures to express those rights, and through all the patient work of devising techniques and styles of*

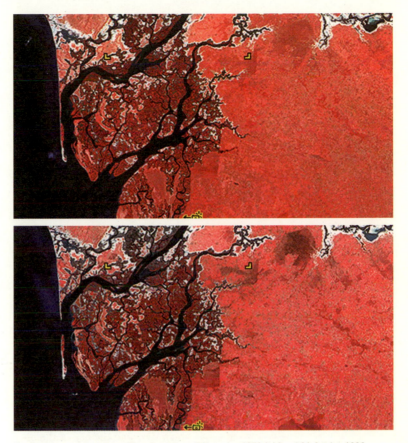

Landsat images of the Saloum River, Senegal, on 5 November 1972 (top) and 31 October 1992 show how much of the mangrove forest (dark red areas) has disappeared in 20 years, even in a protected area

*Source: Landsat 2001*

*development which enhance and preserve our planetary inheritance.'*

This vision of the way forward was reflected in the detailed new images of the planet that appeared in the 1970s as a result of the launch by the United States in

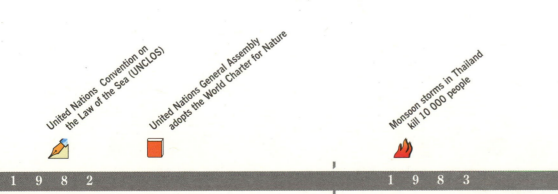

United Nations Convention on the Law of the Sea (UNCLOS)

United Nations General Assembly adopts the World Charter for Nature

Monsoon storms in Thailand kill 10 000 people

1 9 8 2        1 9 8 3

July 1972 of the Landsat satellite. Such images were undoubtedly instrumental in changing human attitudes to the state of the planet's environment. Sadly, the 30-year record that Landsat has provided also shows that attitudes have not yet changed enough (see photos page 7).

In terms of climate change, growing concern about global warming (the Swedish scientist Svante Arrhenius had in 1896 warned the world about the 'greenhouse effect') led to the first World Climate Conference in Geneva in February 1979 (Centre for Science and Environment 1999). It concluded that anthropogenic carbon dioxide emissions could have a long-term effect on climate. The World Climate Programme (WCP) was established the following year, providing the framework for international cooperation in research and the platform for identifying the important climate issues of the 1980s and 1990s, including ozone depletion and global warming.

## The 1980s: defining sustainable development

The defining political events of the 1980s were the breakdown of the Eastern Bloc and the end of the bi-polar world built on the balance of power between Western and communist countries and their allies in the developing world. The changes that were the culmination of reform and perestroika in the Soviet Bloc came on the heels of years of apparently strong economic growth and massive military spending.

### The lost decade

The situation was markedly different in the developing regions of Africa, West Asia, and Latin America and the Caribbean, where most countries registered little growth in income (UNCHS 1996). The sub-Saharan region fell further behind with per capita income falling 1.2 per cent a year during the 1980s (UN 2000) due to a combination of factors, including severe droughts and unfavourable terms of trade. For many developing countries the 1980s became known as the lost decade. Starting with the debt crisis in Latin America in 1982, the situation was particularly difficult in countries where wars led to the displacement of millions of people. The number of refugees doubled from about 9 million in 1980 to more than 18 million by the early 1990s (UNHCR 2000).

Dealing with the cycle of poverty became a particular challenge as population growth in the developing world not only continued but an increasing number of the poor were living in cities. As urban populations grew, cities were finding their physical infrastructure increasingly stressed and unable to cope with demand.

### New issues and new accidents

Catching the scientific world as well as policy makers by surprise, measurements by British researchers of the size of the ozone hole were first reported in 1985 (Farnham, Gardiner and Shanklin 1985). The *Global 2000* report recognized for the first time that species extinction was threatening biodiversity as an essential component of the Earth's ecosystems (US Government 1980). As the interdependence of environment and development became increasingly clear, the United Nations General Assembly adopted the *World Charter for Nature*, bringing attention to the intrinsic value of species and ecosystems (UN 1982).

Besides new discoveries, the 1980s also saw a

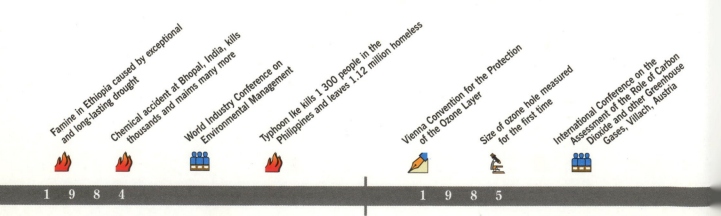

Famine in Ethiopia caused by exceptional and long-lasting drought

Chemical accident at Bhopal, India, kills thousands and maims many more

World Industry Conference on Environmental Management

Typhoon Ike kills 1 300 people in the Philippines and leaves 1.12 million homeless

Vienna Convention for the Protection of the Ozone Layer

Size of ozone hole measured for the first time

International Conference on the Assessment of the Role of Carbon Dioxide and other Greenhouse Gases, Villach, Austria

1 9 8 4        1 9 8 5

By 1990, at least 900 million people in urban areas in Africa, Asia and Latin America were living in poverty

*Source: UNEP, Topham Picturepoint*

range of catastrophic events that left a permanent mark both on the environment and on the understanding of its connection to human health. In 1984, a leak from a Union Carbide plant left 3 000 people dead and 20 000 injured in Bhopal, India (Diamond 1985). The same year, up to 1 million people starved to death in Ethiopia. In 1986, the world's worst nuclear accident happened as a reactor at the Chernobyl nuclear power plant exploded in the Ukrainian Republic of the Soviet Union. The 1989 spill of 50 million litres of oil from the *Exxon Valdez* supertanker into Alaska's Prince William Sound demonstrated that no area, however remote and 'pristine', is safe from the impact of human activities.

## The World Conservation Strategy

The events referred to above confirmed that environmental issues are systemic and addressing them requires long-term strategies, integrated action and the participation of all countries and all members of society. This was reflected in the World Conservation Strategy (WCS), one of the seminal documents which served to redefine environmentalism post-Stockholm. Launched in 1980 by IUCN, the strategy recognized that addressing environmental problems calls for long-term effort and the integration of environmental and development objectives.

The WCS envisaged governments in different parts of the world undertaking their own national

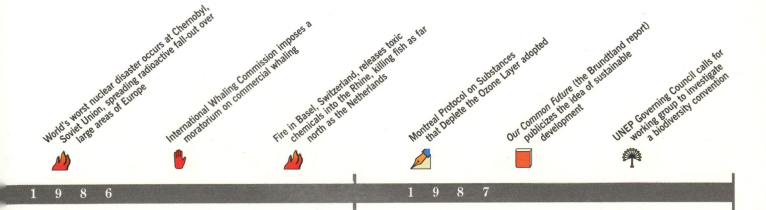

World's worst nuclear disaster occurs at Chernobyl, Soviet Union, spreading radioactive fall-out over large areas of Europe

International Whaling Commission imposes a moratorium on commercial whaling

Fire in Basel, Switzerland, releases toxic chemicals into the Rhine, killing fish as far north as the Netherlands

Montreal Protocol on Substances that Deplete the Ozone Layer adopted

*Our Common Future* (the Brundtland report) publicizes the idea of sustainable development

UNEP Governing Council calls for working group to investigate a biodiversity convention

**1 9 8 6**          **1 9 8 7**

'This is a kind of development that provides real improvements in the quality of human life and at the same time conserves the vitality and diversity of the Earth. The goal is development that will be sustainable. Today it may seem visionary but it is attainable. To more and more people it also appears our only rational option.' — *World Conservation Strategy, IUCN, UNEP and WWF 1980*

conservation strategies, meeting one of the objectives of Stockholm to incorporate environment in development planning. Since 1980, more than 75 countries have initiated multi-sector strategies at national, provincial, state and local levels (Lopez Ornat 1996). These are aimed at addressing environmental problems such as land degradation, habitat conversion and loss, deforestation, water pollution and poverty.

### World Charter for Nature: general principles

- The genetic viability on the earth shall not be compromised; the population levels of all life forms, wild and domesticated, must be at least sufficient for their survival, and to this end necessary habitat shall be safeguarded.
- All areas of the earth, both land and sea, shall be subject to these principles of conservation; special protection shall be given to unique areas, to representative samples of all the different types of ecosystems and to the habitat of rare or endangered species.
- Ecosystems and organisms, as well as the land, marine and atmospheric resources that are utilized by man [sic], shall be managed to achieve and maintain optimum sustainable productivity, but not in such a way as to endanger the integrity of those other ecosystems or species with which they co-exist.
- Nature shall be secured against degradation caused by warfare or other hostile activities.

*Source: UN 1982*

## The World Commission on Environment and Development

However, communicating the message that environment and development were interdependent required a process which carried authority and credibility to the North and South, to government and the business sector, to international organizations and civil society. In 1983, the World Commission on Environment and Development (WCED), also known as the Brundtland Commission, was formed to hold hearings across the globe and produce a formal report of its findings.

The report was issued after three years of hearings with government leaders and the public worldwide on environment and development issues. Public meetings were held in both developed and developing regions, and the process empowered different groups to articulate their views on issues such as agriculture, forestry, water, energy, technology transfer and sustainable development in general. *Our Common Future*, the Commission's final report, defined sustainable development as 'development that meets the needs of the present without compromising the ability of future generations to meet their own needs', making it part of the environment lexicon (WCED 1987).

The Commission highlighted environmental problems such as global warming and ozone layer depletion that were new at the time. It expressed concern that the rate of 'change is outstripping the ability of scientific disciplines and our current capabilities to assess and advise'. The Commission concluded that existing decision-making structures and institutional arrangements, both national and international, simply could not cope with the demands of sustainable development (WCED 1987):

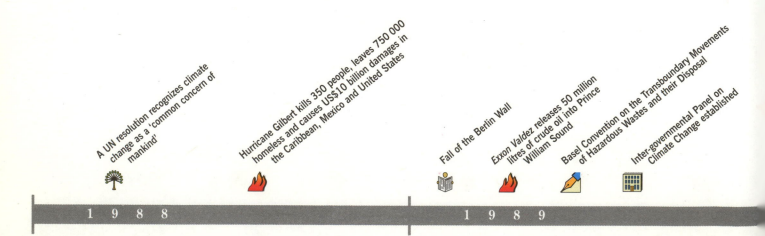

A UN resolution recognizes climate change as a 'common concern of mankind'

Hurricane Gilbert kills 350 people, leaves 750 000 homeless and causes US$10 billion damages in the Caribbean, Mexico and United States

Fall of the Berlin Wall

*Exxon Valdez* releases 50 million litres of crude oil into Prince William Sound

Basel Convention on the Transboundary Movements of Hazardous Wastes and their Disposal

Inter-governmental Panel on Climate Change established

1 9 8 8          1 9 8 9

*'The present decade (1980s) has been marked by a retreat from social concerns. Scientists bring to our attention urgent but complex problems bearing on our survival: a warming globe, threats to the Earth's ozone layer, deserts consuming agricultural land. We respond by demanding more details, and by assigning the problems to institutions ill equipped to cope with them'* (WCED 1987).

Thus were the seeds of broader engagement in environment and development issues sown. As a sign of a strengthening non-governmental sector, many new organizations were formed. In Europe, green parties entered the political arena and the membership of grass-roots environmental organizations increased rapidly.

## Involving the other actors

In the wake of the industrial accidents of the 1980s, the pressure on corporations grew. In 1984, UNEP co-organized the World Industry Conference on Environmental Management, and in 1984 Responsible Care was established by the chemical industry in Canada, one of the first attempts to provide a code of conduct to sound environmental management in the business sector. By the end of the decade, the concept of eco-efficiency was being introduced into industry as a means of simultaneously reducing environmental impact while increasing profitability. Few if any of these interests were shared by corporations based in developing countries, but there were already debates on the implications of industries migrating to 'pollution havens' in the South.

As it became clear that an increasing number of actors would need to grapple with the environmental dimensions of activities previously not recognized as having environmental implications, academic interest in the subject grew. Environment and development became legitimate subjects of study in more of the established social and natural disciplines, but also new disciplines were born to address cross-cutting areas. Environmental economics, environmental engineering and other previously fringe subjects started to become established and legitimate fields of scholarship, developing their own theories but also proving their worth in real world contexts.

The environment and sustainability still did not feature high in the principles and particularly practice of bilateral aid. As an early sign of change, in 1987 the OECD established a Development Advisory Committee charged with the establishment of guidelines for the integration of environment and development in development assistance programmes.

The successful conclusion of the Montreal Protocol in 1987 was held as a promising model for cooperation between North and South, government and business to address global environmental matters. However, dealing with ozone depletion was more straightforward than dealing with other environmental issues that entered the public agenda in the 1980s, notably climate change.

## The Intergovernmental Panel on Climate Change

In 1989, the Intergovernmental Panel on Climate Change (IPCC) was established with three working groups focused on the scientific assessment of climate change, environmental and socio-economic impacts, and response strategies, foretelling the wide range of challenges that humanity would face as it entered the

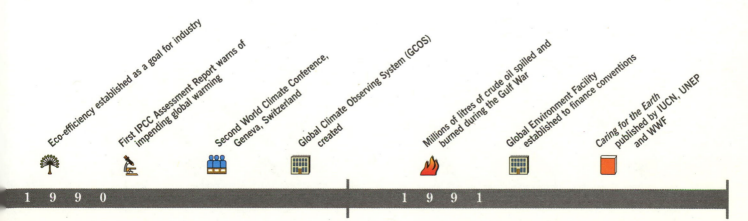

Eco-efficiency established as a goal for industry

First IPCC Assessment Report warns of impending global warming

Second World Climate Conference, Geneva, Switzerland

Global Climate Observing System (GCOS) created

Millions of litres of crude oil spilled and burned during the Gulf War

Global Environment Facility established to finance conventions

Caring for the Earth published by IUCN, UNEP and WWF

1 9 9 0          1 9 9 1

'Indigenous people are the base of what I guess could be called the environmental security system. For many of us, however, the last few centuries have meant a major loss of control over our lands and waters. We are still the first to know about changes in the environment, but we are now the last to be asked or consulted.' — *Louis Bruyère, President of the Native Council of Canada, WCED public hearing, Ottawa, Canada, May 1986*

last decade of the millennium. The establishment of the IPCC by UNEP and the World Meteorological Organization (WMO) helped develop a broad consensus on the science, social impacts and best responses to human-induced global warming. The IPCC has contributed immensely to public understanding of the dangers of global warming, particularly in the industrialized countries. In many developing countries, where climate studies are rare and climate experts almost non-existent, climate change is not regarded in the same light. This has led some organizations in the developing regions to complain about 'an enormous disparity in North-South participation. ... Southern countries have no coordinated national climate programmes, few climate researchers, and hardly any data to compute long-term climate projections' (Centre for Science and Environment 1999).

## Multilateral environmental agreements

Some of the major Multilateral Environmental Agreements (MEAs) of the 1980s are:

- the 1982 United Nations Convention on the Law of the Sea (UNCLOS);
- the 1987 Montreal Protocol on Substances that

Deplete the Ozone Layer (implementing the 1985 Vienna Convention for the Protection of the Ozone Layer); and
- the 1989 Basel Convention on the Control of Transboundary Movements of Hazardous Wastes and their Disposal (Basel Convention).

### Law of the Sea

Although UNCLOS was signed in 1982, it did not come into force until 12 years later, an indication perhaps of the complexity of negotiating MEAs. The convention, which has 136 parties, is a landmark legal undertaking that encompasses a wide range of maritime issues, including environmental protection. Its environmental provisions include:

- the extension of sovereign rights over marine resources, such as fish, within the 200-mile exclusive economic zones (EEZs);
- obligations to adopt measures to manage and conserve natural resources;
- a duty to cooperate regionally and globally with regard to environmental protection and research related to this protection;
- a duty to minimize marine pollution, including land-based pollution; and
- restrictions on marine dumping by ships.

### The Montreal Protocol

The Montreal Protocol to the Vienna Convention on Substances that Deplete the Ozone Layer, which entered into force in 1989 and had 182 parties as of December 2001, is one of the most successful examples of international environmental cooperation. The success of the protocol in part has hinged upon

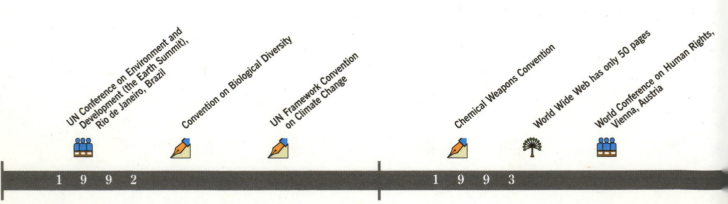

UN Conference on Environment and Development (the Earth Summit), Rio de Janeiro, Brazil

Convention on Biological Diversity

UN Framework Convention on Climate Change

Chemical Weapons Convention

World Wide Web has only 50 pages

World Conference on Human Rights, Vienna, Austria

1 9 9 2          1 9 9 3

the Multilateral Fund as an inducement to participation by developing countries (UNEP 2001a).

Parties to the Montreal Protocol must annually provide statistical data on the production, import and export of those ozone-depleting substances (ODS) that are controlled by the protocol to the secretariat, through national reports. Reporting rates are high, with more than 85 per cent of the parties reporting their data. The implementation of the protocol has been tightened and expanded significantly over the years, through the 1990 London, 1992 Copenhagen, 1997 Montreal and 1999 Beijing Amendments (UNEP 2000).

### The Basel Convention

The Basel Convention, which entered into force in 1992 and had 149 parties as of December 2001, has three key objectives:

- to reduce transboundary movements of hazardous wastes;
- to minimize the creation of such wastes; and
- to prohibit their shipment to countries lacking the capacity to dispose of hazardous wastes in an environmentally sound manner.

The convention arose out of growing concerns over shipments of waste from industrialized to developing states. Concerned about shipments to Africa, member states of the Organization of African Unity (OAU) responded with the 1991 Bamako Convention on the Ban of the Import into Africa and the Control of the Transboundary Movement and Management of Hazardous Waste within Africa. It came into force in April 1998.

## The 1990s: implementing sustainable development

The 1990s were characterized by the search for increased understanding of the concept and significance of sustainable development. This was accompanied by accelerating trends towards globalization, particularly with regard to trade and technology. The conviction grew that there were an increasing number of global environmental problems that required international solutions. The profile of environmental issues was also increasing in the South as new organizations began demanding diagnoses and solutions for developing countries. The Regional Environmental Centre was established in Hungary in 1990 to address environmental issues in post-Soviet Central Europe. There was significant action by

'The solution cannot be that which bans the development of those who need it the most; the fact is that everything that contributes to underdevelopment and poverty is an open violation of ecology.'
— *Cuban President Fidel Castro, UNCED 1992*

private industry to put its house into better environmental shape and explosive growth in the use of the Internet and electronic communications.

The decade started badly for the environment with the loss of thousands of lives in the 1991 Persian Gulf conflict and a partial black-out over some of the area as millions of barrels of oil were wilfully ignited (Bennett 1995). For West Asia, this was a major environmental catastrophe. An oil slick — caused by the release of between 0.5 million to 11 million barrels

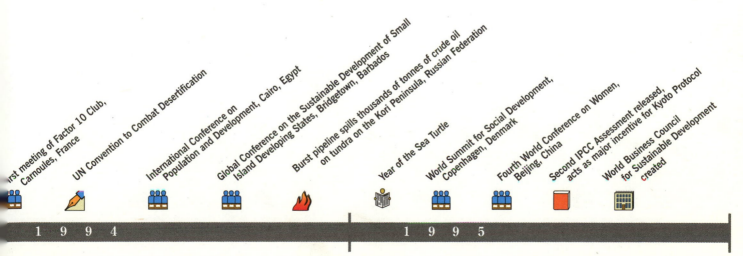

First meeting of Factor 10 Club, Carnoules, France

UN Convention to Combat Desertification

International Conference on Population and Development, Cairo, Egypt

Global Conference on the Sustainable Development of Small Island Developing States, Bridgetown, Barbados

Burst pipeline spills thousands of tonnes of crude oil on tundra on the Kori Peninsula, Russian Federation

Year of the Sea Turtle

World Summit for Social Development, Copenhagen, Denmark

Fourth World Conference on Women, Beijing, China

Second IPCC Assessment released, acts as major incentive for Kyoto Protocol

World Business Council for Sustainable Development created

1994      1995

**Firemen trying to extinguish a burning oil rig in Kuwait in 1991**

*Source: UNEP, Abdel Saurad-Mali, Kuwait, Topham PicturePoint*

of crude oil — is reported to have killed 15 000-30 000 sea birds. In addition, about 20 per cent of mangroves in the Persian Gulf were contaminated and 50 per cent of coral reefs affected (Island Press 1999). The atmosphere was not spared either: about 67 million tonnes of oil were burnt, producing about 2.1 million tonnes of soot and 2 million tonnes of sulphur dioxide (Bennett 1995).

Elsewhere, while technical progress was transforming industrialized society, few in the

developing world were benefiting. The death toll from infectious diseases (such as AIDS, malaria, respiratory diseases and diarrhoea) was 160 times greater than the number killed in 1999 from natural disasters, including earthquakes in Turkey, floods in Venezuela and cyclones in India (IFRC 2000). The International Federation of Red Cross and Red Crescent Societies reported that a 1995 survey of 53 countries showed a 15 per cent decline in health spending per person following economic structural adjustment.

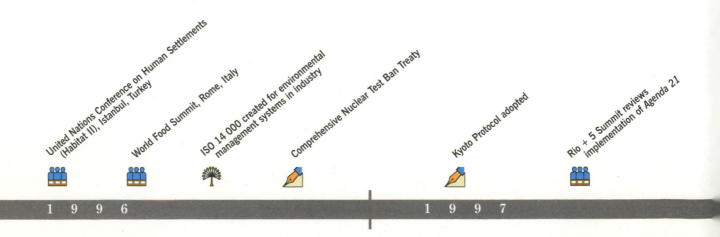

United Nations Conference on Human Settlements (Habitat II), Istanbul, Turkey

World Food Summit, Rome, Italy

ISO 14 000 created for environmental management systems in industry

Comprehensive Nuclear Test Ban Treaty

Kyoto Protocol adopted

Rio + 5 Summit reviews implementation of Agenda 21

1 9 9 6     1 9 9 7

By 1997, near the end of the 20th century, some 800 million people (nearly 14 per cent of the world population) not only went hungry every day but also lacked the basic skills of reading and writing essential to sustainable development (UNESCO 1997).

In terms of governance, events of the late 1980s continued to influence political developments across the globe. No region was immune as dictatorships and military regimes in Africa and Latin America were voted out of power, and the single party governments in some European countries were relegated to opposition benches by a restless electorate. The people had begun to exercise their right to elect their leaders and demand accountability. Despite this radical change in terms of governance, there was little immediate impact on the environment in most countries. In the countries of the former Soviet Union, however, economic recession helped reduce waste emissions and energy consumption. Whether such effects will prove only temporary remains to be seen.

At the institutional level, ideas that had taken shape during the late 1980s, such as multistakeholder participation and increased accountability on environmental and social matters, were given a higher profile by a number of international events. The first of these was a ministerial conference on the environment held in Bergen, Norway, in May 1990, where such ideas were first formally endorsed. This conference was convened to prepare for the UN Conference on Environment and Development (UNCED or the Earth Summit) that was held in June 1992 in Rio de Janeiro, Brazil.

## The Earth Summit

UNCED was attended by an unprecedented number of representatives of state, civil and economic society — 176 governments (UN 1993), more than 100 heads of state compared to the two who attended the 1972 Stockholm Conference (Haas, Levy and Parson 1992), and an estimated 10 000 delegates, 1 400 non-governmental organizations (NGOs) and about 9 000

**'No matter what resolutions are made or not made at a forum such as this, no genuine and lasting environmental improvement can take place without grass-roots involvement on a global scale.'** — *Iceland President Vigdís Finnbogadóttir, UNCED 1992*

journalists (Demkine 2000). It is still the largest such gathering ever held. Prior to the Summit itself, the preparatory events from national and sub-regional to regional and global also involved the participation of hundreds of thousands of people across the world, ensuring that their voices were heard. Sub-regional and regional organizations such the Association of Southeast Asian Nations (ASEAN), the Organization of African Unity, the European Union and many others played a role before and during the Earth Summit. They continue to do so in trying to implement *Agenda 21*, the action programme that resulted from the conference.

The Summit produced at least seven major achievements:

- the Rio Declaration on Environment and Development (containing 27 principles);
- *Agenda 21* — a blueprint for environment and development into the 21st century;
- two major international conventions — the United

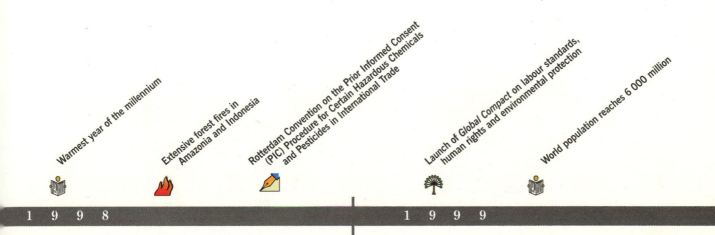

Warmest year of the millennium

Extensive forest fires in Amazonia and Indonesia

Rotterdam Convention on the Prior Informed Consent (PIC) Procedure for Certain Hazardous Chemicals and Pesticides in International Trade

Launch of Global Compact on labour standards, human rights and environmental protection

World population reaches 6 000 million

1 9 9 8          1 9 9 9

Nations Framework Convention on Climate Change (UNFCCC) and the Convention on Biological Diversity (CBD);

- the Commission on Sustainable Development (CSD);
- agreement to negotiate a world desertification convention; and
- the statement of Principles for the Sustainable Management of Forests.

The Rio Principles reaffirmed the issues that had been articulated in Stockholm 20 years earlier, placing human beings at the centre of sustainable

development concerns by stating that humans are 'entitled to a healthy and productive life in harmony with nature'.

The Earth Summit provided a forum to address issues of both environment and development, and to highlight differences in perspective between the North and South. After the Summit, sustainable development took on a life of its own, forcing its way into the deliberations of bodies ranging from city councils to international organizations. More than 150 countries have established national-level institutions to develop an integrated approach to sustainable development — although, in some countries, the national councils of sustainable development have been more political than substantive in nature (Myers and Brown 1997). A wide range of civil society sectors is now involved in agenda setting and strategy building. More than 90 per cent of them have been established in response to Rio, the majority in developing countries.

The emphasis given to sustainable development also had considerable impact on both legal instruments and the institutions that administer them. For example CITES, which was already evolving away from a classic conservation approach, moved further towards an approach that balances conservation with sustainable use. The practical application of sustainable use within CITES provoked substantial and heated debate throughout the decade.

## Agenda 21

*Agenda 21* is an action programme. It was partially based on a series of specialized contributions from governments and international bodies, including *Caring for the Earth: a Strategy for Sustainable Living* (IUCN, UNEP and WWF 1991). *Agenda 21* is now the

---

### Agenda 21

*Agenda 21* lays a solid foundation for the promotion of sustainable development in terms of social, economic and environmental progress. *Agenda 21* has 40 chapters, and its recommendations are divided into four main areas:

- Social and economic issues such as international cooperation to accelerate sustainable development, combating poverty, changing consumption patterns, demographic dynamics and sustainability, and protecting and promoting human health.
- Conservation and management of resources for development, such as protection of the atmosphere, combating deforestation, combating desertification and drought, promoting sustainable agriculture and rural development, conservation of biological diversity, protection of freshwater resources and the oceans, and the sound management of toxic chemicals and hazardous wastes.
- Strengthening the role of major groups, including women, children and youth, indigenous people and their communities, NGOs, local authorities' initiatives in support of *Agenda 21*, workers and their trade unions, business and industry, the scientific and technological community, and farmers.
- Means of implementation, including financial resources and mechanisms, transfer of environmentally sound technology, promoting education, public awareness and training, international institutional arrangements, international legal instruments and mechanisms, and information for decision-making.

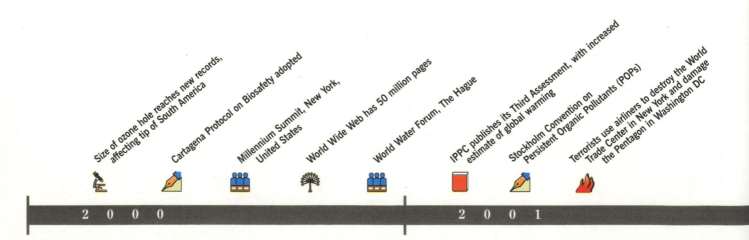

Size of ozone hole reaches new records, affecting tip of South America

Cartagena Protocol on Biosafety adopted

Millennium Summit, New York, United States

World Wide Web has 50 million pages

World Water Forum, The Hague

IPPC publishes its Third Assessment, with increased estimate of global warming

Stockholm Convention on Persistent Organic Pollutants (POPs)

Terrorists use airliners to destroy the World Trade Center in New York and damage the Pentagon in Washington DC

2 0 0 0

2 0 0 1

most significant and influential non-binding instrument in the environmental field, serving as the blueprint for environmental management in most regions of the world (see box left).

The cost of implementing *Agenda 21* in developing countries was estimated by the Earth Summit secretariat to be about US$625 billion a year, with the developing countries meeting 80 per cent, or US$500 billion, of it. Developed countries were expected to foot the remaining 20 per cent, or about US$125 billion annually, by meeting their long-established official development assistance (ODA) target of 0.7 per cent of gross national product (GNP).

Although UNCED was concerned with global approaches, an important outcome was the adoption of many national and regional *Agenda 21* programmes for sustainable development. In the Southern African Development Community (SADC) region, for example, the member states adopted the SADC Policy and Strategy for Environment and Sustainable Development in 1996. The European Union adopted the 5th Environmental Action Plan *Towards Sustainability* (EU 1993).

## The Global Environment Facility
The Global Environment Facility (GEF) was created in 1991 as an experimental partnership involving UNEP, UNDP and the World Bank to generate ecological dividends from local and regional development by providing grants and low-interest loans to developing nations and economies in transition. Following the Summit, it was intended to be the financing mechanism for *Agenda 21*, and was expected to mobilize the necessary resources. It helps fund national, regional and global development projects which benefit the world's environment in four focal areas — climate change, biodiversity, ozone and international waters — as well as local economies and societies.

Following its successful restructuring in March 1994, GEF membership has grown from 34 to more than 155 countries, whose representatives meet in the GEF Assembly of participating states, the GEF's overall supervisory body, every three years.

GEF chief executive officer and chairman Mohamed T. El-Ashry acknowledges that it is too early to assess the impact of the more than 220 GEF-supported projects in terms of sustainable development. A gap between donor pledges and actual contributions to the GEF has raised concerns, particularly among developing countries. Despite the commitment to meet an ODA target of 0.7 per cent of GNP annually, ODA in 1995 stood at 0.29 per cent, its lowest level since 1973 (GEF 1997).

However, foundations, individuals, corporations and bequests committed to sustainable development have brought a new meaning to the word 'charity', contributing a total of US$129 billion in 1994 (Myers and Brown 1997). This figure was estimated to increase by 9 per cent in 1995 to US$143.85 billion.

## Multilateral environmental agreements
### *UN Framework Convention on Climate Change*
The ability of IPCC to provide evidence that climate change posed a real threat encouraged governments at the Summit to sign the UN Framework Convention on Climate Change (UNFCCC). This became the centrepiece of the Summit and entered into force in 1994; it had 186 parties as of December 2001. The development of the convention can be traced back to

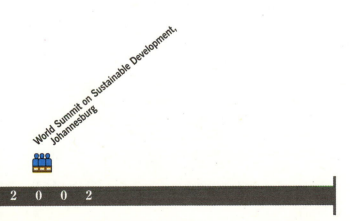

the 1990 Second World Climate Conference in which the ministerial declaration was the vehicle for pushing ahead with policy development and the establishment of the Global Climate Observing System (GCOS).

The primary goal of the UNFCCC is to stabilize greenhouse gas emissions at levels that will prevent dangerous anthropogenic interference with the global climate. The principle of 'common but differentiated responsibilities' that was embraced by this convention has guided the adoption of a regulatory structure. This principle reflected the reality that most emissions of greenhouse gases are from industrialized states.

The Kyoto Protocol, which set actual targets for emissions reductions, was opened for signature in 1997. As of December 2001, 84 Parties had signed and 46 Parties had ratified or acceded to the Protocol (UNFCCC 2001). A notable exception was the United States which announced its decision not to ratify the Protocol in early 2001.

## The Convention on Biological Diversity

The CBD came into force in 1993. It was the first global agreement on the conservation and sustainable use of biodiversity and serves as a blueprint for national action. The Convention establishes three main goals: the conservation of biological diversity, the sustainable use of its components, and the fair and equitable sharing of the benefits from the use of genetic resources. Many biodiversity issues are addressed, including habitat preservation, intellectual property rights, biosafety and indigenous peoples' rights.

The Convention stands as a landmark in international law, noted for its comprehensive, ecosystems approach to biodiversity protection. The treaty has gained rapid and widespread acceptance. By December 2001, a total of 182 governments had ratified the agreement. A supplementary agreement to the Convention, the Cartagena Protocol on Biosafety, was adopted in January 2000 to address the potential risks posed by cross-border trade and accidental releases of living genetically modified organisms. The adoption of the biosafety protocol is a success for developing countries which called for it. The protocol had been signed by 103 parties and ratified by 9 as of December 2001. The CBD has also influenced the enactment of a law which seeks to regulate genetic resources within the Andean Pact nations of Bolivia, Colombia, Ecuador, Peru and Venezuela. The law became effective in July 1996 (Centre for Science and

### The role of developing countries in the CBD negotiations

Unhappy with the early draft of the CBD in November 1991, the Geneva-based South Centre urged developing countries to reject the draft and ... 'insist that any negotiation on biodiversity should be linked to a negotiation on biotechnology, and more generally to IPR (intellectual property rights). This combined trend towards the privatization of knowledge and gene resources is a serious threat to the South's development and should be countered.'

During negotiations, the South:

- stressed national sovereignty over natural resources;
- called for technology transfer to developing countries on a preferential basis;
- pushed for supremacy of CBD over other institutions such as the World Intellectual Property Organization (WIPO) and the General Agreement on Tariffs and Trade (GATT); and
- called for a protocol on biosafety.

*Source: Centre for Science and Environment 1999*

Environment 1999). Despite the success of the convention, negotiations before its adoption were often acrimonious (see box).

## The Convention to Combat Desertification

Though negotiations were not completed until 1994, the UN Convention to Combat Desertification (CCD) developed out of the process associated with the 1992 UNCED. However, its history extends back to the 1970s. It became effective in 1996 and had 177 parties as of December 2001. The CCD has been described as a 'Rio stepchild' (Centre for Science and Environment 1999) because it did not get as much attention as the UNFCCC and CBD. The industrialized countries opposed it because 'they were not willing to undertake any financial responsibility for arresting the process of desertification' which is not perceived as a global problem (Centre for Science and Environment 1999). While it has been projected that a 20-year global effort to combat desertification would cost US$10-22 billion annually, funding countries provided a meagre US$1 billion in 1991 for desertification control worldwide (Centre for Science and Environment 1999).

Although the CCD has modest financial support compared to the UNFCCC and the CBD, the convention is distinctive for two reasons:

- It endorses and employs a 'bottom-up' approach to

international environmental cooperation. Under the terms of the CCD, activities related to the control and alleviation of desertification and its effects are to be closely linked to the needs and participation of local land users and non-governmental organizations.

- It employs detailed regional annexes, sometimes more detailed than the core treaty itself, that address the particularities of the desertification problem in specific regions such as Africa, Latin America and the Caribbean, and the Northern Mediterranean (Raustiala 2001).

The central substantive commitment in the CCD is the obligation to develop 'national action programmes', in conjunction with local stakeholders. These programmes delineate the tasks that the parties will undertake to implement the CCD. For example, parties must make the prevention of desertification a priority in national policies and must promote awareness of desertification among their citizens.

## The Commission on Sustainable Development

The establishment of the CSD in December 1992 was a direct outcome of the Summit. Although the goal of sustainable development was established in the 1980s, it was not until Rio that an international body was assigned the mandate to oversee and help the international community achieve this goal (see box). Although this was a major step, the Commission has been criticized for being a weak response to problems of institutional capacity, and has encountered apathy from high-level government ministers (Long 2000). The integration of economic, social and environmental policies — a requirement of sustainable development spelled out by the Brundtland Commission — continues to challenge institutions at all levels.

## Rio + 5

Five years after UNCED, the international community convened a review summit, known as Rio + 5, in New York where concerns were expressed about the slow implementation of *Agenda 21*. The general conclusion was that while some progress had been made in terms of sustainable development, 'many of the targets of *Agenda 21* are a long way from being met' (UN 1997).

---

### Mandate of the Commission on Sustainable Development

The CSD, which was established in December 1992 under the UN Economic and Social Council, is composed of 53 members elected for terms of office of three years. The Commission meets annually for a period of two to three weeks, meeting first in June 1993. Broadly, the role of the Commission is to:

- review progress at the international, regional and national levels in the implementation of recommendations and commitments contained in the final documents of UNCED — *Agenda 21*, the Rio Declaration on Environment and Development, and the Forest Principles;
- elaborate policy guidance and options for future activities as a follow-up to UNCED and to achieve sustainable development; and
- promote dialogue and build partnerships for sustainable development with governments, the international community and the major groups identified in *Agenda 21* as key actors outside central government which have a major role to play in the transition towards sustainable development.

*Source: UN 2001*

---

'Here in the United States, we must do better. With 4 per cent of the world's population, we produce 20 per cent of its greenhouse gases. So we must do better, and we will.' — *Bill Clinton, President of the United States, Rio + 5, 1997*

---

'It is a matter of deep concern to India that five years after Rio, there is a discernible effort to erode the framework for partnership built at Rio — notably the principle of common but differentiated responsibilities — with efforts to prescribe equal obligations and liabilities on unequal players.' — *Professor Saifuddin Soz, Indian Minister of Environment and Forests, Rio + 5, 1997*

---

## Other important international conferences

The principles of sustainable development were reaffirmed throughout the 1990s at numerous international conferences such as the:

- 1993 World Conference on Human Rights in Vienna;
- 1994 International Conference on Population and Development in Cairo;
- 1994 Global Conference on the Sustainable Development of Small Island Developing States in Bridgetown, Barbados;
- 1995 World Summit for Social Development in Copenhagen;
- 1995 Fourth World Conference on Women in Beijing;

'The five years that elapsed since the Rio Conference have clearly shown that changes in the global political and economic structure have not been followed through by commensurate progress in the fight against poverty and the predatory use of natural resources.' — *President Fernando Henrique Cardoso of Brazil, whose country hosted the 1992 Earth Summit, Rio + 5, 1997*

- 1996 United Nations Conference on Human Settlements (Habitat II) in Istanbul; and
- 1996 World Food Summit in Rome.

## Stakeholder participation in sustainable development

Much of this international activity was mirrored by attempts by the private sector to improve its environmental performance. Action was encouraged by the creation of the World Business Council for Sustainable Development (WBCSD) in 1995 which has done much to encourage industry to look for improvements in profitability by reducing waste of both resources and energy and by reducing emissions. The WBCSD now has hundreds of members, of whom many have managed to effect remarkable savings for both themselves and the environment (Rabobank International 1998). In 1996, the International Organization for Standardization created a new voluntary standard for environmental management systems in industry, the ISO 14 000 (International Organization for Standardization 2001).

By the end of the decade, transnational corporations had greatly improved their environmental image; indeed, their environmental performance was often better than that of many small and medium-sized enterprises (Kuhndt and Van der Lugt 2000). Corporate environmental reporting also became more common during the 1990s and the Global Reporting Initiative was created to establish a common framework for voluntary reporting of the environmental, economic and social performance of an organization (GRI 2001). The GRI seeks to elevate enterprise-level sustainable development reporting to the same level of credibility, comparability and consistency as financial reporting.

Civil society was also active, notably in its attempts to create an Earth Charter which articulates the 'fundamental ethical principles for a sustainable way of life'. Hundreds of groups and thousands of individuals have been involved. The Charter, which was originally meant to have been adopted at the Earth Summit, has been refined in a process spearheaded by the Earth Council and Green Cross International. The Charter is available in 18 languages on the Secretariat's website (Earth Charter 2001).

Civil society has not, however, limited itself to campaigns such as the Earth Charter but has also organized massive demonstrations in different parts of the world, many of them against the perceived threat of globalization. Such attempts are themselves reflections of the globalization process, and of the now extraordinary power of the Internet which has undergone explosive growth. While in 1993, there were only 50 pages on the World Wide Web, these had multiplied by a million by the end of the decade (UN 2000), making radical changes to the way many people live and work — mainly in the rich industrialized countries. Even though 'electrons are cheap', at the end of the 1990s 88 per cent of Internet users lived in industrialized countries, which collectively represented just 17 per cent of the world's population (UNDP 1999). This was a sobering conclusion to the end of the 1990s: in at least one important sense, the voices and concerns of the poor majority — for all the decade's rhetoric — were still being left out of the global conversation.

## The Comprehensive Nuclear Test Ban Treaty

An important milestone in international cooperation with a bearing on the environment came in 1996 with the adoption of the Comprehensive Nuclear Test Ban Treaty (CTBT) by the United Nations General Assembly in New York. The CTBT, which prohibits all nuclear test explosions in all environments, was opened for signature in New York on 24 September 1996, when it was signed by 71 States, including the five nuclear weapon states. As of August 2001, 161 States had signed the Treaty and 79 had ratified it. An elaborate global verification scheme is being developed by the Preparatory Commission of the CTBT for when the Treaty enters into force, which will be 80 days after the 44 States listed in Annex 2 to the Treaty have all ratified; 31 had done so by August 2001 (CTBTO 2001).

## 2000 and beyond: reviewing the agenda

Despite many setbacks, the past 30 years have provided a strong foundation on which to build sustainable development over the coming decades. The prevailing mood in environmental circles is cautiously optimistic about future progress in general — though this is tempered by several important unknowns, including notably the threat of climate change.

### Environmental interest and awareness rekindled

Environmental interest and awareness in 2002 have been stimulated by preparations for the World Summit on Sustainable Development. There have also been a number of other interesting developments which may have far-reaching impacts. One of these is the greater willingness among disparate groups to work together on a common cause. The United Nations Secretary-General Kofi Annan has supported the establishment of the Global Compact (see box), which aims to build synergy between the private sector and three United Nations organizations — UNEP, the International Labour Organization (ILO) and the UN Office of the High Commissioner for Human Rights (UN 1999). For the first time, principles that embrace protection of human rights, sound labour laws and environmental responsibility are addressed by these offices in a single international agreement.

### Chemicals

Thirty years ago, many toxic and persistent chemicals were considered to be not only resources but also pollutants adversely affecting human health and the environment, particularly where they could be accumulated up the food chain or transported long distances over the globe. Today, chemicals are seen as even more essential to development, and as a resource that needs to be managed to protect or even enhance human health and the environment. This sound management of chemicals applies to both those anthropogenically produced and those of natural origin, including those generated through biological processes.

The international community has recently concluded a landmark convention to control the use of a group of persistent toxic organic compounds (see

box). In December, 2000 representatives of 122 governments finalized the text of a legally binding treaty for implementing international action on certain persistent organic pollutants (POPs). The Stockholm Convention on Persistent Organic Pollutants, signed in May 2001 and which had 111 signatories and 2 Parties as of December 2001, sets out control measures

---

### Principles of the Global Compact

**Human Rights**
- Principle 1: support and respect the protection of international human rights; and
- Principle 2: ensure that corporations are not complicit in human rights abuses.

**Labour**
- Principle 3: freedom of association and the effective recognition of the right to collective bargaining;
- Principle 4: the elimination of all forms of forced and compulsory labour;
- Principle 5: the effective abolition of child labour; and
- Principle 6: the elimination of discrimination in respect of employment and occupation.

**Environment**
- Principle 7: support a precautionary approach to environmental challenges;
- Principle 8: undertake initiatives to promote greater environmental responsibility; and
- Principle 9: encourage the development and diffusion of environmentally friendly technologies.

*Source: UN 1999*

---

### Stockholm Convention on Persistent Organic Pollutants

The POPs treaty covers an initial list of 12 chemicals, the so-called 'dirty dozen':

- eight pesticides — aldrin, chlordane, dichlorodiphenyltrichloroethane (DDT), dieldrin, endrin, heptachlor, mirex and toxaphene;
- two industrial chemicals — polychlorinated biphenyls (PCBs) and hexachlorobenzene (which is also a pesticide); and
- two unwanted by-products of combustion and industrial processes (dioxins and furans).

A health-related exemption has been granted for DDT, which is still needed in many countries to control malarial mosquitoes until 2025. Governments may also maintain existing equipment that contains PCBs in a way that prevents leaks to give them time to arrange for PCB-free replacements. PCBs have been widely used in electrical transformers and other equipment.

The Convention also designates GEF as its primary financial mechanism, on an interim basis, through which developed countries will channel new and additional resources to help countries with economies in transition and developing countries to implement their obligations. It also provides for a science-based process, incorporating precaution, to review other chemicals for possible addition by the Conference of the Parties.

*Source: UNEP 2001*

covering 12 chemicals. The control provisions call for eliminating production and use of intentionally produced POPs and eliminating unintentionally produced POPs where this is feasible (UNEP 2001).

Since the Stockholm Conference, the global chemicals industry has grown almost ninefold and an annual growth rate of about 3 per cent is expected to continue over the next three decades, with a considerable increase in trade (OECD 2001). This will increase the risk of exposing an increasing number of people and the environment to new chemicals and the potential for the emergence of new diseases of chemical origin.

Information about the release of chemicals into the environment is now much more widely available than used to be the case. North America has led action in this area, in particular with the US Toxics Release Inventory (TRI 2001) enacted through the Emergency Planning and Community Right-to-Know Act (EPCRA) in the United States in 1986. EPCRA's purpose is to inform communities and citizens of chemical hazards in their areas. The Act requires businesses to report the locations and quantities of chemicals stored on-site to state and local governments. Through EPCRA, the US Congress mandated that a Toxics Release Inventory (TRI) be made public. TRI provides citizens with information about potentially hazardous

chemicals and their use so that communities have more power to hold companies accountable and make informed decisions about how toxic chemicals are to be managed.

## The Millennium Summit

Environmental issues featured prominently during the United Nations Millennium Summit hosted by Secretary-General Kofi Annan in New York in 2000 (see box below). While recognition of the importance of environmental issues at this summit was encouraging, the actual progress report was not. The Secretary-General was blunt in his comments regarding environmental management, stating that the international community was failing to provide future generations the freedom to 'sustain their lives on this planet. On the contrary', he said, 'we have been plundering our children's future heritage to pay for environmentally unsustainable practices in the present' (UN 2000).

## Climate and energy consumption

In early 2001, IPCC announced that the evidence for anthropogenic climate change was getting stronger, that warming was happening faster, and that the consequences looked more severe than first predicted. The expert panel, made up of thousands of scientists

---

### UN Secretary-General's key proposals presented to the Millennium Summit

**Freedom from want: the Development Agenda**

Heads of State or Government are urged to take action in the following areas:

- *Poverty:* to halve, by 2015, the proportion of the world's people (currently 22 per cent) whose income is less than one dollar a day.
- *Water:* to halve, by 2015, the proportion of people who do not have access to safe drinking water (currently 20 per cent).
- *Education:* to narrow the gender gap in primary and secondary education by 2005; and to ensure that, by 2015, all children complete a full course of primary education.
- *HIV/AIDS:* to halt, and begin to reverse, the spread of HIV/AIDS by 2015 by:
  — adopting as an explicit goal the reduction of HIV infection rates in persons 15 to 24 years of age, by 25 per cent within the most affected countries before the year 2005, and by 25 per cent globally before 2010;
  — setting explicit prevention targets: by 2005 at least 90 per cent, and by 2010 at least 95 per cent, of young men and women must have access to HIV-preventive information and services; and
  — urging every seriously affected country to have a national plan of action in place within one year of the Summit.

- *Clearing the Slums:* to endorse and act upon the *Cities Without Slums* plan launched by the World Bank and United Nations to improve the lives of 100 million slum dwellers by 2020.

**A sustainable future: the Environmental Agenda**

Heads of State or Government are urged to adopt a new ethic of conservation and stewardship; and, as first steps:

- *Climate Change:* to adopt and ratify the Kyoto Protocol, so that it can enter into force by 2002, and to ensure that its goals are met, as a step towards reducing emissions of greenhouse gases.
- *Green Accounting:* to consider incorporating the United Nations system of 'green accounting' into their own national accounts, in order to integrate environmental issues into mainstream economic policy.
- *Ecosystem Assessment:* to provide financial support for, and become actively engaged in, the Millennium Ecosystem Assessment, a major international collaborative effort to map the health of the planet.
- *Earth Summit +10:* to prepare the ground for the adoption of concrete and meaningful actions by the world's leaders at the 10-year follow-up to the Earth Summit in 2002.

*Source: UN 2000*

from around the world, predicted that average temperatures would rise between 1.4 and 5.8°C over the 21st century. IPCC states that: 'There is new and stronger evidence that most of the warming observed over the last 50 years is attributable to human activities ... Furthermore, it is very likely that the 20th century warming has contributed significantly to the observed sea level rise, through thermal expansion of sea water and widespread loss of land ice' (IPCC 2001).

The implications of this faster rise in global temperatures cut across broad areas of economic, social and environmental concern and add urgency to the need for controls on factors contributing to global warming. The first and most important of these is energy consumption. Only in Europe is the per capita consumption of fossil fuels falling, and there only slowly.

## El Niño

Increasing attention is also being paid to El Niño as a result of a particularly severe episode during 1997–98 which caused millions of dollars worth of damage. It also gave rise to a major study by several institutions of the lessons learned from that episode and of what could be done to mitigate the effects of future El Niños (see box right).

## Scientific developments

In the early years of the 3rd millennium, scientific advances continue to provide ethical and environmental challenges. A scientific breakthrough whose impact on humankind and ultimately the environment is still uncertain is the mapping of the human genome. The benefits of such mapping include learning the underlying causes of thousands of genetic diseases and predicting the likelihood of their occurrence in any individual. Genetic information might also be used to predict sensitivities to various industrial and environmental agents. While concerns about misuse and loss of personal privacy exist, many of the ramifications of mapping the human genome will be recognized only as science and technology merge in the future applications of this new tool (Human Genome Project 1996).

Also controversial is the increasing use of genetically modified organisms (GMOs).

As described in *GEO-2000* (UNEP 1999), the rapid evolutionary character of microbes and viruses,

### Sea levels during the 1997–98 El Niño

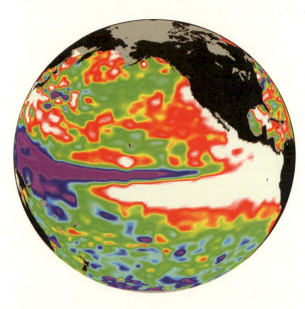

Satellite image records sea levels in the Pacific on 10 November 1997. El Niños are characterized by higher sea levels (red and white areas) on the South American side of the southern Pacific, lower levels (blue areas) on the other side

*Source: Topex/Poseidon NASA*

### Once burned, twice shy: the 1997–98 El Niño

Thousands of human casualties and tens of billions of dollars in economic damage will continue to befall the world's developing countries every two to seven years until an investment is made to improve forecasting and preparedness against El Niño, according to a new international study. The study was developed by teams of researchers working in 16 countries in Latin America, Asia and Africa. Four United Nations organizations collaborated in the preparation of the study – UNEP, the UN University, WMO and the International Strategy for Disaster Reduction – together with the US-based National Center for Atmospheric Research.

More reliable El Niño forecasts and the ability of governments to react quickly to them are critical. In the absence of such capabilities, vulnerable people, infrastructure and economies in many parts of the world will continue to suffer periodically from El Niño events through floods, fires, drought, cyclones and outbreaks of infectious disease.

Few forecasters came close to forecasting El Niño's onset in mid-1997 and none was able to grasp the magnitude of the 'El Niño of the Century' until it was well under way. National and regional forecasters typically provided predictions of El Niño impacts that in many cases were too general to be used with confidence by national and local decision-makers. Losses from the El Niño in 1997-98 included thousands of deaths and injuries from severe storms, heat waves, fires, floods, frosts and drought. Estimates of El Niño-related damage ranged from US$32 to US$96 billion.

*Source: UNU 2001*

coupled with increased transport, presents potential surprises in this millennium. The reality behind this statement was revealed by the discovery of bovine spongiform encephalopathy (mad cow disease) in the United Kingdom and other parts of Europe, and then more dramatically with the spread of foot-and-mouth disease in the United Kingdom.

The effects of increased transport of livestock and feed material across political boundaries intensified the spread of these diseases, leading to the destruction of many farm animals and concern for transmission to and from wild populations. Although foot-and-mouth is commonly found in many developing countries, it is the industrialized nations that feel its effects most acutely. Although the disease is rarely lethal, it is debilitating and reduces productivity. In intensive industrial agricultural systems, where profit

## The costs of global warming

A report by Munich Re, a member of UNEP's financial services initiative, has estimated the potential financial consequences of the IPCC predictions:

- Losses due to more frequent tropical cyclones, loss of land as a result of rising sea levels and damage to fishing stocks, agriculture and water supplies, could cost more than US$300 000 million annually.
- Globally some of the biggest losses would be in the area of energy. The water industry worldwide faces US$47 000 million of extra cost annually by 2050. Agriculture and forestry could lose up to US$42 000 million worldwide as a result of droughts, floods and fires if carbon dioxide levels reach twice their pre-industrial concentrations.
- Flood defence schemes to protect homes, factories and power stations from rising sea levels and storm surges may cost US$1000 million annually.
- Ecosystem losses, including mangrove swamps, coral reefs and coastal lagoons, could amount to more than US$70 000 million by 2050.

*Source: Berz 2001*

margins are low because of overproductivity, the economic impact of the disease cannot be tolerated.

## Globalization

Globalization has been described by some as the new Industrial Revolution. There are fears that it could result in a dangerous polarization between people and countries benefiting from the system and those that are merely passive recipients of its effects.

In its *Human Development Report 1999*, UNDP states that the one-fifth of the world's people living in the highest income countries have 86 per cent of world GDP, 82 per cent of world export markets, 68 per cent of foreign direct investment, and 74 per cent

of telephone lines (UNDP 1999). The bottom one-fifth, in the poorest countries, have about 1 per cent in each category. In the 1990s, more than 80 per cent of foreign direct investment in developing countries and those of Central and Eastern Europe went to just 20 countries, notably China.

The main engines of globalization are the transnational corporations, transnational media organizations, intergovernmental organizations and NGOs (Riggs 2000).

Globalization is more than the flow of money and commodities — it is the growing interdependence of the world's people through 'shrinking space, shrinking time and disappearing borders' (UNDP 1999). This offers great opportunities for enriching people's lives and creating a global community based on shared values. But markets, the UNDP report argues, have been allowed to dominate the process, and the benefits and opportunities have not been shared equitably.

One response to the rapid growth of economic globalization has been massive civil society demonstrations in many parts of the world. The November 1999 demonstration at the World Trade Organization (WTO) meeting in Seattle in which thousands of people campaigned against globalization was a major event. Increased public awareness was also apparent at the World Bank and International Monetary Fund meetings in Prague in September 2000, and at other meetings since.

These demonstrations show that citizens across the globe are insisting on being heard, and are demanding the implementation and enforcement of acceptable trade, labour and environmental standards worldwide. Many international organizations involved in regulating the global economy are now having to adjust their policies to include the participation of civil society in their activities. The irony of globalization and increased public awareness is that consumption by people in industrialized countries continues to grow, and poverty in developing regions continues to worsen.

## Water

Water will play a leading role in the agenda of the new millennium. The World Water Forum held in The Hague in March 2000 led to the adoption of 'water visions' for different regions of the world, helping to define the water agenda for the 21st century. About 6 000 people participated in the global forum but

One of the world's largest dams — the Itaipu hydroelectric plant in Brazil. The future of such projects is called in question by a new report

*Source: Julio Etchart, Still Pictures*

thousands more had been involved in regional preparatory meetings. It is hoped that mass participation in these events will keep issues of water quality and quantity at the forefront of the environment agenda so that the new regional visions can be successfully implemented.

Over the previous decades, large dams had emerged as one of the most significant and visible tools for the management of water resources. In November 2000, the World Commission on Dams released its report *Dams and Development: A New Framework for Decision-Making* which stated that over the past 50 years, dams have fragmented and transformed the world's rivers, displacing 40-80 million people in different parts of the world (WCD 2000). The report questions the value of many dams in meeting water and energy development needs when compared with alternatives. It thus represents a significant change of view of the value of dams, and may pave the way for different approaches to water development in the future.

## Assessments and early warning

The Millennium Ecosystem Assessment (MA), launched on World Environment Day 2001, will examine the processes that support life such as the world's grasslands, forests, rivers and lakes, farmlands and oceans. The US$21 million, four-year effort will involve 1 500 of the world's leading scientists (MA 2001).

'The Millennium Ecosystem Assessment will map the health of our planet, and so fill important gaps in the knowledge that we need to preserve it,' said UN Secretary-General Kofi Annan in announcing the study. 'All of us have to share the Earth's fragile ecosystems and precious resources, and each of us has to play a role in preserving them. If we are to go on living together on this earth, we must all be responsible for it.'

The study was launched to provide decision-makers with authoritative scientific knowledge concerning the impact of changes to the world's ecosystems on human livelihoods and the environment. It will provide governments, the private sector and local organizations with better information about steps that can be taken to restore the productivity of the world's ecosystems.

The MA has been recognized by governments as a mechanism to meet the assessment needs of three international environmental treaties — the UN

Convention on Biological Diversity, the Ramsar Convention on Wetlands and the UN Convention to Combat Desertification.

## Moving forward, making progress

A new spirit of collaboration and participation is apparent in the early years of the 21st century — likened by some to the 'Stockholm spirit of compromise'. With the World Summit on Sustainable Development scheduled for 2002 in Johannesburg, there is renewed hope for adoption of meaningful and effective actions by the world's major decision makers. The following four chapters, presenting global and regional environmental assessments, insights into environmental change and human vulnerability, scenarios for the future and implications for policy making, are intended as a substantive contribution to this debate.

## References: Chapter 1, Integrating Environment and Development, 1972–2002

Bennett, M. (1995). *The Gulf War*. Database for Use in Schools http://www.soton.ac.uk/~engenvir//environment/water/oil.gulf.war.html [Geo-1-002]

Berz, G. (2001). Insuring against Catastrophe. *Our Planet*. 12, 1, 19–20

Bingham, M.J. (1992). Elephants, Rhinos, Tuna, Bears, Oh My! ... Heated Debates at Recent CITES Convention. In Mahony, D.E. (1996). The Convention on International Trade in Endangered Species of Fauna and Flora: Addressing Problems in Global Wildlife Trade and Enforcement. *New England International & Comparative Law Annual* http://www.nesl.edu/annual/vol3/cite.htm [Geo-1-003]

Campbell, T. (1998). *The First E-mail Message: who sent it and what it said*. PreText Magazine http://www.pretext.com/mar98/features/story2.htm [Geo-1-004]

Carson, R. (1962). *Silent Spring*. New York, Houghton Mifflin

Centre for Science and Environment (1999). *Green Politics: Global Environmental Negotiations 1*. New Delhi, Centre for Science and Environment

Chenje, M., Mohamed-Katerere, J. and Ncube, W. (1996). *Environmental Rights and Fairness in Zimbabwe's Environmental Legislation*. Harare, Ministry of Environment and Tourism, Government of Zimbabwe

CITES Secretariat (2001). *The CITES Species*. CITES http://www.cites.org/eng/disc/species.shtml [Geo-1-005]

Clarke, R., and Timberlake, L. (1982). *Stockholm Plus Ten — Promises, Promises? The Decade Since the 1972 UN Environment Conference*. London, Earthscan

Commission to Study the Organization of Peace (1972). *The United Nations and the Human Environment — The Twenty-Second Report*. New York, United Nations

CTBTO (2001). *The Comprehensive Nuclear Test Ban Treaty*. Preparatory Commission for the Comprehensive Nuclear Test Ban Treaty Organization http://pws.ctbto.org/ [Geo-1-006]

Demkine, V. (2000). *Introduction to Environmental Policy*. Kiev, Ukraine, University of Kiev Mohyla Academy

Diamond, S. (1985). The Bhopal Disaster: How it Happened. *The New York Times*, 28 January 1985

Earth Charter (2001). *The Earth Charter*. The Earth Charter Initiative: promoting change for a sustainable future http://www.earthcharter.org/welcome/ [Geo-1-007]

EU (1993). *Towards Sustainability: A European Community Programme of Policy and Action in Relation to the Environment and Sustainable Development*. Brussels, Commission of the European Communities

Farman, J. C., Gardiner, B. G., and Shanklin, J. D. (1985). Large losses of total ozone in Antarctica reveal seasonal $ClO_x/NO_x$ interaction. *Nature*. 315, 207–10

GEF (1997). *The Global Environment Facility: A Self Assessment*. Global Environment Facility http://www.ecouncil.ac.cr/rio/focus/report/english/gef.htm [Geo-1-008]

GRI (2001). *Global Reporting Initiative*. Coalition for Environmentally Responsible Economics (CERES) and UNEP http://www.globalreporting.org [Geo-1-009]

Haas, P., Levy, M. and Parson, T. (1992). Appraising the Earth Summit: how should we judge UNCED's success? *Environment*. 34 (8), 6–11, 26–33

Hardin, G. (1968). The Tragedy of the Commons. *Science*. 162, 1243–48

Human Genome Project (1996). *To Know Ourselves*. US Department of Energy http://www.ornl.gov/hgmis/publicat/tko/08–ethical.html [Geo-1-010]

IEA (1999). *Energy Balances of OECD countries 1960-97, Energy Balances of Non-OECD countries 1971–97*. Paris, Organization of Economic Cooperation and Development, International Energy Agency

IFRC (2000). *World Disasters Report 2000*. Geneva, International Federation of Red Cross and Red Crescent Societies http://www.ifrc.org/publicat/wdr2001/chapter1.asp [Geo-1-012]

IPCC (2001). *Climate Change 2001: The Scientific Basis. Contribution of Working Group I to the Third Assessment Report of the Intergovernmental Panel on Climate Change*. Cambridge, United Kingdom, and New York, United States, Cambridge University Press

Island Press (1999). *The Environmental Impacts of War*. Island Press http://www.islandpress.org/ecocompass/war/war.html [Geo-1-014]

ISO (2001). *The ISO Survey of ISO 9000 and ISO 14000 Certificates*. Geneva, International Organization for Standardization http://www.iso.ch/iso/en/iso9000-14000/index.html [Geo-1-015]

IUCN, UNEP and WWF (1980). *World Conservation Strategy: Living Resource Conservation for Sustainable Development*. Gland, Switzerland, International Union for Conservation of Nature and Natural Resources

IUCN, UNEP and WWF (1991). *Caring for the Earth. A Strategy for Sustainable Living*. London, Earthscan

Kuhndt, M., and Van der Lugt, C. (2000). Der Kalender für effizientes Wirtschaften — Ein innovatives Instrument zur Verbesserung von Umweltleistungen in klein- und mittelst-indigen Unternehmen im globalen Maßstab (The Efficient Entrepreneur Calendar — an innovative tool to improve environmental performance in small and medium-sized enterprises worldwide). *Umweltwirtschaftforum*. Autumn 2000, Springer Publishing

Landsat (2001). *USGS Earthshots: satellite images of environmental change*. US Data Center of the US Geological Survey http://edc.usgs.gov/earthshots/slow/Saloum/Saloum1972.jpeg [Geo-1-016]

Long, B.L. (2000). *International Environmental Issues and the OECD 1950-2000: An Historical Perspective*. Paris, Organization for Economic Cooperation and Development

Lopez Ornat, A. (1996). *Strategies for Sustainability: Latin America*. London, Earthscan in association with IUCN http://www.iucn.org/themes/ssp/lastrategies.pdf [Geo-1-017]

MA (2001). *Millennium Ecosystem Assessment*. United Nations http://www.millenniumassessment.org/en/index.htm [Geo-1-018]

Meadows, D. and Meadows, D. (1972). *The Limits to Growth: A Report for the Club of Rome's Project on the Predicament of Mankind*. New York, Universe Books

Munich Re Group (2000). *Topics 2000: Natural Catastrophes — The Current Position. Special Millennium Issue*. Munich, Munich Re Group

Myers, N. and Brown, N. (1997). *The Role of Major US Foundations in the Implementation of Agenda 21: The Five-Year Follow-up to the Earth Summit*. The Earth Council http://www.ecouncil.ac.cr/rio/focus/report/english/foundatn.htm [Geo-1-019]

OECD (2001). *Environmental Outlook for the Chemical Industry*. Paris, Organization for Economic Cooperation and Development

Rabobank International (1998). *Sustainability: Choices and Challenges for Future Development*. Leiden, The Netherlands, Rabobank International

Ramsar Convention Bureau (2001). *The Ramsar Convention on Wetlands* http://www.ramsar.org [Geo-1-033]

Raustiala, K. (2001). *Reporting and Review Institutions in Ten Multilateral Environmental Agreements*. UNEP/DEWA Technical Report. Nairobi, United Nations Environment Programme

Riggs, F.W. (2000). *Globalization. Key Concepts*. University of Hawaii http://www2.hawaii.edu/~fredr/glocon.htm#TEHRANIAN [Geo-1-020]

SCEP (1970). *Man's Impact on the Global Environment*. Study of Critical Environmental Problems. Cambridge, Massachusetts, MIT Press

Stanley Foundation (1971). *Sixth Conference on the United Nations of the Next Decade*. Conference held 20–29 June 1971, Sianai, Romania

Strong, M. (1999). *Hunger, Poverty, Population and Environment. The Hunger Project Millennium Lecture, 7 April 1999*. Madras,India, The Hunger Project http://www.thp.org/reports/strong499.htm [Geo-1-021]

Topex/Poseidon (1997). *El Ni–o's warm water pool is increasing*. Jet Propulsion Laboratory, NASA http://photojournal.jpl.nasa.gov/tiff/PIA01085.tif [Geo-1-022]

TRI (2001). *Toxics Release Inventory: Community Right-To-Know*. US Environmental Protection Agency http://www.epa.gov/tri/general.htm [Geo-1-023]

UN (1982). *United Nations General Assembly 37th Session, Resolution 37/7*. New York, United Nations

UN (1993). *Report of the United Nations Conference on Environment and Development*. New York, United Nations

UN (1999). *The Global Compact: What It Is and Isn't*. United Nations http://www.unglobalcompact.org/gc/unweb.nsf/content/thenine.htm [Geo-1-024]

UN (2000). *We the Peoples — The Role of the United Nations in the 21st Century*. New York, United Nations http://www.un.org/millennium/sg/report/key.htm [Geo-1-001]

UN (2001). *Mandate of the Commission for Sustainable Development*. United Nations http://www.un.org/esa/sustdev/csdback.htm [Geo-1-025]

UN-ECOSOC (1997). *Overall Progress Achieved since the United Nations Conference on Environment and Development. Report of the Secretary General*. New York, United Nations http://www.un.org/documents/ecosoc/cn17/1997/ecn171997-2.htm [Geo-1-026]

UNCHS (1996). *An Urbanizing World: Global Report on Human Settlements — 1996*. Nairobi, United Nations Commission on Human Settlements

UNDP (1999). *Human Development Report 1999*. New York, United Nations Development Programme http://www.undp.org/hdro/E1.html [Geo-1-027]

UNEP (1981). *In Defence of the Earth*. Nairobi, UNEP

UNEP (1999). *GEO-2000*. United Nations Environment Programme. London and New York, Earthscan

UNEP (2000). *Action on Ozone*. Nairobi, UNEP

UNEP (2001). *The Stockholm Convention on Persistent Organic Pollutants*. UNEP Chemicals/WHO – GEENET http://irptc.unep.ch/pops/newlayout/negotiations.htm [Geo-1-028]

UNEP/CHW (1995). *Evaluation of the Effectiveness of the Basel Convention on the Control of Transboundary Movements of Hazardous Wastes and Their Disposal*. 3/Inf.7. Nairobi, UNEP/CHW

UNEP/UNCTAD (1974). *Patterns of Resource Use, Environment and Development Strategies*. Conference held June 1974, Cocoyoc, Mexico

UNESCO (1997). Address by UNESCO Director-General at the Special Session of the General Assembly: Earth Summit +5, 25 June 1997

UNESCO (2001). *The World Heritage List*. Paris, UNESCO http://www.unesco.org/whc/heritage.htm [Geo-1-029]

UNFCCC (2001). *The Convention and Kyoto Protocol*. Secretariat of the UNFCCC http://www.unfccc.de/resource/convkp.html [Geo-1-030]

UNHCR (2000). *The State of the World's Refugees: Fifty Years of Humanitarian Action*. Oxford, Oxford University Press http://www.unhcr.ch/sowr2000/toc2.htm [Geo-1-031]

United Nations Population Division (1998). *World Population Prospects 1950–2050 (The 1998 Revision)*. New York, United Nations

UNU (2001). *Once Burned, Twice Shy? Lessons Learned from the 1997–98 El Niño*. Tokyo, United Nations University http://www.esig.ucar.edu/un/index.html [Geo-1-032]

US Government (1980). *Entering the Twenty-first Century: The Global 2000 Report*. Washington DC, US Government Printing Office

WCD (2000). *Dams and Development: A New Framework for Decision-Making. The Report of the World Commission on Dams*. London, Earthscan http://www.damsreport.org/wcd–overview.htm [Geo-1-033]

WCED (1987). *Our Common Future: The World Commission on Environment and Development*. Oxford, Oxford University Press

*Chapter*

# 2

# State of the Environment and Policy Retrospective: 1972–2002

State of the environment (SOE) reporting was introduced in the United States with the enactment of the 1969 National Environmental Policy Act (NEPA); it was made a global activity in the declaration adopted at the Stockholm Conference on the Human Environment in 1972. In the early years, the focus was on the state of the biophysical environment — land, freshwater, forests and wildlife, for example. People were generally reported as a threat to the environment. But SOE reporting has over the years become more integrated and now takes into account the complex human–environment interactions in assessing and reporting on the changing state of the environment.

Subsequently, SOE reporting has been established at virtually every level — local, national, sub-regional, regional and global. Many approaches have been used: some focused on media such as land and water, some on sectoral themes such as agriculture and forestry, some on issues such as land degradation and pollution (and some combined these approaches). Other frameworks have included the pressure-state-response (PSR) and later the driving force-pressure-state-impact-response (DPSIR). These different approaches have served their purpose but their inherent weakness is a linear approach to complex ecological processes and human–environment interactions. The reports often down played the fact that people not only have an impact on the environment but also that the environment has an impact on people.

Over time, therefore, a more integrated environmental assessment and reporting framework has emerged; one that aims to show the cause-and-effect of human–nature linkages. It seeks to connect causes (drivers and pressures) to environmental outcomes (state) to activities (policies and decisions) that have shaped the environment over the past three decades, and the impacts such changes now have on people.

The analysis is first by theme — socio-economic trends, land, forests, biodiversity, freshwater, coastal and marine areas, atmosphere, urban areas and disasters — but the holistic nature of the environment is emphasized where necessary. These thematic issues are analysed from first the global level then at GEO regional level: Africa, Asia and the Pacific, Europe, Latin America and the Caribbean, North America, West Asia and the Polar Regions. The global sections highlight many of the major issues under each sector, showing trends over the past three decades. The analysis uses the 1972 Stockholm Conference as the baseline, discussing the evolution of the issue and how the international community has tried to address the problems.

At the regional level, each region identified for analysis — through various consultation processes — two or three key regional issues under each sector or theme. These issues are discussed in the following pages and are listed in the table opposite. The table highlights common issues across the different regions, showing the global nature of the environmental issues facing the world today. In addition, the table identifies some unique regional differences, which have called for unique regional responses. Throughout the report, region-specific sections and graphics are colour-coded for easy identification (see table for regional colours).

Sub-regional differentiation analyses are also provided where appropriate. National level examples are presented to stress certain developments. The ultimate purpose of policy evaluation under integrated assessment is to identify successes and failures in environmental policy development and implementation as guidance for future policy initiatives.

The analyses are supported with graphics and other illustrations developed using data specially compiled for the GEO-3 30-year assessment period. The data were compiled from many different sources and then, wherever possible, aggregated from national to sub-regional, regional and global levels, making comparisons possible at these different levels. The GEO-3 Data Portal, some of the contents of which are available on a CD-ROM available with this report, addressed some of the data issues first identified in *GEO-1* in 1997: the harmonization of national datasets and acquisition of global datasets.

This chapter emphasizes integration across regions, between the state of the environment and policy, between the past and future, between thematic areas, and among sectors, for example, environmental, economic, social and cultural. It also tries to analyse policy (social responses) in relation to specific environmental issues, showing positive and negative policy impacts on the environment and how the environment can drive policy, both retrospectively and proactively. It covers the impacts of public and private sector policies, and regional and global policies, including multilateral environmental agreements. The

## Key environmental issues by GEO region

| | Land | Forests | Biodiversity | Freshwater | Coastal and marine | Atmosphere | Urban areas | Disasters |
|---|---|---|---|---|---|---|---|---|
| **Africa** | • Degradation and desertification<br>• Inappropriate and inequitable land tenure | • Deforestation<br>• Loss of forest quality | • Habitat degradation and loss<br>• Bushmeat trade | • Variability of water resources<br>• Water stress and scarcity<br>• Access to safe water and sanitation<br>• Deteriorating water quality<br>• Wetlands loss | • Coastal area erosion and degradation<br>• Pollution<br>• Climate change and sea-level rise | • Air quality<br>• Climate variability and vulnerability to climate change<br>• Floods and drought | • Rapid urbanization<br>• Solid waste<br>• Water supply and sanitation<br>• Air pollution | • Drought<br>• Floods<br>• Armed conflict |
| **Asia and the Pacific** | • Land degradation<br>• Desertification<br>• Land use change | • Forest degradation<br>• Deforestation | • Habitat loss<br>• Forest loss and degradation<br>• Alien species | • Water scarcity<br>• Pollution | • Degradation of coastal and marine resources<br>• Pollution due to mining and coastal development | • Air quality<br>• Ozone depletion<br>• Greenhouse gas emissions and climate change | • Air pollution<br>• Waste management<br>• Water supply and sanitation | • Floods<br>• Drought<br>• Volcanoes<br>• Earthquakes |
| **Europe** | • Land use<br>• Soil degradation, sealing and contamination<br>• Soil erosion | • Loss of natural forests<br>• Forest degradation<br>• Sustainable forest management | • Agricultural intensification<br>• Genetically modified organisms | • Water quantity and quality<br>• Policy and legislative framework | • Coastal erosion<br>• Pollution | • Air pollution<br>• Stratospheric ozone depletion<br>• Greenhouse gas emissions | • Air quality<br>• Noise pollution<br>• Solid waste | • Storms and floods<br>• Earthquakes<br>• Human-caused disasters |
| **Latin America and the Caribbean** | • Land degradation<br>• Land tenure | • Deforestation<br>• Forest degradation | • Habitat loss and degradation<br>• Overexploitation of resources and illegal trade | • Decreasing water available per capita<br>• Water quality | • Habitat conversion and destruction<br>• Pollution<br>• Overexploitation of fisheries | • Air pollution<br>• Ozone depletion<br>• Air quality | • Solid waste<br>• Water supply and sanitation<br>• Air quality | • Drought<br>• Hurricanes<br>• Floods<br>• Earthquakes<br>• Spills of hazardous substances |
| **North America** | • Land degradation<br>• Pesticides | • Forest health<br>• Old growth forests | • Habitat destruction and degradation<br>• Bio-invasion | • Groundwater<br>• Great Lakes water quality | • Conversion of fragile ecosystems<br>• Overexploitation of marine resources<br>• Pollution | • Stratospheric ozone depletion<br>• Greenhouse gases and climate change | • Urban sprawl<br>• Ecological footprint | • Floods and climate change<br>• Forest fires |
| **West Asia** | • Land degradation<br>• Rangeland deterioration | • Degradation<br>• Overexploitation<br>• Sustainable forest management | • Habitat degradation and loss<br>• Overexploitation of species | • Increasing water demand<br>• Overexploitation of groundwater<br>• Water quality | • Coastal development and urbanization<br>• Overexploitation of resources<br>• Marine pollution | • Air pollution<br>• Ozone-depleting substances<br>• Climate change | • Land conversion<br>• Solid waste | • Drought<br>• Oil discharges<br>• Armed conflict |
| **Polar Regions** | • Degradation<br>• Erosion<br>• Climate change | • Boreal forest issues<br>• Threats to forest tundra | • Climate change<br>• Ozone depletion<br>• Overexploitation | • Alien species<br>• Pollution | • Overexploitation of fisheries<br>• Pollution<br>• Climate change | • Stratospheric ozone depletion<br>• Long-range air pollution<br>• Climate change | • Sanitation and waste | • Floods<br>• Oil discharges<br>• Pest invasion |

analysis takes into consideration not only environmental policy but also the impacts of general policies on environmental issues, such as broader social and economic policy trends with environmental repercussions.

Another important component of this chapter is the use of satellite images to illustrate environmental change over the past 30 years. The images were generated by Landsat, which coincidentally was launched in 1972 — the same year the Stockholm Conference was held. The Landsat images, which are placed in one or sometimes two pages at the end of each section, under the rubric 'Our changing environment', highlight environmental changes at different locations in different regions.

*Note:*
*This table represents the two or three key thematic issues by region which are covered in this chapter. Due to the DPSIR framework used for the analysis, one issue may be covered under two or more themes. For example, forest degradation may be a major driver of biodiversity loss in one region while in another it may be the key issue of concern*

UNEP S. Yoh, Topham Picturepoint

# Socio-economic background

## Global overview

Over the past 30 years, the world has undergone unprecedented social, economic, political and technological change. These interlinked components provide the backdrop against which to view changes in the state of the environment over the same period because they serve a dual purpose as some of the most forceful drivers of that environmental change.

### Human development

There have been some impressive gains in human development, particularly in the developing world: incomes and income poverty have improved, people are living longer, are healthier, more literate and better educated than ever before. Average annual incomes in developing countries have mostly risen: in real terms (constant US$1995) they rose during 1972-99 by 13 per cent in Africa, by 72 per cent in Asia and the Pacific and by 35 per cent in Latin America and the Caribbean; in West Asia they fell by 6 per cent (compiled from World Bank 2001). Nevertheless, the challenges remain daunting in the 21st century, with high levels of deprivation persisting across the world.

Approximately 1.2 billion people, or one-fifth of the world's population, still live in extreme poverty on less than US$1 a day, and 2.8 billion people, or almost half the world's population, on less than US$2 a day (UNDP 2001). Three-quarters of those in extreme poverty live in rural areas (IFAD 2001), and the majority are women. Poverty is not limited to developing countries: more than 130 million people in the developed countries of the Organization for Economic Cooperation and Development (OECD) are considered income-poor (UNDP 2001).

Ill health is related to environmental factors (WHO 1997, Murray and Lopez 1996) and poverty. Medical innovation, progress in basic health care and enabling social policies have resulted in dramatic increases in life expectancy and declines in infant mortality (UN 2000). Overall, a child born today can expect to live eight years longer than one born 30 years ago (UNDP 2001). However, poverty rates in both urban and rural areas, as well as major infectious diseases such as HIV/AIDS, tuberculosis and malaria are a threat to health successes over the past few decades.

Tremendous progress has also been made in terms of education in the past 30 years, and adult literacy

## Progress in human development over the past 30 years

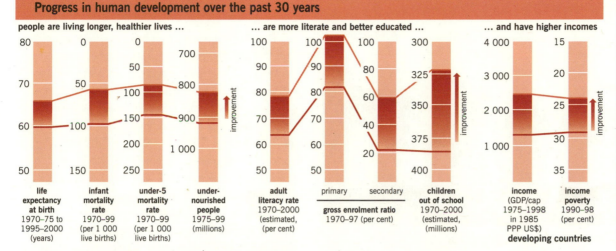

people are living longer, healthier lives ... | ... are more literate and better educated ... | ... and have higher incomes

| life expectancy at birth 1970–75 to 1995–2000 (years) | infant mortality rate 1970–99 (per 1 000 live births) | under-5 mortality rate 1970–99 (per 1 000 live births) | under-nourished people 1975–99 (millions) | adult literacy rate 1970–2000 (estimated, per cent) | primary / secondary gross enrolment ratio 1970–97 (per cent) | children out of school 1970–2000 (estimated, millions) | income (GDP/cap 1975–1998 in 1985 PPP US$) developing countries | income poverty 1990–98 (per cent) |

Bar charts left show that progress in human development has been made on several fronts. Poverty data refer to the share of the population living on less than US$1 a day

*Sources: FAO 2000, UNDP 2001, UNESCO 2000*

rates have increased from an estimated 63 per cent in 1970 to 79 per cent in 1998 (UNESCO 2000). Nevertheless, in 2000 there were still 854 million illiterate adults, of whom 543 million (63.6 per cent) were women, and 325 million children not attending school of whom 56 per cent were girls (UNDP 2001). Improved education (especially among women) together with capacity building is considered to have been critical in slowing down world population growth from an annual peak of 2.1 per cent in the early 1970s to 1.3 per cent in 2000 (UN 1997, UNFPA 2001).

### The Human Development Index (HDI)

The HDI combines indicators of the basic dimensions of human development (longevity, knowledge and a decent standard of living) to measure a country's overall achievements, categorized as high, medium or low human development. Between 1975 and 1999, there was overall progress in human development (see table), demonstrating the potential for poverty eradication and progressive human development in the coming decades. Nevertheless, 8 countries in economic transition and 12 in sub-Saharan Africa have suffered setbacks in the same period (see 'Africa' and 'Europe' in this section).

*Changing structure of human development (millions of people)*

|  | 1975 | 1999 |
| --- | --- | --- |
| High human development | 650 | 900 |
| Medium human development | 1 600 | 3 500 |
| Low human development | 1 100 | 500 |

*Note: numbers of people refer only to countries for which 1975 and 1999 data are available and therefore do not equal total population*
*Source: UNDP 2001*

### The changing population

World population increased from about 3.85 billion people in 1972 to 6.1 billion in mid-2000 (see figure on page 34), and is currently growing by 77 million people a year (UNFPA 2001). Most of the growth is concentrated in developing regions, with nearly two-thirds in Asia and the Pacific. Six countries accounted for 50 per cent of the annual growth: India (21.1 per cent), China (13.6 per cent), Pakistan (4.8 per cent), Nigeria (3.9 per cent), Bangladesh (3.7 per cent) and Indonesia (3.6 per cent) (United Nations Population Division 2001).

The population of industrialized regions, currently 1.2 billion, is expected to change little in the next 50 years while that of the developing regions is projected to increase from 4.9 billion in 2000 to 8.1 billion by 2050 (United Nations Population Division 2001). This difference is mainly due to levels of fertility. Less developed countries recorded fertility at 3.1 children per woman over the period 1995–2000, while developed countries recorded fertility at 1.57 children per woman over the same period — well below the replacement level of 2.1 children per woman (UNFPA 2001).

The gap in life expectancy between the developing and the more developed regions narrowed from 22 years in 1960 to less than 12 in 2000. Between 1995 and 2000, life expectancy in the industrialized regions was estimated to be 75 years, compared to about 63 years in developing regions (United Nations Population Division 2001). As world fertility continues to decline and life expectancy rises, the population of the world will age faster in the next 50 years than during the past half-century (United Nations

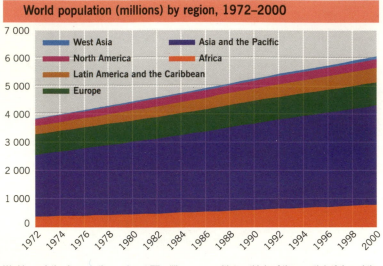

**World population (millions) by region, 1972–2000**

Legend:
- West Asia
- North America
- Latin America and the Caribbean
- Europe
- Asia and the Pacific
- Africa

World population is currently growing at 77 million a year, with two-thirds of the growth in Asia and the Pacific

*Source: compiled from United Nations Population Division 2001*

Population Division 2001). Nevertheless, the emergence of HIV/AIDS in the 1970s has depressed life expectancy in the most affected countries, and the disease is now the fourth most common cause of death worldwide. More than 60 million people have been infected with HIV since the 1970s, and 20 million have died. Of the 40 million living with HIV/AIDS worldwide, 70 per cent are in sub-Saharan Africa where it is the leading cause of death (UNAIDS 2001). Compared to Africa, the relative impact of the

HIV/AIDS epidemic in most other regions of the world is still low.

There have been notable population movements over the past 30 years due to rapid urbanization, international migration and the movement of refugees and displaced persons. The number of people living outside their own countries rose from 84 million in 1975 to an estimated 150 million people at the end of the 20th century (UNDP 1999, UNHCR 2000). The number of refugees rose from 2.7 million in 1972 to a peak of 18.3 million in 1992, and stood at 11.7 million at the end of 1999 (UNHCR 2000). By 2001, an estimated 22 million people 'of concern' were numbered among the world's refugees, returnees and persons displaced within their own countries (UNHCR 2001). The more developed regions are expected to continue being net receivers of international migrants, with an average gain of about two million a year over the next 50 years. Because of low fertility in recipient countries, this migration will have a significant impact on population growth in the developed regions (United Nations Population Division 2001).

## Economic development

The world economy has, on aggregate, expanded considerably over the past three decades, despite significant fluctuations. World gross national product (GNP) more than doubled from approximately US$14 300 billion in 1970 to an estimated US$29 995 billion in 1999 (Costanza and others 1997, World Bank 2001). However, these figures do not include the value of environmental goods and services which are critical to the Earth's life-support systems, and contribute to human welfare but are outside the market. An estimate of the economic value of these ecosystem services is between US$16 000 billion and US$54 000 billion a year, with an average of US$33 000 billion a year. This estimate should be considered a minimum because of the nature of the uncertainties (Costanza and others 1997).

The world economy grew by 3.1 per cent annually in real gross domestic product (GDP) between 1980 and 1990, and 2.5 per cent annually between 1990 and 1998, with annual per capita growth rates of 1.4 and 1.1 per cent respectively (UNCTAD 2000). There has, however, been significant regional variability over this period, with by far the highest growth rates in Asia and the Pacific, which contains more than half the world population. Per capita GDP (in constant

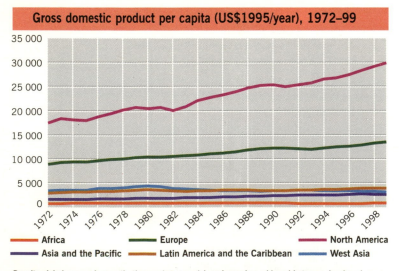

**Gross domestic product per capita (US$1995/year), 1972–99**

Legend:
- Africa
- Asia and the Pacific
- Europe
- Latin America and the Caribbean
- North America
- West Asia

Despite global economic growth, the gap between rich and poor has widened between developed and developing countries; per capita incomes have risen only marginally except in Europe and North America

*Source: compiled from World Bank 2001*

US$1995) almost doubled in Northwest Pacific and East Asia during 1972-99, growing by an annual average of 2.4 per cent a year (compiled from World Bank 2001); by contrast, it fell in sub-Saharan Africa.

Despite global economic growth, the gap between rich and poor has widened both between developed and developing countries and within countries, particularly in Latin America and sub-Saharan Africa (UNDP 2001). Per capita incomes have risen only marginally in most regions, with the exceptions of Europe and North America (see figure on page 34). Currently 3.5 billion people in low-income countries earn less than 20 per cent of the world's income, while the 1 billion people living in developed countries earn 60 per cent (UN 2000). The ratio between income earned in countries with the richest 20 per cent of the population, compared to the world's poorest 20 per cent, has also widened — from 30:1 in 1960, to 60:1 in 1990, to 74:1 in 1997 (UNDP 1999).

Growth in use of energy (see box) and transport are both indicators of economic development, and both have severe impacts on the environment. Private vehicular transportation has become an entrenched lifestyle choice among those who can afford it. Since the 1970s, about 16 million new vehicles have come onto the world's roads annually (UNDP, UNEP, World Bank and WRI 1998) and passenger cars account for 15 per cent of total global energy consumption (Jepma and others 1995).

Inequalities in income are also reflected in similar disparities in material consumption (see 'The Ecological Footprint', page 36). It has been estimated that the richest 20 per cent of the world's population accounts for 86 per cent of total private consumption expenditure, consumes 58 per cent of the world's energy, 45 per cent of all meat and fish, 84 per cent of paper, and owns 87 per cent of cars and 74 per cent of telephones. Conversely, the poorest 20 per cent of the world's population consumes 5 per cent or less of each of these goods and services (UNDP 1998).

For many developing countries poverty, unemployment and low productivity are major concerns. In developing countries as a whole, the informal sector provides 37 per cent of employment, and as much as 45 per cent in Africa (UNCHS 2001). In the 1980s, structural adjustment programmes (SAPs) were introduced by the World Bank to correct underlying economic imbalances and improve economic efficiency through reforms. SAPs have had

## Trends in global energy production and consumption

Energy is a key to socio-economic development. It is also central to achieving the economic, social and environmental goals of sustainable development. Harnessing energy has dramatically expanded people's choices, allowing those with access to enjoy unprecedented productivity, mobility and comfort. But the per capita use of electricity illustrates a major energy divide. The OECD annual average of 8 053 kilowatt-hours (kWh) per capita is nearly 100 times greater than in the least developed countries where it is only 83 kWh per capita (UNDP/UNDESA/WEC 2000).

The annual growth rate in total energy use between 1972 and 1999 averaged 2 per cent a year but this decreased from 2.8 per cent in the 1970s to 1.5 per cent in the 1980s and 2.1 per cent in the 1990s (IEA 1999). This decrease was due to weak economic performance in the transition economies in Europe in the 1990s, compounded by the global financial crisis of 1997-98 (UNDP/UNDESA/WEC 2000).

The human benefits of energy production and consumption frequently have an environmental downside, which may in turn threaten human health and quality of life. Impacts on atmospheric composition, deforestation leading to soil erosion and siltation of water bodies, the disposal of nuclear fuel waste, and occasional catastrophic accidents such as Chernobyl are some of the widely recognized problems.

Globally, per capita consumption has changed relatively little over the past 30 years although total consumption grew by some 70 per cent during 1972–99. At the regional level, per capita consumption has fallen in North America, the greatest consumer, and risen most sharply in West Asia. Reducing fossil fuel energy consumption in areas of high consumption, and achieving more balanced per capita consumption within and between countries, are environmental imperatives for the 21st century.

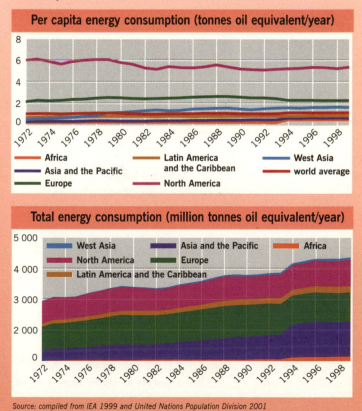

### Per capita energy consumption (tonnes oil equivalent/year)

Legend: Africa; Asia and the Pacific; Europe; Latin America and the Caribbean; North America; West Asia; world average

### Total energy consumption (million tonnes oil equivalent/year)

Legend: West Asia; North America; Latin America and the Caribbean; Asia and the Pacific; Europe; Africa

Source: compiled from IEA 1999 and United Nations Population Division 2001

economic, social and environmental impacts, including negative impacts on social stability and environmental sustainability (Reed 1996). Poverty, unemployment and falling standards of living also emerged as significant problems for countries in economic transition in the 1990s.

One critical issue is that of external debt which stood at US$2 572 614 million in 1999 (World Bank 2001). The Heavily Indebted Poor Countries (HIPCs) initiative was launched in 1996 and by November 2001 debt-reduction packages totalling US$36 000 million had been committed to 24 countries (mainly in Africa) (IMF 2001). However, there has been some disappointment with the initiative, and many of the countries receiving HIPC debt relief still spend more on debt servicing than on basic education or health (Oxfam 2001).

### The Ecological Footprint

The Ecological Footprint is an estimate of human pressure on global ecosystems, expressed in 'area units'. Each unit corresponds to the number of hectares of biologically productive land required to produce the food and wood people consume, the infrastructure people use, and to absorb the $CO_2$ produced from burning fossil fuels; thus the footprint takes into account the total impact people have on the environment.

The world's Ecological Footprint is a function of population size, average per capita consumption of resources, and the resource intensity of the technology used. During 1970–96, the world's Ecological Footprint rose from about 11 000 million area units to more than 16 000 million area units. The world average footprint remained fairly constant during 1985–96 at 2.85 area units per capita.

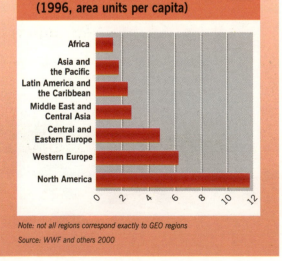

**Regional Ecological Footprints
(1996, area units per capita)**

Note: not all regions correspond exactly to GEO regions
Source: WWF and others 2000

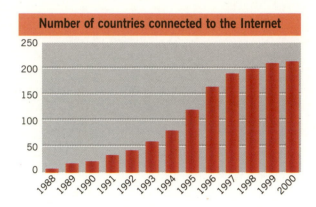

**Number of countries connected to the Internet**

## Science and technology

*The wonders of science and technology have brought to man higher standards of health, longer life, better jobs and education and a more comfortable existence than his forebears knew 100 years ago.*

*Commission to Study the
Organization of Peace 1972*

This perception from the 1970s still holds true today. Science and technology have brought about major breakthroughs over the past 30 years in, for example, the fields of information and communications, medicine, nutrition, agriculture, economic development and biotechnology. Forty-six global hubs of technological innovation have been identified around the world, principally in Europe and North America (Hillner 2000).

Information and communications technology (ICT) particularly has revolutionized the way people live, learn, work and interact (Okinawa Charter 2000). The Internet, mobile phones and satellite networks have shrunk time and space. Satellite communications technology from the mid-1980s gave rise to a powerful new medium with a global reach. Bringing together computers and communications in the early 1990s unleashed an explosion of ways to communicate, process and store, and distribute enormous amounts of information. In 2001, more information could be sent over a single cable in a second than was sent over the entire Internet for a month in 1997 (UNDP 2001).

ICT is advancing rapidly, presenting tremendous opportunities for human development by making it easier for more people to access available information from remote locations, quickly and cheaply. However,

### Number of Internet users (millions)

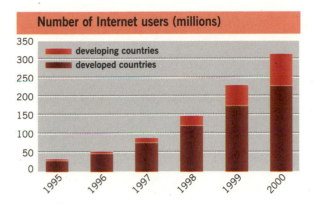

Legend: developing countries; developed countries

(Chart axis values: 350, 300, 250, 200, 150, 100, 50, 0 for years 1995, 1996, 1997, 1998, 1999, 2000)

### Fixed and mobile telephone subscribers (millions)

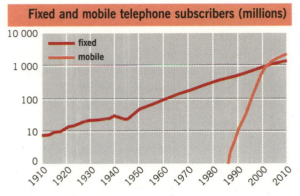

Legend: fixed; mobile

(Chart axis values: 10 000, 1 000, 100, 10, 0 for years 1910, 1920, 1930, 1940, 1950, 1960, 1970, 1980, 1990, 2000, 2010)

Figures on the left demonstrate the explosive growth of the use of the Internet and mobile telephones — but even in 2000 only one-quarter of Internet users were from developing countries

*Source: ITU 2001*

the uneven diffusion of ICT means that access to related technological developments may be an advantage for the minority only. Today, Internet users are predominantly urban and 79 per cent of users live in OECD countries, which contain only 14 per cent of the world's population. Nevertheless, even in developing countries the increase in Internet use has been dramatic — for example, from 3.9 million to 33 million people in China between 1998 and 2002 (UNDP 2001, CNNIC 2002).

Mobile telephones have overcome the infrastructure constraints of fixed lines and the number of subscribers has increased from slightly more than 10 million around the world at the start of the 1990s to more than 725 million at the beginning of 2001, or one mobile phone for every eight inhabitants (ITU 2001).

Additionally, new technologies are helping people to better understand the environment. In July 1972,

the US government launched the first LANDSAT satellite. By 2002, the LANDSAT programme has acquired 30 years of records which constitute the longest continuous record of data on the Earth's continental surfaces (USGS 2001). This has added a new dimension to environmental monitoring and assessment, enabling changes to be tracked, trends monitored and early warning improved (see image below). Images from this facility are included in the pages at the end of sections in Chapter 2.

However, for some developing countries, technology can be a source of exclusion instead of a tool for progress. 'Technology is created in response to market pressures, not the needs of poor people who have little purchasing power. As a result research neglects opportunities to develop technology for poor people' (UNDP 2001). For example, of the 1 223 new drugs marketed worldwide between 1975 and 1996, only 13 were developed to treat tropical diseases

Image below is the most detailed true-colour image of the entire Earth available in March 2002. Many months of satellite-based observations of the land surface, oceans, sea ice, and clouds were pieced together into a seamless, mosaic of every square kilometre the Earth (Antarctica not shown)

*Source: NASA Goddard Space Flight Center Image*

'It is only through the deep concern, information and knowledge, commitment and action of the people of the world that environmental problems can be answered. Laws and institutions are not enough. The will of the people must be powerful enough, insistent enough, to bring about the truly good life for all mankind.' — *Commission to Study the Organization of Peace 1972*

(UNDP 2001). New technologies also come with unforeseen risks to human health and the environment: for example, ozone-layer depletion from the use of CFCs, the side effects of drugs, unintended use of new technologies as weapons, pollution, concerns over the impacts of genetically modified organisms, and technological disasters such as Chernobyl and Bhopal.

## Governance

Governance is an overriding issue which applies at all levels and sectors of society — from local to global, from the private to the public sector — and has impacts on law and human rights, political, parliamentary, democratic and electoral systems, civil society, peace and security, public administration, public information, the media and the corporate world. Awareness of and attention to governance issues have consequently grown in every aspect of modern life,

not least in relation to the environment. 'Good' governance is recognized as a prerequisite for sound policy development and as being even more important for ensuring that policies are effectively implemented.

The 30 years between the Stockholm Conference and the 2002 World Summit on Sustainable Development have witnessed a major overhaul of political systems, including the decolonization of Africa, the end of apartheid in South Africa, the raising of the Iron Curtain, the reunification of Germany and the disintegration of the former Soviet Union. There has been a rapid increase in economic and trade alliances, and in membership of the United Nations, which stood at 190 in March 2002. Perhaps the greatest change has been at the national level where democracy and transparency have become major issues, particularly since the 1990s, and governments have been replaced as a result of popular demand. In the past 10 years, more than 100 developing and transition countries ended military or one-party rule (UNDP 2001). The internationalization of the environment since 1972 has had a bearing on national politics in many of the developed countries, with green parties making their mark, particularly during the 1980s (Long 2000). The past three decades have also seen the massive growth of civil society movements in all the regions of the world, with many

A hand through the Berlin Wall symbolizes the raising of the Iron Curtain in Europe in 1989 — one of the major political events of the past three decades

*Source: UNEP, Joachim Kuhnke, Topham Picturepoint*

organizations taking a more proactive role. Non-governmental organizations are increasingly influencing and sometimes participating in government and private sector decisions.

The power of the people in influencing policy has been recognized since at least the 1970s: 'It is only through the deep concern, information and knowledge, commitment and action of the people of the world that environmental problems can be answered. Laws and institutions are not enough. The will of the people must be powerful enough, insistent enough, to bring about the truly good life for all mankind.' (Commission to Study the Organization of Peace 1972).

The growing integration of finance, economies, culture, technologies and governance through globalization is having profound impacts, both positive and negative, on all aspects of people's life and the environment. With market forces beginning to dominate the social and political as well as economic spheres, there is a danger that power and wealth become concentrated in a minority while the majority become increasingly marginalized and dependent. In the 21st century, the challenge is to institute stronger governance to ensure that globalization operates for the benefit of most people and not just for profits.

## References: Chapter 2, socio-economic background, global overview

CCNIC (2002). *Semiannual Survey report on the Development of China's Internet (January 2002)*. China Internet Network Information Center http://www.cnnic.net.cn/develst/rep200201-e.shtml

Commission to Study the Organization of Peace (1972). *The United Nations and the Human Environment – The Twenty-Second Report*. New York, United Nations

Costanza, R., d'Arge, R., de Groot, R., Farber, S., Grasso, M., Hannon, B., Naeem, S., Limburg, K., Paruelo, J., O'Neill, R.V., Raskin, R., Sutton, P. and van den Belt, M. (1997). The value of the world's ecosystem services and natural capital. *Nature* 387, 253-260

FAO (2000). *The State of Food Insecurity in the World 2000*. Rome, Food and Agriculture Organization of the United Nations

Hillner, J. (2000). Venture capitals. *Wired*, 7 August 2000

IEA (1999). *Energy Balances of OECD countries 1960–97, Energy Balances of Non-OECD countries 1971–97*. Paris, Organization of Economic Cooperation and Development, International Energy Agency

IFAD (2001). *Rural Poverty Report 2001 – The Challenge of Ending Rural Poverty*. Rome, International Fund for Agricultural Development http://www.ifad.org/poverty/index.htm [Geo-2-270]

IMF (2001). *Debt Relief for Poor Countries (HIPC): What has Been Achieved? A Factsheet*. International Monetary Fund http://www.imf.org/external/np/exr/facts/povdebt.htm [Geo-2-271]

ITU (2001). *ITU Telecommunication Indicator Update*. International Telecommunication Union http://www.itu.int/journal/200105/E/html/update.htm#top [Geo-2-272]

Jepma, C. J., Asaduzzaman, M., Mintzer, I., Maya, R.S. and Al-Moneef, M. (1995). A generic assessment of response options. In Bruce, J.P., Lee, H. and Haites, E.F. (eds.), *Climate Change 1995. Economic and Social Dimensions of Climate Change*. Cambridge, Cambridge University Press

Long, B.L. (2000). *International Environmental Issues and the OECD 1950-2000: An Historical Perspective*. Paris, Organization for Economic Cooperation and Development

Murray, C. and Lopez, A. (1996). *A Global Burden of Disease*. Cambridge, Harvard University Press

Okinawa Charter (2000). *Okinawa Charter on Global Information Society*. Ministry of Foreign Affairs of Japan http://www.mofa.go.jp/policy/economy/summit/2000/pdfs/charter.pdf [Geo-2-273]

Oxfam (2001). *Debt Relief: Still Failing the Poor*. Oxfam http://www.oxfam.org/what_does/advocacy/papers/OxfamDebtPaperApril2001.doc [Geo-2-274]

Reed, D. (1996). *Structural Adjustment, the Environment and Sustainable Development*. London, Earthscan http://www.panda.org/resources/programmes/mpo/library/download/books/CH2SD.doc [Geo-2-275]

UN (1997). *Address by Executive Director of the United Nations Population Fund at the Special Session of the General Assembly: Earth Summit + 5*, New York, 25 June 1997

UN (2000). *We the Peoples — The Role of the United Nations in the 21st Century*. New York, United Nations http://www.un.org/millennium/sg/report/key.htm [GEO-1-001]

UNAIDS (2001). *AIDS Epidemic Update*. Joint United Nations Programme on HIV/AIDS (UNAIDS) http://www.unaids.org/epidemic_update/report_dec01/index.html [Geo-2-276]

UNCHS (2001). *State of the World's Cities 2001*. Nairobi, United Nations Centre for Human Settlements (HABITAT)

UNCTAD (2000). *The Least Developed Countries 2000 Report*. Geneva, United Nations Conference on Trade and Development

UNDP (1998). *Human Development Report 1998*. New York, United Nations Development Programme

UNDP (1999). *Human Development Report 1999*. New York, United Nations Development Programme

http://www.undp.org/hdro/E1.html [Geo-2-277]

UNDP (2001). *Human Development Report 2001*. Oxford and New York, Oxford University Press http://www.undp.org/hdr2001/completenew.pdf [Geo-2-278]

UNDP, UNDESA and WEC (2000). *World Energy Assessment*. United Nations Development Programme http://www.undp.org/seed/eap/activities/wea [Geo-2-320]

UNDP, UNEP, World Bank and WRI (1998). *World Resources 1998-99*. New York, Oxford University Press

UNESCO (2000). *World Education Report 2000: The Right to Education — Towards Education for All Throughout Life*. Paris, UNESCO

UNFPA (2001). *Population Issues Briefing Kit 2001*. United Nations Population Fund http://www.unfpa.org/modules/briefkit/ [Geo-2-279]

UNHCR (2000). *The State of the World's Refugees: Fifty Years of Humanitarian Action*. Oxford, Oxford University Press http://www.unhcr.ch/sowr2000/toc2.htm [Geo-1-031]

UNHCR (2001). *Basic Facts*. UNHCR, The UN Refugee Agency http://www.unhcr.ch/cgi-bin/texis/vtx/home?page=basics [Geo-2-280]

United Nations Population Division (2001). *World Population Prospects 1950-2050 (The 2000 Revision)*. New York, United Nations www.un.org/esa/population/publications/wpp2000/wpp2000h.pdf [Geo-2-204]

WHO (1997). *Health and Environment in Sustainable Development*. Geneva, World Health Organization

World Bank (2001). *World Development Indicators 2001*. Washington DC, World Bank http://www.worldbank.org/data/wdi2001/pdfs/tab3_8.pdf [Geo-2-024]

## Socio-economic background: Africa

The African region has a wealth of natural resources, offering myriad opportunities for human, social and economic development. Its diversity of cultures and valuable indigenous knowledge provides the necessary human capital to realize these opportunities. Nevertheless, Africa entered the 21st century facing enormous challenges.

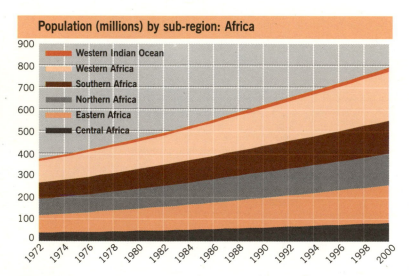

**Population (millions) by sub-region: Africa**

Legend:
- Western Indian Ocean
- Western Africa
- Southern Africa
- Northern Africa
- Eastern Africa
- Central Africa

Rates of population growth in Africa are still high — 2.4 per cent a year compared to a world average of 1.3 per cent

*Source: United Nations Population Division 2001*

## Human development

Of the 49 countries in Africa for which data are available, 20 are classified as having medium human development and 29 low human development (UNDP 2001). Generally, this translates to:

- a low life expectancy — 52.5 years compared to a world average of 66.3 years (United Nations Population Division 2001);
- low levels of education and literacy — about 60 per cent adult literacy in 1999, compared to an estimated world average of 75 per cent (compiled from UNDP, UNEP, World Bank and WRI 2000); and
- widespread poverty — per capita GDP (in US$1995) of US$749 in 1999 compared to a global average of US$5 403 (World Bank 2001a).

Sub-regional differences are most marked between Northern Africa, where rapid progress has been made over the past 30 years, and sub-Saharan Africa. In the former, life expectancy increased by 14 years in the

period from 1970–75 to 1995–2000. However, in sub-Saharan Africa progress has been slow and 12 countries suffered setbacks in human development between 1975 and 1999 (UNDP 2001).

Close to 350 million people, 44 per cent of the total population, live on US$1 or less a day (as high as 70 per cent in Nigeria) and up to 150 million children live below the poverty line (ADB 2000, UNDP 2001). Income distribution is also highly skewed with the poorest 10 per cent of Africans earning less than 5 per cent of the income and the richest 10 per cent earning 25–45 per cent of the income, depending on the country (ADB 2001).

There are also large discrepancies between the status of men and women in Africa, with women prohibited from owning property or land in many societies. Women also generally earn less and do not hold a representative proportion of high-ranking jobs.

Access to health services varies but generally lags behind the international average. Poor economic growth and increasing population pressures on existing facilities have contributed to low investment in the health sector. In 1998, government expenditure on health care per capita (at purchasing power parity) ranged from a high of US$623 in South Africa to only US$15 in Madagascar (UNDP 2001).

## The changing population

Africa has had one of the highest population growth rates in the world over the past 30 years; at the current 2.4 per cent a year, it is much higher than the global average of 1.3 per cent. The population more than doubled from 375 million in 1972 to 794 million in 2000, or approximately 13 per cent of the world's population. Fertility rates in Africa are also among the highest in the world, although they are declining — from 6.8 children per woman in the period 1965–70 to 5.4 children per woman in 1995–2000) (United Nations Population Division 2001).

The HIV/AIDS pandemic, which killed 2.3 million people in Africa in 2001, is having an impact on all aspects of human, social and economic development. The continent has the highest new infection rate and the largest proportion of the population living with HIV/AIDS (8.4 per cent of adults) in the world. In 2001, there were 28.1 million people with HIV/AIDS in sub-Saharan Africa — 70 per cent of the global total. Over the past 20 years, the disease has had a severe impact on life expectancy in the region, and in countries such as Botswana and Malawi average life expectancy is already below 40 years (UNAIDS 2001). Northern African countries are less severely affected. Despite commendable action by many countries, the impact of AIDS on social development, economic growth and on health systems is projected to run to billions of dollars. For example, in South Africa the impact is anticipated to be equal to 0.4 per cent of GDP over the next decade (UNAIDS 2000). The impact on families, communities and societies is incalculable.

## Economic development

The economies of African countries have been largely based on primary products or extraction of natural resources, both exported unprocessed. As a result, economic growth has been below potential, because revenues from the value that is added by processing accrue outside the continent, making African economies extremely vulnerable to external price fluctuations and trade regulations. The first oil crisis, in 1973–74, sparked a series of setbacks and economic recessions that have lasted for more than a quarter of a century. Falling prices for coffee, cocoa and other cash crops during the 1980s had catastrophic impacts on the economies of the region. Between 1970 and 1995, Africa lost half its markets, representing a loss of income of about US$70 billion a year (Madavo 2000).

Africa's dependence on rain-fed agriculture means that production is vulnerable to climatic variability, which can severely affect food and human security, and exports. The focus on mineral extraction, cash crops and timber harvesting has also had detrimental impacts on the environment.

With the additional constraints of a growing population, Africa's economic performance has been poor over the past 25 years. Annual growth of per capita GDP for sub-Saharan Africa was -1 per cent between 1975 and 1999, and incomes have fallen (UNDP 2001). Nevertheless, 34 African countries recorded increases in per capita incomes between 1994 and 1997, and 18 grew at aggregate rates above the 5 per cent a year threshold for reducing poverty (Madavo and Sarbib 1998). There is some speculation that this may signal a sustained economic recovery, partly reflecting the positive results of implementing growth-oriented macroeconomic and structural reforms (Madavo 2000, Madavo and Sarbib 1998).

Since the mid-1990s price controls have largely been lifted, marketing boards abolished, trade taxes rationalized, financial markets liberalized and the process of privatization accelerated (ADB 2000).

National external debt is still a significant barrier to economic growth and poverty reduction in Africa.

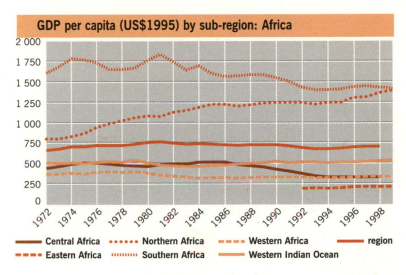

**GDP per capita (US$1995) by sub-region: Africa**

Legend: Central Africa · Northern Africa · Western Africa · region · Eastern Africa · Southern Africa · Western Indian Ocean

For the region as a whole, it increased almost 22-fold from US$16 960 million in 1971 to US$370 727 million by 1999 (World Bank 2001a). In 1970, the debt burden of sub-Saharan Africa was just US$6 000 million, or 11 per cent of GNP; this grew to US$330 000 million or 61 per cent of GNP by 1999 (ADB 2000). Since then there has been a small decline (World Bank 2001b). In Northern Africa, growth of external debt has followed a similar pattern. Recently, more emphasis has been placed on debt relief and increasing foreign direct investment (FDI). Although 20 African countries have had debt-reduction packages approved under the enhanced Heavily-Indebted Poor Countries Initiative (IMF 2001), indebtedness remains an issue of major concern.

## Science and technology

In terms of technological achievement, diffusion of, access to and adoption of science and technology is generally poor in Africa. The region has a number of marginalized countries (such as Ghana, Kenya, Mozambique, Senegal, Sudan and Tanzania) where large parts of the population have not even benefited from the use of old technology such as fixed-line telephones. Nevertheless, Africa has a number of 'dynamic adopters' in the use of new technology,

**While GDP per capita has climbed steadily since 1972 in Northern Africa, it has stagnated or declined in sub-Saharan Africa**

*Note: data for Eastern Africa are unreliable pre-1992*

*Source: estimated from World Bank 2001a*

including Algeria, Egypt, South Africa, Tunisia and Zimbabwe, although the diffusion of old technology is still slow and incomplete even in these countries. The region has two recognized global hubs of technological innovation: in El Ghazala, Tunisia, and Gauteng, South Africa. However, most African countries are not included on the Technology Achievement Index (TAI), and even South Africa, which has the highest score of any African country, has a TAI of 0.340 which is less than half the highest TAI value of 0.744 for Finland (UNDP 2001).

Lack of access to affordable appropriate technologies seriously constrains sustainable development options. In the agricultural sector, for example, many African countries depend on irrigation but the more efficient drip irrigation systems are too costly for most farmers, resulting in wastage of water. Africa also remains marginalized with respect to access to biotechnology for agricultural productivity, pharmaceutical products and disease prevention. Foreign companies may be able to exploit biological species commercially whereas local companies do not have the technology, capital or know-how to do so.

All countries in the region have Internet connections with a total of around 4 million users (2.5 million in South Africa), or one user for every 200 people, compared to a world average of about one user for every 30 people (Jensen 2001). Mobile communications technology has enabled Africa to leapfrog the infrastructure constraints of land-based communications. In 1990, African countries had no or low access to cellular communications; by 1999 the technology had spread dramatically to most countries — for example, availability has risen from 0.1 per 1 000 population to 132 per 1 000 in South Africa (UNDP 2001).

## Governance

Despite significant institutional and political changes over the past 30 years, 'good' governance in Africa is still a partial and fragile feature. Most notable changes have been the end of colonialism, as well as military and one-party rule in most countries, and the rise in participation by non-governmental, community-based and civil society organizations. Nevertheless, corruption is endemic in many countries. For example, 14 African countries scored less than five out of a clean score of ten on a corruption perception index, and four of those scored less than two (TI 2001).

A further barrier to stability, economic growth and social development in the region over the past 30 years has been the escalating incidence of civil conflict. Conflicts, typically arising from ethnic or religious differences or competition for natural resources, have resulted in massive displacement of people and diversion of financial resources away from vital sectors such as health and education. About one in every five Africans still lives in circumstances of civil conflict (Madavo 2000).

### References: Chapter 2, socio-economic background, Africa

ADB (2000). *ADB Statistics Pocketbook 2001*. African Development Bank http://www.afdb.org/knowledge/publications/pdf/statistics_pocket_book.pdf [Geo-2-281]

ADB (2001). *Human Development Indicators*. African Development Bank http://www.afdb.org/knowledge/statistics/statistics_indicators_selected/human/pdf/human_tab3.pdf [Geo-2-282]

IMF (2001). *Debt Relief for Poor Countries (HIPC): What has Been Achieved? A Factsheet*. International Monetary Fund http://www.imf.org/external/np/exr/facts/povdebt.htm [Geo-2-283]

Jensen, M. (2001). *Information & Communication Technologies (ICTs): Telecommunications, Internet and Computer Infrastructure in Africa*. African Internet Connectivity http://www3.wn.apc.org/africa/ [Geo-2-284]

Madavo, C. (2000). *Celebrating the Wealth of Africa*. Speech given at the Official Banquet of the US National Summit on Africa, 18 February 2000. World Bank

http://www.worldbank.org/afr/speeches/cm000218.htm [Geo-2-285]

Madavo, C. and Sarbib, J-L. (1998*). Is There an Economic Recovery in Sub-Saharan Africa?* World Bank http://www.worldbank.org/afr/speeches/ifpri.htm [Geo-2-286]

TI (2001). *Press Release: New Index Highlights Worldwide Corruption Crisis*. Transparency International http://www.transparency.org/cpi/2001/cpi2001.html [Geo-2-321]

UNAIDS (2000). *AIDS Epidemic Update; December 2000*. Joint United Nations Programme on HIV/AIDS (UNAIDS) http://www.unaids.org/wac/2000/wad00/files/WAD_epidemic_report.PDF [Geo-2-287]

UNAIDS (2001). *AIDS Epidemic Update; December 2001*. Joint United Nations Programme on HIV/AIDS (UNAIDS) http://www.unaids.org/worldaidsday/2001/Epiupdate2001/Epiupdate2001_en.pdf [Geo-2-288]

UNDP, UNEP, World Bank and World Resources Institute (2000). *World Resources 2000-2001*. Washington DC, World Resources Institute

UNDP (2001). *Human Development Report 2001*. Oxford and New York, Oxford University Press http://www.undp.org/hdr2001/completenew.pdf [Geo-2-289]

United Nations Population Division (2001). *World Population Prospects 1950-2050 (The 2000 Revision)*. New York, United Nations www.un.org/esa/population/publications/wpp2000/wpp2000h.pdf [Geo-2-204]

World Bank (2001a). *World Development Indicators 2001*. Washington DC, World Bank http://www.worldbank.org/data/wdi2001/pdfs/tab3_8.pdf [Geo-2-024]

World Bank (2001b). *Global Development Finance 2001*. Washington DC, World Bank

## Socio-economic background: Asia and the Pacific

The Asia and the Pacific region occupies 23 per cent of the Earth's land area and is home to more than 58 per cent of its people. The region includes several of the world's largest emerging economies, such as China and those of Southeast Asia. Over the past 30 years, the region has gradually moved from a subsistence lifestyle towards a consumer society, with rapid rates of urbanization and westernization as well as population increase. This transition has not been without adverse social and economic, as well as environmental, impacts.

### Human development

Of the 53 countries in the region, 7 are classified as having a high level of human development, 21 as a medium level, and 5 as a low level (the other countries, mainly small islands in the South Pacific, have not been classified). The Northwest Pacific and East Asia sub-region has made sustained and rapid progress in most areas of human development, while South Asia lags behind with human and income poverty still high. Per capita GDP (in US$1995) ranges from US$506 in South Asia to US$4 794 in Northwest Pacific and East Asia. Life expectancy at birth has improved throughout the region, rising in South Asia from 50 years in 1970–75 to more than 60 years by 1995-2000, and in Northwest Pacific and East Asia from about 61 to nearly 70 years over the same period. Adult literacy rates also show similar improvements increasing from 33 to 55 per cent in South Asia during 1972–99, and from 55 to 84 per cent in Northwest Pacific and East Asia (World Bank 2001).

An estimated three-quarters of the world's poor live in Asia, and poverty is particularly significant in Afghanistan, Bangladesh, Cambodia, India, Lao People's Democratic Republic, Nepal and Pakistan. In South Asia, 40 per cent of the population lives on less than US$1 a day (UNDP 2001). Poverty is not just determined by economics, however. Conventional indicators suggest that many Pacific Island populations are at poverty level (UNESCAP 1999) — however, many communities still enjoy a high degree of subsistence affluence from traditional, non-monetary resource management systems (UNEP 1999).

Poverty for many countries of the region is the result of gross inequalities and institutional failures which allow the benefits of economic growth to be captured by a decreasing number of elites. In addition, urbanization, the shift to a monetary economy and high population growth without commensurate growth in employment opportunities compound the problem. So does the overexploitation of natural resources which threatens viable agricultural or subsistence lifestyles (UNESCAP 1999).

### The changing population

The region's population grew from 2 173 million in 1972 to 3 514 million in 2000 (United Nations Population Division 2001). Population growth rates had declined from 2.3 per cent in 1972 to 1.3 per cent (the same as the world average) by 2000 — although there are significant sub-regional variations. This can be partly attributed to declining fertility levels which have fallen from 5.1 to 2.1 children per woman over the past three decades (United Nations Population Division 2001).

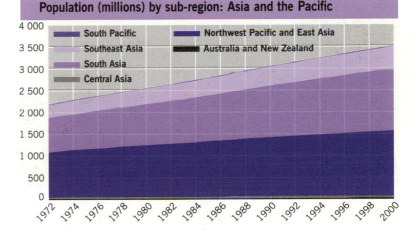

**Population (millions) by sub-region: Asia and the Pacific**

Legend:
- South Pacific
- Southeast Asia
- South Asia
- Central Asia
- Northwest Pacific and East Asia
- Australia and New Zealand

Nevertheless, the region includes some of the most populous countries in the world, with China and India accounting for 38 per cent of the world population. It also contains five of the six countries which account for one-half of global annual population growth — Bangladesh, China, India, Indonesia and Pakistan (United Nations Population Division 2001).

High population growth is reflected in the region's population structures. Most countries have youthful populations, with 30 per cent of Asia's population less than 15 years old (United Nations Population Division 2001). While this could be seen as a positive characteristic in terms of the large number of young

Asia and the Pacific's huge population is dominated by just three sub-regions. Overall, growth has now slowed to the world average of 1.3 per cent a year

*Source: compiled from United Nations Population Division 2001*

Asia and the Pacific's traditional agricultural economy is losing ground to service industries: during the period 1972–99, agriculture's contribution to GDP fell from 23 to 16 per cent while the contribution of the service industries grew from 43 to 50 per cent

*Source: UNEP, Topham Picturepoint*

workers available, in some sub-regions, especially the Pacific Islands, it also has significant negative socio-economic implications, particularly in terms of high unemployment. In addition, large numbers of young people entering their reproductive years compound the pressures of population growth.

Despite gains in life expectancy, an estimated 7.1 million people live with HIV/AIDS (almost 18 per cent of the world total) in Asia and the Pacific. There were about 435 000 deaths and more than 1 million new cases in 2001 (UNAIDS 2001).

## Economic development

During the past 30 years, countries in the region have striven for economic development and higher standards of living. However, annual GDP growth rates decreased from a high of 9.76 per cent in 1970 to 2.54 per cent in 1999, with a negative growth of −1.04 per cent in 1998 due to the Asian economic crisis (World Bank 2001). Overall, however, between 1972 and 1999 per capita real incomes (measured in US$1995) nearly doubled in Northwest Pacific and East Asia, growing by an average of 2.4 per cent annually (see graph on page 45). In South Asia, the growth rate also exceeded 2 per cent (compiled from World Bank 2001). However, growth was very low in the Pacific Islands, and this is consistent with recent studies that indicate a general decline in the standard of living in Pacific island countries (UNESCAP 1999).

Asia and the Pacific accounted for 41.7 per cent of global external debt at US$1 073 977 million in 1999 — a significant burden which has increased more than five-fold from US$189 968 million in 1981 (World Bank 2001).

The economic structure of the region has changed remarkably over the past 30 years, with the importance of agriculture diminishing and the service sector growing. Even in South Asia, the contribution of agriculture to GDP fell from 39 per cent in 1980 to 30 per cent in 1995 while the contribution of the service sector increased from 35 to 41 per cent. (World Bank 1997). These structural changes are also reflected in employment. In 1960, 75 per cent of Asians were employed in agriculture. By 1990 this had fallen to nearer 60 per cent while the share of people working in industry grew from around 15 to 21 per cent (ADB 1997).

In the Pacific, lifestyles have changed from subsistence to cash-driven societies reliant on budgetary assistance. The standard of living for the sub-region's urban dwellers is relatively high when compared with those in other developing countries. However, there are some worrying trends, with indications of rising unemployment, particularly among young people; high drop-out rates from primary schools; low household cash incomes; and a growing incidence of drug abuse and crime (SPC 1998). Many of the small and remote islands of the Pacific have essentially no industry at all, while other countries in the sub-region have small industries related to food or beverage processing, clothing and minor machinery assembly or repair (UNEP 1999).

## Science and technology

The region has at least ten global hubs of technological innovation in Australia, China, India, Japan, Malaysia, Republic of Korea, Singapore and Taiwan (Hillner 2000). Asia accounts for about 30 per cent of global expenditure on research and development, with Japan alone accounting for half of that (UNESCO 2000).

In line with developments in other parts of the world, the spread of new technologies such as the Internet and mobile communications has been unprecedented and is having significant impacts on people's lives and selected national economies. For example, rural information centres have been set up in Pondicherry in India allowing Internet access using solar as well as electric power and wireless as well as wired communications. As a result, farmers and fishermen can access everything from market information to satellite images. Nevertheless, only 0.4 per cent of Indians were using the Internet in 2001 (UNDP 2001). In China, use of the Internet has grown almost ten-fold from 3.9 million users in 1998 to more than 33 million by January 2002 (UNDP 2001, CCNIC 2002); this is still only 2.75 per cent of the entire population, although more than half the population of Hong Kong has access to the Internet (UNDP 2001). The information and communications industry in India generated an estimated US$7 700 million in 1999 — 15 times more than in 1990, with almost US$4 000 million in exports (UNDP 2001). The associated employment and economic development

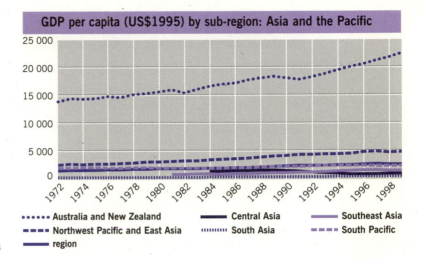

GDP per capita (US$1995) by sub-region: Asia and the Pacific

- ••••• Australia and New Zealand
- ▪▪▪ Northwest Pacific and East Asia
- —— region
- —— Central Asia
- ▪▪▪▪▪▪ South Asia
- —— Southeast Asia
- ▪▪▪ South Pacific

opportunities offer significant potential for addressing poverty in the region.

## Governance

The glowing picture of Asia's future in the early to mid-1990s has been overshadowed by more recent events in Southeast Asia and Korea. There has been a loss of confidence in the region which has ensured that the region's leaders are now more attentive to the need for adaptive governance and fiscal management to guard against future downturns. For countries to prosper again, governments and institutions must encourage new or burgeoning markets and pursue social policies that will simultaneously benefit the economy, the environment and the people.

Although incomes in Australia and New Zealand dwarf those elsewhere, there has been steady growth in the other sub-regions, except in Central Asia and the South Pacific Islands

*Note: data unavailable pre-1984 for Central Asia and pre-1981 for South Asia*

*Source: estimated from World Bank 2001*

### References: Chapter 2, socio-economic background, Asia and the Pacific

ADB (1992). *Environment and Development: a Pacific Island Perspective*. Manila, Asian Development Bank

ADB (1997). *Emerging Asia – Changes and Challenges*. Manila, Asian Development Bank

CCNIC (2002). *Semiannual Survey Report on the Development of China's Internet (January 2002)*. China Internet Network Information Center http://www.cnnic.net.cn/develst/rep200201-e.shtml [Geo-2-290]

Hillner, J. (2000). Venture Capitals. *Wired*, 7 August 2000

SPC (1998). *Pacific Island Populations*. Noumea, Secretariat of the Pacific Community

UNAIDS (2001). *AIDS Epidemic Update; December 2001*. Joint United Nations Programme on HIV/AIDS (UNAIDS) http://www.unaids.org/worldaidsday/2001/Epiupdate2001/Epiupdate2001_en.pdf [Geo-2-291]

UNDP (2001). *Human Development Report 2001*. Oxford and New York, Oxford University Press http://www.undp.org/hdr2001/completenew.pdf [Geo-2-289]

UNEP (1999). *Pacific Islands Environment Outlook*. Nairobi, United Nations Environment Programme

UNESCAP (1999). *Survey of Pacific Island Economies*. Port Vila, UNESCAP, Pacific Operations Centre

UNESCO (2000). *Facts and Figures 2000 – Science & Technology*. UNESCO Institute for Statistics http://www.uis.unesco.org/en/pub/pub0.htm [Geo-2-292]

United Nations Population Division (2001). *World Population Prospects 1950-2050 (The 2000 Revision)*. New York, United Nations www.un.org/esa/population/publications/wpp2000/wpp2000h.pdf [Geo-2-204]

World Bank (2001). *World Development Indicators 2001*. Washington DC, World Bank http://www.worldbank.org/data/wdi2001/pdfs/tab3_8.pdf [Geo-2-024]

## Socio-economic background: Europe

The most important developments in Europe over the past three decades are the political, economic, social and institutional processes resulting from the strengthening and expansion of the European Union (EU) and the transition from centrally planned regimes to more open, market economy based societies (see box below). These changes have had profound effects on developments in all the countries concerned, on sub-regions and on the region as a whole. Although the three sub-regions of Europe (Western, Central and Eastern) do have similarities, there also are distinct differences due to recent and historical events resulting in political, economic and social heterogeneity in the region.

Following the collapse of communism at the end of the 1980s, a new era of pan-European cooperation on environmental issues began within the framework of the 'Environment for Europe' (EfE) process. Included in the broader political agenda of this process was the goal of supporting and strengthening democratization, which gradually replaced state socialism in post-communist countries (see box right). During preparations for the Århus Convention in the 1990s, it became clear that public rights and participation remained an elusive goal, in many of the established Western democracies as well as in Central and Eastern Europe (REC 1998).

### Human development

Europe is predominantly a region of high to medium levels of human development (UNDP 2001). However,

### The enlargement of the European Union

For the ten Central and Eastern European (CEE) countries that have applied to join the EU (the Accession Countries), membership is seen as a means to stabilize the changes resulting from transition, as well as a means to accelerate economic development. For all 13 Accession Countries, EU membership poses tremendous political and economic challenges, including harmonization of laws and institutions to EU requirements. Both the EU and Accession Countries are in transition to more sustainable development but with different starting points.

Note: in early 2002, the Accession Countries were Bulgaria, Cyprus, the Czech Republic, Estonia, Hungary, Latvia, Lithuania, Malta, Poland, Romania, Slovakia, Slovenia and Turkey

### Availability of and access to environmental information

Information, participation and access to justice are essential elements of a true participatory democracy. These themes therefore became central elements in the EfE process, resulting in the endorsement of the Sofia Guidelines in 1995 and the adoption of the Convention on Access to Information, Public Participation in Decision-making and Access to Justice in Environmental Matters (the Århus Convention) at the Environment for Europe Ministerial Conference held in Århus, Denmark, in 1998.

The Århus Convention is based on the notion that the involvement of the public in decision-making, notably by public authorities, tends to improve the quality and implementation of final decisions. It guarantees the right to information, participation and justice in the context of protecting the rights of present and future generations to live in an environment adequate to health and well-being.

while the overall level continues to improve gradually throughout Western and parts of Central Europe, many countries of Eastern Europe have suffered severe setbacks, including a rise in income poverty, since the beginning of the transition process.

The region traditionally has high rates of adult literacy, estimated at 95 per cent or more for Europe as a whole, although rates tend to be slightly lower in southern parts of Western Europe (UNESCO 1998).

In several of the CEE countries (Moldova, Romania, the Russian Federation and Ukraine) half or more of the population had incomes below the official poverty line in the period 1989–95 (UNDP 1999a). This impoverishment is reflected in a drastic fall in real wages and per capita GDP, high rates of inflation and a rise in income inequalities — including between men and women, the latter often being the first to lose their jobs. Relative prices have also changed, with prices of goods and services needed by the poor often rising much faster than others (UN 2000a). While income poverty is clearly more pervasive and severe in Eastern Europe, it is not unknown in Western Europe, with an estimated 17 per cent of the EU population (excluding Finland and Sweden) still experiencing poverty. Vulnerability to income poverty is more widespread: 32 per cent of Europeans experience at least one annual spell of low income over a period of three years, while 7 per cent experience persistent poverty during this period (EC 2001).

The human costs of the transition process have reached beyond income poverty alone. In Europe as a whole, life expectancy has increased in the period 1995–2000 compared to 1975–1980 from 70.3 to 73.1 years (both sexes, compiled from United Nations Population Division 2001). However, in some Eastern European countries life expectancy has decreased over the same period, especially for men — for example from 62 to 58 in the Russian Federation and from 65 to 64 in Ukraine (UNDP 1999b). In addition, in many CEE countries (Belarus, Estonia, Latvia, the Russian Federation and Ukraine), the ratio of men to women is far below the standard ratio. The causes of this 'missing men issue' are multiple and complex but stem mainly from human insecurity: military conflict, poor health, unemployment, loss of pensions and corruption, all of which result in social breakdown and a poor quality of life (UNDP 1999b).

Dismantling of the communist era welfare system also led to social disintegration and inequality in social services in CEE. This decline was associated with a proliferation of fraud, illegal businesses and organized crime (UNDP 1999b). In sharp contrast to conditions before transition, people now find themselves deprived of personal safety and security — often at the mercy of organized criminal forces that have arisen on the basis of collusion with corrupt government officials. The increase in crime reveals a weakness in state authority and in public law enforcement.

## The changing population

Europe's population has increased by 100 million since 1972 to a total of 818 million in 2000, or 13.5 per cent of the global population (see graphic). The most significant demographic change currently taking place in much of the region is the ageing of the population as a result of low fertility rates and increased life expectancy. Fertility rates have declined from 2.3 to 1.4 children per woman over the past 30 years and are as low as 1.1 in Armenia, Bulgaria and Latvia — well below the 2.1 children per woman required to keep population levels stable (United Nations Population Division 2001).

Another trend which is likely to continue, and which is an enormous challenge for the region, is that of population movements throughout Europe. These are related both to conflicts (asylum-seekers, displaced persons and refugees, including transit migration from developing countries) and to the search for more remunerative lifestyles (UNECE and others 1999, UNDP 1999b).

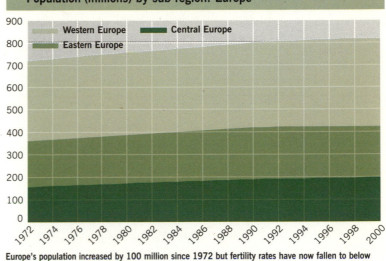

**Population (millions) by sub-region: Europe**

Europe's population increased by 100 million since 1972 but fertility rates have now fallen to below replacement levels in many countries

*Source: compiled from United Nations Population Division 2001*

## Economic development

The economies of Western Europe have recovered from the recession of the early 1990s and were growing at around 2.5 per cent a year by the end of 2000 (UN 2000a). An important factor has been the realization of the single market. Starting with the creation of the European Monetary System in 1979, the completion of the European Single Market became a fact in 1993, and the European Monetary Union became a reality for 300 million people in 12 EU countries with the debut of the Euro on 1 January

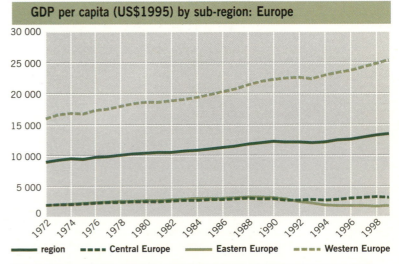

**GDP per capita (US$1995) by sub-region: Europe**

region ▬▬▬ Central Europe ▬ Eastern Europe ▬▬▬ Western Europe

Although GDP per capita has climbed steadily in Western Europe and thus in the region as a whole, there are marked contrasts with GDP per capita levels in Central and Eastern Europe

*Note: data for CEE are unreliable pre-1989. Source: estimated from World Bank 2001*

## Energy consumption in Europe

Although the per capita consumption of fossil fuels in Europe as a whole has hardly changed over 30 years, this is partly the result of negative growth in energy consumption in CEE countries due to economic restructuring. In Western Europe, however, the link between economic growth and energy use has not been broken (EEA 2001). Per capita energy consumption varies considerably throughout Western Europe but is increasing in most countries with the exception of Germany, where it decreased by 5 per cent between 1987 and 1997. While per capita energy consumption in CEE is often lower than the Western European average, energy intensity is three or more times higher (OECD 1999). This is due to the high share of heavy industries, obsolete technologies and low efficiency of energy use. Current and future changes in industrial activity will have major implications for the link between energy use and economic growth. Replacing obsolete technologies with modern cleaner technology provides a potential for a more sustainable development.

2002. The currency is likely to be an instrument of economic stability and growth throughout Europe, which will strengthen economic and political cooperation in the region.

Per capita GDP (measured in constant US$1995) has grown steadily for the region as a whole from about US$9 000 in 1972 to an average of US$13 500 in 1999 (see graph on page 47). Nevertheless, there are major sub-regional differences, ranging from US$25 441 in Western Europe in 1999 to US$3 139 in Central Europe and US$1 771 in Eastern Europe (compiled from World Bank 2001). Between 1980 and 1999, real GDP declined in 14 CEE countries and by more than 50 per cent in four of them — Georgia, Moldova, Ukraine and Yugoslavia (UN 2000a).

Average per capita consumption has increased steadily by an average 2.3 per cent a year in Western Europe over the past 25 years (UN 2000b). Consumption in some CEE countries has started to increase in recent years, as some of the population has achieved increased purchasing power, particularly in Poland (which has experienced a 65 per cent increase since 1991), Hungary and Slovenia (UN 2000b).

## Science and technology

Europe is a leader in the development and use of science and technology. The region has at least 19 hubs of technological innovation, led by Finland and Sweden, with many countries at the cutting-edge of technological innovation. Europe accounts for about 30 per cent of global expenditure on research and development, second after North America and equal to Asia and the Pacific (UNESCO 2001). The growth of information and communications technology, particularly the growth of the Internet linking millions of European homes and workplaces, is probably the single most stunning technological advance in the past 30 years. Internet users increased by 250 per cent between 1998 and 2000, from 539 per 10 000 inhabitants to 1 366 per 10 000 (ITU 2002), although these figures mask distinct sub-regional differences.

The European Space Agency and Canada launched the Envisat environmental satellite in early 2002 to monitor the health of the planet by collecting data on changes to the Earth's land, oceans, ice caps and atmosphere.

## References: Chapter 2, socio-economic background, Europe

EC (2001). *Consultation paper for the preparation of an EU Strategy for Sustainable Development.* COM(2001)264-final. Brussels, European Commission

EEA (2001). *Environmental Signals 2001.* Copenhagen, European Environment Agency

ITU (2002). *ICT Free Statistics Home Page: Internet Indicators by Country for 1998 and 2000.* International Telecommunication Union http://www.itu.int/ITU-D/ict/statistics [Geo-2-293]

OECD (1999). *Environment in the Transition to a Market Economy. Progress in CEE and NIS.* Paris, Organization for Economic Cooperation and Development

REC (1998). *Doors to Democracy: A Pan-European Assessment of Current Trends and Practices in Public Participation in Environmental Matters.* The Regional Environmental Center for Central and Eastern Europe http://www.rec.org/REC/Publications/PPDoors/EUR OPE/summary.html [Geo-2-294]

UN (2000a). *Economic Survey of Europe 2000 No.1.* New York and Geneva, United Nations

UN (2000b). *Economic Survey of Europe 2000 No.2/3.* New York and Geneva, United Nations

UNDP (1999a). *Human Development Report 1999.* New York, United Nations Development Programme http://www.undp.org/hdro/E1.html [Geo-2-295]

UNDP (1999b). *Transition 1999. Human Development Report for Central and Eastern Europe and the CIS, 1999.* New York, United Nations Development Programme

UNDP (2001). *Human Development Report 2001.* Oxford and New York, Oxford University Press http://www.undp.org/hdr2001/completenew.pdf [Geo-2-289]

UNECE, UNPF, Council for Europe and Hungarian Central Statistical Office (1999). *Population in Europe and North America on the Eve of the Millennium: Dynamics and Policy Responses.*

Regional Population Meeting 7-9 December 1998. Geneva, United Nations Economic Commission for Europe

UNESCO (1999). *World Education Indicators 1998,* on CD-ROM. UNESCO Division of Statistics, Paris, 1999.

UNESCO (2001). *Facts and Figures 2000.* Paris, UNESCO Institute for Statistics http://www.uis.unesco.org/en/pub/pub0.htm [Geo-2-292]

United Nations Population Division (2001). *World Population Prospects 1950-2050 (The 2000 Revision).* New York, United Nations www.un.org/esa/population/publications/wpp2000/ wpp2000h.pdf [Geo-2-204]

World Bank (2001). *World Development Indicators 2001.* Washington DC, World Bank http://www.worldbank.org/data/wdi2001/pdfs/tab3 _8.pdf [Geo-2-024]

## Socio-economic background: Latin America and the Caribbean

Latin America and the Caribbean has experienced financial and political turmoil over the past three decades. While some aspects of human development have improved significantly, poverty — especially in rural populations — and inequity persist as major problems, hindering regional efforts to move towards sustainable development.

### Human development

Six of the region's 46 countries (Argentina, Bahamas, Barbados, Chile, Costa Rica and Uruguay) are ranked as having a high level of human development; most of the others are in the medium human development group and only Haiti ranks in the low human development group (UNDP 2001).

Poverty is widespread. It is estimated that about 200 million people, or 40 per cent of the region's population, live in poverty (IADB 2000, ECLAC 2000). The incidence of poverty is higher in rural areas but there are more poor people in urban areas than in rural ones, and almost one-half of the poor are children or youth.

Life expectancy increased from 65.8 to 72.5 years between 1970 and 2000, with important national and sub-national differences that are related to per capita income levels (PAHO 1998). The highest life expectancies are in the Caribbean (74 years) and in South America (73.5 years), although there are variations with sub-regions — life expectancy is 20 years longer in Cuba and Puerto Rico than in Haiti and 10 years longer in Venezuela and Colombia than in Bolivia. Despite this, all countries except Haiti now exceed the life expectancy goal of 60 years proposed for the region in 1977 as part of the World Strategy on Health for All by the Year 2000 (PAHO 1998). More efficient health programmes have also lowered the child mortality rate significantly, from 81.6 per 1 000 births in 1970 to 35.5 per 1 000 in 1995 (World Bank 1999).

Education has also improved in the past two decades. Adult literacy rates are generally high at about 88 per cent in 1999 (UNDP 2001), a leap from 77 per cent in 1980 (PNUMA/OD 2001). However, the highly unequal distribution of income, which is pervasive throughout the region, is mirrored by inequalities in access to schooling, attendance and performance (UIS 2001).

Violence, including homicide, is on the increase in the entire region, particularly in Colombia and Brazil. Furthermore, violence within the family has increased, particularly towards women and children; it is estimated that about half the women in Latin America face at least one episode of family violence in their life (ECLAC 2000). In recent years, the region as a whole has edged towards peace except for a few conflicts such as those between Peru and Ecuador in the 1990s.

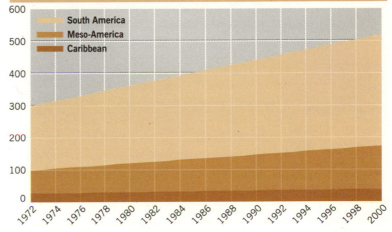

Population (millions) by sub-region: Latin America and the Caribbean

- South America
- Meso-America
- Caribbean

### The changing population

The region's population has increased by about 74 per cent from 299 million in 1972 to an estimated 519 million in 2000. However, the annual population growth rate dropped from 2.48 to 1.52 per cent over the same period, largely as a result of changes in birth patterns — fertility rates halved from 5.6 children per woman in 1970 to 2.7 children per woman by 1999. Population growth rates are now highest in Meso-America, 1.78 per cent, and lowest in the Caribbean, 1.04 per cent (compiled from United Nations Population Division 2001).

### Economic development

Economic growth has fluctuated in the region over the past three decades from a high of 8.4 per cent a year in 1973 to a low of –2.2 per cent a year in 1983 (World Bank 2001). As a result, per capita GDP has grown by an average of only about 1.0 per cent a year, from US$2 827 in 1972 to US$3 819 in 1999 (compiled from World Bank 2001), although some countries have performed better than others. In Chile, for example, per capita GDP more than doubled from US$2 360 to

Although the region's population grew by 74 per cent during 1972–2000, the growth rate dropped from 2.48 to 1.52 per cent a year over the same period

*Source: compiled from United Nations Population Division 2001*

### GDP per capita (US$1995/year): Latin America and the Caribbean

Legend: Meso-America — South America (dashed) — region

For the region as a whole, growth of per capita GDP averaged only about 1.0 per cent a year during 1972–99

Note: reliable data for the Caribbean sub-region are unavailable

Source: estimated from World Bank 2001

US$5 121 while in Nicaragua it almost halved from US$917 to US$472 (World Bank 2001).

Growth in the 1990s was made possible through major economic reforms, particularly trade and investment liberalization. Integration processes, including free trade agreements and customs unions — such as the North American Free Trade Agreement (NAFTA), the Andean Pact, the Southern Common Market of Latin America (MERCOSUR), the Caribbean Community (CARICOM), and the Central American Common Market — have begun to pay dividends. For example, Andean Community exports increased by 37 per cent in value terms in 2000 and intra-regional exports by 29 per cent. Similarly, intra-regional trade in the MERCOSUR countries increased by 21 per cent and under NAFTA by 20 per cent (IADB 2000).

## Inequities in social development

The level of distributive inequity in the region is the highest in the world, and is still increasing in all sub-regions. In the region as a whole, the minimum wage was on average 28 per cent lower in 1998 than in 1980. The limited job creation capacity of the region's economies and the fact that those with university education benefit most from rising demand for labour are among the suspected reasons for the continuing concentration of income but debate continues on the root causes.

The situation with regard to the distribution of land reflects a similar trend, with land ownership highly concentrated in Chile, Mexico and Paraguay, for example. Inequality in access to this basic asset by the rural population is a source of social tension. Numerous conflicts arose during the 1990s due to land access problems and high levels of rural poverty. To address this problem, Costa Rica's government has redistributed almost 2 million hectares (roughly one-third of the country's total land area) through large-scale land title allocation, acquisition and settlement programmes. El Salvador's 'Peace Agreement' has brought agrarian reform and a land-transfer programme (currently, 75.1 per cent of land is owner-occupied in El Salvador).

Source: ECLAC and UNEP (2001)

Nevertheless, except for a few countries such as Chile, the majority have been unable to regain their pre-1980s economic strength and, overall, the region has achieved only modest economic growth over the past 30 years. Exports remain largely based on commodities and primary goods, particularly oil and its derivatives, minerals, agriculture, forestry and related products. In this respect, the region's traditional vulnerability and external dependence have increased further due to the unsustainable nature of these activities in terms of both market access and long-term availability of natural resources (UNEP 2000). In many countries imports continue to grow more rapidly than exports (ECLAC and UNEP 2001).

Per capita energy consumption increased from about 0.7 to 0.9 tonnes of oil equivalent during 1972–99, compared with the global average of 1.1 tonnes of oil equivalent (compiled from IEA 1999 and United Nations Population Division 2001).

The region's external debt burden increased dramatically (21-fold) from US$46 251 million in 1971 to US$982 032 million by 1999, accounting for 38 per cent of global debt (World Bank 2001). Governments started to take on unsustainably high levels of debt in the 1970s with devastating consequences for regional economies during the decades that followed. In the 1980s, rising interest rates in the United States and Western Europe increased debt service payments while efforts to reduce the inflation caused by recession reduced the income from which to service the debt. Hyperinflation occurred in many countries, notably in Argentina and Brazil, as governments resorted to printing money. The 1990s saw an accumulation of large macroeconomic imbalances that led to severe crises in Mexico in 1995, Brazil in 1998 (ECLAC and UNEP 2001) and most recently Argentina in 2001-2002. Argentina alone has a national debt of US$147 880 million, or about 18 per cent of the region's total. Some countries, such as Bolivia and Guyana, have now qualified for debt relief under the Heavily Indebted Poor Countries (HIPC) initiative (World Bank 2001).

In 1999, the unemployment rate in the region reached 8.8 per cent, the highest in the 1990s (ECLAC and UNEP 2001), similar to the rate at the height of the debt crisis in the 1980s. With the exception of Chile and Panama, the number of people working in the informal sector rose in most countries as unemployment rates increased. In the 1990s, seven out of every ten jobs generated in the region's cities were in the informal sector, characterized as non-permanent, with little regulation and no social security (ECLAC and UNEP 2001). The only positive development in terms of labour force trends is the growth in female participation in the labour market. In 1980, little more than one-quarter of the labour force was female in Meso- and South America; by 1997, women made up one-third of the labour force in Meso-America and nearly two-fifths in South America. In the Caribbean, where female participation in the work force has been higher than the rest of the region, the figure reached 43 per cent in 1997 (ECLAC and UNEP 2001). The increase over the past two decades has been larger than in any other region in the world.

## Science and technology

Traditional information and communication technologies continue to spread throughout the region, with a large increase in the distribution of telephones and radios in all sub-regions over the past two decades (see table). There has also been increased usage of mobile phones and computers, with Internet usage growing at more than 30 per cent a year in Latin America (UNDP 2001). Brazil is one of the top ten users of mobile phones, with more than 23 million subscribers in 2000; mobile phones have overtaken fixed lines in a number of countries including Mexico, Paraguay and Venezuela (ITU 2001).

The region, with 8.6 per cent of the world population, has 2.7 per cent of the international scientific community and produced about 2.5 per cent of the scientific publications in 1998. Brazil is considered to be the most successful country in science and technology, investing about 1 per cent of GDP for

| The spread of communications 1980–98 (numbers/1 000 people) | | | | | | |
|---|---|---|---|---|---|---|
| | Telephone lines | | Daily newspapers | | Radios | |
| | 1980 | 1998 | 1980 | 1998 | 1980 | 1998 |
| Meso-America | 23.0 | 86.2 | 54.8 | 54.7 | 181.4 | 298.7 |
| South America | 35.8 | 120.6 | 48.9 | 46.9 | 305.1 | 457.8 |
| Caribbean | 52.9 | 227.4 | 37.9 | 23.7 | 361.4 | 520.3 |
| **Region** | **36.7** | **139.1** | **45.7** | **37.3** | **293.1** | **442.7** |

Source: World Bank 2000

scientific research and development, compared to a regional average of 0.53 per cent (Massarani 2001).

## Governance

Two important political developments have marked the past three decades in the region. The first is the transition from military dictatorships towards democratic governments. All countries now either have a democratically elected government or are in the course of establishing one. The democratization process has made more rapid progress in recent years due to strengthening of local governments and municipalities, reform of the judiciary system and privatization of large state-owned enterprises.

The second important development relates to the participation of civil society and creation of civil society institutions such as non-governmental organizations. The increase in freedom has brought with it greater public concern for the environment and sustainable development but these issues have yet to be fully integrated into political decision-making.

### References: Chapter 2, socio-economic background, Latin America and the Caribbean

ECLAC (2000). *Social Panorama of Latin America 1999-2000*. Santiago, United Nations Economic Commission for Latin America and the Caribbean

ECLAC and UNEP (2001). *The Sustainability of Development in Latin America and the Caribbean: Challenges and Opportunities*. Report prepared for Regional Preparatory Conference of Latin America and the Caribbean for the World Summit on Sustainable Development, Rio de Janeiro, 23-24 October 2001

IADB (2000). *Annual Report 2000*. Washington DC, Inter-American Development Bank

IEA (1999). *Energy Balances of OECD countries 1960–97, Energy Balances of Non-OECD countries 1971–97*. Paris, Organization of Economic Cooperation and Development, International Energy Agency

ITU (2002). *ICT Free Statistics Home Page: Internet Indicators by Country for 1998 and 2000*. International Telecommunication Union http://www.itu.int/ITU-D/ict/statistics [Geo-2-293]

Massarani, L. (2001). *Latin America Falls Short in Science Spending*. SciDev.net http://www.scidev.net/gateways/newsLA.asp?t=N&gw=LA&gwname=Latin%20America# [Geo-2-296]

PAHO (1998). *La Salude en las Américas*. Edición de 1998, Publicacíon Científica No. 569. Washington DC, Pan American Health Organization

PNUMA/OD (2001). *GEO: Estadísticas Ambientales de América Latina y el Caribe*. San José, Costa Rica, PNUMA y Observatorio del Desarrollo, Universidad de Costa Rica

UIS (2001). *Latin America and the Caribbean: Regional Report*. Nîmes, Société Edition Provence

UNEP (2000). *GEO Latin America and the Caribbean Environment Outlook*. Mexico City, United Nations Environment Programme, ROLAC

UNDP (2001). *Human Development Report 2001*. Oxford and New York, Oxford University Press http://www.undp.org/hdr2001/completenew.pdf [Geo-2-289]

United Nations Population Division (2001). *World Population Prospects 1950-2050 (The 2000 Revision)*. New York, United Nations www.un.org/esa/population/publications/wpp2000/wpp2000h.pdf [Geo-2-204]

World Bank (1999). *World Development Indicators 1999*. Washington DC, World Bank

World Bank (2001). *World Development Indicators 2001*. Washington DC, World Bank

## Socio-economic background: North America

The past three decades of the 20th century have brought increasing affluence and power to North America. North Americans not only live long lives in increasingly diverse societies but their production of material wealth and consumption of goods are also among the highest in the world. American capital, technology and goods are fuelling globalization, a defining trend of the new millennium that carries unprecedented opportunities and risks.

### Human development

Based on the Human Development Index (HDI), the region probably has the highest level of human development in the world. With Canada ranked third and the United States sixth, the region has an average HDI value of 0.935, compared to 0.928 for the high-income OECD countries (UNDP 2001).

Despite this, poverty is not unknown in North America. Over the past decade, poverty rates have declined in the United States but increased in Canada. Although debates about the definition, measurement and thus extent of poverty continue, data clearly show that some social groups are more vulnerable than others. Poverty is more likely to affect aboriginal people, some minorities, single parents and children. (Ross, Scott and Smith 2000, Dalaker 2001).

### The changing population

In contrast to other industrialized countries, particularly in Europe, population growth in North America continues, although growth rates have stayed constant at about 1 per cent over the past three decades and the region's share of global population has declined slightly from 6.2 per cent in 1972 to 5.2 per cent (about 314 million) in 2000 (United Nations Population Division 2001). Although birth rates are low, there is continuous immigration mostly from Latin America, the Caribbean, and Asia and the Pacific. This has also resulted in a more diverse population in the region (Blank 2001).

The population is growing older (see charts below). People aged 60 and more accounted for 14 per cent of the population in 1970 and 16 per cent in 2000. By 2025, this is projected to increase to 25 per cent (United Nations Population Division 1998). The gradual 'greying' of the population is a result of declining birth rates and increasing life expectancy as well as the ageing of the post World War II generation. This trend has implications for social security systems and also for global financial flows. As the number of retirees increases, they stop saving and start drawing down their accumulated assets instead.

### Economic development

Since 1972, North America has experienced greater regional integration, increased economic activity and a gradual shift towards the service sector. Some North American companies have become truly transnational and have invested heavily in emerging economies, significantly influencing development patterns elsewhere. Despite periodic setbacks over the past 30 years, North America has strengthened its role as an engine of global economic change (Blank 2001).

Population pyramids for the United States show a clearly discernible ageing trend, even over the single decade 1990–2000

Source: US Census Bureau 2002

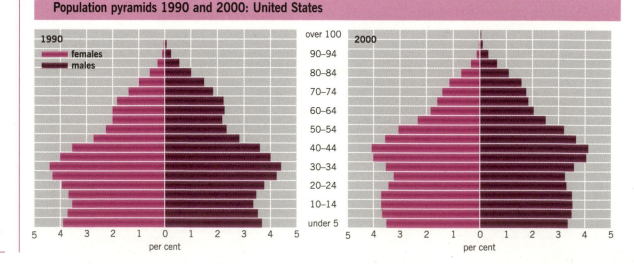

Population pyramids 1990 and 2000: United States

Concerns about the vulnerability of the energy sector largely vanished as the 1973 and 1979 oil crises were followed by economic restructuring and the growth of the service sector (see graph). With the conclusion of a free trade agreement and the emergence of information and biotechnologies, many regional North American economies soared through most of the 1990s and then collapsed in 2000, shaking the stock markets.

In 2001, it was estimated that the 285 million people (including 135 million workers) of the United

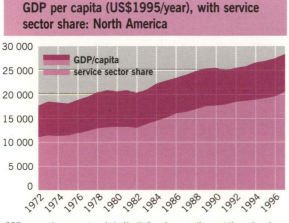

**GDP per capita (US$1995/year), with service sector share: North America**

GDP per capita grew strongly in North America over the past three decades, with the service sector share of the economy growing from 63 to 72 per cent during the period 1972–1997

*Source: World Bank 2000*

States produced about US$10 000 billion in GDP; the 31 million people (including 15 million workers) of Canada about US$670 billion in GDP (US Department of Commerce 2002, US Census Bureau 2002, US Department of Labor 2002, Statistics Canada 2002).

North America not only leads the world in economic output but also consumes the most. Private consumption per capita in the region is about five times the global average, and grew from US$11 461 in 1972 to US$18 167 in 1997, compared to a global average of US$2 315 in 1972 and US$3 257 in 1997 (World Bank 2001, all figures expressed in constant US$1995).

Although representing only around 5 per cent of the global population, the United States and Canada consume nearly 25 per cent of total energy (IEA 2002). While there is evidence of a slight decoupling of energy use and economic growth, per capita energy use has remained consistently higher than in any other of the world's regions (Mathews and Hammond 1999). Use of private vehicles continues to increase, whereas use of public transportation has generally remained constant (see 'Urban areas').

## Science and technology

Over the past three decades, the region has led the world in scientific and technological innovation. North America has 14 global hubs of technological innovation, 13 in the United States and 1 in Canada, and 38 per cent of global expenditure on research and development comes from North America, with a large share of this spending taking place in the United States (UNESCO 2001). An increasing proportion of this investment comes from the private sector, accounting for 67 per cent in the United States and 45 per cent in Canada. Venture capital continues to be a particularly important source of funding for new technology-based firms, particularly in the information, communication and biotechnology sectors. Spending on higher education is among the highest in the world at more than US$19 000/student/year in the United States and more than US$14 500/student/year in Canada in 1998. The region also attracts the largest number of foreign-born scientists (OECD 2001a).

The United States was responsible for 34.8 per cent of all patents filed in 1995, and like Canada publishes a high number of scientific papers per capita. North America is a keen diffuser of information and communication technologies, key assets for a knowledge-based economy. Access to computers and the Internet are among the highest in the world, and access rates continue to grow. The United States is the world's largest Internet market, with almost 100 million regular users at the beginning of 2001. It was also the world's leading mobile market with about 110 million users in 2000, a lead likely to be soon overtaken by China (ITU 2001).

Multi-factor productivity, or the efficiency of the use of capital and labour in the production process, increased rapidly both in Canada and in the United States during the second half of the 1990s (OECD 2001b).

## Governance

As the world moves towards global integration, political, fiscal and administrative power is increasingly devolving to states and provinces in North America. This has led to a 'flatter' corporate structure and decentralized decision-making. At the same time, non-governmental organizations have emerged as important new social actors, many with little formal authority structure.

But growing interconnectedness has also exposed the region to new risks associated with events half way across the world. The events of 11 September 2001 demonstrated not only interconnectedness but also exposure, vulnerability and a need to improve understanding of the major driving forces at global level. The protection of American economic interests and investments has become integrated into the concept of national security (IIP 2001). Protests over liberalized trade in Seattle in 1999 and Quebec City in 2001 were evidence of growing public anxiety about globalization, environmental values, trade and labour rights. At the same time, a trend towards greater corporate accountability and transparency has potentially important implications for regulation and civil society's engagement in influencing the private sector.

The past 30 years also brought an increasingly conscious struggle to balance continued economic growth with environmental and social objectives. Concern about the state of the natural environment has come to the forefront as environmentalism became a recognized social movement. Prodded by the grassroots in the 1970s, environmental laws and

policies were quickly enacted. North America was an early adopter of environmental legislation, public participation and, at least in the case of Canada, the concept of sustainable development (Barr 1993). Impressive gains were made in controlling many conventional pollutants and in continuing a trend in setting aside protected areas.

Environmental concern was increased during the mid-1980s by a new awareness of the global nature of some environmental problems, and membership in environmental NGOs soared. By the 1990s, 'common sense' approaches were advocated as concerns over deficit reduction led to budget cuts to environmental departments and to reliance on market incentives and voluntary programmes (Dowie 1995, Vig and Kraft 1997). After the UN Conference on Environment and Development in 1992, both countries became committed to sustainable development as reflected in stated federal goals in Canada and the efforts by many US states and localities in moving forward on *Agenda 21*.

## References: Chapter 2, the socio-economic background, North America

Barr, J. (1995). *The Origins and Emergence of Quebec's Environmental Movement: 1970-1985.* Master's Thesis. Montreal, McGill University

Blank, R.M. (2001). An overview of trends in social and economic well-being, by race. In Smelser, N.J., Wilson W.J. and Mitchell, F. (eds.), *America Becoming: Racial Trends and their Consequences, Volume 1.* Washington DC, National Academy Press

Dalaker, J. (2001). *Poverty in the United States.* Washington DC, US Census Bureau, US Department of Commerce http://www.census.gov/prod/2001pubs/p60-214.pdf [Geo-2-297]

Dowie, M. (1995). *Losing Ground: American Environmentalism at the Close of the Twentieth Century.* Cambridge, Massachusetts, MIT Press

Hillner, J. (2000). Venture capitals. *Wired*, 7 August 2000

IEA (2002). *Key World Energy Statistics.* Paris, International Energy Agency http://www.iea.org/statist/keyworld/keystats.htm [Geo-2-298]

IIP (2001). *The Americas.* US Department of State International Information Programmes http://usinfo.state.gov/regional/ar/ar.htm [Geo-2-299]

ITU (2002). *ICT Free Statistics Home Page: Internet Indicators by Country for 1998 and 2000.* International Telecommunication Union http://www.itu.int/ITU-D/ict/statistics [Geo-2-293]

Mathews, E. and Hammond, A. (1999). *Critical Consumption Trends and Implications: Degrading Earth's Ecosystems.* Washington DC, World Resources Institute

OECD (2000). *Policy Brief: Economic Survey of Canada, 2000.* Paris, Organization for Economic Cooperation and Development

OECD (2001a). *Education at a Glance: OECD Indicators 2001.* Paris, OECD www1.oecd.org/els/education/ei/eag/chB.htm [Geo-2-325]

OECD (2001b). *OECD Science, Technology and Industry Scoreboard 2001. Towards a Knowledge Based Economy.* Paris, Organization for Economic Cooperation and Development http://www1.oecd.org/publications/e-book/92-2001-04-1-2987/A.1.htm [Geo-2-300]

Ross, D.P., Scott, K. and Smith, P. (2000). *The Canadian Factbook on Poverty.* Ottawa, Canadian Council on Social Development. http://www.ccsd.ca/pubs/2000/fbpov00/hl.htm [Geo-2-301]

Statistics Canada (2002). *Canadian Statistics.* Ottawa, Statistics Canada http://www.statcan.ca/english/Pgdb/Economy/Finance/fin06.htm [Geo-2-323]

UNDP (2001). *Human Development Report 2001.* Oxford and New York, Oxford University Press http://www.undp.org/hdr2001/completenew.pdf [Geo-2-289]

UNESCO (2001). *Facts and Figures 2000.* Paris, UNESCO Institute for Statistics www.uis.unesco.org/en/pub/pub0.htm http://www.uis.unesco.org/en/pub/pub0.htm [Geo-2-292]

United Nations Population Division (1998). *World Population Prospects: The 1998 Revision. Volume II: Sex and Age.* New York, United Nations

United Nations Population Division (2001). *World Population Prospects 1950-2050 (The 2000 Revision).* New York, United Nations www.un.org/esa/population/publications/wpp2000/wpp2000h.pdf [Geo-2-204]

US Census Bureau (2002). *Population Estimates.* US Census Bureau http://eire.census.gov/popest/data/national/populartables/table01.php [Geo-2-302]

US Department of Commerce (2002). *National Income and Product Account Tables.* Bureau of Economic Analysis, US Department of Commerce http://www.bea.doc.gov/bea/dn/nipaweb/TableView Fixed.asp?SelectedTable=3&FirstYear=2000&Last Year=2001&Freq=Qtr [Geo-2-303]

US Department of Labor (2002). *Labor Force Statistics from the Current Population Survey.* Bureau of Labor Statistics, US Department of Labor http://www.bls.gov/cps/home.htm [Geo-2-304]

Vig, N.J. and Kraft, M.E. (eds., 1997). *Environmental Policy in the 1990s: Reform or Reaction.* Washington DC, CQ Press

World Bank (2000). *Entering the 21st Century: World Development Report 1999/2000.* New York, Oxford University Press

World Bank (2001). *World Development Indicators 2001.* Washington DC, World Bank http://www.worldbank.org/data/wdi2001/pdfs/tab3_8.pdf [Geo-2-024]

## Socio-economic background: West Asia

The West Asia region has undergone major demographic development and socio-economic transformation, including substantial agricultural and industrial development, since oil was discovered at the beginning of the 20th century. These trends have intensified during the past 30 years.

### Human development

Most West Asian countries fall into the high (Bahrain, Kuwait, Qatar and the United Arab Emirates) or medium (Jordan, Lebanon, Oman, Saudi Arabia and Syria) category of human development. Yemen is the only country classified as having a low level of human development, and information is not available for Iraq and the Occupied Palestinian Territories (UNDP 2001). Human development rankings were higher for most countries in the 1990s than the early 1980s although many have experienced set-backs over this period, particularly in the 1990s (UNDP 2000).

In some countries, there has been a significant improvement in certain components of human development over the past three decades. For instance, in Oman life expectancy increased from 54.9 years in the early 1970s to more than 70 in 2000 although in Iraq it declined from 66 to 58 years over the same period (WHO 2000). Access to improved water and adequate sanitation is generally high (80–100 per cent) with the exception of Yemen, where the figures are 69 per cent for improved water and 45 per cent for adequate sanitation (UNDP 2000, 2001). Access to safe water also dropped in Iraq during the second half of the 1990s (UNDP 2000).

There is considerable variation in per capita GDP between the countries of West Asia. The highest are on the Arabian Peninsula, ranging from US$6 384 in Saudi Arabia to US$16 483 in Kuwait in 1998. However, in countries such as Kuwait, Qatar and United Arab Emirates, per capita GDP has declined over the past 30 years — for example, from US$36 413 in 1975 to US$12 950 by 1998 in Qatar. These changes are attributed to fluctuations in oil prices. Mashriq countries have much lower levels of per capita GDP, ranging from US$1 095 in Syria to US$2 288 in Lebanon in 1998 (data are not available for Iraq and the Palestinian territories). Yemen is by far the poorest country — average per capita GDP increased

from only US$169 in 1975 to US$471 in 1998 (UNESCWA 1999).

Despite the relatively high per capita GDP in many countries, human and income poverty still exist. Seven West Asian countries (Iraq, Jordan, Lebanon, Oman, Saudi Arabia, Syria and Yemen) score poorly on one or more of the key components used to assess levels of human development. For most of these countries, adult literacy and low life expectancy are the key factors, rather than income poverty which is mainly an issue in Jordan, Oman and Yemen (UNDP 2001). Overall, literacy rates have increased in West Asia over the past two decades — for example to 92 per cent in Lebanon. Female literacy has increased steadily in most countries but it remains below the male literacy rate (UNESCO 2000).

### The changing population

The total population of West Asia (excluding the Occupied Palestinian Territories) has almost tripled from an estimated 37.3 million in 1972 to 97.7 million in 2000, increasing less in the Mashriq than the Arabian Peninsula (see graph on page 56). The

Although the West Asian economy is statistically dominated by the petroleum industry, economic reality for many West Asians is still based on traditional lifestyles

*Source: UNEP, Topham Picturepoint*

West Asian GDP per capita has shown little overall change since 1972. Variations are mainly due to changes in the price of petroleum

*Source: estimated from World Bank 2001*

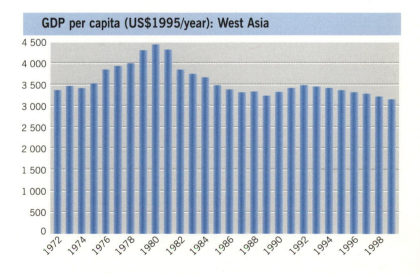

**GDP per capita (US$1995/year): West Asia**

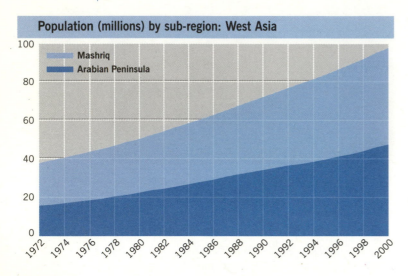

**Population (millions) by sub-region: West Asia**

Legend:
- Mashriq
- Arabian Peninsula

The West Asian population is still increasing at more than 3 per a year — by about 3.6 per cent a year in the Arabian Peninsular sub-region and by about 2.7 per cent a year in the Mashriq sub-region

*Source: compiled from United Nations Population Division 2001*

population of the Occupied Palestinian Territories was 1.13 million in 1972 and 3.19 million in 2000 (United Nations Population Division 2001).

The regional population growth rate was still above 3 per cent in 2000, well above the global average of 1.3 per cent (United Nations Population Division 2001). There are, however, significant variations within the region — the population of the United Arab Emirates has increased more than eightfold since 1970 whereas in other countries the rate has been much lower or even negative. The highest growth rates are currently in the Yemen — 4.1 per cent a year at the end of the 20th century (United Nations Population Division 2001).

The high population growth rates can be partly attributed to national policies. For example, health improvements have brought about a decline in death rates of 50 per cent or more, increased life expectancy from 60.7 to 69.7 years, and more than halved the infant mortality rate from 75 to less than 30 per 1 000 live births. Despite a decrease in fertility rates in both sub-regions from more than 7 to 6.3 and 4.6 children per woman in the Arabian Peninsula and Mashriq respectively, present fertility rates are still much higher than the world average of 2.8 (United Nations Population Division 2001).

In most countries, the population is very young. In the Gulf Cooperation Council countries (GCC, all countries in the Arabian Peninsula except Yemen), 43 per cent of the population is younger than 15 years (Al-Qudsi 1996) and in the Mashriq sub-region the figure ranges from 30 per cent in Lebanon to 48 per cent in Iraq (UNESCWA 1997). Almost 50 per cent of

the Palestinian population is under the age of 15 years, increasing the dependency ratio (those under 15 and more than 64 years, who depend on the working population) to more than 100 per cent, very high by world standards (PCBS 1997).

Despite rapid population growth during the past three decades, GCC countries still suffer from a low population base (Al-Qudsi 1996). While the increase in population has been partly due to high population growth rates, a large influx of foreign workers due to increasing demand for labour by the expanding industrial and service sectors has also been a significant factor. The total workforce in the GCC countries increased from 2 million in 1975 to 8 million by 1995. Foreign workers formed 70 per cent of this total workforce and up to 90 per cent in the United Arab Emirates and Qatar, 83 per cent in Kuwait, 60 per cent in Bahrain and Oman, and 59 per cent in Saudi Arabia (Al-Qudsi 1996).

## Economic development

Economic performance has been greatly affected by fluctuations in oil prices on international markets, internal economic policies and other non-economic factors, including regional wars and internal conflicts (UNESCWA 1999). The economies of the GCC countries depend on oil revenues and related industries while those of the Mashriq countries and Yemen are more diversified.

Total GDP for the region has increased more than

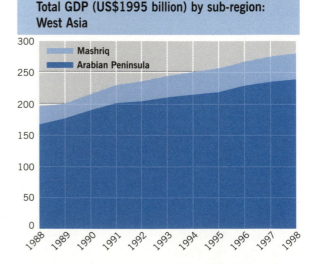

**Total GDP (US$1995 billion) by sub-region: West Asia**

Legend:
- Mashriq
- Arabian Peninsula

In real terms, total GDP increased by 43 per cent in the region as a whole over the decade to 1998 (measured in constant US$1995)

*Source: estimated from World Bank 2001*

threefold from US$85.8 billion in 1975 to US$256.67 billion in 1980 and reached US$307.71 billion by 1998 (UNESCWA 1999). The graph on page 56 shows the growth of total GDP in constant US$1995 for the period 1988–98.

The GCC countries (excluding Iraq) accounted for 85.47 per cent of aggregate nominal GDP for the region in 1997, of which Saudi Arabia had the largest share (US$146.2 billion) followed by the United Arab Emirates (US$49.54 billion) and Kuwait (US$30.37 billion). The Gulf War in 1990 severely damaged the economies of many countries in the region, directly or indirectly.

Economic growth rates have varied considerably within the region. While the real annual GDP growth rate averaged 3.04 per cent in the GCC countries between 1976 and 1998, it was slightly higher in some Mashriq countries — 4.46 per cent in Syria, 5.51 per cent in Jordan and 6.39 in Lebanon (UNESCWA 1999).

The structural composition of GDP in the region has changed markedly in the past three decades due to economic diversification (UNESCWA 1999). GCC countries started restructuring their economies to reduce their dependency on oil by diversifying into agriculture, industry and the service sector, including tourism. The combined share of the industrial sector (including oil) fell from 80 per cent in 1975 to 51 per cent by 1998, while the service sector's contribution increased from 19 per cent in 1975 to 44.5 per cent by 1998. The overall contribution of agriculture increased from 0.89 per cent in 1975 to 4.22 per cent in 1998 (UNESCWA 1999). Although the share of oil in the GDP of the GCC countries has fallen from 62.4 per

### Energy production and consumption: West Asia

West Asia is rich in conventional energy resources and 9 of the 12 countries are oil producers and exporters. Despite being a major producer, the Middle East uses only about 4.3 per cent of total global commercial primary energy. Energy consumption has grown faster in West Asia over the past three decades than anywhere else. Nevertheless, this growth slowed from 6.4 per cent annually in the 1970s to 4.7 per cent in the 1990s (UNDP, UNDESA and WEC 2000). Per capita total final energy consumption has also grown steadily over the past three decades, from 0.5 tonnes of oil equivalent in 1971 to 1.6 tonnes of oil equivalent by 1999 (compiled from IEA 2001).

cent in 1980, it was still high at 33.81 per cent in 1998.

## Science and technology

Achievements in science and technology have been modest. Science and engineering students comprise about one-quarter of tertiary level students in Jordan, Kuwait, Lebanon, Syria and the United Arab Emirates, and as much as 41 per cent in Iraq (World Bank 2001). Nevertheless, lack of financial resources limit their contribution. Priority areas for research include water resources, biotechnology, renewable energy and the development of indigenous technologies.

The diffusion of communication technologies is variable. Distribution of personal computers ranges from almost twice the world average of 7.72 per 100 inhabitants in Bahrain, Kuwait, Qatar and the United Arab Emirates to only 0.19 per 100 inhabitants in Yemen (World Bank 2001). Use of mobile phones has grown rapidly, and is likely to have overtaken fixed lines in Bahrain and the United Arab Emirates, which have the greatest number of subscribers per 100 inhabitants — 54.8 and 30.0 respectively (ITU 2001, 2002).

### References: Chapter 2, socio-economic background: West Asia

Al-Qudsi, S. (1996). Labour market policies and development in the GCC: Is domestic policy of significance? In Delvin, J. (ed.), *Gulf Economies: Strategies for Growth in the 21st Century*. Washington DC, Georgetown University

IEA (2001). *World Energy Outlook: 2001 Insights*. International Energy Agency. http://www.iea.org/weo/insights.htm [Geo-2-305]

ITU (2001). *ITU Telecommunication Indicator Update*. International Telecommunication Union http://www.itu.int/journal/200105/E/html/update. htm#top [Geo-2-322]

ITU (2002). ICT Free Statistics Home Page: Internet Indicators by Country for 1998 and 2000 www.itu.int/ITU-D/ict/statistics/at_glance/ cellular00.pdf [Geo-2-324]

PCBS (1997). *Population and Housing Census*. Palestinian Central Bureau of Statistics http://www.pcbs.org/inside/f_pophos.htm [Geo-2-322]

UNDP (2000). *Human Development Report 2000*.

Oxford and New York, Oxford University Press http://www.undp.org/hdr2000/english/book/back1. pdf [Geo-2-306]

UNDP (2001). *Human Development Report 2001*. Oxford and New York, Oxford University Press http://www.undp.org/hdr2001/completenew.pdf [Geo-2-289]

UNDP, UNDESA and WEC (2000). *World Energy Assessment*. United Nations Development Programme http://www.undp.org/seed/eap/activities/wea [Geo-2-320]

UNESCO (2000). *Adult Literacy Rates by Sex. Region: Arab States*. Paris, UNESCO Institute for Statistics

UNESCWA (1997). *Demographic and Related Socioeconomic Data Sheets for Countries of the Economic and Social Commission for Western Asia as Assessed in 1996*. United Nations

Economic and Social Commission for Western Asia, No.9-1997. New York, United Nations

UNESCWA (1999). *Survey of Economic and Social Developments in the ESCWA Region*. New York, United Nations Economic and Social Commission for Western Asia

United Nations Population Division (1996). *Annual Populations 1950-2050 (the 1996 Revision)*. New York, United Nations

United Nations Population Division (2001). *World Population Prospects 1950-2050 (The 2000 Revision)*. New York, United Nations www.un.org/esa/population/publications/wpp2000/ wpp2000h.pdf [Geo-2-204]

WHO (2000). *WHO Statistical Information System*. World Health Organization http://www-nt.who.int/whosis/statistics/ [Geo-2-307]

World Bank (2001). *World Development Indicators 2001*. Washington DC, World Bank

## Socio-economic background: the Polar Regions

This section covers only the Arctic since the Antarctic has no permanent population. In the past 30 years, the Arctic has emerged as an important geopolitical region composed of eight nations surrounding the Arctic Ocean: Canada, Denmark (Greenland and the Faeroe Islands), Finland, Iceland, Norway, the Russian Federation, Sweden and the United States (Alaska). The Arctic encompasses about 13.4 million $km^2$ with a population of only 3.5 million people, a density of 0.26 people/$km^2$ (AMAP 1997).

### Human development

Seven of the eight Arctic states rank high on the Human Development Index (HDI), including Norway (1st) and Greenland/Denmark (15th) while the Russian Federation at 55th is in the mid-range (UNDP 2001). The Russian Federation is the only Arctic nation with an HDI that has fallen over the past three decades (UNDP 2001). The rankings mask a subtle but critical difference between the Arctic region and the more temperate latitudes of each of the Arctic nations.

The Arctic region has lower life expectancy and higher mortality rates, including higher infant mortality rates, than the national averages of its constituent countries. Life expectancy in northern Norway is five years less than the national average for men and three years less than that for women (AMAP 1997). In Greenland, where more than 80 per cent of the population is Inuit, life expectancy is 69.5 years, almost ten years below that of Iceland (AMAP 1997,

UNDP 2001). At the end of the 1980s, life expectancy for men (54 years) and women (65 years) in the Russian north was 10–20 years less than the national average (AMAP 1997). The rate of infant mortality for indigenous minorities of the Russian North is 30 per 1 000, and reached 47.6 per 1 000 among the Siberian Yup'ik, while infant mortality in Iceland is only 6 per 1 000 live births (AMAP 1997).

High rates of literacy characterize all Arctic areas but the quality of schooling in remote communities is below that of urban centres to the south. Concern for native language retention has led to renewed efforts to offer primary education in native languages as well as native language training in secondary schools and institutes of higher education.

All Arctic peoples share health risks from persistent organic pollutants (POPs), toxic metals, radionuclides, indoor and outdoor air pollutants, water contamination and ultraviolet radiation. Initial studies in Canada showed that levels of POPs in the blood of indigenous people who consume marine mammals were 3–10 times higher than levels in southern Canada. Fear of contaminants, however, may lead to changes in traditional diets that could lead to other health problems (Government of Canada 2000).

### The changing population

The Arctic is home to numerous indigenous peoples. Inuit comprise more than 80 per cent of the population of Greenland and 85 per cent of the population of Nunavut, Canada. With these exceptions, indigenous peoples are minorities in their own homelands due to immigration.

The Arctic has a very youthful population; one-quarter of the population is younger than 15 in Greenland and Iceland, whereas 41 per cent are younger than 16 in Nunavut, Canada (Conference Board of Canada 2002, CIA 1998a and b). There was a dramatic 32 per cent increase in population in Nunavut between 1986 and 1996 due to high birth rates and increased life expectancy (see charts left).

Employment opportunities and housing construction have not kept pace with population growth, resulting in unemployment and serious housing crises in many communities (AMAP 1997). High rates of alcoholism, suicide, homicide and accidental deaths in Arctic populations may also be related to lack of opportunities and a resulting sense of powerlessness (Bjerregaard and Young 1998). By

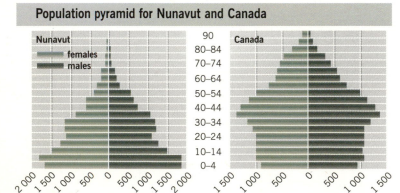

**Population pyramid for Nunavut and Canada**

Arctic populations are young compared to those of the Arctic states themselves

*Note: Nunavut in numbers of people, Canada in 1000s*
*Source: Conference Board of Canada 2002*

the late 1990s, unemployment in the Russian North had reached 25–30 per cent (AMAP 1997), and half a million people had left the region (Weir 2001).

## Economic development

Fishing, tourism, the fur trade, arts and crafts are traditionally important commercial activities in the Arctic, and an estimated 26 per cent of the jobs in Alaska depend on a healthy environment (Colt 2001). The economies of Greenland, the Faeroe Islands, and Iceland are dependent on fishing and fish exports (AMAP 1997) which account for 75 per cent of Iceland's exports (CIA 1998b). The fur industry crashed in the 1970s due to animal rights protests, and European and US bans on marine mammal products (Lynge 1992).

Tourism is increasingly important to Arctic economies. Summer tourist visits to Alaska doubled in the 1990s, reaching almost 1.2 million in 1999 (ADT 2000) and accounted for 3 per cent of Alaska's gross state product in 1998 (Goldsmith 1999). By 1999, tourism brought annual revenues of US$30 million to Nunavut and almost US$1 000 million to Alaska (State of Alaska 2001).

Exploitation of petroleum resources has fuelled economic growth in the Arctic nations. Nearly 85 per cent of Alaska's budget comes from oil revenues (State of Alaska 2001), and further developments are planned. Oil development has expanded to offshore Alaska, and exploration is occurring on the shelf of the Faeroes as well as in the Norwegian sector (Bjorsvik 2000). Oil and gas resources are developed in several regions of the Russian North, of which West Siberia has been assessed as the world's largest petroleum province (Klett and others 1997). Exploration in Northern Canada, the site of half of the country's estimated petroleum potential, has been revitalized in recent years (DIAND 2001).

Mining is another important economic activity for some countries. Alaska's mining industry was valued at more than US$1 000 million/year during 1995–2000 (Knowles 2001a). Gold, lead, zinc and diamond production continue to be important to the Canadian Arctic (BHP Billioton 2002). Lead and zinc mining has ceased in Greenland (Taagholt and Hansen 2001) but a new gold mine has started test production. Russia's Norilsk mining complex was the world's largest nickel producer in 1997 (Norilsk 2002).

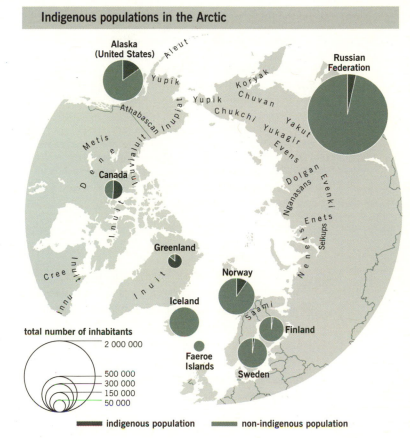

**Indigenous populations in the Arctic**

total number of inhabitants

2 000 000

500 000
300 000
150 000
50 000

■■■ indigenous population    ■■■ non-indigenous population

Map shows location of main indigenous peoples in the Arctic and the percentage of indigenous peoples in the Arctic areas of Arctic states

*Source: CAFF 2001*

## Science and technology

Following the 1972 UN conference in Stockholm, indigenous participation in NGO forums and scientific meetings has led to an appreciation of different forms of traditional knowledge and the inclusion of traditional ecological knowledge in land and resource planning. Today, many scientists welcome the partnership of indigenous and local Arctic residents in research.

Internet access, while unevenly distributed, has revolutionized Arctic communication. However, while computers as well as television, film, video and broadcasting have spread across the Arctic, many of the settlements in the Russian Arctic still have inadequate or no telephone service.

### The importance of subsistence foods

Communities throughout the Arctic depend on domestic reindeer, wild meat, birds, marine mammals, fish and local plants which account for up to 50 per cent of the indigenous diet and 25 per cent of the general population's diet in the Chukotka Autonomous Okrug region of the Russian Federation (AMAP 1997). This subsistence food is critical to indigenous people, and it is one reason why indigenous organizations promote the conservation of natural resources, rights to hunt, fish, trap and gather plants, and a reduction in the pollution transported to the Arctic from the mid-latitudes.

## Alaskan Oil and the Arctic National Wildlife Refuge

The Arctic National Wildlife Refuge (ANWR) in northeastern Alaska is 'America's finest example of an intact naturally functioning community of arctic/subarctic ecosystems' (USFWS 2001). The Refuge is set aside for wilderness protection except for one disputed area that may be open to oil and gas exploration by an Act of the US Congress. This area is estimated to contain 2–12 billion barrels of economically recoverable oil. The US Fish and Wildlife Service (USFWS) reports a 50 per cent chance of finding an amount of oil equal to that consumed by the United States in nine months. Alaska's North Slope oilfields have already produced 13 billion barrels since 1973 and may have only 3 billion barrels remaining.

For the Gwich'in people straddling the Alaska/Canada border, the ANWR is sacred land because it includes calving grounds of the porcupine caribou herd, their chief source of food, clothing, tools, ornaments, and the centre of their culture (Gemmill 2002).

## Governance

In 1972, the Arctic was a highly militarized zone preventing most international cooperation. Only with the establishment of the Arctic Environmental Protection Strategy (AEPS) in 1991 did all eight Arctic nations commit themselves to ongoing cooperation. In 1996, the AEPS developed into the Arctic Council to further environmental protection and sustainable development. The Council is unique among international organizations in granting indigenous organizations special status as 'permanent participants' of the Council (Arctic Council 2002).

Devolution of political authority from central governments to regional and even local governments and huge transfers of land and capital to indigenous peoples have occurred in the Arctic over the past three decades. Comprehensive Claims Agreements now cover all Arctic areas of Canada and include the transfer of millions of square kilometres of land and water, capital, revenues, harvesting exploitation and development rights. The Saami have gained considerable powers of self-determination through the creation of Saami Parliaments in each of the Nordic states. Greenland became semi-autonomous in 1979 with the establishment of the Home Rule Government, which was further strengthened in 1985 (Osherenko and Young 1989). Indigenous people of the Russian North have yet to achieve such a degree of control over their lands and lives despite protection of their rights in the 1993 Constitution and recent legislation (Osherenko 2001, Kryazhkov 1996).

## References: Chapter 2, socio-economic background, the Polar Regions

Arctic Council (2002). Arctic Council www.arctic-council.org [Geo-2-326]

ADT (2000). The State's Role in Guiding Tourism Growth. Alaska Division of Tourism http://www.dced.state.ak.us/cbd/toubus/pptandspeeches.htm [Geo-2-308]

AMAP (1997). Arctic Pollution Issues: A State of the Arctic Environment Report. Oslo, Arctic Monitoring and Assessment Programme

BHP Billioton (2002). Diamonds. http://www.bhpbilliton.com/bb/customerCentre/productGroups/diamonds.jsp [Geo-2-308]

Bjerregaard, P. and Young, T.K. (1998). The Circumpolar Inuit – Health of a Population in Transition. Copenhagen, Munksgaard International

Bjorsvik, B.T. (2000). Exploration Takes Off in Major Fish Spawning Ground, Faroese Oil Exploration Underway. WWF Arctic Bulletin 3, 2000, 14-15

CAFF (2001). Arctic Flora and Fauna: Status and Conservation. Helsinki, Arctic Council Programme for the Conservation of Arctic Flora and Fauna

CIA (1998a). Greenland. World Rover www.worldrover.com/vital/greenland.html [Geo-2-309]

CIA (1998b). Iceland. World Rover www.worldrover.com/vital/iceland.html [Geo-2-310]

Colt, S. (2001). What's the Economic Importance of Alaska's Healthy Ecosystems, Research Summary 61.University of Alaska Anchorage

http://www.iser.uaa.alaska.edu/publications/formal/rsummary/rs61.pdf [Geo-2-311]

Conference Board of Canada (2002). Iqaluit Demographics. Conference Board of Canada www.city.iqaluit.nu.ca/demographics/demographics.htm [Geo-2-312]

DIAND (2001). Oil and Gas in Canada's North. The Canadian frontier — Renewing Exploration in the North. Indian and Northern Affairs Canada http://www.ainc-inac.gc.ca/ps/ecd/env/nor_e.html [Geo-2-313]

Gemmill, F. (2002). Arctic Refuge, Home of the Gwich'in People. National Wildlife Federation http://www.nwf.org/arcticrefuge/gwichin.html [Geo-2-314]

Goldsmith, S. (1999). Alaska Gross State Product University of Alaska Anchorage http://www.iser.uaa.alaska.edu/publications/formal/review97_2000.pdf [Geo-2-315]

Government of Canada (2000). Northern Science and Technology in Canada: Federal Framework and Research Plan April 1, 2000-March 31, 2002. Ottawa, Government of Canada

Kryazhkov, V.A. (1996). Land rights of the small peoples in Russian federal legislation. Polar Geography 20, 2, 85-98

Lynge, F. (1992). Arctic Wars, Animal Rights, Endangered Peoples. Hanover, New Hampshire, New England University Press.

Norilsk (2002). Norilsk Mining Centre - Nickel, Palladium and Copper Production Facility, Russia. The Website for the Mining Industry

http://www.mining-technology.com/projects/norilsk/index.html [Geo-2-316]

Osherenko, G. (2001). Indigenous rights in Russia: is title to land essential for cultural survival? Georgetown International Environmental Law Review 3, 695-734

Osherenko, G. and Young, O. (1989). Age of the Arctic: Hot Conflicts and Cold Realities. Cambridge, Cambridge University Press

State of Alaska (2001). Visitor Information. State of Alaska www.dced.state.ak.us/tourism/learn/learn6.htm [Geo-2-317]

Taagholt, J. and Hansen, J.C. (2001). Greenland: Security Perspectives, Fairbanks, Arctic Research Consortium of the United States

UNDP (2001). Human Development Report 2001. Oxford and New York, Oxford University Press http://www.undp.org/hdr2001/completenew.pdf [Geo-2-289]

USFWS (2001). Potential Impacts of Proposed Oil and Gas Development on the Arctic Refuge's Coastal Plain. Arctic National Wildlife Refuge http://www.defenders.org/wildlife/arctic/fws/drill/usfws4.html [Geo-2-318]

Weir, F. (2001). Russia's Arctic is Now an Economic Gulag, Christian Science Monitor www.csmonitor.com/durable/2001/02/26/p1s4.htm [Geo-2-319]

# OUR CHANGING ENVIRONMENT: Mesopotamian marshlands

Comprising an integral part of the Tigris-Euphrates river system, the marshlands are located at the confluence of the rivers in southern Iraq and into Iran. The desiccation of these vast wetland resources is attributable to two main causes: upstream dams and drainage schemes. An aerial view of the marshlands in 1976 shows them still largely intact. Since then, there has been a 90 per cent decline in marshland area. By the year 2000, only a small section of the Al-Hawizah marsh straddling the Iran-Iraq border remains but even this is rapidly shrinking due to upstream water projects.

The marshlands are a key site for migratory birds. Marshland loss has put an estimated 40 species migrating between Siberia and South Africa at great risk. Several mammals and fish unique to the marshlands are now considered extinct. Coastal fisheries in the Northern Gulf, dependent on the marshlands for spawning grounds, have also been affected.

Many of the Marsh Arabs, who have lived on their fragile, near-floating homes in this rare water world for millennia, have now been forced to flee as a result of the collapse of their habitat. A culture has been destroyed and an indigenous people turned into refugees.

A typical marsh landscape, with villages built on artificial floating islands that enclose an area of swamp which is then filled with reeds and mud. For flood protection, more layers are added each year to strengthen the platform's foundation

In the image below, dense vegetation (mainly *Phragmites* reeds) appears as dark red patches, while red patches along river banks are date palms. By 2000 most of the Central Marshes appear as olive to greyish-brown patches indicating low vegetation on moist to dry ground

Compilation: Hassan Partow, UNEP Division of Early Warning and Assessment
Satellite images: USGS/EROS Data Center
Photograph: Nik Wheeler

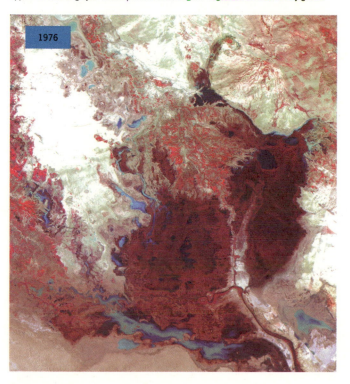

1976

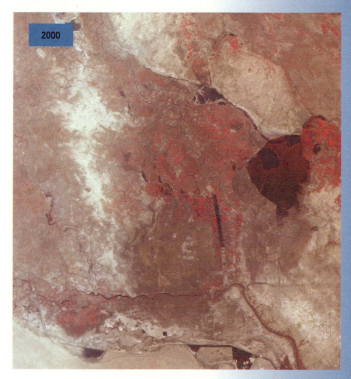

2000

# Land

## Global overview

The land area of the Earth covers a total of more than 140 million km$^2$ — somewhat less than one-third of the Earth's surface. Land resources are finite, fragile and non-renewable. They include soil, which is mainly important for agriculture; land cover, which is important for the environment; and landscapes which are an important component of human habitat and welfare. Besides forming a basis for plant and animal life support systems and agricultural production, land aids in the preservation of terrestrial biodiversity, regulation of the hydrological cycle, carbon storage and recycling, and other ecosystem services. It acts as a store of raw materials, a waste dump and landfill for both solid and liquid waste, and a basis for human settlement and transport activities (FAO 1995a, Wood, Sebastian and Scherr 2000).

The 1992 Earth Summit took a step forward in bringing problems associated with land resources to wider attention. In *Agenda 21* (UNCED 1992), Chapters 10, 12, 13 and 14 relate to land, covering the integrated approach to management of land resources, desertification and drought, mountain region development and sustainable agriculture. In the discussions of deforestation, biological diversity and freshwater resources (Chapters 11, 15 and 18), significant emphasis is placed on land as a productive resource, the importance of sustainable land use, and environmental pollution and conservation. *Agenda 21* has remained a primary basis for land resources policy although a further landmark of awareness of land at the highest policy level is found in the review prepared for the UN Millennium Summit (UN 2000). This review identifies the threats to future global food security arising from problems of land resources.

## Agriculture and food production

Since 1972, the main driving force leading to pressure on land resources has been increasing food production. In 2002, food is needed for some 2 220 million more people than in 1972 (United Nations Population Division 2001). The trend during the decade 1985–95 showed population growth racing ahead of food production in many parts of the world, particularly Africa: in 64 of 105 developing countries studied in this period, food production lagged behind population growth (UNFPA 2001).

Agricultural land (defined as land under arable use plus permanent crops) has increased steadily in developing regions but not in developed ones (see graph). The decrease in developed regions seems to have been driven less by availability of land resources than by economic forces, including overproduction of major commodities and decreasing prices for farm produce.

Policy failure and poor agricultural practices contribute to increased land pressure. For example, the excessive use of fertilizers and other chemicals contributes to soil degradation and water pollution. Between 1972 and 1988, global fertilizer use grew at an annual average of 3.5 per cent or by more than 4 million tonnes a year (FAO 2001). Up to the 1980s, maintenance and improvement of fertility was thought of chiefly in terms of addition of mineral fertilizers, and agricultural subsidies increased the use of fertilizers further. Government policies supported farmers by subsidizing agricultural inputs such as irrigation, fertilizer and pesticides. A study by FAO of 38 developing countries showed that 26 of them subsidized fertilizer use (FAO/IFA 1999).

Pesticides continue to be used indiscriminately (sometimes illegally) in places, and disposed of casually. A survey published by FAO of countries in Africa and the Near East reported stocks of unwanted or banned pesticides amounting to more than 16 500 tonnes at some 1 000 sites in 49 countries (FAO 1995a).

Irrigation has also made, and continues to make, an important contribution to agricultural production but the potential for future growth has changed. The efficiency of many irrigation schemes is low and land degradation problems are widespread. Poorly designed and implemented irrigation schemes can cause waterlogging, salinization and alkalization of soils. Some 25–30 million ha of the world's 255 million ha of irrigated land were severely degraded due to the accumulation of salts, according to 1995 FAO estimates. An additional 80 million ha were reported to be affected by salinization and waterlogging (FAO 1995b). In the 1980s it was estimated that about 10 million ha of irrigated land were being abandoned annually (WCED 1987) although the total irrigated area has continued to rise (see graph).

## Land degradation

Land degradation leads to a significant reduction of the productive capacity of land. Human activities

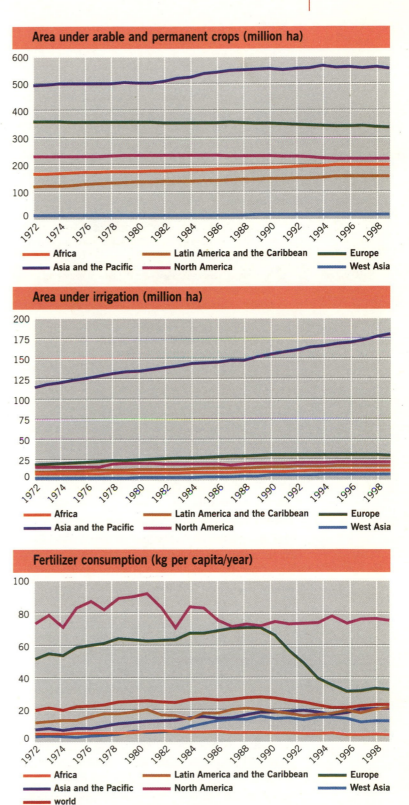

Graphs above show 30-year trends in three major agricultural variables: agricultural area, irrigated area and per capita fertilizer consumption. Fertilizer consumption has fallen in Europe and North America but continues to climb — albeit slowly — elsewhere

*Source: compiled from FAOSTAT 2001 and United Nations Population Division 2001*

## Extent and causes of land degradation

| Degradation extent | Cause |
| --- | --- |
| 580 million ha | **Deforestation** — vast reserves of forests have been degraded by large-scale logging and clearance for farm and urban use. More than 220 million ha of tropical forests were destroyed during 1975–90, mainly for food production. |
| 680 million ha | **Overgrazing** — about 20 per cent of the world's pasture and rangelands have been damaged. Recent losses have been most severe in Africa and Asia. |
| 137 million ha | **Fuelwood consumption** — about 1 730 million $m^3$ of fuelwood are harvested annually from forests and plantations. Woodfuel is the primary source of energy in many developing regions. |
| 550 million ha | **Agricultural mismanagement** — water erosion causes soil losses estimated at 25 000 million tonnes annually. Soil salinization and waterlogging affect about 40 million ha of land globally. |
| 19.5 million ha | **Industry and urbanization** — urban growth, road construction, mining and industry are major factors in land degradation in different regions. Valuable agricultural land is often lost. |

Source: FAO 1996

contributing to land degradation include unsuitable agricultural land use, poor soil and water management practices, deforestation, removal of natural vegetation, frequent use of heavy machinery, overgrazing, improper crop rotation and poor irrigation practices. Natural disasters, including droughts, floods and landslides, also contribute. A Global Assessment of Soil Degradation (GLASOD) was undertaken in the early 1990s (Oldeman, Hakkeling and Sombroek 1990, UNEP 1992) and a land degradation assessment of drylands (LADA) was initiated by GEF and UNEP in 2000 and is now being developed with FAO.

It has been estimated that 23 per cent of all usable land (excluding mountains and deserts, for example) has been affected by degradation to a degree sufficient to reduce its productivity (UNEP 1992, Oldeman, Hakkeling and Sombroek 1990). In the early 1990s, about 910 million ha of land were classified as 'moderately degraded', with greatly reduced agricultural productivity (see illustrations opposite). A total of 305 million ha of soils ranged between 'strongly degraded' (296 million ha) and 'extremely degraded' (9 million ha, of which more than 5 million ha were in Africa). 'Extremely degraded' soils are

beyond restoration (Oldeman, Hakkeling and Sombroek 1990).

Despite these compelling statistics on land degradation, some studies are beginning to question the data, arguing that degradation estimates are overstated. A major reason suggested for the overestimation of land degradation has been underestimation of the abilities of local farmers (Mazzucato and Niemeijer 2001). These authors argue that ' ... experts need to discriminate more carefully between a naturally bad state, a temporary bad state and a degraded state of land'.

Soil erosion is a major factor in land degradation and has severe effects on soil functions — such as the soil's ability to act as a buffer and filter for pollutants, its role in the hydrological and nitrogen cycle, and its ability to provide habitat and support biodiversity. About 2 000 million ha of soil, equivalent to 15 per cent of the Earth's land area (an area larger than the United States and Mexico combined), have been degraded through human activities. The main types of soil degradation are water erosion (56 per cent), wind erosion (28 per cent), chemical degradation (12 per cent) and physical degradation (4 per cent). Causes of soil degradation include overgrazing (35 per cent), deforestation (30 per cent), agricultural activities (27 per cent), overexploitation of vegetation (7 per cent) and industrial activities (1 per cent) (GACGC 1994).

Approaches to soil conservation have been greatly modified since the 1970s. Work used to concentrate on mechanical protection, such as bunds and terraces, largely to control surface run-off. This has been supplemented by a new approach (Shaxson and others 1989, Sanders and others 1999) which calls for greater attention to biological methods of conservation, and the integration of water conservation with soil protection, through improved management of soil-plant-water relationships, including reduced disturbance by tillage (University of Bern and others 2000). Within the international agricultural research system, the Consultative Group on International Agricultural Research, there is now a commitment to natural resource management, and explicit recognition of degraded land and desertification as environmental problems (Shah and Strong 1999).

Despite these developments, there is no clear indication that the rate of land degradation has decreased. As yet, there are no continuously monitored indicators of soil condition that would

## Extent and severity of land degradation

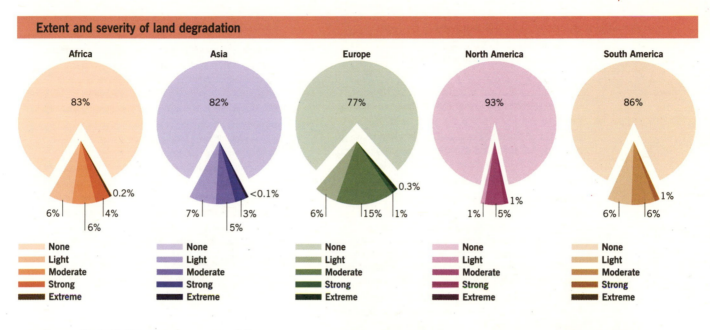

**Africa**
83%
0.2%
6% 4%
6%

None
Light
Moderate
Strong
Extreme

**Asia**
82%
<0.1%
7% 3%
5%

None
Light
Moderate
Strong
Extreme

**Europe**
77%
0.3%
6% 15% 1%

None
Light
Moderate
Strong
Extreme

**North America**
93%
1%
1% 5%

None
Light
Moderate
Strong
Extreme

**South America**
86%
1%
6% 6%

None
Light
Moderate
Strong
Extreme

permit quantitatively based assessments of changes over time, comparable to the monitoring of deforestation.

It has been suggested that soil monitoring should become a basic task of national soil survey organizations (Young 1991) but this proposal has yet to be widely adopted. An international programme was set up to develop a set of land quality indicators (Pieri and others 1995), comparable to those used to monitor economic and social conditions. The programme continues on a modest scale under the Global Terrestrial Observation System.

### Desertification

The UN Convention to Combat Desertification (UNCCD) defines desertification as 'land degradation in arid, semi-arid and dry sub-humid areas' brought about by factors such as climatic variations and human activities. Around 3 600 million ha, or 70 per cent, of the world's drylands (excluding hyper-arid deserts) are degraded (UNCCD 2000a). Many parties to the convention have now prepared national action programmes to strengthen activities to combat desertification and drought (UNCCD 2000b, 2001). However, there is no indication that governments are developing structures through which bottom-up action programmes could be implemented at the local level (CSE 1999). In addition, inadequate resource mobilization is hampering the affected developing countries' efforts to fulfil their commitments under the convention. A recent analysis of the CCD (Toulmin

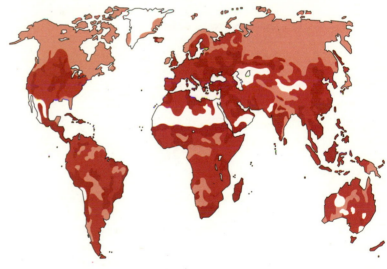

■ Very degraded soil   ■ Degraded soil   ■ Stable soil   □ Without vegetation

2001) argues that the convention model was ill-advised as 'it has tied people into a series of COP [Conference of the Parties] performances which demonstrate no linkage with real problems on the ground'. The desertification problem remains poorly understood as the available data show: estimates of areas affected range from one-third of the world's surface area to about 50 per cent, and people affected from 1 in 6 to 1 in 3 (Toulmin 2001).

### Climate change

The consequences of global climate change on agriculture and ecosystems are highly uncertain. Based on simulation models, the most likely impacts

**Pie charts and map above show the extent of areas of degraded land in the world and the location of degraded soils**

*Note: regions do not correspond exactly with GEO regions*

*Source: UNEP 1992 and GRID Arendal 2001*

## Climate change impacts on land and biodiversity by region

| Region | Adaptive capacity, vulnerability and key concerns |
| --- | --- |
| Africa | Grain yields are projected to decrease for many scenarios, diminishing food security, particularly in small food-importing countries. |
| | Desertification would be exacerbated by reductions in average annual rainfall, run-off and soil moisture, especially in Southern, Northern and Western Africa. |
| | Significant extinctions of plant and animal species are projected and would affect rural livelihoods, tourism and genetic resources. |
| Asia and the Pacific | Decreases in agricultural productivity and aquaculture due to thermal and water stress, sea-level rise, floods and droughts, and tropical cyclones would diminish food security in many countries of arid, tropical and temperate Asia; agriculture would expand and productivity would increase in northern areas. |
| | Climate change would exacerbate threats to biodiversity due to land-use and land-cover change and population pressure in Asia. |
| | In Australia and New Zealand, the net impact on some temperate crops of climate and $CO_2$ changes may initially be beneficial but this balance is expected to become negative for some areas and crops with further climate change. |
| | Some species with restricted climatic niches and which are unable to migrate due to fragmentation of the landscape, soil differences or topography could become endangered or extinct. |
| Europe | There will be some positive effects on agriculture in northern Europe; productivity will decrease in southern and eastern Europe. |
| Latin America | Yields of important crops are projected to decrease in many locations in Latin America, even when the effects of $CO_2$ are taken into account; subsistence farming in some regions of Latin America could be threatened. |
| | The rate of biodiversity loss would increase. |
| North America | Some crops would benefit from modest warming accompanied by increasing $CO_2$ but effects would vary among crops and regions, including declines due to drought in some areas of Canada's Prairies and the US Great Plains, potential increased food production in areas of Canada north of current production areas and increased warm-temperate mixed forest production. |
| Polar | Natural systems in the polar regions are highly vulnerable to climate change and current ecosystems have low adaptive capacity; technologically developed communities are likely to adapt readily to climate change but some indigenous communities, in which traditional lifestyles are followed, have little capacity and few options for adaptation. |
| Small Island States | The projected sea-level rise of 5 mm/year for 100 years would cause enhanced coastal erosion, loss of land and property, dislocation of people. |
| | Limited arable land and soil salinization makes agriculture of small island states, both for domestic food production and cash crop exports highly vulnerable to climate change. |

*Source: IPCC 2001*

## Population controversy

'Many people identify growing population pressures of the poor and the resultant overgrazing, deforestation and unsustainable agricultural practices as major causes of desertification. This theory, however, is based on the assumption that only the poor and their growing populations cause environmental degradation. It misses the impact of a chain of international trade and economic practices which result in low prices for agricultural and livestock commodities for the South; and political compulsions such as debt, which force a country to promote adverse land use practices in order to earn foreign exchange. In its simplistic reaction, the West chooses to provide food, first through aid and then by promoting increased agricultural production. The problem still persists, showing that the solution is far more complex.'

*Source: CSE 1999*

are net favourable effects for the cooler margins of the temperate zone, and adverse consequences for the sub-tropical semi-arid zone (see box). Regional changes in climate have already affected diverse physical and biological systems in many parts of the world. Mid- to high-latitude growing seasons have lengthened. Poleward and altitudinal shifts of plant and animal ranges have been observed (IPCC 2001). Natural systems at risk of climate change include glaciers, atolls, polar and alpine ecosystems, prairie wetlands and remnant native grasslands. Human systems that are vulnerable include agriculture, particularly food security, and forestry.

From the 1990s, the climate change issue directed attention to the role of land as a terrestrial store of carbon. Land degradation almost always involves a loss of soil organic matter. If this trend can be checked or reversed, a considerable potential exists for carbon sequestration through building up the levels of carbon stored in soils and the vegetation cover (IFAD/FAO 1999).

## Human settlements and infrastructure

Urban areas occupy only 1 per cent of the Earth's land area (UNEP 2000). However, urban expansion, including land requirements for industry, transport and for leisure activities in all regions, increases pressures on land resources. In the United States, for example, about 400 000 ha of farmland are lost to urbanization annually and China lost about 5 million ha of farmland to towns and cities during 1987–92 (UNFPA 2001). Land degradation, river siltation and soil pollution, from acid rain and industrial wastes, are some of the environmental issues associated with urbanization and industrialization.

The waste generated by cities is a major source of degradation. It is estimated that about 1.95 million ha of land have been degraded by industry and urbanization (FAO 1996). One cause has been the export by some developed countries of hazardous and toxic wastes to developing regions.

The international response to this was the 1989 Basel Convention on the Control of Transboundary Movements of Hazardous Wastes and their Disposal. The Basel Convention, which entered into force in 1992 (see Chapter 1), aims to reduce transboundary movements of hazardous wastes, minimize the creation of such wastes, and prohibit their shipment to countries lacking the capacity to dispose of hazardous wastes in an environmentally sound manner.

Urbanization has also spawned urban agriculture (see 'Urban areas'), which was hardly recognized internationally in the 1970s but has been expanding globally over the past 15-20 years, 'more rapidly than urban populations, and in many countries more rapidly than their economies' (Smit 1996). Urban agriculture takes place on both public and private land, both legally and illegally. More than 800 million urban dwellers were involved in urban agriculture in 1993 (Smit 1996). For example, in the Brazilian city of São Paulo, agriculture is a major planned land use in the city's metropolitan master plan, which was adopted in the 1990s.

In virtually all regions, urban agriculture has become one of the major food-producing activities. For example, most households in the Southeast Asia and Pacific Island sub-regions practise urban agriculture (Sommers and Smit 1994). About 30 per cent of the Russian Federation's food is produced on 3 per cent of the land in suburban dachas (Sommers and Smit 1994). In Moscow, families engaged in agriculture grew from 20 per cent of the city's population in 1970 to 65 per cent in 1990 (Smit 1996). During 1980–90, urban agriculture in the United States grew by 17 per cent (Smit 1996). In some African urban areas, the response by municipal authorities has been to cut down the crops to enforce land-use by-laws.

The impacts of urban agriculture include air, water and soil pollution, mainly from improper use of

Much good agricultural land is threatened by chemical pollution, particularly — as here in China — by waste products from urban centres. Chemical degradation is responsible for 12 per cent of global soil degradation

Source: UNEP, Zehng Zhong Su, China, Still Pictures

chemicals. Advocates of urban agriculture argue that, in addition to providing food, the activity can contribute to improving the environment through recycling organic matter. Solid wastes can be composted and used to fertilize soils.

## Chemicals and land use

Important recent developments include:

- The Stockholm Convention on Persistent Organic Pollutants (POPs) was adopted in May 2001 (see Chapter 1).
- UNEP, together with FAO and WHO, is promoting more sustainable practices in replacing POP pesticides with integrated pest management. The Global Crop Protection Federation is playing a proactive role in promoting the judicious use of pesticides and the prevention of toxic exposures and misuse of pesticides.

Other actions include pilot projects to demonstrate the technical and economic feasibility of new technologies to destroy obsolete chemicals and pesticides; and the encouragement of donors and industry to increase funding for management and disposal of these substances.

### Urban agriculture in Zimbabwe

In Harare, Zimbabwe, sanctions on urban agriculture were lifted temporarily in 1992. Within two years, the area cultivated had doubled and the number of farmers more than doubled. Municipal costs for landscape maintenance and waste management were down, food prices were down, and hundreds of jobs had been created. Several benefits were gained from just a change in policy. Similar policy-related benefits were documented in Lusaka and Accra in the 1970s (Smit 1996).

## Conclusion

The increase in world population means that pressures on land will continue to be acute, particularly in Africa and Asia. The increased needs for food and other agricultural products must be met mainly by raising and sustaining crop and livestock yields and by more intensive land use. This has to be accompanied by more efficient harvesting and processing of products so as to reduce post-production losses. However, current projections also assume an expansion of the arable area in developing countries, although at half the rate of the previous 30 years (FAO 2001). By 2030, FAO estimates suggest that an additional 57 million ha will be brought into cultivation in Africa, and 41 million ha in Latin America, increases of 25 per cent and 20 per cent respectively (FAO 2001). This expansion must necessarily come either from further conversion of forest and woodland, or by bringing into cultivation fragile areas of the semi-arid zone, both of which raise serious environmental concerns.

Meeting these challenges will stretch the limited resources currently allocated to agricultural research and development, and may call for reallocation of the scarce funding available. It will, in addition, require good governance, land and soil policies, and continued

### Land and the International Year of Mountains: importance of the mountain commons

**Litter on a mountainside in China**

*Source: UNEP, Zhe Hao, Still Pictures*

Mountains can provide crucial resources for social and economic development. Mountain commons provide essential local and downstream environmental products and services such as freshwater supplies, irrigation, hydropower, flood control, biodiversity conservation and tourism. However, with few exceptions, mountain commons are ecologically under-managed and suffer from the classic 'commons syndrome': while all seek to benefit, stakeholders lack coordination, incentives and instruments for joint care.

Satellite imagery shows significant loss of mountain forests and other vegetative cover over the past 20 years. The causes are often inappropriate agriculture and livestock developments in fragile areas. Downstream, poor watershed management causes siltation of rivers and reservoirs, and allows natural disasters to take an unprecedented toll as roads, bridges and sometimes entire communities are washed away.

Whenever mountain ecosystems are degraded by overexploitation, costs to businesses and communities are high. As vegetation is removed, aquifers and wells run drier. Siltation reduces the sustainability of hydropower and irrigation reservoirs. Agricultural run-off spoils the purity of renewable sources of freshwater. Fisheries suffer and urban water supplies dwindle in the dry season. In deforested mountain ranges, floods may become uncontrollable after heavy rain. They cause global damage of tens of billions of dollars every year.

Businesses stand to benefit from joining hands, and from shaping common action programmes to safeguard mountain ecosystems. This is a long-term challenge, and will require a measure of social responsibility and commitment beyond customary business horizons. Local, long-term, strategic private-public partnerships could begin to address and reverse patterns of degradation. In the same way that water-user associations are necessary in downstream water and irrigation management, there is a need for mountain-stakeholder associations. Region-by-region, these would need to equip themselves with supporting institutional, legal, economic and monitoring instruments.

The International Year of Mountains 2002 (IYM) could inspire such processes: it can draw attention to issues and opportunities; it can help network stakeholders across sectoral and company boundaries, it can promote conducive policy and incentive instruments. The business community could now build on recent work under the global water partnership agenda. The Water and Mountain Commons agenda, developed jointly by the Earth3000 NGO and UNEP's Mountain Programme, could become a tangible contribution to IYM. During the Bishkek Global Mountain Summit, the main concluding event of IYM, a special Mountain Marketplace facility will be established to promote private-public partnerships and mountain stakeholders' associations, involving upstream and downstream communities.

efforts to achieve sustainable use of land resources. A prerequisite is the adequate support by governments for national land resource institutions, and for building up the capacities of land resource planners, farmers and managers at local and national levels. Maintenance or improvement of the productive potential of land resources to meet the needs of present and future populations, while at the same time sustaining the vital ecosystem functions and other multiple uses of land, is a fundamental requirement for sustainability.

## References: Chapter 2, land, global overview

CSE (1999). *Green Politics: Global Environmental Negotiations 1*. New Delhi, Centre for Science and Environment

FAO (1995a). *Prevention and disposal of obsolete and unwanted pesticide stocks in Africa and the Near East*. Rome, Food and Agriculture Organization http://www.fao.org/docrep/W8419E/W8419e09.htm#7 [Geo-2-165]

FAO (1995b). *Planning for Sustainable Use of Land Resources: Towards a New Approach. FAO Land and Water Bulletin 2*. Rome, Food and Agriculture Organization

FAO (1996). *Our Land Our Future*. Rome and Nairobi, Food and Agriculture Organization and United Nations Environment Programme

FAO (2000). *Fertilizer Requirements in 2015 and 2030*. Rome, Food and Agriculture Organization ftp://ftp.fao.org/agl/agll/docs/barfinal.pdf [Geo-2-166]

FAO (2001). *Agriculture: Towards 2015/30. Technical Interim Report April 2000*. Rome, Food and Agriculture Organization http://www.fao.org/es/ESD/at2015/chapter1.pdf [Geo-2-167]

FAO/IFA (1999). *Fertilizer Strategies*. Rome and Paris, Food and Agriculture Organization and International Fertilizer Industry Association ftp://ftp.fao.org/agl/agll/ch10/ch104.pdf

FAOSTAT (2001). FAOSTAT Statistical Database. Rome, Food and Agriculture Organization http://www.fao.org/ [Geo-2-068]

GACGC (1994). *World in Transition: The Threat to Soils. Annual Report*. German Advisory Council on Global Change. Bonn, Economica Verlag GmbH

GRID Arendal (1997). *Soil Degradation Map* http://www.grida.no/db/maps/prod/global/tv01_l.gif [Geo-2-168]

IFAD/FAO (1999). *Prevention of land degradation, enhancement of carbon sequestration and conservation of biodiversity through land use change and sustainable land management with a focus on Latin America and the Caribbean. World Soil Resources Reports 86*. Rome, Food and Agriculture Organization

IPCC (2001). *Climate Change 2001: Impacts, Adaptation and Vulnerability. Contribution of Working Group II to the Third Assessment Report of the Intergovernmental Panel on Climate Change*. Cambridge, United Kingdom, and New York, United States, Cambridge University Press

Mazzucato, V. and Niemeijer, D. (2001). *Overestimating Land Degradation, Underestimating Farmers in the Sahel, Drylands Issues Paper*. London, International Institute for Environment and Development http://www.iied.org/pdf/dry_ip101eng.pdf [Geo-2-169]

Oldeman, L. R., Hakkeling, R. T. A. and Sombroek, W. G. (1990). *World Map of the Status of Human-Induced Soil Degradation*. Wageningen, International Soil Reference and Information Centre

Pieri, C., Dumanski, J., Hamblin, A. and Young, A. (1995). *Land quality indicators. World Bank Discussion Paper 315*. Washington DC, World Bank

Sanders, D.W., Huszar, P. C., Sombatpanit, S., and Enters, T. (eds) (1999). *Incentives in Soil Conservation: From Theory to Practice*. Enfield, New Hampshire, Science Publishers for World Association of Soil and Water Conservation

Shah, M. and Strong, M. (1999). *Food in the 21st Century: From Science to Sustainable Agriculture*. Washington DC, CGIAR System Review Secretariat, World Bank

Shaxson, T.F., Hudson, N.W., Sanders, D.W., Roose, E. and Moldenhauer, W.C. (1989). *Land Husbandry: A Framework for Soil and Water Conservation*. Ankeny, Iowa, Soil and Water Conservation Society

Smit, J. (1996). *Cities Feeding People: Report 18 - Urban Agriculture, Progress and Prospect: 1975-2005*. Ottawa, International Development Research Centre

Sommers, P. and Smit, J. (1996). *Cities Feeding People: Report 9 - Promoting Urban Agriculture: A Strategy Framework for Planners in North America, Europe, and Asia*. International Development Research Centre, Ottawa, Canada

Toulmin, C. (2001). *Lessons from the Theatre: Should this be the Final Curtain Call for the Convention to Combat Desertification? WSSD Opinion Series*. International Institute for Environment and Development http://www.iied.org/pdf/wssd_02_drylands.pdf [Geo-2-170]

UN (2000). *We the Peoples — The Role of the United Nations in the 21st Century*. New York, United Nations http://www.un.org/millennium/sg/report/key.htm [Geo-1-001]

UNCCD (2000a). *Fact Sheet 2: The Causes of Desertification*. United Nations Secretariat of the Convention to Combat Desertification http://www.unccd.int/publicinfo/factsheets/showFS.php?number=2 [Geo-2-171]

UNCCD (2000b). *Fact Sheet 4: Action Programmes for Combating Desertification*. United Nations Secretariat of the Convention to Combat Desertification http://www.unccd.int/publicinfo/factsheets/showFS.php?number=4 [Geo-2-172]

UNCCD (2001). *Action Programmes on National (NAP), Sub-Regional (SRAP) and Regional Level (RAP)*. United Nations Secretariat of the Convention to Combat Desertification http://www.unccd.int/actionprogrammes/menu.php [Geo-2-173]

UNCED (1992). *Agenda 21: Programme of Action for Sustainable Development*. Rio de Janeiro, United Nations

UNEP (1992). *World Atlas of Desertification*. London, Arnold

UNEP (2000). The Urban Environment: facts and figures. *Industry and Environment* Vol. 23, No. 2

UNFPA (2001). *Footprints and Milestones: Population and Environmental Change - The State of World Population 2001*. New York, United Nations Population Fund

United Nations Population Division (2001). *World Population Prospects 1950-2050 (The 2000 Revision)*. New York, United Nations www.un.org/esa/population/publications/wpp2000/wpp2000h.pdf [Geo-2-204]

University of Bern, FAO, ISRIC, DLD and WASW (2000). *WOCAT World Overview of Conservation Approaches and Technologies*. FAO Land and Water Digital Media Series No. 9. CD ROM. Rome, Food and Agriculture Organization

WCED (1987). *Our Common Future: The World Commission on Environment and Development*. Oxford, Oxford University Press

Wood, S., Sebastian, K. and Scherr, S.J. (2000). *Pilot Analysis of Global Ecosystems: Agroecosystems*. Washington DC, World Resources Institute and International Food Policy Research Institute http://www.ifpri.cgiar.org/pubs/books/page.htm [Geo-2-174]

Young, A. (1991). Soil monitoring: a basic task for soil survey organizations. *Soil Use and Management*. 7, 126-130

## Land: Africa

Africa's total land area covers 29.6 million km², of which two-thirds is arid or semi-arid (UNEP 1999a). Land is central to development in Africa since the livelihoods of about 60 per cent of the population are dependent on agriculture (Moyo 2000).

The main issues related to land in Africa include increasing degradation and desertification, together with inappropriate and inequitable land tenure systems, which have played a major role in exacerbating degradation. Other widespread problems include a decline in soil fertility, soil contamination, land management and conservation, gender imbalances in land tenure, and conversion of natural habitat to agricultural or urban uses.

### Agriculture

As well as providing subsistence crops for a large proportion of Africa's population, there are increasing demands on the land to produce cash crops for export, facilitating economic growth. These demands are often in conflict, and make coherent policy development and implementation a complex and difficult task. Over the

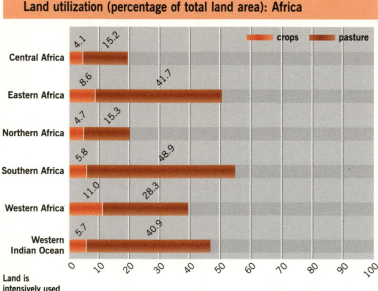

**Land utilization (percentage of total land area): Africa**

Land is intensively used in most African sub-regions, with more than 50 per cent of all land in use in two sub-regions

*Source: compiled from FAOSTAT 2001*

past 30 years, more and more land has been converted to agriculture, most noticeably during the 1980s in response to rising commodity prices. By 1999, about 202 million ha of land in Africa were under cultivation (32 per cent of the potentially cultivable area), and 906 million ha were being used as permanent pasture

(compiled from FAOSTAT 2001). The percentage of agricultural land (cultivated and pasture) varies considerably across Africa, from 54.7 per cent in Southern Africa and 46.6 per cent in the Western Indian Ocean islands to 20 per cent in Northern Africa and 19.3 per cent in Central Africa (see bar chart). The extent to which African economies are dependent on agriculture is reflected in the contribution to GNP (approximately 17 per cent during the 1990s), and to employment — more than 60 per cent of the total labour force in 1996, although this had declined from 70 per cent in 1980 (ADB 2001).

Production has increased considerably over the past 30 years, mostly due to expansion of the area under cultivation, although improvements in cultivation methods and increased use of agro-chemicals have also played a role. Cereal production in Africa was 58 million tonnes in 1975, and this had almost doubled to 106 million tonnes by 1999 (FAOSTAT 2001). Despite this, nutritional intake is still low in many parts of Africa and the number of undernourished people has doubled since 1970 (FAO 2000). The region is a net importer of cereal crops, and the ratio of imports to exports is escalating. In 2000 alone, millions of people in at least 16 African countries experienced food shortages, either due to crop failures or distribution breakdowns associated with civil conflict (FAO 2000). The lack of agricultural technologies suitable for African conditions has also contributed to under-realization of production potential (FAO 2000). Dependence on rain-fed agriculture, now that the potential for the expansion of irrigated agriculture has become limited due to water scarcity, increases the risk of food and economic insecurity, especially in areas of high climate variability. Restricted access to foreign markets, heavy agricultural subsidies in OECD countries, and limited processing before export add to Africa's vulnerability to international price fluctuations, and therefore failure to realize the full potential of its land resources.

### Land degradation

The expansion of agriculture over the past three decades involved the cultivation of marginal areas, or clearance of important natural habitats such as forests and wetlands. Such conversion is a major driving force behind land degradation. In the Western Indian Ocean islands, for example, competition for land is so intense that coastal wetlands have deliberately been destroyed, and inland swamps have been drained and used as construction sites (UNEP 1999b). Many African rural communities survive by moving their cattle and crops as subsiding floodwaters expose enriched bottomlands and floodplains. More than 1.5 million people in Mali, Mauritania, Senegal and Sudan depend on this resource, as do vast numbers of wild herbivores (Maltby 1986). Draining wetlands for agriculture therefore threatens not only habitats and biodiversity but also the livelihoods of pastoralists and wildlife.

Loss of natural habitats has reduced vegetation cover and exposed soils to wind and water erosion. Wind and water erosion is extensive in many parts of Africa with about 25 per cent of the land prone to water erosion and about 22 per cent to wind erosion (Reich and others 2001).

Soil erosion also causes increased rates of siltation of dams and rivers, and increased risk of flooding in rivers and estuaries. In Sudan, for example, the total capacity of the Roseires reservoir — which generates 80 per cent of the country's electricity — has fallen by 40 per cent in 30 years due to siltation of the Blue Nile (Conway 2001).

Soil erosion reduces the productivity of land, requiring farmers to apply more and more fertilizers and other chemicals that help check falling productivity. However, many small-scale farmers cannot afford to buy these inputs and so get low yields.

As a result of the increasing recognition of soil nutrient depletion, a soil fertility initiative for sub-Saharan Africa (where the problem is particularly widespread) was established in 1996 (New Agriculturalist 2001). The objective is to strengthen action by the participating agencies to improve productivity and increase farm incomes through a combination of policy reform and technology adaptation. National soil fertility action plans are currently being prepared in 23 sub-Saharan countries. Organic farming systems offer considerable scope for addressing soil fertility problems as well as raising farm incomes.

Policies on land management have generally failed to address the root causes of land degradation which stem from colonial imbalances in land distribution, lack of incentives for conservation, insecure tenure and the failure to provide for diversified rural production systems (Moyo 1998). The United Nations Convention to Combat Desertification (UNCCD)

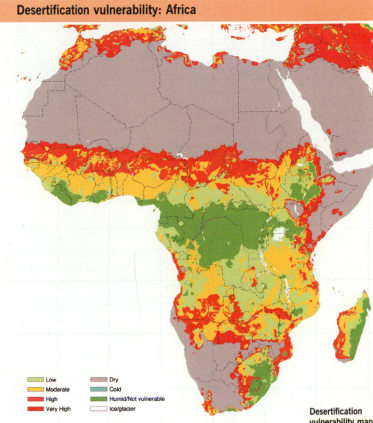

**Desertification vulnerability: Africa**

| Low | Dry |
| Moderate | Cold |
| High | Humid/Not vulnerable |
| Very High | Ice/glacier |

Desertification vulnerability map of Africa locates the 46 per cent of the area at risk, of which 55 per cent is at high or very high risk

*Source: Reich and others 2001*

points out that land degradation is intricately linked to poverty and that addressing this problem requires the participation of the resource users and, where appropriate, providing them with alternative livelihood options. Many African nations have signed and ratified the convention, and 15 countries submitted national action programmes in 2000. The Maghreb Arab Union, Southern African Development Community, the Economic Community of West African States and the Permanent Interstate Committee for Drought Control in the Sahel also submitted sub-regional plans. This has served to raise public awareness about issues of environment and resource sustainability, but the resources required to enforce these plans have frequently been inadequate (UNCCD 2001). A recent study estimated that desertification processes affect 46 per cent of Africa, and 55 per cent of that area is at high or very high risk. The worst affected areas are along desert margins (see map), and in total about 485 million people are affected (Reich and others 2001).

The success of land conservation programmes depends on several factors, and is closely linked with socio-economic conditions. Improving the distribution of wealth, access to resources and economic opportunities are key factors (SARIPS 2000). Peace and political stability are vital to improving resource and food security, as shown by the low per capita food production of countries where there is conflict, and resource security is necessary to implement and sustain conservation programmes. Improving extension services and access to appropriate and affordable technology, rural credit schemes and marketing assistance, and breaking down trade barriers are other essential requirements for sustainable agricultural development.

## Land tenure

Inequitable land distribution patterns are common in Africa — between genders, races and socio-economic classes as well as between private and state-ownership. Parts of the region also have inappropriate land ownership or land tenure policies, and this affects access to land and associated resources, as well as land management practices. In the Western Indian Ocean states, the best land is reserved for commercial crops mainly for export, while the poor and disempowered struggle to make a living from less productive, even marginal areas. South Africa presents an extreme example of inequitable land distribution. Due to apartheid policies abolished only recently, white farmers own 87 per cent of the land (Moyo

2000). The average amount of land held per person in South Africa is slightly more than 1 ha for blacks and 1 570 ha for whites (SARIPS 2000).

Conflicts over land have occurred for centuries but have become more frequent in recent years (most notably in Zimbabwe), especially since independence from European colonialism. During the past decade, there have been a number of land grabs and retrospective claims against the government, largely due to landlessness and displacements. Experiences with land reform in Africa are varied, and have had contrasting results. Some African countries embarked on land reform as early as the 1970s; for example, Kenya proceeded to privatize previously held customary land, resulting in speculation and the loss of land by some poor peasants (Quan 2000). Other countries including Botswana and Lesotho and, to some extent, Zambia have introduced leasehold arrangements in former customary lands to increase security of tenure. Market-driven land reforms have not achieved the desired effect of reducing inequalities, as is evidenced by the South African and Namibian experiences where the delivery of land to the disadvantaged black majority is proceeding at a very slow pace, while the prices of land are increasing.

## References: Chapter 2, land, Africa

ADB (2001). *Statistics Pocket Book 2001.* Abidjan, African Development Bank

Conway, D. (2001). Some water resource management issues in the Nile Basin. In Gash. J. H. C., Odana, E. O., Oyebande, L. and Schulze, R. E. (eds.), *Freshwater Resources in Africa — Proceedings of a Workshop, Nairobi, Kenya, October 1999.* Postdam, BAHC (Biospheric Aspects of the Hydrological Cycle)

FAO (2000). *The State of Food and Agriculture 2000.* Rome, Food and Agriculture Organization

FAOSTAT (2001). *FAOSTAT Statistical Database.* Food and Agriculture Organization http://www.fao.org/ [Geo-2-196]

Maltby, E. (1986). *Waterlogged Wealth.* London, Earthscan

Moyo, S. (1998). Land entitlements and growing poverty in Southern Africa. *Southern Africa Political and Economic Monthly: Southern Review.* Harare, SAPES Trust

Moyo, S. (2000). The land question and land reform in Southern Africa. In Tevera, D. and Moyo, S. (eds.) *Environmental Security in Southern Africa.* Harare, SAPES Trust

New Agriculturalist (2001). Maintaining soil fertility in Africa http://www.new-agri.co.uk/00-1/pov.html

Quan, J. (2000). Land tenure, economic growth and poverty in Sub-Saharan Africa. In Toulmin, C. and Quan, J. (eds) *Evolving Land Rights, Policy and Tenure in Africa.* London, International Institute for Environment and Development and Natural Resources Institute

Reich, P.F., Numbem, S.T., Almaraz, R.A. and Eswaran, H. (2001). Land resource stresses and desertification in Africa. In Bridges, E.M., Hannam, I.D., Oldeman, L.R., Pening, F.W.T., de Vries, S.J., Scherr, S.J. and Sompatpanit, S. (eds). *Responses to Land Degradation. Proceedings of the 2nd International Conference on Land Degradation and Desertification, Khon Kaen, Thailand.* New Delhi, Oxford University Press

SARIPS (2000). *SADC Human Development Report: Challenges and Opportunities for Regional Integration.* Harare, SAPES Trust

UNCCD (2001). *Action Programmes to Combat Desertification: Africa.* United Nations Secretariat of the Convention to Combat Desertification http://www.unccd.int/actionprogrammes/africa/afric a.php [Geo-2-158]

UNEP (1999a). *GEO 2000.* United Nations Environment Programme. London and New York, Earthscan

UNEP (1999b). *Western Indian Ocean Environment Outlook.* Nairobi, United Nations Environment Programme

## Land: Asia and the Pacific

The Asia and Pacific region covers about 23 per cent of the total land area of the Earth. The most critical land issues are degradation (including desertification), land use change and soil contamination. Population growth and high population density, poor land management practices, and emerging inequities in land and resource access have been the major driving forces for change over the past 30 years. Pressures behind degradation problems vary across the region. Overgrazing, overcropping and overuse of inorganic fertilizers are issues in most sub-regions while mining, logging, monocropping and alien invasive species have had dramatic outcomes in the Pacific Island countries (PICs).

### Land degradation

Land degradation processes of particular concern in Asia and the Pacific include erosion, compaction, acidification, declining soil organic matter, weed infestation, soil fertility depletion and biological degradation.

The Global Assessment of Soil Degradation (GLASOD) estimated that about 13 per cent (or 850 million ha) of the land in Asia and the Pacific is degraded (Oldeman 1994) — most of this is in Asia but 104 million ha were estimated to be degraded in the Pacific sub-region where large-scale clearance of forest land has caused a decline in soil structure and fertility and where invasive species are the predominant land cover in many islands.

The most severe water erosion occurs in the Himalayas, Central Asia, China, the South Pacific and Australia, while the GLASOD study indicated that in the South Asian sub-region Afghanistan, India, Iran and Pakistan are the worst affected by wind erosion (Oldeman 1994).

Chemical soil degradation is mainly caused by agricultural mismanagement. In parts of northern India and Bangladesh, soils have been acidified and salinized, and have been losing nutrients, while a significant proportion of land in Cambodia, Malaysia, Thailand and Viet Nam has been degraded by acid sulphates (Oldeman 1994). Poor soil nutrient balances (between phosphorus, nitrogen and potassium) are common in Australia, Bangladesh, Nepal, Pakistan and Sri Lanka.

Saline soils cover 60 million ha of agricultural land

in the region, and Australia in particular is facing severe land salinization problems (MoAFFA 1999). Excessive extraction from groundwater and surface water sources, and rising water tables brought about by faulty irrigation systems, have increased the occurrence of surface water and soil salinity.

Serious soil contamination problems are characteristic of the northern parts of the region, and parts of Australia and New Zealand. The contaminants include cadmium (contained in fertilizer), hexavalent chromium, lead, arsenic, trichloroethylene, tetrachloroethylene and dioxin concentrates. Health issues arising from chronic poisoning from agricultural land were common in the 1970s in the northwest Pacific and northeast Asia (MoE Japan 2000). The major soil polluters in the region are now the chemical

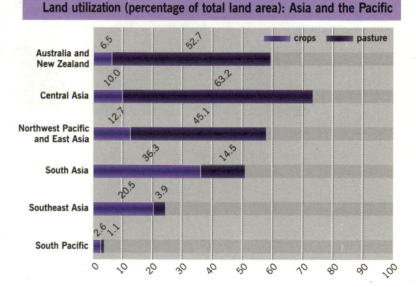

**Land utilization (percentage of total land area): Asia and the Pacific**

*legend:* crops, pasture

- Australia and New Zealand: 6.5 / 52.7
- Central Asia: 10.0 / 63.2
- Northwest Pacific and East Asia: 12.7 / 45.1
- South Asia: 36.3 / 14.5
- Southeast Asia: 20.5 / 3.9
- South Pacific: 2.6 / 1.1

and electroplating industries in Japan and the Republic of Korea but heavy metals are also present in agricultural land (as a result of fertilizer application), and near mines and refineries (due to chemical discharges). Soil contamination from lead and arsenic contamination is prevalent throughout South and Southeast Asia. Irrigation with untreated effluent has also caused contamination and soil acidification in many areas; in Mongolia, for example, waste disposal and wastewater discharges are the main causes of soil contamination (UNDP 2000).

Actions taken to address soil contamination include Japan's Agricultural Land Soil Pollution Prevention Law which, as well as placing restrictions

Land is intensively cropped in South and Southeast Asia, with large areas of pasture in all other sub-regions except the South Pacific. In South Asia, more than one-third of all land is cropped

*Source: compiled from FAOSTAT 2001*

**Removal of vegetation from Western Australia's farming areas has allowed groundwater to rise and salinization to set in**

*Source: UNEP, Peter Garside, Topham Picturepoint*

on contaminating activities, has also instigated remedial projects. By 1999, remedial projects for 79 per cent of the total polluted land area (7 145 ha) had been undertaken (MoE Japan 2000). In the Republic of Korea, the Ministry of Environment established a Soil Contamination Monitoring Network in 1996 to prevent soil contamination adjacent to mines, refineries, military bases, oil storage facilities and waste landfills (Shin-Bom 1996). Australia now has a nationally consistent approach to the assessment of site contamination through the National Environmental Protection Measure (NEPM) for the Assessment of Site Contamination (NEPC 2001).

Many of the failures of physical responses to land degradation problems have stemmed from the competing influences of fiscal and market incentive programmes. The underpricing of resources and subsidization of agricultural inputs such as fertilizers have played important roles in maintaining pressures on land. A major policy failure leading to land degradation is insecure land tenure although in many cases even ownership is insufficient to ensure the sustainable use of land because population pressures have led to the fragmentation and overexploitation of

land holdings. Competing economic and environmental policies have also influenced land use practices in New Zealand. Government subsidies in the 1970s and 1980s resulted in the conversion of large areas of forest and woodlands to pasture and crops, dramatically increasing the risk of erosion in these areas. However, since the removal of these subsidies in the 1980s, large areas of marginal pasture on steep land have been allowed to regenerate to scrub and native forest, reducing the risk of erosion (MoE New Zealand 1997).

## Desertification

Of the 1 977 million ha of drylands in Asia, more than one-half are affected by desertification (UNCCD 1998). The worst affected area is Central Asia (more than 60 per cent affected by desertification) followed by South Asia (more than 50 per cent) and Northeast Asia (about 30 per cent).

Activities to combat desertification include watershed management, soil and water conservation, sand dune stabilization, reforestation programmes, reclamation of waterlogged and saline lands, forest and rangeland management, and soil fertility restoration.

In India, programmes initiated since the early 1990s include the Afforestation Programme, Drought Prone Areas Programme (1994-95), Desert Development Programme, National Watershed Development Project for Rainfed Areas (1990-91), the Indira Gandhi Nahar Project (encouraging local community participation) and the Environmental Action Programme 1993 (MoEF India 2000).

## Land use change

Land degradation problems are directly related to land-use practices, particularly agricultural expansion and intensification. Thailand's land use pattern has changed dramatically over the past 30 years, for example, as forest land declined from 56 to 24 per cent of total land area between 1965 and 1997 (Donner 1978 and GWF 1999). In Japan, the area of agricultural land decreased from 5.8 to 4.9 million ha between 1970 and 1999 as arable land was converted to residential use (NLA 2000).

Attempts to reduce land degradation by controlling land use change have met with little success. The consistent problem has been the inability to intervene with economic planning systems and the dominant sectoral approaches to land management. For the poorer countries, the priorities of jobs, employment and addressing stagnant economies have prevailed over integrated planning. In Australia, community voluntary initiatives starting in the early 1970s were

given due recognition by government in 1988. The National Farmers' Federation and Australian Conservation Foundation jointly proposed the national land management programme called Landcare (Noble and others 1996). This proliferated in the mid-1990s to include Dune Care, RiverWatch, Bushcare and Coastcare programmes.

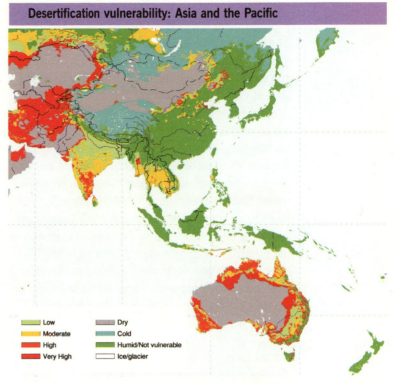

**Desertification vulnerability: Asia and the Pacific**

Low
Moderate
High
Very High
Dry
Cold
Humid/Not vulnerable
Ice/glacier

**More than one-half of the region's drylands are affected by desertification — the worst affected area is Central Asia, followed by South Asia and Australia**

*Source: Reich and others 2001*

**References: Chapter 2, land, Asia and the Pacific**

Donner, W. (1978) *The Five Faces of Thailand: An Economic Geography.* London, C. Hurst and Company

GWF (1999). *State of the Thai Environment.* Bangkok, Green World Foundation

MoAFFA Australia (1999). *Serious Salinity Warning Must Be Heeded* — Tuckey Media Release 24 June 1999. Ministry of Agriculture, Fisheries and Forestry, Australia http://www.affa.gov.au/ministers/tuckey/releases/99/99_71tu.html [Geo-2-157]

MoE Japan (2000). *Policies and Programmes.* Ministry of the Environment, Government of Japan http://www.env.go.jp/en/pol/leaflet1.html [Geo-2-159]

MoEF India (2000). *National Report on Implementation of the United Nations Convention to Combat Desertification.* New Delhi, Ministry of Environment and Forests, Government of India

MoE New Zealand (1997). *The State of New Zealand's Environment 1997.* Wellington, GP Publications

NEPC (2001). National Environment Protection Council, Australia http://www.nepc.gov.au [Geo-2-160]

NLA (2000). *Annual Report on National Land.* National Land Agency of Japan. Tokyo, Printing Bureau, Ministry of Finance

Noble, I., Barson, M., Dumsday, R., Friedel, M., Hacker, R., McKenzie, N., Smith, G., Young, M., Maliel, M. and Zammit, C. (1996). Land resources. In Commonwealth of Australia (ed.), *Australia: State of the Environment 1996.* Collingwood, CSIRO Publishing

Oldeman, L.R. (1994). The global extent of soil degradation. In Greenland, D.J. and Szaboles, T. (eds.), *Soil Resilience and Sustainable Land Use.* Wallingford, Commonwealth Agricultural Bureau International http://www.isric.nl/GLASOD.htm [Geo-2-161]

Reich, P. F., Numbem, S. T., Almaraz, R.A. and Eswaran, H. (2001). Land resource stresses and desertification in Africa. In Bridges, E.M., Hannam, I.D., Oldeman, L.R., Pening, F.W.T., de Vries, S.J., Scherr, S.J. and Sompatpanit, S. (eds.). *Responses to Land Degradation. Proceedings of the 2nd International Conference on Land Degradation and Desertification, Khon Kaen, Thailand.* New Delhi, Oxford Press

Shin-Bom, L. (1996). *South Korea Environmental Report.* ABS Consulting, Government Institutes Division, Rockville, Maryland, United States

UNCCD (1998). *The Social and Economic Impact of Desertification in Several Asian Countries: Inventory Study.* Geneva, Interim Secretariat of the Convention to Combat Desertification

UNDP (2000). *Human Development Report 2000.* Oxford and New York, Oxford University Press

## Land: Europe

The key issues associated with land resources in Europe are land-use planning in relation to agriculture and urban sprawl, and soil degradation due to factors such as contamination and erosion.

Steady population expansion, economic changes and economic growth over the past 30 years have led to competing demands on land for agriculture, forestry, environmental protection and recreation, and for urban and infrastructural development. The average annual rate of land cover change in Western Europe is quite small but at the local level changes can be significant, especially in densely populated areas — 74 per cent of the population of Europe is concentrated in only 15 per cent of its land surface (EEA 1999). At the same time, these areas experience high levels of activity in industry, transport, services and other economic sectors, with concomitant environmental problems.

### Land use

Despite being a minority activity in terms of income and employment, agriculture is the dominant land use in Europe. Since the 1950s, Europe has experienced a continuing trend towards urbanization at the expense of natural, semi-natural and agricultural land. The area under productive agriculture in Western Europe has fallen over the past 30 years — by 6.5 per cent for arable and permanent crops and by 10.9 per cent for permanent pasture (FAOSTAT 2000). However, the decrease has been accompanied by more intensive production methods. This intensification trend seems set to continue, and better integrated spatial and land use planning and management are required to tackle the problems associated with land cover and land use change. During the 1990s, in many parts of Central and Eastern Europe, pressure on land resources began to decrease, due to the collapse of centrally planned economies, the ending of state subsidies to large collective farms and depopulation of rural areas. The economic collapse also led to a sharp decrease in the use of agricultural chemicals, abandonment of huge irrigation projects and agricultural land, and a decrease in numbers of livestock with a generally beneficial effect on the environment. A substantial land area is being reforested, and this trend may accelerate with climate change.

In recent years, increased attention has been given to the restoration and protection of wetlands. About two-thirds of the European wetlands that existed 100 years ago have been lost (EC 1999). Wetlands are the only ecosystem type that is covered by its own international convention, the Ramsar Convention of 1971, under which signatories agree to include wetland conservation in their national planning and to promote sound utilization of wetlands. In 1985, the World Wildlife Fund and the International Union for the Conservation of Nature launched a campaign to promote public awareness about wetlands and their importance. A major goal was to ensure that wetland development goes ahead only when all the implications are understood and when plans have been produced to ensure that the environmental consequences are minimized.

Policies and measures relating explicitly to land use planning and management have generally been the responsibility of national and local level governments in Western Europe, while in Central and Eastern Europe (CEE) there has been an abrupt change from central planning to local or no planning. Since 1989, the agricultural policies of CEE have gradually moved into line with those of the European Union. A number of international policy initiatives also exist relating to land management (see box below).

### International efforts to improve land management

International policy efforts to protect ecosystems and wildlife habitats through global conventions include the Ramsar Convention on wetlands, the biodiversity convention and the European Spatial Development Perspective (ESDP) initiated by the Ministers responsible for Regional/Spatial Planning in the European Union.

The ESDP is intended to improve the spatial coherence of European Community (EC) policies. It examines both the achievements and the inadequacies of the main policy areas that affect the development of EC territory, including competition policy, policies linked to networks in transport and telecommunications, structural funds, agricultural and environment policy, and research, technology and development (EC Committee on Spatial Development 1999).

The Environment for Europe process also focuses attention on the European landscape. The European Biodiversity and Landscape Strategy was launched during the fourth Environment Ministerial Conference in Århus (1998).

These major international programmes all emphasize the need to improve statistical monitoring activities. The European Land Use/Land Cover Statistical Survey project (LUCAS) is a promising example which was approved by the European Parliament in April 2000.

The increase in sealed surfaces together with a decrease in forest cover has led to increased flooding — as here in Portugal — mudflows and landslides

*Source: UNEP, Angelo Sande, Topham Picturepoint*

## Soil degradation

Damage to Europe's soils from human activities is increasing, including sealing of soil surfaces, local and diffuse contamination, and soil erosion. Despite the general recognition that soil degradation is a serious and widespread problem in Europe, it has not been quantified, and its geographical distribution and real extent are not accurately known.

The increase in sealed surfaces due to changes in land use together with a decrease in forest cover has increased the frequency and size of storm run-off, causing flooding, mudflows and landslides (EEA and

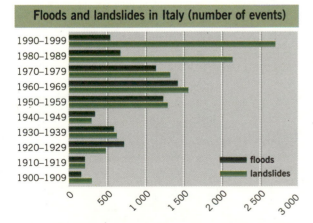

### Floods and landslides in Italy (number of events)

| | floods | landslides |
|---|---|---|
| 1990–1999 | | |
| 1980–1989 | | |
| 1970–1979 | | |
| 1960–1969 | | |
| 1950–1959 | | |
| 1940–1949 | | |
| 1930–1939 | | |
| 1920–1929 | | |
| 1910–1919 | | |
| 1900–1909 | | |

0    500    1 000    1 500    2 000    2 500    3 000

**In the past 20 years floods and landslides have affected more than 70 000 Italians and caused economic damage of nearly €11 000 million. Real impacts are underestimated since data are available for only a few events**

*Source: EEA and UNEP 2000*

UNEP 2000). Increases in damage from flooding have also resulted from the development of floodplains for industry and habitation.

Soil contamination occurs throughout Europe, although soil acidification from acid rain is no longer considered a major problem, having decreased by 50 per cent since the 1980s (EEA 1999). Contamination is particularly severe in urban areas due to industrial activities and inadequate waste disposal as well as in areas with a long tradition of heavy industry, mining and military activities and accidents. Throughout southeastern Europe, land which was already under stress from poor land management practices has been further damaged by military and refugee settlements, land mines (as much as 27 per cent of Bosnia's ploughed land is still mined) and other unexploded devices (REC 2000). In Eastern Europe huge irrigation and hydroelectric projects coupled with poor water management have resulted in salinization and waterlogging of large areas, especially in Azerbaijan, Belarus, the Russian Federation and Ukraine.

Soil erosion in Europe is mainly caused by water and is largely a result of unsustainable agricultural practices, clear cutting of forests and overgrazing. Soil erosion is most serious in the Mediterranean region. It has become irreversible (meaning a loss of more than 1 tonne/ha/year over 50-100 years) in some Mediterranean land areas and in the black soil regions of the Republic of Moldova, the Russian Federation and Ukraine. Erosion is a particular problem in the

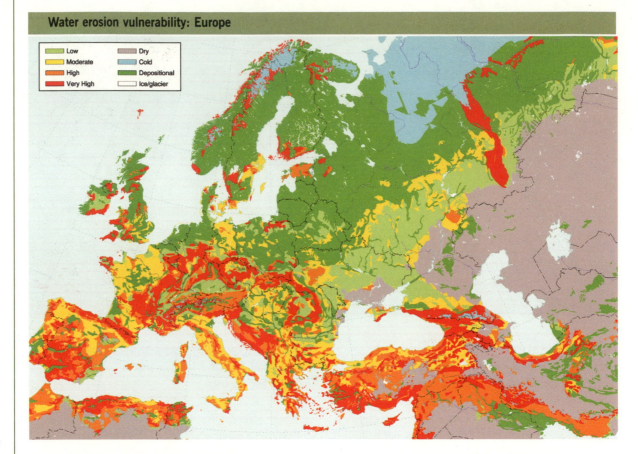

**Water erosion vulnerability: Europe**

Low
Moderate
High
Very High
Dry
Cold
Depositional
Ice/glacier

Soil erosion in Europe is mainly caused by water and is most serious in the Mediterranean region and in the black soil regions of the Republic of Moldova, the Russian Federation and Ukraine

*Source: USDA 2001*

Commonwealth of Independent States: in 12 countries, 475 million ha (79 per cent) of agricultural land are affected by soil erosion to some degree (Interstate Statistical Committee 1999).

Unlike other media, no specific objectives and targets have been set for soil conservation, and it is rarely considered in sectoral planning activities such as transnational transport corridors. At the national level, some countries have produced legislation, policies and guidelines to ameliorate or prevent further soil degradation but policy measures are primarily aimed at combating pollution in other areas, and affect soils only indirectly. Statutory soil monitoring is carried out in a number of countries but rarely specifically for soil protection; policy performance can therefore not be quantified and comparability at the European level remains weak. The development of a common policy framework that recognizes the role of soil, aimed at sustainability, would have multiple benefits and improve Europe's environment as a whole.

## References: Chapter 2, land, Europe

EEA (1999). *Environment in the European Union at the Turn of the Century.* Copenhagen, European Environment Agency

EEA and UNEP (2000). *Down to Earth: Soil Degradation and Sustainable Development in Europe. A Challenge for the 21st Century. Environmental Issues Series No 16.* Copenhagen, European Environment Agency http://reports.eea.eu.int/Environmental_issue_serie s_16/en/envissue16.pdf [Geo-2-163]

EC (1999). *European Spatial Development Perspective. Towards Balanced and Sustainable Development of the Territory of the EU.* Report of the Final Discussion at the Meeting of the Ministers responsible for Regional/Spatial Planning of the European Union, held in Potsdam, May 1999. Brussels, European Commission

FAOSTAT (2000). FAOSTAT Statistical Database. Food and Agriculture Organization http://www.fao.org/ [Geo-2-197]

Interstate Statistical Committee (1999). *Official Statistics of the Countries of the Commonwealth of Independent States.* CD Rom. Moscow, Interstate Statistical Committee of the Commonwealth of Independent States

REC (2000). *Strategic Environmental Analysis of Albania, Bosnia and Herzegovina, Kozová and Macedonia.* Szentendre, Hungary, Regional Environmental Centre for Central and Eastern Europe

USDA (2001). *Water Erosion Vulnerability.* US Department of Agriculture, Natural Resources Conservation Service, Soil Survey Division, World Soil Resources, Washington http://www.nhq.nrcs.usda.gov/WSR/mapindx/erosh 2o.htm [Geo-2-164]

## Land: Latin America and the Caribbean

The Latin America and Caribbean region has the world's largest reserves of arable land with an estimated 576 million ha equal to almost 30 per cent of the total territory (Gómez and Gallopín 1995). The region also contains 16 per cent of the world total of 1 900 million ha of degraded land, taking third place behind Asia and the Pacific and Africa (UNEP 2000).

Priority issues in the region include: loss of agricultural area (caused by factors such as erosion, changes in agricultural practices and growing urbanization); land degradation (associated with compaction, leaching of nutrients and pollution); and land tenure (covering inadequate and inequitable distribution of land as well as lack of tenure rights).

### Expanding the agriculture and livestock boundaries

Agricultural expansion has intensified the use of natural resources and exacerbated many of the processes of land degradation. Over the past three decades, there has been an increase in arable land and grassland at the expense of forests. During 1972–99, the area of permanent arable land and cropland expanded in South America by 30.2 million ha or 35.1 per cent, in Meso-America by 6.3 million ha or 21.3 per cent and in the Caribbean by 1.8 million ha or 32.0 per cent (FAOSTAT 2001). The area under irrigation (see graph) also increased in the same period, resulting in greater agricultural production throughout the region. The expansion of permanent arable land on soils previously covered by forests is still the main cause of deforestation in the Brazilian Amazon (Nepstad and others 1999). Soybean production, mostly for export, has been the main driving force to expand the agricultural boundary in northern Argentina, eastern Paraguay and the central part of Brazil (Klink, Macedo and Mueller 1994).

The expansion of livestock production has also been a major driving force behind land conversion in the region. The process could not have been successful without the strong support of governments through the provision of tax incentives (the 'Legal Amazon' in Brazil), the construction of roads and the availability of skilled and cheap labour. For example, livestock companies in Bolivia leased land to peasants so that they could clear it for cultivation and then return it already cleared when their leases expired (Giglo 2000). Erosion, loss of nutrients, chemical pollution, salinization and the effects of meteorological and geological phenomena are major contributors to the different land degradation processes.

### Land degradation

Erosion is the main cause of land degradation in Latin America, affecting 14.3 per cent of the territory in South America and 26 per cent in Central America (Oldeman 1994). Nutrient depletion is also a serious issue, largely driven by agricultural intensification.

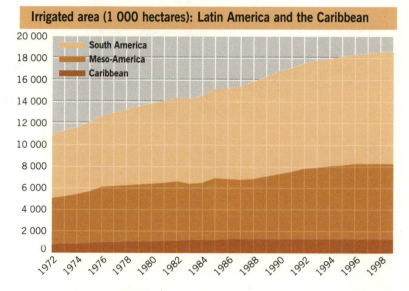

**Irrigated area (1 000 hectares): Latin America and the Caribbean**

In South America, the depletion of nutrients from the soil had affected 68.2 million ha by 1980 (Scherr and Yadav 1997). This depletion has exacerbated poverty which, in turn, has contributed to greater environmental degradation and land deterioration.

Chemical soil pollution is increasingly significant given the intensification of agriculture and the use of pesticides during the past 30 years. Agricultural technology has increased production throughout the region but at a high cost to the environment. Of great concern is the impact of agrochemical pollution on soil and water and, as a consequence, on human health. Soil and water nitrification is linked to the use of chemical fertilizers which increased from 3.7 to 10.9 million tonnes during 1972–97 (FAOSTAT 2001).

Salinization is a particularly significant form of soil degradation because it is difficult to treat and can lead to desertification. Salinization caused by irrigation affects 18.4 million ha in the region, particularly in

The irrigated area in Latin America and the Caribbean has expanded at an average of nearly 2 per cent a year over the period 1972–99

Source: FAOSTAT 2001

## Vulnerability to water and wind erosion: Latin America and the Caribbean

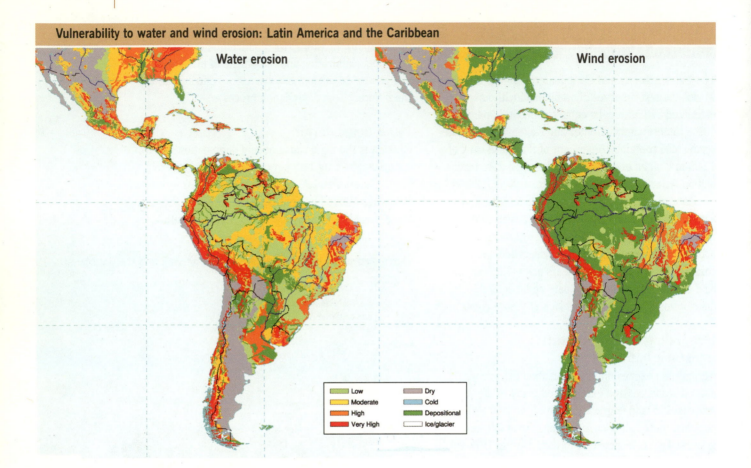

Water erosion

Wind erosion

| | |
|---|---|
| Low | Dry |
| Moderate | Cold |
| High | Depositional |
| Very High | Ice/glacier |

**Erosion is the main cause of land degradation in the region, affecting 14.3 per cent of South America and 26 per cent of Meso-America**

*Source: USDA 2001a and 2001b*

Argentina, Brazil, Chile, Mexico and Peru (AQUASTAT 1997).

The problems of land degradation have been discussed in regional and international fora for several decades. Following the 1992 United Nations Conference on Environment and Development, work on new conventions and agreements started to seek regional and sub-regional solutions. For example, the secretariat of the United Nations Convention to Combat Desertification (UNCCD), together with UNEP and the government of Mexico, established a Regional Coordination Unit for Latin America and the Caribbean to coordinate the work of national focal points in preparing national action programmes. These actions encouraged several countries to set up similar programmes and have led to the creation of monitoring systems (UNEP/ROLAC 1999, Universidad de Buenos Aires 1999). The Amazonian Pact, the Sustainable Development Commission, the Central American Integration System and the Andean Pact are examples of sub-regional mechanisms that have paved the way for agreements and have

promoted monitoring and control systems to prevent land degradation.

## Land tenure

Land tenure problems include the concentration of ownership in a minority of the population and a lack of land titles that has its historical origin in the colonial system of land ownership and the simultaneous existence of large agricultural holdings and smallholdings. About 38 per cent of the rural population are smallholders and they manage 35.1 per cent of the land under permanent cultivation (van Dam 1999). Average farm sizes range from 0.41 ha in Ecuador to a little more than 1.5 ha in Brazil and Peru.

In spite of the numerous agrarian reforms and land distribution schemes introduced in Latin America, land tenure has not changed markedly; there is both a tendency to merge farms to make larger holdings and an increase in the number of smallholdings (van Dam 1999). Both processes have adverse environmental effects. In large farms, the land suffers from erosion and compaction due to mechanization, as well as salinization because of improper irrigation and chemical pollution. Smallholdings increase deforestation, and lead to erosion and loss of soil fertility because they are used intensively without allowing for adequate fallow periods (Jazairy, Alamgir and Panuccio 1992).

The Sub–regional Action Programme for Sustainable Development of the American Puna, under the UNCCD secretariat, is developing an action plan for an area where natural resources are limited and there are problems of increasing poverty, migration and marginality (UNEP/ROLAC 1999). The land tenure question, poor land regulations and the elimination of incentives for agricultural expansion inspired the programme.

## Environmental impact of the land tenure regime on soil conditions in Jamaica

As in the rest of Latin America and the Caribbean, the land tenure regime in Jamaica is inequitable and, on both large properties and smallholdings, few land conservation and recovery methods are used.

In the 1970s, agrarian reform favoured large properties in the form of cooperatives, based on the intensified use of crops, mechanization, an increase in irrigated area and monocropping. The environmental effects included soil erosion and compaction of soils from mechanization, salinization caused by deficient irrigation systems and chemical pollution.

One-quarter of Jamaica's territory was under cultivation in the 1980s, and more than 90 per cent of farms covered 4 ha or less. These smallholdings were concentrated in ecologically fragile mountain areas of low fertility. Agriculture was based on traditional methods, including slash-and-burn cultivation. Physical infrastructure and basic services were lacking, farmers received little or no credit and had little schooling.

The continued expansion of large agricultural properties and the marginalization of peasant farmers has meant that there are now fewer fallow periods and less crop rotation. Deforestation of mountainsides continues and there has been a reduction in the number of draught animals. In zones with smallholdings, soil degradation tends to increase, especially the loss of fertility from erosion, and this is reflected in a marked drop in production.

*Sources: van Dam 1999 and Library of Congress 1987*

## References: Chapter 2, land, Latin America and the Caribbean

AQUASTAT (1997). *Tablas Resumen de America Latina y el Caribe.* Food and Agriculture Organization http://www.fao.org/ag/agl/aglw/aquastat/tables/tab9.htm [Geo-2-176]

FAOSTAT (2001). *FAOSTAT Statistical Database.* Food and Agriculture Organization http://www.fao.org/ [Geo-2-199]

Giglo, N. (2000). *Land and food in Latin America and the Caribbean.* Technical paper. *Mexico City,* DEWA-ROLAC/UNEP

Gómez, I.A. and Gallopín, G.C. (1995). Potencial agrícola de la América Latina. In Gallopin, G.C. (ed.). *El Futuro Ecológico de un Continente: Una Visión Prospectiva de la América Latina.* Mexico City, Universidad de las Naciones and Fondo de Cultura Económica

Jazairy, I., Alamgir, M. and Panuccio, T. (1992). *The State of World Rural Poverty: An Inquiry into its Causes and Consequences.* New York, New York University Press for IFAD

Klink, C. A., Macedo, R.H. and Mueller, C.C. (1994). *Cerrado: Processo de Ocupação e Implicações Pará a Conservação e Utilização Sustentavel de sua Diversidade Biológica.* Brasilia, WWF-Brasil

Library of Congress (1987). *Caribbean Islands: A Country Study.* Library of Congress, Federal Research Division http://memory.loc.gov/frd/cs/cxtoc.html [Geo-2-175]

Nepstad, D. C., Verissimo, A., Alencar, A., Nobre, C., Lima, E., Lefebvre, P., Schlesinger, P., Potter, C., Moutinho, P., Mendoza, E., Cochrane, M. and Brooks, V. (1999). Large-scale impoverishment of Amazonian forests by logging and fire. *Nature* 98, 505-508

Oldeman, L.R. (1994). The global extent of soil degradation. In Greenland, D.J. and Szaboles, T. (eds.), *Soil Resilience and Sustainable Land Use.* Wallingford, Commonwealth Agricultural Bureau International http://www.isric.nl/GLASOD.htm

Scherr, S. and Yadav, S. (1997). *Land Degradation in the Developing World: Issues and Policy Options for 2020, 2020 Vision Policy Brief No. 44.* Washington DC, International Food Policy Research Institute

UNEP (2000). *GEO Latin America and the Caribbean Environment Outlook.* Mexico City, United Nations Environment Programme, Regional Office for Latin America and the Caribbean

UNEP/ROLAC (1999). *Application of the Convention. Examination of Progress in Formulating and Executing Sub-regional and Regional Action Programmes in Latin America and the Caribbean. Summary.* Mexico City, Secretariat of the Convention to Combat Desertification, Regional Coordination Unit for Latin America and the Caribbean

Universidad de Buenos Aires (1999). *Indicadores de la Desertificacion para su Monitoreo con Teledeteccion y Sig en el Valle de Santa Maria (Catamarca).* Universidad de Buenos Aires http://www.rec.uba.ar/pc_98_00/htm/ag13.htm

USDA (2001a). *Water Erosion Vulnerability.* US Department of Agriculture, Natural Resources Conservation Service, Soil Survey Division, World Soil Resources, Washington DC http://www.nhq.nrcs.usda.gov/WSR/mapindx/erosh 2o.htm

USDA (2001b). *Wind Erosion Vulnerability.* US Department of Agriculture, Natural Resources Conservation Service, Soil Survey Division, World Soil Resources, Washington DC http://www.nhq.nrcs.usda.gov/WSR/mapindx/eroswi nd.htm

Van Dam, C. (1999). *La Tenencia de la Tierra en América Latina. El Estado del Arte de la Discusión en la Región Iniciativa Global Tierra, Territorios y Derechos de Acceso.* Santiago, IUCN Regional Office for South America

## Land: North America

About 11 per cent of the world's agricultural croplands are in North America, producing food, fibre and other products both for the region's own needs and for export. Almost 20 per cent of the United States is covered by arable and permanent cropland and 26 per cent by permanent grassland or pastures (OECD 1999). Although only 7 per cent of Canada's land is devoted to agriculture, this represents virtually all the undeveloped land that is amenable to cultivation (Environment Canada 1996). Land degradation, associated with agricultural expansion, intensification and industrialization, is a concern in North America. One of the key issues associated with land degradation is the use of chemical pesticides, which have contributed to increased food production but have also had important environmental and human health effects.

### Conservation programmes

The US Conservation Reserve Program (CRP) was enacted in 1985 and expanded in 1990 to help farmers retire cropland that was environmentally sensitive or susceptible to erosion for 10 years in return for rental and cost-sharing payments and technical assistance. The aim was to reduce erosion and excess production. As of October 1999, 12.5 million ha of cropland were enrolled in the CRP (Zinn 1994, H. John Heinz III Center 1999).

In Canada, the Permanent Cover Program (PCP), first delivered in 1989 by the federal Prairie Farm Rehabilitation Administration, aims to reduce soil deterioration on cropland at high risk of soil damage by maintaining permanent cover of grass and trees. Although the programme has limited funds, only applies for a short period and restricts the amount of land each farmer can retire, some C$2-5 million of soil productivity has been saved by permanent cover on 320 000 ha of land (Tyrchniewicz and Wilson 1994, Vaisey, Weins and Wettlaufer 1996).

## Land degradation

Some of the direct pressures leading to degradation have been agricultural expansion, intensification and overgrazing in arid lands (Dregne 1986, Gold 1999). These practices can cause erosion by water and wind, and chemical and physical degradation (Eswaran, Lal and Reich 2001). Socio-economic drivers include large federal subsidies, increasing global demand for agricultural products and increased trade liberalization (MacGregor and McRae 2000).

Lessons learned from the Dust Bowl experiences of the 1930s led to the adoption of soil conservation strategies such as contour ploughing, no-till methods, reduced summer fallow and increased crop residues. In the late 1970s and early 1980s, both countries reported on the status of their nation's soil. These reports led to the US Soil and Water Resources Conservation Act of 1977 and Canada's 1989 National Soil Conservation Program (Vaisey, Weins and Wettlaufer 1996, USDA 1996). They also adopted strategies that took fragile lands out of agricultural production to protect them from erosion (see box).

Conservation measures have led to significant declines in erosion over the past 30 years. In the United States, 30 per cent of croplands had highly erosion-prone conditions in 1982 compared to 24 per cent in 1992 (H. John Heinz III Center 1999, Huffman 2000, Padbury and Stushnoff 2000).

Data for other indices of land degradation are scarce: consistent US data for the national level of organic matter, the degree of soil compaction and the amount of land affected by salt are lacking (H. John Heinz III Center 1999). Conservation practices in Canada appear to have led to a decline in the rate of organic carbon loss from 70 kg/ha in 1970 to 43 kg/ha in 1990 (Smith and others 2000).

Desertification has generally been stabilized over the past 30 years as plant cover on rangelands has improved, and erosion and waterlogging have been controlled (Dregne 1986, UNCCD 2001). In the mid-1980s, salinization was estimated to affect about 25 per cent of the irrigated land in the United States, and conditions in heavily irrigated agricultural areas of the dry US southwest continue to worsen (de Villiers 2000). In Canada, only 2 per cent of agricultural land has more than 15 per cent of its area affected by salinity (Environment Canada 1996).

Historically, government agricultural policy focused on economic and production goals but sustainability has guided policy reforms in the recent past (MacGregor and McRae 2000). The Canadian Agri-Environmental Indicator project, completed in 2000, contributed to a more informed debate about agricultural sustainability, and the 1985 and 1990 US *Farm Bills* led to more sustainable stewardship by farmers and landowners (McRae, Smith and Gregorich

2000, NRCS 2000). In 1994, the US Task Force on Sustainable Agriculture set out recommendations to achieve environmentally and socially sound agricultural production and, two years later, the Federal Agriculture Improvement and Reform Act was signed expanding on earlier conservation themes (Gold 1999). The Canadian government set out its strategy for sustainable agriculture in 1997 (AAFC 1997).

## Pesticides

North America accounts for 36 per cent of world pesticide use. By far the most common and widespread use of pesticides in North America is agricultural applications, which accounted for 77 per cent of US pesticide use in 1991 (Schmitt 1998). In Canada, the land area treated with chemical pesticides increased 3.5 times between 1970 and 1995 (Statistics Canada 2000).

Since 1979, the total annual amount of pesticides used in the United States has remained fairly steady, while the use of insecticides has declined (Schmitt 1998). Reductions are due to safer pesticide products, new management techniques for controlling crop pests, and training and certification programmes for pesticide users (Fischer 2000).

Pesticides still pose a number of problems. Although the so-called 'soft' pesticides produced since 1975 are shorter-lived than POPs and do not accumulate, they are fast-acting and highly toxic to terrestrial and aquatic invertebrates in the short term. In some places, they have led to increased fish and wildlife kills (OECD 1996, Schmitt 1998). Pests have also become resistant. One report estimates that more than 500 insect pests, 270 weed species and 150 plant diseases are now resistant to one or more pesticides with the result that more frequent applications are needed today to accomplish the same level of control as in the early 1970s (Benbrook 1996).

With increased public concern about the health effects of pesticides and recognition of the special vulnerability of children and indigenous peoples living in the north, pesticide regulations in North America became more stringent during the 1990s. In 1996, the United States passed the 1996 Food Quality Protection Act and Canada's Pest Management Regulatory Agency was instituted in 1995 (OECD 1996, Cuperus, Berberet and Kenkel 1997, PMRA 2001). Heeding

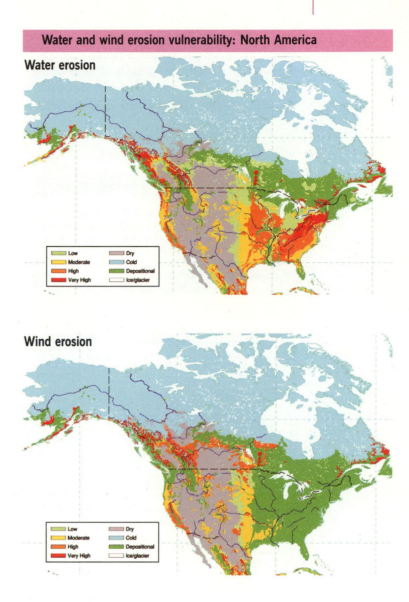

**Water and wind erosion vulnerability: North America**

**Water erosion**

| | | | |
|---|---|---|---|
| Low | | Dry | |
| Moderate | | Cold | |
| High | | Depositional | |
| Very High | | Ice/glacier | |

**Wind erosion**

| | | | |
|---|---|---|---|
| Low | | Dry | |
| Moderate | | Cold | |
| High | | Depositional | |
| Very High | | Ice/glacier | |

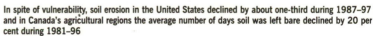

In spite of vulnerability, soil erosion in the United States declined by about one-third during 1987–97 and in Canada's agricultural regions the average number of days soil was left bare declined by 20 per cent during 1981–96

*Source: USDA 2001a and 2001b*

public demand to protect children from lawn pesticides, many North American municipalities now restrict pesticide use on public land and some have instituted total bans. Integrated pest management (IPM) initiatives have also been introduced (NIPMN 2000, Cuperus, Berberet and Kenkel 1997), allowing for greater flexibility than organic agriculture in which chemical pesticides are forbidden.

North America's soil conservation measures and its commitment to the continued phase out of POPs are positive trends. However, there is a lack of reliable data on soil erosion and other measures of land degradation, and improved tracking of pesticide use and impact monitoring are still needed. Strong legislation for point source pollution has diminished

gross emissions to the land but it is now clear that more needs to be done to curb non-point pollution from agricultural inputs.

## References: Chapter 2, land, North America

AAFC (1997). *Agriculture in Harmony with Nature: Strategy for Environmentally Sustainable Agriculture and Agri-food Development in Canada.* Minister of Public Works and Government Services, Canada
http://www.agr.ca/policy/envharmon/docs/strat_e.pdf

Benbrook, C.M. (1996). *Pest Management at the Crossroads.* Yonkers, New York, Consumers Union
http://www.pmac.net/voc.htm [Geo-2-178]

Cuperus, G., Berberet, R. and Kenkel, P. (1997). *The Future of Integrated Pest Management.* University of Minnesota
http://ipmworld.umn.edu/chapters/cuperus.htm [Geo-2-179]

de Villiers, Marq (2000). *Water: The Fate of Our Most Precious Resource.* New York, Mariner Books

Dregne, H.E. (1986). Desertification of arid lands. In El-Baz, F. and Hassan, M.H.A. (eds). *Physics of Desertification.* Dordrecht, Martinus Nijhoff
http://www.ciesin.org/docs/002-193/002-193.html [Geo-2-180]

Environment Canada (1996). The State of Canada's Environment 1996. In Environment Canada (ed.). *Conserving Canada's Natural Legacy.* CD-ROM Ottawa, Environment Canada

Eswaran, H., Lal, R. and Reich, P.F. (2001). Land degradation: an overview. Paper presented at Responses to Land Degradation: the Second International Conference on Land Degradation and Desertification at Khon Kaen, Thailand, 25-29 January 1999

Fischer, J. (2000). Pesticide Hysteria. Toronto, *The Globe and Mail*, 29 August 2000

Gold, M.V. (1999). *Sustainable Agriculture: Definitions and Terms: Special Reference Briefs Series no. SRB 99-02.* National Agricultural Library
http://warp.nal.usda.gov/afsic/AFSIC_pubs/srb9902 .htm [Geo-2-181]

H. John Heinz III Center (1999). *Designing a Report on the State of the Nation's Ecosystem: Selected Measurements for Croplands, Forests, and Coasts and Oceans.* The H. John Heinz III Center for Science, Economics and the Environment
http://www.heinzcenter.org/publications/Coasts.pdf [Geo-2-182]

Huffman, E. (2000). Indicator: soil cover by crops and residue. In McRae, T., Smith, C.A.S. and Gregorich, L.J. (eds). *Environmental Sustainability of Canadian Agriculture: Report of the Agri-Environmental Indicator Project. A Summary.* Ottawa, Agriculture and Agri-Food Canada

MacGregor, R.J. and McRae, T. (2000). Driving forces affecting the environmental sustainability of agriculture. In McRae, T., Smith, C.A.S. and Gregorich, L.J. (eds). *Environmental Sustainability of Canadian Agriculture: Report of the Agri-Environmental Indicator Project. A Summary.* Ottawa, Agriculture and Agri-Food Canada

McRae, T., Smith, C.A.S. and Gregorich, L.J. (eds.) (2000). *Environmental Sustainability of Canadian Agriculture: Report of the Agri-Environmental Indicator Project. A Summary.* Ottawa, Agriculture and Agri-Food Canada

NIPMN (2000). National Integrated Pest Management Network: National Server. National IPM Network
http://www.reeusda.gov/nipmn/ [Geo-2-183]

NRCS (2000). *Summary Report: 1997 National Resources Inventory, Revised December 2000.* US Department of Agriculture, Natural Resources Conservation Service
http://www.nhq.nrcs.usda.gov/NRI/1997/summary_ report/original/body.html [Geo-2-184]

OECD (1996). *Environmental Performance Reviews: United States.* Paris, Organization for Economic Cooperation and Development

OECD (1999). *OECD Environmental Data Compendium.* Paris, Organization for Economic Cooperation and Development.

Padbury, G. and Stushnoff, C. (2000). Indicator: risk of wind erosion. In McRae, T., Smith, C.A.S. and Gregorich, L.J. (eds). *Environmental Sustainability of Canadian Agriculture: Report of the Agri-Environmental Indicator Project. A Summary.* Ottawa, Agriculture and Agri-Food Canada

PMRA (2001). *About PMRA Health Canada*
http://www.hc-sc.gc.ca/pmra-arla/english/aboutpmra/about-e.html

Schmitt, C. J. (1998). Environmental contaminants. In Mac, M.J., Opler, P.A., Puckett Haecker, C.E. and Doran, P.D. (eds). *Status and Trends of the Nation's Biological Resources.* Washington DC, US Department of the Interior and US Geological Survey

Shelton, I.J., Wall, G.J., Cossette, J-M., Eilers, R., Grant, B., King, D., Padbury, G., Rees, H., Tajek, J. and van Vliet, L. (2000). Indicator: risk of water erosion. In McRae, T., Smith, C.A.S. and Gregorich, L.J. (eds). *Environmental Sustainability of Canadian Agriculture: Report of the Agri-Environmental Indicator Project. A Summary* Ottawa, Agriculture and Agri-Food Canada

Smith, C.A.S., Wall, G., Desjardins, R. and Grant, B. (2000). Indicator: Soil Organic Carbon. In McRae, T., Smith, C.A.S. and Gregorich, L.J. (eds). *Environmental Sustainability of Canadian Agriculture: Report of the Agri-Environmental Indicator Project: A Summary.* Ottawa, Agriculture and Agri-Food Canada
http://www.agr.ca/policy/environment/eb/public_htm l/ebe/aei.html [Geo-2-186]

Statistics Canada (2000). *Human Activity and the Environment 2000.* Ottawa, Minister of Industry

Tyrchniewicz, A. and Wilson, A. (1994). *Sustainable Development for the Great Plains: Policy Analysis.* Winnipeg, International Institute for Sustainable Development
http://www.iisd.org/pdf/sd_for_gp.pdf [Geo-2-187]

UNCCD (2001). United Nations Secretariat of the Convention to Combat Desertification
http://www.unccd.int/main.php

USDA (1996). *Part 407 - Sustainable Agriculture (Subpart A - General).* US Department of Agriculture, Natural Resources Conservation Service Electronic Directives System
http://policy.nrcs.usda.gov/national/gm/title180/part 407/subparta/index.htm [Geo-2-188]

USDA (2001a). *Water Erosion Vulnerability.* US Department of Agriculture, Natural Resources Conservation Service, Soil Survey Division, World Soil Resources, Washington DC
http://www.nhq.nrcs.usda.gov/WSR/mapindx/erosh 2o.htm [Geo-2-189]

USDA (2001b). *Wind Erosion Vulnerability.* US Department of Agriculture, Natural Resources Conservation Service, Soil Survey Division, World Soil Resources, Washington DC
http://www.nhq.nrcs.usda.gov/WSR/mapindx/eroswi nd.htm [Geo-2-190]

Vaisey, J.S., Weins, T.W. and Wettlaufer, R.J. (1996). *The Permanent Cover Program - Is twice enough?* Paper presented at Soil and Water Conservation Policies: Successes and Failures, Prague, Czech Republic, 17–20 September 1996

Zinn, Jeffrey (1994). *Conservation Reserve Program: Policy Issues for the 1995 Farm Bill.* National Library for the Environment, Congressional Research Service Reports
http://www.cnie.org/nle/nrgen-21.html [Geo-2-191]

## Land: West Asia

Land degradation and, at its extreme, desertification, continue to be the most significant environmental issues in West Asia (CAMRE, UNEP and ACSAD 1996), especially in countries where the agricultural sector makes a significant contribution to the national economy. There is extensive desert in the region, ranging from 10 per cent in Syria to nearly 100 per cent in Bahrain, Kuwait, Qatar and the United Arab Emirates. Desertification has also affected wide areas of rangelands in Iraq, Jordan, Syria and the countries of the Arabian Peninsula. The causes include a combination of climate, high population growth rates and intensive agriculture. Poverty and inappropriate government policies exacerbate the problem.

Geopolitical instability in and around the countries of West Asia has persuaded governments to adopt policies aimed at achieving national food security. These policies have been accompanied by agricultural protectionism, the erection of trade barriers and government subsidies for agricultural inputs. Subsidies, together with free or cheap irrigation water, have had severe impacts on land and water resources, and have contributed to the unsustainability of agriculture in the region (UNESCWA 1997). As a result, land degradation has become widespread, and it has accelerated as more rangelands were reclaimed and put under cultivation (CAMRE, UNEP and ACSAD 1996). The charts below show the extent and causes of degradation by sub-region.

Forest fires and forest clearance are two of the main causes of vegetation cover loss and soil erosion. Between 1985 and 1993, forest fires destroyed more than 8 000 hectares of forests and affected more than 20 000 ha of coastal forests in Syria, resulting in soil erosion in excess of 20 tonnes/ha/year. At the same time, nearly 2 440 ha of forest land were cleared for agricultural purposes (World Bank and UNDP 1998).

Population growth and other demographic changes have led to losses of land to urbanization, industrialization and non-agricultural purposes. Insufficient development and services in rural areas in the Mashriq sub-region and in Yemen have resulted in a rural influx to urban areas, spreading illegal settlements and squatter houses on the peripheries of major cities at the expense of fertile agricultural land. As well as encouraging intensification of agriculture, national policies aimed at achieving higher levels of food self-sufficiency also resulted in a more than two-fold increase in irrigated area between 1972 and 1999, from 2 991 million ha to 7 191 million ha (FAOSTAT 2001). The largest increase occurred in Saudi Arabia, from 0.437 million ha in 1980 to 1.6 million ha in 1993 (Al-Tukhais 1999). However, despite the large increase in the irrigated land area (see graph on page 86), the increase in food production has not kept pace with population growth.

Poor management and inefficient use of irrigation water have resulted in salinization, alkalization, water logging and nutrient depletion in large areas in the region. Salinization, which is the most important cause of degradation in irrigated soils, has affected about 42.5 per cent of the desert area in West Asia (Harahsheh and Tateishi 2000). About 2 million ha of the cultivated land area in Saudi Arabia and 33.6 per cent of cultivated land of Bahrain are moderately salinized (FAOSTAT 2001). Salinity and waterlogging have affected 8.5 million ha or 64 per cent of the total arable land in Iraq, while 20–30 per cent of irrigated land has been abandoned due to salinization (Abul-Gasim and others 1998). More than 50 per cent of the

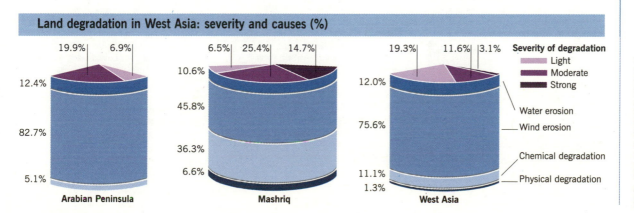

**Land degradation in West Asia: severity and causes (%)**

Arabian Peninsula: 19.9% | 6.9% | 12.4% | 82.7% | 5.1%

Mashriq: 6.5% | 25.4% | 14.7% | 10.6% | 45.8% | 36.3% | 6.6%

West Asia: 19.3% | 11.6% | 3.1% | 12.0% | 75.6% | 11.1% | 1.3%

Severity of degradation
- Light
- Moderate
- Strong

Water erosion
Wind erosion
Chemical degradation
Physical degradation

Charts left show the severity (percentage of total land area) and the causes (percentage of total degradation) for the region and the two sub-regions. **Note the prevalence of wind erosion**

*Source: compiled from Marcoux 1996*

### Irrigated area (million ha): West Asia

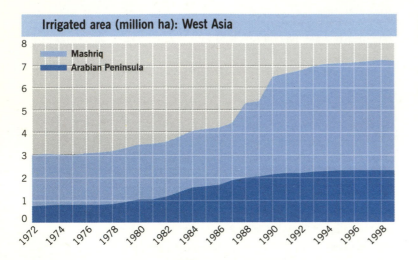

Mashriq
Arabian Peninsula

**Irrigated area in West Asia has grown sharply over the past three decades but agricultural production has not kept pace with population growth**

*Source: compiled from FAOSTAT 2001*

irrigated lands in the Euphrates plains in Syria and Iraq have been badly affected by salinization and waterlogging (UNESCWA 1997).

## Rangelands

Rangelands occupy about 50 per cent of the total area in West Asia. The vegetation cover is characterized by low tolerance, low plant density and coverage, and low species variability and plant productivity per unit area. Drought, overgrazing, uprooting of woody species for use as fuel, tillage, and mismanagement of water resources are the principal causes of rangeland deterioration. It is estimated that about 90 per cent of the rangelands are degraded or vulnerable to desertification. More than 30 per cent of the grazing land in Saudi Arabia is degraded (Shorbagy 1986, Al-Hassan 1991) and deterioration of rangelands has also been reported in several other countries of West Asia (Al-Kuthairi 1992).

The grazing intensity in most West Asian countries has more than doubled over the past four decades, mainly as a result of subsidized feeding, provision of water points and mechanization. Sheep density on some rangelands is more than one mature head per hectare — some four times the natural carrying capacity (Le Houerou 1995). It is estimated that the grazing capacity in the rangelands of the West Bank is exceeded by a factor of 5.7 (Palestinian Authority 2000).

Many West Asian countries are in the process of formalizing their national action plans to combat desertification. A Strategic Regional Action Plan to combat desertification in West Asia has been established within the framework of the UNCCD. Legislation has been enacted and laws and regulations regarding water and land use tightened. A number of range reserves have been established in the region.

### References: Chapter 2, land, West Asia

Abul-Gasim, S. and Babiker, M. (1998). Iraq's Food security: the sand dunes fixation project. *Desertification Control Bulletin*, No. 33, 2–10

Al-Hassan, H.Z. (1991). *Deteriorated Rangelands of Northern Saudi Arabia and Measures to Improve.* MSc. Thesis, Bahrain, Sciences Graduate Programme, Arabian Gulf University (in Arabic)

Al-Kuthairi, A.M. (1992). *Forests and Pastoral Activities in Dhofar Mountains: Study of Strategy for their Rehabilitation.* MSc. Dissertation, Arabian Gulf University, Bahrain

Al-Tukhais, A.S. (1999). *Arabian sheald: a model for sustainable agriculture in the Kingdom of Saudi Arabia.* The Third Conference on Desertification and Environmental Studies: Beyond the Year 2000. November 30-December 4 1999. Riyadh, King Saud University

CAMRE, UNEP and ACSAD (1996). *State of Desertification in the Arab Region and the Ways and Means to Deal with It.* Damascus, Arab Centre for Studies on Dry Areas and Arid Lands

FAOSTAT (2001). *FAOSTAT Statistical Database.* Food and Agriculture Organization http://www.fao.org/ [Geo-2-196]

Harahsheh, H. and Tateishi, R. (2000). *Environmental GIS Database and Desertification Mapping of West Asia.* Paper presented at the Workshop of the Asian Region Thematic Programme Network on Desertification Monitoring and Assessment, Tokyo, 28-30 June 2000

Le Houerou, H.N. (1995). Eco-climatic and bio-geographic comparison between the rangelands of the iso-climatic Mediterranean arid zone of northern Africa and the Near East. In Omar, A.S., and others (eds.). *Range Management in Arid Zones: Proceedings of the Second International Conference on Range Management in the Arabian Gulf.* London, Kegan Paul International

Marcoux, A. (1996). *Population Change-Natural Resources-Environment Linkages in the Arab States Region.* Population Information Network http://www.un.org/popin/fao/arabstat.htm [Geo-2-193]

Palestinian National Authority (2000). State of the Environment Palestine. Gaza, Ministry of Environmental Affairs

Shorbagy, M.A. (1986). *Desertification of natural rangelands in the Arab world. Agriculture and Water, 4.* Damascus, Arab Centre for Studies on Dry Areas and Arid Lands (in Arabic)

UNESCWA (1997). *Economic and Social Commission for Western Asia: Regional Report. Implementation of Agenda 21: Review of Progress made since the United Nations Conference on Environment and Development, 1992.* United Nations Department of Economic and Social Affairs http://www.un.org/esa/earthsummit/ecwa-cp.htm [Geo-2-194]

World Bank and UNDP (1998). *State of the Environment in Syria.* London, Environmental Resource Management

## Land: the Polar Regions

### The Arctic

The Arctic land mass is approximately 14 million km$^2$ (AMAP 1997), of which the Russian Federation and Canada account for nearly 80 per cent, the Nordic countries for around 16 per cent and the United States about 4 per cent (CAFF 1994).

The Arctic consists of three main sub-systems:

- the high polar desert in eastern Canada, which comprises mainly bare soils and rocks with sparse plant communities;
- the tundra, which is a vast, open plain with continuous low vegetation cover; and
- the forest-tundra, which is the transition zone that parallels the boreal forest to the south, and consists of patches of continuous forest cover interspersed with tundra-like open areas (CAFF 2001).

Besides its living resources, the Arctic contains huge deposits of oil, gas and minerals. In the Arctic regions of North America, there has been a recent upsurge of mining and associated infrastructural development. Likewise, in the Russian Federation — a country which covers 12.6 per cent of the Earth's land surface — much land has been seriously degraded by mineral extraction, forestry, fires, air pollution or conversion to agriculture, and erosion is widespread and increasing. In recent years, approximately 70 million ha of tundra have been degraded through destruction of soil and vegetative cover, resulting from prospecting, mineral development, vehicular movement, construction and, at certain locations, overgrazing by reindeer (OECD 1999).

The Russian Federation has established a solid legislative and regulatory base to respond to these threats. Unfortunately, implementation is not guaranteed due to the decline in the Russian economy, especially since 1998. Without an infusion of financial support to implement and enforce the legislative regime, the environmental situation will continue to decline (OECD 1999).

Along with increased resource exploitation, construction of roads and other infrastructure is also changing the face of the Arctic landscape.

In Norway, for example, the area of undisturbed land has been reduced from 48 per cent in 1900 to 11.8 per cent in 1998. Norway is taking political action and is now placing increased emphasis on preservation of wilderness areas and to avoid piecemeal development (Nellemann and others 2001).

Tourism is growing in the Arctic and is already an important component of the economies of the north although it is still in its infancy in northern Russia. In 2000, more than 1.5 million people visited the Arctic (CAFF 2001). There are concerns, however, that tourism is promoting environmental degradation by putting extra pressures on land, wildlife, water and other basic necessities, and on transportation facilities.

Erosion is a serious problem in parts of the Arctic. It is caused by thawing, removal of ground cover and deforestation. In Iceland, for example, more than one-half of the vegetation and soil cover has been lost since the island was colonized by humans, especially in the interior, as a result of deforestation and overgrazing.

Arctic country governments have taken some action to protect their land base. Approximately 15 per cent of the Arctic land mass is protected, although nearly 50 per cent of the protected area is classified as Arctic desert or glacier — the least productive part of the Arctic and the one with the lowest biodiversity and habitat values (CAFF 2001).

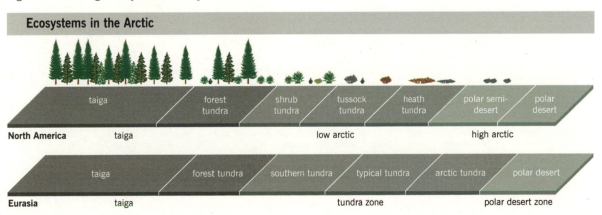

**Ecosystems in the Arctic**

| North America | taiga | forest tundra | shrub tundra | tussock tundra | heath tundra | polar semi-desert | polar desert |

North America: taiga — low arctic — high arctic

| Eurasia | taiga | forest tundra | southern tundra | typical tundra | arctic tundra | polar desert |

Eurasia: taiga — tundra zone — polar desert zone

The Arctic is characterized by three main eco-systems: desert, tundra and the forest-tundra which is the transition zone

*Source: CAFF 2001*

## Antarctica

The ice-free areas of Antarctica comprise less than 2 per cent of the total land area of the continent. These areas are largely found on the continental coastline (particularly in the Peninsula area) and on the islands south of 60°. The ice-free areas are biologically active sites with relatively easy access. They are therefore also the focus of increasing human activities and infrastructure. Threats to Antarctic land arise from this human activity, and threats to the ice sheets arise both as a result of this activity and, more importantly, from global climate change.

The risks associated with human uses of ice-free areas are related to potential local pollution due to oil spills, deposition of combustion products and sewage, habitat loss, terrain modification, disturbance to wildlife due to operations and human presence and introduction of exotic species and disease. However, so far little is known about the long-term and cumulative significance of these impacts.

There are now 70 research stations in Antarctica; half operate throughout the entire year and almost half are located in the Peninsula region (COMNAP 2000b). Few are located in ice-covered areas. Half of today's operative stations were constructed before 1970. In addition to this scientific activity, tourism in Antarctica is also increasing.

Ice covers 98 per cent of the Antarctic continent. The mass balance of this Antarctic ice sheet is of global concern, particularly in view of the impact on sea level of ice melting. The mass of ice is growing over most of East Antarctica although coastal regions tend to be near balance with some losses around some

### The Madrid Protocol on Environmental Protection

The Madrid Protocol on Environmental Protection to the Antarctic Treaty came into force in 1998. The signing of the protocol significantly strengthened the environmental objectives of the Antarctic Treaty. It requires, among other things, that all activities be planned and conducted so as to limit adverse impacts on the Antarctic environment and dependent and associated ecosystems. The Madrid Protocol also defines a framework for protected areas, enabling special protection of unique, important or especially vulnerable areas.

It is yet too early to assess the effectiveness of the provisions of the Madrid Protocol. However, some environmental measures adopted since the Protocol have already proved efficient. For example, in 1992 the National Antarctic operators developed guidelines for fuel handling and emergency response. Since then, a gradual decrease in the number of reported incidents per year has been recorded, indicating that these recommendations are being implemented and are effective (COMNAP 2000a).

of the large ice shelves and coastal ice streams (Budd, Coutts and Warner 1998). The ice masses of Antarctica are therefore increasing rather than decreasing on a continental level (Vaughan and others 1999). However, the ice shelves in the Antarctic Peninsula continue to disintegrate because of regional warming. A total area loss of 6 300 km$^2$ was observed for the Larsen ice shelf between 1975 and 1998 (Skvarca and others 1999) and an additional 1 714 km$^2$ was lost during the 1998-99 season. Iceberg break-up is consistent with global warming but is not a proof of it. Melting of marginal ice shelves in the Antarctic Peninsula is, however, not expected to have significant and direct effects on sea level (IPCC 1998).

### References: Chapter 2, land, the Polar Regions

AMAP (1997). *Arctic Pollution Issues: A State of the Arctic Environment Report.* Oslo, Arctic Council Arctic Monitoring and Assessment Programme

Budd, W.F., Coutts, B. and Warner, R.C. (1998). Modelling the Antarctic and Northern Hemisphere ice-sheet changes with global climate through the glacial cycle. *Annals of Glaciology.* 27, 153-160

CAFF (2001). *Arctic Flora and Fauna: Status and Conservation.* Helsinki, Arctic Council Programme for the Conservation of Arctic Flora and Fauna

CAFF (1994). *The State of Protected Areas in the Circumpolar Arctic - 1994,* CAFF Habitat Conservation Report No. 1, Trondheim, Directorate for Nature Management

COMNAP (2000a). *Assessment of Environmental Emergencies Arising from Activities in Antarctica.*

Working Paper No 16. Tromsø, Norwegian Polar Institute, Committee for Environmental Protection

COMNAP (2000b). *Stations and Bases.* Council of Managers of National Antarctic Programs http://www.comnap.aq/comnap/comnap.nsf/P/Stations/ [Geo-2-192]

IPCC (1998). *Rapid Non-Linear Climate Change – Report of a Workshop, Noordwijkerhout, The Netherlands, 31 March - 2 April, 1998.* Bracknell, UK Meteorological Office

Nellemann, C., Kullerud, L., Vistnes, I., Forbes, B.C., Foresman, T., Kofinas, G.P., Kaltenborn, B.P., Grøn, O., Husby, E., Magomedova, M., Lambrechts, C., Bobiwash, R., Schei, P.J. and Larsen, T.S. (2001). GLOBIO Global Methodology for Mapping Human Impacts on the Biosphere; The Arctic 2050 Scenario and Global Application,

UNEP/DEWA Technical Report No 3 Nairobi, United Nations Environment Programme

OECD (1999). *Environmental Performance Reviews: Russian Federation.* Paris, OECD Centre for Cooperation with Non-Members, Paris, 1999 ISBN 92 64 17145 2

Skvarca, P, Rack, W., Rott, H. and Donangelo, T.I.Y. (1999). Climate trend and the retreat and disintegration of ice shelves on the Antarctic Peninsula: An overview. *Polar Research* 18, 2, 151-157

Vaughan, D.G., Bamber, J.L., Giovinetto, M., Russel, J. and Cooper, A.P.R. (1999). Reassessment of net surface mass balance in Antarctica. *Journal of Climate* 12, 4, 933-946

# OUR CHANGING ENVIRONMENT: Habila, central Sudan

30 October 1979

15 September 1987

21 November 1994

The Habila region was first developed for mechanized rain-fed agriculture in 1968. The intent was to use the fertile cracking clay soils that were not suited to traditional agriculture to address the region's chronic food supply problems, and eventually to produce surpluses for export.

Private investment was encouraged by the government and the land was divided into *feddans* (about 0.4 ha), which were then leased out to private operators. The original leases were to be left fallow after four years and new leases were to be let for adjacent fallow plots. The government controls were intended to ensure the continued viability and productivity of the cracking clay soils.

By 1979, about 147 000 ha were leased under official schemes, and the soils proved well suited to sorghum. However, in the 1970s Sudan launched a programme to become the bread basket of the Arab world. Production was greatly expanded, the proportion of fallow land decreased dramatically, and there was expansion into unsanctioned 'illegal' land.

By 1985, about 45 per cent of mechanized agriculture was located outside sanctioned areas. Farmers interested in quick profits cultivated the land to exhaustion, abandoned it and then recruited more.

By the mid-1990s, periods of persistent drought, internal warfare, unsustainable methods of land use and resultant famines plagued the country. The failed agricultural policy is clearly evident in the 1994 image. There is little evidence of the booming croplands so prominent in 1979.

Images: Chuck Larson, USGS/EROS Data Center
Compilation: UNEP GRID Sioux Falls

UNEP, Rick Collins, Topham Picturepoint

# Forests

## Global overview

The unique nature of forest ecosystems has long been acknowledged. Forest ecosystems play multiple roles at global as well as local levels: as providers of environmental services to nature in general — and humans in particular — and as sources of economically valued products (see box). The 1972 Stockholm Conference recognized forests as the largest, most complex and self-perpetuating of all ecosystems, and emphasized the need for sound land and forest use policies, ongoing monitoring of the state of the world's forests and the introduction of forest management planning. It was recommended that countries should:

- strengthen basic and applied research for improved forest planning and management, with emphasis on environmental functions of forests; and
- modernize forest management concepts by including multiple functions and reflecting the cost and benefits of the amenities that forests provide.

The Conference also called for:

- cooperation of United Nations bodies to meet the needs for new knowledge to incorporate environmental values in national land use and forest management; and
- continuing surveillance of the world's forest cover through the establishment (in countries) of an appropriate monitoring system.

Today, the Stockholm Conference recommendations relating to forests remain valid and unfulfilled, in many ways, because of conflicting interests in managing

### Forest goods and services

- Industrial wood, woodfuel, non-wood forest products such as fibre, food, medicines
- Soil generation, soil and water conservation, purification of air and water, nutrient recycling, maintenance of biological diversity (habitats, species and genetic resources), mitigation of climate change, carbon sequestration
- Employment and income, recreation, protection of natural and cultural heritage

*Sources: UNDP, UNEP, World Bank and WRI 2000, FAO 2001a*

forests for environmental conservation and economic development.

Deforestation over the past 30 years has been the continuation of a process with a long history. By the time of the Stockholm Conference, much of the Earth's forest cover had already been cleared. The historic loss of forests is closely related to demographic expansion and the conversion of forest land to other uses. Major direct causes of forest degradation brought on by humans include overharvesting of industrial wood, fuelwood and other forest products, and overgrazing. Underlying causes include poverty, population growth, markets and trade in forest products, and macroeconomic policies. Forests are also susceptible to natural factors such as insect pests, diseases, fire and extreme climatic events.

A number of assessments of changes in forest cover have been carried out over the past 30 years (including FAO and UNEP 1982, FAO 1995, FAO 1997, FAO 2001b, UNEP 2001 and WRI 1997). While differing in their definitions of forest cover, methodology and specific results, making detailed comparisons unreliable, these assessments have reinforced each other in their overall depiction of declining forest areas and continued degradation of forest ecosystems.

The *1980 Tropical Forest Resources Assessment* by FAO and UNEP was the first comprehensive assessment of tropical forests. The rate of tropical deforestation was calculated at 11.3 million ha a year (FAO and UNEP 1982), vindicating the fears of the

## Forest cover 2000

Stockholm Conference about the alarming rate of global forest loss. Since then, while forest area in developed countries has stabilized and is slightly increasing overall, deforestation has continued in developing countries (FAO-ECE 2000, FAO 2001b, FAO 2001a).

FAO's *Global Forest Resources Assessment 2000* (FAO 2001b), using for the first time a common definition of forests as areas of at least 0.5 ha with tree crown cover of more that 10 per cent, concluded that:

- The total area covered by forest is approximately 3 866 million ha, almost one-third of the world's land area, of which 95 per cent is natural forest and 5 per cent is planted forest; 17 per cent is in Africa, 19 per cent in Asia and the Pacific, 27 per cent in Europe, 12 per cent in North America and 25 per cent in Latin America and the Caribbean

**Forest covered some 3 866 million ha of the planet in the year 2000 — somewhat less than one-third of total land area**

*Note: dark green represents closed forest, more than 40 per cent covered with trees more than 5 metres high; mid-green represents open (10–40 per cent coverage) and fragmented forest; light green represents other woodland, shrubland and bushland*

*Source: FAO 2001b*

## Change in forested land 1990–2000 by region

| | total land area (million ha) | total forest 1990 (million ha) | total forest 2000 (million ha) | % of land forested in 2000 | change 1990-2000 (million ha) | % change per year |
|---|---|---|---|---|---|---|
| Africa | 2 963.3 | 702.5 | 649.9 | 21.9 | -52.6 | -0.7 |
| Asia and the Pacific | 3 463.2 | 734.0 | 726.3 | 21.0 | -7.7 | -0.1 |
| Europe | 2 359.4 | 1 042.0 | 1 051.3 | 44.6 | 9.3 | 0.1 |
| Latin America and the Caribbean | 2 017.8 | 1 011.0 | 964.4 | 47.8 | -46.7 | -0.5 |
| North America | 1 838.0 | 466.7 | 470.1 | 25.6 | 3.9 | 0.1 |
| West Asia | 372.4 | 3.6 | 3.7 | 1.0 | 0.0 | 0.0 |
| **world** | **13 014.1** | **3 960.0** | **3 866.1** | **29.7** | **-93.9** | **-0.24** |

*Source: compiled from FAO 2001b  Note: numbers may not add due to rounding*

(see table on page 91). About 47 per cent of forests worldwide are tropical, 9 per cent subtropical, 11 per cent temperate and 33 per cent boreal.

- At the global level, the net loss in forest area during the 1990s was an estimated 94 million ha (equivalent to 2.4 per cent of total forests). This was the combined effect of a deforestation rate of 14.6 million ha per year and a rate of forest increase of 5.2 million ha per year. Deforestation of tropical forests is almost 1 per cent per year.

- The area under forest plantations grew by an average of 3.1 million ha per year during the 1990s. Half of this increase was the result of afforestation on land previously under non-forest

between permanent large- and small-scale agriculture and areas under shifting cultivation.

A recent study using globally comprehensive and consistent satellite data estimated that the extent of the world's remaining closed natural forests (where crown cover is more than 40 per cent) in 1995 was 2 870 million ha, about 21.4 per cent of the land area of the world (UNEP 2001). About 81 per cent of these forests are concentrated in just 15 countries. Ranked in the highest to lowest order these are: the Russian Federation, Canada, Brazil, the United States, Democratic Republic of the Congo, China, Indonesia, Mexico, Peru, Colombia, Bolivia, Venezuela, India, Australia and Papua New Guinea. The first three countries contain about 49 per cent of the remaining closed forests. More than a quarter of closed forests grow on mountains (see box on page 68).

## Forest products

Wood supply and production remains the focus of most forest inventories. More than one-third of above-ground woody biomass is located in South America, with 27 per cent in Brazil alone. Estimates by FAO (2000) show that global production of total roundwood reached 3 335 million $m^3$ in 1999. Just over half of this was fuelwood, about 90 per cent of which was produced and consumed in developing countries. On the other hand, industrial roundwood production, 1 550 million $m^3$ in 1999, was dominated by developed countries, which together accounted for 79 per cent of total global production. The overall trend for industrial roundwood production was relatively flat during the 1990s. This was a significant change from the rapid growth that occurred prior to 1990.

Commercial logging methods are often destructive and contribute directly or indirectly to deforestation. In West Africa, it was estimated that in obtaining 1 $m^3$ of logs, about 2 $m^3$ of standing trees are destroyed (Serageldine 1990). Logging is especially damaging on steep slopes or in sensitive ecosystems such as transitional forests and mangroves (see box opposite). Where certain species are selected, non-target species can also be damaged. Clearing of forests impacts most severely on local populations, who lose vital sources of food, fuel, construction materials, medicines and areas for livestock grazing. It also exposes soils and shade species to wind, sunlight, evaporation and erosion, accelerating siltation in

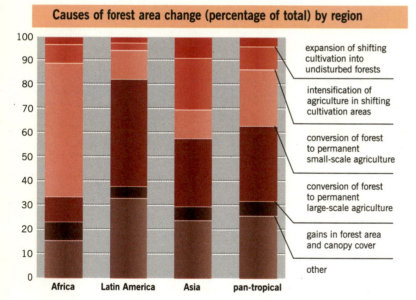

**Causes of forest area change (percentage of total) by region**

- expansion of shifting cultivation into undisturbed forests
- intensification of agriculture in shifting cultivation areas
- conversion of forest to permanent small-scale agriculture
- conversion of forest to permanent large-scale agriculture
- gains in forest area and canopy cover
- other

In the 1990s, almost 70 per cent of deforested areas were changed to agricultural land. In Latin America, most conversion was large scale, whereas in Africa small-scale agricultural enterprises predominated

Notes: 'pan-tropical' refers to data samples from satellite images of tropical areas; regions do not correspond exactly to GEO regions

Source: FAO 2001b

land use, whereas the other half resulted from conversion of natural forest.

- The world's natural forests have continued to be converted to other land uses at a very high rate. During the 1990s, the total loss of natural forests (deforestation plus the conversion of natural forests to forest plantations) was 16.1 million ha per year, of which 15.2 million ha occurred in the tropics.

- In the 1990s, almost 70 per cent of deforested areas were changed to agricultural land, predominantly under permanent rather than shifting systems. In Latin America most conversion was large scale, whereas in Africa small-scale agricultural enterprises predominated. Changes in Asia were more equally distributed

dams, rivers and the coastal zone, as well as causing severe floods.

There is a global trend towards greater reliance on plantations as a source of industrial wood. The development of a significant global plantation estate is quite recent; half of all plantations in the world are less than 15 years old. Asia has led plantation establishment globally; as of 2000, about 62 per cent of all forest plantations were located in that region. Other significant developments include: rising private sector investment in plantations in developing countries; increasing foreign investments in plantations; and an expansion of 'outgrower' schemes whereby communities or small landowners produce trees for sale to private companies (FAO 2001b). Forest plantations typically contain only one, or a few, species, which makes them less biologically diverse and more susceptible to diseases and other disturbances than natural forests.

Forest industries continue to adapt to changes in raw materials, namely the increased supply of plantation wood and of a wider range of species. Recently there has been an emergence of innovative ways to make better use of available supplies and of residues and waste. Such new developments include laminated veneer lumber, glue-laminated timbers and products based on wood fibres. In addition, modern technologies that reduce environmental impacts, through pollution control and other means, are now available to wood-processing industries (FAO 2001a).

In addition, many countries have imposed bans on timber harvesting, either to conserve their forest resources or as a response to devastating natural calamities (such as landslides and flooding) that are attributed, rightly or wrongly, to excessive commercial logging. The effects of logging bans differ widely with the type of policy, the products affected, market conditions, etc. In some situations, logging bans can shift harvesting pressure from one region to another, affect forest-dependent communities, increase or decrease employment opportunities, and disrupt markets (FAO 2001a). There is also increasing interest in forest certification which offers the potential to provide a market incentive for better forest management (see box on page 94).

Trade trends in forest products show an increased proportion of the total production of wood products being exported, increased domestic wood processing prior to export, increased trade among developing

## Where the forest meets the sea

Mangrove forests thrive in intertidal zones of sub-tropical and tropical shores of Africa, Australia, Asia and the Americas. They line about 25 per cent of tropical coastlines. Mangrove forests are among the world's most biologically diverse and productive systems. They provide food and refuge for many species and nutrients for the marine environment. Mangroves also act as nursery grounds for fish and shellfish, and are prime nesting and

Flock of birds in a mangrove forest at Orissa, India

*Source: UNEP, Van Gruissen, Topham Picturepoint*

migratory sites for hundreds of bird species (see photo). In Belize, for instance, more than 500 species of birds have been recorded in mangrove areas. Mangroves also help protect coastlines from erosion, storm damage and wave action, and protect coral reefs and sea grass beds from damaging siltation. Local communities are provided with timber and fuelwood from mangrove forests.

Mangroves are threatened by activities such as overharvesting, freshwater diversion, pollution, prolonged flooding and fluctuating sea levels. In addition, the charcoal and timber industries, tourism and other coastal developments are destroying mangrove forests. The rapidly expanding shrimp aquaculture industry poses the gravest threat — as much as 50 per cent of recent mangrove destruction has been due to clear-cutting for shrimp farms.

Thailand has lost more than half of its mangrove forests since 1960. In the Philippines, mangroves declined from an estimated 448 000 ha in the 1920s to only 110 000 ha in 1990. In Ecuador, the Muisne region has lost nearly 90 per cent of its mangroves. Globally, about half of the world's mangrove forests may have been lost.

*Sources: Quarto 2002, UNDP, UNEP, World Bank and WRI 2000*

countries (particularly in Asia) and trade liberalization at a global level. At the same time some countries are introducing export restrictions to address national environmental and market problems. Forest trade and environment issues have been under consideration by both the World Trade Organization Committee on Trade and Environment and the Intergovernmental Forum on Forests. Impacts of trade on some commercial tree species are currently under review by a working group of the Convention on International Trade in Endangered Species of Wild Fauna and Flora (CITES) (FAO 2001a).

## Forests and climate change

Recent negotiations on the Kyoto Protocol to the UN Framework Convention on Climate Change (UNFCCC) have focused considerable attention on forests in the context of climate change (IISD 2001a and 2001b). Forests both influence and are influenced by climate change: they play an important role in the global carbon cycle, and their management or destruction could significantly affect the course of global warming in the 21st century.

Forests contain somewhat more than half of the carbon that is stored in terrestrial vegetation and soil organic matter with boreal forests accounting for 26 per cent of the total terrestrial carbon stocks. Tropical and temperate forests contain 20 and 7 per cent respectively (Dixon and others 1994). Although considerable uncertainties surround estimates of carbon release from deforestation, removal of forest biomass contributes significantly to net emissions of carbon dioxide to the atmosphere. During the 1980s and 1990s, emissions were estimated to be 1.6-1.7 gigatonnes ($10^9$ tonnes) of carbon a year (Watson and others 2000). If predicted climate changes materialize, the impacts on forests are likely to be regionally varied, dramatic and long-lasting, affecting both the distribution and composition of forests (IPCC 2001a, FAO 2001a).

The Kyoto Protocol may have a profound effect on the forest sector. Parties to the UNFCCC have recently reached agreement on rules and modalities of accounting for carbon sequestered by forests. This may open the way for developed countries to invest in afforestation and reforestation projects in developing countries in exchange for carbon emission reduction units under the Clean Development Mechanism, thereby reducing the cost of implementation of the Protocol (IPCC 2001b).

## Forest certification

Forest management certification has been strongly promoted by civil society over the past decade. It resulted from public disillusionment with the failure of governments and intergovernmental bodies to improve forest management or tackle deforestation effectively, and the lack of discrimination by forest industries about the source of their products.

Forest certification is a voluntary, market-based instrument that enables consumers to identify forest products with high environmental standards. By focusing on quality of forest management rather than the quality of forest products, it contributes to the growing trend to define production and process standards for social and environmental performance in resource management.

Three main certification approaches are in operation:
- Forest Stewardship Council (FSC) accreditation — an international system which requires producers to meet a global set of Principles and Standards for good forest stewardship and provides a trademark for product labelling;
- Certification of the Environmental Management System (EMS) under the International Organization for Standardization (ISO) 14000 series; and
- national certification schemes, some of which also incorporate elements of the FSC and ISO approaches.

By the end of 2000, about 2 per cent of the global forest had been certified for sustainable forest management. About 92 per cent of these forests were located in Canada, Finland, Germany, Norway, Poland, Sweden and the United States. At the same time, only four countries with tropical moist forests (Bolivia, Brazil, Guatemala and Mexico) had more than 100 000 ha of certified forests, with a combined total of 1.8 million ha. An increasing number of large retail 'do-it-yourself' chains in Europe and the United States and some major house-builders in the United States have announced that they will favour certified wood products in the future. Buyers' groups that have committed themselves to trading only in products from certified sources are also on the increase.

Many more millions of hectares are in the process of certification although the concept is still hotly debated in many countries. Producer countries and trade groups tend to consider it restrictive whilst consumer countries with strong environmental lobbies have stressed its potential benefits. Although there is little evidence as yet about the local and market impacts of certification the contribution of this voluntary procedure to good policy is evident. Setting up the system has provided a forum for stakeholders to discuss broader forest policy issues. It has also been successful in moving decision-making powers away from some minorities with vested interests.

*Sources: FAO 2001b and 2001b, Mayers and Bass 1999*

## Forests and biodiversity

Forests are critically important for maintaining biological diversity. Estimated to contain half of the world's total biological diversity, natural forests have the highest species diversity and endemism of any ecosystem type. Tropical forests are particularly richly endowed (CIFOR and others 1998). Forest fragmentation exacerbates the impacts on biodiversity of overall deforestation and forest degradation by blocking migration routes and making access easier for further exploitation by humans and entry by invasive species (UNDP, UNEP, World Bank and WRI 2000). The remnant primary forests need to be identified, mapped, conserved and restored. In the tropics, where most remaining forests are still of natural origin, conservation combined with forest rehabilitation as well as development of local communities in and around the forests, could go a long way to achieve the goal of biological diversity conservation in spite of rising population pressure.

Forest protected areas are one of the keys to the conservation of biological diversity globally. An estimated 12 per cent of the world's forests are under protected area status (as defined by IUCN Categories I to VI). The Americas have the largest proportion, approximately 20 per cent, of forests under protected status. The effectiveness of on-the-ground management is what really matters, however. In many

Forest fires in Australia, Brazil, Ethiopia, Indonesia (photo left), the eastern Mediterranean, Mexico and western United States have raised concern about wildfires, catalysed national policy responses and mobilized initiatives for fire prevention and suppression

Source: UNEP, Paulus Suwito, Topham Picturepoint

parts of the world there is a strong tendency towards 'paper parks' whose existence is largely theoretical and not reflected by substantive and durable conservation reserves on the ground (Vancly and others 2001). Furthermore, those sites that do exist are under increasing pressure from competing land uses.

The depletion of forest-based wildlife as a result of the commercial harvesting and trade of bushmeat is of growing concern. This has reached crisis dimensions in parts of tropical Africa, where many species of primates and antelopes, among others, are threatened (FAO 2001a). This difficult problem is being addressed at the local or national level by various stakeholders, as well as at the international level by CITES.

## Forest damage

Large areas of forest around the world caught fire in 1997 and 1998, when intense El Niño-related drought conditions prevailed. Another serious spate of fires occurred in 1999-2000. The forest fires of the past five years in Australia, Brazil, Ethiopia, Indonesia, the eastern Mediterranean, Mexico and western United States have raised public awareness and concern about

wildfires, catalysed national policy responses and mobilized regional and international initiatives for fire prevention, early warning, detection and suppression. The links between fires and land use policies and practices are now better understood (FAO 2001a).

Extreme weather events are another threat. The storms that struck Europe in December 1999 caused massive damage to forests and to trees outside forests. The total damage in Europe represented six months of the region's normal harvest while, in some countries, the equivalent of several years' harvest was blown down. Changes in forest management, such as increased reliance on natural regeneration, have been proposed in many countries to reduce the potential risk of storm damage in the future (FAO 2001a).

## Forest governance

Forest governance systems are evolving rapidly, together with the respective roles and responsibilities of government, the private sector, indigenous communities and civil society. The concept of sustainable forest management — and efforts to achieve it — continued to gain momentum around the world during the past decade. Broader approaches to forest management, such as integrated ecosystem and landscape management, are becoming more widely accepted and put into practice. These approaches recognize the dynamic nature of ecological and social systems, and the importance of adaptive management and collaborative decision-making. As of 2000, 149 countries were engaged in nine international initiatives to develop and implement criteria and indicators for sustainable forest management, covering nearly 85 per cent of the world's forest. At least 6 per cent of the total forest area in the developing countries is covered by a formal, nationally approved forest management plan, lasting at least five years. Some 89 per cent of the forests in industrialized countries are managed according to formal or informal management plans. An FAO survey of 145 countries found that 96 per cent of the countries had national forest programmes in various stages of development. Model and demonstration forest programmes are widely used to illustrate sustainable forest management in practice (FAO 2001a).

The involvement of local communities in joint forest management is now a significant feature of national forest policies and programmes throughout the world. Faced with inadequate financial and human resources, governments of developing countries are increasingly turning to local communities for assistance in protecting and managing state-owned forests. In some of these management schemes, the community provides the labour and protection, while gaining access to areas that were once restricted. Although several community-based management programmes have been successful, these systems are still evolving (FAO 2001a).

There is also growing awareness of the extent of illegal forest activities, including corrupt practices, and of the immense financial, environmental and social costs that these incur. Corruption, considered a taboo subject until recently, is now openly discussed in major international fora and is being actively tackled by governments, NGOs, the private sector and international organizations. Elements in the fight against crime and corruption include strengthened monitoring and enforcement systems, increased transparency in decision-making, simpler laws and more severe punishment (FAO 2001a).

At the international level, two major international initiatives followed publication of the *1980 Tropical Forest Resources Assessment*. The first was the establishment of the International Tropical Timber Organization (ITTO) in 1983 under UNCTAD, which aimed to bring together producer and consumer countries of tropical timber. ITTO works with projects and has permanent committees on reforestation, industries and markets. While not its original intention, ITTO has become a major platform for issues related to sustainable forest management (ITTO 2000).

The second was the Tropical Forestry Action Plan (TFAP). Launched in 1985 jointly by FAO, United Nations Development Programme (UNDP), World Bank and World Resources Institute, TFAP had four priority areas for action: forestry in land use; fuelwood and energy; conservation of tropical forest ecosystems; and institutions. Towards the end of 1990, TFAP came under major criticism for the way it was managed. Around 1995, TFAP was revamped, made more 'country driven', with a focus on strengthening of planning capacity of governments, and renamed the National Forestry Action Program (Sargent 1990, Persson 2000).

The forest resources assessments of 1980 and 1990 provided important background information for the UNCED process. The findings on deforestation (15.3 million ha annually during 1980-1990) and lack of country capacity in forest resources assessment were timely for framing national capacity building recommendations in *Agenda 21*. The overarching principles governing sustainable forest management, formulated during UNCED in the *Forest Principles* and Chapter 11 in *Agenda 21*, have been further elaborated during the past ten years. Three of the international conventions agreed at UNCED, the UNFCCC already mentioned, the Convention on Biological Diversity and the Convention to Combat Desertification, also have important bearings on the future of forests (FAO 2001a).

A common vision for the management, conservation, and sustainable development of all types of forests has been facilitated by the Intergovernmental Panel on Forests (IPF) (1995-1997) and Intergovernmental Forum on Forests (IFF) (1997-2000), both under the auspices of the United Nations Commission on Sustainable Development (UNCSD). The IPF/IFF process has resulted in nearly 300 agreed proposals for action and in the creation of the United Nations Forum on Forests (UNFF) in October 2000, a permanent high-level intergovernmental body with universal membership. To support the UNFF and to enhance policy coordination and international cooperation, a Collaborative Partnership on Forests (CPF) was formed by 11 international forest-related organizations both within and outside the UN system. The main operative means of the UNFF is its multi-year programme of work and the plan of action for the implementation of the IPF/IFF proposals for action. Although it is possible that UNFF debates will stimulate national policies and trigger action by CPF organizations, the first session of the UNFF in June 2001 failed to create either a clear mandate or accountability for implementing the proposals for action (IISD 2001c).

An important international challenge, to both South and North, is to ensure sustainability of forest goods, services and biological diversity in all forest types.

The recognition of the importance of forest ecosystems and threats to their integrity by the Stockholm Conference was an important step. However, subsequent work has not halted the loss of valued forest. The assessments show continued deforestation and forest degradation. The concerted action required to control and reverse these trends — while also addressing the poverty which is so frequently associated with communities that remain dependent upon forest resources — is long overdue. Dealing successfully with forests as an issue on the international agenda will largely depend on the international community's ability to mobilize political, financial, scientific and technical support for sustainable forest management, particularly in developing countries.

## References: Chapter 2, forests, global overview

CIFOR, Government of Indonesia and UNESCO (1999). *World heritage forests: the World Heritage Convention as a mechanism for conserving tropical forest biodiversity.* Bogor, Indonesia, CIFOR

Dixon, R.K., Brown, S., Houghton, R.A., Solomon, A.M., Trexler, M.C. and Wisniewski, J. (1994). Carbon pools and flux of global forest ecosystems. *Science*, 263, 185-190

FAO/UNEP (1982). *Tropical Forest Resources.* Forestry Paper No. 30, Rome, Food and Agriculture Organization

FAO (1995). *Forest Resources Assessment 1990: Global Synthesis.* Forestry Paper No. 124, Rome, Food and Agriculture Organization

FAO (1997). *State of the World's Forests 1997.* Rome, Food and Agriculture Organization

FAO-ECE (2000). *Forest Resources of Europe, CIS, North America, Australia, Japan and New Zealand.* New York and Geneva, United Nations www.unece.org/trade/timber/ [Geo-2-422]

FAO (2000). *Commodity market review, 1999-2000.* Rome, Food and Agriculture Organization http://www.fao.org [Geo-2-390]

FAO (2001a). *State of the World's Forests 2001.* Rome, Food and Agriculture Organization

FAO (2001b). *Global Forest Resources Assessment 2000.* FAO Forestry Paper 140. Rome, Food and Agriculture Organization http://www.fao.org/forestry/fo/fra/ [Geo-2-391]

IISD (2001a). *COP-6.bis Final Summary.* International Institute for Sustainable Development http://www.iisd.ca/linkages/downloads/asc/enb121 76e.txt [Geo-2-012]

IISD (2001b). Milestones in Climate Change, International Undertaking Talks. *Linkages Journal,* Vol.6, No.11. International Institute for Sustainable Development http://www.iisd.ca/linkages/journal/link0611e.pdf [Geo-2-151]

IISD (2001c). Summary of the First Session of the United Nations Forum on Forests: 11-23 June 2001. *Earth Negotiations Bulletin,* Vol.13, No. 83, International Institute for Sustainable Development

ITTO (2000). *Annual Review and Assessment of the World Timber Situation, 1999.* Yokohama, International Tropical Timber Organization http://www.ittn.or.jp [Geo-2-393]

IPCC (2001a). *Climate Change 2001: Impacts, Adaptation and Vulnerability. Contribution of Working Group II to the Third Assessment Report of the Intergovernmental Panel on Climate Change.* Cambridge. United Kingdom, and New York, United States, Cambridge University Press

IPCC (2001b) *Climate Change 2001:Mitigation. Contribution of Working Group III to the Third Assessment Report of the Intergovernmental Panel on Climate Change.* Cambridge, United Kingdom, and New York, United States, Cambridge University Press

Mayers, J., and Bass, S. (1999). *Policy that Works for Forests and People.* London, International Institute for Environment and Development

Persson, R. (2000). Assistance to Forestry: What we have learned. *International Forestry Review,* 2(3), 218-223

Quarto, A. (2002). *The Mangrove Forest. Background paper.* Mangrove Action Project, The Ramsar Convention on Wetlands http://www.ramsar.org/about_mangroves_2.htm [Geo-2-392]

Sargent, C. (1990). *Defining the Issues: Some thoughts and recommendations on the recent critical comments on TFAP.* London, International Institute for Environment and Development

Serageldine, I. (1991). *La Protection des Forets Ombrophiles de l'Afrique.* Washington DC, World Bank

UNDP, UNEP, World Bank and WRI (2000). *World Resources 2000-2001.* Washington DC, World Resources Institute

UNEP (2001). *An Assessment of the Status of the World's Remaining Closed Forests.* UNEP/DEWA/ TR.01-2. Nairobi, UNEP

Vanclay, J.K., Bruner, A.G., Gullison, R.E., Rice, R.E. and da Fonseca, G.A.B. (2001). The Effectiveness of Parks. *Science,* Vol.293, No.5532, 1007

Watson, T.R., Noble, R.I., Bolin, B., Ravindranath, N.H., Verardo, J.D. and Doken, J.D. (2000). *Land Use, Land Use Change, and Forestry. A special report.* Intergovernmental Panel on Climate Change. Cambridge, United Kingdom, Cambridge University Press

WRI (1997). *The Last Frontier Forests: Ecosystems and Economics on the Edge.* Washington DC, World Resources Institute

## Forests: Africa

Africa's forest cover is estimated at 650 million ha, constituting 17 per cent of the world's forests (FAO 2001a). The major forest types are dry tropical forests in the Sahel, Eastern and Southern Africa, moist tropical forests in Western and Central Africa, sub-tropical forest and woodland formations in Northern Africa and the southern tip of the continent, and mangroves in the coastal zones. They include a number of international biodiversity hotspots (Mittermeier and others 2000). Only 1 per cent of forests in Africa have been planted.

African forests provide many goods and services. A study in Madagascar estimated the value of forest products to the local villages to be US$200 000 over ten years (Kremen and others 2000). In Ghana, it is estimated that 16-20 per cent of the local population's food supply is met from forest products, and as many as 150 animal and plant species are used. The Cross River State rainforest of Nigeria is home to more than 700 species of plants and animals, some 430 of which are used as non-timber forest products (ODA 1994).

Deforestation, both for commercial timber and to make room for agriculture, is the major concern and represents an enormous loss of natural economic wealth to the continent. Selective vegetation removal (during logging and woodfuel collection) contributes to loss of forest quality and biodiversity. Overharvesting of non-timber forest resources, including medicinal plants, adds to this problem. There is also concern that the bushmeat trade, which is prevalent in Central and Western Africa, may be endangering a number of

## Forest extent: Africa

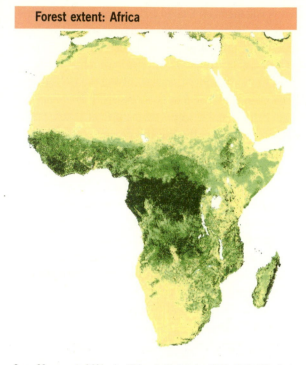

Some 22 per cent of Africa is still forested but during 1990–2000 Africa lost more than 50 million ha, at an annual average rate of 0.7 per cent a year

*Note: dark green represents closed forest, more than 40 per cent covered with trees more than 5 metres high; mid-green represents open (10–40 per cent coverage) and fragmented forest; light green represents other woodland, shrubland and bushland*

*Source: FAO 2001a*

forest-dwelling mammals. The pressures on forests and woodlands are exacerbated by the construction of access roads (by forestry and mining companies), which opens up closed forest areas, making the resources more accessible, and their trade more profitable.

## Change in forested land 1990–2000 by sub-region: Africa

|  | total land area (million ha) | total forest 1990 (million ha) | total forest 2000 (million ha) | % of land forested in 2000 | change 1990-2000 (million ha) | % change per year |
|---|---|---|---|---|---|---|
| Central Africa | 524.3 | 249.4 | 240.3 | 45.8 | -9.1 | -0.37 |
| Eastern Africa | 243.8 | 38.8 | 35.4 | 14.5 | -3.4 | -0.87 |
| Northern Africa | 851.0 | 77.1 | 67.9 | 8.0 | -9.2 | -1.22 |
| Southern Africa | 679.8 | 239.1 | 222.0 | 32.6 | -17.1 | -0.70 |
| Western Africa | 605.6 | 85.1 | 72.5 | 12.0 | -12.6 | -1.53 |
| Western Indian Ocean | 58.9 | 13.0 | 11.9 | 20.1 | -1.1 | -0.90 |
| **Africa** | **2 963.3** | **702.5** | **649.9** | **21.9** | **-52.6** | **-0.7** |

*Source: compiled from FAO 2001b    Note: numbers may not add due to rounding*

## Forest clearance

The annual rate of change in total forest area (land with at least 10 per cent tree cover and 0.5 ha area) from 1990 to 2000 for the whole of Africa was estimated to be -0.74 per cent, equivalent to losing more than 5 million ha of forest a year, an area roughly the size of Togo and the highest rate of any region. Countries with the highest annual deforestation rates are Burundi (9.0 per cent), Comoros (4.3 per cent), Rwanda (3.9 per cent) and Niger (3.7 per cent). In terms of area deforested during 1990–2000, Sudan tops the list with 9.6 million ha, followed by Zambia (8.5 million ha), Democratic Republic of Congo (5.3 million ha), Nigeria (4.0 million ha) and Zimbabwe (3.2 million ha). Only seven countries increased their forest areas over the same period (FAO 2001a).

Economic development strategies and lax implementation of forest protection regulations are the principal pressures on forest resources. Governments in Western and Central Africa have given concessions to private firms for logging selected species. The timber is mostly exported to earn foreign exchange. In countries such as Angola, the Democratic Republic of Congo and Sierra Leone political instability and war have further contributed to deforestation. Forest clearance has negative economic impacts through loss of future export opportunities, tourism revenue and pharmaceutical development options. The annual cost of deforestation in Uganda has been conservatively estimated at US$3-6 million (NEMA 2000).

Weak and ineffective policies have contributed to forest clearance. In Eastern Africa, for example, forestry departments throughout the 1980s were given a low priority, resulting in weak or outdated policies, laws and regulations governing forest management. In Southern Africa, most forestry policies and laws were enacted in the 1970s, and have since become obsolete with small and non-deterrent fines for non-compliance. Policy failures in Western Africa include lack of attention to developing alternative energy sources, inadequate funding of forestry departments, lack of support for private investment in sustainable forest management and reforestation, and out-dated concepts of forest conservation and community participation. However, levels of awareness on forestry issues have been greatly raised through international lobbying, extension services and the activities of NGOs. Several

### Agricultural encroachment in Uganda and Kenya

In Mt Elgon National Park, on the Uganda/Kenya border, agricultural encroachment in the 1970s and 1980s laid bare more than 25 000 ha of virgin forest. In Kibale National Park, Uganda, encroachers cleared more than 10 000 ha of forest. In Mabira Forest Reserve, the Kanani Cooperative Farmers Society entered the forest in 1975. The district administration perceived them as a self-help project rather than as encroachers, and gave cultivation permits to 115 of their members. The permits specified that no more forested land should be cleared, valuable timber tree species should be preserved, and no buildings should be erected. Regulations were not enforced and by 1981 more than 1 800 people had moved in and degraded more than 7 200 ha of the reserve.

In Kenya, between 1995 and 2000, the whole of the indigenous forest in the Imenti Forest Reserve on the slopes of Mt Kenya was illegally converted into cropland. Designated as a forest reserve since 1932, under which no clearance activities were permitted, forest policies clearly failed to provide adequate protection. Landsat images below show loss of forest (red); each image is about 20 km wide.

Sources: NEMA 2000, KWS 1999, Landsat TM 17 March 1995, Landsat ETM 5 February 2000

countries are now correcting these institutional weaknesses, and forest policies are being reviewed, revised or redrafted. Communities have become more involved in policy making, as well as in implementing forest management strategies. International cooperative initiatives have been developed in Southern and Central Africa (FAO 2001b).

Clearing of forests for agriculture has played a significant role in deforestation. In Northern Africa, 13 per cent of forest cover was lost during 1972–92, and in Nigeria deforestation of riparian forests and savannahs for agricultural development was estimated at more than 470 000 ha a year during 1978–96 (DoF Nigeria 1996). In Africa as a whole, 60 per cent of the tropical forest cleared between 1990 and 2000 has been converted into permanent agricultural smallholdings (FAO 2001a).

Some large-scale reforestation programmes have been implemented but most have introduced monocultures without the biological diversity of the natural forests they replace. While some of the more arid countries have increased the size of their forests, reforestation programmes have done little to slow deforestation rates, particularly in moist tropical forests (ADB 2000, FAO 2001a).

Another response has been to designate forests as protected areas. Some 11.7 per cent of African forests have protected area status (FAO 2001a). While the establishment of protected areas has increased the availability and quality of information on forest resources, promoted public awareness and created refuges for endangered species, these areas will meet their objectives only if protection measures are enforced (see box on page 99).

Commercial forestry management has evolved towards a more sustainable philosophy. The forest ecosystem is becoming the focus of management, rather than timber extraction, and non-timber forest resources are given consideration. In Southern Africa, there is a growing realization of the importance of trade in forest products from sustainably managed forests, and a small proportion of forests in Namibia, South Africa and Zimbabwe have been certified by the Forest Stewardship Council (FAO 2001a).

Community-based forest management schemes are also being established, with considerable benefits to community income levels and forest conservation. In Eastern Africa, agroforestry schemes are being introduced to meet the dual need for agricultural production and tree products from smallholdings. In Kenya, afforestation and reforestation at household and commercial scale have been able to supply people with fuelwood, poles, sawn wood, wood-based panels, and pulp and paper.

## Loss of forest quality

Fuelwood collection and charcoal production contribute significantly to degradation of forests and wooded areas such as savannahs. In many countries of Central and West Africa, more than 80 per cent of domestic energy requirements are met from woodfuel (FAO 2001a). In sub-Saharan Africa, traditional fuels accounted for 63.5 per cent of total energy use in 1997 (World Bank 1999). Use of wood for fuel in Eastern Africa amounts to 1-2 kg/person/day, and in Madagascar and Comoros collection of wood for fuel is the largest cause of forest clearance (UNEP 1999). Wood collection often changes the species composition of forest or woodland. In addition, nutrients are removed from the ecosystem, and animals may be deprived of shelter and nesting material (DEA&T 1999). In Zambia, some 430 km$^2$ of woodland are cleared annually to produce more than 100 000 tonnes of charcoal (Chenje 2000). This generates about US$30 million, and is the sole income for about 60 000 people (Kalumiana 1998). Rural electrification is being promoted in some countries but the rural poor often cannot afford the tariffs or the costs of electrical appliances (Chenje 2000).

Commercialization of crafts such as basket making is also causing the disappearance of some plant species. The major source of weaving material in Botswana, Mozambique, Namibia, South Africa and Zimbabwe is fibre from palm leaves and brown dye from *Berchemia* bark. In Botswana, the traditionally conserved *Berchemia* trees are fast becoming scarce (SADC, IUCN & SARDC 2000). Tatamaca, ebony and baobab have almost become extinct from the Western Indian Ocean islands due to selective overexploitation (UNEP 1999).

### References: Chapter 2, forests, Africa

ADB (2000). *Gender, Poverty And Environmental Indicators on African Countries 2001-2002*. Abidjan, African Development Bank

Chenje, M. (ed., 2000). *State of the Environment Zambezi Basin 2000*. Maseru, Lusaka and Harare, SADC/IUCN/ZRA/SARDC

DEA&T (1999). *State of the Environment South Africa*. Pretoria, Department of Environmental Affairs & Tourism

DoF Nigeria (1996). *Preliminary Report on the Assessment of Landuse and Vegetation Changes in Nigeria between 1978 and 1993/95*. Lagos, Federal Department of Forestry

FAO (2001a). *Global Forest Resources Assessment 2000*. FAO Forestry Paper 140. Rome, Food and Agriculture Organization
http://www.fao.org/forestry/fo/fra/ [Geo-2-394]

FAO (2001b). *State of the World's Forests 2001*. Rome, Food and Agriculture Organization

Kalumiana, O.S. (1998). *Woodfuel Sub-Programme of the Zambia Forestry Action Programme*, Lusaka, Ministry of Environment & Natural Resources

Kremen, C., Niles, J.O., Dalton, M.G., Daily, G.C., Ehrlich, P.R., Fay, J.P., Grewal, D. and Guillery, R.P. (2000). Economic Incentives for Rain Forest Conservation Across Scales. *Science*, 9 June 2000, 1828-2832

KWS (1999). *Aerial Survey of the Destruction of Mt. Kenya, Imenti and Ngare Ndare Forest Reserves*. Nairobi, Kenya Wildlife Service

Mittermeier, R.A., Myers, N., Gil, P.R. and Mittermeier, C.G. (2000). *Hotspots; the Earth's Biologically Richest and Most Endangered Terrestrial Ecoregions*. Washington DC, CEMEX and Conservation International

NEMA (2000). *State of the Environment Report for Uganda 2000*. Kampala, National Environment Management Authority

ODA (1994). *Overview of a Planning Process for Sustainable Management of the Forest of Cross River State, Calabar, Nigeria*. UK Technical Report of the Overseas Development Administration. London, ODA

SADC, IUCN & SARDC (2000). *Biodiversity of Indigenous Forests and Woodlands in Southern Africa*. Maseru and Harare, SADC/IUCN/SARDC

UNEP (1999). *Western Indian Ocean Environment Outlook*. Nairobi, United Nations Environment Programme

World Bank (1999). *World Development Indicators 1999*. Washington DC, World Bank
http://www.worldbank.org/data [Geo-2-395]

## Forests: Asia and the Pacific

Asia and the Pacific region accounts for 18.8 per cent of global forests. Within the region, Northwest Pacific and East Asia has the largest forest area (29.3 per cent of the regional total), followed by Southeast Asia (29.1 per cent), Australia and New Zealand (22.3 per cent), South Asia (11.7 per cent), South Pacific (4.8 per cent) and Central Asia (2.7 per cent) respectively. Average per capita availability of forest area in the region in 2000 was 0.2 ha, less than one-third of the world average of 0.65 ha per person (FAO 2001a).

### Forest degradation and deforestation

Deforestation and forest degradation are critical issues, threatening biodiversity, ecosystem stability and the long-term availability of forest products as well as depleting the natural resource base underpinning many national economies (UNESCAP and ADB 2000). Population pressure, heavy dependence on fuelwood, timber and other products, as well as conversion of forests to agricultural, urban and industrial land are the underlying factors for deforestation in the region. Forest degradation and deforestation has also resulted from overgrazing and shifting cultivation. In addition, as forests have become degraded, so fire, pests, diseases and natural disasters have caused greater damage. Construction of irrigation schemes, dams and reservoirs as well as mining are further causes of deforestation (ADB 2000a) while armed conflict has also taken a toll in some countries (UNESCAP and ADB 2000).

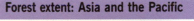

**Forest extent: Asia and the Pacific**

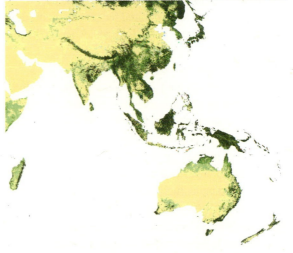

The latest *Global Forest Resources Assessment* (FAO 2001a) showed that, within the region, annual deforestation rates were highest in Southeast Asia at 1 per cent (equivalent to 2.3 million ha per year), whereas Northwest Pacific and East Asia had an increase of 1.85 million ha annually, due mainly to afforestation in China.

More that 40 per cent (and the highest diversity) of the world's mangroves grow along the coasts of South and Southeast Asia. A further 10 per cent grow in the Pacific. Mangrove forests provide numerous benefits to people and the environment but they are disappearing at an alarming rate in this region. More than 60 per cent (some 11 million ha) of Asia's mangroves have already been converted to

Some 21 per cent of Asia and the Pacific is still forested and deforestation, while continuing, is at a relatively low rate — an annual average of 0.1 per cent a year

Note: dark green represents closed forest, more than 40 per cent covered with trees more than 5 metres high; mid-green represents open (10–40 per cent coverage) and fragmented forest; light green represents other woodland, shrubland and bushland

Source: FAO 2001a

### Change in forested land 1990–2000 by sub-region: Asia and the Pacific

| | total land area (million ha) | total forest 1990 (million ha) | total forest 2000 (million ha) | % of land forested in 2000 | change 1990-2000 (million ha) | % change per year |
|---|---|---|---|---|---|---|
| Australia and New Zealand | 795.0 | 164.9 | 162.5 | 20.4 | -2.4 | -0.1 |
| Central Asia | 391.6 | 16.6 | 19.3 | 4.9 | 2.7 | 1.6 |
| Northwest Pacific and East Asia | 1 147.8 | 195.2 | 212.7 | 18.5 | 17.4 | 0.9 |
| South Asia | 640.3 | 86.3 | 85.3 | 13.3 | -1.0 | -0.1 |
| Southeast Asia | 434.5 | 234.7 | 211.4 | 48.7 | -23.3 | -1.0 |
| South Pacific | 53.9 | 36.4 | 35.1 | 65.2 | -1.2 | -0.4 |
| **Asia and the Pacific** | **3 463.2** | **734.0** | **726.3** | **21.0** | **-7.7** | **-0.1** |

Source: compiled from FAO 2001a    Note: numbers may not add due to rounding

aquaculture and more have been cleared to make way for rice farming or urban and industrial land use. Those that remain are exploited for timber, fuelwood, tannin and food items (UNESCAP and ADB 2000).

## Drivers of forest degradation

Many countries are highly dependent on wood to meet national energy needs and this use accounts for some three-quarters of total roundwood production (UNESCAP and ADB 2000). The contribution of fuelwood to total energy consumption varies widely, from less than 5 per cent to more than 85 per cent. In Nepal, for example, fuelwood accounts for 70 per cent of the country's total energy demand (Bhatta and Shrestha 1996). Where fuelwood collection relies primarily on natural forests, it can be a major contributor to forest degradation and depletion. Over-harvesting in steep areas is a particular cause for concern as it may impair the forest's protective functions of safeguarding watersheds and river flow (UNESCAP and ADB 2000).

Commercial logging, as here in Myanmar, is an important cause of deforestation in parts of Asia and the Pacific

Source: UNEP, Aye Myint Than, Topham Picture point

Fire is an important and recurring phenomenon in many forest ecosystems. In Asia and the Pacific, the severity of forest fires has been exacerbated by droughts and by land clearance. As a result, forest fires have become a major cause of deforestation in many countries, especially in East and Southeast Asia. The Indonesian fires of 1996-97 are the best known example but serious forest fires have also occurred in Australia, China and Mongolia in recent years. In response, fire detection and monitoring systems are now in place in several countries and the Association of Southeast Asian Nations (ASEAN) has established a Forest Fire Management Centre in Thailand to provide training and research (FAO 2001a).

Much forest degradation in the Pacific Island countries (PICs) stems from commercial logging. While providing substantial income to some countries, large-scale operations have degraded large proportions of the islands, affecting biodiversity, changing the hydrochemical balance and reducing food availability. New Zealand and Australia have also lost large amounts of their native forest and vegetation. Nearly 70 per cent of New Zealand was covered with native forest before the Europeans arrived in the early 19th century; it now covers only 16 per cent of the land area (MFE New Zealand 1997). In the 1970s and 1980s, the Government of New Zealand introduced subsidies to clear forests for agricultural production and exotic forestry which, compounded with artificially low stumpage fees, encouraged overexploitation of forests. The subsequent removal of these subsidies has resulted in some marginal pasture reverting to scrub and forest.

## Policy responses

The downside of forest clearance and degradation has been widely recognized and many governments have implemented forestry legislation and programmes that aim at conservation and afforestation. Some countries are also opting to control the clearance of land outside conservation and protection areas. Logging bans now exist on 10 million ha but have met with mixed success. In countries such as Cambodia, Indonesia and Thailand, implementation has been inadequate whereas bans in New Zealand and Sri Lanka which have shifted harvesting to alternative sources have proved effective (FAO 2001b). Zero burning policies have been adopted by Thailand and Malaysia. Some countries have introduced economic instruments for the conservation of forest resources. For example, afforestation fees and licences are used in China to strengthen the cultivation, protection and management of forests. In Lao PDR, logging quotas are issued and distributed to the provinces as provincial quotas (ADB 2000b). Government commitment to the protection of forests is best exemplified by the case of Bhutan where, in 1995, it was mandated that the country must keep at least 60 per cent of its total land area under forest cover.

The region contains 60 per cent of the world's plantation forests. Whilst plantation forests are usually a poor substitute for natural forests in terms of maintaining biodiversity, they can supplement and substitute wood and other supplies from natural forests, thereby reducing pressure on and disruption to the latter. They also perform many of the environmental services of natural forests, including carbon sequestration, watershed protection and land rehabilitation, and they provide income and employment. A number of governments are increasing plantations to reap these benefits (see box).

Local community participation in the management of forests has been gaining pace since the late 1970s. In Nepal, regulations for handing over particular forest areas to groups of forest users were drawn up in 1974. Forest users' groups protect, manage, use the forest area, share all benefits among users and possess exclusive rights to forest income (ADB 2000a). Of Nepal's total forestry sector investment, 36 per cent is earmarked for community forestry. In India, Joint Forest Management was introduced in 1990 and about 45 000 village communities in 21 states are involved in managing more than 11 million hectares of degraded forests (MoEF 1999). The community provides any labour required to improve degraded areas and protects the forest while it regenerates. In time the state gains a revitalized forest and the income from selling its products. A portion of the income from selling timber is given to the community in addition to the right to gather non-wood forest products (FAO 2001b)

In Viet Nam, more than 500 000 ha of well-stocked, national forests have been turned over to local communities, mostly of indigenous people, while in the Philippines a system of Integrated Protected Areas attempts to protect biodiversity and involve communities as stakeholders in managing forests.

## Forest plantations: Asia and the Pacific

The Chinese government began afforestation programmes in the 1970s. Forest coverage increased from 13.9 per cent in 1993 to 17.5 per cent in 2000. By 2001, the total afforested area in China had reached 46.7 million ha.
Several countries have ambitious plans for the future:

- Viet Nam has set a target to create 5 million ha of additional forest area in the next 10 years;
- the Philippines Master Plan for Forestry has set a target for 2.5 million ha to be planted between 1990 and 2015;
- China plans to establish 9.7 million ha of plantations between 1996 and 2010; and
- Australia aims to treble its plantation area to 3 million ha by 2020.

Sources: Chan and others (2001), FAO (2001a), UNESCAP and ADB (2000)

The PICs have also emphasized the establishment of community-based conservation areas but some countries still lack formal legislation or institutionalized programmes prohibiting the cutting of trees and forests outside protected areas. For some PICs, where customary management is still very strong, there are traditional practices that protect areas from land clearance.

Both Australia and New Zealand are committed to sustainable forest management. These commitments are formalized in Australia's Nation Forest Policy State of 1992 and New Zealand's Resource Management Act of 1991. In both countries the felling of trees and clearing of bush generally requires formal assessment and approval. In New Zealand, more than 99 per cent of annual roundwood harvests came from plantations in 1997 and several forests have received certification through the Forest Stewardship Council (FAO 2001a).

## References: Chapter 2, forests, Asia and the Pacific

ADB (2000a). *Asian Environment Outlook 2001, Second Discussion Draft*. Manila, Asian Development Bank

ADB (2000b). *Environments in Transition: Cambodia, Lao PDR, Thailand, Vietnam*. Manila, Asian Development Bank

Bhatta, G.R. and Shrestha, D.L. (1996). An overview of woodfuel supply and management status in Nepal. *Wood Energy News*, 11, 1, 7-8

Chan, L., Jian, W., Jijian, Y., Chen, J., Yong, F. and Zhiha, Z. (2001). *China: Timber Trade and Protection of Forestry Resources*. Paper presented at the 5th meeting of the Second Phase of the China Council Working Group on Trade and Environment (CCICED), August 2001

FAO (2001a). *Global Forest Resources Assessment 2000*. FAO Forestry Paper 140. Rome, Food and Agriculture Organization http://www.fao.org/forestry/fo/fra/ [Geo-2-396]

FAO (2001b). *State of the World's Forests 2001*. Rome, Food and Agriculture Organization

MoEF India (1999). *National Forestry Action Programme – India: Vol.1: Status of Forestry in India*. New Delhi, Government of India

MFE New Zealand (1997). *The State of New Zealand's Environment 1997*. Wellington, Ministry for the Environment of New Zealand

UNESCAP and ADB (2000). *State of the Environment in Asia and Pacific 2000*. Economic and Social Commission for Asia and the Pacific and Asian Development Bank. New York, United Nations http://www.unescap.org/enrd/environ/soe.htm [Geo-2-266]

## Forests: Europe

Europe's 1 051 million ha of forests comprise 27 per cent of the world's total forested area and cover 45 per cent of the European landscape. Forest cover ranges from 0.3 per cent in Iceland to 72 per cent in Finland (FAO 2001a). A wide variety of boreal, temperate and sub-tropical forest types are represented, as well as tundra and montane formations. Since the 1970s, afforestation has gradually increased the area under forests: between 1990 and 2000 almost 9.3 million ha were added (FAO 2001a). However, old growth forests and forests of indigenous tree species are decreasing. Forest practices, relying on monocrop plantations and even-aged stands of exotic species, have not been conducive to maintaining biological diversity.

Some countries, particularly those with extensive forest cover (Finland, France, Germany and Sweden), consider their forests in an integrated context with landscapes and biodiversity. In theory, this means a broader, more responsible approach to forest practices. Others, particularly those with little forest cover (for example, Ireland and Spain), are more interested in rapid forest growth for commercial or watershed

protection purposes. Sustainable forest management remains a challenge for many European countries.

### Loss of natural forests and forest degradation

In the Baltic States and western part of the Former Soviet Union (FSU), most deforestation from felling took place in the first half of the 20th century. After World War II, enormous reforestation programmes were carried out alongside industrial logging. In the Russian Federation, there has been a sharp decline in the extraction of forest products in recent years linked to the general decline of industry throughout the FSU. In the late 1990s, total removals amounted to only between one-quarter and one-third of the amounts extracted in the 1970s and 1980s (FAO 2001a).

Significant areas of forest were nationalized as early as 1918 in the FSU and in the 1950s in the countries of Central and Eastern Europe (CEE), and protected categories of forest were established (OECD and World Bank 1993). With increasing poverty in these countries and a loss of traditional communist era livelihoods, protected areas and forests in CEE are now under pressure from illegal tree felling which, in some places, has pushed some rare species to the

*The forested area of Europe increased by more than 9 million ha — or nearly 1 per cent — during 1990–2000*

*Note: dark green represents closed forest, more than 40 per cent covered with trees more than 5 metres high; mid-green represents open (10–40 per cent coverage) and fragmented forest; light green represents other woodland, shrubland and bushland*

*Source: FAO 2001a*

### Forest extent: Europe

### Change in forested land 1990–2000 by sub-region: Europe

|  | total land area (million ha) | total forest 1990 (million ha) | total forest 2000 (million ha) | % of land forested in 2000 | change 1990-2000 (million ha) | % change per year |
|---|---|---|---|---|---|---|
| Central Europe | 209.3 | 48.9 | 50.3 | 24.0 | 1.3 | 0.3 |
| Eastern Europe | 1 789.3 | 870.7 | 875.1 | 48.9 | 4.4 | 0.0 |
| Western Europe | 360.8 | 122.4 | 125.9 | 34.9 | 3.6 | 0.4 |
| **Europe** | **2 359.4** | **1 042.0** | **1 051.3** | **44.6** | **9.3** | **0.1** |

*Source: compiled from FAO 2001a    Note: numbers may not add due to rounding*

brink of extinction. An increasing trend towards privatization in many countries since 1990 is also reducing the area of protected forest (EEA 1995), although vast forested lands in the Komi Republic and the Lake Baikal basin have recently been designated as UNESCO World Heritage Sites, effectively halting planned major logging operations (RFSCEP 2000).

Significant forest degradation has been caused by industrial pollution. Vast tracts of forests in CEE still suffer the lingering consequences of acidification, although $SO_2$ emissions and 'acid rain' have been reduced (see 'Atmosphere' section) and the deteriorating situation appears to have stabilized (EEA 1997 and UNECE and EC 2000). Degraded forests are found in the Russian Federation around industrial centres in the Urals, the Kola Peninsula and Siberia, with more than 500 000 ha damaged in the Siberian region of Norilsk alone (Mnatsikanian 1992). Chernobyl affected about 1 million ha of forests in the Russian Federation as well as large areas in Belarus and Ukraine. They will be excluded from use and public access for the foreseeable future (FAO 2001a).

In the mid-1990s, large areas of forests were lost in the Russian Federation from causes other than logging. Insects were responsible for 46 per cent of the damage, forest fires 33 per cent and unfavourable weather 16 per cent (MoNP Russian Federation 1996). The future of the Russian Federation's 850 million ha of temperate and boreal forests (22 per cent of the world's total and the largest forest area in any one country) is important not just for the country but for the entire region because of its role as a carbon sink (see 'Polar Regions', page 116). All forests in the Russian Federation are state owned and are divided into three groups for management purposes (see box).

Forest clearance for agricultural land, terracing and the creation of fruit orchards has had adverse consequences on the environment and biodiversity in southeastern Europe, especially Albania, Bosnia and Herzegovina, and Macedonia. Forest ecosystems, particularly those close to rural settlements, have been significantly degraded due to overexploitation for fuelwood and overgrazing (REC 2000). The severe energy crisis in the mid-1990s in Armenia and Georgia also caused illegal logging on a large scale for home heating and cooking (Radvadnyi and Beroutchachvili 1999). The affected forests include oak and other tree stands which are characterized by high biological diversity in comparison with other types of forests.

**Managing the world's most extensive forests: forest estate in the Russian Federation**

| GROUP I<br>Protection forests | GROUP II<br>Multipurpose forests | GROUP III<br>Forests for commercial use |
|---|---|---|
| 21 per cent of total forest area | 6 per cent of total forest area | 73 per cent of total forest area |
| Strict felling regimes | Harvesting restricted to amount of annual growth | Clear cutting allowed |
| *Changes in proportion of forest area 1966–88:*<br>increasing | increasing | decreasing |

Source: FAO (2001a)

The harvesting of coastal shrubs and forests has also created problems, especially for birds, which use these habitats for nesting (REC 2000).

Around the Mediterranean, forests have been degraded since historic times, from overgrazing and wood removal, and little undisturbed forest now remains (FAO 2001a). Fire is one of the great enemies of Mediterranean wooded areas due to the climatic conditions (dry air and strong winds) and the combustibility of the plant cover; it is estimated that on average 500 000 ha are burned each year. The fires are almost always caused by humans: in traditional herding areas, 'pastoral fires' are still frequent, especially in scrubland, while elsewhere the majority are due to negligence rather than criminal intent. The number of fires rises rapidly in dry years, especially in tourist areas.

## Striving for sustainable forest management

Sustainable forestry was practised in Central Europe in the 19th century and the culture of sustainable use has survived until today in some parts of the region, particularly in Slovenia. In many parts of Western and Central Europe, however, monocultures, especially those consisting of fast-growing commercially valuable coniferous species, have displaced indigenous broad-leaved forest species; they are unable to support high biodiversity and are more vulnerable to acidification.

All countries in the region are making efforts to decrease wood production from natural forests and enhance biological diversity and other environmental services and protection functions by managing them in a more sustainable manner. To support these efforts, a

## Pan-European criteria for sustainable forest management

'Sustainable management means the stewardship and use of forests and forest lands in a way, and at a rate, that maintains their biodiversity, productivity, regeneration capacity, vitality and their potential to fulfil, now and in the future, relevant ecological, economic and social functions, at local, national and global levels, and that does not cause damage to other ecosystems' (Resolution H1, 2nd meeting, Ministerial Conference on the Protection of Forests in Europe (MCPFE)).

Criteria for sustainable forest management adopted by MCPFE in 1998:

- maintenance and appropriate enhancement of forest resources and their contribution to global carbon cycles;
- maintenance of forest ecosystem health and vitality;
- maintenance and encouragement of productive functions of forests (wood and non-wood);
- maintenance, conservation and appropriate enhancement of biological diversity in forest ecosystems;
- maintenance and appropriate enhancement of protective functions in forest management (notably soil and water); and
- maintenance of other socio-economic functions and conditions.

*Source: MCPFE Liaison Unit (2000)*

framework for Pan-European Forest Certification (PEFC) provides a voluntary mechanism for forest certification and makes provision for mutual recognition of different European national systems and non-European schemes. National PEFC governing bodies have been established in 15 European countries (FAO 2001b).

Another solution to the problem of deforestation is the imposition of fines and other economic instruments on illegal as well as legal cutting. In Croatia, Czech Republic, Hungary, Lithuania and Poland revenue for forest protection and reforestation

activities is generated through timber extraction charges or fines. In Romania, however, the abolition of self-imposed restrictions on wood exports in 1995, combined with increased prices for sawn timber, have led environmentalists to fear increases in illegal cutting and overexploitation (REC 2000).

In addition to national actions, European countries are parties to international collaborative efforts which directly or indirectly address forest issues. Several broad international agreements covering the protection of species, such as the CBD, CITES and RAMSAR Convention, also indirectly protect forests. The European Community Council Directive 92/43/EC on the conservation of natural habitats of wild fauna and flora (the Habitats Directive) entered into force in June 1994. However, two of its requirements — incorporation in national legislation and the submission of national lists of Natura 2000 candidate sites — have not been fulfilled by all Member States.

There have been three Ministerial Conferences on the Protection of Forests in Europe (MCPFEs) since 1990. The second (Helsinki 1993) agreed on a common definition of sustainable forest management (see box). The third (Lisbon 1998) put special emphasis on the socio-economic aspects of sustainable forest management. Resolutions were adopted on People, Forests and Forestry, on Pan-European Criteria (see box) and on Indicators and Operational Guidelines for Sustainable Forest Management (MCPFE Liaison Unit 2000). The resolutions are now being integrated into an overall work programme (FAO 2001a).

## References: Chapter 2, forests, Europe

EEA (1995). *Europe's Environment: the Dobrís Assessment*. Copenhagen, European Environment Agency

EEA (1997). *Air Pollution in Europe in 1997*. Copenhagen, European Environment Agency

FAO (2001a). *Global Forest Resources Assessment 2000*. FAO Forestry Paper 140. Rome, Food and Agriculture Organization http://www.fao.org/forestry/fo/fra/ [Geo-2-397]

FAO (2001b). *State of the World's Forests 2001*. Rome, Food and Agriculture Organization

Mnatsakanian, R. (1992). *Environmental Legacy of the Former Soviet Republics*. Edinburgh, Centre for Human Ecology, University of Edinburgh

MCPFE Liaison Unit (2000). *MCPFE Resolutions*. Ministerial Conference on the Protection of Forests in Europe http://www.mcpfe.org/Basic/FS-MCPFE-Resolution.html [Geo-2-398]

MoNP Russian Federation (1996). *National Report on the State of the Environment in the Russian Federation in 1995*. Ministry of Nature Protection of the Russian Federation. Moscow, Center for International Projects (in Russian)

OECD and World Bank (1993). *Environmental Action Programme for Central and Eastern Europe*. Submitted to the Ministerial Conference, Lucerne, Switzerland. Washington DC, World Bank

Radvadnyi, J. and Beroutchachvili, N. (1999). L'Adjarie, atout et point sensible de la Géorgie. *CEMOTI* No. 27, January–June 1999, 227-283

REC (2000). *Strategic Environmental Analysis of Albania, Bosnia and Herzegovina, Kosovo and Macedonia*. Szentendre, Hungary, Regional Environmental Center for Central and Eastern Europe

RFSCEP (2000). *State of the Environment in Russian Federation in 1999*. State Report. Moscow, Russian Federation State Committee for Environmental Protection

UNECE and EC (2000). *Forest Condition in Europe. Results of the 1999 Crown Condition Survey*. Geneva, United Nations Economic Commission for Europe

## Forests: Latin America and the Caribbean

Forests have many important socio-economic functions in Latin American and Caribbean countries. These include supplying the wood industry with inputs for domestic consumption and export, providing local communities with essential non-wood forest products and providing forest-dwelling indigenous communities with opportunities to continue their traditional livelihoods. They also provide environmental goods and services, acting as natural shields against disasters, affording watershed protection, biodiversity preservation and prevention of soil erosion, and serving as a sink for carbon dioxide.

Latin America and the Caribbean is one of the most important forest regions, with nearly one-quarter of the world's forest cover (FAO 2001a). The region contains 834 million ha of tropical forest and 130 million ha of other forests, both temperate and dry, coastal and montane, covering 48 per cent of the total land area (FAO 2001a). Argentina, Bolivia, Brazil, Colombia, Mexico, Peru and Venezuela contain 56 per cent of the regional total (FAO 2001a). The region's forests contain more than 160 billion m$^3$ of wood, one-third of the world total. Guatemala and Panama are among the world's highest in terms of standing volume per hectare (FAO 2001a).

The Amazon Basin contains the world's most extensive tropical rainforest. It includes at least 20 different rainforest types, and is considered to be the world's richest ecosystem in terms of biodiversity (FAO 2001a).

The rate of deforestation is one of highest in the world at an annual average of 0.48 per cent (varying from 1.2 per cent in Meso-America to 0.4 per cent in

### Forest extent: Latin America and the Caribbean

The most heavily forested region, Latin America and the Caribbean lost nearly 47 million ha during 1990–2000, second only to Africa

*Note: dark green represents closed forest, more than 40 per cent covered with trees more than 5 metres high; mid-green represents open (10–40 per cent coverage) and fragmented forest; light green represents other woodland, shrubland and bushland*

*Source: FAO 2001a*

South America and a net gain of 0.3 per cent in the Caribbean). Of the 418 million ha of natural forest lost worldwide over the past 30 years, 190 million ha were in Latin America (FAO 2001a). Total forest area in the region was reduced by around 46.7 million ha between 1990 and 2000.

### Causes of deforestation and forest degradation

The major problems are deforestation and degradation of the forest ecosystem, including fragmentation and biodiversity loss. These are caused by conversion of forest land to other uses and non-sustainable use of

### Change in forested land 1990–2000 by sub-region: Latin America and the Caribbean

|  | total land area (million ha) | total forest 1990 (million ha) | total forest 2000 (million ha) | % of land forested in 2000 | change 1990-2000 (million ha) | % change per year |
|---|---|---|---|---|---|---|
| Caribbean | 22.9 | 5.6 | 5.7 | 25.0 | 0.1 | 0.3 |
| Meso-America | 241.9 | 82.7 | 73.0 | 30.2 | -9.7 | -1.2 |
| South America | 1 752.9 | 922.7 | 885.6 | 50.5 | -37.1 | -0.4 |
| **Latin America and the Caribbean** | **2 017.8** | **1 011.0** | **964.4** | **47.8** | **-46.7** | **-0.5** |

*Source: compiled from FAO 2001a   Note: numbers may not add due to rounding*

forests. Forest fires, always a natural force in forest ecosystems, have also become a major problem (see box).

The expansion of the agricultural frontier has been one of the main causes of deforestation (FAO 2001a). Commercial farmers have cleared large areas for soybean exports in Brazil, Bolivia and Paraguay, for coffee in Brazil, and for bananas in Central America, Colombia, Ecuador and the Caribbean (Contreras-Hermosilla 2000). Small-scale farmers also cause deforestation by employing slash-and-burn practices to extend their agricultural lands into forests.

Land tenure regulations are part of the problem. In Amazonia and Central America, local communities own significant proportions of forests while in Argentina, Chile and Uruguay virtually all forests are privately owned. Elsewhere, the state is a major forest owner. When legal property rights over land are not clear, people tend to clear and build on areas to establish a claim to them. Forest cover may also be removed to keep areas accessible when forest communities fear that forests may be declared protected areas, limiting community rights to use the forest. This happened in Costa Rica when the government intended to expand its protected area system (Contreras-Hermosilla, 2000).

Deforestation has worsened in some countries because of policies designed to increase economic growth. Subsidies are a contributing factor. For example, subsidies directed towards improving the productivity of existing agricultural lands should ease the pressure for

more land and therefore reduce the pressure for clearing more forests. However, agricultural incentives can result in higher land ownership and more mechanized, capital-intensive methods of production which displace farm workers. Unemployed workers have migrated into forests in the Amazon, in the Cerrados of Brazil, in Santa Cruz, Bolivia, and parts of Paraguay, causing further forest clearance (Contreras-Hermosilla 2000). Livestock expansion and mechanized agriculture account for more loss of forest cover than wood production, which is concentrated in relatively few countries.

Timber exploitation may also cause deforestation by opening up previously forested areas to small-scale farming. In addition, selective logging can eliminate certain tree species, changing forest composition. The construction of roads also contributes to loss of forest cover — 400–2000 ha of forest may be removed for each kilometre of new road built through it. In the Brazilian state of Pará, deforestation due to road construction increased from 0.6 per cent to 17.3 per cent of the state's area during 1972-1985 (Contreras-Hermosilla 2000). In Ecuador, Peru and Venezuela, mining corporations and individual miners clear large areas of forests (MineWatch 1997, Miranda and others 1998). Additionally, biological phenomena such as the proliferation of pests are a cause of irreversible damage to some forests (Monge-Nájera 1997).

## Effects of altering forests
The effects of deforestation, forest degradation and forest fires represent a permanent loss of the potential capacity of forest resources to generate economic benefits (CDEA 1992). These impacts are more severe in some countries than others. Most Caribbean countries have depleted forest resources so much that they must now import forest products, creating an additional need for foreign exchange. In countries with extensive forest resources, such as Brazil, deforestation has had less overall impact, although at the local level the impact can be very significant.

## Improving forest regulations and policies
A number of countries have recently adopted new forest regulations. For example, Bolivia adopted a new forestry law in 1996 (Law 1700) which makes state-owned forests available to private companies through concessions provided that local and indigenous populations are involved (Tomaselli 2000). The

### Forest fires in Latin America and the Caribbean

Fire is a traditional land use tool for opening up new land to agriculture and making hunting easier. Uncontrolled wildfire is now a major concern: forest fires can destroy up to 50 per cent of the forest's surface biomass, with severe effects on forest fauna (UNEP 2000).

Forests were particularly vulnerable to fire in 1997–99 due to seasonal droughts associated with El Niño and decline in forest quality. In Central America, more than 2.5 million ha of land caught fire in 1998 with the greatest losses in Honduras, Guatemala, Mexico and Nicaragua (Cochrane in press). In Mexico alone, there were 14 445 separate fires (FAO 2001a). The same year, large-scale fires also affected many South American countries.

Social and economic costs of fires are high, when full account is taken of medical costs, airport closures, and timber and erosion losses. The damage resulting from the 1998 forest fires in Latin America has been crudely estimated at US$10-15 billion. The first South American Seminar on the Control of Forest Fires was held in Brazil in 1998, and policy makers are starting to realize that emergency response needs to be coupled with better land-use practices. In Mexico, for instance, the Ministries of Agriculture and Forestry have been collaborating since 1998 to reduce the threat of agricultural burning to forests (FAO 2001a).

amount of forest land under protection is also increasing — from less than 10 per cent of total forest area in tropical South America in 1990 to more than 14 per cent in 2000 (FAO 2001a).

Market-based instruments such as certification can also contribute to sustainable forest management, and Bolivia, Brazil, Guatemala and Mexico now have 1.8 million ha of forests certified by the Forest Stewardship Council (see page 94) — far exceeding the area of tropical moist forests certified anywhere else in the world (FAO 2001a). Shade-grown coffee is another example where such instruments have the potential to protect environmental resources and to address local concerns (see box).

The area of plantations increased from about 7.7 million ha in 1990 to about 11.7 million ha in 2000. These plantations, composed of mainly *Pinus* and *Eucalyptus* species, are concentrated in the Southern Cone and in Brazil, Peru and Venezuela (FAO 2001a). Regional policies on forestry plantations are mainly oriented towards recovering degraded land. In some countries, there are a few areas where plantations have played a key part in increasing forest cover and bringing in large amounts of foreign exchange. In other areas, plantations are an economic alternative to other land uses (such as agriculture) and thus help to reduce deforestation. However, plantations contain significantly less biodiversity than native forests (Cavelier and Santos 1999).

Most governments receive international support to formulate environmental policies, strengthen

### Shade-grown coffee — harnessing the market for sustainable development

When North American consumers pay a premium for shade-grown coffee, incentives can be created for Mexican farmers to maintain the biodiversity of the land on which they traditionally grow coffee in the shade of the existing forest canopy. By relying on inherent natural predators and barriers to protect their crops from pests and on the natural fertility of the soil to nurture the plants, they avoid costly and often damaging fertilizers and pesticides. Their diverse agrosystems can continue to provide habitat for migratory songbirds, insects and other fauna that may otherwise be threatened by conversion to large plantations of sun-grown coffee, while preserving the cultural values, livelihoods and integrity of small communities. By realizing the market value of shade-grown coffee, the economic logic for clearing forests is drastically reduced, while incentives to conserve and sustainably use the forest increase (Vaughan, Carpentier and Patterson 2001).

institutions, and establish structures and mechanisms to improve monitoring and evaluation. Most of the internationally supported programmes and projects are linked to global concerns such as biodiversity conservation and climate change. Examples of such initiatives include the PPG 7 Pilot Project in Brazil, the BOLFOR Project in Bolivia (FMT 2002) and the Iwokrama International Centre in Guyana. International organizations are active in the region and efforts to address problems through regional collaboration are gaining ground. The Central American Council for Forests and Protected Areas advises on policies and strategies for sustainable use of forest resources and conservation of biodiversity while the Treaty for Amazonian Cooperation between eight South American countries fosters collaboration on activities in the Amazon Basin (FAO 2001b).

### References: Chapter 2, forests, Latin America and the Caribbean

Cavelier, J. and Santos, C. (1999). Efecto de plantaciones abandonadas de especies exóticas y nativas sobre la regeneración natural de un bosque montano en Colombia. *Revista de Biología Tropical* 47, 4, 775-784

CDEA (1992). *Amazonia Without Myths*. Commission on Development and Environment for Amazonia. Washington DC, Inter-American Development Bank and United Nations Development Programme

Cochrane, M. (in press). *Spreading like Wildfire: Tropical Forest Fires in Latin America and the Caribbean – Prevention, Assessment and Early Warning*. Mexico City, United Nations Environment Programme

Contreras-Hermosilla, A. (2000). *The Underlying Causes of Forest Decline*. Occasional Paper No. 30. Jakarta, Center for International Forestry Research

FAO (2001a). *Global Forest Resources Assessment*

*2000*. FAO Forestry Paper 140. Rome, Food and Agriculture Organization
http://www.fao.org/forestry/fo/fra/ [Geo-2-399]

FAO (2001b). *State of the World's Forests 2001*. Rome, Food and Agriculture Organization

FMT (2002). *Bolivia Sustainable Forestry Project (BOLFOR)*. Forest Management Trust
http://foresttrust.org/Projects_Bolivia.htm [Geo-2-400]

MineWatch (1997). *Mining and oil exploration*. Document submitted to the Latin America and the Caribbean Public Hearing of the World Commission on Forests and Sustainable Development, San José, Costa Rica

Miranda, M., Blanco-Uribe, A., Hernández, L., Ochoa, J. and Yerena, E. (1998). *All That Glitters is Not Gold. Balancing Conservation and Development in Venezuela's Frontier Forests*. Washington DC, World Resources Institute

Monge-Nájera, J. (1997). *Moluscos de Importancia Agrícola y Sanitaria en el Trópico: la Experiencia Costarricense*. San José, Universidad de Costa Rica

Tomaselli, I. (2000). *Investing in the Future: The Private Sector and Sustainable Forest Management – South America Perspective*. Paper prepared for the International Workshop of Experts on Financing Sustainable Forest Management, 22-25 January 2001, Oslo, Norway

UNEP (2000). *GEO Latin America and the Caribbean Environment Outlook 2000*. Mexico, United Nations Environment Programme

Vaughan, S., Carpentier, C.L. and Patterson, Z. (2001). The power of markets and the promise of green goods and services. *Trio*, fall 2001. Commission for Environmental Cooperation
http://www.cec.org/trio/stories/index.cfm?varlan=english&ed=3&id=22 [Geo-2-401]

## Forests: North America

Forests cover about 26 per cent of North America's land area and represent more than 12 per cent of the world's forests. North America has more than one-third of the world's boreal forests as well as a wide range of other forest types. Some 96 per cent are natural forests. After the Russian Federation and Brazil, Canada has more forest than any other country, with 244.6 million ha. The United States is the fourth most forested country, with 226 million ha (FAO 2001). While Canada's forest area remained static during the past decade, in the United States it has increased by almost 3.9 million ha, approximately 1.7 per cent.

Estimates show that North America now grows 255.5 million m³ more timber annually than is harvested (UNECE and FAO 2000). The region accounts for about 40 per cent of the world's production and consumption of industrial wood products (Mathews and Hammond 1999).

The land area under plantation is also increasing in both countries. In Canada, the area regenerated by planting increased from a little less than 100 000 ha in 1975 to nearly 400 000 ha in 1997 (REGEN 2002), while the United States has about 21 million ha of plantations or some 4.5 per cent of its forest land base (UNECE and FAO 2000).

In Canada, 94 per cent of forests are publicly owned, with the provinces responsible for 71 per cent of forest land (NRC 2000). In contrast, some 60 per cent of forests in the United States are privately owned, 35 per cent are publicly owned and managed by the federal government, and the 50 states own and manage 5 per cent (FAO 2001).

### Forest extent: North America

Forests cover about 26 per cent of North America, and their area — though not their quality — is increasing

*Note: dark green represents closed forest, more than 40 per cent covered with trees more than 5 metres high; mid-green represents open (10–40 per cent coverage) and fragmented forest; light green represents other woodland, shrubland and bushland*

*Source: FAO 2001*

## Forest health

In the past, a forest was deemed healthy if it was free from disease and was growing vigorously (NRC 1999). Over the past 20 years, however, the long-term sustainability of the forest ecosystem has become the primary measure of forest health (UNECE and FAO 2000). A forest may be considered healthy when it maintains biodiversity and resilience, provides wildlife habitat, ecological services and aesthetic appeal, and maintains a sustainable supply of timber and non-timber resources (NRC 1999). In many areas, forests are becoming increasingly fragmented, biologically impoverished, and weakened or stressed (Bryant, Nielsen and Tangley 1997).

Human intervention and demand for timber and paper are the primary drivers of forest modification. Poor harvesting practices, the introduction of exotic species and suppression of natural disturbances have created large forested landscapes with an unnatural tree distribution and age structure, which has increased the forest's vulnerability to drought, wind, insects, disease and fire (USDA 1997).

Air pollution is increasingly recognized as a contributing factor to forest degradation (Bright 1999). It has played a role in the major die-off of spruce-fir forests in the southern Appalachians, a region that has been the focus of concern for the US Forest Service (USDA 1997, Mattoon 1998). Although pollution regulation has reduced acid rain in the northeast, there is evidence that reduced growth in some tree species is linked to the long-term effects of acid precipitation (Driscoll and others 2001).

### Timber increments and removals (million m³/year): North America

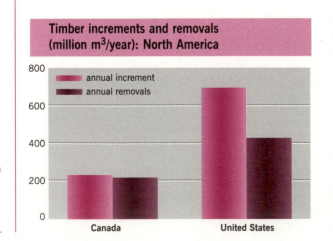

- annual increment
- annual removals

North America currently grows some 255 million m³ more timber than it harvests

*Source: UNECE and FAO 2000*

An emerging issue in maintaining healthy forests is the potential impact of climate change and the connections between climate change and other damaging influences (NRC 1999). North America's forests, particularly its broadleaf ecosystems that appear to have a large capacity for carbon absorption, are unlikely to maintain their absorption attributes in an unhealthy state (Bright 1999). As management practices place greater value on non-timber attributes, as more forested lands are protected from logging, and as a weakened forest's ability to absorb carbon is questioned, it becomes increasingly important to reduce North America's consumption of both wood products and fossil fuels.

## Old growth forests

Old growth forests, which are characterized by stands of large and old trees, a distinct species composition, a multilayered canopy, and a large build up of organic matter (Lund 2000), have many positive attributes. They are a source of high-value timber, contain large amounts of carbon, harbour a large reservoir of genetic diversity, provide habitat for many species, regulate hydrological regimes, protect soils and conserve nutrients, and have substantial recreational and aesthetic value (Marchak, Aycock and Herbert 1999). Much of the interest in old growth forests stems from the powerful images which they project of rich biodiversity and timeless stability. Visitors often sense a form of spirituality and grandeur in such forests and most people place a high value on them.

Old growth forests once occurred in all North American ecosystems although it is now difficult to determine their exact extent. Remnant old growth forests and stands still remain, especially in the Pacific Northwest and down the Pacific coast to California. The classic old growth forest in this area contains redwoods, cedars, Douglas fir, hemlock and spruce. The region probably still contains about half the world's remaining unlogged coastal temperate rainforest, with the greatest share in British Columbia.

The majority of old growth lost in the eastern and lower elevations of North America was due to conversion of land to agriculture and urban environments. In the west (see bar chart) and mountainous regions, loss has been due to harvesting of timber and conversion to younger more vigorously growing stands along with recent catastrophic events such as the eruption of Mount St Helens and the

### Clayoquot Sound

Clayoquot Sound, a 1 000 km$^2$ wilderness on Vancouver Island, became the focus of a well publicized debate over old growth logging. Beginning in 1984, environmentalists and the Nuu-chah-nulth First Nation protested against clear-cutting by blocking logging roads, among other tactics. During 1989–93, government task forces attempted to resolve the conflict and large tracts of coastal temperate rainforest were set aside for protection (MSRM 2002). Claiming that logging was still permitted on 70 per cent of the Sound, the protesters continued their actions, and brought national and international attention to the issue.

In 1995, in recognition that the Nuu-chah-nulth had not been adequately consulted, public negotiations began on a settlement with the First Nation peoples. Recommendations were formulated and adopted by the provincial government (May 1998). A 4 000 km$^2$ model forest was also established.

Progress was subsequently made in resolving the remaining conflicts. One of Canada's largest forest products companies announced in 1998 that it would phase out clear-cutting in British Columbia and design a new strategy focusing on old growth conservation (MacMillan 1998). An agreement was struck between First Nations and environmentalists to set aside most of the western coast of Clayoquot Sound and to promote economic development through small-scale logging, non-timber forest products and ecotourism. With the January 2000 designation of Clayoquot Sound as a UNESCO Biosphere Reserve, industry, environmentalists, governments and First Nations established a new form of governance based on shared responsibility for the ecosystem (ENS 1999, Clayoquot Biosphere Trust 2000).

Yellowstone fires (Harmon 1993, H. John Heinz III Center 2001).

The decline in old growth forest was largely driven by increasing worldwide demand for timber and high prices in the 1970s (Mathews and Hammond 1999). In recent years, losses due to timber harvesting have slowed because of increasing environmental concerns including the desire to preserve natural forests and to prevent further destruction of critical wildlife habitat and biological diversity.

Natural forests are still deemed by some to be essential to Canada's industrial timber supply. Canada harvests about 175 million m$^3$ of timber annually (NRC 2000) from approximately 1 million ha, or 0.5

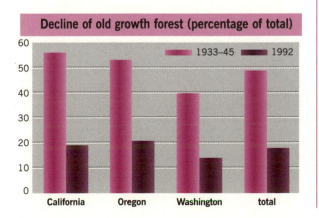

### Decline of old growth forest (percentage of total)

Old growth forests have declined rapidly since the middle of the 20th century

*Source: H. John Heinz III Center 2001*

per cent of the nation's commercial forest base. There is little mature second growth forest and so logging continues mainly from mature natural forests.

The paradigm shift towards the ecosystem approach to managing North America's old growth forests reflects the combined power of scientific knowledge, the action of voluntary groups, public awareness, market pressures on industry, and governmental response (see box on page 111).

## Policy responses

Canada's commitment to sustainable forestry is reflected in its 1998-2003 National Forest Strategy, the Canadian Council of Forest Ministers' set of criteria and indicators of sustainable forest management, and the research performed by the Canadian Forest Services (NRC 2000). The US Forest Service has also incorporated the concept of sustainable forestry and in 1999 it began to develop criteria and indicators for sustainable management (UN 1997).

Many state and provincial initiatives also reflect a shift to sustainable ecosystem management. Largely in response to public pressure, forest management over the past 20 years has incorporated a new emphasis on maintaining wildlife habitat, protecting soils, and retaining natural landscape characteristics. Large tracts of North American forests, including old growth, have been designated as protected areas. Canada has protected about 32 million ha (13 per cent) of its forested lands, and 67 million ha (30 per cent) of forests in the United States have some status of protection (University of Waterloo 1998, FAO 2001).

Export markets increasingly require that timber products be certified as originating in well-managed forests. Many companies and governments are becoming involved (Travers 2000). By 2002, more than 3 million ha of North American forests had been certified by the Forest Stewardship Council (FSC 2002).

## References: Chapter 2, forests, North America

Bright, C. (1999). The Nemesis effect. *World Watch* 12, 3, 12-23

Bryant, D., Nielsen D. and Tangley, L. (1997). *The Last Frontier Forests: Ecosystems & Economies on the Edge.* Washington DC, World Resources Institute

Clayoquot Biosphere Trust (2000). *British Columbia Community Celebrates Designation of Clayoquot Sound as an International Biosphere Reserve.* Canada Newswire http://www.newswire.ca/releases/May2000/05/c2312.html [Geo-2-403]

Driscoll, C. T., Lawrence, G. B., Bulger A., Butler, T. J., Cronan, C. S., Eagar, C., Lamber, K. F., Likens, G.E., Stoddard, J. L. and Weathers, K. (2001). Acidic deposition in the Northeastern United States: sources and inputs, ecosystem effects, and management strategies. *BioScience* 51, 3, 180-98

ENS (1999). Natives, enviros, MacMillan Bloedel sign Clayoquot truce. *Environment News Service*, 17 June 1999

FAO (2001). *Global Forest Resources Assessment 2000.* FAO Forestry Paper 140. Rome, Food and Agriculture Organization http://www.fao.org/forestry/fo/fra/ [Geo-2-402]

FSC (2002). *FSC Regional Total: North America.* Forest Stewardship Council http://www.certified-forests.org/data/nam_table.htm [Geo-2-404]

H. John Heinz III Center (2001). *Designing a Report on the State of the Nation's Ecosystem: Selected Measurements for Croplands, Forests, and Coasts and Oceans.* The H. John Heinz III Center for Science, Economics and the Environment http://heinzctr.org/publications/forests.pdf [Geo-2-405]

Harmon, F. (1993). *Acres of Late-Successional and Old-Growth Forest: The Wealth of Humboldt and the Klamath-Siskiyou Region.* Humboldt University http://www.humboldt.edu/~envecon/Indicators/acresofoldgrowth.htm [Geo-2-406]

Lund, H. G. (2000). *Definitions of Old Growth, Pristine, Climax, Ancient Forests, and Similar Terms.* Forest Information Services http://home.att.net/~gklund/pristine.html [Geo-2-408]

MacMillan (1998). *MacMillan Bloedel to Phase Out Clearcutting: Old-Growth Conservation is Key Goal, Customers to be Offered Certified Products.* Press Release, 10 June 1998

Marchak, M. P., Aycock, L.S. and Herbert, M.D. (1999). *Falldown: Forest Policy in British Columbia.* Vancouver, David Suzuki Foundation and Ecotrust Canada

Mathews, E. and Hammond, A. (1999). *Critical Consumption Trends and Implications: Degrading Earth's Ecosystems.* Washington DC, World Resources Institute

Mattoon, A.T. (1998). Paper forests. *World Watch* 11, 2, 20-28

MSRM (2002). Special Projects – Clayoquot Sound. Government of British Columbia, Ministry of Sustainable Resource Management http://www.luco.gov.bc.ca/specialprojects/clayquot/index.htm [Geo-2-423]

NRC (1999). *Forest Health: Context for the Canadian Forest Service's Science Program.* Science Branch, Canadian Forest Service, Natural Resources Canada http://www.nrcan.gc.ca/cfs-scf/science/context_health/pdf/forhealt_e.pdf [Geo-2-407]

NRC (2000). *The State of Canada's Forests: 1999-2000 Forests in the New Millennium.* Ottawa, Natural Resources Canada http://www.nrcan.gc.ca/cfs/proj/ppiab/sof/sof00/toc.shtml [Geo-2-409]

REGEN (2001). Regneration Treatments in Canada. http://nfdp.ccfm.org/regen/english/regen-frame.htm [Geo-2-410]

Travers, R. (2000). *British Columbia Certification Forum: Seeking Peace in the Woods.* Canadian Environmental Network, Forest Caucus http://www.cen-rce.org/caucus/forest/newsletter/vo2-no2/page10.html [Geo-2-411]

UN (1997). *Natural Resource Aspects of Sustainable Development in the United States of America.* United Nations Department of Economic and Social Affairs http://www.un.org/esa/agenda21/natlinfo/countr/usa/natur.htm#forests [Geo-2-412]

UNECE and FAO (2000). *Forest Resources of Europe, CIS, North America, Australia, Japan and New Zealand (industrialized temperate/boreal counties).* Geneva Timber and Forest Study Papers, No. 17. New York and Geneva, United Nations

University of Waterloo (1998). *Resources on Parks and Protected Areas.* University of Waterloo, Faculty of Applied Health Sciences, Department of Recreation and Leisure Studies http://www.ahs.uwaterloo.ca/rec/parksoption/parkslinks99.htm [Geo-2-413]

USDA (1997). *America's Forests: 1997 Health Update.* US Department of Agriculture, Forest Service http://www.fs.fed.us/foresthealth/fh_update/update97/index.htm [Geo-2-414]

## Forests: West Asia

Forests and woodlands of West Asia occupy only 3.66 million ha or 1 per cent of the region's land area and account for less than 0.1 per cent of the world's total forested area (FAO 2001a). The majority of forest cover (62 per cent) is in the Arabian Peninsula with the remainder scattered in the mountains and hills of northern Iraq, Jordan, Lebanon, Syria and the Occupied Palestinian Territories. The best stands of closed forests are found on the uplands near the Mediterranean. Tracts of mangrove forests grow along the coasts of the Arabian Peninsula. Forest resources are state-owned and administered centrally (FAO 1997).

The forests and woodlands of the region are generally composed of slow-growing species of poor quality and of little economic value (Nahal 1985, FAO 1997). Harsh climatic conditions limit forestry potential and restrict regeneration once forests are degraded (Abido 2000a). Under rainfed conditions, average forest productivity varies from 0.02 to 0.5 $m^3$/ha/year, although it reaches 2.9 $m^3$/ha/year in the natural forests of *Pinus brutia* of northern Syria (Nahal 1985, GORS 1991). By contrast, the productivity of irrigated eucalyptus plantations may exceed 17 $m^3$/ha/year (Abido 2000b). Nevertheless, forests play a vital role in protecting the region's water and soil resources, especially in steep and mountainous terrain, and in areas prone to desertification. They also afford protection from dust storms and stabilize dunes and river banks (FAO 1997).

All countries in the region depend on imports to meet the bulk of their wood product needs. The total value of forest product imports increased nearly fourfold between 1972 and 1996, from US$131 million

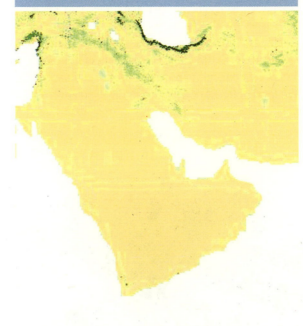

**Forest extent: West Asia**

to more than US$500 million (FAOSTAT 1998) while exports of forest products totalled US$36.6 million between 1996 and 1998 (UNDP, UNEP, World Bank and WRI 2000).

### Degradation and overexploitation

The region's forests and woodlands have suffered from a long history of degradation and overexploitation. Extensive land clearing for human settlements and agriculture in mountainous areas along the coasts of the Mediterranean in Lebanon and Syria has been carried out throughout history (Thirgood 1981). Traditional sheep and goat herding is still practised in *Juniperus excelsa* forest ecosystems in the Anti-Lebanon mountains and on the Syrian steppes where relics of *Pistacia atlantica* trees still remain (Nahal 1995, Abido 2000a).

The least forested region, West Asia has only 0.1 per cent of the world's forest and only 1 per cent of its land area is forested

*Note: dark green represents closed forest, more than 40 per cent covered with trees more than 5 metres high; mid-green represents open (10–40 per cent coverage) and fragmented forest; light green represents other woodland, shrubland and bushland*

*Source: FAO 2001a*

### Change in forested land 1990–2000 by sub-region: West Asia

|  | total land area (1 000 ha) | total forest 1990 (1 000 ha) | total forest 2000 (1 000 ha) | % of land forested in 2000 | change 1990-2000 (1 000 ha) | % change per year |
|---|---|---|---|---|---|---|
| Arabian Peninsula | 300 323 | 2 292 | 2 281 | 0.8 | -11 | -0.05 |
| Mashriq | 72 069 | 1 383 | 1 382 | 1.9 | -1 | -0.01 |
| **West Asia** | **372 392** | **3 675** | **3 663** | **1.0** | **-12** | **-0.03** |

*Source: compiled from FAO 2001a   Note: numbers may not add due to rounding*

Over the past 30 years, natural forest areas have been fragmented and isolated and turned into a mosaic with agricultural fields in Syria, and with urban dwellings in Lebanon and Syria (World Bank and UNDP 1998, GORS 1991, Government of Lebanon 1995). It is difficult to provide a precise estimate of the level of forest degradation in the region over the

**Dragon's blood tree (*Dracaena draco*) growing in arid surroundings in Yemen; more than half Yemen's population depends on limited fuelwood supplies for cooking**

*Source: UNEP, Mohamed Moslih Sanabani, Topham Picturepoint*

past 30 years due to the inaccuracies of earlier estimates and the problems associated with comparing data from different countries due to different calculation methods employed. However, the data that are available indicate a 44 per cent reduction in the region's forest cover from 1972 to 2000.

In Lebanon up to 60 per cent of forests were lost between 1972 and 1994 (Government of Lebanon 1995) while the small area of forest in the Occupied Palestinian Territories decreased by 50 per cent during the 1980s and 1990s (Palestinian Authority 1999, FAOSTAT 1998). However, in the past ten years the total forest area in West Asia has remained almost stable (see table on page 113). Significant changes have occurred only in Yemen, where forest area has decreased by 17 per cent, and in the United Arab Emirates, where plantation forests increased the total area by 32 per cent (FAO 2001a).

Several countries have a high proportion of planted forests (100 per cent in Kuwait, Oman and Qatar, 97.8 per cent in the United Arab Emirates and

approximately 50 per cent in both Jordan and Syria) (FAO 2001b). Afforestation programmes increased the forested area in Jordan by 20 per cent during the 1980s and 1990s (FAOSTAT 1998).

Population growth, urbanization, economic developments (including tourism) and conflict (for example in Iraq, Lebanon and Syria) are among the external factors that significantly affect forests. Fire, overgrazing and overcutting of wood products have contributed locally to forest degradation (FAO 1997). Poverty and inappropriate forest policies are over-riding factors contributing to forest and woodland deterioration in the Mashriq countries and Yemen. Until recently, poor demarcation of public and private lands in and around some forests and protected areas has led to ownership disputes and conflicts, providing the opportunity for some people to increase their private land holdings at the expense of public forests.

Rural communities, especially in mountainous areas, depend heavily on forest resources for their supply of timber, fuelwood, charcoal and non-wood forest products, putting enormous pressure on the limited resources available. It is estimated that 57 per cent of families in Yemen depend on forest resources to satisfy their domestic needs for fuel. The average consumption of 0.5 m$^3$ per person a year far exceeds average annual growth in the country's forests (Government of Yemen 2000). Iraq, Jordan, Lebanon, Saudi Arabia and Syria also use a significant proportion of their wood production for domestic fuel (FAO 2001a). Excessive cutting and wood collection have rendered fragile forest ecosystems prone to soil erosion and desertification (World Bank and UNDP 1998, Government of Lebanon 1995, Government of Yemen 2000). However, rapid urbanization and industrialization in West Asia are resulting in seasonal and permanent rural migration into urban areas (FAO 1997) and this trend is expected to reduce pressure on rural forests in terms of fuelwood collection and grazing.

The average area destroyed each year by forest fires has doubled in parts of the Mediterranean basin since the 1970s (Alexandrian, Esnault and Calabri 1999) and increased by almost 40 per cent in Jordan in the 1980s and 1990s compared to the 1970s (Government of Jordan 1997). In Lebanon, around 550 ha of forest area were lost each year between 1961 and 1997 due to a variety of causes including fire, cutting and urban encroachment. In Syria, as much as

8 000 ha of forests were converted to other land uses by burning between 1985 and 1993, and an additional 2 440 ha of forests were converted to farmland during the same period. Since the 1970s, more than 20 000 ha of coastal forests were burnt in northwestern Syria, resulting in soil erosion of up to 20 tonnes/ha/year on steep slopes (World Bank and UNDP 1998).

## Constraints to sustainable forest management

Traditionally, forests and woodlands were looked on as a source of timber, fuelwood and grazing sites, and forest policy was designed to protect these resources, with forestry departments in the region acting as resource guardians. Since 1992, in most countries forests have been demarcated, forest regulations revised and forest activities incorporated within the countries' national development strategies. These policies include new concepts such as integrated management of forest resources and recognition of the socio-economic values of these resources. However, some policies are still poorly defined, lack measurable objectives, and are not coordinated with land use policies (FAO 1997). Most importantly, the trend of decentralization, which would facilitate public participation in decision-making processes, is rather slow, and policies are rendered ineffective because of lack of financial support. New international initiatives are starting to address the linkages between rural communities and forest resources but the results are not yet available; adoption of community forestry models is still at an early stage (FAO 1997).

West Asian governments have only recently recognized the ecological importance of forests (FAO 1997). There is now a positive trend towards conservation of biological diversity and development of ecotourism industry in the region — for example in Jordan, Lebanon, Oman and Saudi Arabia. Some countries have declared forest reserves but these initiatives have been politically motivated with little involvement of stakeholders, and lack the support of local communities.

If sustainable forest management is to be achieved, further efforts are needed to mobilize resources and involve local communities, NGOs and other stakeholders in forest management.

## References: Chapter 2, forests, West Asia

Abido, M. (2000a). *Forest Ecology*. Damascus, Damascus University Press (in Arabic)

Abido, M. (2000b). Growth performance of *Eucalyptus camaldulensis* Dehn. under irrigated and non-irrigated conditions. *Damascus Journal for Agricultural Sciences* No.16 (in Arabic)

Alexandrian, D., Esnault, F. and Calabri, G. (1999). Forest Fires in the Mediterranean Area. *Unasylva* 197, 50, 35-41

FAO (1997). *State of the World's Forests 1997*. Rome, Food and Agriculture Organization

FAO (2001a). *Global Forest Resources Assessment 2000*. FAO Forestry Paper 140. Rome, Food and Agriculture Organization http://www.fao.org/forestry/fo/fra/ [Geo-2-415]

FAO (2001b). *State of the World's Forests 2001*. Rome, Food and Agriculture Organization

FAOSTAT (1998). *FAOSTAT Statistics Database*. Rome, Food and Agriculture Organization http://www.fao.org/ [Geo-2-068]

GORS (1991). *The Study of Soils and Forests of Coastal Area Using Remote Sensing Techniques (Lattakia Governorate)*. Damascus, General Organization of Remote Sensing (in Arabic)

Government of Jordan (1997). *Arbor Day in Jordan*. Amman, Government of Jordan (in Arabic)

Government of Lebanon (1995). *Lebanon: Assessment of the State of the Environment. Final Report*. Beirut, Ministry of the Environment

Government of Yemen (2000). *Report on the Environmental Status in Yemen*. Yemen, Government of Yemen (in Arabic)

Nahal, I. (1985). *Fuelwood Production in Syria*. FAO Mission Report. Rome, Food and Agriculture Organization

Nahal, I. (1995). Study on sustainable forest resources development in Syria. *University of Aleppo Agricultural Science Series*, 23, 29-67.l

Palestinian Authority (1999). *Palestinian Environmental Strategy*. Palestine, Ministry of Environmental Affairs

Thirgood, J.V. (1981). *Man and the Mediterranean Forest: A History of Resource Depletion*. London, Academic Press

World Bank and UNDP. (1998). *The State of the Environment in Syria*. London, Environmental Resource Management

UNDP, UNEP, WRI and World Bank (2000). *World Resources 2000-2001*. Washington DC, World Resources Institute

## Forests: the Polar Regions

The northern boreal forest system circles the globe through Russia, Scandinavia and North America, covering approximately 13.8 million km$^2$ (UNECE and FAO 2000). It is one of the two largest terrestrial ecosystems on Earth, the other being the tundra — a vast treeless plain that lies north of the boreal forest and stretches to the Arctic Ocean. The boreal forests are an important resource for the Arctic countries and are discussed as an entity here, although they do extend well beyond the Arctic sub-region (see figure).

In contrast to the overall decline in tropical forest cover, boreal forest cover has expanded by more than 560 000 ha since 1990 due to reforestation, afforestation and improved forestry management practices — although in the Russian Federation there are reports of massive clear cuts and unsustainable forest practices (FAO 2001a, Hansen, Hansson and Norris 1996). The main boreal trees are coniferous spruce, pine, fir and larch species. Some species are deciduous and include birch, alder, willow, maple and oak. A large portion of the boreal forest of Canada, Alaska and the Russian Federation remains relatively undisturbed by humans (FAO 2001a, FFS 1998) whereas the long period of forestry activities in Scandinavia has left almost no old growth forest (CAFF 2001).

### Values and uses of boreal forest

The boreal forest is an important contributor to the global resource base and to national and global economies. Wood processing has been a key economic activity of the Nordic countries since industrialization and an important export for Finland and Sweden (Hansen, Hansson and Norris 1996) while the Russian Federation is one of the largest exporters of industrial roundwood in the world. Since 1990, production has been stable or increased in all boreal countries except the Russian Federation, which has experienced a severe decline. For example, roundwood production halved from 227.9 million m$^3$ in 1992 to 115.6 million m$^3$ in 1998, reflecting the country's economic, social and infrastructure problems linked to economic transition (FAO 2001a).

Other uses and products of boreal forests include recreation, hunting, reindeer husbandry, fodder and forage, edible plant products (nuts, wild fruits and berries, mushrooms, maple syrup), medicinal plants,

**Arctic treeline**

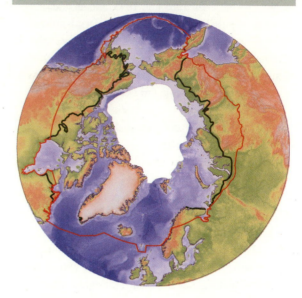

Boreal forest occurs only to the south of the treeline (dark green line). Arctic area, as defined by the Arctic Monitoring and Assessment Programme (AMAP), is limited by the orange line

*Source: GRID Arendal 2002*

Christmas trees and wild floral decorations (FAO 2001a). The forests also provide important wildlife habitat. The environmental functions of the boreal forests include stabilizing fragile northern soils, filtering pollutants and acting as a carbon sink and an indicator of climate change.

### Forest loss and degradation

Major threats to the northern boreal forest include fragmentation (see box opposite), forest fires and insect outbreaks. Spruce bark beetles have killed a significant portion of the spruce forests in Alaska, and decadal outbreaks of the autumn moth *Epirrita autumnata* in Fennoscandia have caused large-scale defoliation (CAFF 2001). Insects can leave dry, dead timber more susceptible to fire, the occurrence of which is already increasing as a result of an increase in temperature and decrease in precipitation. The impacts of insect outbreaks and fires can be severe. For example, in Canada, 6.3 million ha were affected by insect defoliation and 0.6 million ha were burnt in 2000 (Natural Resources Canada 2001).

### Policy and management responses

Some of the Arctic countries have long-established legislation to address the problems associated with forest degradation. Finland enacted the Forest Zones Protection Act in 1922, to prevent soil erosion and protect vulnerable regions of its northern forests while Sweden's 1909 Protection of Nature Act has resulted in the establishment of some 800 crown forest reserves. The more recent 1974 Beech Forest Law and 1993 Deciduous Forests Law strictly regulate the management of these reserves. The Russian Federation adopted the Russian Forest Code in 1997, which established 35 national parks on forest lands, totalling 6.9 million ha (All-Russian Research and Information Centre 1997). A 1999 report of the Canadian Senate recommended dividing boreal forests into three categories to meet competing demands for economic resources, supplying the needs of local communities and preserving biodiversity (see box on page 105). In this way 20 per cent would be managed for timber production, up to 20 per cent would be protected and the remainder would be reserved for multiple use (FAO 2001a). While protected areas in the Arctic have increased, most forests still remain outside these areas (Lysenko, Henry and Pagnan 2000, CAFF 1994).

Reforestation and afforestation are occurring in all boreal countries although many species being used for reforestation are not native to the area. For example, in Iceland, where native forests have been depleted through unsustainable cutting and grazing practices, replanting is conducted with species such as lodgepole pine, Sitka and white spruce, Siberian larch, and poplar (FAO 2001b). New forest management guidelines in many Fennoscandian countries are calling for more natural regeneration and application of forestry management at the landscape level (CAFF 2001). However, regeneration favouring coniferous trees over broadleaf species has changed the tree species composition of some Arctic forests, and resulted in the decline of many invertebrate species that live on deciduous trees (CAFF 2001).

Forest fire management regimes have traditionally suppressed fires, which has resulted in a decrease in fire-dependent species and has also meant that there is more available fuel and consequently a likelihood of fiercer fires once they do occur. Fire is now being increasingly viewed as a management tool since problems of total fire exclusion have been recognized (FAO 2001a).

### Forest fragmentation in the Arctic

Fragmentation, which hinders ecosystem functioning and results in loss of important wildlife habitat, and encroachment are serious threats to Arctic boreal forests, including the forested regions of the Russian Federation (FFS 1998, Lysenko, Henry and Pagnan 2000). In Scandinavia, there has been a long-term trend of converting forest land to other uses, especially agriculture, and ditch digging has increased the leaching of nutrients and run-off from soils. This in turn has caused siltation in rivers and lakes, decreasing their productivity as spawning areas for fish (CAFF 2001).

The coastal areas of Finnmark, Norway, are important calving and summer feeding grounds for the semi-domesticated reindeer of the Saami indigenous people. The maps below illustrate the gradual fragmentation of these areas as a result of expanding road networks. Hydroelectric installations, power lines, military bombing ranges and tourist resorts have had additional impacts (UNEP 2001).

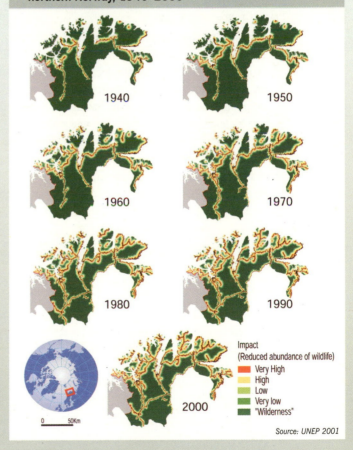

**Spread of road networks in Finnmark, northern Norway, 1940–2000**

1940 1950 1960 1970 1980 1990 2000

Impact (Reduced abundance of wildlife)
- Very High
- High
- Low
- Very low
- "Wilderness"

0 50Km

*Source: UNEP 2001*

### The fragile forest-tundra

Between the northern edge of the boreal forest, where trees actively regenerate, and the treeless tundra is a dynamic transition zone known as 'forest-tundra'. This zone can range from a few kilometres in North America to more than 200 kilometres in Europe

(Stonehouse 1989). It is naturally fragmented and contains patches of relatively heavy forest cover punctuated by areas of lichen-heath as well as areas of very sparse tree growth. It supports more species than either the boreal or the tundra systems since it contains species from both systems (CAFF 2001). The trees of the forest-tundra are often poorly formed and stunted, and regeneration is slow. Traditionally, this has made commercial exploitation of timber impractical although the ecosystem has provided indigenous peoples over the centuries with wood for fuel and construction (CAFF 2001). As world pressure on resources escalates, however, the tundra-forest could become a larger commodity producer. In fact logging operations in Fennoscandia and northwest Russia crept close to the forest-tundra in the 1960s and 1990s (CAFF 2001).

In winter, the forest-tundra provides important habitat for some populations of North American caribou and for European reindeer, in turn supporting the traditional reindeer husbandry activities of indigenous peoples such as the Saami of Scandinavia. The zone also supports sheep farming, fishing and harvesting of non-timber products. Important physical functions of the forest-tundra system are to stabilize and protect fragile soils and nutrients, to prevent erosion, to conserve water resources and watershed capability, to filter pollutants, to act as an indicator of

climate change and, together with the boreal forest proper, to act as a carbon store (see box above).

### Arctic forests and climate change

Any significant change in the area of boreal forests could have a considerable effect on the level of $CO_2$ in the atmosphere. With 26 per cent of total carbon stocks, boreal forests account for more carbon than any other terrestrial ecosystem – 323 gigatonnes (Gt, $10^9$ tonnes) in the Russian Federation, 223 Gt in Canada and 13 Gt in Alaska (Dixon and others 1994).

Conversely, it has been calculated that boreal forests will experience greater temperature increases from climate change than any other forest type. The warming, which is expected to be greater in winter than in summer, will shift climate zones north by as much as 5 km a year. Boreal forests will advance northwards while their southern edges will experience die back or replacement by temperate species. During summer, soils will be drier, and fires and drought more frequent. Local species loss may be significant although few tree species are expected to become extinct (UNEP-WCMC 2002).

Models used to predict the long-term changes in vegetation distribution have not conclusively shown whether the overall area of boreal forest will expand or decrease. However, one of the most comprehensive models of climate change forecasts that the northward expansion of forest will reduce the area of tundra by about 50 per cent by 2100 (White, Cannell and Friend 2000).

### References: Chapter 2, forests, the Polar Regions

CAFF (1994). *The Status of Protected Areas in the Circumpolar Arctic*. CAFF, Habitat Conservation Report No. 1. Trondheim, Directorate for Nature Management

CAFF (2001). *Arctic Flora and Fauna: Status and Conservation*. Helsinki, Arctic Council Programme for the Conservation of Arctic Flora and Fauna

Dixon, R.K., Brown, S., Houghton, R.A., Solomon, A.M., Trexler, M.C., and Wisniewski, J. (1994). Carbon pools and flux of global forest ecosystems. *Science*, 263, 185-190

FAO (2001a). *Global Forest Resources Assessment 2000*. FAO Forestry Paper 140. Rome, Food and Agriculture Organization http://www.fao.org/forestry/fo/fra/ [Geo-2-416]

FAO (2001b). *Forestry Country Profiles: Iceland*. Food and Agriculture Organization http://www.fao.org/forestry/fo/country/index.jsp?lang_id=1&geo_id=127, 6 March 2002 [Geo-2-417]

FFS (1998). *Concept of Sustainable Forest Management in the Russian Federation*. Moscow, Federal Forest Service of Russia (in Russian)

All-Russian Research and Information Centre for Forest Resources (1997). *Forest Code of the Russian Federation*. Moscow, All-Russian Research and Information Centre for Forest Resources

GRID Arendal (2002). *Arctic Environmental Atlas* http://www.maps.grida.no/temp/50647_3_14168.jpg [Geo-2-418]

Hansen, J. R., Hansson, R. and Norris, S. (eds., 1996). *The State of the European Arctic Environment*. EEA Environmental Monograph No. 3, Norsk Polarinstitutt, Meddelelser No. 141. Copenhagen, European Environment Agency and Norwegian Polar Institute

Lysenko, I., Henry, D. and Pagnan, J. (2000). *Gap Analysis in Support of CPAN: The Russian Arctic Habitat*. CAFF Habitat Conservation Report No. 9. Reykjavik, CAFF International Secretariat

Natural Resources Canada (2001). *Natural Resources Statistics. Statistics and Facts on Forestry*. Natural Resources Canada http://www.nrcan.gc.ca/statistics/forestry/default.html [Geo-2-419]

Stonehouse, B. (1989). *Polar Ecology*. London, Blackie

UNECE and FAO (2000). *Forest Resources of Europe, CIS, North America, Australia, Japan and New Zealand (industrialised temperate/boreal countries)*. A UN-ECE/FAO contribution to the Global Forest Resources Assessment 2000. Timber and Forest Study Papers, No.17. New York and Geneva, United Nations

UNEP (2001). *GLOBIO. Global Methodology for Mapping Human Impacts on the Biosphere*. UNEP/GRID-Arendal http://www.globio.info/region/europe/norway/ [Geo-2-421]

UNEP-WCMC (2002). *Climate Change: the Threats to the World Forests*. Cambridge, United Nations Environment Programme, World Conservation Monitoring Centre http://www.unep-wcmc.org/forest/flux/executive_summary.htm [Geo-2-420]

White, A., Cannell, M.R.G. and Friend, A.D. (2000). The high latitude terrestrial carbon sink: a model analysis. *Global Change Biology* 6, 227-246

# OUR CHANGING ENVIRONMENT: Rondônia, Brazil

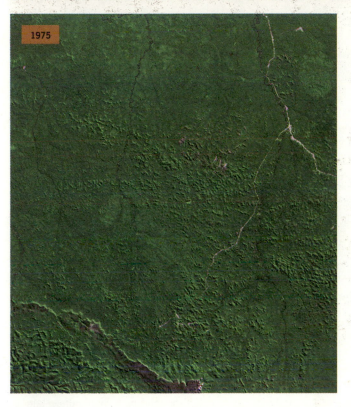

1975

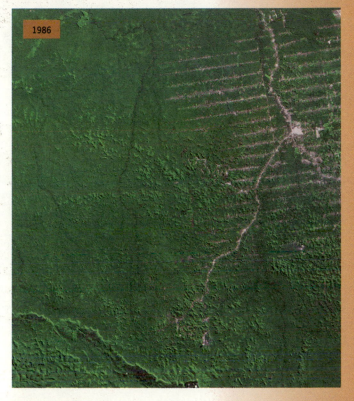

1986

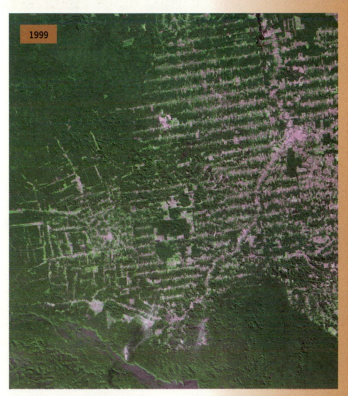

1999

To decentralize the Brazilian population and develop new regions, the Brazilian government completed the Cuiabá-Pôrto Velho highway through the province of Rondônia in 1960. The road provided access to tropical rainforest previously occupied only by indigenous people.

Two main factors increased immigration to the province. First, the World Bank decided in December 1980 to invest in paving the Cuiabá-Pôrto Velho highway, making travel easier. Second, economic hardship near the southern coast encouraged emigration to the area where immigrants hoped to acquire new land. The 1975 and 1986 images show substantial settlement in the Ariquemes area, near the highway. The predominant 'fishbone' pattern on the landscape is the result of logging operations which provide access to new land. Primary land uses are cattle ranching and annual crop farming. More sustainable perennial crops such as coffee, cacao and rubber occupy less than 10 per cent of the agricultural land.

Despite encroachment, programmes are now attempting to preserve the land for multi-use functions providing a wider array of income-producing products for farmers that should eventually result in less impact on the tropical rainforest.

Landsat data: USGS/EROS Data Center          Compilation: UNEP GRID Sioux Falls

UNEP, Soo Wee Ming, Malaysia, Still Pictures

# Biodiversity

## Global overview

### Biodiversity resources

Biodiversity refers to the variability among living organisms from all sources, including terrestrial, marine and other aquatic ecosystems, and the ecological complexes of which they are part. This includes diversity within species (genetic diversity), between species and of ecosystems.

There is no universally accepted classification of ecosystems at the global scale (UNEP 1995) but Olson (1994) defined 94 ecosystem classes based on land cover, vegetation and climate. This framework provides a mechanism for summarizing data at the global level, while recognizing the distinctiveness of ecosystems within each individual region.

Tropical forest ecosystems are the most species-rich environments. Although they cover less than 10 per cent of the world's surface, they may contain 90 per cent of the world's species. Coral reefs and Mediterranean heathland are also highly species-rich. Around 1.75 million species have been named by taxonomists to date (UNEP-WCMC 2000). The total number of species has recently been estimated as 14 million (see table), although this is highly uncertain, due to a lack of information about the number of insect, nematode, bacteria and fungus species.

Living organisms contribute to a wide variety of environmental services, such as regulation of the gaseous composition of the atmosphere, protection of coastal zones, regulation of the hydrological cycle and climate, generation and conservation of fertile soils, dispersal and breakdown of wastes, pollination of

### Estimated number of described species

| Kingdom | Described species |
|---|---|
| Bacteria | 4 000 |
| Protoctists (algae, protozoa, etc.) | 80 000 |
| Animals: vertebrates | 52 000 |
| Animals: invertebrates | 1 272 000 |
| Fungi | 72 000 |
| Plants | 270 000 |
| **Total described species** | **1 750 000** |
| **Possible total including unknown species** | **14 000 000** |

*Source: UNEP-WCMC 2000*

many crops, and absorption of pollutants (UNEP 1995). Many of these services are neither widely recognized nor properly valued in economic terms; however, the combined economic value of 17 ecosystem services has recently been estimated in the range US$16–54 trillion per year (Costanza and others 1997).

Human health and well-being are directly dependent on biodiversity. For example, 10 of the world's 25 top-selling drugs in 1997 were derived from natural sources. The global market value of pharmaceuticals derived from genetic resources is estimated at US$75 000–150 000 million annually. Some 75 per cent of the world's population rely for health care on traditional medicines, which are derived directly from natural sources (UNDP, UNEP, World Bank and WRI 2000).

Biodiversity also provides genetic resources for food and agriculture, and therefore constitutes the biological basis for world food security and support for human livelihoods. A number of wild crop relatives are of great importance to national and global economies. For example, Ethiopian varieties have provided protection from viral pathogens to California's barley crop, worth US$160 million per year. Genetic resistance to disease obtained from wild wheat varieties in Turkey has been valued at US$50 million per year (UNEP 1995).

## Decline and loss of species

Global biodiversity is changing at an unprecedented rate (Pimm and others 1995), the most important drivers of this change being land conversion, climate change, pollution, unsustainable harvesting of natural resources and the introduction of exotic species (Sala and others 2000). The relative importance of these drivers differs between ecosystems. For example, land conversion is most intensive in tropical forests and less intensive in temperate, boreal and Arctic regions; atmospheric nitrogen deposition is largest in northern temperate areas close to cities; introduction of exotic species is related to patterns of human activity — those areas remote from human intervention generally receive fewer introduced species. The ultimate causes of biodiversity loss are human population growth together with unsustainable patterns of consumption, increasing production of waste and pollutants, urban development, international conflict, and continuing inequities in the distribution of wealth and resources.

Over the past three decades, decline and extinction of species have emerged as major environmental issues. The current rate of extinction is many times higher than the 'background' rate — that which has prevailed over long periods of geological time. Estimates based on the fossil record suggest that the background extinction rate in mammals and birds has been one species lost every 500-1 000 years (May, Lawton and Stork 1995).

Information on the conservation status of species is provided by the World Conservation Union (IUCN) which regularly publishes 'Red Lists' of species considered to be threatened with extinction. The latest IUCN Red List (Hilton-Taylor 2000) indicates that about 24 per cent (1 130) of mammals and 12 per cent (1 183) of bird species are currently regarded as globally threatened (see table). Since the Red List assessment in 1996, the number of critically endangered species has increased from 169 to 180 mammals and from 168 to 182 birds (Hilton-Taylor 2000). Analyses suggest that over the next 100 years the extinction rate of vertebrate groups could be as high as 15-20 per cent (Mace 1995). However, species trends derived from Red List data should be interpreted with caution because the criteria for listing have changed over time and some of the changes in status reflect taxonomic revisions (May, Lawton and Stork 1995).

Insufficient information is available to determine precisely how many species have become extinct in

### Globally threatened vertebrate species by region

| | Mammals | Birds | Reptiles | Amphibians | Fishes | Total |
|---|---|---|---|---|---|---|
| Africa | 294 | 217 | 47 | 17 | 148 | 723 |
| Asia and the Pacific | 526 | 523 | 106 | 67 | 247 | 1 469 |
| Europe | 82 | 54 | 31 | 10 | 83 | 260 |
| Latin America and Caribbean | 275 | 361 | 77 | 28 | 132 | 873 |
| North America | 51 | 50 | 27 | 24 | 117 | 269 |
| West Asia | 0 | 24 | 30 | 8 | 9 | 71 |
| Polar | 0 | 6 | 7 | 0 | 1 | 14 |

Note: 'Threatened species' include those categorized by IUCN in 2000 as Critically Endangered, Endangered and Vulnerable (Hilton-Taylor 2000); adding totals for each region does not give a global total because a species may be threatened in more than one region

Source: compiled from the IUCN Red List database (Hilton-Taylor 2000) and the UNEP-WCMC species database (UNEP-WCMC 2001a)

the past three decades. However, the database maintained by the Committee on Recently Extinct Organisms (CREO 2001) lists 58 fish species and 1 mammal species recorded as extinct since 1970; assessments by BirdLife International indicate that 9 bird species have become extinct during this period (BirdLife International 2000).

Much of the relevant information on the status of species is qualitative or anecdotal, and it is therefore difficult to develop a quantitative overview of global trends. To assess trends in species loss or decline, indicators are required that provide quantitative estimates of change over time, using consistent methodologies for sampling and analysis. Ideally, such indicators should be based on data sampled explicitly for this purpose. Few such monitoring programmes have yet been established.

One approach is the Living Planet Index created by UNEP-WCMC in cooperation with WWF (see box). The index is derived from trends in the size of wild populations of species in three habitats — forest, freshwater and marine ecosystems. The prevailing trend of all three indices is downward.

The impact of decline or loss of species on the provision of environmental services is difficult to evaluate because the relationship between species diversity and ecosystem function is still unclear. Some species are known to play more significant roles than others; these have been termed 'keystone' species — loss of one of these species has a particularly disruptive effect (Vitousek and Hooper 1993). Reductions in the number of species affect the provision of all ecosystem services because resource capture (of energy, water and nutrients) is greater in more diverse systems. Some ecosystems, such as arid and arctic areas, appear to be particularly vulnerable to human impacts. In these systems, relatively few organisms share common ecological roles (UNEP 1995). Species diversity may also play a role in buffering ecosystems against the effects of human activity (UNEP 1995).

The past three decades have been marked by the emergence of a concerted response to the biodiversity crisis. Civil society, particularly in the form of a hugely diverse and increasingly sophisticated NGO network, has been a major driving force behind this. A trend towards increased stakeholder participation relating to conservation action is evident as illustrated by the emergence of partnerships between NGOs, governments and the private sector.

A number of international conventions have been developed that deal specifically with conservation of

## The Living Planet Index: a global biodiversity indicator

The Living Planet Index system is based on estimates of population size of individual wild species available in the scientific literature. The index is calculated as a percentage of the population size estimated at 1970; the mean value of the index is calculated as an average of all the species included in the assessment at each time interval (Groombridge and Jenkins 2000, Loh 2000, UNEP-WCMC 2000). The index has been calculated for the forest, marine and freshwater ecosystems (see graphs).

The forest index, based on 319 populations of temperate and tropical species (mostly birds), shows a decline of about 12 per cent during 1970–99. The index for temperate species only shows little change over the period (most deforestation here having taken place before the 20th century). The tropical sample shows a downward trend, consistent with the continuing deforestation in many tropical areas.

The marine index, based on populations of 217 species of marine animals, shows a decline of about 35 per cent in the same period.

Inland water and wetland species, represented by a sample of 194 populations, have declined by 50 per cent. This suggests that inland water ecosystems are more severely degraded than other ecosystem types, a finding consistent with other evidence.

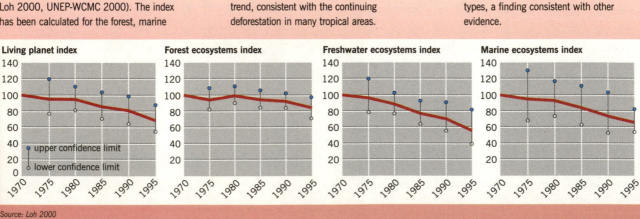

Source: Loh 2000

threatened species. Among the most notable are the 1973 Convention on International Trade in Endangered Species of Wild Fauna and Flora (CITES), and the 1979 Convention on the Conservation of Migratory Species of Wild Animals (CMS) — or the Bonn Convention — which was developed to conserve terrestrial, marine and migratory bird species throughout their range. Inter-governmental agreements such as the African-Eurasian Waterbird Agreement — which aims to develop transboundary strategic measures necessary to conserve the network of critical wetland areas on which migratory waterbirds depend — are the primary tools for the implementation of the CMS.

## Habitat degradation and loss

The focus of conservation action has recently shifted from protecting individual species to conserving habitats and ecosystems. An illustration of how conservation plans are now conceived at broader scales is provided by WWF International which recently developed priorities for action at the scale of ecoregions (large areas of relatively uniform climate that harbour a characteristic set of species and ecological communities). Ecoregions of particular conservation importance include Lake Baikal in Russia, the Australian Great Barrier Reef and the Atlantic forests of Argentina, Brazil and Paraguay.

Loss and degradation of habitat is the most important factor causing loss of species. For example, conversion of forests or grasslands into croplands results in the local extinction of plant and animal species (Sala and others 2000). Worldwide about 1.2 million $km^2$ of land have been converted to cropland in the past 30 years. In a recent global survey, habitat loss was found to be the principal factor affecting 83 per cent of threatened mammals and 85 per cent of threatened birds (Hilton-Taylor 2000, BirdLife International 2000). Habitat modification arises from many different types of land use change including agricultural development, logging, dam construction, mining and urban development.

Over the past three decades, major losses of virtually every kind of natural habitat have occurred. For example, FAO assessments show that between 1980 and 1995 forest cover in developing countries declined by an estimated 2 million $km^2$ — an average annual loss of 130 000 $km^2$ (FAO 1999a). The most important causes of forest loss included conversion to

agriculture and development schemes involving resettlement. As a result, habitats such as the tropical dry forests of Central America have virtually disappeared (UNDP, UNEP, World Bank and WRI 2000). In terms of loss of species, freshwater habitats are the most degraded, with some 20 per cent of freshwater species having become extinct or threatened with extinction in recent decades (UNDP, UNEP, World Bank and WRI 2000). The main causes of extinctions among freshwater fishes are declines in habitat quality (Harrison and Stiassny 1999).

Dryland ecosystems, which cover more than one-third of the world's land area, are particularly vulnerable to degradation. Statistics indicate that more than 250 million people are directly affected by desertification (UNCCD 2001). In 1977, 57 million people failed to produce enough food to sustain themselves as a result of land degradation and by 1984 this number had risen to 135 million (UNEP 1992). Impacts of degradation on dryland biodiversity have not been comprehensively documented but substantial changes have resulted from grazing of livestock, deforestation, introduction of non-native species and conversion to croplands (UNEP 1995). In response, the 1977 United Nations Conference on Desertification adopted a Plan of Action to Combat Desertification. Despite this, assessments by UNEP (1992) indicated that land degradation in many dryland areas had continued to intensify. As a result the United Nations Convention to Combat Desertification was developed, entering into force in 1996. This convention aims to promote effective action through local programmes and international partnerships.

Wetlands are areas where the water table is at or near the surface of the land, or where the land is covered by shallow water, and include areas of marsh, fen and peatland. Wetlands play an important role in regulating water flow and are of exceptional importance as habitats for large numbers of species. Wetland habitats are also of high economic importance for provision of water and fisheries (more than two-thirds of the world's fish harvest is linked to coastal and inland wetland areas). Concern about degradation and loss of wetland habitats led to the development of the Convention on Wetlands of International Importance Especially as Waterfowl Habitat (Ramsar) in 1971. The Ramsar Convention provides a framework for national action and international cooperation for the conservation and wise use of wetlands and their resources (see Chapter 1 for more information).

The designation of protected areas, such as national parks, is one of the most widely used approaches for conserving habitats. In addition to national parks, a total of 167 sites have now been designated as natural heritage sites under the World Heritage Convention. The total area of protected sites has increased continuously during the past three decades from less than 3 million km² in 1970 to more than 12 million km² by the late 1990s (Green and

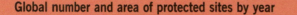

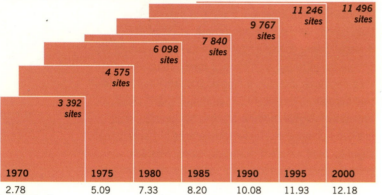

**Global number and area of protected sites by year**

| 1970 | 1975 | 1980 | 1985 | 1990 | 1995 | 2000 |
|------|------|------|------|------|------|------|
| 3 392 sites | 4 575 sites | 6 098 sites | 7 840 sites | 9 767 sites | 11 246 sites | 11 496 sites |
| 2.78 million km² | 5.09 | 7.33 | 8.20 | 10.08 | 11.93 | 12.18 |

**Total area of protected areas has increased from some 2.78 million km² in 1970 to more than 12 million km² by 2000**

*Note: areas of more than 1 000 ha, IUCN categories I-VI*
*Source: compiled from Green and Paine 1997 and UNEP-WCMC 2001b*

Paine 1997), indicating that there are continuing efforts by governments to establish protected areas. Although the effectiveness of protected areas for conserving biodiversity has been questioned, a recent analysis of 93 protected areas around the world indicated that most parks are successful at stopping land clearing and to a lesser extent at mitigating logging, hunting, fire and grazing (Bruner and others 2001).

The most significant response to the biodiversity crisis during the past 30 years has been the Convention on Biological Diversity (CBD) which entered into force in December 1993 and had been signed by 182 Parties by December 2001. The convention has three main goals: the conservation of biodiversity; sustainable use of the components of biodiversity; and sharing the benefits arising from the use of genetic resources in a fair and equitable way (see Chapter 1).

The CBD has resulted in major activity at both national and international levels, and in the increased coordination of cross-sectoral action within and between countries. However, major challenges remain

in increasing capacity to assess biodiversity and its value to people, securing adequate financial resources for conservation actions, and building political support for the changes necessary to ensure biodiversity conservation and sustainable use.

It is clear from national reports that the implementation of the convention is making progress in most countries, as illustrated by preparation of national biodiversity strategies and action plans, increasing efforts to reform institutional and legislative arrangements, integration of biodiversity into sectoral activities and increased recognition by governments of the importance of the identification and monitoring of biological diversity.

It is not yet possible to assess accurately the impacts of the CBD on biodiversity, partly because the CBD has been in force for only a short time. In addition, the parties to the convention have yet to develop any globally applicable criteria and indicators by which overall changes in biodiversity can be measured. It is clear that the convention has had some impact at the policy level in many countries. What remains difficult to assess is the depth of commitment to implementation and how any such policy changes may result in changes in the state of biodiversity. This issue is addressed in the strategic plan for the convention, currently under discussion.

## Climate change and global warming

During the 1990s climate change emerged as one of the major potential threats to biodiversity. The IPCC concluded that climate change could lead to severe adverse impacts on ecosystems, and on the goods and services they provide (IPCC 2001). Some ecosystems might disappear, while others could experience dramatic changes in species composition. Desertification may increase in some areas and some species could also become more vulnerable to extinction (WRI and IUCN 1998).

The impact of climate change on biodiversity to date is unclear. The increasing incidence of coral reef bleaching may be a consequence of recent rises in global ocean temperature (Goreau and others 2000). Reports of coral bleaching have increased greatly since 1989, with all records of mass bleaching occurring after this date. The most significant mass bleaching was associated with the 1997-98 ENSO event, when all ten reef provinces of the world were affected. In some areas, most notably the Indian

Ocean, this event was followed by mass mortality, where up to 90 per cent of all the corals died over thousands of square kilometres (Goreau and others 2000). Climate change has also been implicated in the decline of amphibians in tropical montane forests (Pounds, Fogden and Campbell 1999).

## Nitrogen deposition

Nitrogen deposition has become a major cause of biodiversity loss. It has increased substantially in recent decades, primarily as a result of an increase in the use of fertilizer and the burning of fossil fuels. Increased nitrogen in soil and water can lead to loss of species and shifts in the species composition of plant communities (Wedin and Tilman 1996); for example, the conversion of heathlands to species-poor grasslands in the Netherlands (Vitousek and others 1997). Aquatic ecosystems are the most vulnerable; nitrogen deposition can lead to eutrophication, currently one of the most serious threats to aquatic environments, particularly in inshore waters where many commercial fish and shellfish species breed (Diaz and Rosenberg 1995). Nitrogen deposition has also been associated with the recent increase in toxic algal blooms (Anderson 1994).

## Oil spills

Oil spills have also had a major impact on biodiversity in recent decades. In 1998 alone, a total of 108 000 tonnes of oil were spilled worldwide into marine and inland environments as a result of 215 incidents (Etkin 1999).

## Consumption and international trade

During the past 30 years, consumption of natural resources has increased substantially — for example, the global consumption of forest products such as paper increased threefold (Matthews and others 2000). For many biological resources, such patterns of increasing consumption are unsustainable. The most striking example is marine fisheries. Consumption of fish has increased 240 per cent since 1960. However, the marine catch has now levelled off and shows signs of declining as a result of overexploitation. More than 70 per cent of the world's commercially important fish stocks are described by FAO as either fully fished, overexploited, depleted or slowly recovering (FAO 1999b). Numerous fisheries collapsed during the latter part of the 20th century, including Canada's Grand Banks cod fishery which closed in 1992 with the loss of 40 000 jobs (Milner-Gulland and Mace 1998).

Products derived from wildlife form the basis of an international trade valued at approximately US$10 000 million annually. Additionally, there is an extensive illegal trade in such products (Mahony 1996). In addition to the CITES secretariat, the establishment in 1976 of the Trade Records Analysis for Flora and Fauna in International Commerce (now simply known as TRAFFIC) by IUCN and WWF has strengthened the international community's efforts to monitor illegal wildlife trade and implement CITES' provisions and decisions. The CITES secretariat, Interpol and the World Customs Organization, as well as a number of NGOs, have been establishing networks and organizing training of customs, borders, police, wildlife and other enforcement authorities.

The impact of CITES on biodiversity is difficult to assess, as it is often not possible to ascribe unequivocally any changes in the conservation status of species to the impacts of actions taken under the convention. The continual upgrading of many species to increasingly higher levels of protection suggests ineffectiveness, although some species (such as vicuña) have been downgraded because of successful sustainable use schemes (Milner-Gulland and Mace 1998). In the case of the African elephant, although upgrading from Appendix II to Appendix I in 1989 was highly controversial, it appears to have contributed to a decline in poaching. In contrast, rhinos have been listed on CITES Appendix I since 1973 and yet poaching continues to be a major threat to this species (Milner-Gulland and Mace 1998).

## Invasive species

Invasive species are organisms (usually transported by humans) that successfully colonize native ecosystems. Such species have been a major threat to native species through the effects of predation, alteration of habitat or disruption of ecosystem processes. Notable terrestrial examples include the loss of many endemic land snail species of French Polynesia following the introduction of the predatory snail *Euglandina rosea*, and the decline in New Zealand's native birds due to the introduction of Australian brushtail possum. Aquatic examples include the introduction of the predatory Nile perch *Lates niloticus* to Lake Victoria around 30 years ago, which contributed to the apparent extinction of 250 endemic species of cichlid fishes (Harrison and Stiassny 1999). The number of aquatic introductions rose rapidly during the second half of the 20th century (see graph).

The CBD recognizes the importance of invasive species as a global problem and calls upon contracting parties to prevent the introduction of, control or eradicate those alien species that threaten ecosystems, habitats and species. In response to a recommendation from the CBD in 1996, the Global Invasive Species Programme (GISP) was developed, which is coordinated by the Scientific Committee on Problems of the Environment (SCOPE), in collaboration with IUCN, Centre for Agriculture and Biosciences International and UNEP. The programme will review current knowledge on invasive species and develop new tools and approaches to deal with the problem both locally and globally.

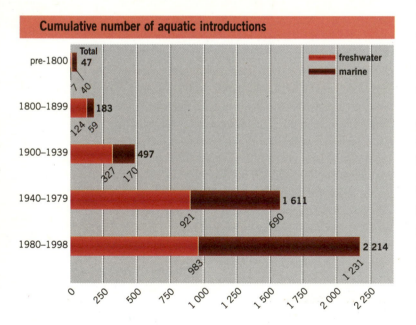

**Cumulative number of aquatic introductions**

Cumulative number of aquatic introductions rose fast in the second half of the 20th century

*Source: FAO 1998 and Wellcome 1988*

## Biotechnology

Biotechnology is increasingly being used for the genetic improvement of crops but concerns have been raised about potential risks to biodiversity. The organisms produced are referred to as genetically modified organisms (GMOs) or living modified organisms (LMOs) and efforts have focused on such crops as tomatoes, grains, cassava, maize and soybeans. In response to this concern, a subsidiary agreement to the CBD was negotiated to address the potential risks posed by cross-border trade and accidental releases of GMOs. Adopted in January

2000, the Cartagena Protocol on Biosafety was developed to ensure that recipient countries have both the opportunity and the capacity to assess risks relating to GMOs, and to ensure their safe transfer, handling and use.

## Conclusion

Assessing the impact of the various multilateral environmental agreements on biodiversity is problematic. This is because there is an absence of baseline data from which to measure changes and the agreements generally do not refer to explicit biodiversity-related targets (either in their texts or in subsequent elaboration) against which to measure impacts. It is also extremely difficult to separate the impacts of one agreement from a host of confounding factors. One exception is the moratorium on commercial whaling imposed by the International Whaling Commission since 1985-86. In this case, there were appropriate baseline data on whale stocks and it is reasonable to assume that subsequent increases in populations, where these have been observed, are a result of the moratorium.

Assessment of the impact of policy responses to pressures on biodiversity is limited by the lack of a comprehensive system for monitoring, for collating relevant data and for presenting information in a consistent manner. The Global Biodiversity Information Facility (GBIF) was recently developed to help address this need by improving collection and presentation of information on biodiversity. GBIF developed from the work of the OECD Megascience Forum Working Group on Biological Informatics that was established in January 1996.

In general, the available data suggest that despite a variety of initiatives, biodiversity continues to decline. Most examples of successful conservation action are those where particular attention, and considerable financial resources, have been focused on individual species or localized areas. Many threats to biodiversity such as habitat loss and invasion by introduced species continue to intensify. In addition, new threats may be emerging, such as climate change and the introduction of LMOs. Overall, it appears that the drivers of biodiversity loss are so pervasive that conservation efforts have at best only slowed the rate of change at the global level.

## References: Chapter 2, biodiversity, global overview

Anderson, D. M. (1994). Red tides. *Scientific American*. August 1994, 62-68

BirdLife International (2000). *Threatened Birds of the World*. Barcelona and Cambridge, Lynx Edicions and BirdLife International

Bruner, A.G., Gullison, R.E., Rice, R.E. and de Fonseca, G.A.B. (2001). Effectiveness of parks in protecting tropical biodiversity. *Science*. 291, 125-28

Costanza, R., d'Arge, R., de Groot, R., Farber, S., Grasso, M., Hannon, B., Limburg, K., Naeem, S., O'Neill, R. V., Paruelo, J., Raskin, R. G., Sutton, P. and van den Belt, M. (1997). The value of the world's ecosystem services and natural capital. *Nature*. 387, 253–60

CREO (2001). *CREO, the Committee on Recently Extinct Organisms*. http://creo.amnh.org/index.html [Geo-2-066]

Diaz, R. J. and Rosenberg, R. (1995). Marine benthic hypoxia: a review of its ecological effects and the behavioral responses of benthic macrofauna. *Oceanography and Marine Biology: An Annual Review*. 33, 245-302

Etkin, D.S. (1999). *International Oil Spill Statistics: 1998*. Arlington, Massachusetts, Cutter Information Corporation

FAO (1998). *Database on Introductions of Aquatic Species (DIAS)*. Food and Agriculture Organization http://www.fao.org/waicent/faoinfo/fishery/statist/fisoft/dias/mainpage.htm [Geo-2-067]

FAO (1999a). *State of the World's Forests 1999*. Rome, Food and Agriculture Organization http://www.fao.org/docrep/W9950E/W9950E00.htm [Geo-2-067]

FAO (1999b). *The State of the World's Fisheries and Aquaculture 1998*. Rome, Food and Agriculture Organization

Goreau, T., McClanahan, T., Hayes, R. and Strong, A.E (2000). Conservation of coral reefs after the 1998 global bleaching event. *Conservation Biology*. 14, 1, 5-15

Green, M.J.B. and Paine, J. (1997). *State of the World's Protected Areas at the End of the 20th Century*. Paper presented at the IUCN World Commission on Protected Areas Seminar 'Protected Areas in the 21st Century: From Islands to Networks'. Cambridge, World Conservation Monitoring Centre

Groombridge, B. and Jenkins, M.D. (2000). *Global Biodiversity: Earth's Living Resources in the 21st Century*. Cambridge, The World Conservation Press

Harrison, I.J. and Stiassny, M.L.J. (1999). The quiet crisis: a preliminary listing of the freshwater fishes of the world that are extinct or "missing in action". In R. D. E. MacPhee (ed.), *Extinctions in Near Time: Causes, Contexts and Consequences*. New York, Kluwer Academic and Plenum Publishers

Hilton-Taylor, C. (2000). *2000 IUCN Red List of Threatened Species*. The World Conservation Union http://www.redlist.org/info/tables/table4a.html [Geo-2-069]

IPCC (2001). *IPCC Third Assessment Report — Climate Change 2001. Working Group II: Impacts, Adaptation and Vulnerability*. Geneva, World Meteorological Organization and United Nations Environment Programme http://www.ipcc.ch/pub/tar/wg2/004.htm [Geo-2-070]

Loh, J. (2000). *The Living Planet Report 2000*. Gland, WWF-The Global Environment Network

Mace, G. M. (1995). Classification of threatened species and its role in conservation planning. In J. H. Lawton and R. M. May (ed.), *Extinction Rates*. Oxford, Oxford University Press

Mahony, D.E. (1996). *The Convention on International Trade in Endangered Species of Fauna and Flora: Addressing Problems in Global Wildlife Trade and Enforcement. New England International and Comparative Law Annual* http://www.nesl.edu/annual/vol3/cite.htm [Geo-2-071]

Matthews, E., Payne, R., Rohweder, M. and Murray, S. (2000). *Pilot Analysis of Global Ecosystems: Forest Ecosystems*. Washington DC, World Resources Institute

May, R. M., Lawton, J. H. and Stork, N. E. (1995). Assessing extinction rates. In J. H. Lawton and R. M. May (ed.), *Extinction Rates*. Oxford, Oxford University Press

Milner-Gulland, E.J. and Mace, R. (1998). *Conservation of Biological Resources*. Oxford, Blackwell Science

Olson, J.S. (1994). *Global Ecosystem Framework-Definitions: Internal Report*. Sioux Falls, South Dakota, United States Geological Service

Pimm, S. I., Russell, G. J., Gittelman, J. L. and Brooks, T. M. (1995). The future of biodiversity. *Science*. 269, 347–50

Pounds, A.J., Fogden, M. P. L. and Campbell, J. H. (1999). Biological response to climate change on a tropical mountain. *Nature* 398, 611–15

Sala, O.E., Chapin III, F.S., Armesto, J.J., Berlow, R., Bloomfield, J., Dirzo, R., Huber-Sanwald, E., Huenneke, L.F., Jackson, R.B., Kinzig, A., Leemans, R., Lodge, D., Mooney, H.A., Oesterheld, M., Poff, N.L., Sykes, M.T., Walker, B.H., Walker, M. and Wall, D.H. (2000). Global biodiversity scenarios for the year 2100. *Science*. 287, 1770-74

UNCCD (2001). *The United Nations Convention to Combat Desertification: An Explanatory Leaflet*. UN Convention to Combat Desertification http://www.unccd.int/convention/text/leaflet.php [Geo-2-098]

UNDP, UNEP, World Bank and WRI (2000). *World Resources 2000-2001*. Washington DC, World Resources Institute

UNEP (1992). *World Atlas of Desertification*. London, Edward Arnold

UNEP (1995). *Global Biodiversity Assessment*. Cambridge, Cambridge University Press

UNEP-WCMC (2000). *Global Biodiversity: Earth's living resources in the 21st century*. Cambridge, World Conservation Press

UNEP-WCMC (2001a). *GEO3 Endangered Animals Snapshot*. United Nations Environment Programme-World Conservation Monitoring Centre http://valhalla.unep-wcmc.org/isdb/geo3.cfm [Geo-2-068]

UNEP-WCMC (2001b). *GEO3 Protected Areas Snapshot*. United Nations Environment Programme-World Conservation Monitoring Centre cfm http://valhall.unep-wcmc.org/wdbpa/GEO3.cfm [Geo-2-053]

Vitousek, P., Aber, J., Howarth, R.W., Likens, G.E., Matson, P.A., Schindler, D.W., Schlesinger, W.H. and Tilman, G.D. (1997). Human alteration of the global nitrogen cycle: causes and consequences. *Issues In Ecology*. 1, 2-16

Vitousek, P. M. and Hooper, D. U. (1993). Biological diversity and terrestrial ecosystem biogeochemistry. In E. D. Schulze and H. A. Mooney (eds.), *Biodiversity and Ecosystem Function*. Berlin, Springer-Verlag

Wedin, D. and Tilman, D. (1996). Influence of nitrogen loading and species composition on carbon balance of grasslands. *Science*. 274, 1720–23

Wellcome, R.L. (1998). *International introductions of inland aquatic species*. Fisheries Technical Paper 294. Rome, Food and Agriculture Organization

WRI and IUCN (1998). *Climate, Biodiversity and Forests*. Issues and Opportunities Emerging from the Kyoto Protocol. Washington DC, World Resources Institute

## Biodiversity: Africa

Five internationally recognized 'biodiversity hot spots' (areas of particularly high species richness and endemism, and under particular threat) are found in the African region (Mittermeier and others 2000). These are the Western Indian Ocean islands, the Cape floristic region, the Succulent Karoo (the most species-rich desert in the world), the Upper Guinea forest and the Eastern Arc mountain forests of Eastern Africa.

### Numbers of threatened vertebrates: Africa

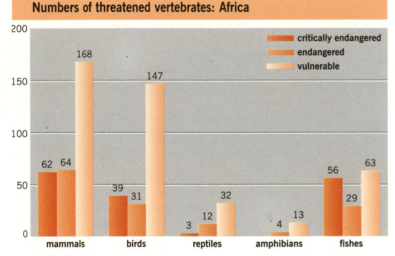

Note: critically endangered (extremely high risk of extinction in immediate future); endangered (very high risk of extinction in near future); vulnerable (high risk of extinction in medium-term future)

The data include all globally threatened vertebrate species with country records in the UNEP-WCMC database (UNEP-WCMC 2001a). Marine species recorded by ocean area are not included

Part of the Mediterranean Basin hot spot, home to 25 000 plant species and 14 endemic genera, is also found in Africa (Quézel and others 1999). The continent possesses several other areas of great importance for biodiversity. These include the highlands of Ethiopia; the forests of the Albertine Rift in Burundi, eastern Congo, Rwanda, and adjacent parts of Kenya and Uganda; the western escarpment of Angola; and the miombo woodlands of interior Southern Africa (Mittermeier and others 2000).

In the past three decades, habitat loss and degradation has been a major issue throughout Africa, particularly in dryland areas. In humid areas, the bushmeat trade has also had a significant impact on biodiversity. Biodiversity resources are extensively used for subsistence and commercial purposes. For example, approximately 70 per cent of the wild plant species in Northern Africa are used as sources of traditional food, forage, medicine and agroforestry, and half have more than one use (Ucko and Dimbleby 1969, UNESCO and UCO 1998, WWF and IUCN 1994). The richness and diversity of ecosystems in

Africa underpins a flourishing tourism industry, which is an important source of foreign exchange for many countries. For instance, Southern Africa's wildlife attracted more than 9 million visitors in 1997 bringing in a total of US$4.1 billion (SADC 2000).

### Habitat degradation and loss

Loss and degradation of habitat have been widespread over the past three decades. FAO's Global Forest Resources Assessment (FAO 2000) estimated the rate of deforestation in Africa during the period 1990–2000 as 0.78 per cent of total forest area a year, representing a yearly loss of some 5.2 million ha. The cause is primarily clearance for agriculture but extraction of timber and fuelwood, fire and overgrazing have also been important factors. Deliberate burning of grasslands is widely practised in many African countries, with 25-50 per cent of land cover in the arid Sudan zone and 60-80 per cent in the humid Guinea zone burned annually (Menaut and others 1991).

Impacts of habitat loss and degradation on biodiversity are difficult to evaluate. However, dramatic contractions in the range of many species have been recorded. For example, in Africa as a whole, elephants declined from about 1 300 000 to 500 000 during the 1980s. Declines were most pronounced in areas characterized by poaching, civil war, high rates of land use change and increases in human population densities (Happold 1995). Central Africa had lost about half of its wildlife habitats by 1986 (McNeely and others 1990). Draining of wetlands for agricultural and urban development, degradation through overgrazing and collection of fuelwood, and pollution through effluent discharge have caused the loss of up to 50 per cent of wetlands in Southern Africa (DEAT 1999) and Western Africa (Armah and Nyarko 1998, Oteng-Yeboah 1998), while some 80 per cent of the Upper Guinea forest has now been cleared (Conservation International 1999).

During 1980–95, the number of recorded extinct plants in Southern Africa increased from 39 to 58, and the number of threatened plants more than doubled (Hilton-Taylor 1996). Recent estimates indicate that more than 700 vertebrate species (see bar chart), around 1 000 species of trees (Hilton-Taylor 2000) and several hundred other plant species (IUCN 1997) are threatened with extinction.

## Protected areas

The main response to loss of natural habitat has been the establishment and extension of protected areas. Overall, approximately 7 per cent of the land area of Africa has been designated as protected. In total, Africa contains 1 254 protected areas (UNEP-WCMC 2001b), including 198 marine protected areas, 50 biosphere reserves, 80 Wetlands of International Importance and 34 World Heritage sites (UNDP, UNEP, World Bank and WRI 2000).

Protected area coverage differs markedly within Africa; for example, a substantially higher proportion of the land area is designated as protected in Southern Africa than in other sub-regions (see graphic). Lack of financial support and weak law enforcement are common problems in African protected areas, resulting in encroachment by human activities and settlements. However, sub-Saharan Africa accounts for 18 per cent of the global mean investment in protected areas (James 1996). Protected areas are being increasingly managed for multiple uses, including tourism and sport hunting.

Some 52 African countries are party to the Convention on Biological Diversity, 48 countries are party to CITES, and 22 are party to CMS. This is reflected at the national level in the development of national action plans and strategies for the environment, biodiversity and conservation. Financial assistance from a range of bilateral and multilateral donors offers opportunities to address the key issues relating to biodiversity and to promote sub-regional cooperation in conservation. Several transfrontier reserves are being established in Southern and Eastern Africa.

During the colonial era, conservation policies were often based on protectionism that ignored the needs of African people, by imposing hunting restrictions and excluding people from reserves. Protected areas fell under this category and have been described as 'fortress conservation' (Adams and Hulme 2001). Policies on wildlife conservation have since changed with communities living adjacent to national parks being considered as partners; a key trend during the past three decades has been the increasing involvement of local people in conservation initiatives. Community-based conservation (CBC) programmes seek to achieve this by allowing people living near protected areas to participate in land management decisions, giving people rights to wildlife resources

and ensuring that local people derive economic benefit from wildlife conservation (Hackel 1999). Some, however, argue that community conservation is no panacea (Adams and Hulme 2001). It has been argued that CBC projects are not primarily established to achieve biodiversity conservation goals but are usually based on the sustainable harvest of living organisms.

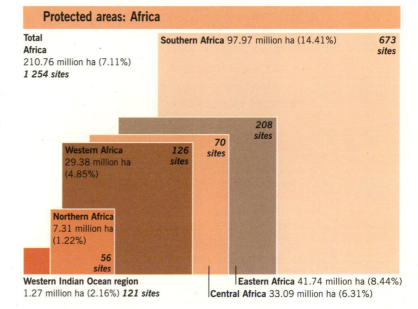

**Protected areas: Africa**

Total Africa 210.76 million ha (7.11%) *1 254 sites*

Southern Africa 97.97 million ha (14.41%) — *673 sites*

*208 sites*

*70 sites*

Western Africa 29.38 million ha (4.85%) — *126 sites*

Northern Africa 7.31 million ha (1.22%) — *56 sites*

Western Indian Ocean region 1.27 million ha (2.16%) *121 sites*

Eastern Africa 41.74 million ha (8.44%)

Central Africa 33.09 million ha (6.31%)

Note: number of protected areas includes those in IUCN categories I-VI

Source: compiled from UNEP-WCMC 2001b

## Impacts of wild harvest

In much of sub-Saharan Africa, the harvest of wildlife for food has a major impact on the populations of many species. Wild food may play an important role in food security for rural people and is also, increasingly, a commercial commodity that is traded nationally and regionally. In many urban areas, meat from wild animals commands a significantly higher price than that from domestic animals, helping to stimulate large-scale harvest. Large quantities of meat are involved: in the Central Africa moist forests alone as much as 1 million tonnes of wildlife (primarily antelope, wild pigs and primates) are killed for food each year. A great deal of the wildlife harvest in Africa is believed to be currently unsustainable and has been implicated in the declines and local extinctions of a range of animal species (Barnett 2000, Oates 1999, Wilkie and Carpenter 1999).

A number of wild plant species are affected by harvest for medicinal purposes. Rural and urban populations all over Africa depend largely on medicinal plants, often collected in the wild, for their health needs. Some species, such as the montane tree *Prunus africana* and the southern African devil's claw *Harpagophytum* species, are also exported in significant quantities. Overharvesting, together with agricultural encroachment and unregulated burning, are believed to be contributing to the decline of many species in the wild. In a survey of medicinal plant use in 17 countries in East and Southern Africa, more than 100 indigenous plant species were identified as conservation or management priorities on a national basis (Marshall 1998).

Over the past 30 years, trade regulation and prohibitions or suspension, mainly through CITES, have been used to control international trade in threatened species with varying degrees of success.

For example, the black rhino, listed in Appendix I of CITES and thereby banned from commercial international trade, is still threatened by illegal hunting, and populations have not recovered to pre-1960s levels. On the other hand, there has been significant recent growth in elephant numbers in Botswana, Namibia and Zimbabwe.

Species re-introduction and plant propagation are also helping. In the Western Indian Ocean islands, successful conservation measures resulted in the Mauritian kestrel population increasing from just four individuals in 1974 to more than 500 in 2000. Similarly, the pink pigeon population now exceeds 350 from a mere 10 wild individuals in 1990 (BirdLife International 2000).

## References: Chapter 2, biodiversity, Africa

Adams, W.M. and Hulme, D. (2001). If community conservation is the answer in Africa, what is the question? *Oryx*. 35, 3, 193-2000

Armah, A.K. and Nyarko, E. (1998). On the faunal biodiversity of the Gulf of Guinea large marine ecosystem. In A. Chidi Ibe and others (eds.), *Integrated Environmental and Living Resource Management in the Gulf of Guinea*. New York, UNIDO, UNDP, NOAA and UNEP

Barnett, R. (2000). *Food for Thought: The Utilization of Wild Meat in Eastern and Southern Africa*. Harare, TRAFFIC East/Southern Africa

BirdLife International (2000). *Threatened Birds of the World*. Barcelona and Cambridge, Lynx Edicions and BirdLife International

Conservation International (1999). *Conservation Priority-Setting For The Upper Guinea Forest Ecosystem, West Africa*. Washington DC, Conservation International

DEAT (1999). *State of the Environment South Africa*. Pretoria, Department of Environmental Affairs and Tourism

FAO (2000). *Forest Resources Assessment Homepage*. Food and Agriculture Organization http://www.fao.org/forestry/fo/fra/main/index.jsp [Geo-2-049]

Hackel, J. D. (1999). Community conservation and the future of Africa's wildlife. *Conservation Biology* 13 (4), 726–34

Happold, D.C.D. (1995). The interactions between humans and mammals in Africa in relation to conservation: a review. *Biodiversity and Conservation*. 4, 395-414

Hilton-Taylor, C. (1996). *Red Data List of Southern African Plants*. Pretoria, National Botanical Institute

IUCN (1997). *1997 IUCN Red List of Threatened Plants*. Gland, IUCN -The World Conservation Union http://www.redlist.org/info/tables/table4b.html [Geo-2-051]

James, A.N. (1996). *National Investments in Biodiversity Conservation*. Gland, IUCN-The World Conservation Union

Marshall, N.T. (1998). *Searching for a Cure: Conservation of Medicinal Wildlife Resources in East and Southern Africa*. Cambridge, TRAFFIC International

McNeely, J.A., Miller, K.R., Reid, W.V., Mittermeier, R.A. and Werner, T.B. (1990). *Conserving the World's Biological Diversity*. Gland and Washington DC, IUCN - The World Conservation Union, World Resources Institute, Conservation International, World Wildlife Fund-US and World Bank

Menaut, J.C., Abbadie, L., Lavenu, F., Loudjani, P. and Podaire, A. (1991). Biomass burning in West African savannas. In J. S. Levine (ed.), *Global Biomass Burning*. Cambridge MA, MIT Press

Mittermeier, R. A., Myers, N., Gil, P.R. and Mittermeier, C.G. (2000). *Hotspots; The Earth's Biologically Richest and Most Endangered Terrestrial Ecoregions*. Washington DC, CEMEX and Conservation International

Oates, J.F. (1999). *Myth and Reality in the Rain Forest: How Conservation Strategies are Failing in West Africa*. Berkeley, California, University of California Press

Oteng-Yeboah, A.A. (1998). Why the emphasis on conservation of biological diversity in the Gulf of Guinea? In A. Chidi Ibe and others (eds.), *Integrated Environmental and Living Resource Management in the Gulf of Guinea*. New York, UNIDO, UNDP, NOAA and UNEP.

Quézel, P., Médail, F., Loisel, R. and Barbero, M. (1999). Biodiversity and conservation of forest species in the Mediterranean Basin. *Unasylva No. 197 - Mediterranean Forests*. 50, 2, 21-28

SADC (2000). *Tourism*. Mbabane, Swaziland, Southern African Development Community

Ucko, P.J. and Dimbleby, G.W. (1969). *The Domestication and Exploitation of Plants and Animals*. London, Gerald Duckworth & Co. Ltd

UNDP, UNEP, World Bank and WRI (2000). *World Resources 2000-2001*. Washington DC, World Resources Institute

UNEP-WCMC (2001a). *GEO3 Endangered Animals Snapshot*. United Nations Environment Programme-World Conservation Monitoring Centre http://valhalla.unep-wcmc.org/isdb/geo3.cfm [Geo-2-052]

UNEP-WCMC (2001b). *GEO3 Protected Areas Snapshot*. United Nations Environment Programme-World Conservation Monitoring Centre cfm http://valhall.unep-wcmc.org/wdbpa/GEO3.cfm [Geo-2-053]

UNESCO and UCO (1998). *Multipurpose Species in Arab African Countries*. Cairo, UNESCO

Wilkie, D.S. and Carpenter, J.F. (1999). Bushmeat hunting in the Congo Basin: an assessment of impacts and options for mitigation. *Biodiversity and Conservation*. 8, 7, 927–55

WWF and IUCN (1994). *Centres of Plant Diversity: A Guide and Strategy for Their Conservation*. Cambridge, IUCN Publications Unit

## Biodiversity: Asia and the Pacific

Species diversity in the region is extremely high. Indonesia is thought to support more species, with more endemic species, than any other country in the world, closely followed by several others, including Australia and China (Groombridge 2000). The tropical waters around the Indo-Australasian archipelago are the world's centre of diversity for a wide range of marine groups, including corals, coral reef fishes and mangroves (Groombridge 2000). Rangelands in western parts of the region, the Tibet plateau and Australia are particularly rich in lizards and snakes adapted to arid conditions (Anderson 1963, Cogger 1992, Zhao and Adler 1993). Many of the rivers and freshwater lakes hold endemic species of fish and aquatic invertebrates (Kottelat and Whitten 1996).

The larger islands are home to a wide range of endemic species while the continental areas often have high species richness together with high rates of endemism. Such 'hot spots' can be identified at a range of scales, from individual mountains to extensive hill ranges. The entire Hindu Kush-Himalayan belt has as many as 25 000 plant species, comprising 10 per cent of the world's flora (Shengji 1998). A few such areas remain relatively unknown: remarkably, even new large mammal species have recently been described in Viet Nam and Laos (see box).

Biological resources have long been of subsistence importance, and have been increasingly exploited for trade. At the global level, around three-quarters of known or suspected species extinctions have occurred on isolated islands (WCMC 1992), many of which were molluscs and birds from the Asia-Pacific region. Some 1 469 vertebrate species in the region are currently considered to be threatened with extinction (see bar chart above). Habitat loss is the principal factor that fragments natural populations and increases their risk of extinction but this often acts in synergy with other pressures such as alien species and unsustainable harvesting (Eder 1996, NBSAP 2000, NIES 1997).

### Alien species

Introduced species have long been recognized as a threat to indigenous species, particularly species endemic to single countries or small islands. For example, native plants on the main islands of New Zealand compete with a range of introduced plants and

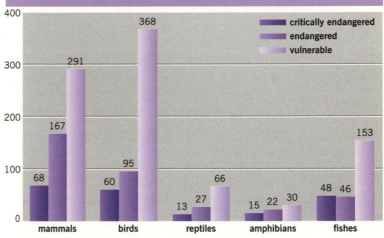

**Numbers of threatened vertebrates: Asia and the Pacific**

are heavily affected by introduced terrestrial mammals, among which brush-tailed possums (from Australia) are a particular threat. Tens of millions of New Zealand dollars were spent annually on possum control in the 1990s to reduce habitat loss and control bovine tuberculosis which can be passed from possums to domestic cattle (MFE 1997). New Zealand birds, reptiles and amphibians are also under pressure from introduced predators such as stoats, rats and cats but much emphasis is now given to invasive species control programmes on small islands, where long-term control may be feasible. The robin *Petroica traversi* was formerly widespread in the Chatham Islands but had been much reduced by the late 19th century. By the 1970s, the species was restricted to Little Mangere Island, where the remaining patch of forest was being destroyed by invasive plants. A conservation programme has now resulted in a population of some 200 birds, all descended from a single pair (MFE 1997).

The brown tree snake *Boiga irregularis* spread widely through Guam, from the 1950s onward, after

Note: critically endangered (extremely high risk of extinction in immediate future); endangered (very high risk of extinction in near future); vulnerable (high risk of extinction in medium-term future)

The data include all globally threatened vertebrate species with country records in the UNEP-WCMC database (UNEP-WCMC 2001a). Marine species recorded by ocean area are not included

---

### New species in Viet Nam

Two large mammals previously unknown to science have been discovered in one small area, the Vu Quang Nature Reserve in Truong Son, Viet Nam. The Vu Quang ox (*Pseudoryx nghetinensis*) was first described in 1993, followed a couple of years later by a giant muntjac deer (*Megamuntiacus vuquangensis*) from the same area. The ox is of particular interest because it does not appear to fit neatly in any of the main bovid groups as currently recognized. It is now known to occur in adjacent parts of Laos. Other new species have also been found, including the world's smallest muntjac deer, the Truong Son muntjac (*Muntiacus truongsonensis*).

*Source: Dung and others 1993*

being accidentally introduced in military aircraft. It has had a severe impact on the native bird fauna, one species of which is believed to be extinct, one is extinct in the wild and one has been assessed as critically endangered. Molluscs in Moorea (Society Islands, French Polynesia) provide a striking example of the potential impacts of introduced species. A carnivorous snail from Florida, *Euglandina rosea*, was introduced to control numbers of the giant African land snail *Achatina fulica* that had become an agricultural pest after itself being introduced to the island. The introduced carnivore subsequently preyed heavily on the endemic native snails in the genus *Partula*, all seven species of which are now extinct in the wild — although they survive in captivity (Wells 1995).

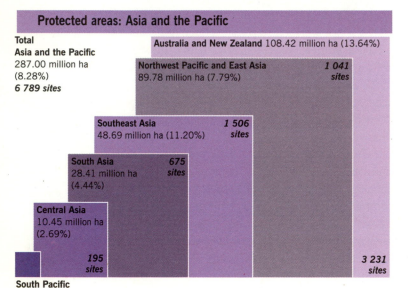

**Protected areas: Asia and the Pacific**

**Total Asia and the Pacific** 287.00 million ha (8.28%) **6 789 sites**

**Australia and New Zealand** 108.42 million ha (13.64%)

**Northwest Pacific and East Asia** 89.78 million ha (7.79%) — *1 041 sites*

**Southeast Asia** 48.69 million ha (11.20%) — *1 506 sites*

**South Asia** 28.41 million ha (4.44%) — *675 sites*

**Central Asia** 10.45 million ha (2.69%) — *195 sites*

*3 231 sites*

**South Pacific** 1.25 million ha (2.31%) *141 sites*

*Note: number of protected areas includes those in IUCN categories I-VI*
*Source: compiled from UNEP-WCMC 2001b*

## Forest loss and degradation

The natural vegetation over much of the region is forest, with grassland, scrub and semi-desert occurring in the more arid regions. Much of the forest cover has been recently cleared by humans so that temperate forests are reduced in China, Japan and New Zealand, while tropical forests are similarly reduced in South Asia and Southeast Asia. More extensive forest cover persists in Borneo, Myanmar and New Guinea (FAO 2000, Groombridge 2000).

Timber and non-timber forest products (rattan, bamboo, resins, waxes, nuts, honey, spices and medicinal plants) provide a livelihood for indigenous people. Timber extraction and clearance for commercial

plantation have caused much of the forest loss, reinforced by increasing human numbers and development pressures.

National policies and plans for management of forest resources exist and there is an increasing amount of plantation forest but serious decline in natural forest cover has occurred in many countries. Indonesia recorded an average annual decrease between 1990 and 2000 of 1.3 million ha (equivalent to a 1.2 per cent annual loss), one of the highest rates of deforestation recorded globally. Malaysia, Myanmar and Thailand all also show major decreases of 237 000, 517 000 and 112 000 ha respectively, with equivalent percentage losses of 1.2, 1.4 and 0.7 (FAO 2000).

This trend is of major concern. If current trends continue, Indonesia's lowland forests will be destroyed by 2005 on Sumatra and by 2010 on Kalimantan (Jepson and others 2001).

## Dams and biodiversity

Although the benefits of dams can be substantial, their negative impacts, including significant biodiversity loss, are common. Analysis by the World Commission on Dams (WCD 2000) has shown that the environmental, hydrological and economic arguments used to support dam construction are often flawed.

Impacts on biodiversity are not well documented but major river systems are drying, groundwater is increasingly overexploited and pollution is a major concern (Fuggle and Smith 2000); as a result biodiversity impacts are likely to be substantial. The Yangtze dolphin *Lipotes vexillifer* and the Chinese alligator *Alligator sinensis* are two large species restricted to the Yangtze basin that are already regarded as globally threatened and are likely to be affected by recent closure of the Three Gorges dam.

A case study of the Pak Mun dam in northeast Thailand reports failures in the decision-making process (Amornsakchai and others 2000). The fish yield from the reservoir was far below the level predicted in the 1981 impact assessment and yields from the original free-flowing river were underestimated. Some 50 fish species dependent on rapids have disappeared and migratory fishes have declined; these biodiversity losses have had serious impacts on households that depend on fishing. The lack of evaluation of the likely impacts on fishes and fisheries is identified as a critical omission from the original impact study (Amornsakchai and others 2000).

More comprehensive impact assessment, better evaluation of biodiversity impacts and greater emphasis on mitigation and remedial measures will be needed for future dams. The work by the World Commission on Dams may provide an opportunity for better-informed debate.

## Response measures

In response to deteriorating biodiversity, many countries are party to international agreements. All except Afghanistan, Brunei Darussalam and Thailand are party to the Convention on Biological Diversity (CBD). The CBD specifies a framework of measures at the national level for the conservation of biodiversity and many countries have prepared National Biodiversity Strategy and Action Plans and submitted National Reports. Most countries are party to CITES and the Ramsar Convention on Wetlands.

National responses aimed at conserving biodiversity have been variable in effectiveness, with

### Conservation in Nepal

The National Parks and Wildlife Conservation Act was implemented in Nepal in 1973, and its amendment in 1993 has provided for the involvement of local people in species conservation. Buffer zone management was introduced in 1996 with the Buffer Zone Management Rules which allow local people to access ecosystem resources in protected zones. Under the Forest Act 1992, 13 plant species have been protected. The government has also given legal protection status to 26 species of mammals, 9 species of birds and 3 species of reptiles. A total of 17 protected areas (eight national parks, four wildlife reserves, one hunting reserve and four conservation areas) constitute about 17 per cent of the total area in the country (MOPE 2000).

many initiatives suffering from a lack of data and common understanding of ecological systems. Protected areas have been set up in different countries but they tend to be geographically limited and disconnected. The proportion of protected area to total area in most countries is lower than the 10 per cent norm recommended by IUCN.

## References: Chapter 2, biodiversity, Asia and the Pacific

Amornsakchai, S., Annez, P., Vongvisessomjai, S., Choowaew, S., Thailand Development Research Institute, Kunurat, P., Nippanon, J., Schouten, R., Sripapatrprasite, P., Vaddhanaphuti, C., Vidthayanon, C., Wirojanagud, W. and Watana, E. (2000). *Pak Mun Dam, Mekong River Basin, Thailand. A WCD Case Study*. Cape Town, World Commission on Dams http://www.dams.org/studies/th/th_exec.htm [Geo-2-054]

Anderson, S.C. (1963). Amphibians and reptiles from Iran. *Proceedings of the California Academy of Sciences*. 31, 16, 417–98

Cogger, H. (1992). *Reptiles and Amphibians of Australia*. Ithaca NY, Reed Books and Cornell University Press

Dung, Vu Van, Pham Mong Giao, Nguyen Ngoc Chinh, Do Thuoc, P. Arctander and J. Mackinnon (1993). A new species of living bovid from Viet Nam. *Nature*, 363, 443–45

Eder, N. (1996). *Poisoned Prosperity: Development, Modernization and Environment in South Korea*. Armonk NY, M.E. Sharpe, Inc

FAO (2000). *Forest Resources Assessment Homepage*. Food and Agriculture Organization http://www.fao.org/forestry/fo/fra/main/index.jsp [Geo-2-055]

Fuggle, R., Smith, W.T., Hydrosult Canada Inc. and Agrodev Canada Inc. (2000). *Large Dams in Water and Energy Resource Development in The People's Republic of China (PRC)*. Cape Town, World Commission on Dams http://www.dams.org/studies/cn/cn_exec.htm [Geo-2-056]

Groombridge, B. and Jenkins, M.D. (2000). *Global Biodiversity: Earth's Living Resources in the 21st Century*. Cambridge, The World Conservation Press

Jepson, P., Jarvie, J.K., MacKinnon, K. and Monk, K.A. (2001). The end for Indonesia's lowland forests? *Science*. 292, 5518, 859–61

Kottelat, M. and Whitten, T. (1996). *Freshwater Biodiversity in Asia*. World Bank Technical Paper. 343, Washington DC, World Bank

MFE (1997). *New Zealand: The State of New Zealand's Environment 1997*. Wellington, Ministry for the Environment of New Zealand

MOPE (2000). *State of Nepal's Environment*. Kathmandu, Ministry of Population and Environment, His Majesty's Government of Nepal

NBSAP (2000). *First National Report for the Convention on Biological Diversity*. Tehran, National Biodiversity Strategy and Action Plan Secretariat http://www.biodiv.org/doc/world/ir/ir-nr-01-en.pdf [Geo-2-058]

NIES (1997). *Research Report for the Establishment of a State Information Database in East Asia*. Ibaraki, Japan, National Institute for Environmental Studies

Shengji, P. (1998). Biodiversity in the Hindu Kush Himalayas. *ICIMOD Newsletter*. 31, Autumn 1998

UNEP-WCMC (2001a). *GEO3 Endangered Animals Snapshot*. United Nations Environment Programme-World Conservation Monitoring Centre http://valhalla.unep-wcmc.org/isdb/geo3.cfm [Geo-2-059]

UNEP-WCMC (2001b). *GEO3 Protected Areas Snapshot*. United Nations Environment Programme-World Conservation Monitoring Centre http://valhalla.unep-wcmc.org/wdbpa/GEO3.cfm [Geo-2-060]

WCD (2000). *Dams and Development: A New Framework for Decision-Making. The Report of the World Commission on Dams*. London, Earthscan http://www.damsreport.org/wcd_overview.htm [Geo-2-061]

WCMC (1992). *Global Biodiversity: Status of the Earth's Living Resources*. London, Chapman and Hall

Wells, S. (1995). The extinction of endemic snails (genus Partula) in French Polynesia: is captive breeding the only solution? In E. A. Kay (ed.), *The Conservation Biology of Molluscs. IUCN Species Survival Commission Occasional Paper No. 9*. Gland, IUCN - The World Conservation Union

Zhao, E., and Adler, K. (1993). *Herpetology of China*. Contributions to Herpetology. 10, St Louis, Missouri, Society for the Study of Amphibians and Reptiles

## Biodiversity: Europe

Europe is home to a wide variety of ecosystems, ranging from the Atlantic coast to the Russian steppes, and from the boreal forest and tundra of Scandinavia to Mediterranean forests and shrubland (EEA 2001). Europe is also an important crossroads for large populations of migratory species shared with Africa, West Asia and North America.

Agricultural land covers some 45 per cent of Europe and most natural habitats are therefore restricted in extent. The impact of agriculture on biodiversity is thus a key issue (Hoffmann 2000). The genetic modification of organisms for agriculture has also emerged as an important issue relating to biodiversity.

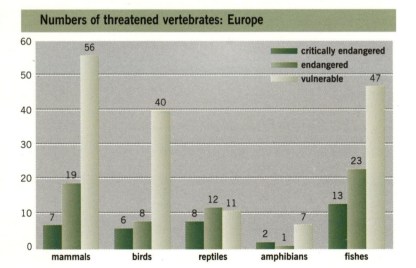

### Numbers of threatened vertebrates: Europe

Note: critically endangered (extremely high risk of extinction in immediate future); endangered (very high risk of extinction in near future); vulnerable (high risk of extinction in medium-term future)

The data include all globally threatened vertebrate species with country records in the UNEP-WCMC database (UNEP-WCMC 2001a). Marine species recorded by ocean area are not included

The landscape has been significantly modified by human activities, including deforestation, agriculture, drainage of wetlands, modifications to coastlines and river courses, mining, road construction and urban development (EEA 2001). As a result, natural habitats have been reduced in size and fragmented, and are therefore less able to support wildlife. Habitats such as lowland forests and wetlands have undergone particularly large declines. Relatively pristine areas remain in some Nordic and Eastern European countries (EEA 2001).

Many large mammals such as the polar bear (*Ursus arctos*), wolf (*Canis lupus*), lynx (*Lynx lynx*) and bison (*Bison bison bonasus*) are now restricted to small remnants of their original habitat while others such as the tarpan (*Equus caballus*) and the saiga

(*Saiga tatarica*) have become extinct (EEA 2001). Some 260 vertebrate species are now considered to be threatened with extinction in Europe (see bar chart). Other species, such as the lark (*Alauda arvensis*) and the hare (*Lepus europaeus*) are directly associated with agricultural landscapes, and have therefore benefited from human activities. Similarly, species such as the seagull (*Larus* spp.) and black kite (*Milvus migrans*) have increased in abundance due to growth in urban waste sites (EEA 2001).

### Agricultural intensification

The direct impacts of agriculture include effects on water quality, land drainage, soil erosion, toxic effects of fertilizers and biocides, and the destruction, degradation and fragmentation of habitat (Hoffmann 2000). This has had a substantial negative impact on biodiversity, and population declines and range contractions have been found to be significantly greater in countries with more intensive agriculture (Donald, Green and Heath 2001). In the United Kingdom, 26 species of farmland birds declined significantly during 1968–95, primarily as a result of agricultural intensification (Siriwardena and others 1998).

Intensive agriculture also often leads to the eutrophication of freshwater habitats, resulting in deoxygenation of water, production of toxins and a general decline in wildlife conservation value (EEA 2001). Some 46 per cent of Ramsar lake sites in Europe have suffered a decline in water quality, largely as a result of eutrophication (EEA 2001). Wetland habitats have also been affected by land reclamation for agriculture. In Spain alone, more than 60 per cent of all inland freshwater wetlands disappeared during a 25-year period (Casado and others 1992).

Nutrient enrichment also has a significant impact on marine ecosystems, particularly in areas such as the Caspian Sea. Such pollution has increased the frequency of algal blooms in the Adriatic, where they foul fishing gear and beaches, and in the North Sea where in 1988 they caused massive mortalities of farmed salmonid fish (EEA 2001).

Key trends over the past three decades include the agricultural 'improvement' of low-intensity farmland, which has led to substantial and mostly irreversible loss of habitats through drainage, fertilization and increased stocking densities (Hoffmann 2000). In addition, hedgerows, field verges and grass tracks have been lost as a result of increased field sizes and mechanization. During the 1970s and 1980s, some 27 200 km of hedgerows were lost annually in England and Wales (Barr and others 1993).

As a result of agricultural mechanization, much of the remaining area of scrub and grassland habitat is now restricted to ground of low agricultural value, such as steep slopes and poor soils (EEA 2001). Agricultural intensification has also resulted in the loss of fallow land and stubble, important habitats for wildlife, particularly birds.

The importance of agriculture to biodiversity has been recognized in several policy responses. A European Commission Biodiversity Action Plan for Agriculture has been developed as part of EC commitments to the Convention for Biological Diversity (CBD) through the 1998 Biodiversity Strategy (Hoffmann 2000). The plan is designed to help integrate biodiversity targets into relevant policy sectors. Strategic questions relating to agricultural policy are mainly addressed within the Common Agricultural Policy (CAP) and a key element of the Biodiversity Strategy is therefore to incorporate biodiversity objectives into CAP (Hoffmann 2000).

In Western Europe, more than 22 million ha of agricultural land are covered by some form of agreement to maintain biodiversity and landscapes (EEA 2000). This exceeds the target set in the EU's fifth environmental action programme. However, the extent varies — from more than 60 per cent of farms in Austria, Finland and Sweden, to 7 per cent or less in Belgium, Greece, Italy and Spain (EEA 2000). The environmental performance of these schemes is open to doubt since many lack precise objectives and have no monitoring provisions (BirdLife International 1995).

Since the early 1980s, grassland and heathland habitats have benefited from a shift in agricultural policies. For example, in Germany and Italy the reform of EU policy has released more than 300 000 ha of arable land for conversion to grassland in lowland areas, as part of the 'set-aside' programme. While initially welcomed as an opportunity to increase the ecological values of such areas, 'set-aside' measures can also have negative results — causing people to abandon traditional farming systems and adopt inappropriate forms of forestry or afforestation (Baldock and Long 1987).

## Biodiversity protection measures

Only 5 per cent of the land area of Europe is currently designated as a protected area (see graphic). The major policy instruments relating to habitat protection are Agenda 2000, Natura 2000, the Emerald Network and the Pan-European Ecological Network. With these it is planned to create a coherent European ecological network of natural and semi-natural habitats and provide or restore corridors between existing protected areas throughout the region.

Agenda 2000 is an action programme designed to strengthen EU policies. The programme will promote

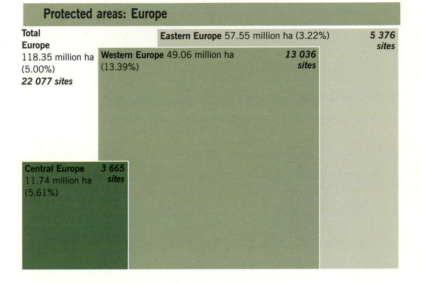

**Protected areas: Europe**

Total Europe 118.35 million ha (5.00%) 22 077 sites

Eastern Europe 57.55 million ha (3.22%) 5 376 sites

Western Europe 49.06 million ha (13.39%) 13 036 sites

Central Europe 11.74 million ha (5.61%) 3 665 sites

new interrelationships between rural areas and biodiversity, involving agri-environmental measures, structural funds, Less Favoured Area measures, afforestation measures, and so on.

In the EU, the Natura 2000 Network (Hoffmann 2000) is expected to become operational within a few years, with more than 10 per cent of EU territory designated for nature conservation purposes. For non-EU countries a less binding programme (the Emerald Network) was set up recently under the Bern Convention. Some eastern European countries have already established Natura 2000 networks.

These developments are key elements in Europe's contribution to the CBD. EU strategy aims to complement biodiversity initiatives at the national level through a series of action plans to integrate biodiversity into other sectoral policies and programmes. Similarly, national biodiversity action plans are being developed throughout much of Europe.

*Note: number of protected areas includes those in IUCN categories I-VI*

*Source: compiled from UNEP-WCMC 2001b*

**Financial support for biodiversity in Central and Eastern Europe**

Economic transition in Eastern Europe has caused biodiversity funding to dry up. In Bulgaria, for example, domestic financing collapsed in the mid-1990s and up to 90 per cent of all biodiversity financing now comes from foreign sources — the EU and bilateral funds, with €4-6 million provided annually by the Netherlands alone; Germany and Switzerland are also major contributors. However, foreign aid rarely exceeds 10-15 per cent of the required funding. Some popular parks in Central Europe are partially financed by park fees but these never cover more than 50 per cent of the costs of park maintenance (OECD 1999).

Countries in Central and Eastern Europe still possess a wealth of well-preserved landscapes, ecosystems and species that are rare or already extinct in Western Europe. Most protected areas in these areas had been designated by the end of the 1970s, often surrounded by large buffer zones and connected by habitat corridors linking sites. However, with economic transition, the system of nature protection came under intense pressure as state financing declined and it is now in jeopardy (see box).

## Genetically modified organisms

Genetically modified organism (GMO) technology could play an important role in increasing agricultural production in Europe. However, the release of GMOs into the environment remains a subject of controversy. Experimental releases of GM crops have been conducted in both Western and Eastern Europe but experience with actual cultivation is still limited.

In Western Europe, the public is generally sceptical about GM foods and organisms. There is strong support for labelling, public consultation and more comprehensive regulation and monitoring. Apart from food safety, concerns have also been expressed about adverse effects on the environment and biodiversity; for example, genetic transfers with native species. While developers of GMOs see a huge market opportunity, food producers are under pressure from consumers who wish to avoid GMOs.

Efforts in Western Europe are currently aiming to inform, involve and consult the public about GMOs, in order to reach a consensus on regulation. In Eastern Europe some NGOs are trying to bring the issue into the open and a regional biosafety process, started in 1995 in Hungary, is also furthering discussion. The European Commission has proposed new legislation to harmonize action and to facilitate agreement on marketing authorization (EC 1998). Current European legislation is consistent with the Biosafety Protocol that was adopted in January 2000 as part of the CBD.

The potential risks of GMOs to biodiversity are the subject of ongoing research. Public awareness also needs to be raised to ensure a well-informed and balanced multi-stakeholder dialogue and decision process.

## References: Chapter 2, biodiversity, Europe

Baldock, D. and Long, T. (1987). *Environment under Pressure: the Influence of the CAP on Spain and Portugal and the IMPs in France, Greece and Italy. A report to WWF*. London, Institute for European Environmental Policy

Barr, C., Bunce, R., Clark, R., Fuller, R., Furse, M., Gillespie, M., Groom, G., Hallam, C., Horning, M., Howard, D. and Ness, M. (1993). *Countryside Survey 1993: Main Report*. London, Department of the Environment

BirdLife International (1995). *The Structural Funds and Biodiversity Conservation: Summary*. Brussels, BirdLife International European Community Office

Casado, S., Florin, M., Molla, S. and Montes, C. (1992). Current status of Spanish wetlands. In M. Finlayson and others (eds.), *Managing Mediterranean Wetlands and their Birds. Wetlands International Publication No 20*. Wageningen, Wetlands International

Donald, P.F., Green, R.E. and Heath, M.F. (2001). Agricultural intensification and the collapse of Europe's farmland bird populations. *Proceedings of The Royal Society of London Series B - Biological Sciences*. 268, 1462, 25-29

EC (1998). *Proposal for a Directive of the European Parliament and of the Council amending Council Directive 90/220 on the Deliberate Release into the Environment of Genetically Modified Organisms*. Brussels, European Commission

EEA (1999). *Environment in the European Union at the Turn of the Century*. Copenhagen, European Environment Agency

EEA (2000). *Environmental Signals 2000*. Environmental Assessment Report. 6, Copenhagen, European Environment Agency

EEA (2001). *Europe's Environment: The Dobris Assessment*. European Environment Agency http://reports.eea.eu.int/92-826-5409-5/en/page002new.html [Geo-2-062]

Hoffmann, L.B. (2000). *CIP: Stimulating positive linkages between biodiversity and agriculture. Recommendations for the EC-Agricultural Action Plan for biodiversity*. Tilburg, European Centre for Nature Conservation

OECD (1999). *Environment in the Transition to a Market Economy: Progress in Central and Eastern Europe and the New Independent States*. Paris, OECD Centre for Cooperation with Non-Members

Siriwardena, G.M., Baillie, S.R., Buckland, S.T., Fewster, R.M., Marchant, J.H. and Wilson, J.D. (1998). Trends in the abundance of farmland birds: a quantitative comparison of smoothed Common Birds Census indices. *Journal of Applied Ecology*. 35, 1, 24-43

UNEP-WCMC (2001a). *GEO3 Endangered Animals Snapshot*. United Nations Environment Programme-World Conservation Monitoring Centre http://valhalla.unep-wcmc.org/isdb/geo3.cfm [Geo-2-064]

UNEP-WCMC (2001b). *GEO3 Protected Areas Snapshot*. United Nations Environment Programme-World Conservation Monitoring Centre http://valhalla.unep-wcmc.org/wdbpa/GEO3.cfm [Geo-2-065]

## Biodiversity: Latin America and the Caribbean

The region contains a wide variety of ecosystem types. Tropical moist and dry broadleaf forests cover 43 per cent of the territory; grasslands and savannas 40.5 per cent; deserts and scrub 11 per cent; temperate forests and tropical and sub-tropical coniferous forests 5 per cent; and mangroves the remaining 0.5 per cent (Dinerstein and others 1995). The region's rivers and lake ecosystems and the marine ecosystems of the Pacific and Atlantic coasts are also productive habitats with high diversity of species. The Caribbean contains 7 per cent of the world's coral reefs (about 20 000 km$^2$) with a great array of marine biodiversity (UNEP 2001).

Seven of the world's 25 biologically richest terrestrial ecoregions are found in the region, containing between them more than 46 000 vascular plant, 1 597 amphibian, 1 208 reptile, 1 267 bird and 575 mammal species (Mittermeier, Myers and Mittermeier 1999, Myers and others 2000).

### Habitat loss and degradation

As a result of habitat conversion and loss, 31 of the 178 ecoregions in the region are in a critical state of conservation, 51 are endangered and 55 are vulnerable (Dinerstein and others 1995). Most endangered ecoregions are found in the northern and central Andes, Central America, the steppe and winter rainfall areas of the southern cone, the Cerrado and other dry forests south of the Amazon basin, and the Caribbean (Dinerstein and others 1995). Myers and others (2000) located 7 of the world's 25 hot spots (where exceptional concentrations of endemic species are undergoing exceptional loss of habitat) in the region.

The Neotropics possess 6 of the 12 countries in the world where globally threatened bird species are concentrated, with Brazil and Colombia having the highest numbers in this category (BirdLife International 2000). Together, Brazil, Colombia, Peru and Mexico account for more than 75 per cent of threatened bird species in the Americas (BirdLife International 2000).

Cloud forests and other humid montane forests have been identified as one of the most threatened habitat types in the region. They are found where persistent cloud cover is in contact with the mountainside, at altitudes of 1 000–3 000 metres and play a critical role in the provision of clean water supplies to human populations in the lowlands. Humid montane forests also harbour the wild relatives and gene pools of many New World crops, including potatoes, maize and beans (Debouck and Libros Ferla 1995).

The principal pressures on cloud forests are clearance for subsistence and commercial agriculture by rural communities, and in some regions for plantations of narcotics. Human population growth and poverty drive these processes but the construction of roads and increased links to commercial markets has also stimulated the production of cash crops. Other major pressures include deforestation for cattle

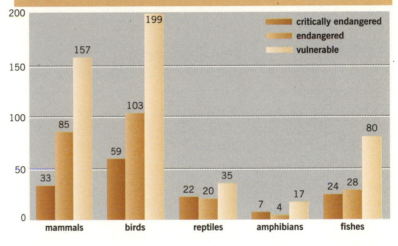

**Numbers of threatened vertebrates: Latin America and the Caribbean**

legend: critically endangered / endangered / vulnerable

mammals: 33, 85, 157
birds: 59, 103, 199
reptiles: 22, 20, 35
amphibians: 7, 4, 17
fishes: 24, 28, 80

ranching, which in the past has often been supported by government policies.

Lowland tropical rainforests have been the focus of particular conservation concern, being the habitat with the highest species richness and with continuing conversion of major areas to other land uses. The Brazilian Amazon is the largest tropical rainforest in the world, which once had a forested area of 4 million km$^2$. By 1998, 86.3 per cent of this area remained, with 377 200 km$^2$ cleared during the preceding 20 years (Fearnside 1999). The mean rate of forest clearing accelerated in the 1990s, and the total area affected by fragmentation, clearing and edge effects is now estimated to comprise one-third of the Brazilian Amazon (Laurance 1998).

Deforestation in the Brazilian Amazon is driven by several processes. A major pressure is the ten-fold population growth in the region since 1960 (Goodman and Hall 1990). In addition, industrial logging and

*Note: critically endangered (extremely high risk of extinction in immediate future); endangered (very high risk of extinction in near future); vulnerable (high risk of extinction in medium-term future)*

*The data include all globally threatened vertebrate species with country records in the UNEP-WCMC database (UNEP-WCMC 2001a). Marine species recorded by ocean area are not included*

mining and their associated networks of roads, which make accessible new areas of forest to colonizers and ranchers, have been major factors in deforestation. Some 6 per cent of the region falls within the strictly protected category. Major efforts have been made in the field of timber certification and forest preservation to reverse the loss of biodiversity (UNEP-ECLAC 2001). Human-ignited fires have also become widespread, especially in logged and fragmented areas (Laurance 1998).

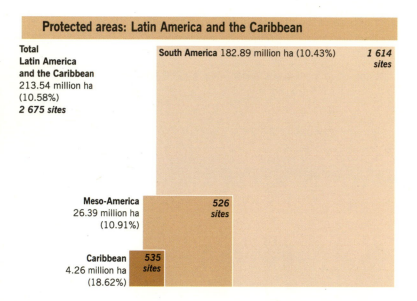

**Protected areas: Latin America and the Caribbean**

Total Latin America and the Caribbean 213.54 million ha (10.58%) 2 675 sites

South America 182.89 million ha (10.43%) 1 614 sites

Meso-America 26.39 million ha (10.91%) 526 sites

Caribbean 4.26 million ha (18.62%) 535 sites

Note: number of protected areas includes those in IUCN categories I-VI

Source: compiled from UNEP-WCMC 2001b

The forests of eastern coastal Brazil are considered among the most endangered habitats on earth and have been given highest priority for biodiversity conservation (Bibby and others 1992). They contain 7 000 endemic plants and 779 endemic vertebrates — 2.7 and 2.1 per cent of the global total, respectively (Myers and others 2000). In the Bahia region, only 0.4 per cent of continuous forest cover remains of the original forest area of 215 436 km$^2$ (Mendonça and others 1994). Threats arise from coastal development and uncontrolled logging, agriculture and charcoal production.

Overall, more than 10 per cent of the region is currently protected (see graphic). In addition, the attractiveness of the cloud forests and recognition of their values by concerned individuals has led to the creation of many private forest reserves in the region, often linked to scientific research programmes and ecotourism ventures. A related trend in the 1990s has been the creation of community-managed montane forest reserves.

A new approach to promoting montane forest conservation in the region is to compensate forest owners for the environmental services their forests provide to society, often financed by the collection of a small surcharge on the users of water originating in the forests. Such schemes are being considered in several Latin American countries and have been tested in Costa Rica (Campos and Calvo 2000). Many forest conservation initiatives have been developed in the Amazon, including land-use planning, the establishment of protected areas linked by corridors and extractive and Amerindian reserves. The largest of these is the Pilot Programme to Conserve the Brazilian Rainforest, with support from the G-7 nations. However, further major infrastructure, industrial agriculture, mining and logging projects are currently planned for the Amazon (Laurance and others 2001).

The CBD has played an important role in terms of the response to biodiversity loss. While some countries have incorporated the CBD's objectives in general legislation, others have done so by means of sectoral laws. The former group includes Brazil, Colombia, Costa Rica, Peru and Venezuela. For example, Brazil established a National Programme on Biological Diversity in 1994 together with an accompanying project for the conservation and sustainable use of Brazilian biological diversity (PROBIO), identifying priority conservation areas and actions through a series of assessments. In Peru, the Law for the Conservation and Sustainable Use of Biological Diversity, which covers most CBD commitments, entered into force in 1997. It is expected that the nine Caribbean countries now preparing national strategies on biodiversity will implement the CBD by means of legislation, development of institutional mechanisms and by providing adequate resources (UNEP 2000). Countries that are modifying their sectoral laws include Cuba, Honduras, Mexico, Nicaragua and Panama. However, legislation for the implementation of the CBD has often been developed without reference to other biodiversity-related conventions such as CITES, the Convention on Migratory Species and Ramsar.

National funding programmes such as the Mexican Fund for Nature Conservation have been established as part of national efforts to implement the CBD. Additional sources of funding include organizations such as the World Bank and the Inter-American Development Bank, together with other international agencies, NGOs and bilateral cooperation agencies.

Between 1988 and 1999, the World Bank Group approved 74 biodiversity projects in the region which were declared consistent with the goals and objectives of the CBD. A substantial amount (more than US$700 million) has been distributed among regional efforts to conserve biodiversity, especially since 1995. As expected, most of the resources went to the largest countries. Brazil alone received 56 per cent of the total but this benefit has not been equally distributed among ecosystems, the majority going to the Amazon and Atlantic rainforests.

## Unsustainable harvesting and illegal trade

Illegal trade in plants and animals is one of the greatest threats to biodiversity in many countries including Brazil, Colombia, Mexico and Peru. It is difficult to measure the extent of this illegal trade and its impact on lesser-known species. Estimates suggest that Brazil accounts for 10 per cent of the global wildlife trade, which is valued at approximately US$10 000 million per year. Despite ongoing efforts, including development and implementation of national strategies to control illegal trafficking in countries such as Colombia, police records on seizures confirm that illegal trade of flora and fauna remains a widespread problem (Government of Colombia 2000, RENCTAS 2000).

National governments are responding to this issue in a number of ways. For example in Colombia, the sale of some wild animals (both live and as animal products) is permitted for domestic and international markets. There are 50 private establishments with legal authorization to capture caiman (*Caiman crocodiles*), iguana (*Iguana iguana*), boa (*Boa constrictor*), black tegu (*Tupinambis nigropunctatus*) and capybara (*Hydro chaeris hidrochaeris*) for processing and marketing. As a result, in the year 2000, 739 000 caimans, 232 000 iguanas, 3 530 boas, 2 700 black tegu and 10 000 capybaras were captured for market in accordance with national regulations and the recommendations of CITES.

### References: Chapter 2, biodiversity, Latin America and the Caribbean

Bibby, C. J., Collar, N. J., Crosby, M. J., Heath, M. F., Imboden, C., Johnson, T. H., Long, A. J., Stattersfield, A. J. and Thirgood, S. J. (1992). *Putting Biodiversity on the Map: Priority Areas for Global Conservation*. Cambridge, International Council for Bird Preservation

BirdLife International (2000). *Threatened Birds of the World*. Barcelona and Cambridge, Lynx Edicions and BirdLife International

Campos, J.J. and Calvo, J.C. (2000). Compensation for environmental services from mountain forests. In M. Agenda (ed.), *Mountains of the World: Mountain Forests and Sustainable Development*. Berne, Mountain Forum

Debouck, D.G and Libros Ferla, D. (1995). Neotropical montane forests: a fragile home of genetic resources of wild relatives of New World crops. In S.P. Churchill and others (eds.), *Biodiversity and Conservation of Neoptropical Montane Forests*. New York, New York Botanical Garden

Dinerstein, E., Olson, D., Graham, D., Webster, A., Primm, S., Bookbinder, M. and Ledec, G. (1995). *A Conservation Assessment of the Terrestrial Ecoregions of Latin America and the Caribbean*. Washington DC, World Bank

Fearnside, P. M. (1999). Biodiversity as an environmental service in Brazil's Amazonian forests: risks, value and conservation. *Environmental Conservation*. 26, 4, 305–21

Goodman, G. and Hall, A. (1990). *The Future of Amazonia: Destruction or Sustainable Development?* London, Macmillan

Government of Colombia (2000). *El Comercio Ilegal de Especes*. Ministerio del Medio Ambiente de Colombia http://www.minambiente.gov.co./biogeo/menu/biodiversidad/especies/comercioilegal.htm [Geo-2-092]

Laurance, W.F. (1998). A crisis in the making: responses of Amazonian forests to land use and climate change. *Trends in Ecology and Evolution*. 13, 411–15

Laurance, W.F., Cochrane, M.A., Bergen, S., Fearnside, P.M., Delamonica, P., Barber, C., D'Angelo, S. and Fernandes, T. (2001). Environment - The future of the Brazilian Amazon. *Science*. 291, 438–39

Mendonça, J. R., de Carvalho, A. M., Mattos Silva, L. A. and Thomas, W. W. (1994). *45 Anos de Desmatamento no Sul da Bahia, Remanescentes da Mata Atlântica - 1945, 1960, 1974, 1990*. Ilhéus, Bahia, Projeto Mata Atlântica Nordeste, CEPEC

Mittermeier, R.A., Myers, N. and Mittermeier, C.G. (1999). *Hotspots. Earth's Biologically Richest and Most Endangered Terrestrial Ecoregions*. Mexico City, CEMEX and Conservation International

Myers, N., Mittermeier, R.A., Mittermeier, C.G., Da Fonseca, G.A.B. and Kent, J. (2000). Biodiversity hotspots for conservation priorities. *Nature*. 403, 853–58

RENCTAS (2000). *Data about the Traffic: Traffic Numbers*. Instituto Brasileiro do Meio Ambiente e dos Recursos Naturais Renováveis - IBAMA (Brazilian Institute for Environment and Renewable Natural Resources) http://www.renctas.org.br/index.html [Geo-2-095]

UNEP (2000). *GEO Latin America and the Caribbean Environment Outlook*. Mexico City, UNEP Regional Office for Latin America and the Caribbean

UNEP (2001). *World Atlas of Coral Reefs*. Nairobi, United Nations Environment Programme

UNEP-ECLAC (2001). *The Sustainability of Development in Latin America and the Caribbean: challenges and opportunities*. Santiago, UNEP-ECLAC

UNEP-WCMC (2001a). *GEO3 Endangered Animals Snapshot*. United Nations Environment Programme-World Conservation Monitoring Centre http://valhalla.unep-wcmc.org/isdb/geo3.cfm, 10 October 2001 [Geo-2-094]

UNEP-WCMC (2001b). *GEO3 Protected Areas Snapshot*. United Nations Environment Programme-World Conservation Monitoring Centre http://valhalla.unep-wcmc.org/wdbpa/GEO3.cfm [Geo-2-096]

## Biodiversity: North America

Habitat destruction and degradation is the most pervasive threat to biodiversity in the region (Wilcove and others 2000). North American wetlands have high biological productivity, providing critical habitats for many species and essential ecological services such as taking up floodwaters and protecting water quality by filtering pollutants (Schmid 2000). Wetland protection is therefore a priority issue for biodiversity conservation in North America. Another key issue is the threat that non-native species pose to native species through predation, competition, parasitism and hybridization.

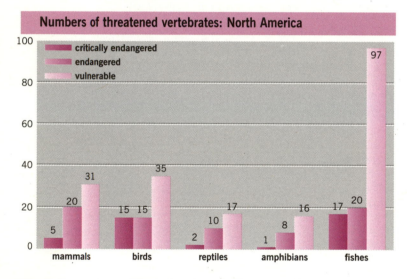

**Numbers of threatened vertebrates: North America**

Note: critically endangered (extremely high risk of extinction in immediate future); endangered (very high risk of extinction in near future); vulnerable (high risk of extinction in medium-term future)

The data include all globally threatened vertebrate species with country records in the UNEP-WCMC database (UNEP-WCMC 2001a). Marine species recorded by ocean area are not included

North America contains many different ecosystems, with biodiversity increasing along a north-south gradient and the Hawaiian Islands containing the highest diversity of species. North America contains a large percentage of the world's wetlands with Canada holding about 24 per cent, accounting for about 16 per cent of its landscape (NRC 2001). Wetlands cover about 264 million ha of North America.

According to Canada's endangered species list, as of May 2001 a total of 352 species were at risk of imminent or eventual extinction (endangered, threatened or of special concern) while in the United States 1 231 species were listed as endangered or threatened (Alonso and others 2001, COSEWIC 2001). Some 309 vertebrate species are threatened with extinction in the region (see bar chart).

To safeguard biological diversity, North America has set aside protected areas. More than 14 per cent of the region's land area is now protected, with 4 521

protected sites covering an area of some 264 million ha (UNEP-WCMC 2001b). Canada has signed and ratified the Convention on Biological Diversity (CBD) and continues to work towards introducing a federal Species At Risk Act. The United States is not yet party to the CBD but has a strong Endangered Species Act. The latter has been used effectively by NGOs to protect substantial areas of habitat for threatened species.

## Wetlands

Wetlands provide food and habitat for about one-third of bird species in the United States and more than 200 species in Canada. They are also home to some 5 000 plant species and 190 kinds of amphibians in the United States and 50 species of mammals and 45 species of waterfowl in Canada. About one-third of North America's threatened and endangered species live in wetlands (NRC 2001).

Prior to the 1970s, government programmes encouraged wetland drainage and filling to allow conversion to agriculture, settlements and industrial sites (US EPA 1997). As a result, North America, excluding Alaska and Canada's undeveloped northern regions, lost more than one-half of its original wetland habitat (EC 1999) with agricultural expansion responsible for between 85 and 87 per cent of the losses (NRC 2001). Since the 1980s, wetland losses have slowed considerably. Changes in agricultural policies, particularly improvements in hydrological conditions and cooperative efforts to conserve wetlands for waterfowl were factors in these achievements (NAWMP 1998). Although more than

### wetlands and waterfowl

Cooperation between governments and NGOs to restore and improve wetlands across North America is an ongoing success story. Ducks Unlimited, a private organization originally established to preserve waterfowl for hunters, began a cooperative programme between its branches in Canada, Mexico and the United States in the 1990s that has improved more than 3.8 million ha of wetlands (Ducks Unlimited 2000).

Canada and the United States signed the North American Waterfowl Management Plan (NAWMP) in 1986 and Mexico joined in 1994. NAWMP is a partnership between government, NGOs, the private sector and landowners for improving wetlands. During 1988–93, more than 850 000 ha of wetlands and associated habitats were protected in Canada alone through NAWMP (NRC 2001).

250 000 ha of wetlands were lost in the United Sates between 1986 and 1997, this was an 80 per cent reduction from the previous decade (US FWS 2000).

At the global level, both countries are parties to the Ramsar Convention on Wetlands of International Importance. North America currently has 53 Wetlands of International Importance — 36 in Canada and 17 in the United States (Ramsar 2000).

More than 70 per cent of Canada's wetland resources are now covered by federal and provincial wetland policies and about 15 US states regulate inland wetlands (NRC 2001, Schmid 2000). In the United States, federal subsidies that allowed wetlands to be converted to agriculture ceased in 1985 and a Wetland Plan was issued in 1993 to make wetland regulation more fair, flexible and effective (US EPA 1999, Schmid 2000). Although past US government authority over wetlands has been fragmented and inconsistent, plans for the restoration of the Florida Everglades are testimony to the success of combined efforts among many levels of government, business and environmental NGOs (Schmid 2000).

The Canadian government does not currently track or report on the status of its wetland resources but Canada was the first nation to adopt a federal policy on wetland conservation. Wetland ecosystems make up about 17 per cent of Canada's national parks, and about 10 per cent are excluded from development (Rubec and Thibault 1998).

The reduction in the rate of wetland loss is a considerable achievement but wetlands are still being lost to development. The future of wetland habitat and the biodiversity it harbours may be compromised by changing conditions such as population growth, expansion of agricultural production, economic growth and changes in hydrological conditions and the flow of people (Wilcove and others 1998).

## Bio-invasion

Bio-invasion is now thought to be the second gravest threat to biodiversity in North America, after habitat destruction and degradation (CEC 2000). Competition or predation by non-native species imperils nearly half of the species listed as threatened or endangered under the US Endangered Species Act (Wilcove and others 1998). In Canada, alien species have been involved in causing risk to about 25 per cent of endangered, 31 per cent of threatened and 16 per cent of vulnerable species (Lee 2001).

### Restoration of the Florida Everglades

The Everglades is the central part of a 23 000 km² watershed covering the lower third of Florida. In the early 1900s, large tracts were drained and water supplies reconfigured. Protected from flooding by levees and canals, South Florida became home to six million people along the Miami-Palm Beach corridor and an important sugarcane, fruit and vegetable producer (UNDP, UNEP, World Bank and WRI 2000).

Originally stretching over 11 650 km², nearly half of the Everglades wetlands have been lost, reducing the amount of freshwater flowing to the coast, disrupting salinity levels and altering the natural capacity of the ecosystem to store and release water. The state of the Everglades deteriorated most rapidly over the past two decades with sea grass die-offs, the invasion of non-native species, nutrient contamination, large algal blooms in Florida Bay and declines in fishing harvests and some bird populations (UNDP, UNEP, World Bank and WRI 2000).

Regional efforts to address the problems began in the early 1980s but it took until 1998 for all parties — the sugar industry, environmentalists, real estate developers and American Indian tribes — to come together in support of a comprehensive plan to restore and preserve the Everglades. Developed by the Army Corps of Engineers, it is the world's most ambitious and extensive wetlands restoration effort, costing the federal government US$7.8 billion. It will take more than 20 years to complete (Alvarez 2000, Army Corps of Engineers 2000).

Invasive aquatic species are particularly threatening to wetland and freshwater ecosystems (see box below) and can also pose serious health risks. For example, human cholera bacteria were found in ballast tanks and in oyster and fin-fish samples in Mobile, Alabama, in 1991 (ANS 2000). Alien aquatic

### Bio-invasion

Bio-invasion is the influx of alien invasive species. Alien species are considered invasive when they become established in natural habitats, are agents of change, and threaten native biological diversity. Alien invasive species include bacteria, viruses, fungi, insects, molluscs, plants, fish, mammals and birds (IUCN 2001).

Species that become invasive can be introduced either intentionally or unintentionally through pathways (or vectors). These include transportation (by water, land and air; in the goods themselves, in dunnage, packing materials or containers, in or on ships, planes, trains, trucks or cars); agriculture; horticulture and plant nursery stock; aquaculture industry; live food fish industry; bait fish; ornamental pond, water garden and the aquarium pet trades. Where there are no natural predators, they can come to dominate ecosystems, and can alter the composition and structure of food webs, nutrient cycles, fire cycles, and hydrology and energy budgets, threatening agricultural productivity and other industries dependent on living resources (Alonso and others 2001).

As an example, purple loosestrife (*Lythrum salicaria*), which was introduced from Europe in the mid-1800s as a garden ornamental, has been spreading in North America at a rate of 115 000 ha a year, invading wetland habitats where it dominates native plants and deprives waterfowl and other species of food sources (Haber 1996, Pimentel and others 1999). When non-indigenous aquatic weeds such as purple loosestrife, Eurasian water milfoil and hydrilla replace native species, they establish dense colonies that can impair navigation, water-based recreation and flood control; degrade water quality and wildlife habitat; accelerate the filling of lakes and reservoirs; and depress property values (Haber 1996).

species are expected to contribute to the extinction of native freshwater species in North America at a rate of 4 per cent a decade over the next century (Ricciardi and Rasmussen 1999).

The high economic costs of damage caused by bio-invasions in North America is causing increasing concern. Both countries have developed monitoring plans and information systems to help control bio-invasion (Haber 1996, Kaiser 1999).

Responses to the challenge of invasive species include legislation, policies, and plans and programmes that focus on preventing the invasion of new species and the eradication or control of established ones.

Canada and the United States cooperate in programmes related to invasive species in the Great Lakes, for example. Despite requirements for ships to exchange ballast water at sea, however, the influx of new species into the Great Lakes continues and is considered to be a serious threat to the integrity of the Great Lakes ecosystem.

As trade increases, new invasions are expected. In addition, it may be that global climate change could create conditions that are even more conducive to bio-invasion (Holmes 1998). North American as well as global cooperation is essential to stem the tide of bio-invasion and the damage it causes.

## References: Chapter 2, biodiversity, North America

Alonso, A., Dallmeier, F., Granek, E. and Raven, P. (2001). *Biodiversity: Connecting with the Tapestry of Life*. Washington DC, Smithsonian Institution and President's Committee of Advisors on Science and Technology

Alvarez, L. (2000). Everglades: Congress Puts Finishing Touches on Massive Restoration Bill. *Naples Daily News*, 4 November 2000. http://www.naplesnews.com/00/11/naples/d54155 3a.htm [Geo-2-072]

ANS (2000). *What are Aquatic Nuisance Species and Their Impacts?* US Fish and Wildlife Service http://www.anstaskforce.gov/ansimpact.htm [Geo-2-073]

Army Corps of Engineers (2000). *Corps Facts: Florida Everglades*. US Army Corps of Engineers http://www.hq.usace.army.mil/cepa/pubs/Everglades .htm [Geo-2-074]

CEC (2000). *Booming Economies, Silencing Economies, and the Paths to Our Future*. Commission for Environmental Cooperation http://www.cec.org/files/english/Trends-e.pdf [Geo-2-075]

COSEWIC (2001). *Canadian Species at Risk*. Committee on the Status of Endangered Wildlife in Canada http://www.cosewic.gc.ca/cosewic/Cosewic_List.pdf [Geo-2-076]

Ducks Unlimited (2000). *Ducks Unlimited: World Leader in Wetlands Conservation*. http://www.ducks.org/conservation [Geo-2-077]

EC (1999). *Freshwater Facts*. Environment Canada http://www.on.ec.gc.ca/glimr/classroom/millennium/ wetlands/wetland-facts-e.html [Geo-2-078]

Haber, E. (1996). *Invasive Exotic Plants of Canada*. National Botanical Services http://infoweb.magi.com/~ehaber/fact1.html [Geo-2-080]

Holmes, B. (1998). The coming plagues — non-native species on the move due to global warming. *New Scientist*. 18 April 1998

IUCN (2001). *IUCN Guidelines for the Prevention of Biodiversity Loss Caused by Invasive Alien Species*. Gland, IUCN

Kaiser, J. (1999). Stemming the tide of invading species. *Science*. 285, 5435, 1836-41

Lee, G. (2001). *Alien Invasive Species: Threat to Canadian Biodiversity*. Ottawa, Natural Resources Canada, Canadian Forest Service

NAWMP (1998). *1998 Update to the North American Waterfowl Managemant Plan*. North American Waterfowl Management Plan http://www.nawmp.ca/eng/pub_e.html [Geo-2-082]

NRC (2001). *The National Atlas of Canada Online: Wetlands*. Natural Resources Canada http://atlas.gc.ca/english/facts/wetlands/ [Geo-2-085]

Pimentel, D., Bach, L., Zuniga, R. and Morrison, D. (1999). *Environmental and Economic Costs Associated with Non-Indigenous Species in the United States*. Cornell University http://www.news.cornell.edu/releases/Jan99/species _costs.html [Geo-2-084]

Ramsar (2000). *The Ramsar Convention on Wetlands*. Ramsar Convention Bureau http://www.ramsar.org/lib_bio_8.htm [Geo-2-085]

Ricciardi, A. and Rasmussen, J.B. (1999). Extinction rates of North American freshwater fauna. *Conservation Biology*. 13, 5, 1220-22

Rubec, C. and Thibault, J.J. (1998). *Managing Canadian Peatlands*. International Symposium on Peatland Restoration and Reclamation, Duluth, Minnesota

Schmid, J.A. (2000). Wetlands as conserved landscapes in the United States. In A. B. Murphy and others (eds.), *Cultural Encounters with the Environment: Enduring and Evolving Geographic Themes*. Boston, Rowman & Littlefield

UNDP, UNEP, World Bank and WRI (2000). *World Resources 2000-2001*. Washington DC, World Resources Institute

UNEP-WCMC (2001a). *GEO3 Endangered Animals Snapshot*. United Nations Environment Programme-World Conservation Monitoring Centre http://valhalla.unep-wcmc.org/isdb/geo3.cfm [Geo-2-086]

UNEP-WCMC (2001b). *GEO3 Protected Areas Snapshot*. United Nations Environment Programme-World Conservation Monitoring Centre http://valhalla.unep-wcmc.org/wdbpa/GEO3.cfm [Geo-2-087]

US EPA (1997). *The Wetlands Program*. US Environmental Protection Agency http://www.epa.gov/OWOW/wetlands/about.html [Geo-2-088]

US EPA (1999). *The Administration Wetlands Plan: An Update*. US Environmental Protection Agency http://www.epa.gov/OWOW/wetlands/facts/fact7.ht ml [Geo-2-089]

US FWS (2000). *Status and Trends of Wetlands in the Conterminous United States 1986 to 1997*. Washington DC, US Fish and Wildlife Service http://wetlands.fws.gov/bha/SandT/SandTReport.ht ml [Geo-2-090]

Wilcove, D.S., Rothstein, D., Dubow, J., Phillips, A. and Losos, E. (1998). Quantifying threats to imperiled species in the United States. *Bioscience*. 48, 8, 607-15

Wilcove, D.S., Rothstein, D., Dubow, J., Phillips, A. and Losos, E. (2000). Leading threats to biodiversity. In B. A. Stein and others (eds.), *Precious Heritage: The Status of Biodiversity in the United States*. New York, Oxford University Press

## Biodiversity: West Asia

### Resources

The region has wide variations in terrestrial and aquatic ecosystems. Main terrestrial habitats include Mediterranean forests, rangelands and deserts. Marine ecosystems include mudflats, mangrove swamps, sea grass and coral reefs. Rivers in the Mashriq and springs in the whole region represent freshwater ecosystems.

The estimated number of endemic vascular species in the region is 800 (Batanouny 1996), and in some hot spots such as the Socotra Islands of Yemen, 34 per cent of the total number of vascular plants are endemic (Al-Saghier 2000, Government of Yemen 2000). There are seven endemic mammal species and ten endemic birds (UNDP, UNEP, World Bank and WRI 1998).

The seas are rich in species diversity with 200 species of crabs, 20 species of marine mammals and more than 1 200 species of fish and more than 330 species of corals in the Red Sea and the Gulf (Fouda, Hermosa and Al-Harthi 1998). More than 11 per cent of the corals are endemic to the Arabian Peninsula sub-region (Sheppard, Price and Roberts 1992). There are up to 12 000 marine species in the Mediterranean, representing 8–9 per cent of the world sea species richness (Bianchi, Dore and Morri 1995). Substantial numbers of vertebrates are threatened with extinction in the region (see bar chart).

Habitat destruction and fragmentation have increased dramatically in most countries over the past three decades due to human population and resource consumption growth. Degradation of unique terrestrial and aquatic ecosystems and loss of genetic resources are the main biodiversity issues in West Asia. Water resource management and the maintenance of inland water biodiversity, as well as overhunting of large mammals and birds, are therefore among the most important issues affecting biodiversity in the region.

### Habitat degradation and loss

Rapid population increases and changes in lifestyle have contributed to the degradation of wetland ecosystems due to increased exploitation of surface and groundwater. In Jordan, groundwater extraction for urban needs increased from around 2 million $m^3$ in 1979 to around 25 million $m^3$ in 1993 (Fariz and Hatough-Bouran 1998) while an additional 25 million $m^3$ per year was used for irrigated agriculture. As well as water extraction, pollution and impacts from refugee camps in the area have led to the deterioration and drying up of the Azraq wetlands natural reserve (Fariz and Hatough-Bouran 1998). As a consequence tourism in Azraq has declined. In the eastern part of the Arabian Peninsula, many of the date palm oases and natural freshwater springs have been lost in the past two decades (Bundy, Connor and Harrison 1989).

By far the most serious wetland change in West Asia over the past three decades has occurred in the lower Mesopotamian marshlands, where serial

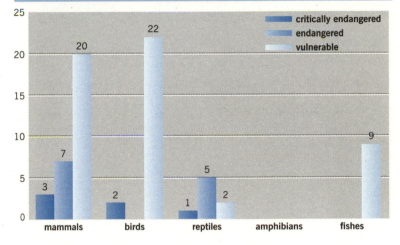

**Numbers of threatened vertebrates: West Asia**

satellite images confirm a loss of around 90 per cent of the area of lake and marshlands (UNEP 2001). This loss may be attributable in part to the large number of dams now present on upstream parts of the Tigris-Euphrates system, but appears to be primarily a result of major hydrological engineering works in southern Iraq, notably the completion of the Major Outfall Drain (or 'Third River') which diverts water to the head of the Gulf. However, despite some negative impacts of damming on indigenous biodiversity, the loss of some habitats such as wetlands has been offset by the creation of large artificial habitats elsewhere in the region. For example, the 630 $km^2$ Assad Lake in Syria on the Euphrates River is considered an important site for migratory and wintering birds in West Asia.

The rapid decline of the lower Mesopotamian marshlands represents one of the most significant environmental events to have occurred globally during the past 30 years. Loss of such an important habitat

*Note: critically endangered (extremely high risk of extinction in immediate future); endangered (very high risk of extinction in near future); vulnerable (high risk of extinction in medium-term future)*

*The data include all globally threatened vertebrate species with country records in the UNEP-WCMC database (UNEP-WCMC 2001a). Marine species recorded by ocean area are not included*

illustrates the pressures on wetlands in the region, which are likely to intensify in future as demand for water continues to increase.

Food self-sufficiency policies in the region have resulted in the cultivation of marginal lands for irrigated intensive agriculture. This has strained water

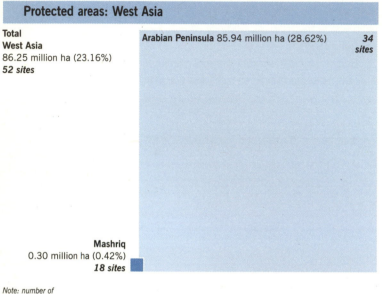

**Protected areas: West Asia**

**Total
West Asia**
86.25 million ha (23.16%)
*52 sites*

Arabian Peninsula 85.94 million ha (28.62%)    *34 sites*

**Mashriq**
0.30 million ha (0.42%)
*18 sites*

*Note: number of protected areas includes those in IUCN categories I-VI*

*Source: compiled from UNEP-WCMC 2001b*

resources and caused salinization, with negative effects on freshwater biodiversity. The breakdown of traditional systems of resource management has also had a major impact on biodiversity. For example, the traditional Al-Hema system, which facilitated the sustainable use of rangelands and other natural resources by setting aside large reserves during times of stress (Abu-Zinada and Child 1991, Daraz 1985) was abandoned in the 1960s in the Arabian Peninsula and Mashriq countries. While about 3 000 hema reserves existed in Saudi Arabia in 1969, only 71 were still in existence under various degrees of protection in 1984 and only nine were on the 1997 Protected Areas list (WCPA 2000).

Coastal and marine biodiversity is threatened by several human activities including pollution (oil spills, industrial and domestic discharges into the sea), physical alteration of habitats (sand dredging and landfills), climate variability and alien species introduced by ballast water (ROPME 1999, UNEP/MAP 1999). The extent of mangroves has been decreasing along the shores of the Gulf over the past 30 years due to unplanned coastal development to the extent that only 125–130 km$^2$ of mangrove patches remain. In Saudi Arabia, more than 40 per cent of the

Gulf coastline has been reclaimed and almost 50 per cent of the mangroves lost (Sheppard, Price and Roberts 1992). In the Arabian Peninsula seas, about 20 000 km$^2$ of coral reefs or 7.9 per cent of the total area of world corals have been exposed to bleaching due to increases in sea water temperature caused by El Niño (UNDP, UNEP, World Bank and WRI 2000). It is feared that global warming will intensify this phenomenon. In the Mashriq sub-region many marine species, including Mediterranean monk seals, marine turtles and marine sponges, are threatened by the continuous deterioration of coastal water quality due to sedimentation, nutrient discharge and eutrophication (Lakkis 1996, Tohme 1996).

## Loss of terrestrial species
A comprehensive decline in the larger terrestrial species has been recorded. This is primarily because of excess hunting resulting from the decline of traditional resource management practices, and the increased availability of four-wheel drive vehicles and automatic weapons (Gasperetti, Harrison and Büttiker 1985, Gasperetti, and Gasperetti 1981, Thouless 1991). While wild goat (*Capra ibex*), and gazelles (*Gazella gazella*, *G. dorcas* and *G. subgutturosa*) are still present in the region they have been much reduced in range and numbers. The leopard, which was formerly widespread, persists in a few isolated areas. The cheetah is on the verge of extinction, if not already extinct, the last confirmed specimen being taken in 1977. The Arabian oryx (*Oryx leucoryx*) was extinct in the wild but has been successfully reintroduced using captive stock. The ostrich is believed extinct, the Arabian bustard (*Ardeotis arabs*) has been reduced in numbers and is possibly extinct in Saudi Arabia, and the Houbara bustard (*Chlamydotis undulata*) now winters in much reduced numbers. Programmes for captive breeding of threatened species have operated since the 1980s, with re-introduction programmes for the Arabian oryx, Houbara bustard and some gazelle species in Jordan, Oman, Saudi Arabia and Syria (GCEP 2000).

## Addressing biodiversity loss
Most countries have ratified the Convention on Biological Diversity. In addition, some have ratified other biodiversity-related conventions such as the Convention on International Trade in Endangered Species (CITES). Countries are also adhering to other

international and regional agreements such as the Mediterranean Action Plan (MAP) and Regional Organization for the Protection of the Environment of the Red Sea and Gulf of Aden (PERSGA). The establishment of protected areas in West Asia has been gaining momentum. Local people are generally unhappy with the existing biodiversity conservation programmes because they are not involved in decision-making (Thouless 1991). However, the situation is improving in some countries such as Lebanon and Jordan (Chatty 1998).

## References: Chapter 2, biodiversity, West Asia

Abu-Zinada, A.H. and Child, G. (1991). *Developing a System of Protected Areas in Saudi Arabia*. 3rd Man and Biosphere Meeting on Mediterranean Biosphere Reserves and the 1st IUCN-CNPPA Meeting for Middle East and North Africa. Conference held 14-19 October 1991, Tunis

Al-Saghier, O.A. (2000). *Conservation and Biodiversity in Socotra*. The Second International Conference on Economics and Conservation of Renewable Natural Resources in Arid Zones. Conference held 12-15 November 2000, Riyadh

Batanouny, K. (1996). *Biological Diversity in the Arab World*. Final Report and Proceedings of the UNEP Workshop on Biodiversity in West Asia, 12-14 December 1995. Bahrain, UNEP-ROWA

Bianchi, C.N., Dore, G. and Morri, C. (1995). *Guida del Subacqueo Naturalista: Mediterraneo e Tropici*. Nuoro, Editrice AFS

Bundy, G., Connor, R.J. and Harrison, C.J.O. (1989). *Birds of the Eastern Province of Saudi Arabia*. London and Dhahran, H.F. Witherby and ARAMCO

Chatty, D. (1998). Enclosures and exclusions: wildlife conservation schemes and pastoral tribes in the Middle East. *Anthropology Today*, Vol. 14, August 1998, 2-7 http://www.fmreview.org/fmr028.htm [Geo-2-195]

Daraz, O. (1985). The hema system of range reserves in the Arabian Peninsula, its possibilities in range improvement and conservation projects in the Near East. In J. A. McNeely and D. Pitt (eds.), *Culture and Conservation: the Human Dimension in Environmental Planning*. London, Croom Helm

Fariz, G. H. and Hatough-Bouran, A. (1998). Population dynamics in arid regions: the experience of the Azraq Oasis Conservation Project. In A. de Sherbinin and V. Dompka (eds.), *Water and Population Dynamics: Case Studies and Policy Implications*. Washington DC, American Association for the Advancement of Science

Fouda, M.M., Hermosa, G. and Al-Harthi, S. (1998). Status of fish biodiversity in the Sultanate of Oman. *Italian Journal of Zoology Speciale*. 65, Supplement 1

Gasperetti, J. and Gasperetti, P. (1981). A note on Arabian ornithology — two endangered species. *Fauna of Saudi Arabia*. 3, 435–40

Gasperetti, J., Harrison, D.L. and Büttiker, W. (1985). The carnivora of Arabia. *Fauna of Saudi Arabia*. 7, 397-445

GCEP (2000). *Jordan Ecology, Ecosystems and Habitats*. Jordan Country Study on Biological Diversity. Nairobi, United Nations Environment Programme

Government of Yemen (2000). *State of Environment in Yemen 2000: Executive Summary*. Sana'a, Yemen Environmental Protection Council

Lakkis, S. (1996). *Biodiversité de la flore et la faune marines du Liban*. National Seminar on Marine Sciences in Lebanon and the Region. Conference held 25-26 November 1996, Batroun, Lebanon

ROPME (1999). *Regional Report of the State of Environment*. Kuwait City, Regional Organization for the Protection of the Marine Environment

Sheppard, C., Price, C. and Roberts, C. (1992). *Marine Ecology of the Arabian Region*. London, Academic Press

Thouless, C.R. (1991). Conservation in Saudi Arabia. *Oryx*. 25, 4, 222–28

Tohmé, H. (1996). *Les Zones Sensibles de la Côte Libanaise, leur Préservation et les Moyens de Conservation*. National Seminar on Marine Sciences in Lebanon and the Region. Conference held 25-26 November 1996, Batroun, Lebanon

UNDP, UNEP, World Bank and WRI (1998). *World Resources 1998-99*. New York and Oxford, Oxford University Press

UNDP, UNEP, World Bank and WRI (2000). *World Resources 2000-2001*. Washington DC, World Resources Institute

UNEP (2001). *The Mesopotamian Marshlands: Demise of an Ecosystem*. United Nations Environment Programme, Division of Early Warning and Assessment - North America http://grid2.cr.usgs.gov/publications/meso.pdf [Geo-2-147]

UNEP-WCMC (2001a). *GEO3 Endangered Animals Snapshot*. United Nations Environment Programme-World Conservation Monitoring Centre http://valhalla.unep-wcmc.org/isdb/geo3.cfm [Geo-2-057]

UNEP-WCMC (2001b). *GEO3 Protected Areas Snapshot*. United Nations Environment Programme-World Conservation Monitoring Centre http://valhalla.unep-wcmc.org/wdbpa/GEO3.cfm [Geo-2-068]

UNEP/MAP and EEA (1999). *State and Pressures of the Marine and Coastal Mediterranean Environment*. Environmental Assessment Report No. 5. Copenhagen, European Environment Agency

WCPA (2000). *North Africa and Middle East*. World Commission on Protected Areas http://wcpa.iucn.org/region/mideast/mideast.html [Geo-2-148]

## Biodiversity: the Polar Regions

The polar regions face threats from climate change, ozone depletion, altered land use and the unsustainable use of natural resources. The ocean areas include some of the largest marine ecosystems on Earth and are threatened by commercial fisheries and the harvesting of marine mammals.

### Arctic

The Arctic has considerable biological diversity (see table below). There are also robust populations of plankton in the marine environment. The Arctic fisheries are an important resource: the Bering Sea fisheries alone provide half the US catch and 2–5 per cent of the global catch (CAFF 2001).

For centuries the Arctic has attracted hunters of mammals such as whales, seals, walruses, polar bears and otters. Many species have been repeatedly driven to near extinction and some are below safe biological limits. Hunting continues but is now more tightly regulated. Even so, marine mammal populations in decline include local populations of the Beluga whale, walrus, Steller's sea lion, harbour seal, northern fur seal and the fin whale. For many more marine mammals, the trend is unknown.

Several bird populations and fish species are in decline. The latter include local populations of Atlantic cod, Arctic cod, Greenland halibut and wolf-fishes. Many

### Polar bear populations in the Arctic

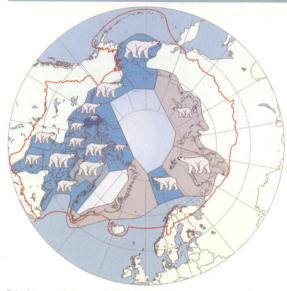

Polar bear populations are stable in the pale blue areas, increasing in the dark blue area. Trends are unknown in grey areas. Largest images of the polar bear denote populations of 3 500, smallest images populations of 500

Source: CAFF 2001

wildlife populations have suffered starvation due to human activity such as overfishing. For example, in the mid-1980s the capelin stock of the Barents Sea collapsed due to overfishing, resulting in the starvation of hundreds of thousands of harp seals. At least 50 000 more were drowned in fishing gear. Norway banned capelin fishing during 1987–90, allowing the capelin population to recover and fishing to resume but at more sustainable levels (NCM 1993).  Puffins have been another casualty. They feed their young mainly on herring fry.  In the late 1970s, some 1.4 million pairs of puffins nested at the southwestern end of the Lofoten Islands. In the 1980s, the colony contracted at a rate of 10–15 per cent a year. By 1995, it was less than half its former size because most puffin chicks starved to death due to the overfishing of herring fry since the 1960s. By the mid-1990s, puffins had still not recovered despite an increase in the herring population due to strict fishing regulations (Bernes 1996).

Reducing exploitation and other responses have had positive impacts on other populations.  For example, an Icelandic fishing ban on Atlantic herring between 1972-75 helped the stock to make a gradual recovery and it is now considered to be within safe biological limits. In the 1940s, the Svalbard population of the barnacle goose had been reduced to only 300 birds. It was then totally protected on its winter ranges in the United Kingdom and a nature reserve

### Biological diversity in the Arctic: number of known species

|  | Global | Arctic | Arctic % |
|---|---|---|---|
| fungi | 65 000 | 5 000 | 7.6 |
| lichens | 16 000 | 2 000 | 12.5 |
| mosses | 10 000 | 1 100 | 11.0 |
| liverworts | 6 000 | 180 | 3.0 |
| ferns | 12 000 | 60 | 0.5 |
| conifers | 550 | 8 | 1.2 |
| flowering plants | 270 000 | 3 000 | 1.2 |
| spiders | 75 000 | 1 000 | 1.2 |
| insects | 950 000 | 3 000 | 0.3 |
| vertebrates | 52 000 | 860 | 1.6 |
| fishes | 25 000 | 450 | 1.8 |
| reptiles | 7 400 | 4 | >0.1 |
| mammals | 4 630 | 130 | 2.8 |
| birds | 9 950 | 280 | 2.8 |

Source: CAFF 2001

was established. Today, there are 23 000 in the
Svalbard population. Similar increases have occurred
in Greenland and Russia (CAFF 2001, Bernes 1996).

Other pressures on Arctic biodiversity are climate
change, and habitat loss and fragmentation. The
warming trend is reducing the ice habitat for species
such as the polar bear and walrus, and is causing more
severe climatic episodes such as ice storms that raise
mortality rates (CAFF 2001, Crane and Galasso 1999).
The Arctic countries have begun a major project
(Arctic Climate Impact Assessment) to develop
recommendations for action on the effects of global
warming in the Arctic. These countries have also
taken several steps to reduce habitat loss and prevent
fragmentation. An important response has been to
increase the number of protected areas from 280 in
1994 to 405 in 2001 and overall coverage from
2 million km² to 2.5 million km². However, this
increase has resulted from the domestic actions of
individual Arctic countries with little circumpolar
collaboration. In 1996, the Arctic countries agreed to
cooperate to implement a Circumpolar Protected Area
Network Strategy and Action Plan but there is little
evidence of progress on implementation (AC 2000).

## Antarctic

The Antarctic terrestrial ecosystem is structurally
simplistic with a small number of species. Marine
biomass in the Southern Ocean can be immense but
species richness is generally low (Wynn Williams
1996). The benthic (bottom) fish fauna of the
continental and upper slope of Antarctica includes 213
species confined to 18 families (Eastman 2000). Seals,
whales and seabirds dominate the higher levels of the
Southern Ocean. Knowledge of Southern Ocean
marine diversity is confined largely to the continental
shelves and slopes. Little is known about the fauna of
the deep sea around Antarctica.

Historic sealing and whaling activities have had a
significant impact on these populations in the
Southern Ocean, at one point threatening extinction of
some species. Today, strict international agreements
govern the harvesting of Antarctic seals (Convention
for the Conservation of Antarctic Seals) and whales
(International Whaling Convention, which also
designated large areas of the Southern Ocean as a
whale sanctuary). Only limited numbers of seals are
taken for scientific purposes, while approximately 440
minke whales are killed each year.

### Protected areas in the Arctic

|  | Number of areas | Total area (km²) | % of country's Arctic land area |
|---|---|---|---|
| Canada | 61 | 500 842 | 9.5 |
| Finland | 54 | 24 530 | 30.8 |
| Greenland | 15 | 993 070 | 45.6 |
| Iceland* | 24 | 12 397 | 12.0 |
| Norway** | 39 | 41 380 | 25.3 |
| Russian Federation* | 110 | 625 518 | 9.9 |
| Sweden | 47 | 21 707 | 22.8 |
| United States (Alaska) | 55 | 296 499 | 50.2 |
| **Total** | **405** | **2 505 943** | **17.0** |

Notes: * large marine components are included; ** most of the area protected is in Svalbord, only about 7 per cent of the Arctic mainland is protected

Source: CAFF 2001

Fish and krill (tiny planktonic crustaceans) are
now primarily the targets of human exploitation in the
Southern Ocean. From 1969-70, when records of
commercial fishing began, to the end of 1998, a total of
8 739 800 tonnes of krill and fish had been taken from
the Southern Ocean (CCAMLR 2000a). In 1982, the
Convention on the Conservation of Antarctic Marine
Living Resources (CCAMLR) was established to
promote the conservation and rational use of marine
living resources south of the Antarctic Convergence.
Southern Ocean fisheries are now managed within the
framework of CCAMLR.

Although there is uncertainty in its assessments,
CCAMLR estimates that the level of illegal, unregulated
and unreported (IUU) fishing in the Southern Ocean —
which has been a major problem for decades — had
decreased in 1998 but has since increased despite
stronger CCAMLR measures to combat IUU fishing.
The high level of illegal catch of Patagonian toothfish
(Dissostichus eleginoides) in the South Indian Ocean has
become a major concern as it threatens the
sustainability of stocks (CCAMLR 2000a). To address
IUU catches, CCAMLR adopted a Catch Documentation
Scheme requiring all landings, trans-shipments and
importations of toothfish into the territories of
contracting parties to be accompanied by a completed
catch document. In 2000, CCAMLR took further steps
to combat IUU fishing by urging all parties to avoid
flagging or licensing vessels with a history of
engagement in illegal practices (CCAMLR 2000b).

CCAMLR regulation has reduced the incidental by-catch of seabirds and marine mammals in legal fisheries to low levels but illegal fishing still takes its toll. For some seabird populations, long-line fisheries represent a major threat. This led to the listing in 1997 of all albatross species on the protected species list of the CMS. Albatross and petrel species, such as the wandering albatross (*Diomedea exulans*) and the Antarctic giant petrel (*Macronectes giganteus*), have also been listed as vulnerable in the IUCN Red List (Hilton-Taylor 2000). The final draft of the Agreement on the Conservation of Albatross and Petrels was recently completed in Cape Town, South Africa.

Changes to the distribution and composition of terrestrial flora and fauna, attributable to recent warming over Antarctica, have been observed over the past three decades. Composition and distribution of marine species is also expected to change with a changing climate. It has been indicated that the marked increase in the number of Adelie penguins (*Pygoscelis adeliae*) in the Ross Sea area in the 1980s showed remarkable synchronization with the climatic variation in the same region (Taylor and Wilson 1990, Blackburn and others 1990). At Palmer Station on Anvers Island, where Adelie penguins are known to have nested only prior to the 1950s, gentoo and chinstrap penguins are now breeding and have expanded their ranges southward in the Peninsula within the past 50 years, in correlation with pronounced regional warming (Emslie and others 1998).

Changes in the extent and thickness of ice affect the timing, magnitude and duration of the seasonal pulse of primary production in the polar regions. It has been suggested that sea ice extent affects krill availability which in turn may affect krill predators. Regional warming and reduced krill abundance may therefore affect the marine food web (Loeb and others 1997). The density and abundance of minke whales has been observed to be lower in seasons with warmer sea surface temperatures, fewer cold-water intrusions, and smaller sea ice extent, possibly owing to the shift in availability of prey (Kasamatsu 2000).

Along the west coast of the Antarctic Peninsula, springtime ozone depletion can lead to a twofold increase in biologically effective UV-B radiation (Day and others 1999). UV exposure affects phytoplankton, including inhibition of primary production. This is a major concern in view of the phytoplankton's key role in the short food chain of the Antarctic marine ecosystem. The spring bloom of phytoplankton coincides with the springtime ozone hole and the subsequent period of high UV-B radiation. Reduction of phytoplanktonic production associated with the ozone hole is estimated to be 6–12 per cent (Smith and others 1992).

## References: Chapter 2, biodiversity, the Polar Regions

AC (2000). *Report from the 3rd Arctic Council Ministerial Meeting.* Barrow, October 2000 http://www.arctic-council.org [Geo-2-149]

Bernes, C. (1996). *The Nordic Arctic Environment — Unspoilt, Exploited, Polluted?* Copenhagen, Nordic Council of Ministers

Blackburn, N., Taylor, R.H. and Wilson, P.R. (1990). An interpretation of the growth of the Adelie penguin rookery at Cape Royds, 1955-1990. *New Zealand Journal of Ecology.* 15 (2), 117–21

CAFF (2001). *Arctic Flora and Fauna – Status and Conservation.* Helsinki, Arctic Council Programme for the Conservation of Arctic Flora and Fauna

Crane, K. and Galasso, J.L. (1999). *Arctic Environmental Atlas.* Washington DC, Office of Naval Research, Naval Research Laboratory

CCAMLR (2000a). Convention for the Conservation of Antarctic Marine Living Resources http://www.ccamlr.org [Geo-2-150]

CCAMLR (2000b). *Report from XIX CCAMLR meeting.* Tasmania, Convention for the Conservation of Antarctic Marine Living Resources

Day, T.A., Ruhland, C.T., Grobe, C.W. and Xiong, F. (1999). Growth and reproduction of Antarctic vascular plants in response to warming and UV radiation reductions in the field. *Oecologia* 119 (1), 24-35

Eastman, J.T. (2000). Antarctic notothenioid fishes as subjects for research in evolutionary biology. *Antarctic Science,* 12 (3), 276-287

Emslie, S.D., Fraser, W., Smith, R.C. and Walker, W. (1998). Abandoned penguin colonies and environmental change in the Palmer Station area, Anvers Island, Antarctic Peninsula. *Antarctic Science* 10 (3), 257–68

Hilton-Taylor, C. (2000). *2000 IUCN Red List of Threatened Species.* The World Conservation Union http://www.redlist.org/info/tables/table4a.html [Geo-2-069]

Kasamatsu, F., Ensor, P., Joyce, G.G. and Kimura, N. (2000). Distribution of minke whales in the Bellingshausen and Amundsen Seas (60 degrees W-120 degrees W), with special reference to environmental/physiographic variables. *Fisheries Oceanography* 9 (3), 214–23

Loeb, V., Siegel, V., Holm-Hansen, O., Hewitt, R., Fraser, W., Trivelpiece, W. and Trivelpiece, S. (1997). Effects of sea-ice extent and krill or salp dominance on the Antarctic food web. *Nature* 387 (6636), 897-900

NCM (1993). *The Nordic Environment — Present State, Trends and Threats.* Copenhagen, Nordic Council of Ministers

Smith, R.C., Prezelin, B.B., Baker, K.S., Bidigare, R.R., Boucher, N.P., Coley, T., Karentz, D., MacIntyre, S., Matlick, H.A., Menzies, D., Ondrusek, M., Wan, Z. and Waters, K.J. (1992). Ozone depletion — ultraviolet radiation and phytoplankton biology in Antarctic waters. *Science* 255 (5047), 952–59

Taylor, R.H. and Wilson, P.R. (1990). Recent increase and southern expansion of Adelie penguin populations in the Ross Sea, Antarctica, related to climatic warming. *New Zealand Journal of Ecology.* 14, 25-29

Wynn Williams, D.D. (1996). Antarctic microbial diversity: the basis of polar ecosystem processes. *Biodiversity and Conservation* 5 (11), 1271–93

# OUR CHANGING ENVIRONMENT: Iguazú National Park

Landsat imagery on this page shows how land-clearing and logging have opened up a previously forested landscape. The protected area of Iguazú National Park, located in Argentina on the border with Brazil and Paraguay, is sharply defined as the dark green enclave on the right of the images, the only remaining original forest in the region. Conservation of this park, a World Heritage site, is critical because it harbours one of the most complete remnant patches of the highly endangered Paranaense forest. The park is rich in fauna and includes 68 species of mammals, 422 of birds, 38 of reptiles and 18 of amphibians, a large number of which are threatened or vulnerable.

Landsat data: USGS/EROS Data Center
Compilation: UNEP GRID Sioux Falls

# Freshwater

UNEP, Still Pictures

## Global overview

### Resources

The total volume of water on Earth is about 1 400 million km$^3$ of which only 2.5 per cent, or about 35 million km$^3$, is freshwater (see table opposite). Most freshwater occurs in the form of permanent ice or snow, locked up in Antarctica and Greenland, or in deep groundwater aquifers. The principal sources of water for human use are lakes, rivers, soil moisture and relatively shallow groundwater basins. The usable portion of these sources is only about 200 000 km$^3$ of water — less than 1 per cent of all freshwater and only 0.01 per cent of all water on Earth. Much of this available water is located far from human populations, further complicating issues of water use.

The replenishment of freshwater depends on evaporation from the surface of the oceans. About 505 000 km$^3$, or a layer 1.4 metres thick, evaporates from the oceans annually. Another 72 000 km$^3$ evaporates from the land. About 80 per cent of all precipitation, or about 458 000 km$^3$/year, falls on the oceans and the remaining 119 000 km$^3$/year on land. The difference between precipitation on land surfaces

and evaporation from those surfaces (119 000 km$^3$ minus 72 000 km$^3$ annually) is run-off and groundwater recharge — approximately 47 000 km$^3$ annually (Gleick 1993). The figure opposite shows one estimate of the average annual water balance of major continental areas, including precipitation, evaporation and run-off. More than one-half of all run-off occurs in Asia and South America, and a large fraction occurs in a single river, the Amazon, which carries more than 6 000 km$^3$ of water a year (Shiklomanov 1999).

### Water scarcity

About one-third of the world's population lives in countries suffering from moderate-to-high water stress — where water consumption is more than 10 per cent of renewable freshwater resources. Some 80 countries, constituting 40 per cent of the world's population, were suffering from serious water shortages by the mid-1990s (CSD 1997a) and it is estimated that in less than 25 years two-thirds of the world's people will be living in water-stressed countries (CSD 1997b). By 2020, water use is expected to increase by 40 per cent, and 17 per cent more water will be required for food production to meet the needs of the growing population (World Water Council 2000a).

The three major factors causing increasing water demand over the past century are population growth, industrial development and the expansion of irrigated agriculture. Agriculture accounted for most freshwater withdrawal in developing economies in the past two decades. Planners have always assumed that growing demand would be met by taming more of the hydrological cycle through building more infrastructure. The damming of rivers has traditionally been one of the main ways to ensure adequate water resources for irrigation, hydropower generation and domestic use. About 60 per cent of the world's largest 227 rivers have been strongly or moderately fragmented by dams, diversions or canals, with effects on freshwater ecosystems (WCD 2000). This infrastructure has provided important benefits in the form, for example, of increased food production and hydroelectricity. There have also been major costs. Over the past 50 years, dams have transformed the world's rivers, displacing some 40-80 million people in different parts of the world (WCD 2000), and causing irreversible changes in many of the ecosystems closely associated with them.

Emphasis on water supply, coupled with weak enforcement of regulations, has limited the effectiveness of water resource management, particularly in developing regions. Policy-makers have now shifted from entirely supply solutions to demand management, highlighting the importance of using a combination of measures to ensure adequate supplies of water for different sectors. Measures include improving water use efficiency, pricing policies and privatization. There is also a new emphasis on integrated water resources management (IWRM), which takes into account all the different stakeholders in water resource planning, development and management (CSD 1997b).

## Irrigated agriculture

Agriculture accounts for more than 70 per cent of freshwater drawn from lakes, rivers and underground sources. Most is used for irrigation which provides about 40 per cent of world food production (CSD 1997a). Over the past 30 years, the area of land under irrigation has increased from less than 200 million ha to more than 270 million ha (FAO 2001). During the same period, global water withdrawals rose from about 2 500 km³ to

### Major stocks of water

| | volume (1 000 km³) | % of total water | % of total freshwater |
|---|---|---|---|
| **Salt water** | | | |
| Oceans | 1 338 000 | 96.54 | |
| Saline/brackish groundwater | 12 870 | 0.93 | |
| Salt water lakes | 85 | 0.006 | |
| **Inland waters** | | | |
| Glaciers, permanent snow cover | 24 064 | 1.74 | 68.7 |
| Fresh groundwater | 10 530 | 0.76 | 30.06 |
| Ground ice, permafrost | 300 | 0.022 | 0.86 |
| Freshwater lakes | 91 | 0.007 | 0.26 |
| Soil moisture | 16.5 | 0.001 | 0.05 |
| Atmospheric water vapour | 12.9 | 0.001 | 0.04 |
| Marshes, wetlands* | 11.5 | 0.001 | 0.03 |
| Rivers | 2.12 | 0.0002 | 0.006 |
| Incorporated in biota* | 1.12 | 0.0001 | 0.003 |
| **Total water** | **1 386 000** | **100** | |
| **Total freshwater** | **35 029** | | **100** |

Source: Shiklomanov 1993

Notes: totals may not add exactly due to rounding

* Marshes, wetlands and water incorporated in biota are often mixed salt and freshwater

### Precipitation, evaporation and run-off by region (km³/year)

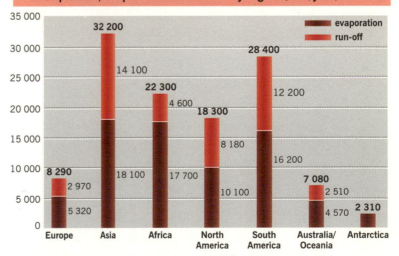

Height of bars shows total precipitation; darker areas represent evaporation while lighter areas show run-off. Total annual precipitation on land is 119 000 km³, of which 72 000 km³ evaporates, leaving some 47 000 km³ of run-off

Notes: regions do not correspond exactly to GEO regions; run-off includes flows to groundwater, inland basins, and ice flows of Antarctica

Source: Shiklomanov 1993

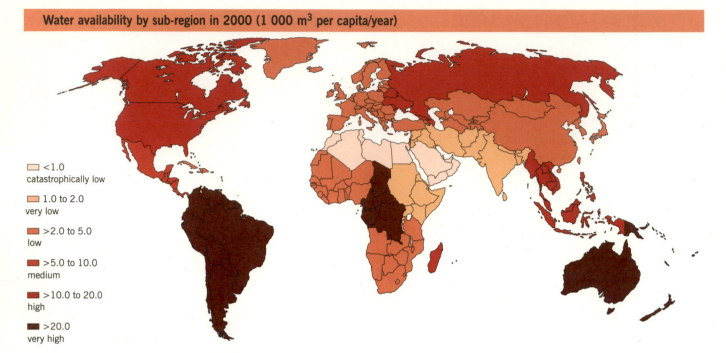

### Water availability by sub-region in 2000 (1 000 m³ per capita/year)

- □ <1.0 catastrophically low
- □ 1.0 to 2.0 very low
- ■ >2.0 to 5.0 low
- ■ >5.0 to 10.0 medium
- ■ >10.0 to 20.0 high
- ■ >20.0 very high

Map shows water availability measured in terms of 1 000 m³ per capita/year

Source: compiled from UNDP, UNEP, World Bank and WRI 2000 and United Nations Population Division 2001

more than 3 500 km³ (Shiklomanov 1999). Poor management has resulted in the salinization of about 20 per cent of the world's irrigated land, with an additional 1.5 million ha affected annually (CSD 1997a), significantly reducing crop production (WCD 2000). The countries most severely affected are mainly in arid and semi-arid regions.

Response measures have included national action programmes, water policy review and reform, promotion of increased water-use efficiency, and

irrigation technology transfer. At the global level, FAO initiated a global information system, AQUASTAT, in 1993 which provides data on the use of water in agriculture (FAO 2001).

### Water and sanitation

For many of the world's poorer populations, one of the greatest environmental threats to health remains the continued use of untreated water. While the percentage of people served with improved water supplies increased from 79 per cent (4.1 billion) in 1990 to 82 per cent (4.9 billion) in 2000, 1.1 billion people still lack access to safe drinking water and 2.4 billion lack access to improved sanitation (WHO and UNICEF 2000). Most of these people are in Africa and Asia. Lack of access to safe water supply and sanitation results in hundreds of millions of cases of water-related diseases, and more than 5 million deaths, every year (see box right). There are also large, but poorly quantified adverse impacts on economic productivity in many developing countries.

The importance of meeting basic human needs for water has always played a major role in water policy. One of the earliest comprehensive water conferences was held in 1977 in Mar del Plata, Argentina. The focus on human needs led to the International Drinking Water Supply and Sanitation Decade (1981–90) and the efforts of the United Nations and other international organizations to provide basic

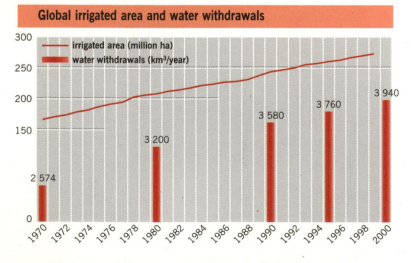

### Global irrigated area and water withdrawals

- — irrigated area (million ha)
- ■ water withdrawals (km³/year)

2 574    3 200    3 580    3 760    3 940

Since 1970 global water withdrawals have mirrored the rise in irrigated area. Some 70 per cent of withdrawals are for agriculture, mostly for irrigation which provides 40 per cent of the world's food

Source: FAO 2001, Shiklomanov 1999

(see table on page 154)

**The costs of water-related diseases**

- two billion people are at risk from malaria alone, with 100 million people affected at any one time, and 1-2 million deaths annually

- about 4 billion cases of diarrhoea and 2.2 million deaths annually: this is the equivalent of 20 jumbo jets crashing every day

- intestinal worms infect about 10 per cent of the population of the developing world

- about 6 million are blind from trachoma

- 200 million people are affected with schistosomiasis

*Sources: CSD 1997a, WHO and UNICEF 2000*

water services (UN 2000). The concept of meeting basic water needs was reaffirmed during the 1992 Earth Summit in Rio de Janeiro and expanded to include ecological water needs. A recent United Nations report (UN 1999) recognized that all people require access to adequate amounts of safe water, for drinking, sanitation and hygiene. Most recently, the Second World Water Forum and Ministerial Conference in The Hague in 2000 (see box below right) produced a strong statement from more than 100 ministers in support of re-emphasizing basic human needs as a priority for nations, international organizations and donors.

Providing urban dwellers with safe water and sanitation services has remained a particular challenge. Some 170 million developing country urban dwellers were provided with safe water and 70 million with appropriate sanitation during the first half of the 1990s but this had limited impact because about 300 million more urban residents still lacked access to safe water supply, while nearly 600 million lacked adequate sanitation by the end of 1994 (CSD 1997b). However, a major area of success in many developing countries is related to investments in wastewater treatment over the past 30 years which have 'halted the decline in – or actually improved – the quality of surface water' (World Water Council 2000b).

## Water quality

Water quality problems can often be as severe as those of water availability but less attention has been paid to them, particularly in developing regions. Sources of pollution include untreated sewage, chemical discharges, petroleum leaks and spills, dumping in old mines and pits, and agricultural

chemicals that are washed off or seep downward from farm fields. More than half of the world's major rivers are 'seriously depleted and polluted, degrading and poisoning the surrounding ecosystems, threatening the health and livelihood of people who depend on them' (World Commission on Water 1999).

In the 1990s, many new efforts were made to monitor water quality and institute better policies and programmes (Meybeck, Chapman and Helmer 1990). For example, water quality monitoring programmes have been established for many international river basins, including the Danube, the Rhine, the Mekong, the Plate and the Nile. The UNEP-Global Environment Monitoring System (GEMS) Water Programme also provides water quality data and information for both assessment and management purposes.

## Groundwater

About 2 billion people, approximately one-third of the world's population, depend on groundwater supplies, withdrawing about 20 per cent of global water (600-700 km$^3$) annually — much of it from shallow aquifers (UNDP and others 2000). Many rural dwellers depend entirely on groundwater.

The issues of groundwater use and quality have until recently received far less attention (particularly in some developing regions) than surface water, and data on groundwater stocks and flows are even less reliable. However, in Europe, much attention has been paid to groundwater quality because many settlements depend on such resources for water supply. Generally, groundwater resources are vulnerable to a variety of threats, including overuse and contamination (see table on page 154).

When use exceeds natural recharge over a long period, groundwater levels drop. Parts of India, China,

**Vision 21: global targets for water supply and sanitation**

To address issues plaguing the provision of water supply and sanitation to the developing world, the Water Supply and Sanitation Collaborative Council (WSSCC) presented the following global targets, called Vision 21, at the Second World Water Forum at The Hague in March 2000:

- by 2015, reduce by one-half the proportion of people without access to hygienic sanitation facilities;

- by 2015, reduce by one-half the proportion of people without sustainable access to adequate quantities of affordable and safe water;

- by 2025, provide water, sanitation and hygiene for all.

*Source: WSSCC 2000*

## Groundwater quality problems

| Problem | Causes | Concerns |
|---|---|---|
| Anthropogenic pollution | Inadequate protection of vulnerable aquifers against human-made discharges and leachates from:<br>● urban and industrial activities;<br><br>● intensification of agricultural cultivation | Pathogens, nitrates, ammonium salts, chlorine, sulphates, boron, heavy metals, DOC, aromatic and halogenated hydrocarbons<br><br>nitrates, chlorine, pesticides |
| Naturally occurring contamination | Related to pH-Eh evolution of groundwater and dissolution of minerals (aggravated by anthropogenic pollution and/or uncontrolled exploitation) | Mainly iron, fluorine and sometimes arsenic, iodine, manganese, aluminium, magnesium, sulphates, selenium and nitrates (from paleo-recharge) |
| Well-head contamination | Inadequate well design and construction allowing direct intrusion of polluted surface water or shallow groundwater | Mainly pathogens |

Source: Foster, Lawrence and Morris 1998

West Asia, the former Soviet Union, the western United States and the Arabian Peninsula are experiencing declining water tables, limiting the amount that can be used and raising the costs of pumping to farmers (Postel 1997, UNEP 1999). Overpumping of groundwater can lead to salt-water intrusion in coastal areas. In Madras, India, for example, saltwater intrusion has moved 10 km inland, contaminating wells (UNEP 1996).

Concern over growing problems related to groundwater resources has galvanized the international community, governments and other stakeholders to start addressing them. For example,

the Second World Water Forum in March 2000 organized a special workshop on groundwater. Some of the recommendations arising from the workshop included the need to raise public awareness and 'improve information availability, quality and accessibility to stakeholders, technical specialists and policy-makers' (World Water Forum 2000).

## Transboundary water management

Water is widely shared among nations, regions, ethnic groups and communities. A total of 261 rivers (see graphic left), covering 45.3 per cent of the total land area (excluding Antarctica), are shared by two or more countries (Wolf and others 1999), making transboundary water resources management one of the most important water issues today.

Disputes over shared water resources have a long history. Water has been used as a tool and weapon of conflict, access to water has been a source of dispute and contention, and major water development projects (for example dam construction) have led to violence and civil strife (Gleick 1998). But shared waters can also be a source of cooperation. This is particularly evident today with the increase in the number of initiatives related to river basin management regimes and institutions committed to bilateral and/or multilateral management of transboundary water resources. This can be traced back to the 1966 Helsinki Rules which laid the foundation for international principles for shared watercourses and

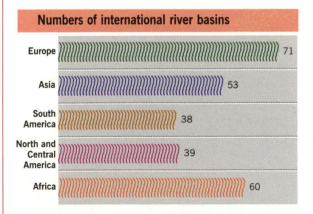

### Numbers of international river basins

|  | |
|---|---|
| Europe | 71 |
| Asia | 53 |
| South America | 38 |
| North and Central America | 39 |
| Africa | 60 |

A total of 261 river basins are shared by two or more countries

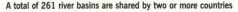

Notes: regions do not correspond exactly to GEO regions; the Jurado, shared by Colombia and Panama, is included in South America
Source: Wolf and others 1999

influenced many specific river treaties. The Rules were subsequently followed up by various international efforts, including particularly the work of the UN International Law Commission, which led in 1997 to the United Nations Convention on the Law of the Non-Navigational Uses of International Watercourses. The impact of this new convention is already being felt with the 14-member Southern African Development Community (SADC) adapting many of its principles in its revised protocol on shared watercourses.

The recognition of river basin organization over the past 30 years has also resulted in the establishment of the International Network of Basin Organizations (INBO) in 1996 (see box), while other initiatives include the 1998 International Conference on Water and Sustainable Development, which declared that 'a common vision of riverine countries is needed for the efficient management and effective protection of transborder water resources'. The conference's priority action programme (Bernard 1999) emphasized the need to:

- facilitate the exchange of accurate and harmonized information among riverine countries;
- promote consultation at all levels, especially within pertinent international institutions and mechanisms; and
- define medium-range priority action programmes of common interest to improve water management and decrease pollution.

## Water and ecosystems

Water development projects during the 20th century have had significant impacts on freshwater ecosystems by eliminating marshes and wetlands, removing water for other uses, altering flows, and contaminating water with industrial and human wastes. In many rivers and lakes, ecosystem functions have been lost or impaired. In some areas, growing water demand has led to reductions in the volume of large rivers, affecting riverine and adjacent coastal areas (CSD 1997a). Reproductive failures and death in various wildlife species, particularly at higher levels in the food chain, have been reported as a result of high withdrawals of water (CSD 1997a).

Wetlands are an important freshwater ecosystem influencing not only species distribution and biodiversity in general but also human settlements

**The International Network of Basin Organizations**

The International Network of Basin Organizations had a total of 125 member organizations in 49 countries in 1998. Its objectives are to:

- establish a network of organizations interested in global river basin management, and facilitate exchanges of experiences and expertise among them;
- promote the principles and means of sound water management in sustainable development cooperation programmes;
- facilitate the implementation of tools for institutional and financial management, for programming and for the organization of data banks;
- promote information and training programmes for the different actors involved in water management including local elected officials, users' representatives and the executives and staff of member organizations;
- encourage education of the population, the young in particular; and
- evaluate ongoing actions and disseminate their results.

*Source: INBO 2001*

and activities. They provide natural flood control, carbon storage, natural water purification, and goods such as fish, shellfish, timber and fibre (UNDP, UNEP, World Bank and WRI 2000). While information on the real extent of wetlands globally remains unreliable, recent estimates show that they may cover at least 12.8 million $km^2$ (Finlayson and others 1999). Human activities, including agriculture and settlements, have caused serious damage to freshwater ecosystems and contributed to the loss of about 50 per cent of the world's wetlands during the 20th century (Finlayson and others 1999). This damage to ecosystems reduces water quality and quantity, leading to a reduction in the effective availability of water for human use.

The total area of wetlands lost during the past 30 years is difficult to assess because of paucity of data and lack of accurate global information on the original extent of wetlands (UNDP and others 2000). However, a 1992 review of Ramsar sites (wetlands designated as 'important' under the Convention on Wetlands of International Importance Especially as Waterfowl Habitat) showed that 84 per cent were either threatened or experiencing ecological changes (Dugan and Jones 1993).

There has recently been a marked shift in water policy as policy-makers recognize that ecosystems require adequate water supplies to sustain normal functions and biodiversity conservation. Since 1992, new water policies have been developed that address the goal of preserving and allocating water for the environment — a change since the 1972 Stockholm

Conference which focused mainly on protecting air and water quality, and paid no attention to water for ecosystems. Although large projects involving dams are becoming less common due to limited sites, rising costs and general opposition, 349 dams more than 60 metres high were under construction in 1998 (UNDP and others 2000, WCD 2000). The remaining large free-flowing rivers are now found only in the tundra regions of North America and the Russian Federation, and in smaller basins in Africa and Latin America. There is now a growing emphasis on increasing water-use efficiency and increased productivity with the limited resources available (Postel 1997, Postel 1999, Gleick 1998). Throughout the world there are great opportunities to meet human needs with less water by:

- using existing technology (such as drip irrigation, low-flow toilets, and better industrial processes);
- changing irrigation technology;
- finding and stopping wasteful leaks;
- changing wasteful practices (such as irrigating during the day, using potable water for landscape irrigation);
- charging proper prices for water; and
- changing human activities (shifting to more water-efficient crops, changing industrial processes away from water-intensive production).

## Policies and institutions for water management

The Commission for Sustainable Development (CSD) has reported that many countries lack adequate legislation and policies for efficient and equitable allocation and use of water resources. Progress is, however, being made with the review of national legislation and enactment of new laws and regulations.

Concern has also been expressed about the growing incapacity of national hydrological services and agencies, particularly in developing countries, to assess their respective water resources. Many agencies have experienced reductions in observation networks and staff despite increases in water demand. A number of response measures have been undertaken including the World Hydrological Cycle Observing System (WHYCOS), which has been implemented in several regions. Its main objective is to contribute to the improvement of national and regional water resource assessment capabilities (CSD 1997b).

Many different kinds of organizations play a role in water policy decisions, from national governments to local community groups. Over the past decades, however, there has been a growing emphasis on increasing the participation and responsibility of small, local groups and an acknowledgement that communities have an important role to play in water policy.

The Ministerial Declaration at The Hague in March 2000 (see box) called for 'Governing water wisely: to ensure good governance, so that the involvement of the public and the interests of all stakeholders are included in the management of water resources' (World Water Forum 2000).

The private sector has recently begun to expand its role in water management. The 1990s saw a rapid increase in the rate and extent of privatization of previously publicly managed water systems. Private water companies are increasingly serving the needs of growing cities by taking over contracts from public agencies to build, own and operate some or even all of a municipal system. At the same time, concerns have

---

### Ministerial Declaration on Water Security in the 21st Century

Some 120 ministers of water attending the Second World Water Forum held at The Hague in March 2000 adopted a declaration aimed at achieving world water security. The declaration noted the following as the main challenges of this new century:

- **Meeting basic needs:** to recognize that access to safe and sufficient water and sanitation are basic human needs and are essential to health and well-being, and to empower people, especially women, through a participatory process of water management.

- **Securing the food supply:** to enhance food security, particularly of the poor and vulnerable, through the more efficient mobilization and use, and the more equitable allocation of water for food production.

- **Protecting ecosystems:** to ensure the integrity of ecosystems through sustainable water resources management.

- **Sharing water resources:** to promote peaceful cooperation and develop synergies between different uses of water at all levels, whenever possible, within and, in the case of boundary and transboundary water resources, between states concerned, through sustainable river basin management or other appropriate approaches.

- **Managing risks:** to provide security from floods, droughts, pollution and other water-related hazards.

- **Valuing water:** to manage water in a way that reflects its economic, social, environmental and cultural values for all its uses, and to move towards pricing water services to reflect the cost of their provision. This approach should take account of the need for equity and the basic needs of the poor and the vulnerable.

- **Governing water wisely:** to ensure good governance, so that the involvement of the public and the interests of all stakeholders are included in the management of water resources.

Source: World Water Forum 2000

been growing about how best to ensure equitable access to water for the poor, finance projects and share risks.

## Conclusion

The development of water supply infrastructure dominated policy options for most of the two decades following 1972 but many innovative approaches to water resources management were introduced in the 1990s.

Major policy trends in this period include:
- recognition of both the social and economic value of water;
- emphasis on efficient allocation of water;
- recognition of catchment management as critical to effective management of water resources;
- greater cooperation by river basin states to ensure equitable distribution of resources;
- improved data collection;
- recognition of the role of all stakeholders in water management;
- adoption of integrated water resources management as a strategic policy initiative; and
- recognition of growing water scarcity due to various factors, including population and industrial growth, and increased pollution.

While developed countries have made significant strides in addressing water quality issues, the situation has actually worsened in developing countries, with many of them experiencing rising water demand and pollution. More countries are facing water stress or scarcity.

## References: Chapter 2, freshwater, global overview

Bernard, A. (1999). *International Cooperation Through River Basin Commissions*. Ramsar Convention Bureau http://www.ramsar.org/cop7_doc_20.2_e.htm [Geo-2-116]

CSD (1997a). *Comprehensive Assessment of the Freshwater Resources of the World. Report of the Secretary-General*. United Nations Economic and Social Council http://www.un.org/documents/ecosoc/cn17/1997/ecn171997-9.htm [Geo-2-117]

CSD (1997b). *Overall Progress Achieved Since the United Nations Conference on Environment and Development. Report of the Secretary-General. Addendum - Protection of the Quality and Supply of Freshwater Resources: Application of Integrated Approaches to the Development, Management and Use of Water Resources*. United Nations Economic and Social Council http://www.un.org/documents/ecosoc/cn17/1997/ecn171997-2add17.htm [Geo-2-118]

Dugan, P.J. and Jones, T. (1993). Ecological Changes in Wetlands: A Global Overview. In M. Moser, R.C. Prentice and J. van Vessems (eds.), *Waterfowl and Wetland Conservation in the 1990s: A Global Perspective*. Slimbridge, United Kingdom, International Waterfowl and Wetlands Research Bureau

FAO (2001). AQUASTAT — FAO's information system on water and agriculture http://www.fao.org/waicent/faoinfo/agricult/agl/aglw/aquastatweb/main/html/background.htm [Geo-2-119]

Finlayson, C.M., Davidson, N.C., Spiers, A.G. and Stevenson, N.J. (1999). Global wetland inventory - current status and future priorities. *Marine and Freshwater Research* 50, 8, 717–28

Foster, S., Lawrence, A. and Morris, B. (1998). *Groundwater in Urban Development: Assessing Management Needs and Formulating Policy Strategies*. Washington DC, World Bank

Gleick, P.H. (1993). *Water in Crisis: A Guide to the World's Freshwater Resources*. New York, Oxford University Press

Gleick, P.H. (1998). *The World's Water 1998-1999*. Washington DC, Island Press

INBO (2001). *INBO Home Page*. International Network of Basin Organizations http://www.oieau.fr/riob/friobang.htm [Geo-2-120]

Meybeck, M., Chapman, D. and Helmer, R. (1990). *Global Freshwater Quality: A First Assessment*. Cambridge, Massachusetts, Basil Blackwell

Postel, S. (1997). *Pillar of Sand: Can the Irrigation Miracle Last?* New York, W.W. Norton and Company

Postel, S. (1999). *Last Oasis: Facing Water Scarcity*. New York, W.W. Norton and Company

Shiklomanov, I.A. (1993). World freshwater resources. In P. H. Gleick (ed.), *Water in Crisis: A Guide to the World's Freshwater Resources*. New York, Oxford University Press

Shiklomanov, I.A. (1999). World Water Resources and their Use. *Database on CD Rom*. Paris, UNESCO

UNDP, UNEP, World Bank and WRI (2000). *World Resources 2000-2001*. Washington DC, World Resources Institute

UNEP (1996). *Groundwater: A Threatened Resource*. Nairobi, UNEP

UNEP (1999). *GEO-2000*. United Nations Environment Programme. London and New York, Earthscan

UN (1999). *Comprehensive Assessment of the Freshwater Resources of the World. Report of the Secretary-General*. United Nations Division for Sustainable Development http://www.un.org/esa/sustdev/freshwat.htm [Geo-2-121]

UN (2000). *Drinking Water Supply and Sanitation Update. Report No UNE/CN 17/2000/13*. New York, Commission on Sustainable Development

United Nations Population Division (2001). *World Population Prospects 1950-2050 (The 2000 Revision)*. New York, United Nations www.un.org/esa/population/publications/wpp2000/wpp2000h.pdf

WCD (2000). *Dams and Development: A New Framework for Decision-Making. The Report of the World Commission on Dams*. London, Earthscan http://www.damsreport.org/wcd_overview.htm [Geo-2-122]

WHO and UNICEF (2000). *Global Water Supply and Sanitation Assessment 2000 Report*. Geneva and New York, World Health Organization and United Nations Children's Fund http://www.who.int/water_sanitation_health/Globassessment/GlasspdfTOC.htm [Geo-2-123]

World Commission on Water (1999). *World's Rivers in Crisis - Some Are Dying; Others Could Die*. World Water Council http://www.worldwatercouncil.org/Vision/6902B03438178538C125683A004BE974.htm [Geo-2-124]

World Water Council (2000a). *World Water Vision Commission Report: A Water Secure World. Vision for Water, Life and the Environment*. World Water Council http://www.worldwatercouncil.org/Vision/Documents/CommissionReport.pdf [Geo-2-125]

World Water Council (2000b). *World Water Vision: Making Water Everyone's Business*. London, Earthscan

World Water Forum (2000). *Ministerial Declaration of The Hague on Water Security in the 21st Century*. World Water Forum http://www.worldwaterforum.net/index2.html [Geo-2-126]

WSSCC (2000). *Vision 21: A Shared Vision for Water Supply, Sanitation and Hygiene and a Framework for Future Action*. Geneva, World Health Organization

## Freshwater: Africa

Africa's renewable water resources average 4 050 km$^3$/year, providing in the year 2000 an average of about 5 000 m$^3$ per capita/year — significantly less than the world average of 7 000 m$^3$ per capita/year and less than one-quarter of the South American average of 23 000 m$^3$ per capita/year (Shiklomanov 1999 and United Nations Population Division 2001).

However, the distribution of both surface water and groundwater is uneven. For example, the Democratic Republic of Congo is the wettest country, with average annual internal renewable water resources of 935 km$^3$ compared to the region's driest country Mauritania, where the annual average is 0.4 km$^3$ (UNDP, UNEP, World Bank and WRI 2000). The spatial distribution of water resources in the region does not coincide with the highest population densities, resulting in many areas (particularly urban centres) being water stressed or dependent on external sources of water.

At least 13 countries suffered water stress or scarcity (less than 1 700 m$^3$ per capita/year and less than 1 000 m$^3$ per capita/year respectively) in 1990 and the number is projected to double by 2025 (PAI 1995). This presents a major challenge to water planners in terms of supply and distribution.

Groundwater is a major source of water in the region, contributing 15 per cent of Africa's resources (Lake and Souré 1997). The major aquifers are found in the northern Sahara, Nubia, Sahel and Chad basins as well as the Kgalagadi (Kalahari). Groundwater is used for domestic and agricultural consumption in many areas, particularly the more arid sub-regions where surface water resources are limited. However, areas heavily dependent on groundwater reserves are also at risk of water shortages, as water is extracted far more rapidly than it is recharged.

### Variability of water resources

Africa experiences large spatial variations in rainfall, with 95 per cent of the total falling in the central and southwestern wet equatorial zone (Lake and Souré 1997). Severe droughts have been recorded in the Sahel and in the Northern, Eastern and Southern sub-regions over the past 30 years.

As a result, a number of inter-basin water transfer schemes have been developed. For example, in South Africa where 60 per cent of the run-off originates from one-fifth of the land area, large volumes of water are transported by inter-basin transfer schemes to major industrial centres such as Johannesburg (Goldblatt and others 2000). However, these schemes can exert significant pressure on the environment as reduced natural flows impact on downstream ecosystems.

Responses to water shortage in the Seychelles and Mauritius include desalinization, water rationing by the hotel and manufacturing industries, and recycling of domestic wastewater. These measures are expected to produce savings of about 240 million m$^3$/year in the long-term (Government of Mauritius and ERM 1998). In Egypt, severe water shortages have also prompted schemes to recycle agricultural drainage water to meet growing agricultural demand.

As in other regions, the major factors influencing water availability in Africa include growing domestic consumption for drinking water and sanitation, irrigated agriculture and industrialization (which also is a source of pollution and affects water quality). Losses from domestic water distribution systems account for significant wastage. Similarly, many irrigation systems are outdated. In South Africa, up to 50 per cent of irrigation water is lost due to leakages (Global Water Partnership 2000). In some countries, however, efforts are being made to improve water use efficiency.

### Access to safe water and sanitation

Some 62 per cent of Africans had access to an improved water supply in 2000. Even so, rural Africans spend much time searching for water and 28 per cent of the global population without access to improved water supplies live in Africa. Women are particularly affected as they are often responsible for the family's water needs. Urban areas are better

---

### Rainfall variability in the Lake Chad basin

**Lake Chad in 1973 and 1997; red colour denotes vegetation on the lake bed**

*Source: NASA 2001*

Over the past 30 years, the surface area of Lake Chad has varied considerably — from 25 000 to 2 000 km$^2$ — due to rainfall variability over the past 30 years. The lake supports globally important wildlife, particularly migratory birds. The economic activities of about 20 million people are based on the lake's resources. A new GEF-funded project in the Lake Chad Basin aims to decrease environmental degradation by improving cooperation between interested and affected parties, with the benefits from project-related activities accruing to the local communities.

*Source: Coe and Foley 2001*

supplied, with 85 per cent of the population having access to improved water supplies. In rural areas, the average is 47 per cent, with 99 per cent of the rural population in Eritrea having no sanitation coverage. The total African population with access to improved sanitation was 60 per cent in 2000. Again, urban populations fared better, with an average 84 per cent having improved sanitation compared to an average 45 per cent in rural areas (WHO and UNICEF 2000).

Poor water supply and sanitation lead to high rates of water-related diseases such as ascariasis, cholera, diarrhoea, dracunculiasis, dysentery, eye infections, hookworm, scabies, schistosomiasis and trachoma. About 3 million people in Africa die annually as a result of water-related diseases (Lake and Souré 1997). In 1998, 72 per cent of all reported cholera cases in the world were in Africa.

Poor water supply and sanitation lead to contamination of surface and groundwater, with subsequent effects on plant, animal and human communities. The economic costs can be high. In Malawi, for example, the total cost associated with water degradation was estimated at US$2.1 million in 1994 (DREA Malawi 1994). These costs included the need for water treatment, the development of human resources and reduced labour productivity. Meeting basic water and sanitation needs is also expensive. In Nigeria, a recent study estimates the future cost of water supply and environmental sanitation to be

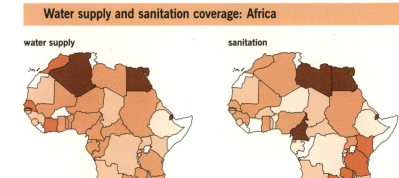

**Water supply and sanitation coverage: Africa**

water supply         sanitation

☐ 0%–25%
☐ 26%–50%
☐ 51%–75%
☐ 76%–90%
■ 91%–100%
☐ missing data

**In the year 2000, 62 per cent of Africans had access to improved water supplies and 60 per cent to sanitation — but coverage was poor in large areas of the continent**

*Source: WHO and UNICEF 2000*

US$9.12 billion during 2001–10 (Adedipe, Braid and Iliyas 2000).

Governments are trying to improve the situation with environmental management policies that include waste management and urban planning, and by making environmental impact assessments compulsory for large projects. One of the major regional policy initiatives was the 1980 Lagos Plan of Action, which urged member states to formulate master plans in the sectors of water supply and agriculture (OAU 1980). The Plan was influenced by the 1977 United Nations Water Conference's Mar del Plata Action Plan and the 1978 African regional meeting on water-related issues. Despite these initiatives, a lack of human and financial resources, and equipment for implementation and enforcement, still limit progress.

## Deteriorating water quality

Freshwater and groundwater pollution is a growing concern in many areas, further limiting access to safe water. Poor water quality leads not only to water-related diseases but also reduces agricultural production, which means that more foodstuffs and agricultural products must be imported. Poor water quality also limits economic development options, such as water-intensive industries and tourism, a situation that is potentially disastrous to developing countries in Africa.

To counter this problem, many countries have established or enforced effluent water standards and rehabilitated wastewater treatment facilities. Other responses include schemes in Central Africa for purification and decontamination of freshwater systems, and public awareness campaigns. Although

### Sludge disposal in Cairo

A study launched in Cairo in 1995 has shown that wastewater treatment can address not only the Egyptian city's water pollution problems but also open new opportunities for business and agriculture. The Greater Cairo Wastewater Project will produce about 0.4 million tonnes of sludge or biosolids annually from wastewater treatment.

The study was initiated under the Mediterranean Environmental Technical Assistance Programme funded by the European Investment Bank and promoted by the Cairo Wastewater Organization. Initial results show that sludge can be effective in growing wheat, berseem clover, forage maize and grape vines. Digested sludge offers significant nitrogen fertilizer replacement value to farmers; no harmful effects of biosolids on crops were detected in field trials; and the benefits of spreading biosolids on newly reclaimed soils are expected to increase with cumulative applications. Farmers in Egypt are prepared to pay for bio-solids due to the scarcity of manure and the high costs of inorganic fertilizers.

*Source: UNCSD 1999*

only recently implemented, these responses have been locally successful in improving access to drinking water and raising awareness.

In Eastern and Southern Africa, the widespread invasion of the water hyacinth (*Eichornia crassipes*) is a further cause of deteriorating water quality. The water hyacinth forms dense mats that block water channels, disrupting flow patterns. Decaying mats of the weed generate bad odours and lead to eutrophication of the water body. Areas afflicted by the water hyacinth include Lakes Victoria and Kariba, and some rivers. Affected countries have begun biological and chemical control programmes, in addition to mechanical clearance, with some success (Global Water Partnership 2000). Watercourses in West Africa are similarly threatened by *Salvinia molesta* and *Typha* species.

## Wetlands

Wetland habitats in Africa cover about 1.2 million km$^2$ (Finlayson and others 1999). However, wetlands are threatened by both pollution and reclamation.

Loss of wetlands in Southern Africa is thought to have contributed to the severity of the flooding in 1999-2000, which affected 30 000 families and 34 000 hectares of farmland (Mpofu 2000). To prevent further wetland degradation, 27 African countries had signed and ratified the 1987 Ramsar Convention as of December 1998, placing 75 sites covering some 14 million ha under protection (Frazier 1999).

## Integrated water resources management

A shift towards integrated water resources management (IWRM) is one of the new policy initiatives that have been adopted in Africa to address the issues raised above. Integrated water resources management is not limited to the national level but also includes basins shared by two or more states. The Nile Basin Initiative, launched in 1999, is a joint programme of action between 10 Nile countries. The objectives are to ensure sustainable resource development, security, cooperation and economic integration. In Southern Africa, the eight basin states of the Zambezi have been cooperating under the Zambezi River System Action Plan but efforts to establish a Zambezi Basin Commission have been slow. Another example of regional cooperation is in the Lake Victoria area, where in 1995 a GEF-funded project was established to focus primarily on fisheries management, pollution control, control of invasive weeds, and catchment land use management.

## References: Chapter 2, freshwater, Africa

Adedipe, N.O., Braid, E.J., and Iliyas, M.H. (2000). *Development of Strategy/Action Plan and Implementation Guidelines for the National Water Supply and Sanitation Policy*. Abuja, UNICEF and Nigerian Federal Ministry of Water Resources

Coe, M. and Foley, J. (2001). Human and Natural Impacts on the Water Resources of the Lake Chad Basin. *Journal of Geophysical Research* 27 February 2001, Vol. 106, No. D4

DREA Malawi (1994). *National Environmental Action Plan Vol. 1*. Lilongwe, Malawi Department of Research and Environmental Affairs

Finlayson, C.M., Davidson, N.C., Spiers, A.G., and Stevenson, N.J. (1999). Global wetland inventory: current status and future priorities. *Marine Freshwater Resources* 50, 717–27

Frazier, S. (ed., 1999). *A Directory of Wetlands of International Importance*. Wageningen, Wetlands International and Ramsar Convention Bureau

Global Water Partnership (2000). *Southern African Vision for Water, Life and the Environment in the 21st Century and Strategic Framework for Action Statement*. Global Water Partnership Southern Africa Technical Advisory Committee http://www.gwpsatac.org.zw/vision/chapter10.html [Geo-2-101]

Goldblatt, M., Ndamba, J., van der Merwe, B., Gomes, F., Haasbroek, B. and Arntzen, J. ( 2000). *Water Demand Management: Towards Developing Effective Strategies for Southern Africa*. Harare, IUCN ROSA

Government of Mauritius and ERM (1998). *Mauritius NEAP II: Strategy Options Report*. Port Louis, Government of Mauritius and Environmental Resources Management

Government of Mauritius (1994). *National Physical Development Plan*. Port Louis, Ministry of Housing, Lands and Country Planning

Lake, W. B. and Souré, M. (1997). *Water and Development in Africa*. International Development Information Centre http://www.acdi–cida.gc.ca/xpress/dex/dex9709.htm [Geo-2-103]

Mpofu, B. (2000). *Assessment of Seed Requirements in Southern African Countries Ravaged by Floods and Drought 1999/2000 Season*. SADC Food Security Programme, Food, Agriculture and Natural Resources http://www.sadc-fanr.org.zw/sssd/mozcalrep.htm [Geo-2-104]

NASA 2001. *A Shadow of a Lake: Africa's disappearing Lake Chad*. NASA Goddard Space Flight Center http://www.gsfc.nasa.gov/gsfc/earth/environ/lakechad/chad.htm [Geo-2-327]

OAU (1980). *Lagos Plan of Action for the Economic Development of Africa: 1980-2000*. Addis Ababa, Organization of African Unity

PAI (1995). *Sustaining Water: An Update*. Washington DC, Population Action International, Population and Environment Programme

Shiklomanov, I.A. (1999). *World Water Resources: Modern Assessment and Outlook for the 21st Century*. St Petersburg, Federal Service of Russia for Hydrometeorology and Environment Monitoring, State Hydrological Institute

UNCSD (1999). *Cairo Sludge Disposal Study*. United Nations Commission on Sustainable Development http://www.un.org/esa/sustdev/success/cairo_st.htm [Geo-2-105]

UNDP, UNEP, World Bank and WRI (2000). *World Resources 2000-2001*. Washington DC, World Resources Institute

United Nations Population Division (2001). *World Population Prospects 1950-2050 (The 2000 Revision)*. New York, United Nations

WHO and UNICEF (2000). *Global Water Supply and Sanitation Assessment 2000 Report*. Geneva and New York, World Health Organization and United Nations Children's Fund http://www.who.int/water_sanitation_health/Globassessment/Glassessment6.pdf [Geo-2-111]

WMO (1997). *Comprehensive Assessment of the Freshwater Resources of the World: assessment of water resources and water availability in the world*. Geneva, WMO

## Freshwater: Asia and the Pacific

The Asia and the Pacific Region accounts for about 36 per cent of global run-off. Even so, water scarcity and pollution are key issues and the region has the lowest per capita availability of freshwater: renewable water resources amounted to about 3 690 m$^3$ per capita/year in mid-1999 for the 30 largest countries in the region for which records are available (UNDP, UNEP, World Bank and WRI 2000 and United Nations Population Division 2001). In absolute terms, China, India and Indonesia have the largest water resources, more than one-half of the region's total. Several countries, including Bangladesh, India, Pakistan and the Republic of Korea, already suffer from water scarcity or water stress. More will do so as populations and consumption increase. Agriculture is the biggest consumer (86 per cent), with smaller amounts going to industry (8 per cent) and domestic use (6 per cent) (compiled from UNDP, UNEP, World Bank and WRI 2000).

### Water scarcity

Many countries do not have sufficient water to meet demand, with the result that aquifer depletion due to overextraction is common. Moreover, the scarcity of water is accompanied by a deterioration in the quality of available water due to pollution and environmental degradation. Dams and reservoirs coupled with deforestation in some watersheds have reduced stream water levels, lowered water tables, degraded riparian wetlands and diminished freshwater aquatic diversity. Excessive demand for groundwater in coastal cities such as Bangkok, Dhaka, Jakarta, Karachi and Manila has led to saline intrusion and ground subsidence.

Government policies and strategies have traditionally been concerned with increasing supply. However, policies have recently become increasingly focused on an integrated approach to water resource management by emphasizing demand management measures such as efficient water use, conservation and protection, institutional arrangements, legal, regulatory and economic instruments, public information and inter-agency cooperation. Common elements in the national policies and strategies now being adopted include integration of water resources development and management into socio-economic development; assessment and monitoring of water resources; protection of water and associated resources; provision of safe drinking water supply and sanitation; conservation and sustainable use of water for food production and other economic activities; institutional and legislative development; and public participation.

In India, a new irrigation management policy aims to improve water application efficiency through the use of modern technologies such as drip/sprinkler irrigation and better on-farm irrigation measures. In the Republic of Korea, where agriculture uses more than 50 per cent of water resources, the government's water resources development plan for the 21st century highlights measures that relate to increased food production with efficient water use (Kwun 1999). Decentralized water management is also being

### Lake Toba–Lake Champlain Sister Lakes Exchange

North–South cooperation between organizations in Indonesia and the United States has contributed to enhanced catchment management in the Lake Toba watershed — the world's largest volcanic crater lake, which covers about 4 000 km$^2$. The Indonesian lake, which suffers from degraded water quality, loss of biological diversity and invasions of troublesome non-native plants and animals, has benefited from institutional cooperation between the Lake Toba Heritage Foundation and the Lake Champlain Basin Programme (LCBP) in Vermont, United States. The Foundation used part of a grant from the United States Agency for International Development to establish a sister lakes relationship with the LCBP. The exchange programme has helped address freshwater management issues in the Lake Toba catchment using experiences from another catchment and region.

The programme demonstrates the following lessons:
- freshwater lakes of the world share similar management challenges;
- some of the greatest challenges have to do with managing a resource shared by multiple jurisdictions in a large geographic area;
- many of the management solutions require successful citizen and stakeholder involvement; and
- management experience can be directly transferred to other countries.

*Source: UNCSD 1999*

encouraged in countries such as China where city or provincial authorities are authorized to manage water resources. In India, multidisciplinary units in charge of developing comprehensive water plans have been established in some states. Stakeholder participation has reduced operational costs in countries such as Pakistan by involving communities in the development of water supply, sanitation, and water pollution prevention facilities and their maintenance.

Progress has also been made in adopting a basin-wide approach. The Indus Basin water-sharing accord

## Improved water supply and sanitation coverage: Asia and the Pacific

improved water supply          improved sanitation

- ☐ 0–25%
- ☐ >25–50%
- ☐ >50–75%
- ■ >75–90%
- ■ >90%
- ☐ missing data

In the year 2000, 81 per cent of Asians had access to improved water supplies but only 48 per cent — the lowest of any region — to sanitation

*Source: WHO and UNICEF 2000*

between India and Pakistan, the acclaimed Water Sharing Treaty between India and Bangladesh, the India–Bhutan cooperation on hydropower development and India–Nepal cooperation in harnessing transboundary rivers are examples of transboundary cooperation on water management in South Asia.

A major challenge is to change the fragmented sub-sectoral approaches to water management that have caused conflict and competition in the past, and to design and implement integrated mechanisms, particularly for projects that transcend sub-sectors.

### Water pollution

Over the years, water pollution has emerged as a major issue. Pollutants include pathogens, organic matter, nutrients, heavy metals and toxic chemicals, sediments and suspended solids, silt and salts.

South Asia — particularly India — and Southeast Asia are facing severe water pollution problems. Rivers such as the Yellow (China), Ganges (India), and Amu and Syr Darya (Central Asia) top the list of the world's most polluted rivers (World Commission on Water 1999). In cities in the developing countries of the region, most water bodies are now heavily polluted with domestic sewage, industrial effluents, chemicals and solid wastes. Most rivers in Nepal's urban areas have been polluted and their waters are now unfit for human use, while drinking water in Kathmandu is contaminated with coliform bacteria, iron, ammonia and other contaminants (UNEP 2001).

Water pollution has affected human health. In the Pacific Islands, especially in some atoll communities, use of polluted groundwater for drinking and cooking has led to health problems such as diarrhoea,

hepatitis, and occasional outbreaks of typhoid and cholera. Groundwater in districts of West Bengal, India, and in some villages in Bangladesh, for example, is contaminated with arsenic at levels as much as 70 times higher than the national drinking water standard of 0.05 mg/litre. While pollution is a factor, arsenic contamination is also due to natural phenomena. According to one report, 'With the majority of the country's 68 000 villages potentially at risk, UN scientists estimate that the arsenic may soon be killing 20 000 Bangladeshis a year' (Pierce 2001).

Inadequate water supply and poor sanitation cause more than 500 000 infant deaths a year as well as a huge burden of illness and disability in the region (UNEP 1999). Some 8–9 per cent of the total Disability Adjusted Life Years (DALYs) are due to diseases related to inadequate water supply and poor sanitation in India and other countries (World Bank 2000). Cholera is prevalent in many countries, particularly those where sanitation facilities are poor such as Afghanistan, China and India (WHO 2000).

Of the global population without access to improved sanitation or water supply, most live in Asia (WHO and UNICEF 2000, see map above). In the Southwest Pacific sub-region, water supply and sanitation appear to be relatively good, with 93 per cent of the population having access to improved sanitation and 88 per cent to improved water supply (WHO and UNICEF 2000). These figures are strongly biased by the large and well-served population of Australia, however. Only an estimated 48 per cent of the Asian population has sanitation coverage (WHO

### Water pollution in Australia

In Australia, the quality of water in many inland waterways has declined due to human activities within catchments (Ball and others 2001). Sediments, nutrients and toxic materials as well as excessive growth of aquatic weeds have affected aquatic ecosystems. Response measures include the Urban Storm Water Initiative, the Industry Partnership Programme and Waterwatch Australia that together aim to monitor and improve the health of urban waterways. A number of state and territory-based programmes have also been introduced, together with community programmes such as Streamwatch and Waterwatch. In addition, local authorities are developing storm water management plans for urban catchments with financial support from state and territory agencies. Storm water is increasingly seen as a resource to be collected and utilized rather than a waste for disposal.

*Source: Australia State of the Environment Committee 2001*

and UNICEF 2000) — less than in any other region of the world. The situation is worse in rural areas, where only 31 per cent of the population have improved sanitation, compared to 78 per cent coverage in urban areas.

During the past decade, several countries have started to address the water quality problem by implementing large-scale programmes and action plans to rehabilitate degraded streams and depleted aquifers. These programmes are typically given legislative or statutory authority such as that provided by Thailand's National Water Quality Act, the Philippine Water Quality Code, India's Environment Protection Act, China's Water Law and the Republic of Korea's Water Quality Preservation Act (UNESCAP 1999). Success stories with respect to rehabilitation and protection of water quality of rivers come from those countries where water policies promote a multisectoral and multidisciplinary approach to the management of water resources.

Clean-up campaigns for rivers, canals, lakes and other water bodies have become widespread. The programmes have often been successful in improving water quality and, occasionally, have led to the adoption of new water quality standards and water use regulations. They have also increased awareness of the need to reduce pollutant loads through wastewater treatment, reuse and recycling of sewage and industrial wastewater, introduction of low-cost technologies, and strict control of industrial and municipal effluent. There have been a number of successes in water reuse and recycling in the industrialized countries of the region.

Water quality has been improved in China, Japan, the Republic of Korea and Singapore as a result of initiatives to address water pollution. In Japan, the government has set environmental quality standards and made remarkable improvements: in 1991, 99.8 per cent of water samples met standards for heavy metals and toxins in Japan (RRI 2000). In 2000, the rate of industrial wastewater treatment across China was 94.7 per cent (SEPA 2001). Action in Singapore means that Singaporeans can now enjoy drinkable piped water straight from the tap.

## References: Chapter 2, freshwater, Asia and the Pacific

Australia State of the Environment Committee (2001). *Coasts and Oceans,* Australian State of the Environment Report 2001 (Theme Report). Canberra, CSIRO Publishing on behalf of the Department of the Environment and Heritage

Kwun, S. (1999). *Water for Food and Rural Development,* Country Paper of the Republic of Korea Regional Consultation Meeting for ICIDVision for Subsector. Kuala Lumpur, 17–19 May 1999

Pierce, F. (2001). Death in a Glass of Water. *The Independent.* 19 January 2001 http://www.independent.co.uk/story.jsp?story=515 08 [Geo-2-106]

RRI (2000). *Japan Environmental Policy.* Resource Renewal Institute http://www.rri.org/envatlas/asia/japan/jp-conc. html#Water [Geo-2-107]

SEPA (2001). *Report of the State of the Environment in China 2000.* Beijing, State Environmental Protection Administration

UNCSD (1999). *Lake Toba–Lake Champlain Sister Lakes Exchange.* United Nations Commission on Sustainable Development http://www.un.org/esa/sustdev/success/watenfed.htm [Geo-2-108]

UNDP, UNEP, World Bank and WRI (2000). *World Resources 2000-2001.* Washington DC, World Resources Institute

UNEP (1999). *GEO-2000.* United Nations Environment Programme. London and New York, Earthscan

UNEP (2001). *Nepal: State of the Environment 2001.* Bangkok, MoPE/HMGN/ICIMOD/ SACEP/NORAD/UNEP

UNESCAP (1999). *ESCAP Population Data Sheet, Population and Development Indicators for Asia and the Pacific, 1999.* Bangkok, United Nations Economic and Social Commission for Asia and the Pacific

United Nations Population Division (2001). *World Population Prospects 1950-2050 (The 2000 Revision).* New York, United Nations www.un.org/esa/population/publications/wpp2000/ wpp2000h.pdf

WHO (2000). *Communicable Disease Surveillance and Response. Global Cholera Update.* World Health Organization http://www.who.int/emc/diseases/cholera/choltbl19 99.html [Geo-2-109]

WHO and UNICEF (2000). *Global Water Supply and Sanitation Assessment 2000 Report.* Geneva and New York, World Health Organization and United Nations Children's Fund http://www.who.int/water_sanitation_health/Globass essment/Glassessment7.pdf [Geo-2-112]

World Commission on Water (1999). *World's Rivers in Crisis - Some Are Dying; Others Could Die.* World Water Council http://www.worldwatercouncil.org/Vision/6902B03 438178538C125683A004BE974.htm [Geo-2-110]

World Bank (2000). *Health and Environment. Environment Strategy Paper.* World Bank http://lnweb18.worldbank.org/essd/essd.nsf/Global View/HealthandENV.pdf/$File/HealthandENV.pdf [Geo-2-113]

## Freshwater: Europe

Water resources are unevenly distributed in Europe. Annual average run-off ranges from 3 000 mm in western Norway to 100-400 mm over much of central Europe and less than 25 mm in central and southern Spain (ETC/WTR 2001). Traditionally, most European countries rely more on surface water than on groundwater, which is often used only for public water supply (EEA 1999a, Eurostat 1997). Data for assessing water quantity trends are rather poor but relatively good for water quality. Water pollution is a serious issue throughout Europe. Though some progress has been made in pollution reduction in Western Europe, the situation is less promising in Central and Eastern Europe (CEE).

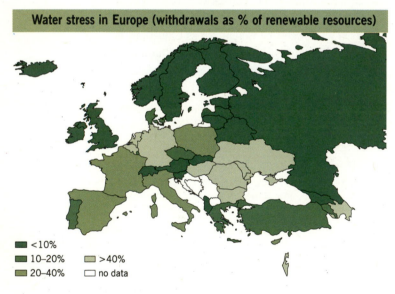

**Water stress in Europe (withdrawals as % of renewable resources)**

■ <10%
■ 10–20%
■ 20–40%
▢ >40%
☐ no data

**Water stress occurs in parts of Europe, notably in the irrigated areas of CEE and the highly industrialized countries of Western Europe**

*Source: compiled from UNDP, UNEP, World Bank and WRI 2000*

### Water quantity

Europe abstracts a relatively small portion of its total renewable water resources. Western Europe abstracts, on average, around 20 per cent (EEA 1999b), although this ranges from less than 5 per cent in the northern countries to more than 40 per cent in Belgium, Germany, and the Netherlands. The Russian Federation, with 9 per cent of the world's water resources, abstracts less than 2 per cent annually (RFEP 2000). However, water quantity problems do occur in areas with low rainfall and high population density, and in large land areas under irrigated agriculture, especially in Mediterranean countries and in CEE.

In the central part of Western Europe, most of the

water supply is used as a coolant in energy production. This water is returned to its source more or less unchanged and can be re-used. In southern countries of Western Europe, where water resources are less abundant, agriculture consumes far more than the other sectors — about 80 per cent, compared to 20 per cent for urban and industrial use (ETC/WTR 2001). Some 80 per cent of the water used for irrigation evaporates.

The amount of water abstracted for public water supply in Western Europe fell by 8–10 per cent between 1985 and 1995 as a result of improved industrial and domestic water use efficiency (ETC/WTR 2001). However, a significant increase in agricultural water use occurred in southern Europe because irrigated farmland has increased by nearly 20 per cent since the mid-1980s. In CEE, there has been a marked decline in water consumption for industrial purposes due to economic restructuring but the demand from urban areas and for irrigated agriculture is growing steadily (EEA 1998).

There is little legislation controlling water use in Europe. Traditionally, quantity problems have been dealt with by increasing storage capacities through reservoirs and water transfer schemes. However, demand reduction measures are now in place in several countries in Western Europe. These, together with greater awareness of water use in general, have reduced public consumption. The domestic and industrial sectors have become increasingly water-efficient. Examples of water conservation measures include: metering; increased charges and taxes; restrictions on garden watering; reducing leakage; user education and widespread use of more efficient appliances such as low and dual flush toilets, and washing machines that consume less water.

Abstraction charges and pricing mechanisms are valuable for improving the sustainability of water use in agriculture and deserve more attention because water prices for agricultural use are often lower than for other users. For instance, a recent study (Planistat 1998) found that in the French Adour-Garonne basin, the drinking water supply is almost entirely self-financing (about 98 per cent) but the irrigation tariff covers only 30–40 per cent of the total cost of the services. Other agricultural reforms include planting crops with lower water demands and introducing more efficient irrigation systems. In CEE, all these less conventional measures are being applied but a major challenge will be to reduce leakage — losses sometimes exceed 50 per cent (EEA 1998).

## Water quality

Overloading with organic matter, nitrogen and phosphorus in the 1970s and 1980s resulted in eutrophication of seas, lakes, rivers and groundwater throughout Europe. The main source of nitrogen is fertilizers in run-off from agricultural land. Most phosphorus comes from households and industry wastewater, though in areas with intensive agriculture in Western Europe, phosphorus from agriculture approaches 50 per cent of the total load (EEA 2001). In Western Europe, fertilizer consumption has fallen since the mid-1980s but eutrophication has continued due to increased nutrient run-off from intensive livestock production. In CEE, use of agrochemicals has declined markedly since the early 1990s, resulting in a reduction of nitrogen-phosphorus fertilizer use by about 50 per cent (Czech Republic 1999, Republic of Hungary 1999).

Pollution of groundwater is another serious problem, mainly associated with nitrates and pesticides from agriculture (EEA 1998). In the Russian Federation alone, more than 2 700 sources of groundwater were identified as polluted in 1999 (RFEP 2000).

Phosphorus discharges from urban wastewater treatment plants in Western Europe have fallen significantly (50–80 per cent) since the early 1980s, largely due to the huge increase in treatment of wastewater (ETC/WTR 2001) and wide-scale introduction of phosphorus-free detergents. By the end of the 1990s, 90 per cent of Western Europeans were connected to sewers and 70 per cent to wastewater treatment plants (ETC/WTR 2001). In CEE, however, 30–40 per cent of households were not yet connected to sewers by 1990 and treatment was inadequate (EEA 1999c). Since 1990, most Accession Countries have started to invest heavily in sewage collection and treatment but its high cost is one of the major financial issues in the accession process (Republic of Slovenia 1999). In the Eastern European countries of the former Soviet Union, little has been done to improve wastewater treatment.

Many lakes that had high phosphorus concentrations in the early 1980s have lower concentrations today. However, only slight changes in phosphorus concentrations have been observed in

---

### How the Volga and the Ural were not cleaned up

In the early 1970s, funds of 1.2 billion roubles were allocated for a clean-up plan for the Volga and the Ural rivers (Bush 1972) — one of the first publicly announced projects to clean up industrial rivers and safeguard the water supply. Many ministries were charged with negligence or slowness in implementing measures to correct the problem and with failing to make full use of the capital investment allotted for water protection measures. The authorities were given until 1980 to implement the measures needed to ensure a complete end to the discharge of untreated wastewater into the Volga-Ural river basins. However, by the end of the 1980s, the pollution level of the Volga and its tributaries was still assessed as 'extremely high', and it continued to increase in the 1990s.

*Source: Interstate Statistical Committee 1999*

---

initially less-affected lakes (EEA 2000). This is mainly due to accumulation and (delayed) release of phosphorus from lake bottoms or continued contamination from small, scattered dwellings and from agricultural sources. Overall, water quality in many European lakes is still poor (ETC/WTR 2001). Heavy pollution in Western European rivers such as the Rhine has declined significantly since 1980 (ETC/WTR 2001) but improvements have been less significant in southern and Central Europe. In Eastern Europe, the situation is different. In the Russian Federation and Ukraine, the two most industrialized countries of the former Soviet Union, discharge of polluted water into rivers increased in the second half of the 1980s and in the 1990s, despite an alleged clean-up campaign for the Volga and Ural rivers as early as 1972 (see box above).

Poor water quality impacts human health. In Europe, however, outbreaks of water-borne diseases affecting less than 20 per cent of the supplied population are rarely detected. Even so, occasional outbreaks of water-borne diseases such as gastro-intestinal infections, affecting much of the population, are reported across Europe, even from countries with high standards of supply (WHO 1999). Lead from old distribution pipes and, in Eastern Europe, contaminated wells can affect the neuro-behavioural development of children (EEA/WHO 1999).

At sub-regional level, various EU Directives tackle water quality issues. Implementation of the Drinking Water and Nitrate Directives has been unsatisfactory in most member states, although the Urban Wastewater Treatment Directive has led to a decrease in organic matter discharges by two-thirds and in nutrients by one-half (ETC/WTR 2001). Further improvements are likely as more countries invest in new infrastructure to comply with the objectives of the Directive. The same will be true for Accession Countries in Central Europe.

The mixed success of these measures can be related to the absence of integrated policies for water management. Policy development currently focuses on sustainable watershed management and freshwater protection through integration of quantity and quality aspects. Integration may be improved by the Water Framework Directive which aims to achieve good surface water status in all European water bodies by 2015 and addresses the issue of integrated management of water resources at the catchment level (EEA 1999a).

## Policy and legislative framework

There are many multilateral and bilateral agreements for the management of transboundary waters. At the pan-European level, the 1992 UNECE Convention of the Protection and Use of Transboundary Watercourses and International Lakes strengthens national measures, obliging parties to prevent, control and reduce water pollution from point and non-point sources. It also includes provisions for monitoring, research and development, consultations, warning and alarm systems, mutual assistance, institutional arrangements, and the exchange and protection of information, as well as public access to information. A Protocol on Water and Health is awaiting entry into force.

At the watershed level, transboundary initiatives include the Convention on Cooperation for the Protection and Sustainable Use of the River Danube and the new Convention for the Protection of the Rhine. The Danube Convention pledges the signatories to work together to conserve, improve and rationally use the surface and ground waters in the Danube Catchment basin; to control hazards originating from accidents in the river area; and to contribute to reducing the pollution loads of the Black Sea from sources in the catchment area. The new Rhine Convention, adopted at the January 2001 Conference of Rhine Ministers, will be the basis for international cooperation of the riparian countries and the EU, replacing the Agreement on the International Commission for the Protection of the Rhine against Pollution (Bern 1963) and the 1976 Convention for the Protection of the Rhine against Chemical Pollution. The new convention fixes targets for international cooperation for sustainable development of the Rhine, further improvement of its ecological state, holistic flood protection and defence. In addition to aspects of water quality and quantity, including flood-related problems, groundwater problems in relation to the Rhine will in future be included in the convention's provisions (ICPR 2001).

## References: Chapter 2, freshwater, Europe

Bush, K. (1972). Steps towards Pollution Control in the USSR. *Radio Liberty Research*, 6 April 1972, pp.1-7

Czech Republic (1999). *State Environmental Policy*. Prague, Ministry of the Environment

EEA (1998). *Europe´s Environment: The Second Assessment*. Copenhagen, European Environment Agency

EEA (1999a). *Groundwater Quality and Quantity in Europe. Environmental Assessment Report No.3*. Copenhagen, European Environment Agency

EEA (1999b). *Sustainable Water Use in Europe – Sectoral Use of Water. Environmental Assessment Report No.1*. Copenhagen, European Environment Agency

EEA (1999c). *Environment in the European Union at the Turn of the Century. Environmental Assessment Report No.2*. Copenhagen, European Environment Agency

EEA (2000). *Environmental Signals 2000. Environmental Assessment Report No. 6*. Copenhagen, European Environment Agency

EEA (2001). *Environmental Signals 2001. Environmental Assessment Report No. 8*. Copenhagen, European Environment Agency

EEA and WHO (1999). *Children in Their Environment: Vulnerable, Valuable, and at Risk*. Background briefing for the 3rd European Ministerial Conference on Environment and Health, Copenhagen, World Health Organization Regional Office for Europe and European Environment Agency

ETC/WTR (2001). European Topic Centre on Water http://water.eionet.eu.int/Databases [Geo-2-114]

Eurostat (1997). *Estimations of Renewable Water Resources in the European Union*. Luxembourg, Statistical Office of the European Communities

ICPR (2001). *Home Page*. International Commission for the Protection of the Rhine http://iksr.firmen-netz.de/icpr/ [Geo-2-115]

Interstate Statistical Committee (1999) *Official Statistics of CIS countries*. CD-ROM. Moscow, Interstate Statistical Committee of the Commonwealth of Independent States

Planistat (1998). *A Study on Water Economics – Integrated Report*. A study for the European Commission – DG XI.B.1. Paris, Planistat Group

Republic of Hungary (1999). *National Environmental Programme 1997-2002* Budapest, Ministry of Environment.

Republic of Slovenia (1999). *National ISPA Strategy of the Republic of Slovenia: Environmental Sector*. Llubljana, Ministry of Environment and Physical Planning

RFEP (2000). *Government Report on the State of the Environment in the Russian Federation in 1999*. Moscow, State Committee of the Russian Federation on Environmental Protection

UNDP, UNEP, World Bank and WRI (2000). *World Resources 2000-2001*. Washington DC, World Resources Institute

United Nations Population Division (2001). *World Population Prospects 1950-2050 (The 2000 Revision)*. New York, United Nations www.un.org/esa/population/publications/wpp2000/wpp2000h.pdf

WHO (1999). *Overview of Environment and Health in Europe in the 1990s*. Report prepared for the 3rd European Conference on Environment and Health. Geneva, World Health Organization

## Freshwater: Latin America and the Caribbean

The Latin America and Caribbean Region is rich in renewable water resources with more than 30 per cent of the world's total. However, three hydrographic regions — the Gulf of Mexico Basin, the South Atlantic Basin and the La Plata Basin — covering 25 per cent of the region's territory, are home to 40 per cent of the population and contain only 10 per cent of the region's water resources (WWC 2000).

Most water-related problems transcend national boundaries although there are marked differences between sub-regions and countries. The major challenges are: decreasing per capita water availability due to population growth, urban expansion, deforestation and climate change; deteriorating water quality arising from untreated sewage, excessive use of fertilizers and pesticides, and industrial pollution — particularly from the mining and energy industries; and outdated institutional and legal frameworks.

### Availability and use

Water availability varies greatly, with South America being the richest sub-region. Some countries suffer from water shortages, and loss of aquatic biodiversity and habitats, with some Caribbean islands approaching or below water scarcity levels (WWC 2000). Sharp differences also exist within countries.

In most Caribbean small island states, rainfall is the sole source of freshwater (Antigua and Barbuda, the Bahamas and Barbados use desalinated water). In South America, groundwater reserves are of great importance and are estimated at 3 million km³ (GWP 2000). Mexico is particularly dependent on groundwater, which accounts for one-third of all reported freshwater extraction and for two-thirds of urban drinking water (CATHALAC 1999, WWC 1999).

Agriculture and industry are the major consumers of water in the region, followed by domestic consumption. Irrigated agriculture is one of the fastest expanding uses of freshwater. The amount of land under irrigated agriculture increased from 10 million ha in 1970 to more than 18 million ha in 1998 (FAOSTAT 2001). Water withdrawals for irrigation range from 56 per cent of total withdrawals in the Caribbean to 78 per cent in Mesoamerica. There is a general lack of efficiency in irrigation technology and

practice (World Bank 1999). Some recent institutional reforms have attempted to address this. In Mexico, for example, ownership of public irrigation systems has been transferred to 386 Water User Associations resulting in a dramatic improvement in cost recovery, system maintenance, yield and water use efficiency (Saleth and Dinar 1999).

Industry also uses large amounts of water. In South America, it is estimated that annual industrial withdrawals reach 15 km³ with 80 per cent of this demand coming from Argentina and Brazil alone

**Water availability in 2000 (1 000 m³ per capita/year)**

- 1.0 to 2.0 very low
- >2.0 to 5.0 low
- >5.0 to 10.0 middle
- >10.0 to 20.0 high
- >20.0 very high
- no data

Map shows water availability measured in terms of 1 000 m³ per capita/year

Source: compiled from UNDP, UNEP, World Bank and WRI 2000 and United Nations Population Division 2001

(ACAA 2001). In Brazil, virtually all the country's electricity comes from hydropower. The mining sector, especially in Chile and Peru, requires increasing quantities of water. For some regions such as the Andes, this may well lead to the need to import water in the near future. In Venezuela and Trinidad and Tobago, the petroleum sector is an important consumer.

The demand for water for domestic use is also on the increase. However, inequity among users, even in water-rich countries, is rampant. Many of the poor in both rural areas and urban communities have neither access to clean water nor sanitation services (WWC 2000). In 1995, 27 per cent of the population had

'In 1998, Hurricane Mitch caused US$58 million of damage in Honduras alone. The devastation included the destruction of 85 000 latrines and 1 683 rural water mains. As a result, 75 per cent of the population — about 4.5 million people — lost access to drinking water. Devastation such as that caused by Hurricane Mitch may last for months or even years.' — *WHO and UNICEF 2000*

either no domestic water supply or no easy access to it. In the same year, 41 per cent of the water was untreated and 31 per cent of the population had no sewage services (PAHO 1998). By 2000, 85 per cent of the population had an improved water supply and 78 per cent had improved sanitation coverage — but this still meant that 78 million people had no access to improved water supply and 117 million had no access to improved sanitation services (WHO and UNICEF 2000). Large disparities also exist between rural and

### The Tegucigalpa Model: water supply for peri-urban settlements

Community participation, a cost-sharing and cost-recovery system, hygiene education and training have contributed to improving water supply and sanitation in many peri-urban communities in the Honduran capital of Tegucigalpa. Rapid urbanization over the past 20 years increased Tegucigalpa's population to 850 000, with more than half of the people living in 225 peri-urban communities. Surface water is almost non-existent, and groundwater is often too deep and polluted. The provision of basic services such as water and sewage systems is difficult and costly.

The programme on water supply for peri-urban settlements, which is a partnership involving UNICEF, with the National Autonomous Water and Sewage Authority (SANAA) Executive Unit for Settlements in Development (UEBD) and communities, provided water supply to 150 000 people in 80 communities and sanitation coverage to about 5 000 in four communities between 1987 and 1996. One of the strengths of the programme is community participation and investment. The community has to provide labour and construction materials, contribute financially through water tariffs and recover the full investment cost. The community must establish a Water Board to collect tariffs, administer the water system and take care of the operation and simple maintenance activities. A cost-sharing and cost-recovery system exists and this includes the use of a revolving fund: the community's contribution is about 40 per cent of the cost of the water system, while SANAA and UNICEF contribute 25 per cent and 35 per cent respectively.

*Source: UNCSD 1999*

urban areas. Natural disasters provide an additional, unexpected factor that can seriously undermine efforts to improve water and sanitation services.

Attempts have been made to improve water supply and sanitation in many urban areas and to set tariffs that reflect the real value of water. Although the efficiency of privatization and the use of economic instruments such as water pricing remain highly contentious (WWC 2000), some countries, such as Jamaica, have started using economic instruments (UNECLAC 2000).

Limited information on water utility infrastructure and operation is a major constraint in government efforts to improve regulations related to the urban water sector. While the role of governments has shifted from provider of a water service to regulator representing the public, many governments still do not have sufficient information on water utility operation, and this limits their regulatory functions. Although the rate of technological change in the water sector is generally slower than in other sectors, the need to transfer technology is critical to efforts to save water and introduce improved control strategies.

To increase the efficiency of the sanitation sector, as well as to attract capital, national and international initiatives have been suggested, including the creation of local or regional markets such as the Guarani Aquifer project (see box on page 169). In Brazil, there have been notable advances in legislation, especially with a 1997 federal law that put in place a national water resources policy and established a national water resources management system.

## Water quality

Water pollution problems in Latin America and the Caribbean did not become a serious issue until the 1970s. Over the past 30 years, however, there has been a significant decrease in the quality of surface water and groundwater. Agriculture and the release of untreated urban and industrial sewage have become the major sources of pollution.

The excessive use of fertilizers in agriculture has enhanced algal growth and eutrophication in lakes, dams and coastal lagoons. Rising levels of nitrates have been observed in rivers, including the Amazon and the Orinoco, as well as in underground sources in the region. In Costa Rica, levels of nitrates approaching or surpassing international guidelines

## The Guarani Aquifer System

The Guarani Aquifer System is one of the world's largest aquifers, covering about 1.2 million $km^2$ in the southeast of South America. The permanent reserves of the system in Brazil are conservatively estimated at about 48 000 $km^3$ with an annual recharge of 160 $km^3$. Groundwater extraction of about 20 per cent of current annual recharge rates would be enough to supply 300 litres per day per capita to 360 million inhabitants.

Argentina, Brazil, Paraguay and Uruguay are working together to develop an integrated plan for the protection and sustainable management of the system under a project funded by the Global Environment Facility and the World Bank — the Project for Environmental Protection and Sustainable Development of the Guarani Aquifer System. The Organization of American States, other international donors and agencies are also participating. Success would be an important step towards ensuring long-term availability of freshwater and aquifer resources for people in these countries.

have been found in both metropolitan and rural sources (Observatorio del Desarrollo 2001).

Untreated sewage from urban centres remains a major cause of pollution. In the region as a whole, only about 13 per cent of collected sewage receives any kind of treatment (PAHO 1998). Increasing pollution from urban run-off and the release of untreated sewage into water bodies serving urban areas has added to the difficulties of meeting the increasing

demand for water in cities, especially those located in areas such as Lima and Mexico City where water is scarce (WWC 2000).

Industrial activities, and the resulting pollution, have contributed substantially to water quality problems. Animal waste from tanneries, slaughterhouses and meat packing plants, for example, pollutes aquifers with coliform bacteria (WWC 2000).

Another water quality problem that is becoming more prevalent, especially in the Caribbean, is the salinization of water in coastal areas due to overextraction. This is particularly severe given the rising demand for water in the Caribbean, mainly to service the tourism industry (UNEP 1999).

## Institutional and legal frameworks

In most countries, water resources continue to be managed on a sectoral basis with little integration either between sectors or with other environmental management procedures. Such an approach ignores vital interactions with much wider ecosystems and other functions, and ecological services related to water. There has been a trend towards transferring water services from the public to the private sector during the past decade and to decentralizing legal and administrative responsibilities. As a result, laws and regulations designed to protect freshwater resources are often lacking or poorly enforced (WWC 2000).

## References: Chapter 2, freshwater, Latin America and the Caribbean

ACAA ( 2001). *Usos e Impactos* Atlas Continental del Agua en America http://www.atlaslatinoamerica.org/usos_impac/amer_sur.htm

CATHALAC (1999). *Vision on Water, Life and the Environment for the 21st Century. Regional Consultations. Central America and Caribbean.* Panama City, Water Centre for the Humid Tropics of Latin America and the Caribbean (CATHALAC).

FAOSTAT (2001). FAOSTAT Statistical Database. Food and Agriculture Organization http://www.fao.org/ [Geo-2-068]

GWP (2000). *Water for the 21st Century: Vision to Action – South America.* Stockholm, Global Water Partnership South American Technical Advisory Committee

Observatorio del Desarrollo (2001). El agua en Costa Rica: abundante pero vulnerable *Boletín Información para la Toma de Decisiones*, Año 3, No. 6, Abril-Mayo

PAHO (1998). *Health in the Americas. Volume I,* PAHO Scientific Publication No. 569. Washington DC, Pan American Health Organization

Saleth, R.M. and Dinar, A. (1999). *Water Challenge and Institutional Response (A Cross-Country Perspective), Policy Research Working Paper 2045.* Washington DC, World Bank Development Research Group Rural Development and Rural Development Department

UNCSD (1999). *The Tegucigalpa Model: Water Supply for Peri-urban Settlements.* United Nations Commission for Sustainable Development http://www.un.org/esa/sustdev/success/tegu_mod.htm

UNDP, UNEP, World Bank and WRI (2000). *World Resources 2000-2001.* Washington DC, World Resources Institute

UNECLAC (2000). *Water Utility Regulation: Issues and Options for Latin America and the Caribbean.* ECLAC, LC/R. 2032. Santiago de Chile, United Nations Economic Commission for Latin America and the Caribbean

UNEP (1999). *Caribbean Environment Outlook.* Nairobi, United Nations Environment Programme

WHO and UNICEF (2000). *Global Water Supply and Sanitation Assessment 2000 Report.* Geneva and New York, World Health Organization and United Nations Children's Fund http://www.who.int/water_sanitation_health/Globassessment/GlasspdfTOC.htm

World Bank (1999). *Annual Review – Environment Matters,* Washington DC, World Bank

World Bank (2001). *World Development Indicators 2001.* Washington DC, World Bank http://www.worldbank.org/data/wdi2001/pdfs/tab3_8.pdf [Geo-2-024]

WWC (1999). *Vision on Water, Life and the Environment for the 21st Century. Regional Consultations: North America.* Marseille, World Water Council

WWC (2000). *Water in the Americas for the Twenty First Century, Roundtable Meeting of the Americas, July 26-28 2000, Final Report,* Montreal, World Water Council

## North America

North America holds about 13 per cent of the world's renewable freshwater (excluding glaciers and ice caps). At the end of the 1990s, North Americans used 1 693 cubic metres of water per person per year (Gleick 1998), more than in any other region. In the United States, recent conservation measures have led to declines in consumption: during 1980–95, water withdrawals declined by nearly 10 per cent while the population increased by 16 per cent (Solley, Pierce and Perlman 1998). In Canada, on the other hand, water withdrawal increased by 80 per cent during 1972–91 while the population grew by 3 per cent (EC 2001a).

Although point source water pollution has been reduced in the United States since the 1970s, non-

### Health risks from groundwater pollution

A number of recent reports of localized well contamination have alerted the public to the health risks associated with contaminated groundwater (EC 1999a). In May 2000, for example, seven Canadians died and more than 2 000 became sick in Walkerton, Ontario, from *E. coli* contamination in the town's water supply. Livestock manure was one of the factors implicated in the accident, exacerbated by others such as infrastructure failure, high-risk well location, human error and extreme rainfall (ECO 2000).

The tragedy alerted the Canadian provinces to the need to correct serious drinking water problems related to contaminants from animal waste entering groundwater supplies and, in the case of some, to the roles played by earlier budget cuts, staff reductions and greater reliance on municipalities for regulating environmental services (Gallon 2000).

point sources, such as agricultural run-off and urban storm drainage, have grown causing serious pollution problems. Nutrient enrichment problems are of particular concern.

Most of the continent's (unfrozen) freshwater resources lie in groundwater. Groundwater contamination and declining aquifer levels are now priority issues (Rogers 1996, EC 1999a).

Thirty years ago, one of the gravest issues facing North America's freshwater resources was the precarious state of the Great Lakes Basin. The clean-up effort is a notable story of cooperation among nations and local users.

### Groundwater

By the mid-1990s, groundwater was supplying up to 50 per cent of the North American population and more than 90 per cent of rural dwellers (EPA 1998, Statistics Canada 2000).

The many hazardous compounds used in industry and agriculture are now threatening groundwater quality. Contaminants from non-point sources are present in many shallow wells throughout large regions of North America (Moody 1996). Agriculture is the worst offender, with artificial fertilizer use in the region increasing from 15 to 22.25 million tonnes a year over the past 30 years (IIFA 2001).

Although nitrogen contamination rarely exceeds levels of potential health risk, it is a chronic problem for the population in the Prairie Provinces that rely on wells for water, and it affects groundwater to some extent in 49 US states (OECD 1996, Statistics Canada 2000). Consumed in high concentrations, nitrates can cause infant methaemoglobinaemia or blue-baby syndrome (Sampat 2000).

During 1993–95, low concentrations of pesticides were also detected in shallow groundwater in 54.4 per cent of US sites tested. Although concentrations of pesticides rarely exceed drinking water standards, some scientists suggest that their combined effects on health and the environment are not adequately assessed (Kolpin, Barbash and Gilliom 1998).

Underground storage tanks containing, for example, petroleum products, acids, chemicals and industrial solvents, are leading sources of groundwater contamination (Sampat 2000). The tanks are often inappropriate containers for these substances or have been improperly installed. In 1998, more than 100 000 petroleum tanks in the United States were found to be leaking. State Underground Tank Remediation Funds have helped clean-up many US sites (US EPA 1998).

Septic tank systems, the largest source of waste discharged to the land, contain many organic contaminants and are suspected to be one of the key sources of rural well contamination. Between one-third and one-half of US septic systems may be operating poorly (Moody 1996).

The long-term availability of groundwater in arid agricultural regions is a priority issue. In general, groundwater levels stopped declining during the 1980s but depletion of stored groundwater still accounted for about 10 per cent of all freshwater withdrawals in the United States in the mid-1990s (OECD 1996). Agriculture relied on groundwater resources for 62 per cent of its irrigated farmland in 1990 (OECD 1996, Sampat 2000).

During the late 1980s and early 1990s, all US states enacted groundwater legislation (TFGRR 1993,

Gobert 1997). The Canadian federal government has initiated new national legislation on the environment, trade and groundwater issues (EC 1999a). Although groundwater management has traditionally focused on surface and groundwater separately, interactions between them have direct effects on water quality and availability, and on the health of wetlands, riparian ecology and aquatic ecosystems in general (Cosgrove and Rijsberman 2000).

## Great Lakes water quality

The Great Lakes basin is one of the Earth's largest freshwater systems, containing 18 per cent of the world's fresh surface water (EC 2001a). Less than 1 per cent of the water is renewed annually by precipitation, surface water run-off and groundwater inflow.

Over the years, the lakes have been subject to a polluting mix of effluents due to inadequate sewage treatment, fertilizer and wastewater effluent. By the early 1970s, beaches were smothered with algae and water was unfit for drinking unless extensively purified. Lake Erie suffered from excess phosphorus, algal blooms and serious declines in fish populations. Aboriginal communities were the most affected. Newspaper headlines in 1970 declared that 'Lake Erie is Dead' (EC 1999b, EC 2001c).

Other clues pointed to more insidious problems. In the early 1970s, eggshells of the double-crested cormorant, which is high on the aquatic foodchain and subject to the effects of bioaccumulation, were some 30 per cent thinner than normal (EC 1999b). Some species of bird populations crashed.

The International Joint Commission (IJC) released a report on the pollution problem in the lower Great Lakes in 1970. The IJC, an independent organization of Canadian and US representatives, has been in charge of assessing water quantity and quality along the boundary between Canada and the United States since 1909 (IJC 2000a). The report led to the 1972 signing of the Great Lakes Water Quality Agreement (GLWQA) and the beginning of concerted efforts to restore water quality. In 1978, the GLWQA was renewed to introduce the ecosystem approach and to address persistent chemical discharges (IJC 1989).

In 1987, targets or strategies for phosphorus load reductions, airborne pollutants, pollution from land-based activities and the problems of contaminated sediment and groundwater were set. Remedial Action

Plans (RAPs) were developed to clean up 43 areas of concern (see map).

Municipal phosphorus loadings to Lakes Erie and Ontario have been reduced by almost 80 per cent since the early 1970s, slowing algal growth and decreasing the extent of oxygen depletion in bottom waters. Once thought 'dead', Lake Erie now has the world's largest walleye fishery (EC 1999b, EC 2001c).

Discharge of a number of persistent toxic chemicals was also reduced. Since the late 1980s, government regulations achieved an 82 per cent reduction in chlorinated toxic substances discharged from pulp-and-paper mills. Since 1972, there has been an overall reduction of 71 per cent in the use,

generation and release of seven priority toxic chemicals and a significant reduction in chemical spills (EC 1999b, EC 2000, EC 2001c).

DDE and PCB residues, once exceptionally high in cormorant eggs in the Great Lakes basin, decreased by as much as 91 per cent and 78 per cent respectively between the early 1970s and 1998 (EC 2001b). Cormorant populations are breeding successfully again and other bird populations are increasing (EC 1998, EC 1999b).

Rapid urban and industrial development, however, continued to cause environmental damage to the watershed during the 1990s. Sediment contamination in harbours and river mouths threatened to contaminate fish and posed problems related to dredging and sediment disposal (IJC 1997). Evidence revealed that pollutants carried in the air settle on the

In 1987, Remedial Action Plans were developed to clean up 43 areas of concern in the Great Lakes basin in both Canada and the United States

Source: EC 2000

lakes, contributing significantly to water pollution (US EPA 1997). Up to 96 per cent of PCBs in the Great Lakes come from the atmosphere (Bandemehr and Hoff 1998). The Great Lakes Binational Toxics Strategy was launched in 1997 to eliminate these chemical contaminants (BNS 1999, EC 2000b).

Although exposure to persistent toxic contaminants has decreased, some studies show that children of mothers who ate large quantities of Great Lakes fish had development problems (Health Canada 1997). Recent IJC reports warn of slow progress with some problems, such as the clean-up of sediments containing persistent toxic chemicals and exotic invasive species (IJC 2000b).

The Great Lakes will face other environmental challenges in the future. Global warming could lower lake levels by a metre or more by the middle of this century, causing severe economic, environmental and social impacts. Water shortages throughout North America may also increase pressure to divert or remove water in bulk from the lakes, threatening the sustainable use of surface and groundwater resources (IJC 2000c, IPCC 2001).

## References: Chapter 2, freshwater, North America

Bandemehr, A. and Hoff, R. (1998). *Monitoring Air Toxics: The Integrated Atmospheric Deposition Network of the Great Lakes* (unpublished report to the CEC Secretariat). Montreal, Commission for Environmental Cooperation

BNS (1999). *The Great Lakes Binational Toxics Strategy*. Binational Toxics Strategy http://www.epa.gov/glnpo/p2/bns.html [Geo-2-129]

Cosgrove, William J. and Rijsberman, Frank R. (2000). *World Water Vision: Making Water Everybody's Business*. World Water Council. London, Earthscan

EC (1998). Toxic Contaminants in the Environment: Persistent Organochlorines. *Environment Canada National Environmental Indicator Series, State of the Environment Reporting Program*. 98-1

EC (1999a). *Groundwater — Nature's Hidden Treasure: Freshwater Series A-5*. Environment Canada, Minister of Public Works and Government Services http://www.ec.gc.ca/water/en/info/pubs/FS/e_FSA5.htm [Geo-2-130]

EC (1999b). *Rising to the Challenge: Celebrating the 25th Anniversary of the Great Lakes Water Quality Agreement*. Ottawa, Environment Canada

EC (2000a). *Binational Remedial Action Plans (RAPs)*. Environment Canada http://www.on.ec.gc.ca/glimr/raps/intro.html [Geo-2-131]

EC (2001a). *The Management of Water*. Environment Canada http://www.ec.gc.ca/water/index.htm

EC (2001b). *Tracking Key Environmental Issues*. Environment Canada http://www.ec.gc.ca/TKEI/air_water/watr_qual_e.cfm [Geo-2-132]

EC (2001c). *Great Lakes Water Quality Agreement*. Environment Canada http://www.ijc.org/agree/quality.html [Geo-2-134]

ECO (2000). *Changing Perspectives: Annual Report 1999/2000*. Toronto, Environmental Commissioner of Ontario

Gallon, Gary (2000). The Real Walkerton Villain. *The Globe and Mail*, 20 December 2000

Gleick, P.H. (1998). *The World's Water 1998-1999*. Washington DC, Island Press

Gobert, Christopher (1997). Groundwater Contamination: A Look at the Federal Provisions. *The Compleat Lawyer*. Spring 1997 http://www.abanet.org/genpractice/lawyer/complete/98julschneid.html [Geo-2-135]

Health Canada (1997). *State of Knowledge Report on Environmental Contaminants and Human Health in the Great Lakes Basin*. Ottawa, Minister of Public Works and Government Services

IIFA (2001). *Fertilizer Nutrient Consumption, by Region, 1970/71 to 1998/99*. International Industry Fertilizer Association http://www.fertilizer.org/ifa/ab_act_position3.asp [Geo-2-136]

IJC (1989). *Great Lakes Water Quality Agreement of 1978*. International Joint Commission http://www.ijc.org/agree/quality.html [Geo-2-137]

IJC (1997). *Overcoming Obstacles to Sediment Remediation in the Great Lakes Basin*. International Joint Commission http://www.ijc.org/boards/wqb/sedrem.html [Geo-2-138]

IJC (2000a). *International Joint Commission: United States and Canada*. http://www.ijc.org/agree/water.html [Geo-2-139]

IJC (2000b). *Open Letter to Great Lakes Leaders and the Great Lakes Community*. Washington DC and Ottawa, International Joint Commission

IJC (2000c). *Protection of the Waters of the Great Lakes: Final Report to the Governments of Canada and the United States*. International Joint Commission http://www.ijc.org/boards/cde/finalreport/finalreport.html [Geo-2-140]

IPCC (2001b). *Climate Change 2001: Impacts, Adaptation and Vulnerability. Contribution of Working Group II to the Third Assessment Report of the Intergovernmental Panel on Climate Change*. Cambridge, United Kingdom, and New York, United States, Cambridge University Press

Kolpin, Dana W., Barbash, Jack E. and Gilliom, Robert J. (1998). Occurrence of Pesticides in Shallow Ground Water of the United States: Initial Results from the National Water-Quality Assessment Program. *Environmental Science and Technology*. 32, 1998 http://water.wr.usgs.gov/pnsp/ja/est32/ [Geo-2-141]

Moody, David W. (1996). *Sources and Extent of Groundwater Contamination*. North Carolina Cooperative Extension Service, Publication Number: AG-441-4 http://www.p2pays.org/ref/01/00065.htm [Geo-2-142]

OECD (1996). *Environmental Performance Reviews: United States*. Paris, Organization for Economic Cooperation and Development

Rogers, Peter (1996). *America's Water: Federal Roles and Responsibilities*. Cambridge, Massachusetts, MIT Press

Sampat, Payal (2000). Groundwater Shock: The Polluting of the World's Major Freshwater Stores. *World Watch*. 13, 1, 13-22

Solley, Wayne B., Pierce, Robert R. and Perlman, Howard A. (1998). *Estimated Use of Water in the United States in 1995*. US Department of Interior, US Geological Survey http://water.usgs.gov/watuse/pdf1995/html/ [Geo-2-143]

Statistics Canada (2000). *Human Activity and the Environment 2000*. Ottawa, Minister of Industry

TFGRR (1993). *Groundwater Issues and Research in Canada: a report prepared for the Canadian Geoscience Council*. Task Force on Groundwater Resources Research http://wlapwww.gov.bc.ca/wat/gws/gissues.html [Geo-2-145]

US EPA (1997). *Deposition of Air Pollutants to the Great Waters: Second Report to Congress*. EPA-453/R-977-011. Research Triangle Park, North Carolina, US Environmental Protection Agency

US EPA (1998). *National Water Quality Inventory: 1998 Report to Congress*. US Environmental Protection Agency http://www.epa.gov/305b/98report/98summary.html [Geo-2-144]

## Freshwater: West Asia

The Arabian Peninsula is characterized by an arid climate with annual rainfall of less than 100 mm. There are no reliable surface water supplies. The sub-region depends entirely on groundwater and desalination plants to meet its water requirements. Large increases in demand have placed the meagre resources available under increasing pressure. The Mashriq sub-region is mostly arid and semi-arid. About 70 per cent of the sub-region receives less than 250 mm of rain a year. The Mashriq has two shared rivers originating outside the area, the Euphrates and Tigris, and many smaller ones. Agreements or understandings about how to share these water resources have been reached among Arab countries but agreements over the Euphrates are yet to materialize between Iraq and Syria on one side and Turkey on the other.

### Increasing water demand

The major cause of the increasing demand for water is rapid population growth. The region's population increased from 37.3 million in 1972 to 97.7 million in 2000 (United Nations Population Division 2001). A high annual population growth rate of more than 3 per cent in the Mashriq sub-region has seen the annual per capita share of available water resources decreasing from 6 057 $m^3$ in 1950 (Khouri 2000) to 1 574 $m^3$ in 2000 (see box above) .

Domestic water demand has also been rising due to an increase in per capita consumption. In many countries, water rationing is used to limit demand. For example, Jordan restricts water supplies in Amman to only three days a week. In Damascus, water can be used for less than 12 hours a day.

Agriculture is the main user of water in West Asia, accounting for nearly 82 per cent of the total water consumed compared to 10 per cent and 8 per cent for the domestic and industrial sectors, respectively. In the Arabian Peninsula, agriculture utilizes about 86 per cent of the available water resources, and about 80 per cent in the Mashriq (Khouri 2000). To satisfy water demand, especially for irrigation, groundwater abstraction has increased dramatically during the past three decades.

In the Gulf Cooperation Council (GCC) countries, the total annual water supply increased from 6 km³ in 1980 to 26 km³ in 1995, with 85 per cent of the water

### Water stress index: West Asia

|  | Mashriq | Arabian Peninsula | West Asia region |
|---|---|---|---|
| population (millions, 2000) | 50.7 | 47.0 | 97.7 |
| available water (km³/year) | 79.9 | 15.3 | 95.2 |
| water used (km³/year) | 66.5 | 29.6 | 96.1 |
| **water stress index (%)** | **83.3** | **>100** | **>100** |
| per capita available (m³/year) | 1574 | 326 | 974 |

Source: ACSAD 2000 and United Nations Population Division 2001

used for agricultural purposes (Zubari 1997). In 1995, the GCC countries had water resources equivalent to 466 m³/year per capita and a per capita water use of 1 020 m³/year, producing an average annual water deficit of about 554 m³ per capita, provided mainly by mining groundwater reserves (Zubari 1997).

The water stress index in West Asia (expressed as a percentage of water used to available water resources) is more than 100 per cent in five of the seven countries in the Arabian Peninsula, and is critical in the remaining two. These countries have already exhausted their renewable water resources and are now exploiting non-renewable reserves. In the Mashriq, except in Jordan, the water stress index is lower (see table above). While per capita water resources in 9 of the 12 countries in West Asia are below 1 000 m³/year, they are also below 500 m³/year

### Water uses in West Asia

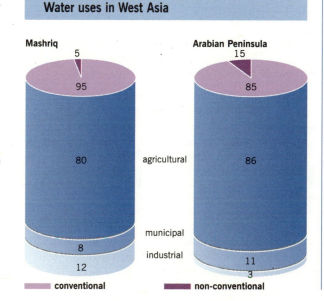

**Mashriq**

5
95
80
8
12

**Arabian Peninsula**

15
85
86
11
3

agricultural

municipal

industrial

conventional   non-conventional

Origins and uses of water resources in the West Asian sub-regions; the Arabian Peninsular depends mainly on groundwater, the Mashriq countries on surface water — but both use most of their water in agriculture

Source: Khouri 2000

## Available water resources in West Asia (million m³/year)

| | Mashriq | Arabian Peninsula | West Asia region |
|---|---|---|---|
| surface water | 68 131 | 6 835 | 74 966 |
| groundwater | 8 135 | 6 240 | 14 375 |
| desalination | 58 | 1 850 | 1 908 |
| agricultural drainage reuse | 3 550 | 392 | 3 942 |
| **total** | **79 873** | **15 318** | **95 191** |

Source: Khouri 2000

in seven countries. The overall value of the water stress index for West Asia is more than 100 per cent (see table on page 173).

Over the past three decades, the adoption of food self-sufficiency policies has encouraged agricultural expansion. Governments offered subsidies and incentives which resulted in a large-scale expansion of farming, increasing water demand which was satisfied mainly by mining deep aquifers. Furthermore, unregulated pumping, absence or minimal irrigation water tariffs, lack of enforcement measures against unlawful drilling, poor irrigation practices and lack of farmer awareness have resulted in excessive water usage.

Intensive agriculture and heavy application of agrochemicals have also contributed to the contamination of water resources. For example, the concentration of nitrates in Gaza's tap water exceeds WHO guidelines (10 mg/litre) and nitrate concentrations are increasing at a rate of 0.2-1.0 mg/litre per year in the country's coastal wells. Adherence to WHO standards would place half of

## Water use for irrigation in West Asia

Subsidies and incentives have led to a large expansion of the private agricultural sector in West Asia, and to the extension of supplementary irrigation into some rainfed farming areas. For example, the total irrigated area in Syria has nearly doubled over the past three decades, increasing from 625 000 ha (10.9 per cent of arable land) in 1972 to 1 186 000 ha (25.2 per cent of arable land) in 1999 (FAOSTAT 2001). In Iraq, the percentage of irrigated land increased from 30.3 per cent in 1972 to 67.8 per cent in 1999 (FAOSTAT 2001). Irrigation efficiency — the percentage of water that actually reaches the crop — does not exceed 50 per cent in the region, and sometimes falls as low as 30 per cent, leading to high water losses (ACSAD 1997).

The water used in wheat farming in Saudi Arabia during 1980-95 was about 254 km³ (Al-Qunaibet 1997), equivalent to 13 per cent of the country's total fossil groundwater reserves of 1 919 km³ (Al Alawi and Razzak 1994).

these coastal wells off limits as drinking water (PNA 2000).

## Overexploitation of groundwater

Excessive use of groundwater has resulted in sharp declines in groundwater levels and quality deterioration due to seawater intrusion. For instance, in Saudi Arabia water levels declined by more than 70 metres in the Umm Er Radhuma aquifer during 1978-84, and this decline was accompanied by a salinity increase of more than 1 000 mg/litre (Al-Mahmood 1987). In the United Arab Emirates, excessive groundwater pumping has created cones of depression 50-100 km in diameter in several areas. These cones have caused groundwater levels to fall, shallow wells to dry up, and saltwater intrusion. Groundwater salinity in most areas of the Syrian and Jordanian steppe has increased to several thousand milligrammes per litre. overexploitation of coastal aquifers in the coastal zone of Lebanon has caused seawater intrusion with a subsequent rise from 340 to 22 000 mg/litre in some wells near Beirut (UNESCWA 1999).

## Water quality

Water quality degradation is often a consequence of both water scarcity and overexploitation. Water quantity and quality are both major issues in the Mashriq countries. Effluent, agrochemicals and industrial discharges have seriously affected aquatic life, causing public health hazards. Discharge from tanneries into the Barada River in Syria has caused levels of biological oxygen demand (BOD) to increase 23-fold above normal (World Bank 1995). Close to Homs, in Syria, the winter BOD levels of the Orontes River are 100 times higher than where the river enters the country from Lebanon.

Health impacts due to poor water quality are a major concern. Water-borne diseases, especially diarrhoea, are second only to respiratory diseases as a cause of mortality and morbidity among children in the region (World Bank 1995).

## Policy developments

West Asia is developing policies to increase both water supply and conservation. In Jordan, priority is given to the sustainability of water resources without mining groundwater resources; the country is constructing dams and facilities to store all available water resources (Al-Weshah 2000). Many countries have started to invest in more efficient irrigation technology. Improvements in irrigation efficiency in the Jordan Valley increased average yields for vegetables from 8.3 tonnes per hectare in 1973 to 18.2 tonnes per hectare in 1986 (World Bank 1995). Wastewater reuse is another important conservation tool for non-potable uses, including irrigation, and for reducing environmental degradation and improving public health. Reuse of treated wastewater has increased in Mashriq countries from zero in 1973 to about 51 million m$^3$/year in 1991 (Sarraf 1997). But comprehensive water policies to manage water resources are still lacking in many countries.

The problem of water scarcity and quality deterioration in the region is attributed to:

- fragmentation and weakness of water authorities, leading to inefficient water management and to conflicts over use between different sectors;
- rapid and unplanned urbanization, including rural to urban migration;
- political and military conflicts negatively affecting the development of the water sector;
- escalating sectoral water demands;
- food self-sufficiency policies;
- poor irrigation practices;
- lack of sanitation causing pollution; and
- lack of mechanisms for strengthening water legislation and enforcement procedures.

Lack of hydrographic data is a serious issue. Most studies are based on short record data or even on educated guesses.

In the past three decades, water authorities in the region have concentrated their efforts on supply augmentation and, to a lesser extent, on demand management and conservation. Although their effectiveness is not yet proven, programmes related to demand management, conservation and protection have been implemented in both sub-regions. These programmes include the reduction of fuel and agricultural subsidies, metering of groundwater wells, future plans for an irrigation water tariff, subsidies for modern irrigation techniques, and public awareness campaigns.

In the GCC countries, these policies have been only partially successful in alleviating water scarcity caused by increasing demand and food self-sufficiency policies. In fact, the food self-sufficiency policies of the past three decades have not been successful. The deficit in food production is growing and is aggravated by the scarcity of land and water resources that are already overexploited. Water security will become one of the major constraints to further development in the region in the next 30 years unless there are major changes to agricultural and water policies.

## References: Chapter 2, freshwater, West Asia

ACSAD (1997). *Water resources and their utilization in the Arab world, 2nd Water Resources Seminar.* Conference held in Kuwait, 8-10 March 1997

ACSAD (2000). *Alternative Policy Study: Water Resource Management in West Asia.* Nairobi, United Nations Environment Programme http://www.grida.no/geo2000/aps-wasia/index.htm [Geo-2-146]

Al-Alawi, Jamil and Abdul Razzak, M. (1994). Water in the Arabian Peninsula: Problems and Perspectives. In Peter Rogers and Peter Lydon (eds.). *Water in the Arab World: Perspectives and Prognoses.* Cambridge, Massachusetts, Harvard University Press

Al-Mahmood, M.J. (1987). *Hydrogeology of Al-Hassa Oasis.* M.Sc. Thesis, Geology Department, College of Graduate Studies, King Fahd University of Petroleum and Minerals, Saudi Arabia

Al-Qunaibet, M.H. (1997). Water Security in the Kingdom of Saudi Arabia. In Al-Zubari, W. and Mohammed Al-Sofi (eds.). *Proceedings of the 3rd Gulf Water Conference, 8-13 March 1997,* Muscat

Al-Weshah, R. (2000). *Hydrology of Wadi Systems in Jordan.* Damascus, Arab Network on Wadi Hydrology, ACSAD/ UNESCO

FAOSTAT (2001). FAOSTAT Statistical Database. Food and Agriculture Organization http://www.fao.org/ [Geo-2-068]

Khouri, J. (2000). *Sustainable Management of Wadi Systems in the Arid and Semi Arid zones of the Arab Region.* International Conference on Wadi Hydrology. Conference held in Sharm El-Sheikh, Egypt, 21-23 November 2000

PNA (2000). *State of Environment, Palestine.* Jerusalem, Ministry of Environmental Affairs, Palestine National Authority

Sarraf, S. (1997). Water Resources of the Arab Countries: A Review. In ACSAD, *Water resources and their utilization in the Arab world, 2nd Water Resources Seminar.* Conference held in Kuwait, 8-10 March 1997

UNESCWA (1999). *Updating the Assessment of Water Resources in ESCWA Member States, ESCWA/ ENR/ 1999/ WG.1/7.* Beirut, United Nations Economic and Social Commission for West Asia

United Nations Population Division (2001). *World Population Prospects 1950-2050 (The 2000 Revision).* New York, United Nations www.un.org/esa/population/publications/wpp2000/wpp2000h.pdf

World Bank (1995). *Towards Sustainable Development: an Environmental Strategy for the Middle East and North Africa Region.* Washington DC, World Bank

Zubari, W.K. (1997). *Towards the Establishment of a Total Water Cycle Management and Re-use Program in the GCC Countries.* The 7th Regional Meeting of the Arab International Hydrological Programme Committee, 8-12 September 1997, Rabat, Morocco

## Freshwater: the Polar Regions

### Arctic

The Arctic holds much of the world's freshwater supply and its landscape is dominated by freshwater systems. The two main permanent ice fields are the ice pack of the Arctic Ocean (8 million $km^2$) and the Greenland ice cap (1.7 million $km^2$), which together hold 10 per cent of the world's freshwater. The Greenland ice cap produces about 300 $km^3$ of icebergs a year. The Arctic has several of the world's largest rivers. They pour 4 200 $km^3$ of freshwater into the Arctic Ocean annually along with about 221 million tonnes of sediment (Crane and Galasso 1999, AMAP 1997).

Low temperatures, low nutrient, short light availability and a brief growing season limit the primary productivity of Arctic freshwater systems. This in turn restricts the animal life that can be supported. Nevertheless, the river systems are

### Major river systems in the Arctic

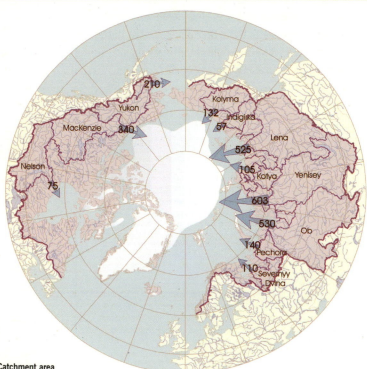

Catchment area of the Arctic Ocean, showing major rivers with their annual discharges in cubic kilometres

*Source: CAFF 2001*

heavily populated by several fish species such as the Arctic charr, and the North Atlantic and Pink salmon. In recent years, the overall warming trend plus increased recreational and commercial fisheries use have put pressure on these populations. Accidental

### The decline of Barrow's Goldeneye

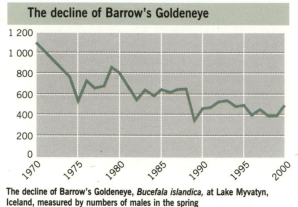

The decline of Barrow's Goldeneye, *Bucefala islandica*, at Lake Myvatyn, Iceland, measured by numbers of males in the spring

*Source: CAFF 2001*

introduction of alien species and increased fish farming is another source of concern (Bernes 1996). Eutrophication is a recent problem in several lakes in Scandinavia where human settlements have raised nutrient levels.

Northbound rivers are major pathways of pollutants from sources far inland, especially in the Russian Federation. In the spring, these contaminants are deposited into the freshwater systems and eventually into the marine environment and can be transported thousands of kilometres from their sources via the Arctic's marine circulation patterns. Contaminants include chemicals from agricultural, industrial and petroleum production, radionuclides from nuclear testing and military activities, and water soluble salts (Crane and Galasso 1999). The Arctic countries adopted a circumpolar Regional Programme of Action for Protection of the Arctic Marine Environment against Land-based Activities (based on the Global Programme of Action for the Protection of the Marine Environment from Land-based Activities) as well as National Programmes of Action in some countries, including the Russian Federation. These instruments are too recent to assess long-term effectiveness (PAME 1998).

Opposition to damming is strong in the Nordic countries. During 1975-2001, the Cree people fought the government of Quebec over environmental damage to their lands. In a surprise move in October 2001, however, the Cree reversed their stand and signed an agreement in principle to allow the government of Quebec to build another large power development project on the Eastmain-Rupert river system in exchange for a cash settlement. In 2000, a hydroelectric power project that would have flooded an important wetland was rejected (Arctic Bulletin

2001). In 2001, Iceland's National Planning Agency rejected plans for a hydroelectric power project that would have dammed two of the three main rivers flowing from Europe's largest glacier and destroyed a vast wilderness.

Since the 1970s, surface air temperatures appear to have increased on average 1.5°C per decade over continental Siberia and western portions of North America, both of which are major sources of freshwater into the Arctic basin. The opposite trend is occurring in Greenland and Canada's eastern Arctic where there is a negative trend of –1°C per decade (AMAP 1997). The warming trend has resulted in thawing of the continuous permafrost in Alaska and northern Russia (Morison and others 2000, IPCC 2001).

Arctic countries have partially responded to threats to their freshwater systems by establishing protected areas and designating important wetland areas under the Convention on Wetlands of International Importance. Nearly half the protected area in the Arctic is the Greenland ice cap and glaciers which store freshwater.

## Antarctic

Although the Antarctic ice cap is the world's largest body of freshwater, there are also seasonal streams and rivers, and numerous lakes and ponds in Antarctica. Other sources of freshwater are captured in the glaciers that occur in many coastal Antarctic regions. All these freshwater features are potentially threatened by pollution, including contaminates introduced by Antarctic scientists and tourists.

Freshwater lakes are found mainly in the coastal regions, on many of the sub-Antarctic Islands, and in the rare ice-free areas. Many are exposed to potential contamination from human activities. Observations at selected lakes, however, show that contamination resulting from research activities and station operations is generally near or below detection levels. In the Larsemann Hills of East Antarctica, trace metal concentrations appear to be higher in lakes situated in the vicinity of stations than those further away. The concentration levels still complied with drinking water standards (Gasparon and Burgess 2000). It is expected that the Protocol on Environmental Protection to the Antarctic Treaty will minimize the impacts of human activities on these lakes.

In 1970, observations revealed the existence of large lakes under the ice sheet in the central regions of the continent. Lake Vostok, which is about 220 km long, 70 km wide and holds about 2 000 km$^3$ of water, is the largest of the approximately 70 sub-glacial lakes known today (Dowdeswell and Siegert 1999). The global significance of sub-glacial lakes is that they have not been exposed to the atmosphere for the past 500 000 years and therefore maintain a unique archive of the past environment. There are also indications that Lake Vostok could contain viable micro-organisms (Karl and others 1999, Priscu and others 1999). A number of technologies for entering the lake without contaminating it are being considered (Russian Federation 2001).

### References: Chapter 2, freshwater, the Polar Regions

Arctic Bulletin (2001). *WWF Arctic Programme* No. 3.01, Oslo

AMAP (1977). *Arctic Pollution Issues: A State of the Arctic Environment Report.* Arctic Council Arctic Monitoring and Assessment Programme, Oslo

Bernes, C. (1996). *The Nordic Arctic Environment – Unspoilt, Exploited, Polluted?* Nordic Council of Ministers, Copenhagen

CAFF (2001). *Arctic Flora and Fauna: Status and Conservation.* Conservation of Arctic Flora and Fauna. Helsinki, Edita

Crane, K. and Galasso, J.L. (1999). *Arctic Environmental Atlas.* Office of Naval Research, Naval Research Laboratory, Washington DC

Dowdeswell, J.A. and Siegert, M.J. (1999). The dimensions and topographic setting of Antarctic subglacial lakes and implications for large-scale water storage beneath continental sheets. *Geological Society of America Bulletin* 111, 2

Gasparon, M. and Burgess, J.S. (2000). Human impacts in Antarctica trace-element geochemistry of freshwater lakes in the Larsemann Hills, East Antarctica. *Environmental Geology* 39 (9), 963–76

IPCC (2001). *Climate Change 2001: The Scientific Basis. Contribution of Working Group I to the Third Assessment Report of the Intergovernmental Panel on Climate Change.* Cambridge, United Kingdom, and New York, United States, Cambridge University Press

Karl, D.M., Bird, D.F., Bjorkman, K., Houlihan, T., Shackelford, R. and Tupas, L. (1999). Microorganisms in the accreted ice of Lake Vostok, Antarctica. *Science* 286 (5447), 2144–47

Morison, J., Aagaard, K. and Steele, M. (2000). Recent Environmental Changes in the Arctic: a review. *Arctic (Arctic Journal of the Arctic Institute of North America)* 53, 4, December 2000

PAME (1998). *Regional Programme of Action for the Protection of the Arctic Marine Environment from Land-Based Activities.* Arctic Council Programme for the Protection of the Arctic Marine Environment

Priscu, J.C., Adams, E.E., Lyons, W.B., Voytek, M.A., Mogk, D.W., Brown, R.L., McKay, C.P., Takacs, C.D., Welch, K.A., Wolf, C.F., Kirshtein, J.D., and Avci, R. (1999). Geomicrobiology of subglacial ice above Lake Vostok, Antarctica. *Science* 286 (5447), 2141–44

Russian Federation (2001). *Expert Conclusions for the Project 'Justification and development of the ecologically clean technology for penetrating the subglacial Lake Vostok'.* Working Paper 29, 4th Antarctic Treaty Consultative Meeting, 9-20 July 2001, St. Petersburg

# OUR CHANGING ENVIRONMENT: Three Gorges dam, China

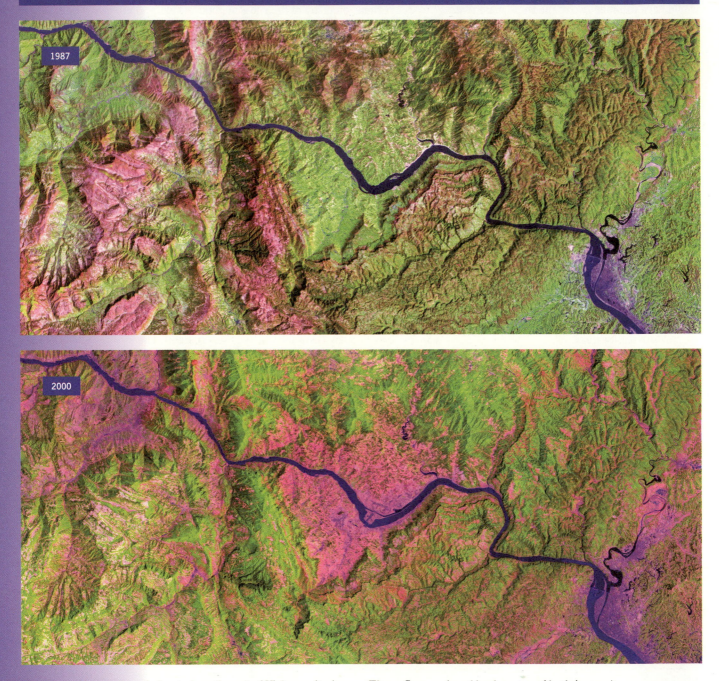

The Three Gorges Dam is located northwest of Yichang city in Hubei Province, China, a sub-tropical region that supports evergreen and deciduous mixed forest.

In the images, vegetation appears natural green, water bodies blue, bare land pink and built-up areas bluish-violet.

The images show the great changes that have taken place to farmland and to the original bush forest. In the area round the Three Gorges dam (dead centre of both images), a formerly vegetated area has been largely replaced by a man-made landscape. Soil erosion in this area has been intensified, as can be seen in the year 2000 image.

**Imagery and text: China National Environmental Monitoring Centre**

# OUR CHANGING ENVIRONMENT: Jilin Province, China

Nenjiang plain is located in the northeast of China, in the semi-arid mid-temperate zone. The plain is nowhere more than 100 metres above sea level. Much of the region consists of wetlands which are important for protecting biodiversity and marshland resources. The images show the vast marshland zone to the east of Baicheng City in Jinlin Province. Water bodies appear blue-black. The large area of water on the lower right of the image is Yueliangpao. The two images show how marshland has been lost and replaced by farmland, which appears red in the image. also indicated the loss of biodiversity in this region. Land salinization is beginning to occur along the banks of the river (white areas).

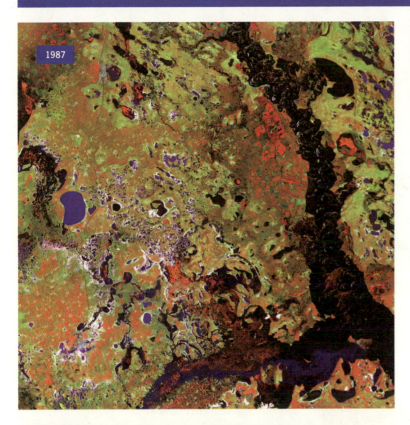

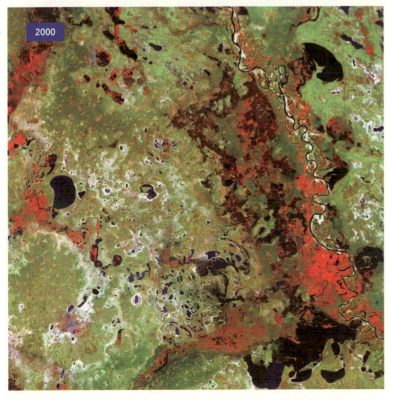

**Imagery and text: China National Environmental Monitoring Centre**

UNEP, Hideyuki Ihasi, Japan, Still Pictures

# Coastal and marine areas

## Global overview

Progress in protecting the marine and coastal environment over the past 30 years has generally been confined to relatively few, mostly developed countries, and to relatively few environmental issues. Overall, coastal and marine environmental degradation not only continues but has intensified. The major threats to the oceans that were recognized in 1972 — marine pollution, the overexploitation of living marine resources and coastal habitat loss — still exist, despite national and international actions to address these problems.

There have, however, been significant changes in perspective, and new concerns have emerged. The exploitation of living marine resources and loss of habitats are now recognized as being at least as great a threat to ocean health as marine pollution. The perspectives of developing countries were embodied in the Founex Report on Development and Environment that was produced in preparation for the 1972 Stockholm Conference. Their response in 1972 was that degradation was a developed-country problem; for them poverty, not pollution,

was the problem (Brenton 1994, Caldwell 1996).

Marine and coastal degradation is caused by increasing pressure on both terrestrial and marine natural resources, and on the use of the oceans to deposit wastes. Population growth and increasing urbanization, industrialization and tourism in coastal areas are root causes of this increased pressure. In 1994, an estimated 37 per cent of the global population lived within 60 km of the coast — more people than inhabited the planet in 1950 (Cohen and others 1997). The effects of population are multiplied by both poverty and human consumption patterns.

### Marine pollution

Prior to 1972, the crash of some seabird populations caused by DDT, outbreaks of Minamata disease in Japan from mercury-contaminated seafood, and the *Torrey Canyon* and other oil spills focused the attention of the Stockholm Conference on marine pollution. Policy responses included bans on production and use of some substances, regulations to reduce discharges, and the prohibition of ocean dumping, as well as a significant scientific effort to improve the status of knowledge about these pollutants. These responses are enshrined in a number of international agreements, including the 1972 London Dumping Convention and its 1996 Protocol, the 1989 Basel Convention on the Control of Transboundary Movement of Hazardous Wastes and their Disposal, and the 1995 Global Programme of Action for the Protection of the Marine Environment from Land-based Activities. Marine pollution is also an important focus of UNEP's Regional Seas Programmes that have been established in many parts of the world.

Globally, sewage remains the largest source of contamination, by volume, of the marine and coastal environment (GESAMP 2001a), and coastal sewage discharges have increased dramatically in the past three decades. In addition, because of the high demand for water in urban neighbourhoods, water supply tends to outstrip the provision of sewerage, increasing the volume of wastewater.

Public health problems from the contamination of coastal waters with sewage-borne pathogens were well known in the 1970s, and in many developed countries improved sewage treatment and reduction of the disposal of industrial and some domestic contaminants into municipal systems have significantly improved water quality. In the developing world, however, the provision of basic sanitation, as well as urban sewer systems and sewage treatment, has not kept pace. High capital costs, the explosive pace of urbanization, and in many cases limited technical, administrative and financial capacities for urban planning and management and ongoing operation of sewage treatment systems are barriers to efficient sewage treatment (GESAMP 2001a). Removal of these barriers, as well as alternative approaches, is urgently needed.

Recent evidence suggests that bathing in waters well within current microbiological standards still poses significant risk of gastrointestinal disease, and that sewage contamination of marine waters is a health problem of global proportions (see box, GESAMP 2001a, WHO 1998).

A primary concern at the Stockholm Conference was the introduction of nutrients to coastal and marine waters. Human activities now account for more than half of global nitrogen fixation (Vitousek and others 1997a), and the supply of fixed nitrogen to the oceans has greatly increased. Sewage discharges are often the dominant local source near urban areas but global inputs are dominated by agricultural run-off and atmospheric deposition. The highest rates of riverine

| Disease burden of selected common and marine-related diseases | | |
| --- | --- | --- |
| disease | DALYs/year (millions) | economic impact (US$billion) |
| malaria | 31.0 | 124.0 |
| diabetes | 11.0 | 44.0 |
| trachea, brachia and lung cancer | 8.8 | 35.0 |
| stomach cancer | 7.7 | 31.0 |
| intestinal nematodes | 5.0 | 20.0 |
| upper respiratory tract infections | 1.3 | 5.2 |
| trachoma | 1.0 | 4.0 |
| dengue fever | 0.75 | 3.0 |
| Japanese encephalitis | 0.74 | 3.0 |
| diptheria | 0.36 | 1.4 |
| **diseases related to marine contamination** | | |
| related to bathing and swimming | 0.4 | 1.6 |
| seafood consumption (hepatitis) | 1.8 | 7.2 |
| seafood consumption (algal toxins) | 1.0 | 4.0 |
| **sub-total** | **3.2** | **12.8** |

Note: one DALY (Disability-Adjusted Life Year) equals one person-year of productive life lost through death or disability

Source: GESAMP 2001a

transport of dissolved inorganic nitrogen to estuaries from all sources occur in Europe and in South and East Asia (Seitzinger and Kroeze 1998). Nitrogen levels are exacerbated by widespread loss of natural interceptors such as coastal wetlands, coral reefs and mangrove forests.

At the time of Stockholm, agricultural nutrient run-off was 'not yet a major global problem'. Most fertilizer use was in developed countries but the rapid increase of fertilizer use in developing countries was already foreseen (SCEP 1970). Fertilizer use has stabilized in developed countries but is increasing in developing ones (Socolow 1999), a trend expected to continue. Fertilizer use has undoubtedly been enhanced by widespread subsidies, which reflect the high political priority of increasing food production and reducing food costs.

Atmospheric inputs, derived primarily from vehicle and industrial emissions and in some areas evaporation from animal manure and fertilizer, dominate anthropogenic nitrogen inputs to some coastal areas. They are expected to rise with increasing industrialization and vehicle use, especially in developing regions (GESAMP in prep.). Atmospheric nitrogen inputs to the nitrogen-limited

## Seasonal zones of oxygen-depleted waters

Red dots on the map indicate seasonal zones of oxygen-depleted waters resulting from human activities

Source: Malakoff 1998 after Diaz and Rosenberg 1995

elevated growth and subsequent decay of phytoplankton has caused widespread areas of seasonally oxygen-depleted water (see map). Phytoplankton blooms can have major economic impacts on fisheries, aquaculture and tourism (see table below left).

At the time of the Stockholm Conference concerns for ocean health centred on pollution by POPs (particularly DDT and PCBs), heavy metals and oil (Goldberg 1976, Matthews and others 1971, UN 1972a, SCEP 1970). Some response measures have been effective, for example, introduction of unleaded gasoline helped to reduce lead levels in Bermuda (Wu and Boyle 1997, Huang, Arimoto and Rahn 1996); national regulations and international agreements such as the Convention on the Prevention of Pollution from Ships (MARPOL) resulted in the reduction of operational oil discharges from ships; and North American seabird populations affected by DDT recovered after this chemical was banned in the region.

In other cases, improved information has clarified some concerns. High levels of mercury in tuna and swordfish, for example, have been shown to have natural sources; the most dramatic effects of oil spills have proved to be localized and relatively transient; and heavy metal contamination, except for lead and mercury, has been found to be highly localized and has relatively minor impacts except at high concentrations. There are, however, other continuing concerns about these pollutants. The chemical residues of oil spills may have subtle long-term effects (Heintz, Short and Rice 1999), and chronic, small releases cause seabird mortality and other environmental effects (GESAMP in prep.). The effects of heavy metal contamination can be severe and are a significant concern in the Arctic (AMAP 1998).

open oceans will also increase, with potential significant impacts on primary production and the carbon cycle.

Marine and coastal eutrophication from elevated nitrogen inputs has emerged as a worrying trend not foreseen three decades ago. There is increasing evidence that blooms of toxic or otherwise undesirable phytoplankton are increasing in frequency, intensity and geographic distribution (Richardson 1997). Severe eutrophication has occurred in several enclosed or semi-enclosed seas, including the Black Sea (Zaitsev and Mamaev 1997, Balkas and others 1990). Elsewhere,

The most serious concerns globally relate to POPs, many of which are transported globally via the atmosphere and are ubiquitous in the oceans. There is growing evidence that long-term, low-level exposures to some POPs cause reproductive, immunological, neurological and other problems in marine organisms, and possibly in humans, but the evidence for widespread ecological or human health impacts at current levels of contamination remains equivocal.

Another threat to the oceans, and in particular to living organisms, is non-biodegradable litter which enters the sea. Each year, large numbers of seabirds, sea turtles and marine mammals are killed by

## Economic losses from red tides in fisheries and aquaculture

| date | location | species | loss (US$million) |
|---|---|---|---|
| 1972 | Japan | yellowtail | ~47 |
| 1977 | Japan | yellowtail | ~20 |
| 1978 | Japan | yellowtail | ~22 |
| 1978 | Republic of Korea | oyster | 4.6 |
| 1979 | Maine, United States | many | 2.8 |
| 1980 | New England, United States | many | 7 |
| 1981 | Republic of Korea | oyster | >60 |
| 1985 | Long Island, United States | scallops | 2 |
| 1986 | Chile | red salmon | 21 |
| 1987 | Japan | yellowtail | 15 |
| 1988 | Norway and Sweden | salmon | 5 |
| 1989 | Norway | salmon, rainbow trout | 4.5 |
| 1989–90 | Puget Sound, United States | salmon | 4-5 |
| 1991 | Washington State, United States | oyster | 15-20 |
| 1991–92 | Republic of Korea | farmed fish | 133 |
| 1996 | Texas, United States | oyster | 24 |
| 1998 | Hong Kong | farmed fish | 32 |

Source: Worldwatch Institute 1999

entanglement in or ingestion of non-biodegradable litter.

Human-induced changes in the natural flow of sediment have emerged since the Stockholm Conference as a major threat to coastal habitats. Urban and industrial development drives the construction of residential and industrial infrastructure which, depending on its nature, can alter sediment flow. In addition, agriculture, deforestation and construction typically mobilize sediments. Deltas, mangrove forests, beaches and other coastal habitats are sustained by the supply of sediment, while other habitats, such as coral reefs and seagrass beds, may be smothered or deprived of light. Sedimentation is one of the major global threats to reefs, particularly in the Caribbean, Indian Ocean, and South and Southeast Asia (Bryant and others 1998, Wilkinson 2000).

## Fisheries

The Stockholm Conference projected that annual harvests could approximately double from 1970 levels to 'rather more than 100 million tonnes' (UN 1972b), although the depletion of some fisheries by overexploitation was also recognized. In the same year the world's largest fishery, the Peruvian anchovy, crashed spectacularly, a result of years of unsustainable harvests precipitated by a strong El Niño event. Harvests from marine capture fisheries did rise but failed to reach 100 million tonnes, fluctuating around 80-90 million tonnes from the mid-1980s (see graph). Contrary to indications that the global fisheries catch is stable, a recent study reveals that catches have actually been declining for more than a decade (Watson and Pauly 2001). The study shows that vast overreporting of catches by some countries combined with the large and wildly fluctuating catch of the Peruvian anchovy, have painted a false picture of the health of the oceans. Aquaculture production, by contrast, has risen sharply but is entirely dominated by Asia and the Pacific (see graph).

The Stockholm Conference recommended two basic approaches to fisheries management: improving management information through research, assessment and monitoring, and international cooperation. Despite great improvement in the quality and scope of fisheries information, better fisheries management has generally not been achieved. There has been an almost inexorable global trend towards increasingly intense exploitation and depletion of fisheries stocks (see figure), three-quarters of which

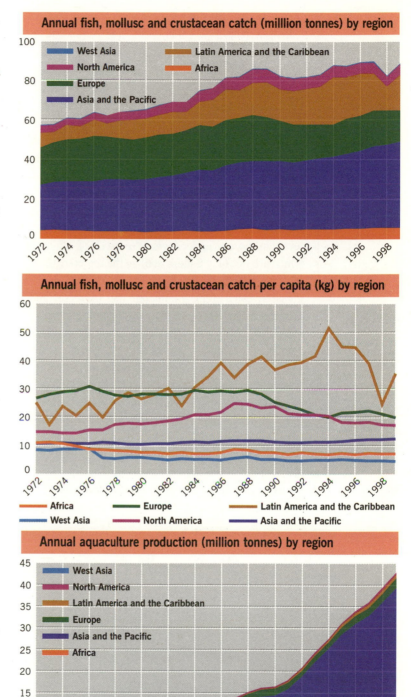

Global fish, mollusc and crustacean catch seems to have stabilized at around 90 million tonnes but per capita values have declined in Europe and North America; note Latin American variations due to fluctuations in the Peruvian anchovy fishery. Aquaculture production has risen steeply for more than a decade, and is dominated by Asia and the Pacific

*Source: compiled from Fishstat 2001 and United Nations Population Division 2001*

are maximally exploited (FAO 2001), and many have collapsed. Global agreements aimed at sustainable fisheries exploitation include the adoption in 1995 of an Agreement on the Conservation and Management of Straddling and Highly Migratory Fish Stocks, and the Code of Conduct for Responsible Fisheries developed by the FAO.

Thirty years ago fisheries issues were considered almost entirely in economic and political terms. Today fisheries activities are increasingly recognized as environmental problems in the broader sense. The global expansion in yields has been delivered by fishing on progressively smaller species at lower levels in the marine food web (the knock-on effects of which are not fully understood) as the top predators have been depleted (Pauly and others 1998). The global by-catch of many million tonnes (Alverson and others 1994) includes not only charismatic animals such as dolphins and turtles but many other species. Effects on marine and coastal ecosystems are poorly known but are probably substantial (Jennings and Kaiser 1998, McManus, Reyes and Nañola 1997). Negative ecosystem impacts also result from some types of fishing gear (such as that used for bottom trawling) and destructive practices (such as blast fishing) which cause physical damage to the habitat. Recognition of the complex inter-relationships between fisheries and marine ecosystems, and the

**Percentage of world fish stocks that are under- or even moderately exploited is falling; depleted, overexploited and recovering stocks are becoming more common**

*Source: FAO 2001*

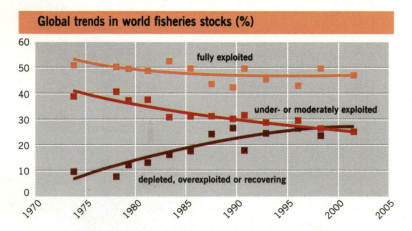

**Global trends in world fisheries stocks (%)**

fully exploited

under- or moderately exploited

depleted, overexploited or recovering

need for ecosystem considerations in the management of capture fisheries, is reflected in the FAO Reykjavik Declaration (2001) on Responsible Fisheries in the Marine Ecosystem.

While seafood is the primary source of protein for many coastal people, especially the poor, the global

demise of fisheries has not been driven only by nutritional needs. Much of the catch is for luxury foods, or is processed into livestock feed. The 'tragedy of the commons' — the absence of a rational reason to restrain harvests that are freely available to all — is one root cause of overfishing while at the other end of the spectrum is so-called 'Malthusian overfishing' (Pauly 1990), when the desperately poor have no choice but to glean the last of the resource. Many attempts to manage fisheries sustainably have degenerated into a 'division of the spoils' (Caldwell 1996). Political imperatives to maintain employment, international competitiveness or sovereign rights of access have led to fisheries subsidies estimated at up to US$20 billion annually (Milazzo 1998), although these are probably now declining.

## Physical alteration

The Stockholm Conference and contemporary reports recognized the importance of estuaries and other coastal habitats but the primary concern was the effects of pollution on them. Direct physical alteration and destruction of habitats is now viewed as arguably the most important single threat to the coastal environment (GESAMP 2001a). The driving force for physical alteration is ill-planned, and accelerating, social and economic development in coastal areas, which itself results from such increasing pressures as population, urbanization and industrialization, maritime transport and tourism.

Habitat alteration results from activities such as port dredging, landfill, coastal solid waste dumps, coastal construction and road building, the cutting of coastal forests, beach and reef mining, and trampling, anchor and diver damage from tourism and recreation, to name some prominent examples. Failure to consider the economic value of these habitats exacerbates the problem. Mangrove forests, for example, are generally regarded as wastelands ripe for 'reclamation', despite an economic value estimated at around US$10 000/ha/year (Costanza and others 1998). Globally, about one-half of the wetlands and more than one-half of mangrove forests have been lost over the past century (OECD and IUCN 1996), largely because of physical alteration. An estimated 58 per cent of the world's coral reefs are threatened, with direct physical destruction among the most important causes (Bryant and others 1998).

**Part of the fishing industry's inadvertent by-catch — a seal ensnared in broken fishing net**

Source: UNEP,
L. K. Nakasawa,
Topham Picturepoint

## Global climate and atmospheric change

The rapid global warming caused by human-induced changes in the atmosphere that is projected by the IPCC would have dramatic effects on the ocean (IPCC 2001), threatening valuable coastal ecosystems and the economic sectors that depend upon them. Other potential impacts are complex and poorly understood. Polar warming, and melting of the ice caps, could slow down the global atmosphere/ocean 'heat engine', potentially altering the flow of major ocean currents (Broecker 1997). The warming of the ocean's surface layers, and an increased input of fresh water, could reduce the upwelling of nutrients that supports much of the ocean's productivity. On the other hand, the highly productive upwelling on the eastern side of some oceans could intensify if, as some projections predict, relatively greater warming occurs there (Bakun 1996). The IPCC predicts that storms and other extreme weather events will increase in frequency and intensity (IPCC 2001), increasing natural disturbances to coastal ecosystems and perhaps reducing their ability to recover.

There is particular concern about the possible effects of global warming on coral reefs. During the intense El Niño of 1997-98, extensive coral bleaching occurred on coral reefs worldwide (Wilkinson 1998, Wilkinson and others 1999). While some reefs quickly recovered, others, particularly in the Indian Ocean, Southeast Asia and the far western Pacific, suffered significant mortality, in some cases more than 90 per cent (Wilkinson 1998, 2000).

Some models predict a long-term shift to an increased frequency and intensity of El Niño events or similar conditions. If this occurs, bleaching could also become more frequent and intense, with irreversible damage to reefs. There is evidence that a long-term decline of reefs in the remote Chagos archipelago in the Indian Ocean is related both to El Niño events and to a long-term rise in surface temperature (Sheppard 1999). Mass bleaching of reefs in various parts of the world was also observed in 2000, a possible sign that bleaching is becoming more frequent. Reefs may also be threatened by a higher concentration of $CO_2$ in seawater which impairs the deposition of their limestone skeletons.

### Jellyfish in the Black Sea

The effect of a jellyfish invasion on the Black Sea is one of the best documented examples of the far reaching economic and ecological consequences that can follow the introduction of an alien species into an environment favouring its almost unlimited expansion.

*Mnemiopsis leidyi,* a comb jellyfish, originates on the eastern seaboards of both North and South America. It abounds in ports and harbours, and is pumped in ballast water into cargo ships. These jellyfish can live for 3–4 weeks without food, by reducing the size of their bodies, so they can easily survive the 20-day voyage to the Black Sea. They were first found in the Black Sea, off the south-east Crimea, in 1982.

Damaging human activities — including overfishing, pollution, water extraction and barrages on rivers running into the sea — had set the stage for its entrance. Overfishing and eutrophication seem to have combined to remove top predators such as turbot, bluefish and monk seals and to cut the numbers of plankton-eating fish severely, opening up a niche for the jellyfish. Meanwhile plankton proliferated.

Hermaphroditic and self-fertilizing, the numbers of jellyfish exploded from 1988 onwards. The populations of plankton crashed as the invaders ate them. Fish stocks collapsed, partly because the jellyfish deprived them of their food and ate their eggs and larvae. The catch of the former states of the Soviet Union plummeted from 250 000 to 30 000 tonnes a year, and it was much the same story in Turkey. At least US$300 million was lost in falling fishery revenues between the mid-1980s and the early 1990s, with grave economic and social consequences. Fishing vessels were put up for sale, and fishermen abandoned the sea.

*Source: GESAMP 2001b*

Proposed protection measures to address a sea-level rise caused by climate change have shifted away from solid constructions such as seawalls in favour of a mix of soft protection measures (such as beach nourishment and wetland creation), adaptive planning (such as new building codes), and managed retreat, including cessation of new coastal construction (IPCC 2001). Some proposals to address global climate change are themselves a cause for concern, particularly those to short-circuit the natural transfer of $CO_2$ from the atmosphere to the ocean by fertilizing large areas of the ocean surface with nitrogen or iron to enhance phytoplankton growth, or to inject $CO_2$ directly into deep waters. The effects of these large-scale measures cannot be predicted but are potentially enormous.

Small island developing states (SIDS) and low-lying coastal areas are particularly vulnerable to the effects of rising sea levels and more extreme weather. Furthermore, they are essentially entirely coastal and therefore more dependent upon coastal and marine resources. Recognition of this special vulnerability in *Agenda 21* of the UN Conference on Environment and Development (UNCED) led to the adoption in 1994 of the Barbados Programme of Action on the Sustainable Development of Small Island States.

## The introduction of exotic species

Another serious problem is the introduction of marine species to distant habitats where they can multiply uncontrollably, sometimes with devastating effects on the economy and marine biodiversity. Such invasions are occurring around the world with increasing frequency. The most common medium for species introductions is in ships' ballast water, with about 3 000 species of animals and plants transported every day (GESAMP 2001a). Efforts to control species introductions in ships' ballast include the development of new regulations by the International Maritime Organization for ballast water management which is expected to be adopted by 2003.

## Conclusion

The Stockholm Conference marked a sea change in our approach to environmental issues by linking environment and development issues. This step towards a holistic approach has been particularly important with regard to the coastal and marine environment which is inevitably affected by different sectors of human activity. The need for a cross-sectoral, holistic approach to managing marine and coastal environments, and their watersheds, is now widely recognized and has been formalized as the discipline of Integrated Coastal Management (ICM).

The Global International Waters Assessment (GIWA) implemented by UNEP is focusing on transboundary water bodies, including marine and coastal areas. This systematic assessment of the environmental conditions and problems, and their social causes, in international waters, includes the development of scenarios of the future condition of the world's water resources and analysis of policy options. Recognition of the increasing degradation of the coastal and marine environment is also reflected by a request of the UNEP Governing Council in 2001 for the conduct of a feasibility study for the establishment of a regular process for global marine assessment.

## References: Chapter 2, coastal and marine areas, global overview

Alverson, D. L., Freeberg, M. H., Pope, J. G. and Muraski, S. A. (1994). *A Global Assessment of Fisheries Bycatch and Discards*, FAO Fisheries Technical Paper No. 339. Rome, Food and Agriculture Organization

AMAP (1998). *AMAP Assessment Report: Arctic Pollution Issues*. Oslo, Arctic Monitoring and Assessment Programme

Balkas, T., Dechev, G., Mihnea, R., Serbenescu, O. and Unluata, U. (1990). *State of the Marine Environment in the Black Sea Region,* UNEP Regional Seas Reports and Studies No. 124. Nairobi, United Nations Environment Programme

Bakun, A. (1996). *Patterns in the Ocean: Ocean Processes and Marine Population Dynamics*. San Diego, University of California Sea Grant Program

Brenton, T. (1994). *The Greening of Machiavelli. The Evolution of International Environmental Politics*. London, Royal Institute of International Affairs

Broeker, W. S. (1997). Thermohaline circulation, the Achilles Heel of our climate system: Will man-made $CO_2$ upset the current balance? *Science* 278,1582-1588

Bryant, D., Burke, L., McManus, J. and Spalding, M. (1998). *Reefs at Risk. A Map-based Indicator of Threats to the World's Coral Reefs*. Washington DC, World Resources Institute

Caldwell, L.K. (1996). *International Environmental Policy: From the Twentieth to the Twenty-first Century*, 3rd edn, Durham and London, Duke University Press

Cohen, J.E., Small, C., Mellinger, A., Gallup, J. and Sachs, J. (1997) Estimates of coastal populations. *Science* 278, 1211-1212

Costanza, R., d'Arge, R., de Groot, R., Farber, S., Grasso, M., Hannon, B., Limburg, K., Naeem, S., O'Neill, R.V., Paruelo, J., Raskin, R.G., Sutton, P. and van den Belt, M. (1998). The value of the world's ecosystem services and natural capital. *Ecological Economics* 25, 3-15

Diaz, R.J. and Rosenberg, R. (1995). Marine benthic hypoxia: A review of its ecological effects and the behavioural responses of benthic macrofauna. *Oceanography and Marine Biology Annual Review* 33, 245-303

FAO (2001). *The State of World Fisheries and Aquaculture 2000*. Rome, Food and Agriculture Organization

Fishstat (2001). *FISHSTAT Plus, Universal software for fishery statistical time series*. FAO Fisheries, Software version 2.3 http://www.fao.org/fi/statist/fisoft/fishplus.asp [Geo-2-237]

GESAMP (in prep.). *Estimates of Oil Entering the Marine Environment from Sea-based Activities*. GESAMP Reports and Studies No. 66 http://gesamp.imo.org/no66/index.htm [Geo-2-268]

GESAMP (2001a). *Protecting the Oceans from Land-Based Activities. Land-based Sources and Activities Affecting the Quality and Uses of the Marine, Coastal and Associated Freshwater Environment*. GESAMP Reports and Studies No. 71. Nairobi, United Nations Environment Programme

http://gesamp.imo.org/no71/index.htm [Geo-2-238]

GESAMP (2001b). *Sea of Troubles*. GESAMP Reports and Studies No. 71. IMO/FAO/UNESCO-IOC/WMO/WHO/IAEA/UN/UNEP Joint Group of Experts on the Scientific Aspects of Marine Environmental Protection. Arendal, GESAMP

Goldberg, E.G. (1976). *The Health of the Oceans*. Paris, UNESCO Press

Heintz, R.A., Short, J. W. and Rice, S. D. (1999). Sensitivity of fish embryos to weathered crude oil: Part II. Increased mortality of pink salmon (*Oncorhynchus gorbuscha*) embryos incubating downstream from weathered *Exxon Valdez* crude oil. *Environmental Toxicology and Chemistry* 18, 494-503

Huang, S., Arimoto, R. and Rahn, K.A. (1996). Changes in atmospheric lead and other pollution elements at Bermuda. *Journal of Geophysical Resources*101, 21 033-21 040

IPCC (2001). *Climate Change 2001: Impacts, Adaptation and Vulnerability. Contribution of Working Group II to the Third Assessment Report of the Intergovernmental Panel on Climate Change*. Cambridge, United Kingdom, and New York, United States, Cambridge University Press

Jennings, S. and Kaiser M.J. (1998). The effects of fishing on marine ecosystems. *Advances in Marine Biology* 34, 201-351

McManus, J.W., Reyes, R.B.J. and Nañola, C.L.J. (1997). Effects of some destructive fishing methods on coral cover and potential rates of recovery. *Environmental Management* 21, 69-78

Malakoff, D. (1998). Death by suffocation in the Gulf of Mexico. *Science* 281, 190-192

Matthews, W.H., Smith, F.E. and Goldberg, E.D. (eds., 1971). *Man's Impact on Terrestrial and Oceanic Ecosystems*. Cambridge MA, Massachusetts Institute of Technology

Milazzo, M. (1998). *Subsidies in World Fisheries: A Re-examination*. World Bank Technical Paper No. 406, Fisheries Series. Washington DC, World Bank

OECD and IUCN (1996). *Guidelines for Aid Agencies for Improved Conservation and Sustainable Use of Tropical and Sub-tropical Wetlands*. Paris, Organization for Economic Cooperation and Development

Pauly, D. (1990). On Malthusian overfishing. *Naga: ICLARM Quarterly* 13, 3-4

Pauly, D., Christensen, V., Dalsgaard, J., Froese, R. and Torres Jr, F. (1998). Fishing down Marine Food Webs. *Science* 279, 860–63

Richardson, K. (1997). Harmful or exceptional phytoplankton blooms in the marine ecosystem. *Advances in Marine Biology* 31, 301-385

SCEP (1970) *Man's Impact on the Global Environment. Assessment and Recommendations for Action*. Report of the Study of Critical Environmental Problems (SCEP). Cambridge MA and London, Massachusetts Institute of Technology

Seitzinger, S. and Kroeze, C. (1998). Global distribution of nitrous oxide production and N inputs in freshwater and marine and coastal ecosytems. *Global Biochemical Cycles* 12, 93-113

Sheppard, C.R. (1999). Coral decline and weather patterns over 20 years in the Chagos Archipelago, central Indian Ocean. *Ambio* 28, 472-482

Socolow, R.H. (1999). Nitrogen management and the future of food: lessons from the management of energy and carbon. *Proc Natl Acad Sci* 96, 6001-6008

UN (1972a). *United Nations Conference on the Human Environment. A/CONF.48/8. Identification and Control of Pollutants of Broad International Significance*. (Subject area III). New York, United Nations

UN (1972b). *United Nations Conference on the Human Environment. A/CONF.48/7. Environmental Aspects of Natural Resources Management* (Subject area II). New York, United Nations.

United Nations Population Division (2001). *World Population Prospects 1950-2050 (The 2000 Revision)*. New York, United Nations www.un.org/esa/population/publications/wpp2000/wpp2000h.pdf [Geo-2-204]

Vitousek, P.M., Aber, J., Howarth, R.W., Likens, G.E., Matson, P.A., Schindler, D.W., Schlesinger, W.H. and Tilman, G.D. (1997). Human alteration of the global nitrogen cycle: causes and consequences. *Issues in Ecology* 1, 1-14

Watson, R. and Pauly, D. (2001). Systematic distortions in world fisheries catch trends. *Nature* 29 November 2001

WHO (1998) *Guidelines for Safe Recreational-Water Environments: Coastal and Freshwaters*. Draft for consultation. Geneva, World Health Organization

Wilkinson, C.R. (1998). The 1997-1998 mass bleaching event around the world. In C.R. Wilkinson (ed.). *Status of Coral Reefs of the World: 1998*. Townsville, Australian Institute of Marine Science

Wilkinson, C.R. (ed., 2000). *Status of Coral Reefs of the World: 2000*. Townsville, Australian Institute of Marine Science

Wilkinson, C., Lindén, O., Cesar, H., Hodgson, G., Rubens, J. and Stong, A.E. (1999). Ecological and socioeconomic impacts of 1998 coral mortality in the Indian Ocean: An ENSO impact and a warning of future change? *Ambio* 28, 188–96

Worldwatch Institute (1999). *State of the World 1999: Chapter 5, Charting a New Course for Oceans*. Washington DC, Worldwatch Institute and W.W.Norton http://secure.worldwatch.org/static/titles/sow.html?4hVWj6Hx;;72 [Geo-2-269]

Wu, J. and Boyle, E.A. (1997). Lead in the Western North Atlantic Ocean: Completed response to leaded gasoline phaseout. *Geochimica et Cosmochimica Acta* 61, 3279–83

Zaitsev, Y. and Mamaev, V. (1997). *Marine Biological Diversity in the Black Sea*. New York, United Nations Development Programme

## Coastal and marine areas: Africa

Africa's 40 000 km of coastline are characterized by a diversity of ecosystems and an abundance of natural resources. The ecosystems include mangrove swamps, estuaries, rocky shores, coastal wetlands and coral reefs; they moderate storm impacts and protect coastal features, recycle nutrients, absorb and break down wastes, provide human and wildlife habitat and maintain biodiversity, and present opportunities for recreation, tourism, transport, trade, and employment.

**Africa's coral reefs — an important source of tourist revenue — are under threat from both coastal development and from potential global warming**

Source: UNEP, David Fleetham, Still Pictures

Coastal and marine resources include fish and shellfish, seaweed, wood and fibre, and oil and gas. Mangrove forests extend from Mauritania to Angola on the west coast and from Somalia to South Africa on the east coast, supporting a diversity of species, many extensively used by local communities. Commercial fisheries contribute significantly to GDP and employment (particularly in small islands). Oil and gas reserves, and other mineral deposits, are also important resources for coastal countries. The growing population and its demands on these resources, however, is causing widespread degradation and pollution of marine and coastal habitats and resources. An additional cause for concern is the threat of sea level rise.

### Resource degradation

Coastal and marine habitats are being physically eroded and biologically degraded through unsustainable rates of resource extraction (including intensive commercial fishing, mining of sand dunes and clearing of mangrove forests). The harvesting methods are also damaging, as in coral extraction and the use of dynamite in fishing. Activities further inland, such as damming of rivers, increased use of fertilizers and clearing of natural vegetation, also affect the coastal zone. Population growth and migration to the coast, together with rapidly expanding tourism and industrial activities, encourage high rates of infrastructure development, modifying the physical and ecological environment of the coastal zone. Lack of formal protection, sustainable development policies and inadequate resources to implement coastal and marine management have contributed to the pressures, although the situation in many countries is now changing.

Coastal drift (erosion and deposition of dunes, beaches and shoreline) is a natural phenomenon but human action can alter natural patterns. Clearing of forests and natural vegetation inland leads to increased soil erosion and increased sediment load in rivers. Sediment is eventually deposited on the seabed, smothering benthic communities and coral reefs. In contrast, when rivers are dammed upstream, sediment settles before reaching the river mouth, thus depriving coastal zones of sediment. In Western Africa, damming of the Upper Niger, Benue and Volta rivers has altered the flow reaching the Niger Delta, and local subsidence is proceeding at 25 mm per year (World Bank 1996). In Ghana, construction of the Akosombo dam in 1965 accelerated coastal erosion west of Accra to 6 metres per year, and in Togo and Benin coastal retreat has exceeded 150 metres over the past 20 years (UNEP 1999).

In Northern Africa, 40-50 per cent of the population in the Mediterranean countries lives in coastal areas (UNEP 1996), with population densities reaching 500-1 000 inhabitants/$km^2$ along the Nile Delta (Blue Plan 1996). In Western Africa, about one-third of the total population is concentrated on a coastal band 60-km wide between Senegal and Cameroon, and large-scale urban growth has occurred from Accra to the Niger Delta, an environmentally sensitive portion of the African coastline.

The coastal zone is also receiving increasing numbers of tourists — in South Africa, for example, the industry grew at 7 per cent a year during the late 1990s (SADC 2000). According to FAO (1998), 38 per cent of Africa's coastal ecosystems are under high levels of threat from development-related activities. The exceptional demand for infrastructure development often results in uncoordinated and poorly planned or sited construction which can in turn cause habitat loss, destabilization or mining of dunes for construction materials, and draining of coastal wetlands. Economic costs are further inflated as governments and investors have to spend large budgets on mitigation and rehabilitation.

The demand for fisheries resources is also increasing. The marine fisheries of Africa have developed significantly over the past 30 years, and most demersal stocks are now thought to be fully exploited (FAO 1996, FAO 1997). The fishery sector contributes more than 5 per cent to GDP in Ghana, Madagascar, Mali, Mauritania, Mozambique, Namibia, Senegal and Seychelles, and the shrimp fishery on the Sofala Bank in Mozambique contributes 40 per cent of the country's foreign exchange (FAO 1997). From 1973 to 1990, fisheries supplied some 20 per cent of the animal protein intake of the population of sub-Saharan Africa. However, per capita fish catch (see figure) has been fairly static since 1972, except in Southern Africa where it has fallen sharply (FAO 1996, FAO 1997). The Cape rock lobster and abalone catches have declined steadily since the 1950s, causing concern over the sustainability of these populations and leading to the setting of annual catch limits (FAO 1997).

In Southern Africa, declining catches, together with a decrease in the mean sizes of fish caught, have led to calls for the protection of line fish stocks. Today fisheries management measures include minimum size limits, bag limits, use of appropriate fishing gear, closed seasons, control agreements with foreign fleets and establishment of marine reserves. In Western Africa, a Sustainable Fisheries Livelihoods Programme aims to develop social and human capital in fisheries-dependent communities, whilst enhancing natural habitats in those communities.

### Addressing coastal and marine degradation

The Convention for the Protection, Management, and Development of the Marine and Coastal Environment of the Eastern African Region (Nairobi Convention) of 1985 is a UNEP Regional Seas Programme initiative, under which the erosion-associated impacts on ecosystems and species are dealt with proactively. Although all affected countries are party to the convention, it is not legally binding, and has received insufficient funding for application of many of the activities.

National efforts to regulate coastal development include the introduction of integrated coastal management policies, requirements for environmental impact assessments to be conducted, and establishment of marine national parks. The Indian Ocean Commission has facilitated the development of a Regional Sustainable Development Policy and a coral reef monitoring and action programme. In Central and Southern Africa, most countries have, or are preparing, Integrated Coastal Zone Management Plans. Africa is the top regional recipient of GEF biodiversity funds, about one-third of which are directed towards projects in coastal, marine and freshwater ecosystems.

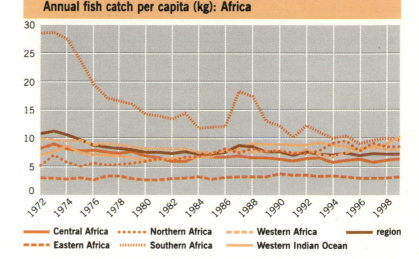

**Annual fish catch per capita (kg): Africa**

Legend: Central Africa, Northern Africa, Western Africa, region, Eastern Africa, Southern Africa, Western Indian Ocean

## Coastal and marine pollution

The waters of the Western Indian Ocean are major sea routes for an estimated 470 million tonnes of oil every year (Salm 1996). More than 100 million tonnes of oil are transported annually through the Red Sea alone (World Bank 1996). This level of shipping incurs a high risk of disastrous oil spills. Furthermore, oil tankers frequently empty ballast and wash engines on the high seas, causing residues of degraded oil to end up on the shore. Port petroleum and oil handling activities also pose threats to the marine and coastal environment. Accidental leakage from ships, refineries and transport systems are common, especially in Mombasa.

Clean-up and disposal of oily wastes is difficult and expensive. Several oil spills off the South African coast have affected African penguins and other marine life. In response, national and regional oil spill contingency plans have been established in several African regions.

*In Africa and most of its sub-regions, the per capita fish catch has stagnated for some 30 years — but in Southern Africa it has fallen sharply*

*Note: fish catch includes marine and freshwater catches but excludes crustaceans and molluscs*

*Source: compiled from Fishstat 2001 and United Nations Population Division 2001*

Effluent from fish processing plants, abattoirs, and chemical and manufacturing industries is frequently discharged into the sea. In Mozambique, for example, more than 100 factories in and around Maputo do not have waste treatment plants and drain toxic wastes, poisons, non-degradable substances and organic matter into coastal waters (Chenje and Johnson 1996). Most of Tanzania's textile mills release dyes, bleaching agents, alkalis and starch directly into Msimbazi Creek in Dar es Salaam (Chenje and Johnson 1996). Residues of fertilizers and pesticides washed down in rivers are prevalent in Western Africa, around cities such as Lagos, Abidjan, Conakry and Dakar. Contaminated shellfish can severely reduce economic returns on the catch and may also expose people to gastric and other infections as a result of swimming in contaminated waters or eating the contaminated food. Domestic solid and liquid waste is also a source of marine and coastal pollution, as municipalities frequently do not have the capacity to deal with the large volumes of waste produced. Solid waste is often dumped on beaches from where it can be blown or washed out to sea.

National responses to marine and coastal pollution have included public health legislation and municipal cleaning of coastal areas. International initiatives include the Convention for the Prevention of Pollution from Ships (MARPOL) and the Convention for Co-operation in the Protection and Development of the Marine and Coastal Environment of the West and Central African Region (Abidjan Convention).

However, difficulties have been experienced in monitoring and enforcement, mainly because of the size of the territories requiring policing and a lack of efficient surveillance systems.

Other responses have had more success. In Northern Africa, regional emergency plans for containment and clean-up of oil spills have been put in place for the Mediterranean region and the Red Sea. The GEF's US$6 million Industrial Water Pollution Control in the Gulf of Guinea project, which aims to improve the health of the coastal waters between Guinea-Bissau and Gabon, has been instrumental in the adoption of the Accra Declaration, a regional policy for long-term sustainable development in the region.

## Climate change and sea level rise

Current predictions for sea level rise over the next 100 years indicate that human settlements in the Gulf of Guinea, Senegal, Gambia, Egypt and along the East African coast, including the Western Indian Ocean islands, would be at high risk of flooding and land recession (IPCC 2001a). The Nile delta, for example, would suffer enormous economic losses due to salt-water contamination and inundation. The delta accounts for 45 per cent of national agricultural production and 60 per cent of national fish production. Sea temperature is also predicted to increase due to global climate change, which would damage coral reef ecosystems and the economic activities that they support (IPCC 2001a).

### References: Chapter 2, coastal and marine areas, Africa

Blue Plan (1996). *A Blue Plan for the Mediterranean People: From Thought to Action*. Cairo, The Blue Plan Regional Activity Centre

Chenje, M. and Johnson, P. (eds.) (1996). *Water in Southern Africa*. Harare and Maseru, SADC, IUCN and SARDC

FAO (1996). *Fisheries and Aquaculture in Sub-Saharan Africa: Situation and Outlook in 1996*. Fisheries Circular No. 922 FIPP/C922. Rome, Food and Agriculture Organization

FAO (1997). *Review of The State of World Fisheries Resources: Marine Fisheries*. Fisheries Circular No. 920 FIRM/C920. Rome, Food and Agriculture Organization

FAO (1998). *Coastal Environments Under Threat*. FAO Factfile. Food and Agriculture Organization http://www.fao.org/NEWS/FACTFILE/FF9804-E.HTM [Geo-2-239]

Fishstat (2001). *FISHSTAT Plus, Universal software for fishery statistical time series*. FAO

Fisheries, Software version 2.3 http://www.fao.org/fi/statist/fisoft/fishplus.asp [Geo-2-237]

IPCC (2001a). *Climate Change 2001: Impacts, Adaptation and Vulnerability. Contribution of Working Group II to the Third Assessment Report of the Intergovernmental Panel on Climate Change*. Cambridge, United Kingdom, and New York, United States, Cambridge University Press

PRE/COI (1998). *Rapport Régional sur les Récifs*. Quatre Bornes, Mauritius, Programme Régional Environment, Commission de l'Océan Indien

SADC (2000). *Tourism*. Mbabane, Southern African Development Community

Salm, R.V. (1996). The Status of Coral Reefs in the Western Indian Ocean with Notes on the Related Ecosystems. In UNEP (ed.), *The International Coral Reef Initiative (ICRI) Western Indian Ocean. An Eastern African Regional Workshop Report, 29 March- 2 April 1996, Mahé, Seychelles*. Nairobi, United Nations Environment Programme

UNEP (1996). *The State of the Marine and Coastal Environment in the Mediterranean Region*. MAP Technical Report Series No. 100. Athens, United Nations Environment Programme

UNEP (1999). *Overview of Land-base Sources and Activities Affecting the Marine, Coastal, and Associated Freshwater Environments in the West and Central Africa Region*. UNEP Regional Seas Reports and Studies No. 171. Nairobi, United Nations Environment Programme

United Nations Population Division (2001). *World Population Prospects 1950-2050 (The 2000 Revision)*. New York, United Nations www.un.org/esa/population/publications/wpp2000/wpp2000h.pdf [Geo-2-204]

World Bank (1996). *Development in Practice: Toward Environmentally Sustainable Development in Sub-Saharan Africa, A World Bank Agenda*

## Coastal and marine areas: Asia and the Pacific

In the past 30 years, depletion of coastal resources such as fisheries, mangroves and coral reefs has emerged as a critical issue in Asia and the Pacific. Increasing urbanization, industrialization and tourism, coupled with a growing coastal population, have degraded coastal areas, reduced water quality and increased pressures on marine resources. These pressures are exacerbated by poverty. For example, in Viet Nam poor people have become increasingly dependent on marine resources for their livelihoods (MoSTE Viet Nam 1999), and significant beach pollution occurs in the vicinity of Sihanoukville and Kep, both important tourist destinations (ADB 2000). Similar trends have been observed in almost all countries of the region.

### Fisheries and aquaculture

Fish production and aquaculture are practised extensively in the region. Overexploitation of fish stocks and poor aquaculture practices are of concern in Bangladesh (DoE, SACEP and UNEP 2001), India (ESCAP and ADB 2000), Pakistan (ESCAP 1996), Sri Lanka, many Pacific Island countries (PICs) and some other countries. Overexploitation of shrimp resources in coastal waters has reduced exports from capture fisheries and encouraged the growth of aquaculture in almost all countries of the region.

Mangrove clearance for shrimp culture has emerged as a major issue in recent years. It is estimated that more than 60 per cent of Asia's mangroves have already been converted to aquaculture farms (ESCAP and ADB 2000). Besides encroaching on mangroves, aquaculture has led to the release of nutrients, pathogens and potentially hazardous chemicals into marine waters. In India, prawn farms have been constructed in low-lying coastal areas, depriving impoverished farmers of agricultural land, causing salinization of groundwater in coastal villages and polluting waterways with excess nutrients (Subramaniam 1994 in ESCAP and ADB 2000).

A number of countries including Australia, India, Maldives, New Zealand, Philippines and Sri Lanka have developed legislation to address problems associated with pollution and overexploitation of fish stocks. Governments have also initiated steps for

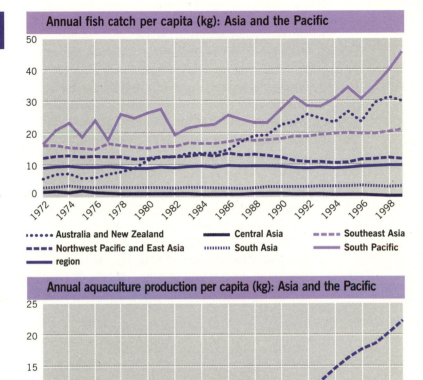

**Annual fish catch per capita (kg): Asia and the Pacific**

······ Australia and New Zealand · ——— Central Asia · ‒ ‒ ‒ Southeast Asia · ‒ ‒ ‒ Northwest Pacific and East Asia · ········ South Asia · ——— South Pacific · ——— region

**Annual aquaculture production per capita (kg): Asia and the Pacific**

······ Australia and New Zealand · ——— Central Asia · ‒ ‒ ‒ Southeast Asia · ‒ ‒ ‒ Northwest Pacific and East Asia · ········ South Asia · ——— South Pacific · ——— region

fisheries management by reducing fishing subsidies and regulating fishing access rights. The South Pacific tuna fishery offers a model of international cooperation for open sea fishing that may prove to be the first sustainable, multinational ocean fishery in the world. Despite these positive initiatives, the pelagic and near-shore fisheries continue to be overexploited by multinational corporations as well as local fishermen, and negotiations are required to ensure that the benefits of sustainable exploitation remain with Pacific communities.

### Coral reefs and coastal resources

Coral reefs are under stress in many areas, especially those near shallow shelves and dense populations. More than half of the world's coral reefs are located in the PICs, and large areas are already degraded. The causes range from global, large-scale changes in the

*While regional fish catch has changed little over 30 years, aquaculture production has increased markedly*

*Note: fish catch includes marine and freshwater catches but excludes crustaceans and molluscs*

*Source: compiled from Fishstat 2001 and United Nations Population Division 2001*

ocean environment and global warming to tourism and recreation, high population density and economic development in coastal areas since the late 1980s.

Most coral reefs in South Asia were adversely affected by coral bleaching in mid-1998. Extensive damage to reefs has been reported from the Andaman Islands, the Gulf of Mannar in India, Lakshadweep, Maldives, Sri Lanka and the PICs. Increasing water temperatures and increased levels of dissolved carbon dioxide in seawater have resulted in the widespread death of stony corals throughout the tropics (Wilkinson 2000). An important development in coral reef conservation and management was the establishment of the Global Coral Reef Monitoring Network (GCRMN) for South Asia in July 1997 by the International Coral Reef Initiative (ICRI) to facilitate monitoring, training, networking and management of coral reefs.

## Marine and coastal pollution

Pollution has considerably degraded the coastal and marine environment, including estuaries, of the region over the past 30 years. Increased wastes from land-based urban, industrial and agricultural activities as well as from offshore oil and gas exploitation are discharged untreated in the coastal region (MoSTE Viet Nam 1999).

The most significant sources of pollution include oil from ships, sewage and other domestic wastes, and industrial effluents. The main route of marine transport of oil from the Gulf is across the Arabian Sea, and accidental oil spills have been frequently reported along oil transport routes, at points of discharge and loading of oil carriers. The shipping of oil coupled with increasing emphasis on offshore oil exploration makes the northern Indian Ocean extremely vulnerable to oil pollution. Oil spills also cause severe pollution in ports in Bangladesh, Indonesia, Malaysia and Pakistan (DoE Malaysia 1996, 1998). In addition, the cleaning of oil tanks in and around ports has led to the frequent formation of tar-balls on the southwestern beaches of Sri Lanka. In the PICs, marine pollution from ships is a threat that is likely to increase as trade and economies develop further.

The enhanced use of agrochemicals on land and discharge of chemicals into seawater is a common problem. An estimated 1 800 tonnes of pesticides enter the Bay of Bengal every year (Holmgrem 1994). In the Sea of Japan, a survey has revealed high

concentrations of mercury, the source of which could have been wastewater from chemical plants (MSA 1997), while the Russian Federation admitted in 1993 that the former Soviet Union had dumped nuclear wastes there 'for decades' (Hayes and Zarsky 1993). In spite of international regulations, marine pollution in the Sea of Japan and the Yellow Sea has continued to worsen.

Tourism and other recreational activities also pose a threat to coastal ecosystems in many countries. The construction of tourism infrastructure has both a direct and indirect adverse impact on coastal environments through infilling, dredging and re-suspension of contaminated silts, discharge of

### Managing ballast water discharges in Australia

The annual discharge of ballast water in Australian coastal waters is about 150 million tonnes from international vessels and 34 million tonnes from coastal vessels. A major incursion of black-striped mussels in Darwin Harbour in early 1999 prompted the establishment of a National Task Force on the Prevention and Management of Marine Pest Incursions. A major recommendation of the task force was the establishment of a single national management regime for vessels. Its recommendations are implemented through the National Introduced Marine Pests Coordination Group which was established under the Ministerial councils for environment, fisheries and aquaculture, and transport. The Consultative Committee on Introduced Marine Pest Emergencies, a mechanism for emergency responses to introduced marine pests, was introduced in 2000.

Since 1990 the Australian Quarantine and Inspection Service (AQIS) has adopted voluntary guidelines and measures to manage ballast water. In July 2001, Australia introduced mandatory ballast water management for international vessels entering its waters. Vessels are assessed by AQIS: high risk vessels are required to fully exchange ballast water at sea, while low risk vessels are allowed to exchange within coastal waters.

*Source: Environment Australia 2001*

untreated or partially treated sewage, operational leaks, and discharge of hydrocarbons and waste dumping. Sand dunes, an important component of coastal ecosystems in the region, have also been eroded as a result of tourism activities.

Sediment load in the coastal zones of South Asia is high, mainly as a result of soil erosion caused by poor land-use practices and construction activities. Annually, about 1.6 billion tonnes of sediment reach the Indian Ocean from rivers flowing from the Indian sub-continent. The total sediment load of the river system of Bangladesh alone amounts to about 2.5 billion tonnes, of which the Brahmaputra carries 1.7 billion tonnes and the Ganges 0.8 billion tonnes (UNEP 1987). Coastal erosion is severe in many areas including the Andaman coast, the Gulf of Thailand, Japan and the PICs.

## Policy responses

The gradual move towards integrated planning and development of coastal and marine areas, through national, regional and global initiatives, is an encouraging trend. Many countries have adopted the two major international agreements on marine pollution: the London Convention of 1972 and the International Convention for the Prevention of Marine Pollution from Ships (MARPOL) of 1973, with its 1978 Protocol.

ESCAP has instituted studies relating to a Coastal Environmental Management Plan for a number of countries in South Asia, including Bangladesh, Pakistan and Sri Lanka. The Plan requires intensive multidisciplinary studies encompassing socio-economic dynamics, industry, agriculture, fishery, forestry, water resources, energy, ecology and health, as well as close collaboration between the scientific community and governments, other institutions and experts. Mechanisms for implementing coastal environmental management continue to be developed, and Sri Lanka appears to have made more progress than other countries.

Another major multilateral effort that aims at marine and coastal environmental protection at the regional level is UNEP's Regional Seas Programme initiated in 1974. At the sub-regional level the South Asian Seas Action Plan was adopted in 1995 and includes Bangladesh, India, Maldives, Pakistan and Sri Lanka. In 1995, 108 governments across the world adopted the Global Programme of Action for the Protection of the Marine Environment from Land-based Activities. Many countries have also introduced national legislation and projects to address marine pollution.

## References: Chapter 2, coastal and marine areas, Asia and the Pacific

ADB (2000). *Environments in Transition: Cambodia, Lao PDR, Thailand, Vietnam.* Manila, Asian Development Bank

DoE Malaysia (1996). *Malaysia Environmental Quality Report 1996.* Kuala Lumpur, Malaysia Department of Environment

DoE Malaysia (1998). *Malaysia Environmental Quality Report 1998.* Kuala Lumpur, Malaysia Department of Environment

DoE, SACEP and UNEP (2001). *Bangladesh State of the Environment Report.* Dhaka, Department of Environment Bangladesh

Environment Australia (2001). The National Taskforce on the Prevention and Management of Marine Pest Incursions. http://www.ea.gov.au/coasts/imps/taskforce.html [Geo-2-267]

ESCAP (1996). *Coastal Environmental Management Plan for Pakistan.* Bangkok, United Nations Economic and Social Commissions for Asia and the Pacific

ESCAP and ADB (2000). *State of the Environment in Asia and Pacific 2000.* Economic and Social Commission for Asia and the Pacific and Asian Development Bank. New York, United Nations http://www.unescap.org/enrd/environ/soe.htm [Geo-2-266]

Fishstat (2001). *FISHSTAT Plus, Universal software for fishery statistical time series.* FAO Fisheries, Software version 2.3 http://www.fao.org/fi/statist/fisoft/fishplus.asp [Geo-2-237]

Hayes, P. and Zarsky, L. (1994). Environmental Issues and Regimes in Northeast Asia. *International Environmental Affairs* Vol. 6, No. 4, Fall 1994 http://www.nautilus.org/papers/enviro/neaenv.html [Geo-2-240]

Holmgren, S. (1994). *An Environmental Assessment of the Bay of Bengal Region.* BOPG/REP/67. Madras, Bay of Bengal Programme,

MSA (1997). *Report of Marine Pollution.* Tokyo, Maritime Safety Agency

MoSTE Viet Nam (1999). *State of the Environment of Viet Nam: 1999 Report.* Hanoi, Ministry of Science, Technology and Environment

UNEP (1987). *Environmental Problems of the South Asian Seas Region: An Overview.* UNEP Regional Seas Reports and Studies No 82. Nairobi, United Nations Environment Programme

UNEP (1999). *GEO-2000.* United Nations Environment Programme. London and New York, Earthscan

United Nations Population Division (2001). *World Population Prospects 1950-2050 (The 2000 Revision).* New York, United Nations www.un.org/esa/population/publications/wpp2000/wpp2000h.pdf [Geo-2-204]

Wilkinson, C.R. (ed., 2000). *Status of Coral Reefs of the World: 2000.* Townsville, Australian Institute of Marine Science

## Coastal and marine areas: Europe

Europe is almost surrounded by semi-closed and closed seas, such as the Adriatic, Mediterranean, Black, Azov, Caspian, Baltic and White seas. Coastal landscape features range from dunes, cliffs, lagoons and river deltas to very diverse islands, with numerous important marine and bird areas, including 449 Ramsar sites in Western Europe. The Danube has the largest delta in Europe, encompassing about 580 000 ha (113 000 ha of which are permanently covered by water). The limited water exchange of the semi-closed and closed seas with the open ocean makes these seas very sensitive to pollution, which increased dramatically between the 1970s and 1990s, although this trend has been halted and even reversed in a few places in the past ten years. The open coasts of the Atlantic show impacts from land-based pollution, offshore oil and gas, and shipping operations and accidental oil spills.

### Infrastructure development

Some 85 per cent of European coasts are at high or moderate risk from development-related pressures (Bryant and others 1995). The rapid development of tourism, increasing transport, intensive agricultural and industrial activities, and continuing urbanization have all put pressures on coastal areas. As a result of infrastructure development and other construction activities, as well as natural causes, coastal erosion is a major issue in some areas, with 25 per cent of the European coast subject to erosion (CORINE 1998). The challenges for coastal areas are to cope with further economic development and hence growing environmental pressures.

Tourism is important for the coastal areas of Europe, considering that they host two-thirds of the region's tourism (Europe attracts 60 per cent of all international tourism). The Mediterranean is the world's leading destination, accounting for 30 per cent of international tourist arrivals and for one-third of the receipts from international tourism. The number of tourists on the Mediterranean coast is expected to rise from 135 million in 1990 to 235-353 million in 2025 (EEA 1999a). Tourism is growing at a rate of 3.7 per cent a year (EUCC 1997) and its demands consume increasing amounts of land. Similar developments can be observed in other important tourist areas along the Baltic, North Sea and northeast Atlantic coasts. Tourism accounts for 7 per cent of pollution and makes a huge contribution to water scarcity, water consumption by this sector being three to seven times higher than for local populations (EEA 2001).

### Pollution

Although shipping is considered to be an environmentally friendly mode of transport, it can have major negative environmental impacts if standards are not observed or enforced. Maritime transport increased in the EU by 35 per cent between 1975 and 1985 but has since levelled off (EUCC 1997). This has had an impact on $SO_2$ emissions: maritime transport now accounts for 10-15 per cent of total $SO_2$ emissions (EEA 1999b). It is estimated that 30 per cent of all merchant shipping and 20 per cent of global oil shipping (see map) crosses the Mediterranean every year (MAP and REMPEC 1996b).

Pollution from land-based sources is still serious in many areas. Many of the 200 nuclear power plants operating throughout Europe (EEA 1999b) are located in coastal regions or along major rivers, because of the large volume of cooling water needed. Since the 1960s, radioactive discharges from the nuclear fleets of the former Soviet navy have affected remote areas of the Arctic and Pacific Oceans (Yablokov 1993). About 150

Although the number of incidents related to oil transportation has risen over the past two decades, the proportion that actually results in oil spills is decreasing

*Source: MAP and REMPEC 1996a*

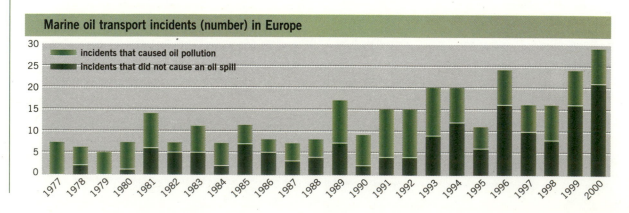

**Marine oil transport incidents (number) in Europe**

incidents that caused oil pollution
incidents that did not cause an oil spill

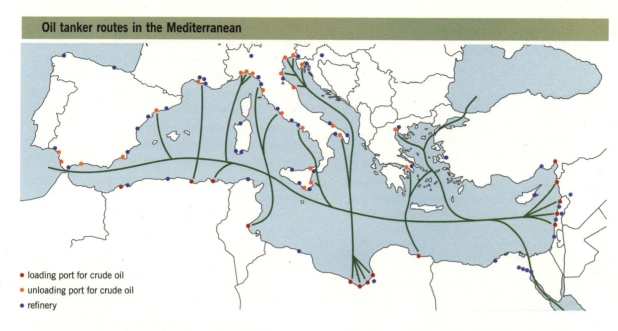

**Oil tanker routes in the Mediterranean**

- ● loading port for crude oil
- ● unloading port for crude oil
- ● refinery

Some 30 per cent of all merchant shipping and 20 per cent of global oil shipping crosses the Mediterranean every year

Source: MAP and REMPEC 1996b

decommissioned nuclear submarines are rusting in harbours on the Kola Peninsula, Kamchatka and the Russian Far East, representing a potential environmental threat. Although the Helsinki Commission (HELCOM) reports that there is no environmental threat from chemical munitions or radioactive substances in the Baltic marine environment, citizens groups are still concerned (HELCOM 2001). Discharges from nuclear reprocessing plants originating from the United Kingdom and France are also a matter of concern in the maritime area of the North Sea and the Atlantic (OSPAR 2001).

Pollution by heavy metals and persistent organic pollutants, and contamination by microbes and other substances, occur in all European seas. However, there have been some significant improvements:

- Inputs of hazardous heavy metals and organic substances into the northeast Atlantic fell significantly between 1990 and 1998 after increasing for several decades. Atmospheric inputs of heavy metals into the North Sea also fell, showing the effect of air pollution abatement policies in the surrounding countries (EEA 2001).
- Between 1985 and 1998, nitrate concentrations decreased by 25 per cent (against a 50 per cent target) in the coastal areas covered by the Convention for the Protection of the Marine Environment of the North-East Atlantic (OSPAR Convention) and the Baltic Marine Environment Protection Commission (EEA 2000).

- The reduced phosphate content of detergents and other measures such as wastewater treatment in catchment areas have resulted in an average decrease of phosphate concentrations in some regions, including the Skagerrak, Kattegat, the German Bight and the Dutch coastal zone (EEA 2000).

Wastewater treatment still needs to be improved, however. High population concentrations also result in high levels of wastewater, which is often not sufficiently treated — for example, in the Mediterranean, Adriatic and Black seas. Until the end of the 1980s, large cities on the shores of the Baltic Sea such as St Petersburg (4 million inhabitants) and Riga (800 000 inhabitants) had no wastewater treatment plants (Mnatsakanian 1992).

Solid waste is also a problem in some European seas. A recent study showed that the main sources of solid waste on the coast, sea surface and sea bed in the Mediterranean region are direct disposal from households, tourist facilities and run-off from coastal landfill sites.

## Policy measures

Global, regional and national measures are being taken to reduce the input of polluting substances into marine waters. International agreements such as OSPAR, HELCOM and the Mediterranean Action Plan (MAP) provide a binding legal framework. In the OSPAR and Baltic Sea areas, for example, targets have been set to

## Hazards and contingency planning for oil spills

The main principles for international cooperation in preparedness for and response to marine pollution incidents are defined by the Emergency Protocol to the Barcelona Convention. In order to assist coastal states in its implementation, the Regional Marine Pollution Emergency Response Centre for the Mediterranean Sea (REMPEC) was established in Malta in 1976. Since 1977, REMPEC has systematically collected reports on incidents causing or likely to cause pollution of the sea by oil. Some 311 incidents were recorded between August 1977 and December 2000, 156 of which actually resulted in the spillage of oil. Spill response operations in the Mediterranean between 1981 and 2000 were regularly conducted either by national or local authorities or by the spill clean-up contractors under their supervision. To date, nearly 2 000 people have participated in a training programme developed by REMPEC to assist coastal states in developing their own capabilities for effective responses to pollution incidents. The only case that necessitated mutual assistance between neighbouring countries (France and Italy) was the spill from the tanker *Haven* near Genoa in Italy, with the loss of 144 000 tonnes of oil in 1991.

*Source: REMPEC 2000*

reduce emissions, losses and discharges of hazardous wastes with the ultimate aim of achieving concentrations near background values for naturally occurring substances and close to zero for synthetic substances by 2020 (HELCOM 1998).

Some states have difficulties in implementing their obligations under these agreements, and this reduces the effectiveness of regional MEAs such as MAP and the Black Sea Convention. Assistance programmes from wealthier states may play an important role in improving implementation and compliance in relation to regional and sub-regional MEAs.

Enforcement has improved significantly in some

CEE countries, and the introduction of economic instruments has had an impact. For example, the European Bank for Reconstruction and Development (EBRD) has made funding available for infrastructure improvements in the transition countries in cooperation with HELCOM. However, the slow transformation of large, polluting, state-owned enterprises continues to present obstacles.

The recently adopted European Water Framework Directive provides a strong instrument for the control of pollutants and monitoring in the catchment and coastal areas and improvement of water quality for all EU States and incoming accession States.

A recent example of a non-binding agreement at the global level is the Global Programme of Action for the Protection of the Marine Environment from Land-based Activities (GPA). Its implementation will require new forms of collaboration between governments, organizations and institutions concerned with marine and coastal areas at all levels — national, regional and global. Although still in its early stages, the interest and commitment shown by governments in Europe are encouraging.

The main challenge in coastal areas is the implementation of Integrated Coastal Zone Management which aims at harmonizing the various, sometimes conflicting, uses of the coastal zone. In regions such as the Baltic Sea, bordered by several independent nations, transboundary and international cooperation is a basic requirement.

## References: Chapter 2, coastal and marine areas, Europe

Bryant, D., Rodenburg, E., Cox, T. and Nielsen, D. (1995). *Coastlines at Risk: An Index of Potential Development-Related Threats to Coastal Ecosystems*. WRI Indicator Brief. Washington DC, World Resources Institute

CORINE (1998). *CORINE Coastal Erosion Atlas*. Luxembourg, Office for Official Publications of the European Communities

EEA (1999a). *State and Pressures of the Marine and Coastal Mediterranean Environment*. Environmental Assessment Series No. 5. Copenhagen, European Environment Agency

EEA (1999b). *Environment in the European Union at the Turn of the Century*. Environmental Assessment Report No 2. Copenhagen, European Environment Agency

EEA (2000). *Environmental Signals 2000*. Environmental Assessment Report No 6. Copenhagen, European Environment Agency

EEA (2001). *Environmental Signals 2001*. Environmental Assessment Report No 8. Copenhagen, European Environment Agency

EUCC (1997). *The European Coastal Code – EUCC, Draft 2. A contribution to Action Theme 5 of the Pan-European Biological and Landscape Diversity Strategy*. Leiden, European Union for Coastal Conservation

HELCOM (1998). *Recommendations 19/5 HELCOM Objective with Regard to Hazardous Substances*. Helsinki, Helsinki Commission

HELCOM (2001). *Environment of the Baltic Sea area 1994 -1998*. Baltic Sea Environmental Proceedings No. 82A. Helsinki, Helsinki Commission

MAP and REMPEC (1996a). *List of alerts and accidents in the Mediterranean*. Athens, UNEP Mediterranean Action Plan

MAP and REMPEC (1996b). *An Overview of Maritime Transport in the Mediterranean*. Athens, United Nations Environment Programme

Mnatsakanian, R. (1992). *Environmental Legacy of the Former Soviet Republics*. Edinburgh, Centre for Human Ecology, University of Edinburgh

OSPAR (2001). *Liquid Discharges from Nuclear Installations in 1999* http://www.ospar.org/eng/html/welcome.html [Geo-2-241]

REMPEC (2001). *Alerts and Accidents*. Regional Marine Pollution Emergency Response Centre for the Mediterranean Sea http://www.rempec.org/accidents.html

Yablokov, A.V. (1993). *Facts and Problems Related to Radioactive Waste Disposal in Seas Adjacent to the Territory of the Russian Federation*. Materials for a report by the Government Commission on Marrwe Related to Radioactive Waste Disposal at Sea, Created by Decree No. 613 of the Russian Federation President October 24, 1992. Moscow, Office of the President of the Russian Federation

## Coastal and marine areas: Latin America and the Caribbean

The key environmental problems facing the coastal and marine areas of the Latin American and Caribbean Region are related to habitat conversion and destruction, pollution produced by human activities and overexploitation of fisheries resources. The underlying causes of these problems are linked to the development of coastal areas for tourism, infrastructure and urbanization, and to the conversion of coastal habitats for uses such as agriculture and aquaculture. In addition to diminished natural productivity of coastal areas, most coastal and offshore fisheries are severely overexploited. These problems are expected to be significantly exacerbated by climate change and sea-level rise (UNEP 2000), particularly in the Caribbean. The state of coastal areas throughout the region is illustrated in the table on the right. Coastal areas that are heavily populated and exploited require intensive management and infrastructure to sustain coastal ecological systems. However, complicating coastal zone management are multiple physical and political jurisdictions dividing ecological boundaries and scales.

### Exploitation of coastal and marine resources

The region's coastal zones are the foundation of its economy and sustainability — 60 of the 77 largest towns are on the coasts, and 60 per cent of the population lives within 100 km of the coast (Cohen and others 1997). Development of residential areas and tourism infrastructure has greatly changed the features of coastal areas in the region. Physical alterations of coastlines due to urban growth and the construction of ports and industrial infrastructure are among the major factors that impact the region's coastal and marine ecosystems.

Tourism represents around 12 per cent of the GDP of the region, much of which is concentrated along the coasts. Some 100 million tourists visit the Caribbean each year and contribute 43 per cent of GDP and one-third of export revenue (WTTC 1993). The direct and indirect effects of tourism on coastal and marine areas can be seen in the increasing conversion of coastal habitats and subsequent impacts. For example, overextraction of ground water by expanding tourism infrastructure results in the intrusion of brackish or salt water into coastal aquifers, eventually contaminating the groundwater system and coastal soil.

### Management status of principal coastal and marine areas

| Conditions of use | Management and infrastructure support | Biogeographical zones |
|---|---|---|
| Intensively used and heavily populated coastal areas; Intensive fishing pressure from both coastal populations and offshore fisheries; High density or concentration of oil terminals, ports and shipping lanes | Intensively managed – high infrastructure support – regulatory, conservation and education efforts | Some areas of the tropical northwestern Atlantic, including Cancun, Mexico. Southeast Atlantic: Brazil |
| | Moderate management – regulatory efforts with limited enforcement, limited conservation and education efforts | Most areas of the tropical northwestern Atlantic, such as Puerto Rico, parts of US Virgin Islands, Barbados and most islands of the Lesser Antilles; Warm temperate northeastern Pacific, including Mexico; Galapagos Islands |
| | Little to no region-wide management | Most areas of the tropical eastern Pacific, warm temperate southwestern Atlantic, including Argentina, Brazil, Uruguay; Some areas of tropical eastern Pacific |
| Moderately used coastal resources | Intensively managed | Areas of the warm temperate southeastern Pacific, including Peru and Chile — especially those related to coastal shelf fisheries |
| | Moderate management | Cold temperate South America, including Chile and Argentina |
| | Light management | Tropical southwestern Atlantic: Brazil |
| Lightly used coastal resources | Intensive management | Only a few examples of lightly used, intensive management in high profile remote marine protected areas |
| | Moderate management to little to no management | Very few areas under this category — even large, remote areas such as the Orinoco River delta are affected by land use alterations in the delta and upland watershed areas, even though use of the estuarine resources may be low; Also Juan Fernandez and Desventuradas Islands |

### Pollution

Pollution is mainly caused by discharge of municipal and industrial solid waste and wastewater, run-off from agricultural fields, and maritime transport (especially of hazardous substances), as well as oil and gas extraction, refining and transport. Regional capacity for wastewater treatment is low; some 98 per cent of domestic wastewater is discharged into the northeast Pacific and 90 per cent into the wider Caribbean without treatment (UNEP 2001).

The effects of pollutants from land-based activities are exacerbated in large watersheds, and in turn may affect distant states. The transboundary effects of five major watersheds are especially notable: the Mississippi, the Amazon, the Plata, the Orinoco and the Santa Marta. Satellite images have shown large sediment discharges from coastal rivers and some large islands travelling across thousands of kilometres of ocean. During a fish kill episode in the Windward Islands in February 2000, pathological bacteria were detected that previously had been reported only in continental freshwater systems (Caribbean Compass 1999). It was suggested that the pathogens had been transported in sediments originating in floods in the Orinoco basin.

Maritime transport is a significant source of coastal and marine pollution in the region especially the release of oil through dumping of bilge water and

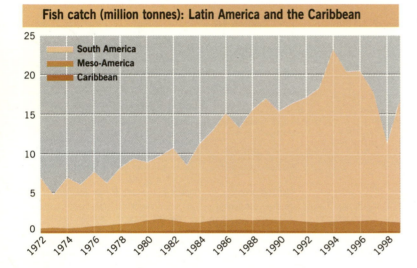

**Fish catch (million tonnes): Latin America and the Caribbean**

- South America
- Meso-America
- Caribbean

Regional fish catch peaked in 1994 but collapsed later as a result of a strong El Niño event

*Note: includes inland fisheries but excludes molluscs, crustaceans and aquaculture*

*Source: compiled from Fishstat 2001*

tank rinsing. Other threats from maritime transport include discharge of sewage, garbage and hazardous chemicals, and introduction of exotic or invasive species to new areas through loading and off-loading of ballast water.

The ports in the region are the second most important destination for containerized goods from the United States, and the Panama Canal is a principal link for global maritime trade. Between 1980 and 1990, maritime transport in the region increased from 3.2 to 3.9 per cent of global trade, and significant increases are expected to continue as a result of trade liberalization and privatization of regional ports (UNCTAD 1995). Without counter measures, environmental problems related to maritime transport are expected to worsen in the future.

The marine and coastal areas of Latin America and the Caribbean are among the most productive petroleum-producing areas in the world. The most important pressure on the marine and coastal environment in specific localities is the risk of oil spills from oil and gas exploration, production and

distribution systems. The world's largest recorded oil spill was the Ixtoc submarine oil blow-out in the Bay of Campeche, Mexico, on 3 June 1979 with a total estimated outflow of oil greater than the volume from the *Exxon Valdez* spill. In 1999 and 2001, significant coastal spills and pipeline ruptures in Brazil and Colombia caused both active public concern and new restrictions to control future spills. All oil and gas exploration operations have the potential to cause severe damage to the coastal and marine environment as a result of large and small spills, and chronic leaks.

## Fisheries

Overexploitation of fisheries resources and the problems of by-catch and discards have become features of the regional fisheries regime. The catch from the region's seas has generally increased over the past 30 years (see figure). Total fish catch (including inland fisheries but excluding molluscs, crustaceans and aquaculture) reached a regional peak of more than 23 million tonnes in 1994 (nearly 30 per cent of the global total). From 1985 to 1995, many South American countries doubled or tripled their catch, and Colombia's catch increased five-fold. However, in 1998 the regional catch dropped considerably to 11.3 million tonnes (15.9 per cent of the global total), due to adverse climatic factors caused by the El Niño.

A recent study that established geographic priorities for marine conservation in the Central Caribbean ecoregion indicated that excessive exploitation was a threat in 34 of the 51 local production systems (Sullivan and Bustamante 1999). The region also faces the problem of large quantities of by-catch and discards that include turtles, marine mammals, marine birds and other smaller but ecologically important species. At present, the region has no system to record indicators on the health of resources and ecosystems that would gear actions to the recovery of overexploited species and their environment (UNEP 2001).

Measures to halt overexploitation of fisheries have been implemented in some countries. In January 2000, the Government of the Bahamas and local NGOs agreed to the establishment of five 'No Take' marine reserves near the offshore islands of Bimini, Berry, South Eleuthera, Exuma and northern Abaco. The objective is to establish, with full community participation, a complete system of such reserves, to aid in the prevention of overfishing and loss of marine biodiversity. This would result in the protection of 20 per cent of the coastal and marine environment (NOAA 2001).

## Policy responses

International policy responses to the problems described above have been many and varied. Most of them are based on fisheries conventions, international shipping conventions, or the large number of agreements tied to the United Nations Convention on the Law of the Sea. At the same time, institutional and organizational weaknesses in the countries of the region, and the myriad authorities responsible for marine and coastal management, make the implementation of policies a difficult task.

The following are among the most important multilateral agreements and action plans:

- The Convention on the Protection and Development of the Marine Environment of the Wider Caribbean ('The Cartagena Convention') (1983) and its protocols (on oil spills and protected areas and land-based pollution).
- UNEP's Regional Seas Programme, and the international project for the elimination of barriers to implement ballast water controls and management measures for developing countries, proposed for the period 2000-2002 by the International Maritime Organization (IMO).
- The International Coral Reefs Action Network (ICRAN), an important effort to halt the degradation of coral reefs, which is supported by the United Nations Foundation (UNF).
- The Caribbean Planning for the Adaptation of Global Climate Change (CPACC) project which

assists the 12 Caribbean CARICOM countries to prepare for the negative impacts of possible global climate change, especially with respect to the rise in sea level, by measuring their vulnerability and planning for the adaptation and development of their capacity to deal with the problem.

Few of the conventions mentioned, however, have been in force long enough, and with adequate established infrastructure, to assess their strengths and weaknesses. It is clear, however, that regional environmental monitoring processes need to be geared to assessing environmental conditions as well as monitoring implementation activities designed to restore sustainability of coastal and marine areas and their resources.

**Capacity for wastewater treatment is low; 98 per cent of domestic wastewater is discharged into the northeast Pacific and 90 per cent into the wider Caribbean without treatment**

*Source: UNEP, David Tapia Munoz, Topham Picturepoint*

### References: Chapter 2, coastal and marine areas, Latin America and the Caribbean

Caribbean Compass (1999). *Fish Kill Theories Abound, but Still No Answers.* Caribbean Compass, November 1999 http://www.caribbeancompass.com/fish.htm [Geo-2-264]

Cohen, J.E., Small, C., Mellinger, A., Gallup, J. and Sachs, J. (1997). Estimates of coastal populations. *Science* 278, 1211–12

Fishstat (2001). *FISHSTAT Plus, Universal software for fishery statistical time series.* FAO Fisheries, Software version 2.3 http://www.fao.org/fi/statist/fisoft/fishplus.asp [Geo-2-237]

NOAA (2001). *Wetland Areas in the Bahamas.* US Department of Commerce, National Oceanic and Atmospheric Administration. http://www.oar.noaa.gov/spotlite/archive/spot_cmrc.html [Goe-2-242]

Sullivan, K. and Bustamante, G. (1999). *Setting Geographic Priorities for Marine Conservation in Latin American and the Caribbean.* Arlington, United States, The Nature Conservancy

UNCTAD (1995). *Review of Maritime Transport 1994.* Geneva, United Nations Conference on Trade and Development

UNEP (2000). *GEO Latin America and the Caribbean Environment Outlook* Mexico City, United Nations Environment Programme, Regional Office for Latin America and the Caribbean

UNEP (2001). *Municipal Waste Water as a Land-Based Source of Pollution in Coastal and Marine Areas of Latin America and the Caribbean.* Mexico City, United Nations Environment Programme, Regional Office for Latin America and the Caribbean

WTTC (1993). *Travel and Tourism: A New Economic Perspective.* London, World Travel and Tourism Council

## Coastal and marine areas: North America

Almost 25 per cent of Canada's and about 55 per cent of the United States' populations live in coastal areas (CEQ 1997, EC 1999). The US coastal population is growing at four times the national average, with some of the highest levels of urban growth taking place in small coastal cities (CEC 2000a). This is of concern because coastal ecosystems are among the richest storehouses of marine biodiversity and provide important ecosystem goods and services. Conversion of these fragile systems to urban uses can lead to physical degradation, exploitation of marine resources and pollution.

### Annual fish catch (million tonnes): North America

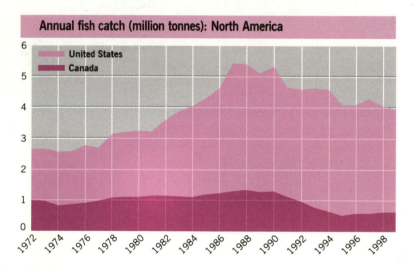

North American fisheries have been in severe decline since the late 1980s, with at least one-third of all species overfished

*Note: fish catch includes marine and freshwater catches but excludes crustaceans and molluscs, and aquaculture production*

*Source: compiled from Fishstat 2001*

Issues of particular concern for the region are the excessive input of nitrogen from land-based activities and the precipitous decline in fisheries (see graph): 21 of the 43 ground-fish stocks in Canada's North Atlantic are in decline and nearly one-third of US federally managed fisheries are overfished (CEC 2000a).

### Pacific Northwest salmon fishery

The Pacific Northwest supports rich fishery resources, of which salmon is of primary importance. Historically abundant in many Pacific coastal and interior waters, salmon runs and species diversity have been shrinking since the late 19th century, due to dam construction (particularly in the United States), rockslides, poor management and overfishing (DFO 1999a). By the late 1980s, both countries had imposed severe restrictions on harvests of some salmon species but, despite these and other measures, by the early 1990s salmon catch and value showed significant declines; by 1999, 24 sub-

species of west coast salmon had been listed under the US Endangered Species Act and Canada had closed or curtailed salmon harvests for some species in a number of its major rivers (Carlisle 1999, TU and TUC 1999).

Complicating the issue have been the two international borders that separate British Columbia's waters from Alaska's and those of the northwest United States (DFO 1999a, TU and TUC 1999). During their life cycle, salmon of US origin travel through Canada's waters and vice versa, resulting in a history of intercepting fishery practices that has encouraged unsustainable harvests (DFO 1999a). The 1985 Pacific Salmon Treaty attempted to resolve this issue but broke down in 1992 because of disagreements. A 1999 amendment to the treaty based on sustaining wild stocks, sharing costs and benefits, and a common basis to assess stocks, monitor fish and evaluate performance is more promising (DFO 1999b, NOAA 1999).

The combined effects of fishing, climate change (see box below) and habitat conditions have prompted a number of status reviews, renewed fishing agreements and new management approaches. For example, in 1998 Canada initiated the Pacific Fisheries Adjustment and Rebuilding Program to conserve and rebuild Pacific salmon stocks and to revitalize Pacific salmon fisheries. It has also implemented a precautionary approach to salmon management, resulting in significant harvest reductions to protect stocks at risk (DFO 1999c). In December 2000, the United States released a comprehensive, long-term

### Impacts of climate change on Pacific salmon and other wild fish stock

Both Canada and the United States are concerned about the potential effects of climate change on salmon populations and other wild fish stocks in North America's coastal and oceanic waters. Studies by Canadian government scientists that simulated expected changes from a doubling of $CO_2$ in the atmosphere indicate that the resulting change in climate could virtually eliminate salmon habitat from the Pacific Ocean (NRC 1998). A 1994 Environment Canada study of the impact of climate change on Fraser River salmon reported that altered flow regimes, aquatic temperatures, river hydrology and seasonal run-off will intensify competition among water users in the watershed (Glavin 1996). A recent US report on climate change impacts notes that a projected narrowing in the annual water temperature range in many estuaries may cause species' ranges to shift and increase the vulnerability of some estuaries to introduced species (US GCRP 2000).

## Pacific Northwest salmon catch value (US$million/year)

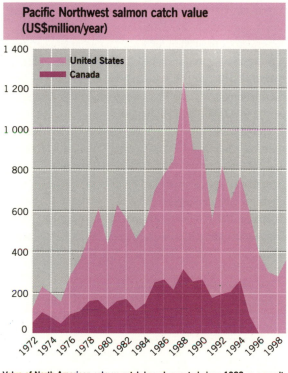

Value of North American salmon catch has plummeted since 1988 as a result of declining stocks and attempts to protect stocks

*Source: DFO 2000b, NMFS 2000*

federal strategy to help restore the 14 salmon sub-species in the Columbia River Basin listed on the Endangered Species Act.

As those dependent on salmon for income struggle to survive (see graph), both countries are taking additional measures to help restore these and other wild fish stocks to the region's coastal and marine waters and to enhance and maintain global biological diversity. Recent restrictions have indeed improved the ocean survival of some important stocks but it remains to be seen if all Pacific salmon species rebound (DFO 2000a, 2001).

## Nutrient loading

Nutrient inputs to marine and coastal ecosystems have increased dramatically over the past three decades due to large increases in population density, fossil fuel use, sewage inputs, livestock production and fertilizer use (EC 2000). These activities release nitrogen and phosphorus, which can enhance plant growth in aquatic systems and lead to oxygen depletion and multiple effects on the ecosystem including destroyed fish habitat, coastal pollution and harmful algal blooms (EC 1999, 2000).

In many parts of North America, nutrients from non-point sources come mainly from fertilizer and manure run-off. Over the past 30 years, fertilizer use has increased by almost 30 per cent while a trend towards rearing livestock in intensive feedlots has led to the release of large amounts of manure to surface and coastal waters (Mathews and Hammond 1999). Atmospheric inputs of nitrogen derived from manure, as well as from vehicles and electric utility power plants, are also significant (NOAA 1998a).

Since the early 1970s, anti-pollution legislation has greatly reduced point sources of nitrogen and phosphorus, principally from the discharge of municipal sewage and industrial wastes and the control of phosphates in laundry detergents (NOAA 1998a, EC 2000). However, most municipal wastewater discharged into Canada's coastal waters is still either untreated or only partially treated (EC 2000). Canadian estuaries in the North Atlantic are less severely affected by nutrient loading than more southerly ones due in part to a cooler climate and significant flushing of coastal waters (NOAA 1998b). Along the north Atlantic coast, non-point sources of nitrogen are some ninefold greater than inputs from wastewater treatment plants (EC 2000).

In 1998, more than 60 per cent of US coastal rivers and bays were moderately to severely degraded by nutrient contamination, and nitrogen was found to be the single greatest environmental threat in some 'trouble' spots on the Atlantic coast (NOAA 1998b, Howarth and others 2000). The US Clean Water Act and the 1972 Coastal Zone Management Act directed states to develop management plans for non-point contamination sources and provided funding and incentives to implement them (NRC 2000). The 1987 US National Estuary Program aims to minimize regional nutrient contamination (see box).

Nutrient enrichment is probably a contributing factor in the recent dramatic increase in the intensity, frequency and spatial extent of algal blooms or red

### Chesapeake Bay

The 1987 Chesapeake Bay Program was set up under the US National Estuary Program. It is a federal-state-local partnership to reduce nitrogen and phosphorus loading to the Bay by 40 per cent. This region has a population of more than 15 million people, and important commercial fish and shellfish harvests, and is a major stopover for migratory birds. By the late 1990s, only the phosphorus reduction goal had been met. Progress in reducing nutrients is being hampered by population growth and development.

tides, causing increased economic losses and health impacts. The number of coastal and estuarine locations in the United States with major recurring incidents of Harmful Algal Blooms (HABs) doubled between 1972 and 1995 (US Senate 1997).

The impacts of HABs can include human illness and death from eating contaminated fish or shellfish, mass mortalities of wild and farmed fish, and changes in marine food webs. In response to incidents of human illness from contaminated shellfish, both Canada and the United States have developed testing and water quality programmes to identify phytoplankton toxins and to provide information about them to the public.

Ocean acts in both countries (1997 in Canada and 2000 in the United States) establish frameworks for improving the stewardship of North America's coastal and ocean waters (EC 1999). Since 1996, the North American Commission for Environmental Cooperation has been facilitating regional implementation of the Global Programme of Action for the Protection of the Marine Environment from Land-based Activities in North America (CEC 2000b).

As yet, there is no regional strategy to address nutrient loading in North America's coastal waters, and coordination among the various agencies responsible for their management is inadequate (NRC 2000). Evidence suggests that the situation can be reversed, but the need remains for increased political action and changes in the activities in the watersheds and airsheds that feed coastal streams and rivers.

### References: Chapter 2, coastal and marine areas, North America

Carlisle, J. (1999). Nature, Not Man, is Responsible for West Coast Salmon Decline. National Center for Public Policy Research http://www.nationalcenter.org/NPA254.html [Geo-2-243]

CEC (2000a). Booming Economies, Silencing Environments, and the Paths to Our Future. Montreal, Commission for Environmental Cooperation

CEC (2000b). North American Agenda for Action 1999-2001: a Three-Year Program Plan for the Commission for Environmental Cooperation. Montreal, Commission for Environmental Cooperation

CEQ (1997). Environmental Quality: the 25th Anniversary Report of the Council on Environmental Quality. Washington DC, US Government Printing Office

DFO (1999a). 1999 Agreement Between Canada and the U.S. Under the Pacific Salmon Treaty. Fisheries and Oceans Canada http://www.ncr.dfo.ca/pst-tsp/agree/toc_e.htm [Geo-2-244]

DFO (1999b). Canada and US Reach a Comprehensive Agreement under the Pacific Salmon Treaty: News Release, 3 June 1999, Fisheries and Oceans Canada http://www.dfo-mpo.gc.ca/COMMUNIC/NEWSREL/1999/hq29_e.htm [Geo-2-245]

DFO (1999c). Pacific Fisheries Adjustment and Restructuring Program. Backgrounder, Fisheries and Oceans Canada http://www.ncr.dfo.ca/COMMUNIC/BACKGROU/1999/hq29%28115%29_e.htm [Geo-2-246]

DFO (2000a). Fisheries and Oceans Announces Rebuilding Efforts Result in Astounding Recovery of Upper Adams and Nadina Sockeye Runs. News Release, 14 December 2000, Fisheries and Oceans Canada http://www-comm.pac.dfo-mpo.gc.ca/english/release/p-releas/2000/nr00138e.htm [Geo-2-247]

DFO (2000b). Annual Summary Commercial Statistics, Salmon Landings in BC (1951-95). Fisheries and Oceans Canada http://www-sci.pac.dfo-mpo.gc.ca/sa/Commercial/SummaryPDF/comsal.htm [Geo-2-249]

DFO (2001). Remarkable Rebuilding of Upper Adams Sockeye Run Continues. News Release, 28 May 2001, Fisheries and Oceans Canada http://www-comm.pac.dfo-mpo.gc.ca/english/release/p-releas/2001/nr054e.htm [Geo-2-248]

EC (1999). Canada's Oceans: Experience and Practices Canadian Contribution to the Oceans and Seas Dialogue. Paper read at Seventh Session of the United Nations Commission on Sustainable Development (UN CSD), 19-30 April, New York

EC (2000). Nutrient Additions and Their Impacts on the Canadian Environment. Ottawa, Environment Canada.

Fishstat (2001). FISHSTAT Plus, Universal software for fishery statistical time series. FAO Fisheries, Software version 2.3 http://www.fao.org/fi/statist/fisoft/fishplus.asp [Geo-2-237]

Glavin, T. (1996). Dead Reckoning: Confronting the Crisis in Pacific Fisheries. Vancouver, Greystone Books

Howarth, R., Anderson, D., Cloern, J., Elfring, C., Hopkinson, C., Lapointe, B., Malone, T., Marcus, N., McGlathery, K., Sharpley, A. and Walker, D. (2000). Nutrient Pollution of Coastal Rivers, Bays, and Seas. Issues in Ecology No. 7, Ecological Society of America http://esa.sdsc.edu/issues7.htm [Geo-2-263]

Mathews, E. and Hammond, A. (1999). Critical Consumption Trends and Implications: Degrading Earth's Ecosystems. Washington DC, World Resources Institute

NMFS (2000). Fisheries Statistics & Economics, Commercial Fisheries, Annual Landings. National Marine Fisheries Service http://www.st.nmfs.gov/: [Geo-2-254]

NOAA (1998a). 1998 Year of the Ocean. Perspectives on Marine Environmental Quality Today. US National Oceanic and Atmospheric Administration http://www.yoto98.noaa.gov/yoto/meeting/mar_env_316.html [Geo-2-255]

NOAA (1998b). Oxygen Depletion in Coastal Waters: NOAA's State of the Coast Report. US National Oceanic and Atmospheric Administration http://state-of-coast.noaa.gov/bulletins/html/hyp_09/hyp.html [Geo-2-256]

NOAA (1999). United States Announces Agreement With Canada On Pacific Salmon. US National Oceanic and Atmospheric Administration http://www.nwr.noaa.gov/1press/060399_1.html [Geo-2-257]

NRC (1998). Sensitivities to Climate Change: Fisheries. Natural Resources Canada http://sts.gsc.nrcan.gc.ca/adaptation/sensitivities/map5.htm [Geo-2-258]

NRC (2000). Clean Coastal Waters: Understanding and Reducing the Effects of Nutrient Pollution. Washington DC, National Academy Press http://books.nap.edu/books/0309069483/html/9.html#page_middle [Geo-2-259]

TU and TUC (1999). Resolving the Pacific Salmon Treaty Stalemate. Seattle, Trout Unlimited USA and Trout Unlimited Canada

US Senate (1997). Animal Waste Pollution in America: An Emerging National Problem. US Senate Committee on Agriculture, Nutrition and Forestry http://www.senate.gov/~agriculture/Briefs/animalw.htm [Geo-2-260]

US GCRP (2000). Climate Change Impacts on the United States: the Potential Consequences of Climate Variability and Change. Socioeconomic Data and Applications Center, CIESIN, Columbia University http://sedac.ciesin.org/NationalAssessment/ [Geo-2-261]

# Coastal and marine areas: West Asia

The coastal zones of West Asia are under various degrees of stress as a result of major demographic shifts from rural to coastal urban areas, intense urbanization of coastal zones and dumping of untreated waste. Furthermore, regional wars and internal conflicts have introduced new dimensions to the region's environmental problems and have stressed both financial and natural resources.

Actions at national and regional levels, the latter through the Regional Organization for the Conservation of the Marine Environment of the Red Sea and Gulf of Aden (PERSGA countries) and the countries of the Regional Organization for the Protection of the Marine Environment (ROPME countries, under the UNEP Regional Seas Programme's Kuwait Action Plan) focus on the key environmental issues that have emerged in the region: physical alterations, overexploitation of marine resources and marine pollution (UNEP and PERSGA 1997, UNEP 1999, UNEP MAP 1996).

## Coastal development and physical alteration

Rapid urbanization has occurred in most of the countries of the region over the past three decades, particularly in the smaller countries such as Bahrain, Iraq, Jordan and Lebanon. By the early 1990s, some of the GCC countries had developed more than 40 per cent of their coastline (Price and Robinson 1993), and recent estimates indicate coastal investments in the region to be worth US$20–40 million/km of coastline (UNEP 1999).

In Lebanon, more than 60 per cent of the population of about 3.5 million live and work along a very narrow coastal strip (Government of Lebanon 1997, Grenon and Batisse 1989). Some 64 per cent of the population of all the Gulf Cooperation Council (GCC) countries except Saudi Arabia live along the western coasts of the Gulf and the Arabian Sea (ROPME 1999). More than 90 per cent of the population of Bahrain and 37 per cent of Kuwaitis live along the coast.

Coastal populations are expected to increase — for example, the population of Aqaba is predicted to more than double from 65 000 to 150 000 by 2020 (UNEP and PERSGA 1997). Increasing urbanization,

accompanied by ill-planned coastal tourism and/or industrial projects, has resulted in the degradation of coastal and marine environmental quality. The Mashriq sub-region and the smaller states of the region are also unable to deal with the large quantities of domestic litter generated along the coasts, due to space limitations and inadequate waste disposal systems.

Dredging and land reclamation are also intensifying in most countries. Major landfilling has occurred along the western coasts of the Gulf countries such as Bahrain, Saudi Arabia and the United Arab Emirates. These activities have led to destruction of marine habitats and ecologically productive areas, coastal erosion, and loss of coastal stretches in many countries.

### Coastal and marine action plans in West Asia

Three major action plans in the region are aimed at preserving the coastal and marine environment and promoting the sustainable development of the coastal zones:

● the Mediterranean Action Plan: Lebanon, Syria and the Mediterranean countries of Europe and North Africa;
● the Kuwait Action Plan: Bahrain, Kuwait, Iran, Iraq, Oman, Qatar, Saudi Arabia and the United Arab Emirates; and
● the Red Sea and Gulf of Aden Action Plan: Jordan, Saudi Arabia and Yemen.

The Red Sea and Gulf of Aden Action Plan was specifically formulated to protect the region from the impacts of land-based activities. The Mediterranean Action Plan was updated in 1995 together with the Barcelona Convention and its protocols.

The need for environmental impact assessments and integrated coastal zone management has been recognized by most countries since the early 1990s and a number of coastal and marine action plans have been developed (see box above). A new methodology for integrated coastal zone management was developed by UNEP's Mediterranean Action Plan (MAP), and a Coastal Area Management Project (CAMP) for the south of Lebanon was launched in 2001 by MAP and the Lebanese Ministry of Environment. Nevertheless, with the exception of a regional programme under MAP aimed at safeguarding 100 historical sites notably in the Mashriq region, no concerted effort has been undertaken to protect other historical sites, including submarine structures, from the ravages of dredging and landfill activities.

## Fisheries and marine resources

The fisheries of West Asia are diverse and continue to provide protein and revenue. However, per capita fish catches have been falling (see graph), albeit slowly, because of adverse climatic and ecological conditions, and unsustainable fishing practices. The most visible

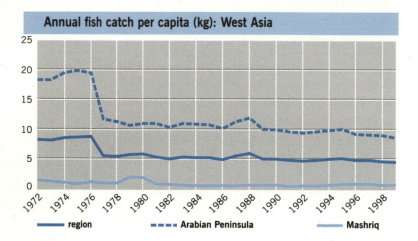

**Annual fish catch per capita (kg): West Asia**

— region  ---- Arabian Peninsula  — Mashriq

**West Asian fisheries have not kept pace with population growth, with the per capita catch falling slowly over 30 years**

*Note: fish catch includes marine and freshwater catches but excludes crustaceans and molluscs, and aquaculture production*

*Source: compiled from Fishstat 2001*

signs of deterioration are the overexploitation and loss of shrimp nursery grounds. Furthermore, fish kill phenomena have often been observed along the shores of the Gulf Area and the Arabian Sea (ROPME 2000). Fishery regulations are lacking or not enforced, particularly in the Mashriq, and regional cooperation for improved fisheries management is weak. However, a range of policy measures, including the introduction of fishing licences, gear and area restrictions, closed seasons and the banning of certain fisheries, have recently been implemented in the GCC countries.

Initial steps have been taken in several countries to supplement fish protein by aquaculture and/or importation. As aquaculture is expected to increase in both the sub-regions, measures will need to be taken to prevent the accidental introduction of alien species into the wild, which could have adverse impacts on coastal and marine ecosystems.

## Marine pollution

The Mashriq and GCC countries have different sets of pollution-related pressures to contend with. Whereas in the GCC countries the challenges are from oil-related industries and desalinization plants, in the Mashriq the challenge is primarily from major rivers that discharge domestic and municipal wastes, agricultural chemicals and hazardous industrial substances into the sea.

Due to heavy oil traffic in the Gulf, and the Gulf's unique geographical location and sensitive biological nature, this sea could become the most polluted in the world unless strict measures are implemented and enforced. The Gulf and the Red Sea are the oil tanker highways of the world: more than 10 000 vessels a year pass through the Straits of Hormuz, about 60 per cent of which are oil tankers (ROPME 1999), and some 34 offshore oil and gas terminals exist in the region (UNEP 1999). About 1.2 million barrels of oil are spilled in the region every year from routine discharge of ballast water (UNEP 1999). Since 1996, facilities for treating oil-contaminated ballast water have been established in the ROPME area, and a task force involving the GCC secretariat, the International Maritime Organization, UNDP, UNEP and the EU was set up through the Marine Emergency Mutual Aid Centre. A regional steering committee was established and a schedule for implementation of oil reception facilities is now under way (Al-Janahi 2001).

More than 360 million tonnes of oil are transported annually in the Mediterranean Sea (EEA 1999) which, though constituting only 0.7 per cent of the global sea surface, receives 17 per cent of global marine oil pollution (ESCWA 1991). Around 2 000 vessels, of which 250–300 are oil tankers, cruise the Mediterranean daily. It is estimated that more than 22 000 tonnes of oil entered the Mediterranean during 1987–96 as a result of shipping incidents (EEA 1999).

Regional wars have also contributed to the degradation of coastal and marine resources. The Iran/Iraq war (1980–88) contributed 2-4 million barrels of spilled oil (Reynolds 1993) and 6-8 million barrels were spilled into the Gulf and the Arabian Sea during the Second Gulf War (ROPME 2000).

The region has made some advances in combating accidental oil spills, particularly in the PERSGA and ROPME countries but in the Mashriq countries and some countries in the PERSGA region, there are no mechanisms to deal with major catastrophes (UNEP and PERSGA 1997). For example, there are no emergency contingency plans to deal with accidents to the 30-odd oil pipelines in Lebanon (Government of Lebanon 1997).

Most countries in the region have recognized pollution from land-based sources as a major threat to the coastal and marine environment. Sewage disposal is a major issue. Most coastal cities in the Mashriq sub-region have outdated sewerage systems, and the discharge of untreated sewage into coastal zones, mainly close to the major cities, continues to be common practice in most of the Mashriq and some parts of the GCC countries. Elsewhere, as in Bahrain, Kuwait, United Arab Emirates and western Saudi Arabia, all sewage is treated prior to discharge and some is recycled. The risk of eutrophication in semi-closed and closed areas is constantly present since most of the seas in the region are oligotrophic (poor in nutrients).

Discharges from desalinization plants of brine, chlorine and heat continue to pose another serious threat to the environment. Nearly 43 per cent of the world's desalinated water is produced in GCC countries (UNEP and PERSGA 1997) and the trend is increasing.

Soil erosion and sedimentation pose another threat to the coastal zone. With an annual estimated soil loss of about 33 and 60 tonnes/ha in Lebanon and Syria respectively, the amount of eroded soil discharged into the Mediterranean from both countries may reach 60 million tonnes annually (EEA 1999). In the absence of adequate river basin management programmes, riverine and estuarine water quality will continue to deteriorate with harmful effects on public health. It is expected that, following the completion of new dams in eastern Turkey, there will be a change in water quantity and quality of the Euphrates River flowing into Syria and Iraq, which in turn will have a major impact on the agricultural areas and estuaries of the Shatt Al-Arab waterways.

Although there is great variation in levels of heavy metals in the region, screening tests show acceptable values in most areas (UNEP MAP 1996, ROPME 1999). Some countries have begun setting standards for environmental quality through international and regional agreements. For example, Lebanon has recently started to develop environmental and developmental indicators and standards within the framework of the Barcelona Convention. Pollution from land-based activities has also been incorporated into protocols in both the Mediterranean and the Kuwait Action Plans.

## References: chapter 2, coastal and marine areas, West Asia

Al-Janahi, A.M. (2001). The preventative role of MEMAC in oil pollution emergencies. *Environment 2001 Exhibition and Conference*. Abu Dhabi, 3-7 February 2001

EEA (1999). *State and Pressures of the Marine and Coastal Mediterranean Environment*. Environmental Assessment Series No. 5. Copenhagen, European Environment Agency

ESCWA (1991). Discussion paper on general planning, marine and coastal resources, and urbanization and human settlements. Arab Ministerial Conference on Environment and Development, 10-12 September 1991, Cairo

Fishstat (2001). *FISHSTAT Plus, Universal software for fishery statistical time series*. FAO Fisheries, Software version 2.3 http://www.fao.org/fi/statist/fisoft/fishplus.asp [Geo-2-237]

Government of Lebanon (1997). *Report on the Regional Environmental Assessment: Coastal Zone of Lebanon*. Beirut, ECODIT-IAURIF (Council for Development and Reconstruction)

Grenon, M. and Batisse, M. (eds., 1989). *Futures for the Mediterranean basin: the Blue Plan*. Oxford, Oxford University Press

Price, A., and Robinson, J. (1993). The 1991 Gulf war: coastal and marine environment consequences. *Marine Pollution Bulletin* 27, 380

Reynolds, R. (1993). Physical oceanography of the Gulf, Strait of Hormuz, and the Gulf of Oman: results from the Mt Mitchell expedition. *Marine Pollution Bulletin* 27, 35-59

ROPME (1999). *Regional Report of the State of the Marine Environment*. Kuwait, Regional Organization for the Protection of the Marine Environment

ROPME (2000). *Integrated Coastal Areas management: guidelines for the ROPME region*. ROPME/GC-10/001. Kuwait, Regional Organization for the Protection of the Marine Environment

UNEP (1999). *Overview on Land-based Sources and Activities Affecting the Marine Environment in the ROPME Sea Area*. UNEP Regional Seas Reports and Studies No.168. The Hague and Kuwait, UNEP GPA Coordination Office and Regional Organization for the Protection of the Marine Environment

UNEP MAP (1996). *Etat du milieu marin et littoral de la région méditerranéenne*. No.101 de la Série des Rapports Techniques du PAM. Athens, UNEP Mediterranean Action Plan

UNEP and PERSGA (1997). *Assessment of land-based sources and activities affecting the marine environment in the Red Sea and Gulf of Aden*. UNEP Regional Seas Reports and Studies No.166. The Hague, UNEP GPA Coordination Office

## Coastal and marine areas: the Polar Regions

### THE ARCTIC

The Arctic marine environment covers approximately 20 million km$^2$ and includes the Arctic Ocean and several adjacent water bodies. Nearly half of the ocean floor is continental shelf, the highest percentage among all oceans. Movements of Arctic waters play a significant role in the global ocean regime (AMAP 1997), and in regulating the global climate (see figure).

### The global ocean circulation

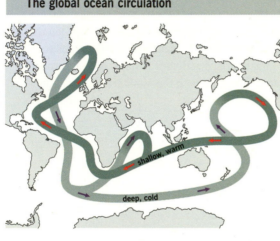

*When warm, salty North Atlantic water reaches the cold Arctic, it becomes denser as it cools, and therefore sinks to deeper layers of the ocean. This process of forming deep water is slow but takes place over a huge area. Every winter, several million cubic kilometres of water sink to deeper layers, which move water slowly south along the bottom of the Atlantic Ocean*

*Source: AMAP 1997*

The Arctic marine environment is rich in fish biodiversity and abundance. The commercial fisheries of the Barents and the Bering systems are among the most productive in the world (Kelleher, Bleakly and Wells 1995), with the Bering Sea accounting for 2–5 per cent of the world's fisheries catches (CAFF 2001, Bernes 1996). Resident and migratory marine mammals include whales, seals and sea lions. The polar bear is also often classified as a marine mammal because it frequents sea ice in search of prey. Many of the indigenous communities of the Arctic have traditionally depended on these marine resources for their livelihood. Other natural resources include vast oil and gas reserves along the continental shelves as well as important mineral deposits. However, there are growing concerns about the negative impacts of development activities on the ecology of the Arctic especially in ice-prone areas and critical habitats.

### Resource degradation

Overexploitation of fisheries is a major concern in the Arctic. Since the 1950s, there have been spectacular crashes of populations of commercially important species such as the cod and Atlantic salmon off the coasts of Canada and Greenland, and herring in the Norwegian and Icelandic waters. Despite strict conservation measures including no-catch zones, recovery has been slow and uncertain. Other species such as the haddock stocks between northern Norway and Svalbard have declined more steadily (Bernes 1993, 1996, CAFF 2001).

Between the 16th and 20th centuries, massive overexploitation of several whale species occurred. Although some species have recovered to sustainable levels, others have not and are still subject to strict domestic or international regulations (for example, the bowhead whale through International Whaling Commission quotas). Illegal exploitation, including of endangered species, and overly generous quotas are a constant threat (CAFF 2001).

### Pollution

Contaminants are another source of pressure on the Arctic marine environment. The annual spring influx of meltwater carries contaminants which accumulate in the estuaries and deltas and also enter the mixed layer where they are transported to the North American coast. Airborne contaminants from industrial and agricultural activities at lower latitudes are also deposited in the ocean where they can accumulate in sea ice. These contaminants are bioaccumulated in sea mammals and in turn are taken up by Arctic peoples (AMAP 1997, Crane and Galasso 1999).

### Stocks of Arctic fisheries (thousands of adults)

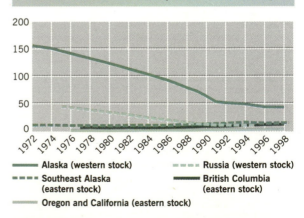

Legend:
- Alaska (western stock)
- Russia (western stock)
- Southeast Alaska (eastern stock)
- British Columbia (eastern stock)
- Oregon and California (eastern stock)

*Stocks of commercially important species such as the cod, Atlantic salmon and herring have declined in many of the Arctic fisheries; despite strict conservation measures, recovery has been slow and uncertain*

*Source: CAFF 2001*

Radioactive contamination is a further threat, sources including former nuclear weapons testing, the Chernobyl accident, and ocean dumping of radioactive solid wastes which was common until the London Dumping Convention came into effect.

## Climate change

Most of the major changes observed in the Arctic marine environment are believed to be attributable to global warming. For example, the Arctic pack ice is showing noticeable thinning from an average thickness of 3.12 m in the 1960s to 1.8 m in the 1990s (CAFF 2001). There has been an observed 2.8 per cent/decade negative trend in the ice seasonal cover over the period November 1978 to December 1996. Changes in seasonal patterns of sea ice will affect ocean currents and weather patterns. It is predicted that globally the largest temperature increase will occur in the Arctic (IPCC 2001).

## Policy responses

Arctic countries are taking steps to protect the marine environment. Since the late 1980s they have increasingly engaged in circumpolar cooperation on the marine environment through fora such as the International Arctic Science Committee and the intergovernmental Arctic Council. Cooperative initiatives have included:

- adoption of a Regional Programme of Action for Protection of the Arctic Marine Environment against Land-based Activities in 1998;
- establishment of a trilateral Russian/United States/Norway Arctic Offshore Oil and Gas Regime that aims to develop a safety and environmental regime for Russian offshore oil and gas operations;
- production of circumpolar guidelines for regulations of offshore oil and gas activities (PAME 1997);
- development of a circumpolar protected areas network to include a marine component (CAFF 2001); and
- sponsorship of a circumpolar marine workshop with IUCN which developed a set of recommendations to improve the protection and management of the Arctic marine environment (CAFF, IUCN and PAME 2000).

Given the current warming trend and interest in resource exploitation in the Arctic, it is expected that there will be further exploitation of the Arctic marine environment and increased competition for strategic advantages (Morison, Aagaard and Steele 2000). However, if the UNCLOS rules for defining limits to resources on the sea bed (International Seabed Authority 2001) are applied to the Arctic sea, the wide continental shelves will transfer almost all the Arctic sea bed to national control under the Arctic States (by 2001 only the Russian Federation and Norway had ratified UNCLOS).

## THE ANTARCTIC

The Southern Ocean represents approximately 10 per cent of the world's oceans. Vast areas of the Southern Ocean are subject to seasonal sea ice which expands from around 4 million $km^2$ in the austral summer to 19 million $km^2$ in the winter (Allison 1997).

The extent of Antarctic sea ice has been estimated using Southern Ocean whaling records dating back to 1931 (de la Mare 1997). Research suggests a decline in sea ice cover of almost 25 per cent early in this period. However, satellite observations suggest that there has been little change in Antarctic sea ice distribution during the 1970s and 1980s (Chapman and Walsh 1993, Bjørgo, Johannessen and Miles 1997); on the contrary, it seems that the Antarctic sea ice extent increased slightly during these decades (Cavalieri and others. 1997). One climate model suggests an ultimate reduction in Antarctic sea ice of about 25 per cent with a doubling of $CO_2$, with these changes relatively evenly distributed around the entire continent (IPCC 1998).

## Resource degradation

There is little doubt that current fisheries activities constitute the single greatest environmental problem in the Southern Ocean. Antarctic fisheries began in the late 1960s with exploitation of the marbled rock cod, a species decimated in the first two years of the fishery. Krill and mackerel ice fish have also formed the basis of substantial fisheries. Fin fish catches declined in the 1980s but the development of longlining for toothfish (*Dissostichus eleginoides* and *D. mawsoni*) has caused a resurgence of exploitation (Constable and others 1999). Southern Ocean fisheries are regulated and managed by the Commission on the Conservation of Antarctic Marine Living Resources (CCAMLR).

## Pollution

Hydrocarbon contamination of the Southern Ocean is very low and difficult to resolve against natural background levels (Cripps and Priddle 1991). A few spill incidents have been reported in Antarctica during the past decade (COMNAP 2000), the largest of which occurred when the *Bahia Paraiso* ran aground in the Antarctic Peninsula in 1989, leaking 600 000 litres of fuel.

Small diesel spills have been shown to have minor, localized and short-term impacts on the Antarctic marine and coastal environment (Green and others 1992, Cripps and Shears 1997). However, a large hydrocarbon spill in the proximity of breeding grounds, rookeries or important species habitats could have significant impacts. This is an issue of growing concern as the level of vessel operations, including tourist vessels, in Antarctic waters is expected to increase.

## Policy responses

The Antarctic Treaty Consultative Parties have urged those countries which have not yet become Parties to the Protocol on Environmental Protection to the Antarctic Treaty, particularly those with Antarctic tourist activities organized in their territory, to adhere to the environmental provisions of the Protocol as soon as possible. In 1999, the Antarctic Treaty Parties gave priority to the development of safety and environmental guidelines for Antarctic shipping, pending the finalization of the IMO Code of Practice for ships operating in the Polar Regions.

Following the decision by Australia and France not to sign the Antarctic Minerals Convention (CRAMRA) in 1989, the Antarctic Treaty Parties negotiated and then agreed to the Protocol on Environmental Protection to the Antarctic Treaty — the Madrid Protocol — in 1991. The Protocol includes provisions that establish environmental principles that govern the conduct of all activities carried out in Antarctica, prohibit mining, establish a Committee for Environmental Protection (CEP) and require development of contingency plans to respond to environmental emergencies. Annex IV of the Protocol includes specific measures relating to the prevention of marine pollution.

## References: chapter 2, coastal and marine areas, the Polar Regions

Allison, I. (1997). Physical processes determining the Antarctic sea ice environment. In *Australian Journal of Physics* 50, 4, 759-771

AMAP (1997). *Arctic Pollution Issues: A State of the Arctic Environment Report*. Arctic Council Arctic Monitoring and Assessment Programme http://www.amap.no/assess/soaer0.htm#executive summary [Geo-2-262]

Bernes, C. (1993). *The Nordic Environment – Present State, Trends and Threats*. Copenhagen, Nordic Council of Ministers

Bernes, C. (1996). *The Nordic Arctic Environment – Unspoilt, Exploited, Polluted?* Copenhagen, Nordic Council of Ministers

Bjørgo, E., Johannessen, O.M. and Miles, M.W. (1997). Analysis of merged SMMR-SSMI time series of Arctic and Antarctic sea ice parameters 1978-1995. *Geophysical Research Letters*, 24, 4, 413-416

CAFF (2001). *Arctic Flora and Fauna: Status and Conservation*. Helsinki, Arctic Council Programme for the Conservation of Arctic Flora and Fauna

CAFF, IUCN and PAME (2000). *Circumpolar Marine Workshop: Report and Recommendations*. Cambridge and Gland, IUCN

Cavalieri, D.J., Gloersen, P., Parkinson, C.L., Comiso, J.C. and Zwally, H.J. (1997). Observed hemispheric asymmetry in global sea ice changes. *Science* 287, 5340, 1104–06

Chapman, W.L. and Walsh, J.E. (1993). Recent variations of sea ice and air-temperature in high-latitudes. *Bulletin of the American Meteorological Society*, 74, 1, 33-47

COMNAP (2000). *Revised Working Paper on an Assessment of Environmental Emergencies Arising from Activities in Antarctica*. Working paper (SATCM XII/WP 5) submitted to the third meeting of the Committee on Environmental Protection, The Hague, September 2000

Constable, A.J., de la Mare, W.K., Agnew, D.J., Everson, I. and Miller, D. (1999). *Managing Fisheries to Conserve the Antarctic Marine Ecosystem*. Montpellier, ICES/SCOR

Crane, K. and Galasso, J.L. (1999). *Arctic Environmental Atlas*. Washington DC, Office of Naval Research, Naval Research Laboratory

Cripps, G.C. and Priddle, J. (1991). Hydrocarbons in the Antarctic marine environment. *Antarctic Science*, 3, 3, 233-250

Cripps, G.C. and Shears, J. (1997). The fate in the marine environment of a minor diesel fuel spill from an Antarctic research station. *Environmental Monitoring and Assessment*, 46, 3, 221-232

de la Mare, W.K. (1997). Abrupt mid-twentieth century decline in Antarctic sea-ice extent from whaling records. *Nature*, 389, 6646, 57-60

Green, G., Skerratt, J.H., Leeming, R. and Nichols, P.D. (1992). Hydrocarbon and coprostanol levels in seawater, sea-ice algae and sediments near Davis Station in Eastern Antarctica. *Marine Pollution Bulletin*, 25, 9-12, 293-302

IPCC (1998). *The Regional Impacts of Climate Change: An Assessment of Vulnerability*. Cambridge, Cambridge University Press

IPCC (2001) *IPCC Third Assessment Report — Climate Change 2001. Working Group I: The Scientific Basis. Summary for Policy Makers*. Geneva, World Meteorological Organization and United Nations Environment Programme, Geneva.

Kelleher, G., Bleakly, C. and Wells, S. (1995). *A Global Representative System of Marine Protected Areas*. Gland, IUCN World Commission on Protected Areas

Morison, J., Aagaard, K. and Steele, M. (2000) Recent environmental changes in the Arctic: a review. *Arctic Journal of the Arctic Institute of North America*, 53, 4, December 2000

PAME (1997) *Regional Programme of Action for the Protection of the Arctic Marine Environment from Land-Based Activities*. Akureyri, Iceland, Arctic Council Programme for the Protection of the Arctic Marine Environment

## OUR CHANGING ENVIRONMENT: Pine Glacier, Antarctica

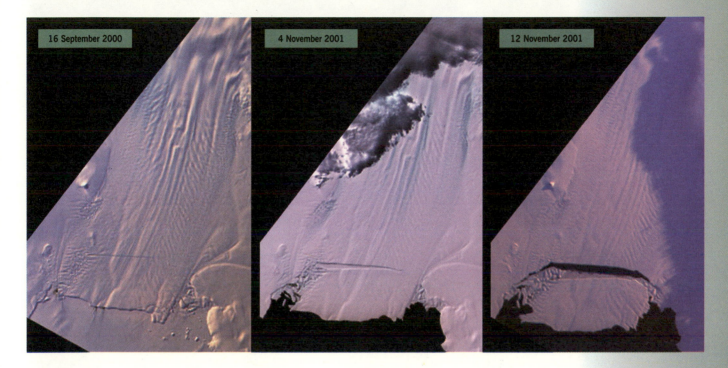

16 September 2000    4 November 2001    12 November 2001

The images above show the break-off of a large iceberg from the Pine Island Glacier in West Antarctica. This event occurred sometime between 4 and 12 November 2001, and provides powerful evidence of rapid changes under way in this area of Antarctica. The iceberg measures about 42 x 17 km.

Pine Island Glacier is the largest discharger of ice in Antarctica and the continent's fastest moving glacier. It is located in an area of the West Antarctic ice sheet that is believed to be the most susceptible to collapse, making the evolution of this glacier of great interest to the scientific community.

In mid-2000, a large crack formed across the glacier, and then began to grow rapidly. Data indicated the crack was growing some 15 metres a day. The images show that the last 10-km segment that was still attached to the ice shelf snapped off in a matter of days.

The first image in this set was captured in late 2000, early in the development of the crack. The second and third views were acquired in November 2001, just before and just after the formation of the new iceberg.

The newly hatched iceberg represents nearly seven years of ice outflow from Pine Island Glacier released to the ocean in a single event. The climatic significance of this calving event is not yet clear. However, when combined with previous measurements from this instrument and data from other instruments cataloguing the retreat of the glacier's grounding line, its accelerating ice flow, and the steady decrease in the sea ice cover in front of the glacier, it provides scientists with additional evidence of rapid change in the region.

Text and imagery: NASA/GSFC/LaRC/JPL, MISR Team

UNEP, Angelo Dotto, Italy, Still Pictures

# Atmosphere

## Global overview

Over the past three decades, anthropogenic emissions of chemical compounds into the atmosphere have caused many environmental and health problems. Some chemicals, such as chlorofluorocarbons (CFCs), are produced deliberately and end up in the atmosphere by accident from equipment or goods. Others, such as sulphur dioxide ($SO_2$) and carbon monoxide (CO), are unavoidable by-products of burning fossil fuels. Urban air pollution, acid rain, contamination by toxic chemicals (some of them persistent and transported over long distances), depletion of the stratospheric ozone layer and changes in the global climatic system are all important environmental threats to ecosystems and human well-being.

### Air pollution and air quality

The World Health Organization (WHO) lists six 'classic' air pollutants: CO, lead, nitrogen dioxide ($NO_2$), suspended particulate matter (SPM) — including dust, fumes, mists and smoke — $SO_2$ and tropospheric ozone ($O_3$) (WHO 1999).

The burning of fossil fuels and biomass is the most significant source of air pollutants such as $SO_2$, CO, certain nitrous oxides such as NO and $NO_2$ (known collectively as $NO_x$), SPM, volatile organic compounds (VOCs) and some heavy metals. It is also the major anthropogenic source of carbon dioxide ($CO_2$), one of the important greenhouse gases. Between 1973 and 1998, total energy supply increased by 57 per cent (see graph opposite), the majority provided by oil, natural gas and coal with nuclear and hydropower and other renewable resources playing a minor role (IEA 2000). The fuels used vary from region to region — for example, natural gas dominates in the Russian Federation, while coal provides 73 per cent of the energy consumed in China (BP Amoco 2000). Biomass is an important source of energy in the developing world and is the main source of indoor air pollution in such countries (Holdren and Smith 2000).

Acid precipitation has been one of the most important environmental concerns over the past decades especially in Europe and North America (Rodhe and others 1995), and more recently also in China (Seip and others 1999). Significant damage to forests in Europe became a high priority environmental issue around 1980, while thousands of lakes in Scandinavia lost fish populations due to acidification from the 1950s to the 1980s. In some parts of Europe, the anthropogenic $SO_2$ emissions which lead to acid precipitation have been reduced by nearly 70 per cent from their maximum values (EEA 2001); there have also been reductions of some 40 per cent in the United States (US EPA 2000). This has resulted in a significant recovery of the natural acid balance, at least in Europe. On the contrary, as a result of the growing use of coal and other high sulphur fuels, increasing $SO_2$ emissions in the Asia and Pacific Region are a serious environmental threat (UNEP 1999).

Air pollutant emissions have declined or stabilized in most industrialized countries, largely as a result of abatement policies developed and implemented since the 1970s. Initially governments tried to apply direct control instruments but these were not always cost-effective. In the 1980s, policies were directed more towards cost-effective pollution abatement mechanisms that relied on a compromise between the cost of environmental protection measures and economic growth. The Polluter Pays Principle has become a basic concept in environmental policy planning.

Recent policy developments, at both national and regional levels, are based on economic and regulatory instruments, and technology improvement and transfer to enhance emission reductions. In the international arena, one of the most important political developments has been the Convention on Long-Range Transboundary Air Pollution (CLRTAP), adopted in 1979. Through a series of protocols establishing reduction objectives for the main air pollutants, this treaty has catalysed European, Canadian and US governments to implement national emission abatement policies (ECE 1995). The most recent protocol is the 1999 Protocol to Abate Acidification, Eutrophication and Ground-Level Ozone that sets up new reduction commitments for $SO_2$, $NO_x$, VOCs and ammonia ($NH_3$) (ECE 2000).

Stricter environmental regulation in the industrialized countries has triggered the introduction of cleaner technology and technological improvements, especially in the power generation and transport sectors. In the latter, a significant reduction in harmful emissions has been achieved due to the improved engine combustion cycle, increased fuel efficiency and the widespread introduction of catalytic converters

### Impacts associated with air pollution

Harmful substances emitted to the air affect both human health and ecosystems. Indoor and outdoor air pollution are estimated to be responsible for nearly 5 per cent of the global burden of disease. Air pollution aggravates and, possibly, even causes asthma and other allergic respiratory diseases. Adverse pregnancy outcomes, such as stillbirth and low birth weight, have also been associated with air pollution (Holdren and Smith 2000). It has been estimated that in developing countries about 1.9 million people die annually due to exposure to high concentrations of SPM in the indoor air environment of rural areas, while the excess mortality due to outdoor levels of SPM and $SO_2$ amounts to about 500 000 people annually. Evidence is also emerging that particles with median aerodynamic diameter less than 2.5 $\mu m$ ($PM_{2.5}$) affect human health significantly (WHO 1999).

Acid deposition is one of the causes of acidification of soil and water that results in declining fish stocks, decreasing diversity in acid-sensitive lakes and degradation of forest and soil. Excessive nitrogen (as nitrate and/or ammonium) promotes eutrophication, particularly in coastal areas. Acid rain damages ecosystems, provokes defoliation, corrosion of monuments and historic buildings and reduces agricultural yields.

(Holdren and Smith 2000). Lead emissions from gasoline additives have now declined to zero in many industrial countries (EEA 1999, US EPA 2000). In developing countries, however, the sources of emissions are more varied and include highly polluting

### World energy supply by fuel (million tonnes oil equivalent/year)

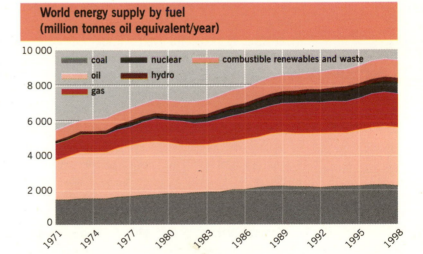

World energy supply is still dominated by the fossil fuels — coal, oil and gas

Source: IEA 2000

power plants, heavy industry, vehicles and the domestic combustion of coal, charcoal and biomass. While the emission of pollutants can be significantly reduced for a small cost, few developing nations have made even small investments in pollution reduction measures, even though the environmental and population health benefits of such measures are evident (Holdren and Smith 2000, World Bank 1997).

Though measurable progress in industrial emission abatement has been achieved at least by the developed countries, transport has become one of the major sources of air pollution (particularly $NO_x$ and many carbon compounds) in many countries. High concentrations of these compounds in urban air can, under certain climatic conditions, result in photochemical smog that severely affects human health. In many urban centres and their surrounding areas, high concentrations of tropospheric $O_3$ are an additional problem. Anthropogenic tropospheric ozone may be produced by reactions between $NO_x$ and VOCs on warm sunny days, especially in urban and industrial areas and in regions prone to stagnant air masses. This can have far-reaching implications since molecules of $O_3$ have been found to travel large distances (up to 800 km) from emission sources (CEC 1997). Tropospheric $O_3$ concentrations over large areas of Europe and some areas of North America are so high that not only is human health threatened but vegetation is also affected. For example, in the United States ground-level ozone has been estimated to cost more than US$500 million a year as a result of reductions in agricultural and commercial forest yields (US EPA 2000).

Urban air pollution is one of the most important environmental problems. In most European and North American cities, the concentrations of $SO_2$ and SPM have decreased substantially in recent years (Fenger 1999, US EPA 2000). However, in many developing countries, rapid urbanization has resulted in increasing air pollution in many cities (Fenger 1999), WHO air quality guidelines are often not met and, in megacities such as Beijing, Calcutta, Mexico City and Rio de Janeiro, high levels of SPM prevail (World Bank 2001).

A final issue of global concern is that of persistent organic pollutants (POPs). These substances are known to decay slowly and they can be transported over long distances through the atmosphere (see illustration above). High concentrations of some POPs are found in polar areas (Schindler 1999, Masclet and others 2000, Espeland and others 1997) with potentially serious regional environmental impacts. These compounds can also accumulate in animal fats, representing a health risk. The Stockholm Convention on Persistent Organic Pollutants, adopted in May 2001, sets out control measures covering handling of pesticides, industrial chemicals and unintended by-products. The control provisions call for eliminating the production and use of intentionally produced POPs, and eliminating unintentionally produced POPs where feasible (UNEP 2001).

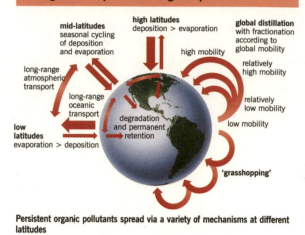

**Migration of persistent organic pollutants**

Persistent organic pollutants spread via a variety of mechanisms at different latitudes

Source: Wania and Mackay 1996

## Stratospheric ozone depletion

The protection of the Earth's ozone layer has presented one of the major challenges over the past 30 years, spanning the fields of environment, trade, international cooperation and sustainable development. The thinning of the ozone layer threatens human health through diseases such as skin cancer, eye cataracts and immune deficiency, affects flora and fauna, and also influences the planet's climate. Ozone depletion is brought about by a number of chemicals known as ozone-depleting substances (ODS), the most notorious of which are the chlorofluorocarbons (CFCs). In 1974, the results of studies linking stratospheric ozone depletion to the release of chloride ions in the stratosphere from CFCs were made publicly available (Molina and Rowland 1974). ODS are used in refrigerators, air conditioners, aerosol spray, insulating and furniture foams, and fire-fighting equipment, and their production peaked in the late 1980s as the demand for such goods grew (see graph on page 213).

The depletion of the Earth's ozone layer has now reached record levels, especially in the Antarctic and recently also in the Arctic. In September 2000, the Antarctic ozone hole covered more than 28 million square kilometres (WMO 2000, NASA 2001). Current average ozone losses are 6 per cent in the northern mid-latitudes in winter and spring, 5 per cent in southern mid-latitudes all year round, 50 per cent in the Antarctic spring and 15 per cent in the Arctic spring. The resulting increases in harmful ultraviolet

## World production of major chlorofluorocarbons (tonnes/year)

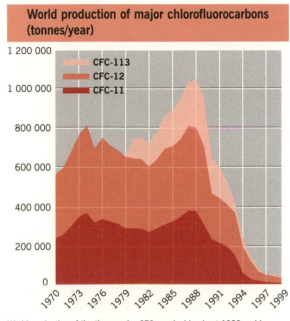

Legend:
- CFC-113
- CFC-12
- CFC-11

Y-axis: 0, 200 000, 400 000, 600 000, 800 000, 1 000 000, 1 200 000

X-axis: 1970, 1973, 1976, 1979, 1982, 1985, 1988, 1991, 1994, 1997, 1999

World production of the three major CFCs peaked in about 1988 and has since declined to very low values

*Source: AFEAS 2001*

irradiation amount to 7 per cent, 6 per cent, 130 per cent and 22 per cent respectively (UNEP 2000a).

However, due to continuous efforts by the international community, the global consumption of ODS has decreased markedly and the ozone layer is predicted to start recovering in the next one or two decades and to return to a pre-1980 level by the middle of the 21st century if all the future control measures of the Montreal Protocol are adhered to by all countries (UNEP 2000a).

International cooperation has been the key to protecting the stratospheric ozone layer. Nations agreed in principle to tackle a global problem before its effects became evident or its existence scientifically proven — probably the first example of acceptance of the precautionary approach (UNEP 2000a).

International action began in earnest in 1975 when the UNEP Governing Council called for a meeting to coordinate activities on protecting the ozone layer. A Coordinating Committee on the Ozone Layer was established the following year to undertake an annual scientific review. In 1977, the United States banned use of CFCs in non-essential aerosols. Canada, Norway and Sweden soon enacted similar control measures. The European Community (EC) froze production capacity and began to limit use of aerosols.

These initiatives, though useful, provided only a temporary respite. After falling for several years, CFC consumption began increasing again in the 1980s, as non-aerosol uses, such as foam blowing, solvents and refrigeration, increased. Stricter control measures were needed and UNEP and several developed countries took the lead, calling for a global treaty on stratospheric ozone layer protection (Benedick 1998).

The Vienna Convention for the Protection of the Ozone Layer was finally agreed by 28 countries in March 1985. It encouraged international cooperation on research, systematic observation of the ozone layer, monitoring of ODS production, and the exchange of information. In September 1987, 46 countries adopted the Montreal Protocol on Substances that Deplete the Ozone Layer (by December 2001, 182 parties had ratified the Vienna Convention and 181 the Montreal Protocol).

The original Protocol required only a 50 per cent cut in consumption of five widely used CFCs by December 1999, and a freeze in the consumption of three halons. Regular scientific assessments were the basis for subsequent amendments and adjustments made to the Protocol in London (1990), Copenhagen (1992), Vienna (1995), Montreal (1997) and Beijing (1999). By the year 2000, 96 chemicals were subject to control (Sabogal 2000).

Most ODS — including all the substances specified in the original Protocol — were phased out in industrialized countries by the end of 1995. The

The ozone hole reached a record size in September 2000 — 28.3 million $km^2$, three times the size of the United States. Dark blue areas denote high levels of ozone depletion

*Source: NASA 2001*

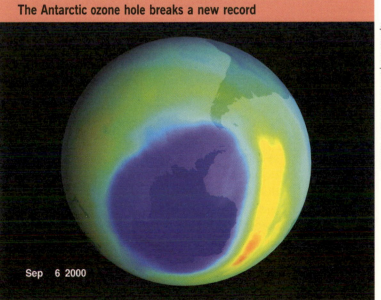

### The Antarctic ozone hole breaks a new record

Sep 6 2000

reprinted with permission from Paul A. Newman

Protocol provides a 10-year grace period for developing countries and the financial mechanism (the Multilateral Fund to the Montreal Protocol) to meet the costs to these countries of phasing out ODS, thus realizing the principle of common but differentiated responsibility. By 2000, the Multilateral Fund had disbursed more than US$1.1 billion for capacity building and projects to phase out ODS in 114 developing countries.

Almost every party to the Montreal Protocol has now taken measures to phase out ODS with the result that, by 2000, the total consumption of ODS had been reduced by 85 per cent (UNEP 2000b).

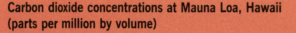

**Carbon dioxide concentrations at Mauna Loa, Hawaii (parts per million by volume)**

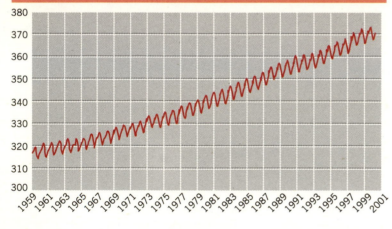

Records from Mauna Loa, Hawaii, show how $CO_2$ concentrations have increased — the increase is largely due to anthropogenic emissions that result from burning fossil fuel

*Source: Keeling and Whorf 2001*

## Greenhouse gases and climate change

Scientists have known about the natural 'greenhouse effect' for more than a century (Arrhenius 1896): the Earth maintains its equilibrium temperature through a delicate balance between the incoming solar energy (short wavelength radiation) it absorbs and the outgoing infra-red energy (long wavelength radiation) that it emits and some of which escapes into space. Greenhouse gases (water vapour, carbon dioxide, methane and others) allow solar radiation to pass through the Earth's atmosphere almost unimpeded but they absorb the infra-red radiation from the Earth's surface and then re-radiate some of it back to the Earth. This natural greenhouse effect keeps the surface temperature about 33°C warmer than it would otherwise be — warm enough to sustain life.

Since the industrial revolution, the concentration of $CO_2$, one of the major greenhouse gases, in the atmosphere has increased significantly (see graph left, which reflects growth since direct measurements started in 1957). This has contributed to the enhanced greenhouse effect known as 'global warming'.

The $CO_2$ concentration in the atmosphere is currently about 370 parts per million (ppm) — an increase of more than 30 per cent since 1750. The increase is largely due to anthropogenic emissions of $CO_2$ from fossil fuel combustion and to a lesser extent land-use change, cement production and biomass combustion (IPCC 2001a). Although $CO_2$ accounts for more than 60 per cent of the additional greenhouse effect accumulated since industrialization, the concentrations of other greenhouse gases such as methane ($CH_4$), nitrous oxide ($N_2O$), halocarbons and halons have also increased. In comparison to $CO_2$, $CH_4$ and $N_2O$ have contributed about 20 per cent and 6–7 per cent respectively to the additional greenhouse effect. Halocarbons have contributed about 14 per cent. Many of these chemicals are regulated under the Montreal Protocol (see above). However, those which have negligible ozone-depleting potential are not controlled under the Montreal Protocol. Although they have accounted for less than 1 per cent of the additional greenhouse effect since industrialization, their concentrations in the atmosphere are increasing (IPCC 2001a).

Greenhouse gas emissions are unevenly distributed between countries and regions. In general, industrialized countries are responsible for the majority of historical and current emissions. OECD countries contributed more than half of $CO_2$ emissions in 1998, with an average per capita emission of about three times the world average. However the OECD's share of global $CO_2$ emissions has decreased by 11 per cent since 1973 (IEA 2000).

In assessing the possible impact of rising atmospheric concentrations of greenhouse gases, IPCC concluded in 2001 that 'there is new and stronger evidence that most of the warming observed over the last 50 years is attributable to human activities'. The overall warming amounts to about 0.6 (±0.2)°C over the 20th century; the 1990s are 'very likely' to have been the warmest decade and the year 1998 the warmest year in the instrumental record, since 1861. Much of the rise in sea level over the past 100 years (about 10 to 20 cm) has probably been related to the concurrent rise in the global temperature (IPCC 2001a).

Ecosystems, human health and economy are all sensitive to changes in climate — including both the magnitude and rate of climate change. Whereas many regions are likely to experience adverse effects of climate change — some of which are potentially irreversible — some effects could be beneficial for some regions. Climate change represents an important additional stress on those ecosystems already affected by increasing resource demands, unsustainable management practices and pollution.

Some of the first results of the changing climate can serve as indicators. Several vulnerable ecosystems such as coral reefs are seriously endangered by increased sea temperature (IPCC 2001b) and some populations of migratory birds have been declining because of unfavourable variations in climatic conditions (Sillett, Holmes and Sherry 2000). Climate change is furthermore likely to affect human health and well-being through a variety of mechanisms. For example, it can adversely affect the availability of freshwater, food production, and the distribution and seasonal transmission of vector-borne infectious diseases such as malaria, dengue fever and schistosomiasis. The additional stress of climate change will interact in different ways across regions. It can be expected to reduce the ability of some environmental systems to provide, on a sustained basis, key goods and services needed for successful economic and social development, including adequate food, clean air and water, energy, safe shelter and low levels of diseases (IPCC 2001b).

The United Nations Framework Convention on Climate Change (UNFCCC) adopted at UNCED in 1992 (see Chapter 1) has the ultimate objective of 'stabilization of greenhouse gas concentrations in the atmosphere at a level that would prevent dangerous anthropogenic interference with the climate system' (UNFCCC 1992). The Convention further defines several principles of fundamental importance, for example that parties should take precautionary measures and act 'on the basis of equity and in accordance with their common but differentiated responsibilities'. Being a framework treaty, the UNFCCC contained only a non-binding recommendation for industrialized countries to return to the 1990 emission levels of $CO_2$ and other greenhouse gases (not controlled by the Montreal Protocol) by the year 2000 (UNFCCC 1992). However, most of them have not returned anthropogenic

emissions of greenhouse gases to 1990 levels (UNFCCC 2001). In general, global emissions of almost all anthropogenic greenhouse gases, particularly $CO_2$, continue to increase (IEA 2000). This reflects the inadequacy of national and international policies and measures to address climate change.

In its *Second Assessment Report*, the IPCC stated that the 'balance of evidence suggests that there is a discernible human influence on global climate' (IPCC 1996). This unequivocal statement provided the scientific basis for the adoption of the Kyoto Protocol

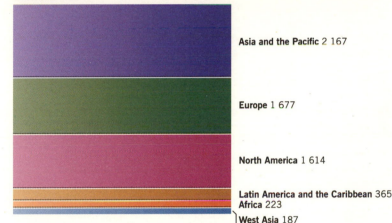

**Carbon dioxide emissions by region, 1998 (million tonnes carbon/year)**

World total 6 234

Asia and the Pacific 2 167

Europe 1 677

North America 1 614

Latin America and the Caribbean 365
Africa 223

West Asia 187

to the UNFCCC in December 1997. The protocol contains, for the first time, greenhouse gas reduction targets for most industrialized countries. The targets, however, range from an obligation to reduce emissions by 8 per cent (for the European Union and many Central European countries) to a permission to increase emissions by 10 per cent (Iceland) and 8 per cent (Australia). Overall, industrialized countries are required to reduce their aggregated emissions to at least 5 per cent below the 1990 level in the period 2008–12. No new obligations were introduced for developing countries. The Kyoto Protocol also allows collective implementation of obligations by means of applying the so-called 'Kyoto mechanisms'. These mechanisms aim at providing 'geographical flexibility' and reducing the costs of complying with the Kyoto targets. For example, one of them — the Clean Development Mechanism — allows industrialized countries to receive emission credits for carrying out

Anthropogenic greenhouse gas emissions are unevenly distributed between regions — most emissions come from industrialized regions. Figures include emissions from fuel consumption, gas flaring and cement production

*Source: compiled from Marland, Boden and Andres 2001*

projects aimed at reducing emissions of greenhouse gases in developing countries (UNFCCC 1997).

The cost estimates for industrialized countries to implement the Kyoto Protocol range between 0.1 and 2 per cent of GDP in 2010 (IPCC 2001c) with most impact being felt by the economies most dependent on fossil fuels. In view of anticipated economic losses, some industrialized nations have prejudiced the Kyoto commitments and the Kyoto Protocol as a whole. Debates on rules and modalities of the implementation of the protocol continued until the 6th Conference of the Parties to the UNFCCC held in November 2000 in The Hague. As negotiating parties still failed to reach

## The background to international cooperation on climate change

Scientists began to attract policy-makers' attention to global warming as an emerging global threat in the early 1970s (SCEP 1970). However their appeals were originally ignored and, as economies grew, more fossil fuels were burnt, more forested areas were cleared for agriculture and more halocarbons were produced. It took a further 20 years of continuous effort by scientists, NGOs, international organizations and several governments to get the international community to agree to coordinated action to address climate change.

The Stockholm Conference is generally regarded as the starting point for international efforts on climate variations and climate change (UN 1972). In 1979, the first World Climate Conference in Geneva expressed concern about the atmospheric commons. This event was attended primarily by scientists and received little attention from policy-makers. In the 1980s, a series of conferences and workshops were held in Villach, Austria, where scenarios for future emissions of all of the significant greenhouse gases were considered. At the 1985 Villach meeting, an international group of scientific experts reached a consensus on the seriousness of the problem and the danger of significant warming (WMO 1986).

As a result of growing public pressure and the implications of the Brundtland Commission (WCED 1987), the problem of global climate change moved onto the political agenda of several governments. A diplomatic breakthrough came at the 1988 Toronto Conference on the Changing Atmosphere from which emerged a recommendation calling on developed nations to reduce $CO_2$ emissions by 20 per cent from 1988 levels by the year 2005. A few months later, IPCC was jointly established by WMO and UNEP to review knowledge of the science, impact, economics of, and the options for mitigating and/or adapting to climate change. The IPCC studies, especially the three extensive *Assessment Reports* in 1990, 1995 and 2001, covered all the different facets of climate change.

consensus, the conference was suspended and parties decided to resume negotiations in 2001. The pivotal point in the global discussion occurred in March 2001 when the US government decided not to introduce any legal restrictions, as implied by the Kyoto Protocol, on anthropogenic emissions of greenhouse gases. The US administration thus declared its opposition to the Protocol, stating that it believed it to be 'fatally

flawed', as it would damage the US economy and it exempted developing countries from fully participating (Coon 2001). This decision meant that the United States — a major emitter of $CO_2$ —would not ratify the Kyoto Protocol.

The Kyoto Protocol would never have come into force if other developed countries had adopted the same position. However, at the resumed 6th Conference of the Parties (COP-6 Part II) in Bonn, Germany, in July 2001, the parties (except the United States) successfully completed negotiations aimed at setting the operational details for commitments on reducing emissions of greenhouse gases. They also reached agreement on actions to strengthen implementation of the UNFCCC itself. The political decision — or Bonn Agreement — was formally adopted by the COP on 25 July 2001. Many saw it as an 'historic' political agreement that saved the Kyoto Protocol and paved the way to its ratification, though it was clearly recognized that this was just a small step towards solving the global problem. Discussions also resulted in a Political Declaration by the European Union, Canada, Iceland, Norway, New Zealand and Switzerland on funding for developing countries. This Declaration includes an undertaking to provide an annual contribution of US$410 million by 2005 (IISD 2001a).

Shortly after COP-6 Part II, the climate change negotiators in Marrakesh (COP-7 held October-November 2001) finalized outstanding issues related to the political deal concluded in Bonn such as a compliance system, the 'Kyoto mechanisms', accounting, reporting and review of information under the Kyoto Protocol, and others (the so-called 'Marrakesh Accords'). The agreement reached in Marrakesh not only allows for ratification of the Kyoto Protocol in the near future but also will serve as the foundation for a comprehensive, multilateral approach that will and must continue beyond this Protocol (IISD 2001b).

Meeting the Kyoto targets will be just a first step in coping with the problem of climate change because it will have a marginal effect on the greenhouse gas concentration in the atmosphere. Even if, in the long term, a stabilization of atmospheric greenhouse gas concentrations is achieved, warming will continue for several decades, and sea levels will continue to rise for centuries with serious consequences for millions of people (IPCC 2001a, b).

## References: Chapter 2, atmosphere, global overview

AFEAS (2001). *Product Data*. Alternative Fluorocarbons Environmental Acceptability Study http://www.afeas.org/prodsales_download.html [Geo-2-008]

Arrhenius, S. (1896). On the influence of carbonic acid in the air upon the temperature of the ground. *Philosophical Magazine*. 41, 251, 237-77

Benedick, R.E. (1998). *Ozone Diplomacy: New Directions in Safeguarding the Planet*. Cambridge, Massachussetts, Harvard University Press

BP Amoco (2000). *The Statistical Review of World Energy — 1999*. London, British Petroleum http://www.bp.com/downloads/68/fullstat99.pdf [Geo-2-009]

CEC (1997). *Continental Pollutant Pathways: An Agenda for Cooperation to Address Long-Range Transport of Air Pollution in North America*. Montreal, Commission for Environmental Cooperation http://www.cec.org/pubs_info_resources/ecoregion/eco98/index.cfm?varlan=english [Geo-2-010]

Coon, C.E. (2001). *Why President Bush is Right to Abandon the Kyoto Protocol*. The Heritage Foundation Backgrounder, 1437. Washington DC, The Heritage Foundation http://www.heritage.org/library/backgrounder/bg1437.html [Geo-2-011]

ECE (1995). *Strategies and Policies for Air Pollution Abatement*. Geneva, United Nations Economic Commission for Europe

ECE (2000). *Convention on Long-Range Transboundary Air Pollution*. United Nations Economic Commission for Europe http://www.unece.org/env/lrtap/ [Geo-2-018]

EEA (1999). *Environment in the European Union at the Turn of the Century*. Copenhagen, European Environment Agency

EEA (2001). *Environmental Signals 2001*. Environmental Assessment Report No. 8. Copenhagen, European Environment Agency

Espeland, O., Kleivane, L., Haugen, S. and Skaare, J.U. (1997). Organochlorines in mother and pup pairs in two Arctic seal species: Harp seal (*Phoca groenlandica*) and hooded seal (*Cystophora cristata*). *Marine Environmental Resources*. 44, 315-30

Fenger, J. (1999). Urban air quality. *Atmospheric Environment*. 33, 4877-900

Holdren, J.P. and Smith, K.R., eds. (2000). Energy, the Environment and Health. In *World Energy Assessment: Energy and the Challenge of Sustainability*. New York, United Nations Development Programme

IEA (2000). *Key World Energy Statistics from the IEA*. Paris, International Energy Agency

IISD (2001a). *COP-6.bis Final Summary*. International Institute for Sustainable Development http://www.iisd.ca/linkages/download/asc/enb12176e.txt [Geo-2-012]

IISD (2001b). Milestones in Climate Change, International Undertaking Talks. */linkages/journal/* 6, No. 11. International Institute for Sustainable Development http://www.iisd.ca/linkages/journal/link0611e.pdf [Geo-2-151]

IPCC (1996). *Climate Change 1995. The Science of Climate Change. Contribution of Working Group I to the Second Assessment Report of the Intergovernmental Panel on Climate Change*. Cambridge, United Kingdom, Cambridge University Press

IPCC (2001a). *Climate Change 2001: The Scientific Basis. Contribution of Working Group I to the Third Assessment Report of the Intergovernmental Panel on Climate Change*. Cambridge, United Kingdom, and New York, United States, Cambridge University Press

IPCC (2001b). *Climate Change 2001: Impacts, Adaptation and Vulnerability. Contribution of Working Group II to the Third Assessment Report of the Intergovernmental Panel on Climate Change*. Cambridge, United Kingdom, and New York, United States, Cambridge University Press

IPCC (2001c). *Climate Change 2001: Mitigation. Contribution of Working Group III to the Third Assessment Report of the Intergovernmental Panel on Climate Change*. Cambridge, United Kingdom, and New York, United States, Cambridge University Press

Keeling, C.D. and Whorf, T.P. (2001). Atmospheric $CO_2$ records from sites in the SIO air sampling network. In CDIAC (ed.), *Trends: A Compendium of Data on Global Change*. Oak Ridge, Oak Ridge National Laboratory, US Department of Energy

Masclet, P., Hoyau, V., Jaffrezo, J.L. and Cachier, H. (2000). Polycyclic aromatic hydrocarbon deposition on the ice sheet of Greenland. Part I: Superficial snow. *Atmospheric Environment* 34, 3195–207

Marland, G., Boden, T.A. and Andres, R.J. (2001). *Global, Regional, and National Fossil Fuel $CO_2$ Emissions*. US Department of Energy, Carbon Dioxide Information Analysis Center http://cdiac.esd.ornl.gov/trends/emis/em_cont.htm [Geo-2-016]

Molina, M. J. and Rowland, F. S. (1974). Stratospheric sink for chlorofluoromethanes: chlorine atom catalyzed destruction of ozone. *Nature*. 249, 810-4

NASA (2001). *Largest-ever ozone hole observed over Antarctica*. NASA Goddard Space Flight Center http://www.gsfc.nasa.gov/gsfc/earth/environ/ozone/ozone.htm [Geo-2-017]

Rodhe, P., Grennfelt, P., Wisniewski, J., Ågren, G., Bengtsson, G., Johansson, K., Kauppi, P., Kucera, V., Rasmussen, L., Rosseland, B., Schotte, L. and Sellden, G. (1995). Conference summary statement. In P. Grennfelt, Rodhe, H., Thörnelöf, E. and Wisniewski, J. (ed.), *Acid Reign '95? Proceedings from the 5th International Conference on Acidic Deposition: Göteborg, 26-30 June 1995*. 1. Water, Air, and Soil Pollution, 1-14. Kluwer Academic Publishers

Sabogal, N. (2000). The Depletion of the Stratospheric Ozone Layer. *Meteorolog. Colomb*. 2, 73-9

SCEP (1970). *Man's Impact on the Global Environment*. Study of Critical Environmental Problems. Cambridge, Massachussetts, MIT Press

Schindler, D. (1999). From acid rain to toxic snow. *Ambio*. 28, 350-5

Seip, H.M., Aagaard, P., Angell, V., Eilertsen, O.,

Kong, G., Larssen, T., Lydersen, E., Mulder, J., Muniz, I.P., Semb, A., Tang, D., Vogt, R.D., Xiao, J., Xiong, J. and Zhao, D. (1999). Acidification in China: assessment based on studies at forested sites from Chongqing to Guangzhou. *Ambio*. 28, 522-8

Sillett, T.S., Holmes, R.T. and Sherry, T.W. (2000). Impacts of a global climate cycle on population dynamics of a migratory songbird. *Science*. 288, 2040-2

UN (1972). *Report of the United Nations Conference on the Human Environment. Stockholm, 5-16 June 1972. A/CONF.48/14/Rev.1*. New York, United Nations

UNEP (1999). *GEO 2000*. United Nations Environment Programme. London and New York, Earthscan

UNEP (2000a). *Action on Ozone*. Nairobi, United Nations Environment Programme

UNEP (2000b). *Report of the Twelfth Meeting of the Parties to the Montreal Protocol*. UNEP Ozone Secretariat http://www.unep.org/ozone/12mop-9.shtml [Geo-2-019]

UNEP (2001). *Text of the Stockholm Convention on Persistent Organic Pollutants for Adoption by the Conference of Plenipotentiaries*. Nairobi, United Nations Environment Programme http://irptc.unep.ch/pops/POPs_Inc/dipcon/meetingdocs/conf-2/en/conf-2e.pdf [Geo-2-020]

UNFCCC (1992). *United Nations Framework Convention on Climate Change*. New York, United Nations

UNFCCC (1997). *Kyoto Protocol to the United Nations Framework Convention on Climate Change. FCCC/CP/1997/L.7/Add.1*. Bonn, UNFCCC Secretariat

UNFCCC (2001). Greenhouse Gas Inventory Database (GHG). The Secretariat of the United Nations Framework Convention on Climate Change http://ghg.unfccc.int/ [Geo-2-152]

US EPA (2000). *Latest Findings on National Air Quality: 1999 Status and Trends*. Washington DC, United States Environmental Protection Agency

Wania, F. and Mackay, D. (1996). Tracking the distribution of persistent organic pollutants. *Environ. Sci. Technol*. 390A-6A

WCED (1987). *Our Common Future: The World Commission on Environment and Development*. Oxford, Oxford University Press

WHO (1999). *Guidelines for Air Quality*. Geneva, World Health Organization

WMO (1986). *Report of the International Conference on the Assessment of the Role of Carbon Dioxide and of Other Greenhouse Gases in Climate Variations and Associated Impacts — Villach, 9-15 October 1985*. Geneva, World Meteorological Organization

WMO (2000). *Antarctic Ozone Bulletin #5/2000*. Geneva, World Meteorological Organization

World Bank (1997). *Clear Water, Blue Skies. China's Environment in the New Century*. Washington DC, World Bank

World Bank (2001). *World Development Indicators 2001*. Washington DC, World Bank

## Atmosphere: Africa

The African continent is climatically diverse. Humid tropical conditions prevail in Western and Central Africa and in the Western Indian Ocean islands; most Southern African countries experience arid and semi-arid conditions, while semi-deserts and deserts are features of Northern Africa. The region experiences a high degree of variability and uncertainty in climatic conditions. Climate variability is therefore the single most important atmospheric phenomenon in Africa.

In comparison to other regions, African countries emit negligible amounts of air pollutants and anthropogenic greenhouse gases. For example, Africa contributes less than 3.5 per cent of global emissions of $CO_2$ (Marland, Boden and Andres 2001). Nevertheless, anthropogenic atmospheric pollution is a problem in Northern and Southern Africa, and in some large cities.

### Climate variability in Africa

In the past 30 years, Africa has experienced at least one major drought episode in each decade. In Eastern Africa there were serious droughts in 1973-74, 1984-85, 1987, 1992–94 and in 1999-2000 (DMC 2000). The last Sahelian drought persisted for a decade, from 1972-73 to 1983-84. Severe droughts were recorded in Southern Africa in 1967 to 1973, 1982-83, 1986-87, 1991-92 and 1993-94 (Chenje and Johnson 1994).

The Western Indian Ocean islands are subject to tropical storms on average ten times a year during November to May. The El Niño Southern Oscillation (ENSO), which affects much of Africa, has been associated with more frequent, persistent and intense warm phases over the past 30 years (IPCC 2001a). The 1997-98 ENSO event triggered higher sea surface temperatures in the southwest Indian Ocean, and flooding and landslides across most of Eastern Africa (Ogallo 2001).

### Air quality

South Africa contributed 42 per cent of the total regional emissions of $CO_2$ in 1998 (Marland, Boden and Andres 2001); some Northern African countries, where total energy consumption increased by 44 per cent from 1980 to 1998 (OAPEC 1999), also contribute significantly. Subsidizing electricity production, promoting industrial development economic strategies and increased consumption have contributed to rising emissions in some areas. For example, in Mauritius total energy consumption doubled between 1990 and 1998, and $CO_2$ emissions rose 23 per cent from 1991 to 1995 (UNCHS 1996).

A rapid increase in the number of private cars, and the poor condition of many commercial and private vehicles, are additional causes of concern. Vehicle emissions are the major source of lead contamination, and contribute to dust, noise and smoke pollution. Policies are in place in Algeria, Mauritius and Morocco to encourage conversion to newer, less polluting vehicles (Government of Mauritius 1990), and unleaded petrol has been promoted or even subsidized in Egypt, South Africa and Tunisia (World Bank 2001a). Industrial processes are also significant sources of atmospheric pollution, especially in large urban centres where the pollutants sometimes combine to create atmospheric smog.

In Northern Africa, the Western Indian Ocean islands, Southern Africa and some large cities (such as Lagos), the incidence of respiratory disease is increasing, reflecting a deterioration of air quality. The main causes are the indoor burning of coal, wood, kerosene (paraffin), dung and refuse for household needs, and vehicular and industrial emissions. In sub-Saharan Africa, traditional fuels accounted for 63.5 per cent of total energy use in 1997 (World Bank 2001b).

Many countries have prepared National Environmental Action Plans (NEAPs) or National Strategies for Sustainable Development (NSSDs) which address, among other things, sources and impacts of atmospheric pollution. Ghana, Kenya, South Africa, Uganda and Zambia are among those that have introduced legislation making Environmental Impact Assessments (EIAs) compulsory for developments such as roads, mines and industrial operations with potentially high atmospheric emissions (Government of Ghana 1994, Government of Kenya 1999, Republic of South Africa 1989, Government of Uganda 1995, Government of Zambia 1990).

### Climatic variability and vulnerability to climate change

Climatic variability and associated floods and droughts result in increased risks of crop failure and therefore reduced food security, as well as higher incidences of malnutrition and disease. In Ethiopia, for example, the 1984 drought affected 8.7 million people, 1 million people died and millions more suffered from malnutrition and famine. This drought also caused the death of nearly 1.5 million livestock (FAO 2000). The 1991-92 drought in Southern Africa caused a 54 per cent reduction in cereal harvest and exposed more than 17 million people to the risk of starvation (Calliham, Eriksen and Herrick 1994). More than

100 000 people died in the Sahelian drought of the 1970s and 1980s (Wijkman and Timberlake 1984). Crop failure and livestock losses lead to increased dependence on imports and foreign aid, reducing economic performance and the ability to cope with future environmental disasters.

In 1997 and 1998, parts of Eastern Africa suffered from high rainfall and flooding due to ENSO disturbances, and in 1999 and 2000 Southern Africa and the Western Indian Ocean islands experienced devastating cyclones and floods. Flood water is an ideal habitat for bacteria and mosquitoes. In Uganda, the ENSO-induced floods of 1997-98 caused more than 500 deaths from cholera, and a further 11 000 people were hospitalized (NEMA 1999).

The sea temperature rise of 1.0–1.5°C due to the ENSO disturbances is thought to have resulted in bleaching of up to 30 per cent of the coral in Comoros, 80 per cent in Seychelles (PRE/COI 1998), and 90 per cent in Kenya and Tanzania (Obura and others 2000).

The region's vulnerability to natural disasters is compounded by the anticipated impacts of global climate change. According to IPCC, Africa is the most vulnerable region in terms of predicted decreases in water and food security, because widespread poverty limits adaptive capacity (IPCC 1998). Changes in rainfall could also have serious consequences for those parts of Africa that depend on hydroelectricity.

The anticipated sea level rise resulting from global climate change may threaten many coastal settlements and islands including the Western Indian Ocean islands. The extent of sea level rise is still uncertain but the latest IPCC (2001a) estimates are in the range 10–94 cm by the year 2100. Even if anthropogenic greenhouse gas emissions were stabilized immediately, sea level would continue to rise for many years. IPCC also predicts that the intensity of cyclones, rain and wind will probably increase (IPCC 2001a), and the cyclone zone in the Western Indian Ocean could expand to include Seychelles (UNEP 1999).

Changes to rainfall and temperature patterns could also alter biodiversity, with many species not being able to adapt or migrate to more suitable areas. WWF forecasts that an anticipated 5 per cent decrease in rainfall in Southern Africa will affect grazing species such as hartebeest, wildebeest and zebra, threatening wildlife in the Kruger National Park, South Africa, the Okavango delta in Botswana and Hwange National Park in Zimbabwe. There are also fears that malaria

could spread to new areas such as parts of eastern Namibia and northern South Africa (WWF 1996).

The region's ability to adapt to climate change will depend on several factors, including population growth and consumption patterns, which will affect demand for food and water, and the location of populations and infrastructure in relation to vulnerable coastal areas, which will determine economic losses due to sea level rise. Many countries will need to change their

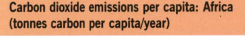

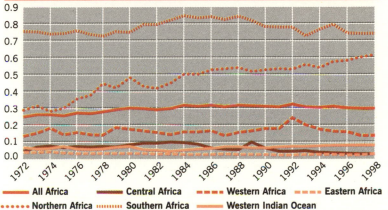

| | |
|---|---|
| All Africa | Central Africa |
| Western Africa | Eastern Africa |
| Northern Africa | Southern Africa |
| Western Indian Ocean | |

agricultural practices, particularly to reduce dependency on rainfed agriculture, and to avoid cultivation in marginal areas. Rural communities that currently depend on biomass for energy may be forced to seek alternative sources if climate change brings about changes to vegetation type and distribution.

## Policy issues

Almost all African countries have ratified the UNFCCC and many are in favour of the Kyoto Protocol. African countries stand to benefit from mechanisms of international cooperation proposed under the Protocol. Countries that are rich in natural forests (as in Western and Central Africa) may also enter into emissions reduction transfer agreements with industrialized countries, contributing to their own economies and assisting development. On the whole, African countries have an interest in a decision on mechanisms that ensures they facilitate sustainable development in Africa, produce gains in the climate system, contribute towards Africa's adaptation to climate change and result in projects that accelerate socio-economic growth (IISD 2000). Algeria, Cape Verde, Côte d'Ivoire, Egypt, Ghana, Lesotho, Mali,

Africa contributes less than 3.5 per cent of global emissions of $CO_2$; Northern and Southern Africa are responsible for more than 80 per cent of the region's emissions

*Source: compiled from Marland, Boden and Andres 2001*

Mauritius, Niger, Senegal, Seychelles and Zimbabwe have all produced National Communications to the UNFCCC (UNFCCC 2001), giving detailed inventories of emissions as well as sinks. South Africa emits the most carbon in Africa but, being classified as a developing country, is not formally required to control emissions of greenhouse gases. However, a National Committee on Climate Change has been established to oversee research, communication and the development of policy on climate change.

In both Northern and Southern Africa, options for further exploitation of alternative sources of energy (such as solar, wind, small-scale hydropower and biomass) are being explored. Such initiatives are likely to be most successful in remote areas, where connections to centralized power sources are expensive, and electricity demand is for domestic use only.

One of the main challenges for most African countries with regard to climatic and atmospheric changes is the need to adapt development processes to the changes in the environment. Mitigation and adaptation mechanisms need to be developed to cope with the impacts of changes in weather patterns and intensified droughts and floods associated with El Niño events (IPCC 2001b). On the other hand, African countries may contribute to the implementation of the UNFCCC and Kyoto Protocol by adopting energy efficient and renewable energy technologies. The Kyoto mechanisms and international institutions to be created to realize these mechanisms provide for active participation of African countries. Failure to realize the potentialities of the Kyoto Protocol may result in further exposure to the adverse effects of climate change (IISD 2000). Localized indoor and outdoor pollution must be controlled and abated through the introduction of cleaner industrial processes, improved transport systems and waste management. For example, a waste management strategy that envisages reducing illegal dumping and burning of solid waste has been developed in South Africa (DEAT 1998).

## References: Chapter 2, atmosphere, Africa

Calliham, D.M., Eriksen, J.H. and Herrick, A.B. (1994). *Famine Averted: The United States Government Response to the 1991/92 Southern Africa Drought: Evaluation Synthesis Report.* Washington DC, Management Systems International

Chenje, M. and Johnson, P. (eds. 1994). *State of the Environment in Southern Africa.* Maseru and Harare, SADC, IUCN and SARDC

DEAT (1998). *Strategy for Integrated Pollution Control and Waste Management.* Pretoria, South Africa, Department of Environmental Affairs and Tourism of the South African Government

DMC (2000). *DEKAD 19 Report (1-10 July, 2000). Ten-Day Bulletin.* Nairobi, Drought Monitoring Centre

FAO (2000). *Agricultural Development and Related Aspects in the Horn of Africa.* ACC Inter-Agency Task Force on the UN Response to Long Term Food Security. Rome, UN Food and Agriculture Organization

Government of Ghana (1994). *Environmental Protection Agency Act, 1994.* Accra

Government of Kenya (1999). *Environment Management and Coordination Act 1999.* Nairobi

Government of Mauritius (1990). *National Environmental Action Plan for Mauritius.* Ministry of Environment, Port-Louis

Government of Uganda (1995). *National Environment Statute.* Statute No 4, Kampala

Government of Zambia (1990). *Environmental Protection and Pollution Control Act 1990.* Act No. 12 of 1990. Lusaka

IISD (2000). *Climate Change Capacity Project–Africa. Report of the Workshop July 17-21, 2000 Dakar, Senegal.* International Institute for Sustainable Development, Winnipeg, Canada http://iisd.ca/climate/cccp_africa.htm [Geo-2-153]

IPCC (1998). *The Regional Impacts of Climate Change: An Assessment of Vulnerability.* Cambridge, United Kingdom, Cambridge University Press

IPCC (2001a). *Climate Change 2001: The Scientific Basis. Contribution of Working Group I to the Third Assessment Report of the Intergovernmental Panel on Climate Change.* Cambridge, United Kingdom, and New York, United States, Cambridge University Press

IPCC (2001b). *Climate Change 2001: Impacts, Adaptation and Vulnerability. Contribution of Working Group II to the Third Assessment Report of the Intergovernmental Panel on Climate Change.* Cambridge, United Kingdom, and New York, United States, Cambridge University Press

Marland, G., Boden, T.A. and Andres, R.J. (2001). *Global, Regional, and National Fossil Fuel $CO_2$ Emissions.* US Department of Energy, Carbon Dioxide Information Analysis Center http://cdiac.esd.ornl.gov/trends/emis/tre_afr.htm [Geo-2-001]

NEMA (1999). *State of the Environment Report for Uganda.* Kampala, National Environment Management Authority

OAPEC (1999). *Annual Statistical Report 1999.* Kuwait, Organization of Arab Petroleum Exporting Countries http://www.oapecorg.org/images/A%20S%20R%201999.pdf [Geo-2-002]

Obura, D., Suleiman, M., Motta, H. and Schleyer, M. (2000). Status of Coral Reefs in East Africa: Kenya, Mozambique, South Africa and Tanzania. In C. Wilkinson (ed.), *Status of Coral Reefs of the World: 2000.* Townsville, Australia, Australian Institute of Marine Science and Global Coral Reef Monitoring Network

Ogallo, L. A. (2001). Unusual floods and droughts in East Africa. *World Climate News.* June 2001, 19, 3-4

PRE/COI (1998). *Rapport Régional sur les Récifs.* Quatre Bornes, Mauritius, Programme Régional Environment, Commission de l'Ocean Indien

Republic of South Africa (1989). *Environment Conservation Act.* Act No. 73 of 1989, Pretoria

UNCHS (1996). *An Urbanizing World: Global Report on Human Settlements 1996.* Nairobi, United Nations Centre for Human Settlements (HABITAT)

UNEP (1999). *Western Indian Ocean Environment Outlook.* Nairobi, United Nations Environment Programme

UNFCCC (2001). *Table of National Communications.* UNFCCC Secretariat http://www.unfccc.de/resource/natcom/nctable.html [Geo-2-003]

Wijkman, A. and Timberlake, L. (1984). *Natural Disasters: Acts of God or Acts of Man?* London, Earthscan

World Bank (2001a). *Middle East and North Africa Region Environment Strategy Update.* Washington DC, World Bank

World Bank (2001b). *World Development Indicators 2001.* Washington DC, World Bank http://www.worldbank.org/data/wdi2001/pdfs/tab3_8.pdf [Geo-2-024]

WWF (1996). *Climate Change and Southern Africa. Summary.* World Wide Fund for Nature http://www.panda.org/resources/publications/climate/Africa_Issue/africa.htm [Geo-2-004]

# Atmosphere: Asia and the Pacific

A serious environmental issue in the Asia and Pacific region is the rapid degradation of the quality of air. Depletion of the ozone layer and the consequences of global climate change are also serious.

## Air quality

Air pollution levels in the most populated cities are amongst the highest in the world, producing serious human health impacts and affecting aquatic and terrestrial ecosystems. Transport is a significant, often major, source of urban air pollution. The other sources include industrial emissions, burning of solid and liquid fuels for power generation, and burning of biomass and other fuels such as charcoal for household use. In a few cities, pollution levels have decreased. For example, in Japan, high fuel prices, technological advances and strict standards have reduced $SO_2$ and particulate emissions, and eliminated lead emissions from transport. However, $NO_x$ emissions in Tokyo and Osaka have not declined sufficiently because of an increasing number of vehicles. This situation is common in cities with growing levels of private transport (UN-ESCAP/ADB 2000).

Traffic has become a major air polluter in the big cities, although most Asian countries have low per capita vehicle ownership in comparison to the world average (World Bank 2000). However, the motorized fleet (see bar chart) has been growing rapidly; for example, the number of private motor vehicles in Sri Lanka doubled during 1975–92 (Government of Sri Lanka 1994) and in India the number of cars has been doubling every seven years for the past 30 years (ADB 1999). This fact, combined with poor roads, fuel quality and vehicle maintenance, makes vehicular air pollution an alarming issue.

Many countries have developed their own air quality standards for principal pollutants as well as emission standards for power plants, selected industries and vehicles. To reduce pollution, many countries have introduced unleaded petrol, mandatory catalytic converters and low sulphur motor fuels. Alternative technologies such as electric vehicles and compressed natural gas operated vehicles are also being considered, especially in India and the Islamic Republic of Iran. Tax incentives for gas or battery operated vehicles have been introduced in Nepal and Pakistan.

Except for developed countries of the Northeast

## Urban air pollution in Asia

The air in Asia's cities is amongst the most polluted in the world. Of the 15 cities in the world with the highest levels of particulate matter, 12 are located in Asia (ADB 1999). Furthermore, six of these cities also have the highest levels of atmospheric $SO_2$. Levels of air pollution substantially exceed the international guidelines for air quality recommended by WHO. Cities such as Beijing, Calcutta, Jakarta, New Delhi, Shanghai and Tehran are notorious for high levels of suspended particulates, with New Delhi recording the maximum of 420 $\mu g/m^3$ (ESCAP/ADB 2000 and ADB 2001). Tehran has also recorded $SO_2$ levels four times the guidelines prescribed by WHO (World Bank 2001).

Asian and parts of the South Pacific sub-regions, concern over the environment began to create a demand for improved environmental protection in the 1980s. The 1990s have seen significant progress in establishing the institutions and policy tools needed to address urgent environmental problems. However, continuous growth in energy consumption and reliance on fuels such as coal and oil with a relatively high carbon content will inevitably increase emissions unless more aggressive policies are introduced.

Indoor air pollution is often a more severe health hazard than outdoor air pollution. Most rural inhabitants in the region use twigs, grass, dried animal dung, crop residues, wood, charcoal and kerosene as household fuels. Coupled with inadequate ventilation, this results in highly contaminated indoor air. Given the high levels of harmful emissions and the number of people using traditional cooking fuels — Asia produces nearly half of the world's woodfuel (FAOSTAT 2001) — the scale of exposure is large. Health effects include acute respiratory infection in children, chronic obstructive lung disease, adverse pregnancy outcomes and lung cancer in women. Acute respiratory diseases are prevalent in the rural and/or hilly areas of Afghanistan, Bangladesh, Bhutan, India, Nepal, Pakistan and Sri Lanka where indoor air

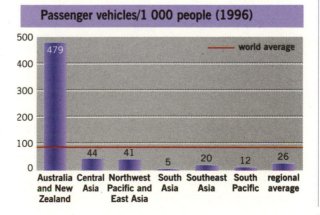

**Passenger vehicles/1 000 people (1996)**

|  |  |
|---|---|
| Australia and New Zealand | 479 |
| Central Asia | 44 |
| Northwest Pacific and East Asia | 41 |
| South Asia | 5 |
| Southeast Asia | 20 |
| South Pacific | 12 |
| regional average | 26 |

world average

Despite the heavy air pollution in Asia's cities, the number of vehicles per capita is well below the global average in all sub-regions except Australia and New Zealand

*Source: World Bank 2000*

pollution is high. About 40 per cent of the global infantile mortality caused by pneumonia occurs in Bangladesh, India, Indonesia and Nepal; many of these deaths are caused by pollutants from burning traditional fuels (ADB 2001). In India, household solid fuel use is estimated to cause about 500 000 premature deaths a year in women and children under five. There are indications that tuberculosis and blindness may be associated with indoor air pollution. Indoor air pollution is blamed for 5–6 per cent of the national burden of diseases in women and children in India (Holdren and Smith 2000).

The key areas for intervention are: use of cleaner fuels such as low-propane gas and kerosene; development of high-grade biomass fuels; improvements in stove design and better dissemination of stoves; improvements in housing; and improvements in environmental awareness and education. To address the problem of indoor air pollution in India, around 3 million biogas plants and more than 22 million improved cooking stoves have been installed in rural and remote areas of the country,

### The Asian brown cloud

In spring 1999, scientists working on the project Indian Ocean Experiment (INDOEX) discovered a dense brownish pollution haze layer covering most of South and Southeast Asia and the tropical region of the Indian Ocean. The researchers tracked the haze over an area of about 10 million km$^2$, and believe it forms over much of the Asian continent. The haze is a mixture of pollutants, mainly soot, sulphates, nitrates, organic particles, fly ash and mineral dust, formed by fossil fuel combustion and rural biomass burning. It reduces the sunlight reaching the tropical Indian Ocean surface, thousands of kilometres from its source, by as much as 10 per cent, with a larger reduction over the Indian sub-continent. Simulations with global climate models indicate that the haze could have major impacts on the monsoon circulation, regional rainfall patterns and vertical temperature profile of the atmosphere.

A programme called ABC (Asian Brown Cloud) has been initiated with support from UNEP. The main aim of the first phase of this programme is to study the impact of the Asian haze on a number of parameters, including monsoon change, water balance, agriculture and health. Scientists plan to establish a network of ground-based monitoring stations throughout Asia to study the composition and seasonal pattern of the haze. UNEP has pledged to facilitate the continued research programme and, in the longer-term, to help coordinate policy responses to address the problem.

*Source: UNEP (2001) and C4 and UNEP (in press)*

resulting in a saving of the equivalent of 21 million tonnes of firewood per annum (Times of India 2000).

Haze and acid rain have been the emerging regional issues over the past decade, especially in Asia because of China and India's overwhelming dependence on coal. Around 0.28 million ha of forest land are reported to be damaged by acid rain in the Sichuan basin of China. $SO_2$ emissions in Asia are estimated to have increased from about 26.6 to about 39.2 million tonnes during 1985–1997 (Streets and others 2000). In China, a reduction of 3.7 million tonnes or 15.8 per cent in $SO_2$ emissions was achieved during 1995–2000 (SEPA 2001). At least two-thirds of acid depositions in the region are caused by coal-fired power plants with outdated pollution control equipment.

Haze problems are also prevalent in the region due to forest fires in Southeast Asia. The most serious episode occurred in 1997, when the effects of forest fires in Indonesia extended to neighbouring countries including Brunei Darussalam, Papua New Guinea, Philippines, Singapore and Thailand (UNEP 1999). A Haze Technical Task Force was established by ASEAN Senior Officials on Environment in 1995 and, in 1997, a Regional Haze Action Plan was approved (ASEAN 2001).

The Acid Deposition Monitoring Network (EANET), with the participation of ten East Asian countries, began a preparatory phase of monitoring acid deposition in April 1998. In October 2000, the network decided to begin regular monitoring from January 2001 (EANET 2000). In South Asia, the Malé Declaration on Control and Prevention of Air Pollution and its likely Transboundary Effects, was adopted by eight South Asian countries in 1998.

## Ozone depletion

Depletion of the stratospheric ozone layer has emerged as a serious concern in the region. Data from Australia and New Zealand show that ultraviolet levels there appear to be rising by about 10 per cent per decade (McKenzie, Connor and Bodeker 1999). It follows that the average exposure time for an individual in Australia to develop sunburn has been reduced by approximately 20 per cent over the past 20 years.

India and China are the largest regional producers and users of CFCs. China's consumption of ODS increased more than 12 per cent per year during 1986–94. India is the second largest producer and the fourth largest consumer of CFCs in the world (UNEP 1998). The Multilateral Fund of the Montreal Protocol and GEF have been helping the region meet the goals of the Montreal Protocol. China has made a commitment to phase out the consumption of ODS by 2010. It has already banned the establishment of new

CFC- and halon-related production facilities, and developed general and sector-specific plans with the help of the World Bank and the Multilateral Fund. The latter has approved a World Bank project which will help India phase out CFC production by 2010.

The countries of Central Asia have also made considerable progress. Azerbaijan, Turkmenistan and Uzbekistan are working towards the phase out of the use of ODS during 2001–03 (Oberthur 1999).

## Greenhouse gas emissions and climate change

Per capita use of commercial energy increased annually by 1.9 per cent in South Asia and 3 per cent in East Asia and the Pacific during 1980–98 (World Bank 2001).

$CO_2$ is the main anthropogenic greenhouse gas. Methane emissions are also high in South Asia, accounting for approximately 50 per cent of the total global anthropogenic emission of $CH_4$ (UNDP, UNEP and WRI 1992). In New Zealand, $CH_4$ emissions are an order of magnitude higher than the global per capita average, primarily due to the large number of ruminant animals (MFE 1997).

Areas under most threat from climate change include marine ecosystems, coastal systems, human settlements and infrastructure (IPCC 1998). Countries in the Northwest Pacific and East Asia sub-regions and the Pacific Island countries may be particularly vulnerable to phenomena such as sea level rise because many of their human settlements and industrial facilities are located in coastal or lowland areas. For the small island developing states, climate change and extreme weather events may have dramatic impacts on terrestrial biodiversity, subsistence cropping and forest food sources. The densely populated and intensively used low-lying coastal plains, islands and deltas in South Asia are especially vulnerable to coastal erosion and land loss because of inundation and sea flooding, upstream movement of the saline/freshwater front and sea water intrusion into freshwater aquifers (IPCC 1998).

GEF and UNDP are promoting projects to help countries in the region assess their emissions and formulate strategies to reduce them. For example, countries participating in the Asia Least Cost Greenhouse Gas Abatement Strategies project have identified a number of options in the energy sector to reduce greenhouse gas emissions (GEF 2000).

### References: Chapter 2, atmosphere, Asia and the Pacific

ADB (1999). *Urban Sector Strategy*. Manila, Asian Development Bank

ADB (2001). *Asian Environment Outlook 2001*. Manila, Asian Development Bank

ASEAN (2001). *Second ASEAN State of the Environment Report, 2001*. Jakarta, ASEAN Secretariat

C4 and UNEP (in press). *The South Asian Brown Cloud: Climate and Other Environmental Impacts* A UNEP Assessment Report. Nairobi, United Nations Environment Programme

EANET (2000). *Report of the Second Intergovernmental Meeting on the Acid Deposition Monitoring Network in East Asia (EANET)*. Niigata, Japan, Interim Network Centre, Acid Deposition and Oxidant Research Centre

ESCAP/ADB (2000). *State of the Environment in Asia and Pacific 2000*. New York, United Nations

FAOSTAT (2001). *FAOSTAT Statistics Database*. Rome, Food and Agriculture Organization of the United Nations http://www.fao.org [Geo-2-068]

GEF (2000). *GEF Contributions to Agenda 21: the First Decade*. Washington DC, Global Environment Facility

Government of Sri Lanka (1994). *State of the Environment, Sri Lanka*. Prepared for submission to the South Asian Co-operative Environmental Programme. Colombo, Government of Sri Lanka, Ministry of Forestry and Environment

Holdren, J.P. and Smith, K.R., eds. (2000). Energy, the Environment and Health. In *World Energy Assessment: Energy and the Challenge of Sustainability*. New York, United Nations Development Programme

IPCC (1998). *The Regional Impacts of Climate Change: An Assessment of Vulnerability*. Cambridge, United Kingdom, Cambridge University Press

McKenzie, R., Connor, B. and Bodeker, G. (1999). Increased summertime UV radiation in New Zealand in response to ozone loss. *Science*. 285, 1709-11

MFE (1997). *New Zealand: The State of New Zealand's Environment 1997*. Wellington, Ministry for the Environment of New Zealand

Oberthur, S. (1999). *Status of the Montreal Protocol Implementation in Countries with Economies in Transition*. Nairobi, UNEP and GEF

Streets, D.G, Tsai, N.Y., Akimoto, H. and Oka, K. (2000). Sulfur Dioxide Emissions in Asia in the Period 1985-1997. *Atmospheric Environment*. 34, 4413-24

SEPA (2001). *Year 2000 Report on the State of the Environment in China*. Beijing, State Environmental Protection Administration of China

Times of India (2000). Indian Ocean Haze traced to Chulha smoke, aerosols. *Times of India*. 17 October 2000, 9

UNDP, UNEP and WRI (1992). *World Resources 1992–93*. New York and Oxford, Oxford University Press

UNEP (1998). *OzoneAction*. 28, October 1998

UNEP (1999). *GEO 2000*. United Nations Environment Programme. London and New York, Earthscan

UNEP (2001). More Knowledge of Interactions between Asian Brown Haze, Global Warming and Ozone Urgently Needed Says UNEP. UNEP News Release 01/46 http://www.unep.org/Documents/Default.asp?DocumentID=197&ArticleID=2813 [Geo-2-154]

World Bank (2000). *World Development Indicators 1999*. Washington DC, World Bank

World Bank (2001). *World Development Indicators 2001*. Washington DC, World Bank

## Atmosphere: Europe

### Air pollution

Air pollution was one of the threats to human health and ecosystems that was recognized early in Europe. A treaty (the 1979 ECE Convention on Long Range Transboundary Air Pollution, CLRTAP) was signed as early as the late 1970s and entered into force in 1983 to curb anthropogenic emissions of harmful substances.

### Health effects of air pollution related to road traffic in Austria, France and Switzerland

A recent health impact assessment of air pollution in Austria, France and Switzerland revealed that car-related pollution kills more people than car accidents in these three countries. Long-term exposure to air pollution from cars causes an extra 21 000 premature deaths from respiratory or heart disease per year in adults over 30. In comparison, the total annual deaths from road traffic accidents in these countries are 9 947. Each year air pollution from cars in the three countries causes 300 000 extra cases of bronchitis in children, 15 000 hospital admissions for heart disease, 395 000 asthma attacks in adults and 162 000 in children, and some 16 million person-days of restricted activities for adults over 20 years old because of respiratory disorders. The total cost of this health impact is €27 billion per year or 1.7 per cent of the combined GNP of the three countries. This is the equivalent of €360/person/year (Kunzli and others 2000).

The main sectors and activities driving air pollution in Western Europe in the past three decades have been energy, transport, industry, agriculture, solvent use, and storage and distribution of fossil fuels. In Central and Eastern European (CEE)

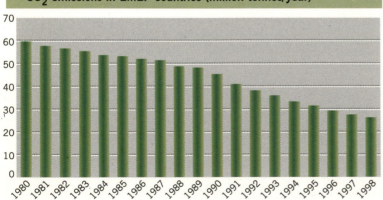

**SO$_2$ emissions in EMEP countries (million tonnes/year)**

Over the period 1980–98, SO$_2$ emissions in countries that are members of the Co-operative Programme for Monitoring and Evaluation of the Long-Range Transmission of Air Pollutants in Europe (EMEP) have been reduced by 56 percent

*Source: Vestreng and Støren 2000*

countries, the power and heavy industry sectors have traditionally been the major polluters, with transport only significant in major cities. In the early 1990s, economic recession was a driver in the decrease of air pollution in CEE but at the same time there was a sharp growth in the use of private cars. For example, even during the worst recession years (1990 to 1994), the number of private cars in Armenia, Russia and Ukraine increased by more than 100 per cent (FSRFHEM 1996). This rapid increase in private car ownership has made transport an increasingly important contributor to CEE's air quality problems.

Emissions of most key air pollutants have declined over the whole of Europe since the early 1980s. By the end of 2000, emissions of sulphur compounds had been reduced to less than one-third of 1980 levels in Western Europe, and to two-thirds of those levels in CEE (EEA 2001a, UNEP 1999). A significant recovery of natural acid balance of water and soils has been observed in Europe, mainly due to reductions in SO$_2$ emissions, although the emissions are still too high to avoid serious effects in sensitive ecosystems. Average figures, however, mask a wide variation among countries and sub-regions. For instance, SO$_2$ emissions increased by 7 per cent in Greece and 3 per cent in Portugal between 1990 and 1998 while reductions of 71 per cent and 60 per cent were observed in Germany and Finland respectively (EEA 2000). NO$_x$ and NH$_3$ emissions have not decreased significantly in Western Europe except for NO$_x$ in Germany and the United Kingdom but NO$_x$ has been reduced in many CEE countries (Czech Environmental Institute and Ministry of the Environment 1996, EEA 2001b, GRID-Budapest 1999, GRID-Warsaw 1998, Interstate Statistical Committee 1999, OECD 1999a, UNECE/EMEP/MSC 1998). A lack of monitoring of emissions of heavy metals, POPs and SPM, especially in CEE countries, means that no convincing trends can be observed but it is clear that particulate matter and tropospheric ozone precursors still represent serious problems (EEA 2000).

In Western Europe, emissions of SO$_2$, NO$_x$ and NH$_3$ have shown a clear de-coupling from GDP growth, pointing towards some degree of effectiveness of measures taken (EEA 2001a). In some of the CEE countries that are likely to be in the first wave of accession to the European Union (EU), economic restructuring and environmental actions also appear to have had an effect in reducing air pollution. In other

CEE countries, the fall in industrial output due to the recession appears to have been the main factor in air pollution reduction (OECD 1999a and b, UNECE 1999). In countries such as Russia and Ukraine, emissions per unit of GDP have actually increased but the effect has been masked by the overall fall in GDP (SCRFEP 1999).

It is clear that the reductions in emissions are at least partly due to national and local measures that have been taken to achieve targets set by CLRTAP and its Protocols, and to EU Directives linked to air emissions such as the Limitation of Emissions of Certain Pollutants into the Air from Large Combustion Plants Directive (1988) and various directives on vehicle emissions, the change to unleaded petrol and higher quality diesel fuels and improved engine design. Despite this clear progress, many air pollution reduction targets have still not been met. In Western Europe, only the EU and CLRTAP targets for $SO_2$ were met well before the target date (the end of 2000) with less progress on $NO_x$, $NH_3$ and VOCs. Two recent European measures are expected to achieve further reductions in air pollutants: a proposal for an EU Directive on National Emission Ceilings for Certain Atmospheric Pollutants (NECD) and the CLRTAP Protocol to Abate Acidification, Eutrophication and Ground-level Ozone. In many European countries, additional measures will be required to achieve the NECD and CLRTAP Protocol targets. In Western Europe 'non-technical' measures for controlling pollution such as road pricing and tax incentives have become more important (EC 2000) but in many CEE countries it is unlikely that currently weak environmental protection bodies can enforce an effective air pollution reduction strategy in the near future (OECD 1999b).

## Stratospheric ozone depletion

The thickness of the ozone layer over Europe has decreased measurably since the 1980s. Though the average ozone loss in northern mid-latitudes is 6 per cent in winter and spring, at certain times the loss can be more significant. For example, in the spring of 1995 after an unusually cold Arctic winter, stratospheric ozone concentrations over Europe were 10–12 per cent lower than in the mid-1970s. The winter of 1995–96 was even colder and ozone concentrations over the United Kingdom fell by almost 50 per cent in the first week in March, the lowest ever recorded

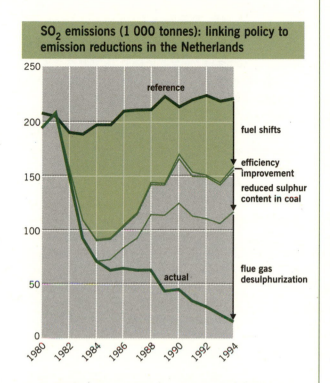

**$SO_2$ emissions (1 000 tonnes): linking policy to emission reductions in the Netherlands**

there (UNEP 2000). As a result, an increase in ultraviolet radiation occurred in Europe between 1980 and 1997, with a clearly higher increase in the northeast (EEA 1999, Parry 2000).

As a result of implementing the Vienna Convention and its Montreal Protocol, ODS production in Western Europe has decreased by almost 90 per cent while the production of hydrochlorofluorocarbons (HCFCs) has increased (EC 1999, UNEP 1998). The political and economic transition in CEE has delayed the phase out of ODS production and consumption but there is progress. Large amounts of donor assistance were channelled via the GEF in the 1990s to upgrade technologies in favour of ozone-friendly substances. An important milestone for the Countries with Economies in Transition (CEIT) was the ceasing of production of ODS listed in Annexes A and B to the Montreal Protocol by the Russian Federation, the major regional producer, in December 2000 (UNEP 2001).

## Greenhouse gas emissions

Although many European countries are enthusiastic proponents of a global climate change treaty, the region is still a major emitter of anthropogenic greenhouse gases. Most $CO_2$ emissions come from fossil fuel combustion (ETC/AE 2000, OECD 1999b). The energy sector (power and heating) is the main

In the Netherlands, a shift in fuel from oil to natural gas produced a net decrease in $SO_2$ emissions until the mid-1980s when greater use of coal reversed the trend. Since 1983, the sulphur content of coal has been reduced, while flue gas desulphurization units began to be fitted to Dutch power plants in 1986, with 96 per cent equipped by 1996

*Note: the reference line above is based on electricity produced*

*Source: EEA 2000*

contributor (32 per cent of the EU's $CO_2$ emissions), while transport, combustion, manufacturing and heavy industry also play a major role (ETC/AE 2000).

Greenhouse gas emissions in the EU decreased by 2 per cent between 1990 and 1998 (EEA 2001a), mainly as a result of stabilization of $CO_2$ emissions and reduction of emissions of $N_2O$ and methane. Most of this decrease was attributable to Germany (as a result of increased efficiency of new power plants, energy saving in households and industries, and economic restructuring in the former East Germany) and the United Kingdom (following a switch from coal to gas). In Western Europe generally, there has been a clear de-coupling between emissions, economic growth and energy consumption thanks to a combination of increases in energy efficiency, and effects of policies and measures to reduce greenhouse gas emissions (ETC/AE 2000). However, meeting the Kyoto Protocol targets will still be difficult (EEA 2001a).

Economic transformation in CEE has contributed to a significant decrease of anthropogenic greenhouse gas emissions. In 2000, $CO_2$ emissions in nine of those countries were 8 per cent lower than in 1990 (ETC/AE 2000). In some of the CEE countries, economic restructuring and environmental actions appear to have had an effect in reducing $CO_2$ (OECD 1999a) while in most CEE countries recession and a decline in industrial output appears to have been the main factor in $CO_2$ reduction (OECD 1999a and b, UNECE 1999).

## References: Chapter 2, atmosphere, Europe

Czech Environmental Institute and Ministry of the Environment (1996). *Environment Year Book of the Czech Republic 1995*. Prague, Czech Statistical Office

EC (1999). *Statistical Factsheet — Ozone-depleting Substances*. Brussels, European Commission

EC (2000). *A Review of the Auto-Oil II Programme. (COM 2000) 626 final*. Brussels, European Commission

EEA (1999). *Environment in the European Union at the Turn of the Century*. Environmental Assessment Report No. 2. Copenhagen, European Environment Agency

EEA (2000). *Environmental Signals 2000*. Environmental Assessment Report No. 6. Copenhagen, European Environment Agency

EEA (2001a). *Environmental Signals 2001*. Environmental Assessment Report No. 8. Copenhagen, European Environment Agency

EEA (2001b). *Databases on Air Quality and Emissions of Air Pollutants and Greenhouse Gases in Europe*. European Topic Centre on Air and Climate Change http://etc-acc.eionet.eu.int/databases [Geo-2-004]

ETC/AE (2000). *European Community and Member States Greenhouse Gas Emission Trends 1990-1998*. Topic report No. 6/2000. European Topic Centre for Air Emissions. Copenhagen, European Environment Agency

FSRFHEM (1996). *Review of Environmental Pollution in the Russian Federation in 1995*. Moscow, Federal Service of the Russian Federation for Hydrometeorology and Environmental Monitoring

GRID-Budapest (1999). *State of the Environment in Hungary*. Budapest, GRID-Budapest

GRID-Warsaw (1998). *State of the Environment in Poland*. State Inspectorate for Environmental Pollution http://pios.gov.pl/raport/ang [Geo-2-006]

Interstate Statistical Committee (1999). *Official Statistics of the Countries of the Commonwealth of Independent States. CD Rom*. Moscow, Interstate Statistical Committee of the Commonwealth of Independent States

Kunzli, N., Kaiser, R., Medina, S., Studnicka, M., Chanel, O., Filliger, P., Herry, M., Horak Jr, F., Puybonnieux-Texier, V., Quenel, P., Schneider, J., Seethaler, R., Vergnaud, J-C. and Sommer, H. (2000). Public-health impact of outdoor and traffic-related air pollution: a European assessment. *The Lancet*. 356, 795-801

OECD (1999a). *Environment in the Transition to a Market Economy: Progress in Central and Eastern Europe and the New Independent States*. Paris, OECD Centre for Cooperation with Non-Members

OECD (1999b). *Environmental Data*. Paris, Organization for Economic Cooperation and Development

Parry, M.L. (2000). *Assessment of Potential Effects and Adaptations for Climate Change in Europe: Summary and Conclusions*. Norwich, Jackson Environment Institute, University of East Anglia

SCRFEP (1999). *National Report on the State of the Environment in the Russian Federation in 1999*. Moscow, State Committee of the Russian Federation for Environmental Protection

UNECE and EMEP/MSC-W (1998). *Transboundary Acidifying Air Pollution in Europe, Report 1/98*. Oslo, Norwegian Meteorological Institute

UNECE (1999). *Economic Survey of Europe, 2000*. Geneva, United Nations Economic Commission for Europe

UNEP (1998). *Production and consumption of ozone-depleting substances 1986-1996*. Nairobi, United Nations Environment Programme

UNEP (1999). *GEO 2000*. United Nations Environment Programme. London and New York, Earthscan

UNEP (2000). *Action on Ozone*. Nairobi, United Nations Environment Programme

UNEP (2001). *Report of the 21st Meeting of the Open-Ended Working Group of the Parties to the Montreal Protocol. 24-26 July 2001*. United Nations Environment Programme http://www.unep.org/ozone/pdf/21oewg-4.pdf [Geo-2-007]

Vestreng, V. and Støren, E. (2000). *Analysis of UNECE/EMEP Emission Data. MSC-W Status report 2000*. EMEP/MSC_W Note 1/00. Research Note No. 37. Oslo, Norwegian Meteorological Institute

# Atmosphere: Latin America and the Caribbean

Air pollution is one of the most critical environmental issues in the Latin America and Caribbean Region because of its impact on human health, especially in urban areas. Rapid urbanization, population growth, industrialization and a growing number of motor vehicles are the main causes of air pollution. The region is also prone to the negative impacts of stratospheric ozone layer depletion.

## Air quality

Some three-quarters of the population of Latin America and the Caribbean live in cities. Several megacities such as Buenos Aires, Mexico City, Rio de Janeiro and São Paulo, each with a population of more than 10 million, are located in the region and economic growth in these urban centres has caused increases in air pollution (particularly CO, $NO_X$, $SO_2$, tropospheric $O_3$, hydrocarbons and SPM) and associated human health impacts (UNEP 2000). Today the problem extends beyond large cities and also affects medium-size cities and small islands (Dalal 1979, Romieu, Weitzenfeld and Finkelman 1990). The transport sector is a major source of urban air pollution — 70 per cent of emissions in Buenos Aires (PAHO 1998) and Mexico City (INEGI 1998) are transport-related, with the number of cars in Mexico City increasing fourfold between 1970 and 1996 (ECLAC 2000a). Industry, agriculture and the municipal sector also contribute to air pollution. In Santiago, the most significant sources of air pollution are transport, and small and medium-size enterprises (IMO 1995). In addition, unfavourable topographic and meteorological conditions in some cities aggravate the impact of pollution: the Valley of Mexico obstructs the dispersal of pollutants from its metropolitan area as do the hills surrounding Santiago (ECLAC 2000b).

The growth of industry, agriculture and transport sectors over the past 30 years has been accompanied by a steady increase in $CO_2$ emissions — estimated at 65 per cent between 1980 and 1998 (UNEP 2001a). In 1991–92, the region was estimated to be responsible for some 11 per cent of global anthropogenic emissions of $CO_2$ — 4.5 per cent of global industrial emissions and 48.5 per cent of emissions from land-use change (UNDP, UNEP, World Bank and WRI 1996). Deforestation is thought to be the principal

### Air pollution increases mortality

In 1992, it was estimated that 76 million urban people were exposed to air pollutant concentrations exceeding WHO guidelines. In São Paulo and Rio de Janeiro, air pollution was estimated to be responsible for 4 000 premature deaths annually (CETESB 1992). Studies in Brazil, Chile and Mexico have shown that a 10 $mg/m^3$ increase of concentration of $PM_{10}$ (particles of $10\mu$ or less in diameter) in the air coincides with a 0.6 to 1.3 per cent increase in mortality in those over the age of 65 (PAHO 1998).

cause of emissions in the region, particularly in the Amazon basin (UNEP 1999). Deforestation and livestock breeding (the latter is significant in Argentina, Chile and Uruguay) also result in a huge regional methane emission — some 9.3 per cent of the world total (UNFCCC-SBI 2000).

The average annual per capita carbon emission from industry in the region was 0.73 tonnes in 1998, somewhat lower than the world average of 1.06 tonnes (Marland, Boden and Andres 2001). Mexico is the region's largest carbon emitter.

Industrial pollutants originate mostly from fuel combustion processes in the power generation sector, although emissions of heavy metals such as lead and mercury are also important (PAHO 1998). In oil-producing countries, emissions from the refining process are also significant — for example, in Mexico City, almost 60 per cent of $SO_2$ emissions originate from industry, including oil refineries in the metropolitan area (INEGI 1998). In many countries,

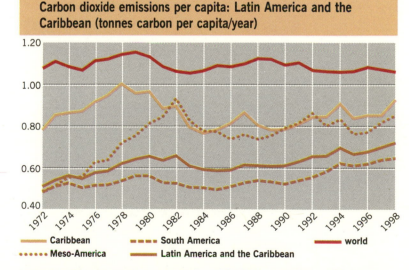

**Carbon dioxide emissions per capita: Latin America and the Caribbean (tonnes carbon per capita/year)**

Legend: Caribbean — South America — world — Meso-America — Latin America and the Caribbean

Average industrial carbon emission in Latin America and the Caribbean in 1998 was 0.73 tonnes/year, compared to the global average of 1.06 tonnes

*Source: compiled from Marlan, Boden and Andres 2001*

## Dealing with air pollution in Mexico City

In Mexico City, one of the biggest megacities in the world, studies have shown a close correlation between urban air pollution and the acceleration of pulmonary diseases, ageing processes in the lungs and respiratory infections (Loomis and others 1999, PAHO 1998, WHO 1999). A comprehensive programme to cope with air pollution in the Valley of Mexico was launched in 1990 aimed at improving the quality of fuel, promoting public transport, reducing emissions from vehicles, industry and services, and reforestation. The 1995-2000 Programme to Improve Air Quality in Mexico City (Proaire) introduced new activities in the field of monitoring, education and public participation. Other initiatives included the establishment of the Valley of Mexico Environmental Trust Fund, which is maintained with tax revenue from petrol and finances air quality improvement activities, the Automatic Environmental Monitoring Network, Environmental Emergency Programmes, 'A Day Without a Car' Programme, a reforestation programme and environmental education in the metropolitan area of Mexico City (ECLAC 2000a).

mining activities result in local deterioration of air quality (PAHO 1998).

Other sources of air pollution have local and sub-regional impacts, including pesticide use in agriculture and airborne particles resulting from soil erosion and biomass combustion. Studies conducted in Colombia and Ecuador in the early 1990s revealed that more than 60 per cent of agricultural workers involved in production for foreign markets had symptoms of acute pesticide poisoning (headaches, allergies, dizziness, dermatitis, blurred vision) while others experienced serious chronic effects (stillbirths, miscarriages, and respiratory and neurological problems). Neighbouring inhabitants can also be affected, as has been found for Nicaraguan cotton fields and Costa Rican coffee plantations (UNDP, UNEP, World Bank and WRI 1998, UNEP 2000).

Forest fires are another important contributor to air pollution, sometimes having a significant long-distance effect (CCAD and IUCN 1996, Nepstad and others 1997). In 1997, for example, the smoke from fires in Guatemala, Honduras and Mexico drifted across much of the southeastern United States, prompting the Texas authorities to issue a health warning to residents (UNEP 2000).

In Latin America and the Caribbean, about one-fifth of the population uses biomass as a major household fuel, resulting in indoor air pollution. This mainly affects women, children and the elderly who stay indoors for long periods. In Colombia and Mexico, for example, women using biomass for cooking are up to 75 times more likely to contract chronic lung disease than the average person (UNDP, UNEP, World

Bank and WRI 1998). Air pollution is blamed for 2.3 million annual cases of infantile chronic respiratory sickness and 100 000 cases of chronic adult bronchitis in the region (ECLAC 2000b).

In recent decades, significant efforts have been made to cope with air pollution, especially in urban areas (see box left) through strategies that include emission controls, changes in fuels and contingency controls. In Santiago, SPM emissions — and the number of days when alerts were sounded or emergencies declared — have been reduced considerably over the past decade, with concentrations of $PM_{10}$ and $PM_{2.5}$ decreasing by 24.1 per cent and 47.4 per cent respectively between 1989 and 1999 (CAPP 2000). This is largely due to implementation of a plan initiated in 1990 which included control of household and industrial emissions, developing monitoring capacity, removing highly polluting buses, controlling bus circulation and emissions, introducing car catalytic converters, improving motor fuel quality, and paving streets (ECLAC 2000c, O'Ryan and Larraguibel 2000).

Notwithstanding the progress achieved, urban air pollution is a serious concern even in some small and medium-sized cities because of the continued growth of the transport and industrial sectors, coupled with a lack of adequate monitoring and regulations. The growth of vehicles due to rising real incomes and the removal of tariffs could nullify the progress made in improving air quality. By 2010, 85 per cent of the population are expected to be living in urban areas, and combating air pollution and preventing its negative health impacts will be a priority in every country.

## Global atmospheric issues

Ozone depletion is a significant issue for the region, especially those countries closest to the Antarctic ozone hole such as Argentina and Chile. Following ratification of the Montreal Protocol, governments in collaboration with private sector and other stakeholders adopted regulations, established institutions and took measures to phase out ODS — Brazil halted production in 1999 (MMA 2001). Countries such as Argentina, Mexico (currently the main regional producer of ODS) and Venezuela that still produce CFCs have developed policies and measures to reduce both production and consumption of ODS. In contrast to other developing regions, the Latin American and Caribbean Region has reduced total production of CFCs from the 1986 level by approximately 21 per cent (UNEP 2001b).

Global climate change may seriously affect the region given its ecological and socio-economic vulnerability. Changes in the water cycle may pose a danger to arid and semi-arid zones and thus affect the production of cereals and livestock as well as hydroelectric power generation in countries such as Argentina, Chile, Costa Rica and Panama. Coastlines and coastal ecosystems in Central America, Argentina, Uruguay and Venezuela may be affected, and the coastal infrastructure may be damaged. Many of the large metropolitan areas are highly vulnerable to sea level rise, especially major ports. In the Caribbean, the small island states will probably be the first to suffer from sea level rise. There may also be impacts on health caused by an increase in epidemic disease vectors, along with other gastrointestinal infections (PAHO 1998).

Countries in the region do not have commitments under the UNFCCC or Kyoto Protocol. Mitigation and adaptation activities include energy-saving measures in transport, agriculture and waste management sectors, developing renewable energy sources and developing carbon sinks, mostly forests. Wind energy is exploited in several countries including Barbados, Costa Rica and Jamaica. A 2-MW demonstration plant using ocean thermal energy conversion has been built in Jamaica (UNEP 2000).

## References: Chapter 2, atmosphere, Latin America and the Caribbean

CAPP (2000). *Estado del Medio Ambiente en Chile - 1999: Informe País*. Santiago, Centro de Análisis de Políticas Públicas, Universidad de Chile

CCAD and IUCN (1996). *Reducción del Efecto Invernadero Mediante la Limitación y Absorción del $CO_2$ en América Central: Propuesta Plan de Prevención y Combate de Incendios Forestales en América Central*. San José, Costa Rica, Comisión Centroamericana de Ambiente y Desarrollo, Consejo Centroamericano de Bosques y Áreas Protegidas, Unión Mundial para la Naturaleza, Oficina para Mesoamérica San José, Costa Rica

CETESB (1992). *Relatorio de Qualidadde do Ar em São Paulo*. São Paulo, Compahia de Tecnologia de Saneamento Ambiental

Dalal, R.C. (1979). Composition of Trinidad Rainfall. *Water Resource Research*. 15, 1217-23

ECLAC (2000a). *De la Urbanización Acelerada a la Consolidación de los Asentamientos Humanos en América Latina y el Caribe*. Regional Conference for Latin America and the Caribbean preparatory to the extraordinary session on the examination and general evaluation of the application of the Habitat Programme, CEPAL/HABITAT, LC/G.2116

ECLAC (2000b). *Conciencia Ciudadana y Pollution Atmosférica: Estado de Situación en la Ciudad de México*. CEPAL, LC/R. 1987. Santiago, Economic Commission for Latin America and the Caribbean

ECLAC (2000c). *Conciencia Ciudadana y Contaminacion Atmosférica: Estado de Situación en el Area Metropolitana de Santiago de Chile*. CEPAL, LC/R. 2022. Santiago, Economic Commission for Latin America and the Caribbean

IMO (1995). *Global Waste Survey - Final Report*. Manila, International Maritime Organization

INEGI (1998). *Estadisticas del medio ambiente. Mexico, 1997*. Aguascalientes, Instituto Nacional de Estadistica, Geografia e Informatica

Loomis, D., Castillejos, M., Gold, D.R., McDonnell, W. and Borja-Aburto, V.H. (1999). Air pollution and infant mortality in Mexico City. *Epidemiology*. 10, 118-23

Marland, G., Boden, T.A. and Andres, R.J. (2001). *Global, Regional, and National Fossil Fuel $CO_2$ Emissions*. US Department of Energy, Carbon Dioxide Information Analysis Center http://cdiac.esd.ornl.gov/trends/emis/tre_amd.html [Geo-2-046]

MMA (2001). *Programa Brasileiro de Eliminação da Produção e do Consumo das Substâncias que Destroem a Camada de Ozônio*. Ministério de Medio Ambiente, Brasil http://www.mma.gov.br/port/ascom/imprensa/maio 2000/informma54.html [Geo-2-047]

Nepstad, D.N., Klink, C.A., Uhl, C., Vieira, I.C., Lefebvre, P., Pedlowski, M., Matricardi, E., Negreiros, G., Brown, I.F., Amaral, E., Homma, A. and Walker, R. (1997). Land-use in Amazonia and the Cerrado of Brazil. *Ciencia e Cultura - Journal of the Brazilian Association for the Advancement of Science*. 49, 1/2, 73-86

O'Ryan, R. and Larraguibel, L. (2000). *Contaminacion del Aire en Santiago: Estado Actual y Soluciones*. Santiago, Universidad de Chile

PAHO (1998). *Health in the Americas. 1998 Edition*. Scientific Publication No. 569. Washington DC, Pan-American Health Organization

Romieu, I., Weitzenfeld, H. and Finkelman, J. (1990). Urban air pollution in Latin America and the Caribbean: Health Perspectives. *World Health Statistics Quarterly* 43, 153-67

UNDP, UNEP, World Bank and WRI (1998). *World Resources 1998–99*. Washington DC, World Resources Institute

UNEP (1999). *GEO 2000*. United Nations Environment Programme. London and New York, Earthscan

UNEP (2000). *GEO Latin America and the Caribbean Environment Outlook*. Mexico City, United Nations Environment Programme, Regional Office for Latin America and the Caribbean

UNEP (2001a). *GEO: Environmental Statistics for Latin America and the Caribbean (work in progress). Estadísticas ambientales de América Latina y el Caribe (trabajo en proceso)*. Mexico City, United Nations Environment Programme, Regional Office for Latin America and the Caribbean

UNEP (2001b). *Report of the Secretariat on Information Provided by the Parties in Accordance with Article 7 of the Montreal Protocol on Substances that Deplete the Ozone Layer*. 13th Meeting of the Parties to the Montreal Protocol, 16–19 October 2001, Colombo, Sri Lanka. UNEP/OzL.Pro.13/3 http://www.unep.org/ozone/13mop-before.shtml [Geo-2-155]

UNFCCC-SBI (2000). *National Communications from Parties not Included in Annex I to the Convention. Second Compilation and Synthesis of Initial National Communications from Parties not Included in Annex I to the Convention. Note by the Secretariat. FCCC/SBI/2000/15, 24 October*. Bonn, United Nations Framework Convention on Climate Change, Scientific Body for Implementation

WHO (1999). *Air Quality Guidelines*. Geneva, World Health Organization

## Atmosphere: North America

### Air quality

Over the past 30 years, there have been notable air quality improvements at both regional and local levels in the region. Levels of many air pollutants have been gradually reduced — the trends in the United States (see graph) are representative of the region.

Acid rain control programmes contributed to the dramatic decline in sulphur emissions since 1995 with reductions of 10–25 per cent in some parts of the north-eastern United States (US EPA 2000a). Recent evidence, however, suggests that many sensitive areas are still receiving acid deposition that exceeds their assimilation capacity, and damage caused by acid deposition may be more fundamental than was previously believed (CEC 2000, Munton 1998).

New concerns have arisen over ground level ozone and fine particulate matter, whose emissions have not decreased as markedly as other common pollutants.

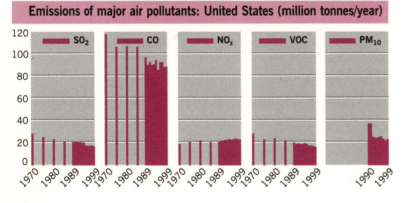

**Emissions of major air pollutants: United States (million tonnes/year)**

Emissions of many air pollutants have been reduced over the past 30 years, particularly for CO, VOCs and SO₂

*Source: US EPA 2001*

### Ground-level ozone

Ground-level $O_3$ is a common, pervasive and harmful air pollutant (see box). Fossil fuel combustion is the major source of $NO_x$, with the transportation sector alone responsible for 60 per cent of $NO_x$ emissions in Canada (Hancey 1999) and 53 per cent in the United States (US EPA 2000b).

Between 1984 and 1991, Canada's ozone guideline of 0.082 ppm over a one-hour period was exceeded at least once in all major cities (EC 2000a). In the United States, tens of millions of people lived in areas where the one-hour ozone standard of 0.120 ppm was regularly exceeded (US EPA 2000b). Control measures in the 1970s focused primarily on reducing VOCs and, in some cases, $NO_x$ emissions from factories and vehicles in the regions that were most affected. In

### Ground-level ozone in North America

Research over the past decade has demonstrated that $O_3$ is responsible for far greater impacts on health than was previously thought. Even average concentrations of $O_3$ can exacerbate asthma and other respiratory diseases, and inhibit or interfere with the immune system, especially in young children, the elderly and outdoor sports enthusiasts (OMA 2000). Research in both Canada and the United States repeatedly documents a strong correlation between hospitalization and worker absenteeism, and episodic high $O_3$ levels (CEC 1997).

many cases, however, controls failed to reduce ozone concentrations sufficiently to meet national health standards (US EPA 1997a).

Ozone molecules have been found to travel large distances from emission sources — the typical transport range of tropospheric $O_3$ is 240–800 kilometres (CEC 1997). Between 30 and 90 per cent of eastern Canada's $O_3$ comes from the United States, while the province of Ontario, the region in Canada that suffers from the worst $O_3$ problem, is a source of $NO_x$ downwind into northeastern United States (EC 2000a).

Fossil fuel power plants are the largest point sources of $NO_x$ — significant amounts of $O_3$ are formed and transported within the plumes of power plants. In addition, while VOCs have decreased in the United States over the past 30 years, $NO_x$ emissions increased between 1970 and 1999 by 17 per cent (US EPA 2000b). These findings led to a new approach in which North America recognized the need for aggressive strategies to reduce regional $NO_x$ emissions and for cooperation between the two countries.

Under the Canada/US Air Quality Agreement (1991), both countries set targets to reduce $NO_x$ emissions and in October 2000 they signed an annex to the agreement to reduce border emissions of $NO_x$ from fossil fuel power (EC 2000b). They have also engaged in the 1995 North American Research Strategy for Tropospheric Ozone and signed the 1999 CLRTAP Protocol to Abate Acidification, Eutrophication and Ground-Level Ozone.

Recognition that exposure to ozone at concentrations below 0.08 ppm results in severe health effects has prompted revisions in both Canadian and US ozone health standards (EC 2000a, US EPA 1997b). Although levels of SPM have decreased by 40 per cent since 1980, recent research has revealed serious health concerns at concentrations well within allowed levels attributable to the finer airborne particles released mainly from vehicles

## Impact of air pollution on health in North America

Air pollution is emerging as a key contributor to some respiratory and cardiovascular diseases. Around 80 million US citizens are exposed to levels of air pollution that can impair health and more than 2 per cent of all deaths annually can be attributed to air pollution (UNDP, UNEP, World Bank and WRI 1998). Air pollution is also linked to an alarming rise over the past two decades in the prevalence of asthma among children and young adults. More than 5.5 million children in North America are affected by asthma. The impact of environmental pollution on children's health is a priority issue in North America.

and power plants. Consequently, North American standards for particulate matter have been adjusted (EC 1999, EC 2000a, OMA 2000).

### Stratospheric ozone layer depletion

North America's northern regions have been subject to serious stratospheric ozone depletion. With the 1987 Montreal Protocol on Substances that Deplete the Ozone Layer, both countries committed themselves to actions to protect the stratospheric ozone layer. In Canada, strict regulations passed in 1990 and reformulated in 1999 reduced production faster than the protocol required, from a high of 27 800 tonnes/year in 1987 to 900 tonnes/year in 1996 (EC 2001). In the United States, the use and trade of ODS is controlled through a marketable permit system and a tax on ODS. The subsequent price increase of ODS encouraged the use of alternatives. Both countries reduced their non-essential CFC consumption to zero by 1996 (Potts 2001).

### Greenhouse gases and climate change

Since 1972 North America's climate has warmed considerably, reflecting a global trend. About half of the average rise in North America's surface temperature during the past century — more than 0.6 °C — occurred since the late 1970s (see graph). North America emits more greenhouse gas than any other region, accounting for around 5 per cent of the world's population but nearly 26 per cent of global anthropogenic emissions of $CO_2$ in 1998 (Marland, Boden and Andres 2001). North America has one of the world's most energy-consuming economies. The transportation sector is the largest source of $CO_2$ emissions, accounting for 30.1 per cent of Canada's emissions in 1995 (EC 1998a) while in 1993 cars and light trucks were responsible for more than 20 per cent of US $CO_2$ emissions (Glick undated). In 1997,

the US transport sector accounted for around 5 per cent of global anthropogenic $CO_2$ emitted and more than one-third of total world transportation energy use (NRC 1997, O'Meara Sheehan 2001).

Two sharp price shocks in the oil market in the 1970s helped to increase awareness that oil is not a renewable resource. Energy-saving standards for vehicle bodies, engines and fuel efficiency in new passenger cars were introduced in the 1970s and strengthened in the 1980s (OECD 1996, CEQ 1997). However, a combination of factors conspired to drive energy use up during the 1980s. Progress in total and per capita energy efficiency slowed and $CO_2$ emissions continued to rise (CEQ 1997, EC 1997, OECD 1998).

Renewed efforts subsequent to the UNFCCC commitments also failed to curb $CO_2$ emissions in the 1990s. In 1998, emissions were 14 and 11 per cent

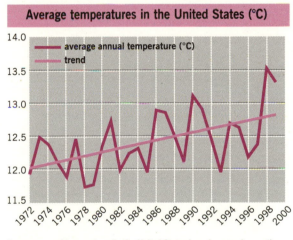

**Average temperatures in the United States (°C)**

Average annual temperatures in the United States have increased more than 0.6°C since the late 1970s

Source: DOC, NOAA and NCDC 2000

above 1990 levels in Canada and the United States respectively (US EPA 2000a, SRP 2000). Renewable energy production from hydropower, wind, solar, biomass and geothermal sources is increasing but still contributes only a small fraction of energy needs, supplying about 7 per cent of US domestic energy demand in 2000 (US EIA 2001).

In the transport sector, progress made in car fuel efficiency and emission controls has been partially offset by increases in the number of automobiles, in distances travelled, and a trend since 1984 toward light-duty trucks and sport-utility vehicles (CEQ 1997, EC 1998a). For example, between 1990 and 1995 there was a 15 per cent increase in automobile travel in Canada, a decrease in urban transit usage and a 6 per cent increase in total fossil fuel use (EC 1998b). In 1994, nearly 60 per cent of US households owned two or more cars and 19 per cent owned three or more (De Souza 1999). Cheap parking and other hidden subsidies, such as funds for highway development and low fuel prices, have encouraged car dependency (Miller and Moffat 1993, EC 1998a).

Under the 1997 Kyoto Protocol, Canada agreed to reduce greenhouse gas emissions to 6 per cent and the United States to 7 per cent below 1990 levels between 2008 and 2012. However, in early 2001, the United States announced that implementing the Kyoto treaty would be too harmful to the economy and that it would pursue other ways of addressing climate change (US EIA 2001). At the July 2001 UNFCCC conference in Bonn a compromise was struck allowing carbon-absorbing forests to be used against emissions with the result that Canada may obtain more than 20 per cent of its target with such credits (MacKinnon 2001).

## References: Chapter 2, atmosphere, North America

CEC (1997). *Long-Range Transport of Ground Level Ozone and its Precursors*. Montreal, Commission for Environmental Cooperation

CEC (2000). *Booming Economies, Silencing Environments, and the Paths to Our Future*. Montreal, Commission for Environmental Cooperation
http://www.cec.org [Geo-2-026]

CEQ (1997). *Environmental Quality — The World Wide Web: The 1997 Annual Report of the Council on Environmental Quality*. Washington DC, The White House, Council on Environmental Quality

De Souza, R-M. (1999). *Household Transportation Use and Urban Air Pollution: A Comparative Analysis of Thailand, Mexico, and the United States*. Washington, DC, Population Reference Bureau

DOC, NOAA and NCDC (2000). *Climate of 1999 Annual Review*. Asheville, North Carolina, US Department of Commerce, National Oceanic and Atmospheric Administration, National Climatic Data Center
http://ceq.eh.doe.gov/nepa/reports/statistics/tab6x1.html [Geo-2-156]

EC (1997). *Global Climate Change: The Greenhouse Gas Emissions Outlook to 2020*. Environment Canada
http://www.ec.gc.ca/climate/fact/greenhou.html [Geo-2-027]

EC (1998a). Canadian Passenger Transportation, National Environmental Indicator Series. In *SOE Bulletin No. 98-5*. Ottawa, Environment Canada, State of the Environment Reporting Program

EC (1998b). Cars more efficient, but Canadians driving more. *Science and the Environment Bulletin*. June 1998

EC (1999). *Canada Signs International Agreement on Acid Rain and Smog Reductions*. Environment Canada
http://www.ec.gc.ca/press/acidrn_n_e.htm [Geo-2-029]

EC (2000a). *Clean Air*. Environment Canada
http://www.ec.gc.ca/air/introduction_e.cfm [Geo-2-030]

EC (2000b). *Canada and the United States Reach a Draft Agreement to Reduce Transboundary Smog*. Environment Canada
http://www.ec.gc.ca/press/001013_n_e.htm [Geo-2-031]

EC (2001). *Stratospheric Ozone*. Environment Canada
http://www.ec.gc.ca/ind/English/Ozone/Bulletin/stind1_e.cfm [Geo-2-032]

Glick, P (undated). *Global Warming: The High Costs of Inaction*. The Sierra Club: Understanding Green Markets Project
http://www.sierraclub.org/globalwarming/resources/inaction.asp [Geo-2-033]

Hancey, C. (1999). *Particulate Matter, Ground-Level Ozone, and the Canada-Wide Standards Regulatory Process*. The Sierra Club
http://www.sierraclub.ca/national/climate/ground-level-ozone.html [Geo-2-034]

MacKinnon, Mark (2001). Pollution Pact Hailed as Crucial First Step. *The Globe and Mail*, 24 July 2001, A1

Marland, G., Boden, T.A. and Andres, R.J. (2001). *Global, Regional, and National Fossil Fuel $CO_2$ Emissions*. US Department of Energy, Carbon Dioxide Information Analysis Center
http://cdiac.esd.ornl.gov/trends/emis/tre_amd.htm [Geo-2-035]

Miller, P. and Moffet, J. (1993). *The Price of Mobility: Uncovering the Hidden Costs of Transportation*. New York, Natural Resources Defence Council

Munton, D. (1998). Dispelling the myths of the acid rain story. *Environment* 40, 6, 27-33

NRC (1997). Vehicle emissions. *National Research Council*. XLVII, 3, 10

O'Meara Sheehan, M. (2001). Making better transportation choices. In L. Starke (ed.), *State of the World 2001*. New York, W.W. Norton

OECD (1996). *Environmental Performance Reviews: United States*. Paris, Organization for Economic Cooperation and Development

OECD (1998). *Environmental Indicators: Towards Sustainable Development*. Paris, Organization for Economic Cooperation and Development

OMA (2000). *The Illness Costs of Air Pollution*. Ontario Medical Association
http://www.oma.org/phealth/icap.htm [Geo-2-036]

Potts, J. (2001). *Ozone Depletion and the Illegal Trade of Ozone Depleting Substances. Unpublished report*. Montreal, Commission for Environmental Cooperation

SRP (2000). *The Sustainability Report*. Sustainability Reporting Program
http://www.sustreport.org [Geo-2-037]

UNDP, UNEP, World Bank and WRI (1998). *World Resources 1998–99*. Washington DC, World Resources Institute

US EIA (1999). *International Energy Annual 1999*. United States Energy Information Administration
http://www.eia.doe.gov/emeu/iea/tablef8.html [Geo-2-038]

US EIA (2001). *Energy Information Brief — United States of America*. Washington DC, US Energy Information Administration
http://www.eia.doe.gov/emeu/cabs/usa.html [Geo-2-039]

US EPA (1997a). *Regional Approaches to Improving Air Quality*. US Environmental Protection Agency
http://www.epa.gov/oar/oaqps/airtrans/groundoz.html [Geo-2-040]

US EPA (1997b). *National Ambient Air Quality Standards for Ozone: Final Rule. Federal Register, 62, 38856-96*. Washington DC, US Environmental Protection Agency

US EPA (2000a). *National Air Quality and Emissions Trends Report, 1999*. US Environmental Protection Agency
http://www.epa.gov/oar/aqtrnd98/html/ [Geo-2-042]

US EPA (2000b). *National Air Quality and Emissions Trends Report, 1998*. US Environmental Protection Agency
http://www.epa.gov/Ozone/title6/phaseout/phasfrm.txt [Geo-2-041]

US EPA (2001). *Average Annual Emissions, All Criteria Pollutants*. US Environmental Protection Agency
http://www.epa.gov/ttn/chief/trends/trends99/tier3_yrsemis.pdf [Geo-2-043]

## Atmosphere: West Asia

### Air quality

The level of industrialization in West Asia is low in comparison with Europe and the United States but population growth, urbanization and an increase in oil-related industries and other industrial activities have resulted in air pollution 'hot spots'. In the major cities and industrial compounds of West Asia, concentrations of the main air pollutants often exceed WHO guidelines by a factor of two to five (World Bank 1995).

The burning of fossil fuels is the main cause of atmospheric air pollution and the main source of anthropogenic $CO_2$ emissions. It accounts for all West Asia's commercial primary energy production which increased from 665.5 million tonnes of oil equivalent (mtoe) in 1972 to 974.2 mtoe in 1997, while energy consumption increased from 27.0 to 229.5 mtoe over the same period (compiled from IEA 1999).

The main sources of air pollution in the Gulf Cooperation Council (GCC) countries are oil refineries, oil gathering centres, oil platforms, petrochemical and fertilizer plants, and motor vehicles. In the Mashriq countries, outdated technologies especially in power generation plants, fertilizer plants, smelters and cement factories have caused deterioration of air quality not only in industrial sites but also in nearby settlements. Amongst the air pollutants emitted, SPM is of great concern with levels well above maximum allowable concentrations. The economic loss due to the impact of poor air quality on human health in Syria is estimated at about US$188 million per year (World Bank and UNDP 1998). However, recent trends in West Asia, and especially in the GCC countries, are towards adopting cleaner production approaches in

**Energy consumption and production: West Asia (million tonnes oil equivalent/year)**

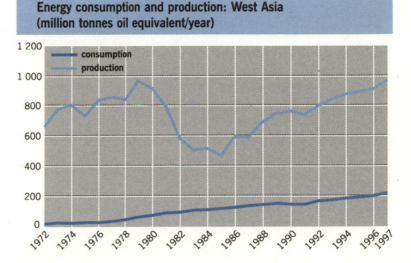

industry, especially in the large oil, petrochemical, fertilizer and metal industries.

The increasing number of vehicles, poor traffic management, ageing cars and congested roads in major cities add to the level of air pollution. Many vehicles are in poor condition and about 30 per cent are older than 15 years and produce significantly higher emissions of hydrocarbons and $NO_x$ than new ones (World Bank and UNDP 1998). Furthermore, leaded petrol is still in use in many countries, compounding health problems in cities and along major highways (World Bank 1995). To cope with this problem, some countries have taken measures to phase out leaded gasoline. Unleaded gasoline has been introduced to the GCC countries and Lebanon, and is the only fuel produced in Bahrain since July 2000 (BAPCO 2000).

Along with atmospheric pollution caused by human activities, seasonal sand and dust storms contribute to air pollution in West Asia in general and along the northern coasts of the Arabian (Persian) Gulf in particular (ROPME 1999). The dust storms absorb pollutants such as pesticides and can transport them for long distances with adverse effects on the environment, the economy and quality of life. It is estimated that the annual amount of dust fall-out along the coastal area of Kuwait may reach 1 000 tonnes/km$^2$ with an overall mean concentration of 200 $\mu$g/m$^3$ (Khalaf and others 1980, EPA 1996).

Transboundary air pollution is an emerging issue in the region. Stricter measures and regulations to control emissions, to promote the use of modern and efficient technologies, and towards restructuring the price of

West Asian energy production has now exceeded its previous maximum in 1979; consumption continues to increase at around 3.5 per cent a year

Source: compiled from IEA 1999

### The cement industry pollutes the atmosphere

The cement industry, the major industrial source of $CO_2$ emissions in the Mashriq sub-region, also emits large amounts of dust, covering nearby vegetation, endangering human health and ecosystems. In Lebanon, the cement industry is responsible for 77.2 per cent of all industrial emissions (Government of Lebanon 1998). In Syria, particulate emissions from one cement company near Damascus result in SPM levels exceeding guidelines within a radius of 3 km. This has caused thoracic and respiratory diseases among workers and nearby communities (CAMRE and UNEP 1997).

energy resources must be taken to curb air pollution. Energy efficiency programmes in the power, petroleum, transportation, industrial, agriculture and residential sectors are needed to reduce energy consumption and associated emissions of greenhouse gases.

## Stratospheric ozone depletion

The West Asia states (with the exception of Iraq) acceded to the Vienna Convention and the Montreal Protocol and its amendments. All countries in the region are users but not producers of ODS and programmes regulating the import and use of ODS have been developed at both national and regional levels. Regulations for specifications and ODS emissions have been enacted, and ozone offices and coordinating committees have been established to monitor the activities of companies related to the consumption, handling and storage of these chemicals. Companies are gradually phasing out the use of ODS and most countries have frozen the consumption of ODS as required by the Montreal Protocol. Further efforts are needed to phase out methyl bromide which is still consumed in Jordan, Lebanon and Syria.

## Climate change

The West Asia region is likely to be affected by climate change. The Arabian Peninsula and a number of islands (such as Bahrain) will probably be prone to sea level rise. Temperature variations and changes in rainfall patterns will affect water resources and food production capacity. Climate change impacts are considered a high priority in some countries, especially in island countries such as Bahrain.

Following ratification of the UNFCCC, National Climate Change Committees were established and some countries have started to monitor air quality and meteorological parameters. National inventories of greenhouse gases have been completed for several countries (Bahrain, Jordan and Lebanon) and work is underway in other countries. These inventories produced figures that were higher by 59, 72 and 25 per cent respectively (AGU and MoHME 2000, GCEP 1997, Government of Lebanon 1998) than those reported by UNDP, UNEP, World Bank and WRI (1998).

Per capita $CO_2$ emissions in West Asia increased from 4.7 tonnes/year in 1972 to 7.4 tonnes/year in 1998, echoing regional trends in population growth, development and industrialization. Emissions in the very high per capita emitting countries (Kuwait, Qatar and the United Arab Emirates) dropped during this period (Marland, Boden and Andres 2001). This decline was one of the results of national policies that included such measures as programmes for cleaner energy development, introduction of new efficient technologies and establishment of air quality standards.

### References: Chapter 2, atmosphere, West Asia

AGU and MoHME (2000). *Bahrain Inventory of Greenhouse Gas Emissions Report under UNEP/GEF Project 2200-97-46*. Manama, Bahrain, Arabian Gulf University and the Ministry of Housing, Municipalities and Environment

BAPCO (2000). *BAPCO Site for Information on the Introduction of Unleaded Gasoline. Frequently Asked Questions*. Bahrain Petroleum Company http://www.unleadedbahrain.com/english/faq.htm#3 [Geo-2-044]

CAMRE and UNEP (1997). *Study on the Application of the General Guidelines for the Identification of the Environment Impacts of Industry: Case Study on Adra Factory for Cement and Construction Materials in Syria*. Damascus, Environmental and Scientific Research Centre, General Commission for Environmental Affairs

EPA (1996). *Environment Protection Authority Annual Report*. Kuwait City, Environment Protection Authority

GCEP (1997). *Initial Communication Report under the UN Framework Convention on Climate Change*. Amman, Jordan, General Cooperation of Environment Protection

Government of Lebanon (1998). *The First National Inventory of Greenhouse Gas Emission by Sources and Removals Sinks, Final Report*. Beirut, United Nations Environment Programme, Global Environment Facility, Ministry of Environment, Lebanon

IEA (1999). *Energy Balances of Non-OECD countries 1971–97*. Paris, Organization of Economic Cooperation and Development, International Energy Agency

Khalaf, F., Kadib, A., Gharib, I., Al-Hashash, M., Al-Saleh, A., Al-Kadi, A., Desouki, M., Al-Omran, L., Al-Ansari, L., Al-Houti and Al-Mudhian, L. (1980). *Dust Fallout (Toze) in Kuwait: Mineralogy, Granulometry and Distribution Pattern. Report No. KISR/PPI 108/EES-RF-8016*. Kuwait City, Kuwait Institute for Scientific Research

Marland, G., Boden, T.A. and Andres, R.J. (2001). *Global, Regional, and National Fossil Fuel $CO_2$ Emissions*. US Department of Energy, Carbon Dioxide Information Analysis Center http://cdiac.esd.ornl.gov/trends/emis/tre_amd.htm [Geo-2-035]

ROPME (1999). *Regional Report of the State of Environment*. Kuwait City, Regional Organization for the Protection of the Marine Environment

UNDP, UNEP, World Bank and WRI (1998). *World Resources 1998-99*. London and New York, Oxford University Press

World Bank (1995). *Middle East and North Africa Environmental Strategy: Towards Sustainable Development*. Washington DC, World Bank

World Bank and UNDP (1998). *State of the Environment in Syria*. London, Environmental Resources Management

## Atmosphere: the Polar Regions

The key atmospheric issues in the Arctic and Antarctic are the depletion of the stratospheric ozone layer, the long-range transport of air pollutants and warming associated with global climate change. These problems are mainly due to anthropogenic activities in other parts of the world.

Seasonal stratospheric ozone depletion over Antarctica, and more recently over the Arctic, has been one of the major regional environmental concerns since it was noticed in 1985 (Farman and others 1985). The depth, area and duration of the Antarctic ozone hole has steadily increased, reaching an all-time high of around 29 million km$^2$ in September 2000 (WMO 2000, NASA 2001).

In the Arctic, average yearly stratospheric ozone levels in the 1990s had declined by 10 per cent from the late 1970s, increasing the risk of snow blindness and sunburn.

The recovery of the stratospheric ozone layer in the polar regions depends primarily on the implementation of the Montreal Protocol on the Substances that Deplete the Ozone Layer. Therefore the efforts of nations to phase out the use of ODS, even though they are located far from the poles, are of the utmost importance (UNEP 2000).

Natural ecosystems in polar regions have low adaptive capacity and are highly vulnerable to climate change. Climate change is expected to be more extreme in the polar regions than anywhere else (a warming trend of as much as 5°C over extensive land areas has been noted in the Arctic, although there are some areas in eastern Canada where temperatures have declined) and will probably have major physical, ecological, social and economic impacts in both the Arctic and the Antarctic (IPCC 2001a and b). Whether due to a natural oscillation or global climate change, the atmospheric temperature of Antarctica is undergoing changes. A marked warming trend is evident in the Antarctic peninsula with spectacular loss of ice shelves and an increase in the cover of higher terrestrial vegetation although, as in the Arctic, there are also areas of marked cooling — at the South Pole for example (Neff 1999).

Climate change is almost certainly responsible for the decrease in extent and thickness of Arctic sea ice, permafrost thawing, coastal erosion, changes in ice

**Monthly mean ozone levels at Halley Bay, Antarctica (Dobson units)**

○ September
● October

Monthly mean ozone levels at the Halley Bay site during the onset of the Antarctic spring

*Source: BAS 2000*

sheets and ice shelves, and the altered distribution and abundance of species in polar regions (IPCC 2001a). Other impacts of the warming trend include a recorded 15 per cent increase in Arctic precipitation, increased storm episodes, earlier springs and a later onset of freezing conditions, and decreased marine salinity (AMAP 1997). Permafrost thawing can itself add to climate change problems — for example, emissions of methane from tundra may increase while reductions in the extent of highly reflective snow and ice cover will magnify warming. These effects may continue for centuries, long after greenhouse gas concentrations are stabilized, and may cause irreversible impacts on ice sheets, global ocean circulation and sea-level rise (IPCC 2001a).

'The permafrost zone covers 58 per cent of the territory of the Russian Federation. Many human settlements, industrial plants and infrastructure are located in this zone. Given the current warming trend, the border of the permafrost zone could move 300–400 km northward by 2100.' — *Interagency Commission 1998*

Since most industrial countries are in the Northern Hemisphere, the Arctic is more exposed to anthropogenic air pollution than the Antarctic. Prevailing winds carry polluting substances — including heavy metals, POPs and sometimes radionuclides — into the Arctic where they can stay airborne for weeks or months and be transported over long distances (Crane and Galasso 1999). Over much of the Arctic, levels of certain types of pollutants are so high that they cannot be attributed to sources

### Long-range transport of pollutants to polar regions

Some persistent toxic substances, including POPs and mercury, can become volatile in warm air and be transported by air masses. After deposition, they can re-enter the atmosphere again and continue their journey, becoming long-distance contaminants. The process can continue until they reach the cooler polar areas where they condense on to particles or snow flakes in the air, which eventually land on the ground. Due to low solubility in water and high solubility in fats, they are easily incorporated into fat-rich polar food webs, and accumulate in biota. Due to the combination of harsh climate conditions with physico-chemical properties of persistent toxic substances, the polar regions, the Arctic in particular, create a sink for these substances, which may result in their levels being higher than in the source regions (AMAP 1997). The implementation of the recently adopted Stockholm Convention on Persistent Organic Pollutants, signed in May 2001, may lead to a reduction in deposition of POPs in the polar regions.

within the region; they come from much further south.

Major sources of anthropogenic radionuclides in the Arctic include fall-out from nuclear tests, releases from nuclear fuel reprocessing plants, and fall-out from the 1986 Chernobyl nuclear power plant accident. A significant increase of radioactivity in Arctic indigenous people was registered after the Chernobyl accident, particularly amongst those who consumed significant quantities of foods that concentrate radio-caesium, such as reindeer meat, freshwater fish, mushrooms and berries. The phenomenon was mainly observed in 1986–89 in Norwegian and Swedish Saami and up to 1991 in the indigenous population of the Kola Peninsula, in the Russian Federation. Since then the levels have been gradually falling back towards the pre-accident levels (AMAP 1997).

Within the Arctic, the Russian Federation's industrial complexes have been a major source of atmospheric pollution. Emissions of sulphur compounds and heavy metals from smelters have caused major forest degradation on the Kola Peninsula and have decreased the number of species in the region. The areas severely affected by air pollution around the Nickel-Pechenga and Varanger smelters increased from around 400 km$^2$ in 1973 to 5 000 km$^2$ in 1988 (AMAP 1997). Since 1990, emissions from Russian smelters have decreased or stabilized mainly because of the economic slowdown.

The level of air pollution in the Arctic is so high that 'Arctic haze' has become a major problem. The term was coined in the 1950s to describe an unusual reduction in visibility that the crews of North American weather reconnaissance planes observed during flights in the high latitudes in the Arctic. The haze is seasonal, with a peak in the spring, and originates from anthropogenic sources of emission outside the Arctic. The haze aerosols are mainly sulphurous (up to 90 per cent) originating from coal burning in the northern mid-latitudes, particularly in Europe and Asia. The particles are about the same size as the wavelength of visible light, which explains why the haze is so apparent to the naked eye.

Improvement in the state of the polar environment depends primarily on policies and measures implemented by people inside and outside of the polar areas. The Arctic countries have taken a number of steps to improve air quality. These include signing the Convention on Long-Range Transboundary Air Pollution (CLRTAP) and the relevant protocols to it,

### Radioactive contamination after Chernobyl

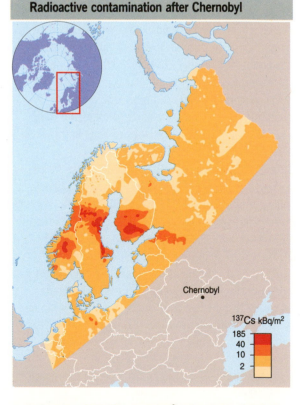

Chernobyl

$^{137}$Cs kBq/m$^2$

185
40
10
2

Levels of caesium 137 (1 000 becquerels/m$^2$) in Scandinavia, Finland and the Leningrad region of Russia following the Chernobyl explosion in 1986

Source: AMAP 1997

## The significance of Arctic haze

The discovery of Arctic haze put paid to the earlier notion that aerosol pollution could only be local or regional. The cold, dry air in the polar regions allows particles to remain airborne for weeks rather than days, which in turn allows sulphur contaminants to spread from industrial sources in Eurasia across the entire Arctic and into North America. The haze particles can facilitate the transport of metals and other contaminants to and within the polar region and result in the deposition of these pollutants in precipitation over major ocean areas surrounding the Arctic (AMAP 1997).

ecosystems and of some traditional indigenous communities. Despite increasing activity in both the domestic and international arenas, only preliminary steps have been taken to address the problem of global climate change. The main regional challenge is therefore enhancing the potential for adaptation to change that should help mitigate adverse impacts. The Arctic countries have initiated an Arctic Climate Impact Assessment to be completed in 2003. It will be integrated into the regional studies of the IPCC (ACIA 2001).

and supporting the development of the Stockholm Convention on Persistent Organic Pollutants. In addition, domestic regulatory measures taken in the United States and Canada have reduced emissions of some POPs, heavy metals and sulphur compounds. Actions to address stratospheric ozone depletion rely on the successful implementation of the Montreal Protocol by all nations (UNEP 2000).

Given the predicted increase in the global mean temperature, climate change will impose significant pressures on the polar regions in the 21st century. These impacts are likely to be exacerbated by the high vulnerability and low adaptive capacity of polar

## References: Chapter 2, atmosphere, the Polar Regions

ACIA (2001). *Arctic Climate Impact Assessment.* http://www.acia.uaf.edu

AMAP (1997). *Arctic Pollution Issues: A State of the Arctic Environment Report.* Oslo, Arctic Monitoring and Assessment Programme

BAS (2000). BAS Ozone Bulletin 01/00. British Antarctic Survey. http://www.nerc-bas.ac.uk/public/icd/jds/ozone/bulletins/bas0100.html [Geo-2-100]

Crane, K. and Galasso, J.L. (1999). *Arctic Environmental Atlas.* Washington DC, Office of Naval Research, Naval Research Laboratory

Farman, J.C., Gardiner, B.J. and Shanklin, J.D. (1985). Large losses of total ozone in Antarctica reveals seasonal $ClO_x/NO_z$ interaction. *Nature* 315, 207-10

Interagency Commission (1998). *The Second National Communication to the UNFCCC.* Moscow, Interagency Commission of the Russian Federation on Climate Change Problems

IPCC (2001a). *Climate Change 2001: Impacts, Adaptation and Vulnerability. Contribution of Working Group II to the Third Assessment Report of the Intergovernmental Panel on Climate Change.* Cambridge, United Kingdom, and New York, United States, Cambridge University Press

IPCC (2001b). *Climate Change 2001: The Scientific Basis. Contribution of Working Group I to the Third Assessment Report of the Intergovernmental Panel on Climate Change.* Cambridge, United Kingdom, and New York, United States, Cambridge University Press

NASA (2001). *Largest-ever ozone hole observed over Antarctica.* NASA Goddard Space Flight Center http://www.gsfc.nasa.gov/gsfc/earth/environ/ozone/ozone.htm [Geo-2-017]

Neff, W.D. (1999). Decadal time scale trends and variability in the tropospheric circulation over the South Pole. *Journal of Geophysical Research-Atmospheres,* 104, 27217-51

UNEP (2000). *Report of the Twelfth Meeting of the Parties to the Montreal Protocol.* UNEP Ozone Secretariat http://www.unep.org/ozone/12mop-9.shtml [Geo-2-019]

WMO (2000). *Antarctic Ozone Bulletin 5/2000.* Geneva, World Meteorological Organization

# OUR CHANGING ENVIRONMENT: Chomutov, Czech Republic

1979

Pollution from coal-fired powerplants near Chomutov, Czech Republic, swept for many years over the Krusne Hory Mountains into Germany — that is, from the lower right to the upper left in the images shown on the left.

The green rectangular shapes are strip mines which supply low-grade, sulphur-rich brown coal for electricity generation. The burning of this low-grade coal not only pollutes the air but also inflicts severe damage on forests throughout Eastern Europe.

In the early 1980s, trees growing high up on the mountains began to die. The effects are shown in the central left portion of the two images. In the 1979 image, the dark areas represesent healthy, dense forest. In the 2000 image, these dark areas are replaced by areas of light grey, in which the trees have died and mostly bare soil has been left. Extensive clear-cutting of dead and dying trees has since occurred. Efforts to replace the damaged forests been widely unsuccessful.

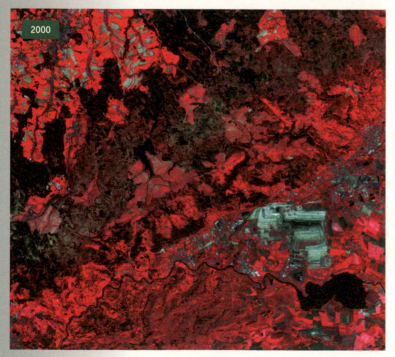

2000

Landsat data: USGS/EROS Data Center
Compilation: UNEP GRID Sioux Falls

# OUR CHANGING ENVIRONMENT: Kilimanjaro, Tanzania

Mt Kilimanjaro, located some 300 km south of the equator in Tanzania, is Africa's highest mountain. Its permanent ice and snow looming some 5 000 metres above an undulating savanna plain have always fascinated people and attracted many visitors to both Tanzania and Kenya.

But the glaciers of Kilimanjaro are vanishing due to regional warming, probably linked to global warming. The map shows the diminishing extent of the glaciers between 1962 and 2000. Over these 38 years, Kilimanjaro has lost some 55 per cent of its glaciers. According to the Byrd Polar Research Center of Ohio State University 'Kilimanjaro has lost 82 percent of the ice cap it had when it was first carefully surveyed in 1912'.

Map shows the extent of the glacier in 1962 (yellow outline, based on geological survey) and in 2000 (black outline, based on Landsat imagery and aerial survey)

view of the south eastern side of Kibo (highest peak of Kilimanjaro)

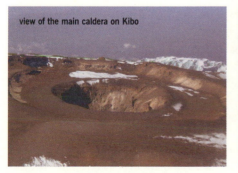

view of the main caldera on Kibo

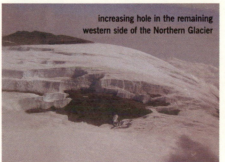

increasing hole in the remaining western side of the Northern Glacier

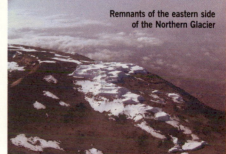

Remnants of the eastern side of the Northern Glacier

Landsat data: USGS/EROS Data Center
Photographs: Christian Lambrechts, UNF/UNEP/KWS/University of Bayneuth/WCST

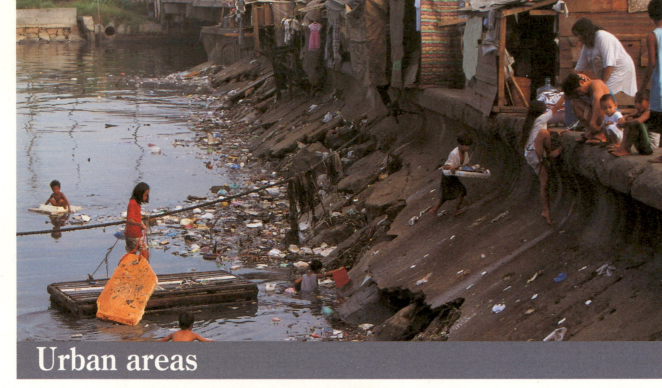

UNEP Hartmut Schwarzbach, Philippines, Still Pictures

# Urban areas

## Global overview

Nearly half of the world's population (47 per cent) lives in urban areas, a figure which is expected to grow by 2 per cent per year during 2000–15 (United Nations Population Division 2001a). The accumulation of people, their consumption patterns, travel behaviour and their urban economic activities have a large impact on the environment in terms of resource consumption and waste discharges. However, cities also offer opportunities to manage a growing population in a sustainable way.

## Urbanization

Increasing levels of urbanization are caused by natural growth of the urban population and migration of the rural population towards cities. Over the past half-century, a great rural-to-urban population shift has occurred and the process of urbanization (the concentration of people and activities into areas classified as urban) is set to continue well into the 21st century. Driving forces include the opportunities and services offered in urban areas — especially jobs and education — while in some parts of the world,

notably Africa, conflict, land degradation and exhaustion of natural resources are also important (UNEP 2000).

Cities play a major role not only as providers of employment, shelter and services but also as centres of culture, learning and technological development, portals to the rest of the world, industrial centres for the processing of agricultural produce and manufacturing, and places to generate income. There is a strong positive link between national levels of human development and urbanization levels (UNCHS 2001b). However, the implications of rapid urban growth include increasing unemployment, environmental degradation, lack of urban services, overburdening of existing infrastructure and lack of access to land, finance and adequate shelter (UNCHS 2001b). Managing the urban environment sustainably will therefore become one of the major challenges for the future.

Levels of urbanization are closely correlated with national income — the more developed countries are already mostly urbanized — and in almost every country, urban areas account for a disproportionate share of the gross national product (GNP). Bangkok, for example, produces 40 per cent of Thailand's output, whereas only 12 per cent of its population lives in this city (UNCHS 2001b). Worldwide, cities produce on average 60 per cent of a country's GNP.

The rapid increase of the world's urban population coupled with the slowing of rural population growth has led to a major redistribution of the population over the past 30 years. By 2007, one-half of the world's population will live in urban areas compared to little more than one-third in 1972, and the period 1950 to 2050 will see a shift from a 65 per cent rural population to 65 per cent urban (United Nations Population Division 2001a). By 2002, some 70 per cent of the world's urban population will be living in Africa, Asia or Latin America (UNCHS 2001a).

The most striking current changes are the levels of urbanization in less developed nations: rising from about 27 per cent in 1975 to 40 per cent in 2000 — an increase of more than 1 200 million people (United Nations Population Division 2001b). Furthermore, there is every indication that the trend will continue for the next 30 years, adding 2 000 million people to the urban population of the presently less-developed nations. Within these global averages, there are complex regional differences in urban growth and change. The annual percentage change in the urban population by region shows a general slowing in the rate of urbanization for all regions except North America — see figure below right (United Nations Population Division 2001b).

There has been a dramatic increase in the number

### Distribution of global population (%) by size of settlement, 1975 and 2000

| | rural areas | | <1 million | | 1-5 million | | >5 million | |
|---|---|---|---|---|---|---|---|---|
| | 1975 | 2000 | 1975 | 2000 | 1975 | 2000 | 1975 | 2000 |
| world | 62.1 | 53.0 | 25.1 | 28.5 | 8.0 | 11.6 | 4.8 | 6.9 |
| developed regions | 30.0 | 24.0 | 46.8 | 48.1 | 13.9 | 18.5 | 9.3 | 9.5 |
| developing regions | 73.2 | 60.1 | 17.6 | 23.7 | 6.0 | 10.0 | 3.2 | 6.3 |

Source: United Nations Population Division 2001a

and size of megacities (cities with more than 10 million inhabitants) and urban agglomerations in the second half of the 20th century, as well as a change in the geographical distribution of these cities: in 1900, nine of the ten largest cities were in North America and Europe, whereas today only three (Los Angeles, New York and Tokyo) are located in the developed world. However, most of the world's urban population still lives in small and medium-sized cities (see table) which, in most countries, are now growing faster than the very large cities (United Nations Population Division 2001b).

## Links to the global economy

Globalization has been progressing for decades but under the impact of new information technologies the speed of globalization has quickened and its reach has

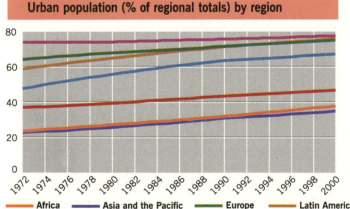

**Urban population (% of regional totals) by region**

Nearly half the world population now lives in urban areas. Africa, and Asia and the Pacific, are the world's least urbanized regions, North America, Europe, and Latin America the most urbanized

Source: compiled from United Nations Population Division 2001b

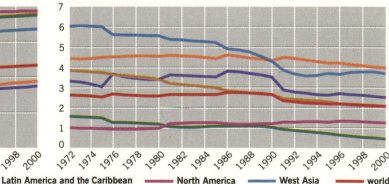

**Annual percentage increase in the urban population**

While all regions are still urbanizing, the rate at which most are doing so is falling, although rates are changing little in Africa and are actually increasing in North America

Source: compiled from United Nations Population Division 2001b

Satellite image of global city lights prepared from a long time series of images of the Earth at night. The Eastern United States, Europe, and Japan are brightly lit by their cities while the interiors of Africa, Asia, Australia and South America remain dark and largely rural

*Source: Mayhew and Simmon 2000*

broadened. These technologies are reinforcing the importance of knowledge and information in economic transformation, while reducing the relative importance of traditional manufacturing and industrial development based on raw materials. In urban areas, this has manifested itself in the growth of the service sector in both absolute and relative terms. Technology has increased the already dominant economic role and importance of urban areas, not just those in the more developed economies but globally (Economist 2000, World Bank 2000), indicating the growing importance of cities in the global economy. In India, software development and related information-communication services is the leading sector for economic growth. This new growth sector — which has grown more rapidly and become internationally more competitive than any of the country's traditional industrial sectors — is concentrated in large urban areas because of the superior infrastructure and educational levels of human resources offered by cities.

In the 1970s, a new phase of globalization started with the deregulation of labour markets, liberalization of financial markets, and privatization of government functions. One of the results was increasing competition for foreign direct investment and employers found themselves able to shift the location of their production facilities more easily, which worsened job and income security in some urban areas but benefited others.

Between the 1970s and mid-1990s, some Asian countries clearly benefited from this development and showed spectacular economic growth and growth in general well-being. However, during 1997–98 the economic crisis in Asia struck not only these economies but also some in other regions. The human impacts of the crisis were severe; poverty in Asia increased and there were massive lay-offs, particularly of women, the young and the unskilled.

The Asian crisis showed that urban areas are highly vulnerable to global economic impacts. Although globalization has often increased opportunities for jobs and knowledge, it has also increased social inequalities and poverty. Benefits are not equally shared, resulting in large groups of people living in slums in developing countries unconnected to water and sanitary services, and unemployment, poor health and social exclusion in the developed world (UNCHS 2001b).

## Urban poverty

Poverty is among the major drivers of environmental degradation. The urban poor, who are unable to compete for scarce resources or protect themselves from harmful environmental conditions, are most affected by the negative impacts of urbanization. The growth of large cities, particularly in developing countries, has been accompanied by an increase in urban poverty which tends to be concentrated in certain social groups and in particular locations. Causes include an increasing gap between incomes and land prices, and the failure of housing markets to provide for low-income groups (UNCHS 2001a).

Land development processes tend to serve middle and higher income classes, forcing the poor to settle (illegally) in high densities on marginal lands within cities or in the urban periphery, sometimes in areas at risk from environmental hazards such as floods and landslides, and without access to basic services such as water and sanitation.

Urban poverty is on the increase. It is estimated that one-quarter of the population lives below the poverty line and that female-headed households are disproportionately affected (UNCHS 2001a). Worldwide, there is a clear correlation between their poverty and lack of control over resources and lack of full citizenship (UNCHS 2001b).

## Urban environment

Urban areas do not have only local environmental impacts but also large so-called 'ecological footprints' (WWF 2000). In their immediate vicinity, cities have a variety of impacts: conversion of agricultural or forest land for urban uses and infrastructure, reclaiming of wetlands, quarrying and excavation of sand, gravel and building materials in large quantities and, in some regions, deforestation to meet fuel demand. The use of biomass fuel also causes indoor and outdoor air pollution. Other effects can be felt further afield such as pollution of waterways, lakes and coastal waters by untreated effluent. Air pollution from cities has an impact on residents' health as well as on vegetation and soils at a considerable distance. Urban transport contributes to air pollution and the large concentration of cars and industries in cities causes the lion's share of urban global greenhouse gas emissions.

Cities are often located in prime agricultural areas. If this land is converted for urban uses, this puts additional pressure on nearby areas that may be less suitable for agriculture. Urbanization in coastal areas often leads to the destruction of sensitive ecosystems and can also alter the hydrology of coasts and their natural features such as mangrove swamps, reefs and beaches that serve as barriers to erosion and form important habitats for species.

Low to medium density residential areas (urban sprawl) around urban centres are common in the developed world. Well developed infrastructure and the increasing use of the car have facilitated this trend. Urban sprawl has an especially damaging effect

---

### Facts about cities

- In cities of the developing world, one out of every four households lives in poverty; 40 per cent of African urban households and 25 per cent of Latin American urban households are living below locally defined poverty lines

- Fewer than 35 per cent of cities in the developing world have their wastewater treated

- Between one-third and one-half of the solid wastes generated within most cities in low and middle income countries are not collected

- 49 per cent of the world's cities have established urban environmental plans

- 60 per cent of the world's cities involve civil society in a formal participatory process prior to the implementation of major public projects

- Buses and minibuses are the most common (used by most people) mode of transport in cities; cars are the second most common and walking the third

- 5.8 per cent of children in cities of the developing world die before reaching the age of five years

- some 75 per cent of the world's countries have constitutions or national laws that promote the full and progressive realization of the right to adequate housing

- One out of every four countries in the developing world has constitutions or national laws which prevent women from owning land and/or taking mortgages in their own names

- 29 per cent of cities in the developing world have areas considered as inaccessible or dangerous to the police

Sources: GUO 2001 and Panos 2001

---

### The ecological footprints of cities

An ecological footprint is the area of productive land and aquatic ecosystems required to produce the resources used, and to assimilate the wastes produced, by a defined population at a specified material standard of living, wherever that land may be located.

London Trust Co-founder Herbert Girardet has calculated that the ecological footprint of London — with 12 per cent of the UK population and covering just 170 000 ha — comes to some 21 million ha or 125 times the surface area of the city itself, equivalent to all the productive land in the United Kingdom.

William Rees — Professor of Community and Regional Planning at the University of British Columbia — has made an ecological footprint analysis of his home city of Vancouver, Canada. This indicates that Vancouver appropriates the productive output of a land area nearly 174 times larger than its political area to support its lifestyle. Other researchers have found that the aggregate consumption of wood, paper, fibre and food by the inhabitants of 29 cities in the Baltic Sea drainage basin appropriates an area 200 times larger than the cities themselves.

Scientists have calculated that a typical North American city with a population of 650 000 people would require 30 000 $km^2$ of land, an area roughly the size of Vancouver Island in Canada, to meet its domestic needs without including the environmental demands of industry. A similarly sized city in India would require only 2 900 $km^2$.

Sources: Global Vision 2001 and Rees 1996

on the environment associated with the increase in use of private motorized transport. Furthermore, low density development occupies proportionally larger areas of land per capita.

Water is a key issue in urban areas. The intensity of demand in cities can quickly exceed local supply. The price of water is typically lower than the actual cost of obtaining, treating and distributing it, partly because of government subsidies. As a result, households and industries have little incentive to

contaminated land management (Butler 1996). Another problem emerging in developed countries is the lack of suitable landfill sites to cater for the increasing demand for solid waste disposal.

Worsening environmental conditions can have serious effects on human health and welfare, particularly for the poor (Hardoy, Mitlin and Satterthwaite 1992). Poor sanitation creates environmental and health hazards particularly by direct exposure to faeces and drinking water

**Population of selected major cities of the world by region (millions)**

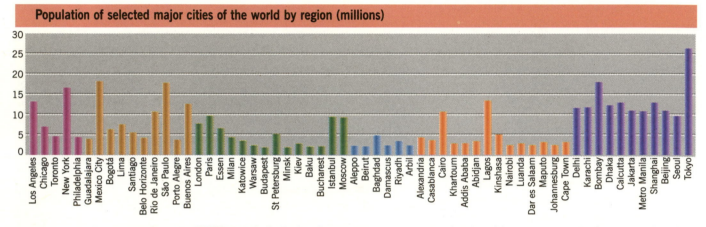

Ten of the world's megacities are in Asia and the Pacific — Tokyo, with more than 26 million inhabitants, is currently the world's largest city

*Source: United Nations Population Division 2001a*

conserve water (UNEP 2000). Pollution from urban run-off, sewage and untreated discharges of industries has adversely affected many water bodies, leaving many cities with unsafe water supply.

Although local environmental problems tend to diminish with increasing income levels, other environmental problems tend to become worse (McGranahan and others 2001). The most obvious are high levels of energy use and increasing levels of consumption and waste production. Urban residents rely heavily on fossil fuels and electricity, and wealthy cities tend to use more energy and produce more waste.

Inadequate waste collection and waste management systems are the cause of serious urban pollution and health hazards, especially in cities in developing countries. Cities in industrialized countries are now also facing the consequences of past environmentally damaging production techniques and inadequate waste disposal. This has resulted in many different forms of pollution and in particular the formation of brownfields: abandoned, vacant or underused former industrial areas where redevelopment is hampered by environmental problems and lack of adequate information on

contamination. Air and water pollution cause chronic and infectious respiratory disease, water-borne diseases such as diarrhoea and intestinal worm infections, increased mortality rates particularly among children and premature deaths — especially among the poor (OECD-DAC 2000, Listorti 1999, Satterthwaite 1997, McGranahan 1993, Hardoy, Cairncross and Satterthwaite 1990). However, worldwide epidemiological and demographic information suggests that survival rates are better in cities than in rural areas because of better access to health services (UNCHS 2001b). The urban poor are particularly exposed because of their location and because they have limited resources with which to compensate for these problems by buying potable water, securing medical care or escaping floods.

There are many other less quantifiable but nonetheless important environmental impacts, such as loss of green space in urban areas, destruction of special local ecosystems, noise pollution, and aesthetically unpleasant sights and smells. These not only constitute a genuine loss of well-being but they can also erode civic pride and lower morale, leading to indifference and cynicism locally and to a negative image externally.

The relatively disproportionate urban environmental footprint is acceptable to a certain extent because, for some issues, the per capita environmental impact of cities is smaller than would be made by a similar number of people in a rural setting. Cities concentrate populations in a way that reduces land pressure and provides economies of scale and proximity of infrastructure and services (Hardoy, Mitlin and Satterthwaite 2001). Urban areas therefore hold promise for sustainable development because of their ability to support a large number of people while limiting their per capita impact on the natural environment (UNCHS 2001b).

Environmental problems occur because of the concentration of environmentally negative impacts. Good urban planning can reduce these impacts. Well-planned, densely populated settlements can reduce the need for land conversion, provide opportunities for energy savings and make recycling more cost-effective. If cities are properly managed, with adequate attention paid to social development and the environment, the problems present as a result of rapid urbanization, particularly in developing regions, can be avoided. A first step in this direction would be for national governments to incorporate a clear urban component in their economic and other policies.

Successes in urban environmental management include increases in resource efficiency, reductions in waste generation, improving urban infrastructure for water supply, the management and conservation of water resources in urban areas by improved waste water treatment and through legislation, setting up of recycling schemes, development of more effective waste collection systems, strict legislation for the treatment of hazardous waste, waste collection through public-private partnership, adoption of energy technologies by industry and households, and restoration of brownfields.

## Urban governance

Many urban environmental problems are the result of poor management, poor planning and absence of coherent urban policies rather than of urbanization itself. Through experience, it has been learned that no amount of finance, technology or expertise can secure environmentally sustainable development — or protect the environment — if the fundamentals of governance are not participatory, democratic and pluralistic. For example, many developing countries

**Young boys sifting through waste on a dump outside a city in Viet Nam**

Source: UNEP, Thiyen Nguyen, Viet Nam, Still Pictures

### Nairobi's garbage

The Dandora garbage dump in Nairobi provides a livelihood for many scavengers. In 1992 Father Alex Zanoteteli started the Mukuru Recycling Centre, helping the scavengers work together to collect different types of garbage more efficiently and sell to middlemen for better prices. The project now has 140 members and with the help of Habitat's Settlements, Infrastructure and Environment Programme has organized itself into a cooperative, with several different projects. One buys waste from individual scavengers, sorts it and sells it to recycling industries — in addition to running a dairy project. Another gathers waste from commercial buildings in the city; it earns small fees for cleaning up the commercial buildings and income from selling the waste to paper and other recycling industries. A third manufactures fuel briquettes from paper and other waste such as sawdust and coffee husks. A fourth manufactures compost from organic waste. The centre is about to establish a facility for recycling plastic.

Source: Panos 2001

## The rise of urban farming

Growing food in and around cities has become a major industry, vital to the well-being of millions of poor and some not-so-poor urban residents. It is estimated that 15 per cent of all the food consumed in urban areas is grown by urban farmers and that this percentage will double within 20 years. Some 800 million people are estimated to be involved in urban farming worldwide (see 'Land'). The following examples from different regions illustrate the potential of urban agriculture.

### Africa

The cultivation of food crops is economically significant in many African urban areas, where city dwellers pay 10 to 30 per cent more for their food than do rural inhabitants. In Kenya and Tanzania, two out of three urban families engage in farming, and nearly every open space, utility service reserve, road, valley or garden in the towns has been taken up for crop planting. In Cairo, one-quarter of all households raise small livestock which provide 60 per cent of household incomes.

Women play a vital role in urban agriculture, many of whom engage in cultivation as a survival strategy. This process of the 'ruralization' of African cities is not a consequence of mass rural-urban migration but is a response to fluctuations in the economies of developing countries' cities. Urban cultivation is not practised exclusively or even primarily by recent migrants. Most farmers originate from poor households that are fully entrenched in the urban economy.

### Latin America and the Caribbean

Every available space — including roofs and balconies — has been given over to urban food production in Cuba's capital, Havana. Intensive urban farming methods including hydroponics help secure fresh food for urban dwellers. The city council facilitates the integrated management of wastewater for food production.

Regional standards for wastewater treatment are developed by the Pan American Centre for Sanitary Engineering and Environment Sciences in Lima, Peru. Systems of wastewater management and re-use at different levels of purity, from woodlots to aquaculture, are promoted and utilized in several countries in the region.

### Europe

Some 72 per cent of all urban households in the Russian Federation raise food, and Berlin has more than 80 000 urban farmers. The St Petersburg Urban Gardening Club has become famous for its promotion of roof top gardening. Its research shows that in just one district (St Petersburg has 12) it is possible to grow 2 000 tonnes of vegetables per season from 500 roof tops. Many crops are grown including radishes, lettuce, onions, cucumbers, tomatoes, cabbage, peas, beets, beans and flowers. The growth of chicory for salads is encouraged as a source of vitamins in the winter. Rooftop gardening is popular because the gardens are secure and cannot be attacked by vandals. The St Petersburg Urban Gardening Club publishes books and has its own web site.

*Source: UNCHS 2001a and 2001b*

The past 30 years have seen significant political change with profound implications for urban areas and for the urban and global environment. These include:

- the collapse of central planning;
- the extension of democracy;
- decentralization and demands for empowerment and self-determination;
- increasing pluralism in politics and society; and
- pressures for participation, accountability and transparency in government.

These trends appear to be strengthening, reinforced by globalization and especially by the impact of freer and faster flows of information and knowledge.

Efforts to improve urban governance involve activities such as promoting participatory processes; developing effective partnerships with and among all actors of civil society, particularly the private and community sectors; securing greater effective empowerment of local government, including greater autonomy in finance and legislation; and reform of unresponsive organizations and bureaucratic structures.

They also involve city-to-city cooperation and exchange of experiences and lessons learned. The International Council for Local Environmental Initiatives works with 286 local governments in 43 countries to improve local energy management and reduce greenhouse gas emissions (Skinner 2000). Initiatives such as the Stockholm Partnership for Sustainable Cities have been developed to introduce sustainability into city planning through partnership between cities and business. Habitat's Local Agenda 21 initiatives have been proved effective in implementing sustainable development policies that involve community members and government (Tuts and Cody 2000).

Because of the importance of specific local circumstances and political realities, there is no viable approach to solving urban environmental problems that can be applied in every city. A first step is to develop a local environmental agenda to assess the local situation regarding environmental issues so that this information can be used in city planning. Whereas the emphasis in 1970 was largely focused on public policy and regulation, the focus of the early 1990s was on markets and technical solutions. At the turn of the century, urban environmental management appears to

have extensive regulations on pollution, most of which are seldom if ever applied effectively because of the lack of proper institutions, legal systems, political will and competent governance (Hardoy, Mitlin and Satterthwaite 2001). Unfortunately, particularly where economic and social change is rapid, established political and administrative institutions have proved highly resistant to change.

be focusing more on changing cultures — corporate, economic and political (Elkington 1999).

## Conclusion

Given the expected scale of urban population growth in the coming decades, continued growth in the number of urban poor will pose a fundamental challenge for global sustainability (Environment and Urbanization 1995a and 1995b, Pearce and Warford 1993). A major concern is the development of megacities and large urban areas in the developing world, because of the speed and scale of urbanization and the incapacity of these cities to provide sufficient housing and basic urban services.

Improved urban environmental management could help avoid many negative environmental impacts, particularly if governments adopt clear urban policies as an integral part of their economic policies. However, urban growth is not yet well managed in most of the rapidly urbanizing areas, and this leads to major environmental and health problems, mainly associated with poverty.

Urbanization will continue to play a major role in the economy, environment and people's lives. The challenge is to learn how to live with urbanization while using its benefits and guiding undesirable and negative impacts in manageable directions.

## References: Chapter 2, urban areas, global overview

Butler, B. E. (1996). Consultation with national experts: managing contaminated land. *UNEP Industry and Environment*, 19, 2

Economist (2000). Internet Economics: a Thinker's Guide. *The Economist*, 1 April, 64-66

Elkington, J. (1999). The Next Wave. *Tomorrow – Global Environment Business Magazine*, 6

Environment and Urbanization (1995a). Urban Poverty I: Characteristics, Causes and Consequences, *Environment and Urbanization - Special Issue*, 7, 1

Environment and Urbanization (1995b). Urban Poverty II: From Understanding to Action, *Environment and Urbanization, Special Issue*, 7, 2

Global Vision (2001). Sustainable City http://www.global-vision.org/city/footprint.html [Geo-2-201]

GUO (2000). *Monitoring the Implementation of the Habitat Agenda*. The Global Urban Observatory. Nairobi, United Nations Centre for Human Settlements (Habitat)

Hardoy, J. E., Cairncross, S. and Satterthwaite, D. (eds., 1990). *The Poor Die Young: Housing and Health in Third World Cities*. London, Earthscan

Hardoy, J.E., Mitlin, D. and Satterthwaite, D. (2001). *Environmental Problems in an Urbanizing World*. London, Earthscan

Hardoy, J. E., Mitlin, D. and Satterthwaite, D. (1992). *Environmental Problems in Third World Cities*. London, Earthscan

Listorti, J. A. (1999). Is environmental health really a part of economic development – or only an afterthought? *Environment and Urbanization*, 11, 1

Mayhew, C., and Simmon, R. (2001). *Global City Lights*. NASA GSFC, based on data from the US Defense Meteorological Satellite Program http://photojournal.jpl.nasa.gov/cgi-bin/PIAGenCatalogPage.pl?PIA02991 [Geo-2-202]

McGranahan, G. (1993). Household environmental problems in low-income cities: an overview of problems and prospects for improvement. *Habitat International*, 17, 2, 105-121

McGranahan, G., Jacobi, P., Songore, J., Surjadi C. and Kjellen, M. (2001). *The Cities at Risk: From Urban Sanitation to Sustainable Cities*. London, Earthscan

OECD-DAC (2000). *Shaping the Urban Environment in the 21st Century: From Understanding to Action, A DAC Reference Manual on Urban Environmental Policy*. Paris, Organization for Economic Cooperation and Development

Panos (2001). *Governing our Cities: will people power work?* London, Panos Institute

Pearce, D. W. and Warford, J.J. (1993). *World without End: Economics, Environment and Sustainable Development*. New York and Oxford, Oxford University Press for the World Bank

Rees, W. (1996). Revisiting Carrying Capacity: Area-Based Indicators of Sustainability. *Population and Environment: a Journal of Interdisciplinary Studies*, 17, 2, January 1996

Satterthwaite, D. (1997). Sustainable cities or cities that contribute to sustainable development? *Urban Studies*, 34, 10, 1667-1691

Skinner, N. (2000). Energy management in practice: communities acting to protect the climate. *UNEP Industry and Environment* 23, 2, 43-48

Tuts, R. and Cody, E. (2000). Habitat's experience in Local Agenda 21 worldwide over the last ten years: approaches and lessons learned. *UNEP Industry and Environment*, 23, 2, 12-15

UNCHS (2001a). *Cities in a Globalizing World: Global Report on Human Settlements 2001*. London, Earthscan

UNCHS (2001b). *State of the World's Cities 2001*. Nairobi, United Nations Centre for Human Settlements (Habitat)

UNEP (2000). The urban environment: facts and figures. *UNEP Industry and Environment*, 23, 2, 4-11

United Nations Population Division (2001a). *World Urbanization Prospects: The 1999 Revision. Key Findings*. United Nations Population Division. http://www.un.org/esa/population/pubsarchive/urbanization/urbanization.pdf [Geo-2-203]

United Nations Population Division (2001b). *World Population Prospects 1950-2050 (The 2000 Revision)*. New York, United Nations www.un.org/esa/population/publications/wpp2000/wpp2000h.pdf [Geo-2-204]

World Bank (2000). *Entering the 21st Century: World Development Report 1999/2000*. New York, Oxford University Press

WWF (2000). Living Planet Report 2000 http://www.panda.org/livingplanet/lpr00 [Geo-2-250]

## Urban areas: Africa

While the majority (62.1 per cent ) of the African population is still rural, urban growth rates at nearly 4 per cent a year are the most rapid in the world, and nearly twice the global average (United Nations Population Division 2001). Growth rates are predicted to average 3.5 per cent per year over the next 15 years, meaning that Africa's share of the world's urban population will increase from 10 to 17 per cent between 2000 and 2015 (United Nations Population Division 2001).

North Africa is the most urbanized sub-region with an average urban population of 54 per cent, followed by West Africa (40 per cent), Southern Africa (39 per cent), Central Africa (36 per cent) and the Western Indian Ocean islands (32 per cent). The least urbanized sub-region is Eastern Africa with only 23 per cent of the population living in urban areas (United Nations Population Division 2001). Malawi has the highest urban growth rate of any country in Africa, which at 6.3 per cent is three times the world rate.

Not only are there more people living in cities but the cities themselves are becoming larger, and more numerous. There are now 43 cities in Africa with populations of more than one million inhabitants, a figure which is expected to increase to almost 70 by 2015 (United Nations Population Division 2001).

Africa's high urban growth rate is a result of rural-urban migration, population growth and, in some areas, conflict. People leave rural areas because of declining agricultural productivity, lack of employment opportunities and lack of access to basic physical and social infrastructure. The expectation of higher

incomes and standards of living in urban areas is seldom realized, however, and urban poverty is widespread and growing. In Moroni, Comoros, 40 per cent of the population lives in poverty (RFIC 1997), and in Southern Africa up to 45 per cent of urban households grow crops or raise livestock in urban environments in order to supplement their livelihoods (UNDP 1996). Environmental disasters and conflicts have also caused many people to flee rural areas and seek refuge in urban centres. In Mozambique, about 4.5 million rural people were displaced to urban areas due to civil strife in the 1980s (Chenje 2000), while the third largest settlement in Sierra Leone is a displaced persons camp (UNCHS 2001b).

Because of slow economic growth in many African countries, lack of sound development policies and an increasing number of small households, infrastructure development has been unable to keep pace with the burgeoning need for shelter and services for growing urban populations. As a result, many African cities have an increasing number of overcrowded, informal settlements, or 'shanty towns', characterized by inadequate housing and poor provision of infrastructure such as roads, street lights, water supplies, sanitation and waste management services. Often these settlements are developed on fragile environments such as steep slopes, natural drainage waterways and flood-prone areas. Inadequate housing and settlement design can also contribute to declining security and increasing levels of crime in African cities (Shaw and Louw 1998).

Governments and authorities have attempted to meet the demand for housing and services through increased construction. South Africa, for example, has

*Graph below shows growth of urban populations in the African sub-regions since 1972; the map shows current level of urbanization as a percentage of total population*

*Source: compiled from United Nations Population Division 2001*

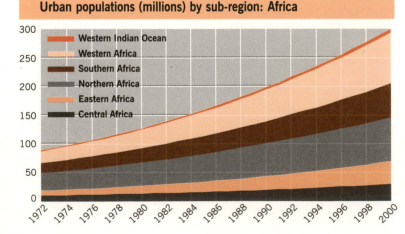

**Urban populations (millions) by sub-region: Africa**

Western Indian Ocean
Western Africa
Southern Africa
Northern Africa
Eastern Africa
Central Africa

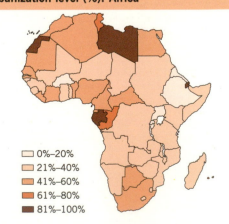

**Urbanization level (%): Africa**

☐ 0%–20%
☐ 21%–40%
☐ 41%–60%
☐ 61%–80%
☐ 81%–100%

produced more than one million low-cost houses during the past six years (DoH South Africa 2000). However, lack of awareness of resource-efficient construction practices has resulted in excessive use of natural resources and generation of large amounts of construction waste that is rarely recycled (Macozoma 2000). In addition, new settlements have mostly been on open land on the urban periphery rather than on little used land within the cities, thus requiring expansion of infrastructure rather than more intensive use of existing networks. Attention is now shifting to integrated development planning, and housing policies that support environmentally sustainable housing have been developed in some countries.

Key environmental issues in urban areas in Africa are related to the provision of services for waste, water and sanitation, and urban air pollution.

## Waste services, water supply and sanitation

The volume of solid waste generated in urban areas is increasing with the growing population, higher consumption levels and the use of more packaging in the retail industry. Rates of waste generation are outstripping the capacities of local authorities to collect, treat and dispose of waste. Across Africa, only 31 per cent of solid wastes in urban areas are collected

(UNCHS 2001b). Inadequate urban infrastructure leads to untreated waste and waste remaining uncollected or improperly disposed of. In Accra, for example, although there is a system of collection from waste points in most residential areas, collection is erratic and legal intermediary dumps overflow (McGranahan and others 2001). Burning of solid waste is common in many countries but the toxic fumes thus released contribute to air pollution. Only 2 per cent of African waste is recovered and recycled (UNCHS 2001b) due to lack of economic incentives and markets for recycled materials. The most commonly recycled materials are paper, textiles, glass, plastic and metal. Composting is carried out to some extent in Egypt, Morocco and Tunisia.

The proliferation of unplanned settlements in the urban areas of Africa has been accompanied by inadequate provision of potable water and sanitation. On average, 85 per cent of African urban populations had access to improved water sources in the year 2000, although this ranged from 100 per cent in Botswana, Djibouti, Mauritius, Morocco and Namibia, to just 29 per cent in Guinea-Bissau and 31 per cent in Chad (WHO and UNICEF 2000). The average urban population with access to improved sanitation was 84 per cent, ranging from 100 per cent in Mauritius and Morocco to 12 per cent in Rwanda and 14 per cent in Congo (WHO and UNICEF 2000). The numbers of people with these services have increased over the past 10 years (see bar chart below) but the percentages have hardly changed.

In order to improve the performance of municipal governments and public utilities, public-private partnerships are being increasingly promoted to provide water management and sanitation services.

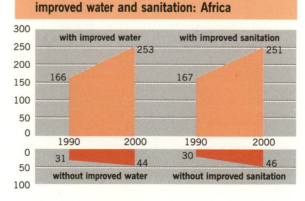

**Urban population (millions) with and without improved water and sanitation: Africa**

| | with improved water | with improved sanitation |
|---|---|---|
| 1990 | 166 | 167 |
| 2000 | 253 | 251 |
| | without improved water | without improved sanitation |
| 1990 | 31 | 30 |
| 2000 | 44 | 46 |

Some 85 per cent of urban Africans now have improved water and sanitation

*Source: WHO and UNICEF 2000*

The use of traditional fuels in dense informal settlements is leading to damaging levels of air pollution, particularly harmful to children

*Source: UNEP, Dilmar Cavalher, Topham Picturepoint*

These partnerships have met with mixed success. While private participation in water supply and sanitation services brings in new investment capital, management and organizational skills, and technical know-how, there is a perceived bias towards meeting the demands of upper and middle-income groups.

## Air pollution

A growing concern in many urban centres, particularly large cities, is the level of air pollution, mainly from vehicle exhausts, industrial emissions, and domestic use of woodfuel, coal, paraffin and refuse for heating and cooking. In Cairo, fumes from the 1.2 million vehicles, combined with suspended particulate matter and sand blown into urban areas from the neighbouring desert create an almost permanent haze over the city. Levels of suspended particulate matter

and lead pollution are among the highest in the world, creating a high risk of respiratory disorders to the 10.6 million inhabitants (UNCHS 1996, SEI 1999). In recognition of this risk, only unleaded fuel is now sold in Cairo, and the rest of the country is expected to follow suit by the end of 2002.

In dense, informal settlements, the use of traditional fuel sources contributes to rising ambient levels of sulphur dioxide, nitrogen oxides, carbon monoxide, ozone and suspended particulate matter. Exposure to these pollutants is associated with increased risk of acute respiratory infections, particularly among children. Electrification of households, promotion of low-smoke fuels, and improved ventilation of houses are some of the measures that have been adopted to reduce health risks.

### References: Chapter 2, urban areas, Africa

Chenje, M. (ed.) (2000). *State of the Environment Zambezi Basin 2000*. Maseru, Lusaka and Harare, SADC, IUCN, ZRA and SARDC

DoH South Africa (2000). *South African Country Report to the Special Session of the United Nations General Assembly for the Review of the Implementation of the Habitat Agenda*. Pretoria, Department of Housing

Everatt, D. (1999). *Yet Another Transition? Urbanization, Class Formation, and the End of National Liberation Struggle in South Africa*. Washington DC, Woodrow Wilson International Centre for Scholars

Macozoma, D. (2000). *Strategies for the Management of Construction Waste*. In Proceedings of The Institute of Waste Management Biennial Conference and Exhibition. 5-7 September 2000, Somerset West, South Africa

McGranahan, G., Jacobi, P., Songore, J., Surjadi C. and Kjellen, M. (2001). *The Cities at Risk: From Urban Sanitation to Sustainable Cities*. London, Earthscan

RFIC (1997). *Plan de Développement Urbain de Moroni. Document de Synthèse*. Mohéli, Comores, Ministère de l'aménagement du territoire, de l'urbanisme et du logement

SEI (1999). *Regional Air Pollution in Developing Countries (RAPIDC) Newsletter*, No 2, June 1999. York, United Kingdom, Stockholm Environment Institute

Shaw and Louw (1998). *Environmental Design for Safer Communities: Preventing Crime in South Africa's Cities And Towns*. ISS Monograph Series No. 24. Pretoria, Institute for Security Studies http://www.iss.co.za/Pubs/Monographs/No24/Contents.html [Geo-2-251]

UNCHS (1996). *An Urbanizing World: Global Report on Human Settlements 1996*. New York and Oxford, Oxford University Press

UNCHS (2001a). *Cities in a Globalizing World: Global Report on Human Settlements 2001*. London, Earthscan

UNCHS (2001b). *State of the World's Cities 2001*. Nairobi, United Nations Centre for Human Settlements (Habitat)

UNDP (1996). *Balancing Rocks: Environment and Development in Zimbabwe*. Harare, United Nations Development Programme

United Nations Population Division (2001). *World Urbanization Prospects: The 1999 Revision. Key Findings*. United Nations Population Division. http://www.un.org/esa/population/pubsarchive/urbanization/urbanization.pdf [Geo-2-203]

WHO and UNICEF (2000). *Global Water Supply and Sanitation Assessment 2000 Report*. Geneva, World Health Organization and United Nations Children's Fund http://www.who.int/water_sanitation_health/Globassessment/GlobalTOC.htm

## Urban areas: Asia and the Pacific

Urbanization in Asia and the Pacific is predicted to grow at an average rate of 2.4 per cent per annum between 2001 and 2015. The current level of urbanization ranges from a low of 7.1 per cent in Bhutan to 100 per cent in Singapore and Nauru. Australia and New Zealand is the most urbanized sub-region (85 per cent) and South Pacific the least (26.4 per cent). In seven countries in the region (Australia, Japan, Nauru, New Caledonia, New Zealand, Republic of Korea and Singapore) the level of urbanization is more than 75 per cent, while the 12 megacities in the region — Beijing, Calcutta, Delhi, Dhaka, Jakarta, Karachi, Metro Manila, Mumbai, Osaka, Seoul, Shanghai and Tokyo — accommodate 12 per cent of the urban population (United Nations Population Division 2001 and UNESCAP and ADB 2000).

In some of the larger cities, excluding those in Australia and New Zealand, up to 60 per cent of the inhabitants live in informal settlements, with a population density of up to 2 500 persons per hectare (Ansari 1997). These settlements suffer from a lack of infrastructure and services such as water supplies, sewerage, drainage, roads, health care and education.

The major urban environmental issues in the region are air pollution and inadequate services.

### Urban air pollution

Air pollution is common, particularly in developing country cities, due to the growing number of motor vehicles and increasing industrial activity. In countries such as India, Indonesia, Nepal, Malaysia and Thailand vehicles with two-stroke engines, such as motorcycles and three-wheel taxis, comprise more than one-half of all motor traffic and pollute heavily. Poor maintenance of vehicles, poor fuel quality and poor road conditions also contribute. The burning of biomass such as firewood and agricultural wastes is a further source of air pollution in many poor areas (World Bank 2000).

Motor vehicles cause serious environmental problems in developed countries as well. In Australia and New Zealand, there is a high dependence on private motor vehicles which leads not only to the need to clear land for roads but also to increasing emissions of carbon dioxide, lead, zinc and copper (Hughes and Pugsley 1998, MoE New Zealand 1997).

A range of policy measures and technologies including catalytic converters, unleaded fuel and alternative fuels such as compressed natural gas are being introduced to improve the quality of urban air. New coal-fired power plants in many Asian countries now use electrostatic precipitators which can reduce emissions of particulates by more than 99 per cent. Subsidies are provided for the use of renewable technologies such as wind turbines and solar photovoltaics. In China, the city of Beijing has implemented 68 atmospheric pollution prevention measures which are resulting in significant reductions in $SO_2$, $NO_2$ and SPM levels (SEPA 1999).

### Waste management

Much of the solid waste generated in urban centres remains uncollected and is either deposited in surface waters and empty lots, or burned in streets. This problem has worsened over the past 30 years. Collected waste is mainly disposed of in open dumps, many of which are neither properly operated nor

Graph and map show high level of urbanization in Australia and New Zealand compared with other sub-regions. Urbanization is proceeding fast in all other sub-regions except Central Asia

*Source: compiled from United Nations Population Division 2001*

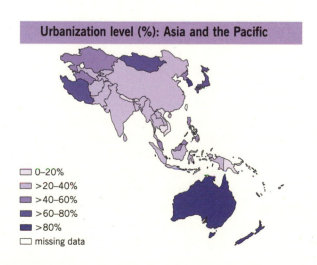

**Urbanization level (%): Asia and the Pacific**

- ☐ 0–20%
- ☐ >20–40%
- ☐ >40–60%
- ☐ >60–80%
- ☐ >80%
- ☐ missing data

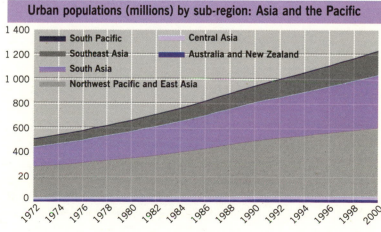

**Urban populations (millions) by sub-region: Asia and the Pacific**

- South Pacific
- Southeast Asia
- South Asia
- Northwest Pacific and East Asia
- Central Asia
- Australia and New Zealand

maintained, and which pose a serious threat to public health. Only a few Asian cities such as Hong Kong and Singapore, and those in Australia, Japan and New Zealand, have adequate solid waste disposal facilities but even these cities have problems in dealing with increasing volumes of waste (ADB 2001).

In the mid-1990s, Metro Manila generated 6 300 tonnes of solid waste daily but its landfills could accommodate only a little more than half that amount (ADB 1996). The island of Kiribati has severe population density problems caused by internal migration and has little land for waste disposal. As on many atoll islands, solid waste is discharged into coastal waters.

Serious health and environmental problems can be caused by poor waste disposal. In the Pacific Islands, freshwater is scarce, and solid waste disposal methods that contaminate water are frequently a source of intestinal diseases and ear and eye infections. In India, an outbreak of bubonic plague in 1994 was linked to inadequate solid waste disposal (Tysmans 1996).

The disposal and treatment of industrial, toxic and hazardous waste also causes serious problems. Dumping of hazardous waste is common in South and Southeast Asia. Countries such as Bangladesh, India and Pakistan have become dumping grounds for significant quantities of hazardous waste from industrialized countries, and are facing growing protests about waste-related pollution.

A large number of stakeholders are involved in national waste management policies and strategies. Waste management services have been privatized in

### Sustainable commuting in Singapore

With a total land area of 650 km$^2$ and a population of 4.1 million, Singapore faced serious challenges of limited space and high population density when designing its transit system. A combination of buses, mass rapid transit (MRT) lines, light rapid transit lines and taxis, Singapore's public transportation system currently supports about 5 million of the total 7 million trips made every day, with 3 million on buses, 1 million on the MRT and another 1 million in taxis.

Singapore has implemented a strict vehicle quota system, under which a certificate must be acquired before registering a vehicle. This allows the government to restrict the increase in vehicle numbers. An electronic road pricing system charges a fee to cars during peak hours, encouraging motorists to use public transportation or less busy roads. Vehicle inspection centres carry out mandatory testing of cars more than three years old and exhaust emissions to ensure they meet the limits set by the Ministry of Environment. The government has also introduced tax incentives to encourage the use of electric and hybrid vehicles.

*Source: Swee Say 2001*

countries such as Japan, the Republic of Korea, Malaysia and Thailand. This appears to be an effective means of improving these services, while providing additional employment. However, much waste is generated by small producers, who are difficult to service with traditional methods.

## Water and sanitation

For most cities, providing an adequate and safe supply of water for domestic and industrial uses is a major problem. In spite of significant investments, the sewage systems in many major cities still cannot support a high-density urban environment with the result that sewage is often discharged directly to drains or waterways, or disposed of in individual septic tanks that are poorly maintained.

Afghanistan has by far the lowest percentage of urban population with access to improved water sources (19 per cent) and sanitation (25 per cent) in the region. However, in absolute terms China and India have by far the largest number of urban people (more than 20 million each) without access to a safe water supply (WHO and UNICEF 2000).

Sanitation services are less developed than water supply, with 23 per cent of urban residents still lacking adequate sanitation (compared to only 7 per cent lacking access to improved water sources). These figures are compiled from the sample of 38 Asian and

By the year 2000, improved water supplies had been provided to a larger proportion of the urban population (95 per cent) than had improved sanitation (65 per cent)

*Note: data are available for many more countries in 2000 than in 1990 so the improvement appears exaggerated*

*Source: compiled from WHO and UNICEF 2000*

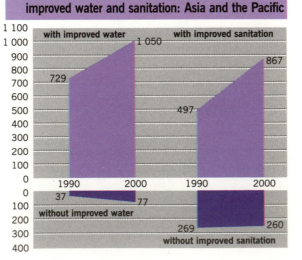

**Urban population (millions) with and without improved water and sanitation: Asia and the Pacific**

with improved water — 1990: 729, 2000: 1 050
with improved sanitation — 1990: 497, 2000: 867
without improved water — 1990: 37, 2000: 77
without improved sanitation — 1990: 269, 2000: 260

Pacific countries for which statistics are available for the year 2000 (WHO and UNICEF 2000). More than 50 per cent of the urban population in Afghanistan and Mongolia still have no access to improved sanitation.

Another major urban environmental issue is flooding and land subsidence. For example, in Bangkok monsoon run-off frequently exceeds the Chao Phraya river drainage capacity — a problem exacerbated by the progressive filling of the 'khlongs' (canals) as urban areas expand. Furthermore, excessive groundwater extraction has produced remarkable land subsidence in Bangkok. Land subsidence increases the probability and worsens the impacts of flooding. Similar conditions are reported in other river basins (ADB 2001).

## Addressing urban environmental problems

Several governments are promoting decentralized and participatory development to help mobilize resources for improving urban infrastructure. However, the process of decentralization is severely constrained by a lack of institutional capacity among local governments, limited resource mobilization at the local level, and limited access to long-term financing for investment programmes (World Bank 1998). Although decentralization and local autonomy are gaining more momentum, excessive controls are still exercised by higher levels of governments resulting in

a mismatch between the responsibilities of local governments and their resources (UNCHS 2001).

In addition to national actions, international and regional programmes have been developed to support urban environmental management in the region. These include the Regional Action Plan on Urbanization, Asia-Pacific Initiative 2000, Land Management Programme, the Local Leadership and Management Training Programme, and Action Planning for Sustainable Urban Development (Local Agenda 21).

Urbanization is one of the most significant issues facing Asia and the Pacific. Uncontrolled growth, inappropriate waste disposal practices, lack of adequate drinking water supply and sanitation facilities, flooding and land subsidence are crucial issues facing urban areas today. In response, investment in domestic wastewater systems, solid waste management schemes, and water supply schemes have been accelerated in many countries. Urban areas offer opportunities for employment, better education and health facilities but they find it increasingly difficult to provide the physical infrastructure required for adequate services to underpin human health and well-being.

### References: Chapter 2, urban areas, Asia and the Pacific

ADB (1996). *Megacity Management in the Asian and Pacific Region*. Manila, Asian Development Bank

ADB (2001). *Asian Environment Outlook 2001*. Manila, Asian Development Bank

Ansari, J.H. (1997). Floods: Can Land Use Planning Help? *Journal of the Institute of Town Planners, India,* Vol.16, No.1 (171), 4-6

Hughes, P. and Pugsley, C. (1998). *The Cities and Their People: New Zealand's Urban Environment*. Wellington, Office of the Parliamentary Commissioner for the Environment

MoE New Zealand (1997). *The State of New Zealand's Environment 1997*. Wellington, Ministry for the Environment

SEPA (1999). *Report on the State of the Environment in China 1999*. State Environmental Protection Administration http://www.sepa.gov.cn/soechina99/air/air.htm [Geo-2-207]

Swee Say, L. (2001). Transport and Energy. Commuting Sustainably. *Our Planet,* 12, 1 http://www.ourplanet.com/imgversn/121/say.html [Geo-2-208]

Tysmans, J. B. (1996). *Plague in India 1994 – Conditions, Containment, Goals*. University of North Carolina http://www.unc.edu/depts/ucis/pubs/carolina/Plague.html#policy [Geo-2-209]

UNCHS (2001). *State of the World's Cities 2001*. Nairobi, United Nations Centre for Human Settlements (Habitat)

UNESCAP and ADB (2000). State of the Environment in Asia and Pacific 2000. Economic and Social Commission for Asia and the Pacific and Asian Development Bank. New York, United Nations http://www.unescap.org/enrd/environ/soe.htm [Geo-2-266]

United Nations Population Division (2001). *World Urbanization Prospects: The 1999 Revision. Key Findings*. United Nations Population Division. http://www.un.org/esa/population/pubsarchive/urbanization/urbanization.pdf [Geo-2-203]

WHO and UNICEF (2000). *Global Water Supply and Sanitation Assessment 2000 Report*. Geneva, World Health Organization and United Nations Children's Fund http://www.who.int/water_sanitation_health/Globassessment/Global7-2.htm [Geo-2-210]

World Bank (1998). *Building Institutions and Financing Local Development: Lessons from Brazil and the Philippines*. Impact Evaluation Report No.18727: Philippines, Brazil. Washington DC, World Bank

World Bank (2000). *Indoor Air Pollution Energy and Health for the Poor. Issue No 1*. Washington DC, World Bank

## Urban areas: Europe

In Europe, the urban population increased steadily throughout the 1960s and 1970s and there was also a massive outflow from the inner cities to the suburbs. Since the 1970s, the trend has been a continued 'sprawling' of cities due to expanding infrastructure, higher household income, diminishing size and increasing number of households, and demographic ageing. Between 1980 and 1995, the urban population in Western Europe increased by 9 per cent (United Nations Population Division 2001) but the number of households in the area increased by 19 per cent (EEA 2000).

The level of urbanization in Europe is currently 74.6 per cent with an expected annual growth of 0.3

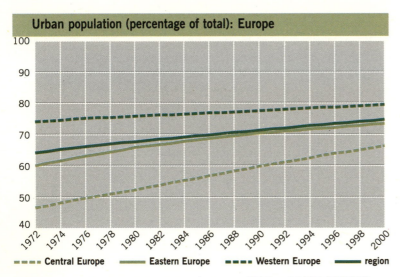

**Urban population (percentage of total): Europe**

Legend: ----- Central Europe    ——— Eastern Europe    ----- Western Europe    ——— region

**Europe's population is currently 76 per cent urbanized, a figure which is expected to stabilize at 82 per cent**

*Source: United Nations Population Division 2001*

per cent per year between 2000 and 2015 (UNCHS 2001a). It is expected that Europe will stabilize at an urbanization level of about 82 per cent. Currently, one-half of the population of Europe lives in small towns of 1 000–50 000 people, one-quarter in medium-sized towns of 50 000–250 000 people and one-quarter in cities of more than 250 000 people (UNCHS 2001b). Further urbanization in Europe is not expected to change this pattern significantly.

The problems of urban development and its impact on the environment have been challenging for European policy-makers. Compounding the problem in CEE and NIS countries is the fact that, in the past ten years, national governments have transferred a wide array of urban (environmental) responsibilities to local or regional authorities but have not provided adequate resources to fulfil these responsibilities. Local

authorities all over Europe have begun to implement Local Agendas 21 and local Habitat Agendas; a significant number have adopted the Charter of European Cities and Towns, which emphasizes integrated approaches towards sustainability and better collaboration between cities. A review of the implementation of the Habitat Agenda shows that progress has been made in Europe in improving the efficiency of water use through advanced technological processes and the establishment of water resource management plans and policies (UNCHS 2001c). Efforts have also been made to reduce air and water pollution through reductions and prevention of discharges of the most polluting and hazardous substances, as well as reuse and recycling incentives. However, increased air pollution generated by motor vehicles remains a strong concern. In Eastern Europe, the use of obsolete communal heating systems and coal burning is a major cause of pollution problems. Two other key issues in Europe are noise pollution and solid waste.

### Urban air quality

Across Europe, transport and mobility are becoming major issues for most cities. In the urban areas of Western Europe, half of all car trips are for less than 6 km while 10 per cent are for less than 1 km. The major factor affecting the increase in traffic is increasing travel distances to work, shopping, schools and leisure activities. These distances are increasing because origins and destinations (residential areas, industrial areas, shopping areas and so on) are being located further apart and often primarily linked with roads. Also, as a result of globalization, increasing competition forces people to find work in different locations and different jobs at different times of the day. Alternatives to the car such as public transport, walking and cycling facilities are often poorly developed or ill-adapted to newly emerging urban patterns (EEA 2001). Major exceptions are Denmark and the Netherlands where infrastructure for alternatives to the car is well developed.

The increase in vehicle traffic has significant implications for urban air quality, although this has been partially offset by a reduction in major air pollutant emissions from transport in Western European countries. Nevertheless, considerable numbers of people in urban areas are still exposed to high pollution levels, leading to some health-related

## Growth of urban sprawl along the French Riviera, 1975–90

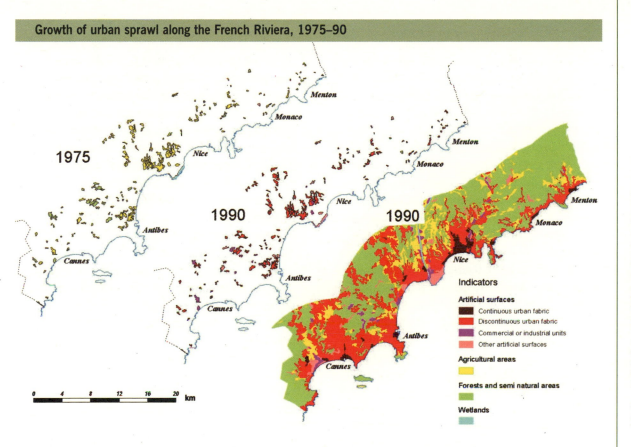

**Indicators**

**Artificial surfaces**
- Continuous urban fabric
- Discontinuous urban fabric
- Commercial or industrial units
- Other artificial surfaces

**Agricultural areas**

**Forests and semi natural areas**

**Wetlands**

Maps show growth of urban sprawl along a 10-km strip of the French Mediterranean coast between 1975 and 1990. Two maps on the left identify agricultural and forested areas that were urbanized during 1975–90. Near map shows the end result — some 35 per cent of the strip is now built on

*Source: Blue Plan 2001*

issues. Projections for 2010 show that 70 per cent of the urban population are still likely to be exposed to particulate matter levels in excess of threshold values, 20 per cent to excess $NO_2$ and 15 per cent to excess benzene (EEA 2001).

The number of exceedance days for $NO_2$ in CEE cities is much lower than in EU cities, and far below the number allowed by EU directives. However, with affluence levels and the number of vehicles increasing, photochemical smog — associated with increasing $NO_x$, hydrocarbons and carbon monoxide — has recently become a problem. The move towards lead-free petrol and mandatory catalysers on private vehicles is now helping improve urban air quality in these countries.

### Noise pollution

Of the 75 per cent of European citizens who reside in urban communities, more than 30 per cent live in dwellings with significant exposure to road noise. This is in spite of major reductions of noise limits from individual sources, such as cars and lorries. However, new vehicle standards have a noticeable effect on noise levels only when vehicle renewal is well

advanced, which can take up to 15 years (EEA 1999).

The dramatic increase in air travel since 1970 has led to a significant increase in noise around airports. However, since the mid-1990s aircraft noise pollution has been reduced by a factor of nine compared with aircraft from 1970. Noise pollution around some European airports is restricted by legislation prohibiting night-time movements, while in CEE the application of economic instruments in the form of fines levied for aircraft noise pollution has been an effective deterrent (REC 1999). It is anticipated that the projected air traffic growth to 2010 can be accommodated at most main airports without significant increases in noise exposure (EEA 1999).

To date, noise policy has been primarily concerned with fixing maximum sound levels for vehicles, aircraft, machines and plants (for example EC 1996). A new directive concerning environmental noise will harmonize EU noise measurements and monitoring, and require countries to make noise maps publicly available as a basis for the development of action plans. In major CEE cities, noise abatement measures are becoming an integral part of new urban development schemes.

## Solid waste

There is a strong correlation between economic growth and waste generation, especially waste from urban-based consumption. In the EU, waste generation per capita from household and commercial activities, which constitutes only part of the total amount of municipal waste, already exceeds the target of 300 kg per capita per year set in the EU's fifth environmental action plan (EEA 2001) by 100 kg. Most European countries have recycling schemes, particularly for paper and glass — although this development has been only a partial success because the generation of waste paper and glass has also increased.

Sludge from urban wastewater treatment plants is estimated to have increased in the EU from 5.2 to 7.2 million tonnes dry solids during 1992–98, and further growth is expected (EEA 2001). Such volumes are increasingly difficult to absorb through incineration, dumping in landfills and recycling in agriculture. The problem is being compounded by the fact that sludge is often contaminated with heavy metals and other toxic chemicals, which even in minute concentrations can affect human health (Hall and Dalimier 1994).

In most European countries, landfilling is still the most common treatment route for waste, even though there is an increasing shortage of available sites. This is because, in both Western and Eastern Europe, recycling is rarely economically viable. However, 'producer responsibility' for the environmentally sound disposal of packaging and products is achieving widespread acceptance (UNEP 1996).

Different approaches have been adopted in different countries. Germany is shifting responsibility for managing packaging waste to industry as a mandate, while in France agreements are mostly voluntary although stringent reporting is required (UNEP 1996). In France, municipalities remain responsible for waste collection but industry has been made responsible for the recycling of only certain materials. In the United Kingdom, all companies involved in the packaging chain are required to meet a share of the total responsibility: 47 per cent for retailers, 36 per cent for packers and fillers, 11 per cent for converters, and 6 per cent for raw material manufacturers (PPIC 1998).

Air quality, noise pollution and waste are not the only urban environmental problems in Europe. Other problems include traffic congestion, utilization of green space, management of water resources and, particularly in CEE, an ageing urban infrastructure such as deteriorating apartment housing and inadequately maintained water mains. To deal with these often interrelated problems, focus is shifting from issue-based approaches to more integrated models for sustainable urban development. Legislation is still one of the major implementation instruments for improving the urban environment. However, instruments such as economic incentives mechanisms, awareness creation through information campaigns and strategic investments are also being used to address environmental concerns (UNCHS 2001c).

### References: Chapter 2, urban areas, Europe

Blue Plan (2001). *Urban Sprawl in the Mediterranean Region.* Sophia Antipolis, Greece, UNEP, MAP and Blue Plan http://www.planbleu.org/indexa.htm [Geo-2-211]

EEA (1999). *Environment in the European Union at the Turn of the Century.* Environmental Assessment Report No 2. Copenhagen, European Environment Agency

EEA (2001). *Environmental Signals 2001.* Environmental Assessment Report No 6. Copenhagen, European Environment Agency

EC (1996). *Future Noise Policy - Green Paper.* COM(96)540 Final. Brussels, European Commission

Hall, J. and Dalimier, F. (1994). *Waste Management – Sewage Sludge.* DGXI Study Contract B4-3040/014156/92. Brussels, European Commission

PPIC (1998). *Producer Responsibility - An Overview.* The Paper Federation of Great Britain http://www.ppic.org.uk/htdocs/info/factsheets/produ cer.htm [Geo-2-212]

REC (1999). *Sourcebook on Economic Instruments for Environmental Policy in Central and Eastern Europe.* Szentendre, Hungary, Regional Environmental Centre for Central and Eastern Europe

UNCHS (2001a). *Cities in a Globalizing world: Global Report on Human Settlements 2001.* London, Earthscan

UNCHS (2001b). *State of the World's Cities 2001.* Nairobi, United Nations Centre for Human Settlements (Habitat)

UNCHS (2001c). *Synthesis of National Reports on the Implementation of the Habitat Agenda in the Economic Commission for Europe (ECE) Region.* United Nations Commission on Human Settlements (Habitat) http://www.unchs.org/istanbul+5/ece.PDF [Geo-2-213]

UNEP (1996). *International Source Book on Environmentally Sound Technologies for Municipal Solid Waste Management.* UNEP International Environment Technology Centre http://www.unep.or.jp/ietc/Issues/Urban.asp [Geo-2-214]

United Nations Population Division (2001). *World Urbanization Prospects: The 1999 Revision. Key Findings.* United Nations Population Division. http://www.un.org/esa/population/pubsarchive/ urbanization/urbanization.pdf [Geo-2-203]

## Urban areas: Latin America and the Caribbean

Latin America and the Caribbean is the most urbanized region in the developing world. Between 1972 and 2000 the urban population rose from 176.4 million to 390.8 million, prompted by better services and job opportunities compared to rural areas. During this period, the percentage of the population living in urban areas increased from 58.9 to 75.3 per cent, accounting for 79.8 per cent of the population in South America, 67.3 per cent in Central America and 63.0 per cent in the Caribbean (compiled from United Nations Population Division 2001). This urban–rural ratio is similar to that seen in highly industrialized countries.

With the exception of Brazil, urbanization patterns typically involve a single, very large city per country. In addition to an expansion of existing urban areas, urbanization has also taken place in some rural districts — 61 per cent of the inhabitants of the Amazon region now live in urban areas. Deep inequalities persist in most of the countries in the region and much poverty is concentrated in urban areas. For example, one-third of the population of São Paulo and 40 per cent of the population of Mexico City live at or below the poverty line. Between 1970 and 2000, the number of urban poor in the region rose from 44 million to 220 million people (UNCHS 2001a).

Although environmental problems are not limited to the largest cities, their impact is most evident there. Urban environmental problems include the concentration of domestic and industrial solid wastes, lack of sewage and air pollution.

### Solid waste

Three decades ago, solid waste production was 0.2–0.5 kg/day per capita; it is now about 0.92 kg/day per capita. In 1995, the region's urban population generated 330 000 tonnes of solid waste per day (CELADE 1999, Acurio and others 1997). Buenos Aires, Mexico City and São Paulo alone generate approximately 51 000 tonnes of garbage per day (see figure right). Although solid waste collection has almost 90 per cent coverage, there is no adequate disposal mechanism for 43 per cent of this waste (PAHO 1998).

The increase in solid waste cannot be explained by urban growth alone. Changes in lifestyle patterns play a major role and waste generation is significantly higher in the more affluent parts of cities. The problem with urban waste is not only the quantity but also the composition, which has changed from dense and almost completely organic to bulky and increasingly non-biodegradable. Increasing amounts of plastic, aluminium, paper and cardboard are being discarded by households and industries. Hazardous waste such as hospital waste, expired drugs, chemicals, batteries and contaminated sludge pose potential risks to human health and the environment alike when handled improperly. Although some countries have a legal framework for waste control, almost all lack the physical infrastructure and human resources necessary to enforce it (UNEP 2000).

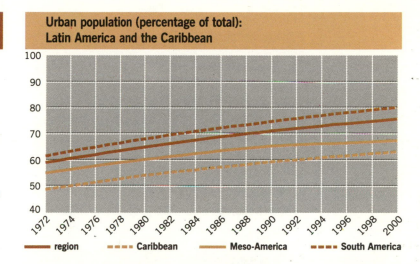

**Urban population (percentage of total): Latin America and the Caribbean**

Legend: region — Caribbean — Meso-America — South America

Graph shows the high levels of urbanization in the region, particularly in South America

Source: compiled from United Nations Population Division 2001

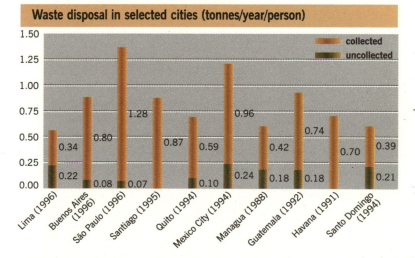

**Waste disposal in selected cities (tonnes/year/person)**

Legend: collected / uncollected

Lima (1996): 0.34 collected, 0.22 uncollected
Buenos Aires (1996): 0.80 collected, 0.08 uncollected
São Paulo (1996): 1.28 collected, 0.07 uncollected
Santiago (1995): 0.87 collected
Quito (1994): 0.59 collected, 0.10 uncollected
Mexico City (1994): 0.96 collected, 0.24 uncollected
Managua (1988): 0.42 collected, 0.18 uncollected
Guatemala (1992): 0.74 collected, 0.18 uncollected
Havana (1991): 0.70 collected
Santo Domingo (1994): 0.39 collected, 0.21 uncollected

Collected and uncollected waste in selected cities in Latin America and the Caribbean; however, much of the collected waste is improperly disposed of. Figures in brackets show year of survey

Source: PAHO and IADB 1997

## Water supply and sanitation

Although in the past 30 years the proportion of the urban population with access to drinking water and sewage system services has increased, many people are still affected by a lack of basic services. In the year 2000, 93 per cent of urban households had access to improved water sources and 87 per cent to improved sanitation — ranging from 50 per cent in Haiti to 100 per cent in the British Virgin Islands, Montserrat and Suriname (WHO and UNICEF 2000).

Groundwater pollution resulting from inadequate sewage treatment endangers public health (PAHO

### A model for public transport systems

The Mayor of Curitiba, Brazil, describes his city as 'a model for developed and developing countries alike'. Its urban transport system, constructed in the 1970s, encouraged residential and business development, and harmonized with the plans for the city. In 1973, the Research and Urban Planning Institute of Curitiba developed special buses designed for mass transit. Further adapted and enlarged to respond to growing population needs in the 1980s and 1990s, the system now transports two million people per day. The integrated transit network provides four alternate modes of transport, integrated within the 12 municipalities of the metropolitan region. The mass use of Curitiba's transit system has reduced the number of vehicles on the road, thereby reducing air pollution, lowering the incidence of smog and lessening the threat of respiratory illness.

Curitiba became the first city in Brazil to use a special fuel made up of 89.4 per cent diesel, 8 per cent anhydrous alcohol and 2.6 per cent soybean additive. This fuel is less polluting and cuts particle emissions by up to 43 per cent. The mixture of alcohol and soybean additive also brings social and economic benefits, maintaining employment in rural areas: every billion litres of alcohol used generates approximately 50 000 new jobs.

*Source: Taniguchi 2001*

1998) and poses a serious challenge to the region's policy-makers. Currently, less than 5 per cent of municipal wastewater in the region is treated (UNEP 2000). There is a clear demand for wastewater treatment systems to reduce water pollution. Pollution of surface and groundwater makes water in urban areas an increasingly contentious issue (Dourojeanni and Jouravlev 1999, PAHO 1998, CEPAL 1994).

The public sector lacks the capacity to operate and maintain existing water and sanitation systems, let alone invest in new ones — especially in the poorest areas where urbanization has occurred most recently. This has led to greater private sector participation since the 1980s and decentralization of the responsibility for providing services to local government (Pirez 2000, CEPAL 1998). However, Latin America still lacks a management model to ensure equity and environmental sustainability in services (Pirez 2000, Idelovitch and Ringskog 1995).

## Air quality

Over the past 30 years, air quality has deteriorated seriously in many urban centres and exposes millions of people to pollutant levels above the limits recommended by the World Health Organization (CEPAL 2000). Air pollution affects the health of more than 80 million inhabitants in the region and results in the annual loss of some 65 million working days. It is the main cause of almost 2.3 million cases a year of respiratory disease in children and more than 100 000 cases of chronic bronchitis in adults (CEPAL 2000).

Two factors have contributed to the increase in urban air pollution: an increase in the number of motor vehicles and an increase in travel time due to road congestion (CEPAL 2000). Motor vehicles produce 80–90 per cent of the lead in the environment, even though unleaded gasoline has been available for some time in most countries in the region (World Bank 2001). Deficient public transport as well as the separation of homes from workplaces in cities, resulting in more frequent and longer journeys, have also contributed to the increase in emissions (CEPAL 2000). The large distance between the home and the workplace stems from the absence of national urban policies combining economic, environmental and social goals. Nevertheless, the region also has some good examples of urban planning since the 1970s (see box). A combination of physical and meteorological factors associated with the location of large cities has also influenced the pollution rate (CEPAL 2000) — for example, the metropolitan area of Mexico City is located in a valley that captures pollutants causing smog.

In the past ten years, there has been substantial progress in air quality management in a number of cities. Air pollution in large cities such as Buenos Aires, Mexico City, Rio de Janeiro, São Paulo and Santiago has been reduced by means of strategies that include emission controls, changes in fuels and contingency controls. However, these programmes have not yet been extended to medium-sized cities in most of which the information needed to implement such measures is not available (ECLAC and UNEP 2001).

## Effects of policies

The economic policies predominating in the region during the 1980s made the introduction of environmental measures difficult as a limit was put on social spending on basic services and sanitation. Although the 1990s were marked by the continuation or persistence of environmental problems typical of poverty and the formation of large cities, the decade also saw the introduction of a number of positive changes including greater citizen participation and the development of public and private networks defending the environment and promoting environmental education. These changes contradict the catastrophic projections for the state of the urban environment that were made in the 1970s (CEPAL 1995, Villa and Rodríguez 1994, CEPAL 2000). However, there is a serious need for substantive evolution from sectoral and fragmented management of cities towards comprehensive and multi-sectoral (national) urban policies and strategies where environmental issues are integrated into all the dimensions of urban management.

## References: Chapter 2, urban areas, Latin America and the Caribbean

Acurio, G., Rossin, A., Teixeira, P. and Zepeda, F. (1997). *Diagnóstico de la Situación del Manejo de Residuos Sólidos Municipales en América Latina y el Caribe*. Serie Ambiental No. 18. Washington DC, Pan-American Health Organization

CELADE (1999). *Boletín Demográfico No. 63*. Santiago, Centro Latinoamericano de Demografía

CEPAL (1994). Financiamiento de la infraestructura de saneamiento: situación actual y perspectivas en América Latina. In *Gestión Urbana y de Vivienda, II Reunión regional MINURVI*. Santiago, United Nations Economic Commission for Latin America and the Caribbean

CEPAL (1995). *Alojar el Desarrollo:Ttarea para los Asentamientos Humanos*. Latin American and the Caribbean Regional Meeting preparatory to the United Nations Conference on Human Settlements. Santiago, United Nations Economic Commission for Latin America and the Caribbean

CEPAL (1998). *Progresos Realizados en la Privatización de los Servicios Públicos Relacionados con el Agua: Reseña por Países de Sud América*. LC/R.1697. Santiago, United Nations Economic Commission for Latin America and the Caribbean, Environment and Development Division

CEPAL (2000). *De la Urbanización Acelerada a la Consolidación de los Asentamientos Humanos en América Latina y el Caribe*. Santiago, United Nations Economic Commission for Latin America and the Caribbean and United Nations Centre for Human Settlements (Habitat) http://www.urb-al.com/es/reader/EspacioRegional.pdf [Geo-2-236]

CEPAL (2000b). *Conciencia Ciudadana y Contaminación Atmósferica: Estado de Situación en la Ciudad de México*. LC/R. 1987. Santiago, United Nations Economic Commission for Latin America and the Caribbean

CEPAL (2000c). *Conciencia Ciudadana y Contaminación Atmósferica: Estado de Situación en el Area Metropolitana de Santiago, Chile*. LC/R 2022. Santiago, United Nations Economic Commission for Latin America and the Caribbean

Dourojeanni, A. and Jouravlev, A. (1999). *Gestión de Cuencas y Ríos Vinculados con Centros Urbanos*. Santiago, United Nations Economic Commission for Latin America and the Caribbean, Division of Naural Resources and Infrastructure

ECLAC and UNEP (2001). *The Sustainability of Development in Latin America and the Caribbean: Challenges and Opportunities*. Regional Preparatory Conference of Latin America and the Caribbean for the World Conference on Sustainable Development, Rio de Janeiro, 23–24 October 2001

Idelovitch, E. and Ringskog, K. (1995). *Private Sector Participation in Water Supply and Sanitation in Latin America*. Washington DC, World Bank

PAHO (1998). *La Salud en Las Américas: Edición de 1998*. Washington DC, Pan-American Health Organization

PAHO and IADB (1997). *Diagnóstico de la Situación del Manejo de Residuos Sólidos Municipales en América Latina y el Caribe*. Washington DC, Pan-American Health Organization and Inter-American Development Bank

Pirez, P. (2000). *Servicios Urbanos y Equidad en América Latina*, Serie Medio Ambiente y Desarrollo. Santiago, United Nations Economic Commission for Latin America and the Caribbean

UNCHS (2001). *State of the World's Cities 2001*. Nairobi, United Nations Centre for Human Settlements (Habitat)

UNEP (2000). *GEO Latin America and the Caribbean Environment Outlook 2000*. Mexico City, United Nations Environment Programme, Regional Office for Latin America and the Caribbean

United Nations Population Division (2001). *World Urbanization Prospects: The 1999 Revision. Key Findings*. United Nations Population Division. http://www.un.org/esa/population/pubsarchive/urbanization/urbanization.pdf [Geo-2-203]

Taniguchi, C. (2001). Transported to the Future, *Our Planet*. United Nations Environment Programme http://www.ourplanet.com/imgversn/121/tanig.html [Geo-2-215]

Villa, M. and Rodríguez, J. (1994). *Grandes Ciudades de América Latina: Dos Capítulos*. Santiago, Centro Latinoamericano de Demografía

WHO and UNICEF (2000). *Global Water Supply and Sanitation Assessment 2000 Report*. Geneva, World Health Organization and United Nations Children's Fund http://www.who.int/water_sanitation_health/Globassessment/Global8-2.htm [Geo-2-216]

World Bank (2001). *Eliminación del Plomo y Armonización de Combustibles en América Latina*. World Bank http://www.worldbank.org/wbi/airelimpio/newsevents/launching/agenda/transportemissions/lallemen.html [Geo-2-217]

## Urban areas: North America

North America is a highly urbanized region. In the period 1972–2000, the percentage of North America's population living in cities increased from 73.8 to 77.2 per cent (United Nations Population Division 2001). Urbanization is related to many of the environmental issues highlighted in this report, including the conversion of agricultural land, habitat degradation and biodiversity loss, regional air pollution, global climate change, coastal degradation, an increased urban-wildlife interface and water pollution.

By the 1970s, the post-war exodus from central cities had led to a settlement pattern characterized by low-density suburbs surrounding city cores, commonly referred to as 'urban sprawl'. Addressing the multiple problems associated with urban sprawl has become a priority in many North American municipalities. Urban populations use high levels of energy and other resources and dispose of large amounts of waste. Because of their significant contribution to both regional and global pollution, and to declines in the Earth's natural resources, North American cities have disproportionately large 'ecological footprints'.

### Urban sprawl

Urban sprawl is defined as low-density, automobile-dependent residential development (Dowling 2000). It is equated with intrusion into rural or undeveloped land on the periphery of a city or town, beyond the edge of service and employment areas (Chen 2000). Sprawling sub-divisions in post-war North America have been fuelled by economic expansion and encouraged by incentives for home ownership, single-use zoning, government subsidies, and investments in highways and suburban infrastructure (ULI 1999, Sierra Club 2000a). As tax-paying, middle-income families left urban centres, many cities turned into impoverished city cores surrounded by car-dependent suburbs serviced by malls.

In the United States, a cycle of public transit decline, increased car use and longer commuting distances took place over the 1970s and 1980s; this was mirrored by Canada during the 1990s. Between 1981 and 1991, the number of car-kilometres travelled by Canadian and US citizens grew by 23 and 33.7 per cent respectively (EC 1998, Raad and Kenworthy 1998). The trend of increased urban car use and stagnant or declining transit use is illustrated below left.

Encouraged during the 1990s by new road building and low fuel prices, the US suburban population grew by 11.9 per cent between 1990 and 1998, compared with 4.7 per cent for central cities (Pope 1999, Baker 2000, HUD 2000). Today, one-half of US sprawl appears to be related to population increase and the other half to land-use and consumption choices that increase the amount of urban land occupied per resident (Kolankiewicz and Beck 2001).

Suburban developments have been built over vast areas of North America's forests, wetlands, recreational wilderness and agricultural land. As these landscape features are lost, so are the services they provide, such as wildlife habitat, flood and run-off control, and soil productivity (Parfrey 1999). Between 1982 and 1992, an average of 5 670 km$^2$ a year of prime farmland in the United States was developed for urban use (NRCS 2000). Today, an average of 9 320 km$^2$ of land is being converted annually, with a substantial portion for suburban homes on lots of 0.5 ha (HUD 2000). In Canada, the urban areas occupying land that could be used for crop production increased from about 9 000 km$^2$ in 1971 to 14 000 km$^2$ in 1996 (Statistics Canada 2000).

Urban sprawl has environmental, social and economic consequences including traffic congestion, deteriorating inner cities that are often fragmented along class and racial lines, and suburban problems of

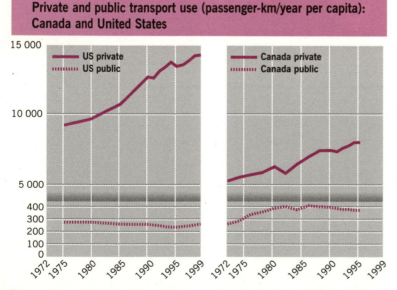

**Private and public transport use (passenger-km/year per capita): Canada and United States**

Legend: US private, US public, Canada private, Canada public

The per capita use of private vehicles in urban areas has grown in both the United States and Canada while the use of public transport has stagnated or dwindled

*Sources: compiled from EC 1998, Wendell Cox 2000 and United Nations Population Division 2001*

isolation and lack of sense of community (Raad and Kenworthy 1998, Dowling 2000). Canadian cities are much less affected by sprawl than their US counterparts (Parfrey 1999, Baker 2000, Sierra Club 2000b).

Increasingly, state and local governments are implementing smart growth and sustainable development plans (see box). Studies show that where urban density is highest, car use per capita is the lowest (Raad and Kenworthy 1998). Successful 'infill' projects in which decaying properties or vacant lots are developed to help cities rebound are now more common. On the other hand, in many places it is still less expensive in the short term for developers to buy and build on land outside city zones (Chen 2000).

At the federal level, initiatives to help address sprawl-related problems include the US 1998 Transportation Equity Act (TEA-21) and the Livable Communities Programme. Most activity addressing urban sprawl takes place at the planning level of government, however. Many of Canada's major urban regions are instituting long-range transportation plans aimed at reducing car dependency and adopting sustainability strategies for higher density, mixed use urban development (Raad and Kenworthy 1998).

There are still many hurdles on the path to sustainable cities: powers to address urban sprawl are generally split among federal, state/province and local governments, and their proper roles are still undefined (Stoel Jr 1999, Dowling 2000); effective compliance regimes to ensure implementation are lacking (Raad and Kenworthy 1998); to some, smart growth implies the loss of individual freedom and property rights fueling an anti-smart growth lobby (Stoel Jr 1999); vested interests of the car manufacturing industry are strong, while suburban sprawl is so entrenched in the North American landscape and psyche that reversing the trend is a formidable challenge.

## Ecological footprint

As suburbs have grown, many of North America's compact central cities have been replaced by a mixture of widely dispersed shopping malls, housing developments and highways (Miller 1985). This pattern of urbanization is one of the principal forces driving the global increase in energy demand (UNDP, UNEP, World Bank and WRI 1996). North American cities consume large amounts of energy and raw materials, and produce large amounts of waste and

### Compact urban development and smart growth

Over the past 10 years, a 'smart growth' movement has emerged in North America to combat urban sprawl. Smart growth is characterized by a mix of residential, office and retail land uses close to civic buildings clustered in a town centre. 'Smart' growth is emphasized rather than 'no' growth, and reform codes and ordinances are sought that permit smart growth characteristics and that create urban growth boundaries (ULI 1999). Smart growth is promoted by a broad coalition including environmental NGOs, social justice activists, local government officials, urban planners and affordable housing advocates. The movement promotes high-density neighbourhoods that reduce car use.

Compact development techniques advocated by smart growth and sustainable city initiatives include building within an already urbanized area, redeveloping on cleaned-up contaminated sites or 'brownfields', and cluster development on reduced-size lots. Such developments use less land area and help reduce travel distances, encourage walking and cycling, stimulate public transit, preserve open green spaces, wildlife habitat and farmland, and reduce impervious surface areas thereby improving drainage and water quality (US EPA 2001).

pollution. And with only five per cent of the world's population, North America is a major consumer of the world's natural resources and a major producer of its wastes. As a result, its impact on the global environment is larger than that of any other region.

North America also produces more municipal solid waste than any other region. Municipal solid waste generated in the United States continues to increase but much more slowly than before 1970; at the same time, waste recovery is increasing and discards to land fills are decreasing (see figure below). Lightweight but high-volume materials such as paper and plastic are replacing dense and heavy materials in the waste

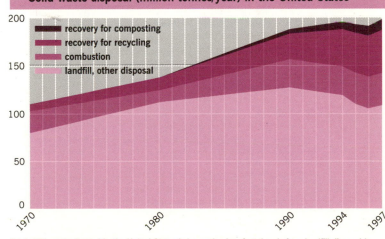

**Solid waste disposal (million tonnes/year) in the United States**

- recovery for composting
- recovery for recycling
- combustion
- landfill, other disposal

Total solid waste disposal in the United States is increasing less fast than before, landfill disposal is decreasing and recycling increasing

Source: Franklin Associates 1999

stream which increases waste volumes (PCSD 1996a). The continued use of older technologies, coupled with a consumer lifestyle based on the desire for mobility, convenience and product disposability, has limited the further advancement of resource efficiency and waste reduction (UN 2001).

*Agenda 21* identified unsustainable consumption and production, especially by industrialized countries, as the major cause of global environmental deterioration (UN 2001). Since 1993, the issue of sustainable patterns of consumption and production has become a part of policy debate. Both federal governments promote eco-efficiency through a number of programmes. The US President's Council on Sustainable Development has recommended national goals for natural resources stewardship, population planning and sustainable consumption

(PCSD 1996a, b). Industry is increasingly restructuring its processes and re-sourcing raw materials to reduce their environmental impact; there is also a perceptible rise in the number of 'green' or socially and environmentally conscious consumers (Co-op America 2000).

North America's urban industrial society is at the same time the provider of a quality of life envied by many of the world's developing countries and, given its large ecological footprint, a region with a disproportionate environmental impact on the planet. When cities are planned to be compact, they are more efficient and sustainable. North America's smart growth and sustainable city programmes could reduce the region's ecological footprint but they are still in their infancy and progress is slow.

## References: Chapter 2, urban areas, North America

Baker, L. (2000). *Growing Pains/Malling America: The Fast-Moving Fight to Stop Urban Sprawl*. Emagazine.com, Volume XI, Number III http://www.emagazine.com/may-june_2000/0500feat1.html [Geo-2-218]

Chen, D. (2000). The Science of Smart Growth. *Scientific American*. 283, 6, 84-91

Co-op America (2000). *Forty-four Million Americans Can't be Wrong. The Market is Ready for Socially Responsible Business*. Co-op America http://www.coopamerica.org/business/B44million.htm [Geo-2-219]

Dowling, T. J. (2000). Reflections on Urban Sprawl, Smart Growth, and the Fifth Amendment. *University of Pennsylvania Law Review*. 148, 3, 873

EC (1998). *Canadian Passenger Transportation, National Environmental Indicator Series, SOE Bulletin No. 98-5*. Ottawa, Environment Canada, State of the Environment Reporting Program

Franklin Associates (1999). *Characterization of Municipal Solid Waste in The United States: 1998 Update*. United States Environmental Protection Agency http://www.epa.gov/epaoswer/non-hw/muncpl/msw98.htm [Geo-2-220]

HUD (2000). *The State of the Cities 2000: Megaforces Shaping the Future of the Nation's Cities*. US Department of Housing and Urban Development http://www.hud.gov/pressrel/socrpt.pdf [Geo-2-221]

Kolankiewicz, L. and Beck, R. (2001). *Weighing Sprawl Factors in Large US Cities*. Sprawl City http://www.sprawlcity.org/studyUSA/index.html [Geo-2-222]

Miller, T. G. (1985). *Living in the Environment: An Introduction to Environmental Science*. 4th ed. Belmont CA, Wadsworth Publishing Company

NRCS (2000). *Summary Report: 1997 National*

Resources Inventory, Revised December 2000. United States Department of Agriculture, Natural Resources Conservation Service http://www.nhq.nrcs.usda.gov/NRI/1997/summary_report/original/body.html [Geo-2-223]

Parfrey, E. (1999). *What is 'Smart Growth'?* Sierra Club http://www.sierraclub.org/sprawl/community/smartgrowth.asp [Geo-2-224]

PCSD (1996a). *Population and Consumption: Task Force Report*. Washington DC, President's Council on Sustainable Development

PCSD (1996b). *Eco-Efficiency: Task Force Report*. Washington DC, President's Council on Sustainable Development.

Pope, C. (1999). *Solving Sprawl: The Sierra Club Rates the States. 1999 Sierra Club Sprawl Report*. Sierra Club http://www.sierraclub.org/sprawl/report99/ [Geo-2-225]

Raad, T. and Kenworthy, J. (1998). The US and us: Canadian cities are going the way of their US counterparts into car-dependent sprawl. *Alternatives*. 24, 1,14-22

Sierra Club (2000a). *Sprawl Costs Us All: How Your Taxes Fuel Suburban Sprawl. 2000 Sierra Club Sprawl Report*. Sierra Club http://www.sierraclub.org/sprawl/report00/sprawl.pdf [Geo-2-226]

Sierra Club (2000b). *Smart Choices or Sprawling Growth: A 50-State Survey of Development*. Sierra Club http://www.sierraclub.org/sprawl/50statesurvey/intro.asp [Geo-2-227]

Statistics Canada (2000). *Human Activity and the Environment 2000*. Ottawa, Minister of Industry

Stoel Jr., T. B. (1999). Reining in Urban Sprawl. *Environment*. 41, 4, 6-11, 29-33

ULI (1999). *Smart Growth: Myth and Fact*. Urban Land Institute http://www.uli.org/Pub/Media/A_issues/A_SmL4_Myth.pdf [Geo-2-228]

UN (2001). *Commission on Sustainable Development Acting as the Preparatory Committee for the World Summit on Sustainable Development Organizational Session: Report of the Secretary-General*. E/CN.17/2001/. New York, United Nations Economic and Social Council

UNDP, UNEP, World Bank and WRI (1996). *World Resources 1996-97*. London and New York, Oxford University Press

United Nations Population Division (2001). *World Urbanization Prospects: The 1999 Revision. Key Findings*. United Nations Population Division. http://www.un.org/esa/population/pubsarchive/urbanization/urbanization.pdf [Geo-2-203]

US EPA (2001). *Our Built and Natural Environment: a Technical Review of the Interactions between Land Use, Transportation and Environmental Quality*. Washington DC, US Environmental Protection Agency http://www.smartgrowth.org [Geo-2-252]

Wendell Cox (2000). *US Urban Personal Vehicle & Public Transport Market Share from 1945. The Public Purpose, Urban Transport Fact Book* http://www.publicpurpose.com/ut-usptshare45.htm [Geo-2-229]

## Urban areas: West Asia

The majority of the West Asian population lives in urban areas, with the notable exception of Yemen, where the predominantly rural population is expected to grow by 2.7 per cent between 2000 and 2015 (UNCHS 2001). The past 30 years have brought about significant economic, political and technological changes, which have influenced the way urban areas are structured and function in West Asia. Three crucial factors have shaped the urban landscapes of the region (UNESCWA 1999):

- the 1970s oil boom and the sharp fluctuations of oil revenues during the following two decades;
- the large-scale movement of people within the region because of armed conflict and civil strife; and
- the forces of globalization that have played and continue to play a vital role since the beginning of the early 1990s, integrating West Asian nations into the global economy and increasing the role of information technology.

Rapid economic growth, which occurred in most countries in the region over the past three decades, was accompanied by population growth and increased urbanization. There has been a massive migration of the population from rural to urban areas in nearly all countries as well as immigration of foreign workers into urban areas, especially in the Gulf Cooperation Council (GCC) countries. Between 1972 and 1980, the total urban population increased from 17.8 million

(44.7 per cent of the total population) to 27 million (55.8 per cent of the total population). The average annual growth rate of the urban population in this period was 5.6 per cent, substantially more than that of the general population, which was 3.6 per cent. Urbanization has continued to increase at a faster rate than the total population (United Nations Population Division 2001a) although there are marked differences in the level and pace of urbanization between the sub-regions and among the countries of the region.

Spectacular growth and urban transition occurred in Oman, where the urban population increased from 11.4 per cent of the total population in 1970, to 84 per cent by 2000. All the countries of the Arabian Peninsula now have a level of urbanization above 84 per cent, except Yemen with a level of urbanization of only 24.7 per cent (see map). By the year 2000, almost the entire population of Bahrain (92.2 per cent), Kuwait (97.6 per cent) and Qatar (92.5) were living in urban areas (United Nations Population Division 2001a).

The average annual growth rate of urban populations in West Asia has slowed over the past three decades, from 6.1 per cent in 1972 to 3.7 per cent in 2000. The impact of the Second Gulf War on urbanization rates was particularly significant, resulting in the repatriation of millions of foreign workers.

Although urban areas are increasingly home to most of the West Asian population, the proportion of people living in cities with more than 1 million residents is still small. In 1975, only two cities (Baghdad and Damascus) had a total population of

**Map and graph show high level of urbanization in West Asia, with the exception of the still largely rural Yemen**

*Source: compiled from United Nations Population Division 2001a*

### Urbanization level (%): West Asia

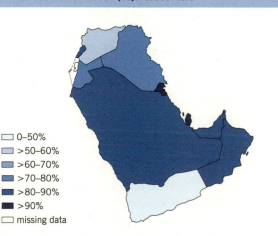

- 0–50%
- >50–60%
- >60–70%
- >70–80%
- >80–90%
- >90%
- missing data

### Urban population (millions) by sub-region: West Asia

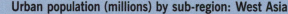
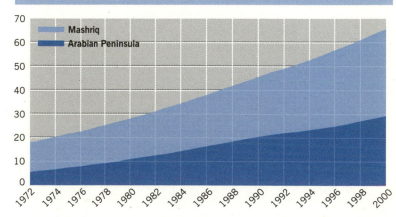

Mashriq
Arabian Peninsula

Rapid urbanization in West Asia is occurring at the expense of both rural lifestyles and smaller-scale village settlements, such as this one in Iran

*Source: UNEP, Mohammad R. L. Mofrad, Topham Picturepoint*

more than 1 million, accounting for a quarter of the total urban population of the region. The number of large cities has doubled every ten years, reaching 12 in the year 2000, but their population as a share of the total urban population has still remained between 25 and 37 per cent. The absolute number of people living in these cities, however, increased from 3.88 million to 23.8 million between 1975 and 2000.

Urbanization is inextricably linked with the economic transition that is taking place in the region from agrarian and nomadic societies to one that is based on manufacturing and services. Economic development has brought dramatic improvement in the well-being of the West Asian people including longer life expectancies, higher incomes and decreased child mortality rates (United Nations Population Division 2001b). However, despite these positive impacts, many cities are now going through a transition process marked by some negative influences. In parts of the region (Mashriq), the pace and scale of change often strains the capabilities of national and local governments to provide adequate services to the urban poor. In such situations, human

health and well-being are at risk (UNDP, UNEP, World Bank and WRI 1998). Growth of urban populations is also synonymous with growth in urban poverty. Most of the large cities are crowded and have high levels of air pollution from increasing traffic, energy consumption and industrial production.

## Land conversion

As urban areas expand, prime agricultural land, coastal habitats and forests are transformed into land for housing, roads and industry. Coastal ecosystems, including wetlands, tidal flats, saltwater marshes and mangrove swamps, are especially threatened by urban land conversion. Land conversion activities range from draining and filling of marshes and wetlands to large-scale reclamation projects that extend shorelines into the sea. In Lebanon and most of the countries of the GCC, these activities have been carried out for decades. Between 1970 and 1985, Dubai City increased in size from 18 $km^2$ to 110 $km^2$ (Doxiadis Associates 1985), part of which was achieved through coastal reclamation. Continuing reclamation along the coastal areas of Bahrain for urban development has resulted in a continuous change in the shape of the island. The area of Bahrain increased from 661.9 km$^2$ in 1975 to 709.2 km$^2$ (an increase of 7.15 per cent) in 1998; land was mainly allocated for housing, industrial and recreational purposes (CSO 1999). The trade-offs between preserving existing marshes, wetlands and coastlines, on the one hand, and the conversion of such areas into land suitable for urban purposes, on the other, are often decided by considerations based on the positive impacts of urbanization on human development and the need to satisfy the ever-growing demands of urban growth.

## Solid waste

It is estimated that municipal waste generation in the region increased from 4.5 million tonnes a year in 1970 to 25 million tonnes a year in 1995 (Kanbour 1997). The per capita waste generation rates at country level were 430, 750, 511, 551 and 510 kg a year in Bahrain, Dubai, Kuwait, Oman and Qatar respectively (Kanbour 1997) — more than double the annual waste generation rates of 285 and 185 kg in the Mashriq countries of Iraq and Syria. Municipal waste management varies between countries but, in the GCC countries, waste collection and disposal systems are fairly efficient compared to those of the Mashriq. Plants for composting municipal solid wastes and sewage sludge have been established in several countries, and their numbers are increasing (Kanbour 1997).

Because of the availability of abundant energy and investment capital, industrial growth has occurred rapidly, especially in the GCC countries. In the Mashriq countries, the highly unregulated transition from an agrarian to an industrial society has resulted in widespread social and economic disruption,

unemployment, pollution and increased exposure to health hazards. Land degradation, and pollution of river systems and coastal areas, are widespread because of uncontrolled rapid industrialization. In most countries of the Arabian Peninsula, industrial growth involves the transformation of raw materials (oil) into industrial products. Not only are these industries resource-intensive but industries such as electricity generation, chemicals and petroleum refining, mining and printing also produce a large amount of hazardous and toxic wastes, which have potential health effects (Hardoy, Mitlin and Satterthwaite 2001). Some of the countries of the region lack adequate facilities to handle hazardous wastes, and this leads to dumping on fallow or public land, in rivers, coastal waters or in sewers designed for discharge of municipal wastes only.

## The demands of cities

The nexus of people and economic activity (including manufacturing, services and commerce) in urban areas of the region requires resources far in excess of what the local area can supply. Cities must draw their supplies of food, fuel and water from distant places. By the year 2030, 142.6 million people will be living in the urban areas of West Asia. These will require land, energy, water and food. As their incomes rise, they will consume greater quantities of goods and in the process will generate greater quantities of waste. The scale of urban consumption and waste generation, and the negative impacts associated with them, varies from city to city, depending largely on a city's wealth and size (UNDP, UNEP, World Bank and WRI 1996). Not surprisingly, the highest levels of resource use and waste generation occur in the wealthy cities of the GCC countries.

## References: Chapter 2, urban areas, West Asia

CSO (1999). *Statistical Abstract 99*. Bahrain, Directorate of Statistics – Central Statistics Organization http://www.bahrain.gov.bh/english/stats/Abstracts/99/index.asp. [Geo-2-253]

Doxiadis Associates (1985). *Comprehensive Development Plan for Dubai Emirate. Vol.2*. Athens, Doxiadis Associates

Hardoy, J.E., Mitlin, D. and Satterthwaite, D. (2001) *Environmental Problems in an Urbanizing World*. London, Earthscan

Kanbour, F. (1997) *General Status of Urban Waste Management in West Asia*. UNEP Regional Workshop on Urban Waste Management in West Asia, Manama, Bahrain, 23–27 November 1997

UNESCWA (1999). *Survey of Economic and Social Developments in the ESCWA Region*. New York, United Nations Economic and Social Commission for Western Asia

UNCHS (2001). *Cities in a Globalizing World: Global Report on Human Settlements 2001*. London, Earthscan

UNDP, UNEP, World Bank and WRI (1996). *World Resources 1996-97*. New York, Oxford University Press

UNDP, UNEP, World Bank and WRI (1998). *World Resources 1998-1999*. New York, Oxford University Press

United Nations Population Division (2001a). *World Urbanization Prospects: The 1999 Revision. Key Findings*. United Nations Population Division. http://www.un.org/esa/population/pubsarchive/urbanization/urbanization.pdf [Geo-2-203]

United Nations Population Division (2001b). *World Population Prospects 1950-2050 (The 2000 Revision)*. New York, United Nations www.un.org/esa/population/publications/wpp2000/wpp2000h.pdf [Geo-2-204]

## Urban areas: the Polar Regions

While the Antarctic is uninhabited, the Arctic has 3.75 million permanent residents, according to the Arctic Council. Most settlements have remained modest in size, with populations of less than 5 000 people. The vast majority of Arctic residents today are non-indigenous immigrants. This shift in demographic make-up has been accompanied by a steady increase in urbanization, with migration from smaller settlements to larger urban settings, a general trend throughout the Arctic (see box).

On the other hand, North America attempted to avoid permanent settlements around mines and oil

### Urban growth in the Arctic

Greenland has experienced urban growth since the 1970s (Rasmussen and Hamilton 2001). Roughly one-quarter of Greenland's population lives in Nuuk, the capital. This concentration of the urban population in one city is found in other Arctic countries: 40 per cent of Iceland's growing population lives in Reykjavik, one-third of the Faroe Islands' people lives in Torshavn, and almost 40 per cent of the population of Canada's Northwest Territories' lives in Yellowknife.

Anchorage in Alaska is the only North American Arctic city with a population of more than 100 000. The rapidly growing population of Anchorage reached 262 200 in 2001, while the population of the next largest city of Arctic Alaska, Fairbanks, declined slightly over the past decade to 30 500.

Norway has pursued a policy of discouraging migration from its northern counties, providing significant support to stimulate jobs, industry, higher education and research in the North. While this policy has not stemmed the decline in small settlements, Tromsø, the largest city in the Scandinavian Arctic, grew to 49 600 in 2001 despite its location at nearly 70° N.

fields by using shift workers rather than moving families north. Facilities were deliberately located away from indigenous villages, and since the 1980s agreements and partnerships have been developed with indigenous organizations to reduce environmental and social impacts, and to increase local employment (Osherenko and Young 1989).

The Russian Federation has 11 cities with populations of more than 200 000 above 60° N (Weir 2001). All grew around resource exploitation, including fishing, wood processing, mining and fuel extraction (CIA 1978). The population of Murmansk, Russia's only ice-free port in the Arctic, grew to 440 000 in 1989. Economic incentives were used to attract people to work in extractive industries in the Russian north, accompanied by the development of urban centres with multi-story apartment blocks, built on permafrost with few or no road or railway connections.

Since the demise of the Soviet Union, the influx into the Russian Arctic has begun to reverse. Following market reforms, contraction of social safety nets, reduced government subsidies, devaluation of the currency and general economic decline in post-Soviet Russia, cities have been unable to support large populations. In the formerly prosperous coal-mining city of Vorkuta, coal production recently dropped to only 2 per cent of what it had been 10 years earlier, the municipal budget had a 100 per cent deficit and the population declined by nearly 30 000 (Weir 2001, World Gazetteer 2001). Tens of thousands left cities such as Norilsk and Murmansk between 1989 and 2001, and in some places the population declined by more than 50 per cent. The Russian Government — with World Bank assistance — provided housing credits and other aid to those seeking to relocate from the Arctic (Weir 2001, World Gazetteer 2001).

The rapid growth of the Arctic population (see 'The socio-economic background') and its increasing concentration in urban settlements has significant implications for the fragile ecosystems of the north. The pressures of urbanization in the Arctic are comparable to those elsewhere but are magnified by the challenges of the climate and remoteness. For example, with winter temperatures dipping as low as –60°C in parts of the Arctic, and with an almost continuous state of darkness for months on end, per capita energy use is very large, adding to the pollution burden of the Arctic. Except for Iceland, which has thermal power, urban centres rely on diesel fuel, hydroelectric or nuclear power. Road networks are expanding and this is leading to increased land use conflicts with wildlife and indigenous people. Habitat fragmentation and sanitation and waste disposal pose perhaps the greatest urban environmental problems.

### Habitat fragmentation

Traditionally, dozens of small groups of semi-nomads orbiting around a small settlement practised a form of extensive land use that fed and supported significantly larger populations. Nomadic indigenous economies use different types of environments at different times of the year, and thus minimize the possibility that a particular resource will be exploited to exhaustion. In this way, indigenous land use in the Arctic encompasses most of the space between isolated urban cities (Anderson 1995).

By contrast, industrial developments such as mining employ an intensive land use strategy, creating expanding rings of pollutants such as heavy metals and sulphur dioxide. This has depopulated tundra and taiga environments formerly used by herders and hunters, and disrupted population dynamics and the migration routes of wild reindeer. Intensive resource development is also a driving force for the formation of road and utility networks.

The habitat fragmentation that arises as a consequence of such developments has both ecological and social impacts. Wild deer migrate in unpredictable ways mixing with domestic herds and causing domestic reindeer to run off with wild herds. Then, as herders lose the reindeer they depend upon for transport and are unable to hunt wild reindeer, they have to depend on social welfare payments. Land privatization further exacerbates problems as indigenous people find their access to resources restricted or barred (Anderson 2000).

A single species (*Rangifer terandus*), that includes the caribou and reindeer, is a primary resource for many indigenous peoples. It has therefore been suggested that urban industrial areas should be isolated from the main Arctic areas of reindeer pasture, and from the main migration routes and calving areas of caribou in North America. Prime areas of reindeer herding should be set aside for reindeer herding and ecosystem protection (Konstantinov 1999). Herders must drive domestic reindeer long distances to reach slaughterhouses located in towns. This reduces the quantity and quality of meat produced, and also degrades land near towns. Herders have recommended re-establishing a network of trade posts (many existed in the mid-1930s), equipped with modern slaughterhouses in tundra locations central to herders (Golovnev and others 1998).

## Sanitation and waste

The safe disposal of waste presents a challenge in the Arctic since the cold climate prevents normal decomposition. Many communities incinerate waste but this contributes to pollution and has aesthetic impacts.

While larger cities have sewage systems, many smaller communities have yet to provide all their citizens with sewage treatment or septic systems. In 1994, half the rural households in Alaska had only 'honey buckets' for the disposal of human waste. By 2001, 70 per cent of rural households had clean water and sewage disposal, and the State aims to relegate the honey bucket to the museum by 2005 (Knowles 2001). Poor housing, water quality and sanitation facilities are

### The interplay of rural and urban populations

Constant contact and exchange occurs between rural and urban populations in the Arctic. While physical boundaries are clear, social and economic boundaries are porous. Hunters and herders come to villages (and in the Russian Arctic are even listed on the census roles of villages) and villagers visit and send their children to the tundra and to fish camp during vacations. This interchange, economic interdependence and constant motion of people is well noted in the Russian and American Arctic as well as in Greenland. The notion that urban groups of indigenous minorities do not lead a traditional life is certainly questionable and, in some cases, wrong (Bogoyavlenskiy 2001).

reported as serious concerns throughout Russia's north and in small communities in Alaska. Many small settlements and parts of larger cities in the Russian Arctic have no indoor plumbing. Funding from federal and regional municipalities is slowly catching up with the need for medical, sanitation, and consumer goods and services in the North.

### References: Chapter 2, urban areas, the Polar Regions

Anderson, D.G. (1995). *Northern Sea Route Social Impact Assessment: Indigenous Peoples and Development in the Lower Yenisei Valley*, INSROP Working Paper No. 18. Lysakker, Norway, Fridtjof Nansen Institute

Anderson, D.G. (2000). *Identity and Ecology in Arctic Siberia: The Number One Reindeer Brigade.* Oxford, Oxford University Press

Bogoyavlenskiy, D.D. (2001). *Historic-demographic note on the Nenets of the Komi Republic.* www.raipon.org/english/library/ipw/number5/article1 9.html [Geo-2-231]

CIA (1978). *Polar Regions Atlas.* Washington DC, Central Intelligence Agency

Golovnev, A.V., Osherenkon, G., Pribylskii, Y.P. and Schindler, D.L. (1998). *Indigenous Peoples and Development of the Yamal Peninsula.* INSROP Working Paper No. 112. Lysakker, Norway, Fridtjof Nansen Institute

Knowles, G. T. (2001). *2001 State of the State/Budget Address.* Governor Tony Knowles on the Web www.gov.state.ak.us/SPEECH/sos01.html [Geo-2-232]

Konstantinov, Y. (1999). *The Northern Sea Route and Local Communities in Northwest Russia: Social Impact Assessment for the Murmansk Region.* INSROP Working Paper No. 152. Lysakker, Norway, Fridtjof Nansen Institute

Osherenko, G. and Young, O.R. (1989). *The Age of the Arctic: Hot Conflicts and Cold Realities.* Cambridge, Cambridge University Press

Rasmussen, R. O. and Hamilton, L. (2001). *The Development of Fisheries in Greenland. With focus on Paamiut/Frederikshaab and Sisisimiut/ Holsteinsborg.* North Atlantic Regional Studies, Research Paper 53. Roskilde, Denmark, Institute of Geography and Development Studies

Weir, F. (2001). *Russia's Arctic is now an economic gulag. The Christian Science Monitor Electronic Edition,* 26 February 2001 www.csmonitor.com/durable/2001/02/26/p1s4.htm [Geo-2-233]

World Gazetteer (2001). *The World Gazetteer.* http://www.gazetteer.de/home.htm [Geo-2-234]

# OUR CHANGING ENVIRONMENT: Everglades, United States

South Florida, the southeastern tip of the United States, was once a 23 000 km² unbroken marshland of sawgrass and small tree islands. The Kissimmee-Okeechobee-Everglades region formed a system of rivers, lakes and wetlands that controlled water flow, mitigated seasonal flooding, filtered sediment, and provided habitats for hundreds of species.

In 1948, the federal government started draining the Everglades and building dikes and canals for agricultural uses. There was a large loss of biodiversity, with some 10 million alligators killed between 1960 and 1965. Populations of herons, egrets, storks and spoonbills had, by 1979, decreased by 90 per cent. By 1998, 68 species were endangered or threatened with extinction.

Agricultural intensification produced sugar cane, tropical fruit and winter vegetables. However, that benefit is now threatened by encroachment from urban areas. Since 1998, the US Army Corps of Engineers has been attempting to restore the natural function of the Everglades. The estimated cost is US$7.8 billion, which covers only the first stage of the restoration effort, which is expected to require more than three decades.

1973, north

2000, north

1973, south

2000, south

Landsat data: USGS/EROS Data Center
Compilation: UNEP GRID Sioux Falls

# OUR CHANGING ENVIRONMENT: Santa Cruz, Bolivia

1975

1992

2000

The area round Santa Cruz de la Sierra in Bolivia has been rapidly deforested since the mid-1980s as a result of resettlement of people from the Altiplano (the Andean high plains) and a large agricultural development project called Tierras Baja. The pie or radial patterned fields (see photo below) are part of the resettlement scheme. In the middle of each unit is a small community centre including a church, bar/cafe, school and soccer field. The rectilinear, light-coloured areas are fields of soybeans cultivated for export. The dark strips running through the fields (bottom photo) are wind breaks, used to prevent erosion of the fine soils. Landsat images show the development of new agricultural settlements east of Santa Cruz in an area of tropical dry forest.

Landsat data: USGS/EROS Data Center
Text and photographs: Compton Tucker, NASA GSFC

# Disasters

## Global overview

Disasters can occur as a consequence of the impact of a natural or a human-caused hazard. Natural hazards comprise phenomena such as earthquakes, volcanic activity, landslides, tsunamis, tropical cyclones and other severe storms, tornadoes and high winds, river

---

**'A disaster is a serious disruption of the functioning of society, causing widespread human, material or environmental losses which exceed the ability of affected society to cope on its own resources.'** — *Source: UNDHA 2001*

---

and coastal flooding, wildfires and associated haze, drought, sand and dust storms, and infestations. Human-caused hazards may be intentional, such as the illegal discharge of oil, or accidental such as toxic spills or nuclear meltdown. All of these can expose people, ecosystems, flora and fauna to threats. The poor are the most vulnerable to disasters because they have fewer resources and capacity to prevent or cope with the impacts.

## Natural disasters

People and the environment are increasingly suffering from the effects of natural disasters. There are a number of reasons for this such as high population growth and density, migration and unplanned urbanization, environmental degradation and possibly global climate change. The sheer scope of the socio-economic impacts of natural disasters has brought about a shift in the political approach to dealing with the concept of risk in modern societies.

Comparing the past two decades, the number of people killed in natural and non-natural disasters was higher in the 1980s (86 328 annually) than in the 1990s (75 252 annually). However, more people were affected by disasters in the 1990s — up from an average of 147 million a year in the 1980s to 211 million people a year in the 1990s. While the number of geophysical disasters has remained fairly steady, the number of hydrometeorological disasters (those caused by water and weather) has increased (see figure on page 271). In the 1990s, more than 90 per cent of those killed in natural disasters lost their lives in hydrometeorological events such as droughts, windstorms and floods. While floods accounted for more than two-thirds of people affected by natural disasters, they are less deadly than many other types of disaster, accounting for only 15 per cent of deaths (IFRC 2001).

The social and economic costs of disasters vary widely and are difficult to estimate on a global basis. Insurance claims tend to be misleading as an estimate of the economic impact of disasters. Considering insured damage claims for the 1999 floods in Austria, Germany and Switzerland, at least 42.5 per cent of damage was covered by disaster insurance. But in Venezuela the same year, only 4 per cent of flood damage was covered (CRED-OFDA 2002). There is a need for reliable and systematic data on disasters to help assess their socio-economic and environmental impacts in both the short and the long term. But although communities in developing countries suffer from numerous local-scale disasters such as wildfires, small floods, droughts and pest infestations, these are often not reflected in disaster statistics.

The most expensive disasters in purely financial and economic terms are floods, earthquakes and windstorms but events such as drought and famine can be more devastating in human terms. While earthquakes accounted for 30 per cent of estimated damage, they caused just 9 per cent of all fatalities due to natural disasters. In contrast, famine killed 42 per cent, but accounted for just 4 per cent of damage over the past decade (IFRC 2001). In 1999, global financial losses from natural catastrophic events were estimated to exceed US$100 billion — the second highest figure on record. A total of 707 large events were recorded compared to 530 to 600 events in previous years. It is even more striking that the number of major catastrophic events over the past decade has increased threefold in comparison with the 1960s, while the rate of economic losses has increased by a factor of almost nine over the same period (Munich Re 2001).

Between 1995 and 1997, the impacts of natural hazards cost the United States at least US$50 billion a year, or the equivalent of about US$1 billion a week (IDNDR 1999a). The economic losses of the United States because of the 1997-98 El Niño event were estimated at US$1.96 billion or 0.03 per cent of GDP. Ecuador suffered equivalent financial losses but this represented 11.4 per cent of its GDP. The floods in China in 1991, 1994-95 and 1998 caused losses ranging from US$20 to 35 billion (CNC-IDNDR 1999).

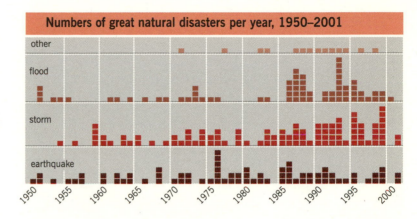

**Numbers of great natural disasters per year, 1950–2001**

Graph shows increasing trend in frequency of 'great' natural disasters. Catastrophes are classed as great if the ability of the region to help itself is overtaxed, making inter-regional or international assistance necessary, as is usually the case when thousands of people are killed, hundreds of thousands made homeless or when a country suffers substantial economic losses

Source: Munich Re 2001

## Recent disasters caused by extreme natural events

**The year 2000**

● Mongolian herders had their hardest winter for 30 years — 2.4 million livestock died and 45 per cent of the country's population was affected.

● In February and March, floods killed 650 people and left more than half a million homeless in Mozambique. Heavy rains also affected Botswana, Swaziland and Zimbabwe.

● Cyclones Eline (mid-February) and Gloria (early-March) left 184 000 people in need of immediate relief support out of the total of 737 000 affected in Madagascar. In early April, a third cyclone, Hudah, hit the north of the island.

● Floods in September and October in Southeast Asia, especially Viet Nam and Thailand, killed approximately 900 people and left 4 million homeless or with insufficient shelter. Losses estimated at US$460 million.

● Hurricane Keith in October killed eight and affected 62 000 people in Belize. Direct losses estimated at US$520 million.

● In mid-October, heavy rains caused floods in the Italian and Swiss Alps killing 38 people and causing economic losses estimated at US$8.5 billion.

● Similar floods killed six people and caused US$1.5 billion loss in the United Kingdom in November.

**The year 2001**

● In mid- to late January, heavy rains over Zambezia Province caused the Licungo River to flood in Mozambique. Nearly 500 000 people were affected by the floods.

● In March, floods devastated a wide area of northeastern Hungary, northwestern Romania and western Ukraine. Tens of thousands of people were forced to move.

● Flash floods unexpectedly struck parts of Pakistan on 23 July. The cities of Islamabad and Rawalpindi were the worst affected. 132 people were killed.

● In mid-November, as many as 576 Vietnamese had been killed by natural disasters, mainly floods and typhoons. Material losses amounted to more than US$200 million.

● A persistent multi-year drought in Central and Southwest Asia had affected about 60 million people by November 2001.

● After several months of drought, devastating floods tore through the Algerian capital Algiers on 10 November, killing 751 people. Thousands were injured, and about 40 000 people were left homeless.

Source: ReliefWeb (2002), Munich Re 2001

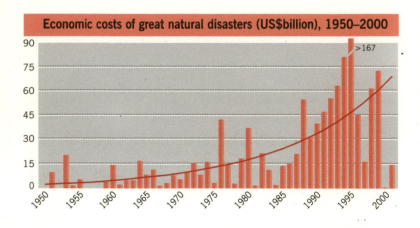

**Economic costs of great natural disasters (US$billion), 1950–2000**

In comparison with the 1960s, economic losses during the 1990s increased by a factor of almost nine

*Note: chart shows only the cost of 'great' natural catastrophes — see figure on page 271 for definition*

*Source: Munich Re 2001*

The annual loss from natural disasters over the period from 1989 to 1996 is estimated to range from 3 to 6 per cent of China's GDP, averaging 3.9 per cent. In December 1999, the Anatol, Lothar and Martin storms generated losses in northern Europe amounting to US$5–6 billion (Munich Re 2001). Less developed countries with limited economic diversity and poor infrastructure must not only rely mostly on external relief if a disaster happens but their economies need more time to recover. In developed economies, governments, communities and individuals have greater capacities to cope with disasters, the economic losses are to some extent absorbed by a diversified economy, and most assets are insured.

Among the least developed countries, 24 of the 49 face high levels of disaster risk; at least six of them have been affected by between two and eight major disasters per year in the past 15 years, with long-term consequences for human development (UNDP 2001). Since 1991, more than half of all the disasters reported occurred in countries with medium levels of human development (see 'Socio-economic background'). However, two-thirds of those killed came from countries with low levels of human development, while just 2 per cent came from highly developed countries. The effect of development on disasters is dramatic: on average, 22.5 people die per reported disaster in highly developed countries, 145 die per disaster in countries with medium human development, and 1 052 people die per disaster in countries with low levels of development (IFRC 2001).

A number of experts link the current trend in extreme weather events with an increase of the global mean temperature. Many parts of the world have suffered major heat waves, floods, droughts and other extreme weather events. While individual events,

such as El Niño-related phenomena (see box), cannot be directly linked to human-induced climate change, the frequency and magnitude of these types of events are predicted to increase in a warmer world. The changes in the global mean temperature are 'very likely' to affect parameters such as precipitation patterns, wind velocities, soil moisture and vegetation cover which appear to influence the occurrence of storms, hurricanes, floods, drought and landslides (IPCC 2001). For example, the extent of damage from storm surges can be directly linked to sea level variations.

Climate change and variability alone do not explain the increase in the impacts related to disasters. 'Natural' can be a misleading description for disasters such as the droughts, floods and cyclones which afflict much of the developing world. Identifying human-induced root causes, and advocating structural and political changes to combat them, is long overdue (IFRC 2001). For example, destruction of the natural environment because of logging or inappropriate land uses for short-term economic gain is one of the major

---

**Socio-economic effects of the 1997–98 El Niño**

The 1997-98 El Niño event affected virtually every region: Eastern Africa suffered drought and unusually high rainfall; Southeast Asia and North America, abnormally warm periods; South Asia, drought; Latin America and the Caribbean, unusually high rainfall and drought; and the Pacific Islands unusually high rainfall. The global socio-economic impacts were varied:

● More than 24 000 people died because of high winds, floods or storm tides that occurred during intense storms.
● More than 110 million people were affected and more than 6 million people were displaced as community infrastructures, including housing, food storage, transport and communications, were lost during storms.
● Direct economic losses exceeded US$34 billion.
● Waterlogging of fields reduced agricultural production in many regions; in others, the absence of storms and rain led to prolonged dry spells, loss of crops and reduction in water supplies.
● Wildfires were more frequent and widespread during extended dry periods.
● Increased incidence of disease followed the prolonged disruption to weather and rainfall patterns that resulted in contamination of water supplies or a more favourable environment for disease-carrying insect vectors.

*Sources: WMO 1999, UNU 2001*

factors promoting floods or mudslides such as those that hit Venezuela in December 1999. Similarly, the migration of population to urban and coastal areas increases human vulnerability as population densities increase, infrastructure becomes overloaded, living areas move closer to potentially dangerous industries, and more settlements are built in fragile areas such as floodplains or areas prone to landslides. As a result, natural catastrophes affect more people and economic losses are increased. For example, despite the fact that seismic activity has remained constant over recent years, the effects of earthquakes on the urban population appear to be increasing.

## Human-induced disasters

A number of major accidents involving chemicals and radioactive materials have drawn attention worldwide to the dangers of mismanagement, particularly in the transport, chemical and nuclear power sectors. These events often have impacts that transcend national boundaries; they also emphasize the fact that issues of technological safety concern more than just the developed countries.

Some disasters have resulted in the introduction of voluntary or mandatory regulations designed to prevent similar occurrences. Public concern following the explosion in 1976 at a pesticide plant in Seveso, Italy, with the release of 2,3,7,8-tetrachlorodibenzo-p-dioxin (TCDD), led to the introduction in 1982 of a European Directive on the major-accident hazards of certain industrial activities. Similarly, other major accidents, such as the methyl isocyanate leak at Bhopal, India, in 1984 and the Switzerland-Sandoz warehouse fire in Basel in 1989, stimulated legislation

### The 1999 earthquake in Izmit, Turkey

On 17 August 1999, an earthquake with a magnitude of 7.4-7.8 on the Richter scale hit the city of Izmit, Turkey, and the surrounding areas. Damage from the earthquake was estimated at more than US$13 billion. More than 15 000 people were killed, 25 000 others were injured and 600 000 people were left homeless. The earthquake was blamed for increasing the national account deficit of some US$3 billion in 1999-2000 (equivalent to about 1.5 per cent of the GNP).

A significant part of the damage could have been avoided had local building codes been effectively implemented. Many new buildings had not been properly designed, had not been built on foundations strong enough to resist earthquakes, and had not been sited in areas where the effects of earthquakes would have been diminished.

*Source: ISDR 1999*

in many countries to prevent and control chemical incidents. Influenced by the Bhopal accident, in particular, the International Labour Office developed in 1993 the Convention Concerning the Prevention of Major Industrial Accidents No. 174 and the Prevention of Major Industrial Accidents Recommendation No. 181. These documents call for an international exchange of relevant information, development of policies aimed at addressing the major accident risks, hazards and their consequences, and recognition that a major accident could have serious impacts on human life and the environment.

Major nuclear accidents such as those at Three Mile Island in the United States in 1979 and at Chernobyl in 1986 have not only catalysed action to strengthen nuclear safety and emergency preparedness but also forced many countries to

**Apartment block split in two by the 1999 earthquake in Izmit, Turkey**

*Source: Alexander Allmann, Munich Re*

abandon or severely restrict development of the nuclear power sector. Following the Chernobyl accident, two major international treaties were adopted — the Convention on Assistance in the Case of Nuclear Accident or Radiological Emergency and the Convention on the Early Notification of a Nuclear Accident. Most recently, the 1994 Convention on Nuclear Safety, committing parties to a higher level of nuclear safety, and the 1997 joint Convention on the Safety of Spent Fuel Management and on the Safety of Radioactive Waste Management were adopted.

The 1989 *Exxon Valdez* oil spill in Alaska resulted in enormous environmental and economic damages and catalysed the development of the 'Valdez Principles' — a voluntary code of conduct for corporate behaviour towards the environment — by the Coalition for Environmentally Responsible Economics (CERES). The 'Valdez Principles' guide corporations in the establishment of environmentally sound policies and require the raising of corporate environmental safety standards and the taking of responsibility for environmental harm that may be caused by them (Adams 1994).

## International policy responses

Until the 1970s, the international community considered disasters as exceptional circumstances, when local coping capacities were exhausted and external emergency relief was required. The term disaster management was generally equivalent to disaster response and tended to be within the exclusive competence of organizations such as the Red Cross and Red Crescent Societies or national civil defence institutions.

In 1971, the United Nations Disaster Relief Office, now the United Nations Office for the Coordination of Humanitarian Affairs (UNOCHA), was established to mobilize and coordinate relief activities from all sources in times of disaster. The concept of disaster preparedness was developed during the 1970s and 1980s, and included training and some cross-sectoral activities to increase capacity for rescue, relief and rehabilitation during and after a disaster. But even the most pessimistic forecasts could not have foreseen the upward spiral in negative socio-economic consequences of natural disasters in the closing decades of the 20th century.

The 1990s was declared the International Decade for Natural Disaster Reduction (IDNDR), one of the

### China committed to risk reduction

The Chinese government is shifting the focus of its disaster policies from improving response capabilities to reducing hazards and risks. During the past ten years, national coordination has been vested in the Chinese National Committee (CNC) for the IDNDR, an inter-ministerial organization composed of representatives from 28 ministries, departments and commissions. Since 1989, CNC has been working on the National Natural Disaster Reduction Plan of the People's Republic of China (1998-2010). It has also helped to develop and coordinate policies and plans for national and local disaster reduction activities.

Motivated by the seriousness of the 1991 floods in China, the Chinese authorities recognized the need 'to integrate disaster reduction into the comprehensive plan for national economy and social development'. The Chinese National Centre for Natural Disaster Reduction has now been established within the Chinese Academy of Sciences. The centre compiles and analyses data on disasters, and passes the results to the State Council for decision-making responsibilities.

China experienced its worst floods in more than 100 years in 1999, which affected more than 300 million people. The floods galvanized more political commitment for the integration of risk and disaster prevention programmes into national social and economic planning. However, China believes that there were fewer losses during the 1999 floods in the Yangtze River Valley, despite higher water levels, because of the US$7.6 billion invested in water conservancy measures since the costly 1998 floods.

*Source: CNC-IDNDR 1999*

principal goals of which was to inculcate a culture of disaster prevention through the wider application of known scientific and technological mechanisms by a better-informed population. In the words of United Nations Secretary-General Kofi Annan, 'We must, above all, shift from a culture of reaction to a culture of prevention. The humanitarian community does a remarkable job in responding to disasters. But the most important task in the medium and long-term is to strengthen and broaden programmes which reduce the number and cost of disasters in the first place. Prevention is not only more humane than cure, it is also much cheaper' (IDNDR 1999b). The IDNDR successfully placed risk reduction higher on the political agenda, as well as setting out a number of priorities to be undertaken by countries and regions in the 21st century.

An increasing number of governments and international organizations are promoting risk reduction as the only sustainable solution for reducing the social, economic and environmental impacts of disasters. Risk reduction strategies include:

- vulnerability mapping;
- identification of areas that are safe for settlement and development;
- adoption of building codes based on disaster resilient engineering and on local hazard risk assessments; and
- enforcing these plans and codes by economic and other incentives.

At the global level, the UN has established an International Strategy for Disaster Reduction (ISDR), a global platform aimed at helping all communities to become resilient to the effects of natural disasters and to proceed from protection against hazards to the management of risk through the integration of risk prevention into sustainable development. The strategy — based on the IDNDR experience and developments such as the 1994 Yokohama Strategy and Plan of Action for a Safer World and the 1999 Strategy 'A Safer World in the 21st Century: Disaster and Risk Reduction' — reflects a cross-sectoral and interdisciplinary approach to disaster reduction.

Implementation of the strategy, which is based on the establishment of partnerships between governments, non-governmental organizations, UN agencies, the scientific community and other

### Prevention and preparedness to reduce the costs of disasters

The fundamental goal of the UNEP disaster management programme is to reinforce the centrality of environmental concerns in disaster management. The other cornerstone is the adoption of preventive strategies and practical measures to reduce the potential loss of human lives and property, as well as destruction of the environment.

The success of this approach depends on increasing public awareness of the risks that natural, technological and environmental hazards pose to societies, and on educating people about the value of existing approaches for prevention and preparedness. UNEP contributes to this process through its programmes on environmental law, early warning and assessment, and Awareness and Preparedness for Emergencies at Local Level (APELL).

UNEP's APELL programme, developed in conjunction with governments and industry, recognizes that the incidence and effects of environmental disasters can be reduced by prevention and preparedness initiatives at the local level. The APELL concept has been successfully introduced to more than 30 countries and in more than 80 industrial communities worldwide. The UNEP strategy includes the promotion of cleaner production processes and technologies, and helping countries establish cleaner production centres.

A major objective of the UNEP early warning and assessment programme is to evaluate the increasing vulnerability of human society due to widespread environmental and climatic change in order to emphasize the need for sound integrated environmental management, and to provide early warning of emerging threats for preparedness and response.

stakeholders in the disaster reduction community, is an integral part of efforts aimed at promoting the overall goal of sustainable development. It is also an indispensable element in the search for solutions designed to counter the increasing threat posed by natural hazards (ISDR 1999).

### References: Chapter 2, disasters, global overview

Adams, J. (1994). Corporate Crime/Our Crime: What citizens have done and can do to curtail corporate 'crime'. In Context, 38, 45 http://www.context.org/ICLIB/IC38/Adams.htm [Geo-2-329]

CNC-IDNDR (1999). Natural Disaster and Disaster Relief in China; the China National Report on International Decade for Natural Disaster Reduction. Beijing, Chinese National Committee IDNDR

CRED-OFDA (2002). EM-DAT: The OFDA/CRED International Disaster Database. Centre for Research on the Epidemiology of Disasters http://www.cred.be/emdat [Geo-2-330]

IDNDR (1999a). Progress and Challenges in Reducing Losses from Natural Disasters http://www.usgs.gov/themes/sndr/sndr09.html [Geo-2-331]

IDNDR (1999b). Despite Dedicated Efforts, Number and Cost of Natural Disasters Continue To Rise. Press Release, United Nations International Strategy for Disaster Reduction http://www.unisdr.org/forum/press3.htm [Geo-2-332]

IFRC (2001). World Disasters Report 2001. International Federation of Red Cross and Red Crescent Societies http://www.ifrc.org/publicat/wdr2001/ [Geo-2-334]

IPCC (2001). Climate Change 2001: The Scientific Basis. Contribution of Working Group I to the Third Assessment Report of the Intergovernmental Panel on Climate Change. Cambridge, United Kingdom, and New York, United States, Cambridge University Press

ISDR (1999). Les retombées socio-économiques du seisme d'Izmit en Turquie. United Nations International Strategy for Disaster Reduction http://www.unisdr.org/unisdr/izmit.htm

ISDR (2001). The Concept of Disaster Reduction Embodied in the ISDR. United Nations International Strategy for Disaster Reduction http://www.unisdr.org/unisdr/aboutisdr.htm [Geo-2-333]

Munich Re (2001). Topics 2000: Natural Catastrophes — The Current Position. Special Millennium Issue. Munich, Munich Re Group

ReliefWeb (2002). Natural Disasters. ReliefWeb: Project of the United Nations Office for the Coordination of Humanitarian Affairs http://www.reliefweb.int/w/rwb.nsf

UNDHA (2001). United Nations Department of Humanitarian Affairs: Internationally agreed glossary of basic terms related to Disaster Management. United Nations International Strategy for Disaster Reduction http://www.unisdr.org/unisdr/glossaire.htm [Geo-2-335]

UNDP (2001). Disaster Profiles of the Least Developed Countries. Geneva, United Nations Development Programme Emergency Response Division

UNU (2001). Once Burned, Twice Shy? Lessons Learned from the 1997-98 El Niño. Tokyo, United Nations University http://www.esig.ucar.edu/un/index.html [Geo-1-032]

WMO (1999). The 1997-1998 El Niño Event: a Scientific and Technical Retrospective. Geneva, World Meteorological Organization

## Disasters: Africa

Extreme hydrometeorological events such as flooding and drought are common across Africa, while geophysical events such as earthquakes occur predominantly in Northern Africa, along the Atlas mountain range, and in the African Rift Valley, which also experiences volcanic activity. The El Niño Southern Oscillation causes significant climatic disturbances in most parts of Africa, either inducing drought or flooding, or increasing sea temperatures leading to cyclones.

These natural events become disasters where large numbers of people or infrastructure are affected, as has occurred over the past 30 years due to high population growth rates, especially in urban centres and drought-prone areas — 34 per cent of Africa's population lives in arid areas compared to just 2 per cent of Europe's population (Findlay 1996).

Impacts of disasters include loss of lives and livelihoods, damage to infrastructure and communications, interruption of economic activities, and increased risk of disease outbreaks. In many places, these impacts are worsened by poverty and marginalization, and overcrowding. Inadequate, old and deteriorating infrastructure and lack of economic security to provide for times of hardship also

compromise people's coping capacities and therefore magnify the impacts of disasters. There is growing concern that the frequency and severity of disasters are increasing at a time when early warning systems are inadequate and disaster management is weak (DMC 2000).

### Natural disasters

Africa has experienced some of the worst droughts and famines in terms of number of people killed or number affected (see table), with particularly severe droughts in 1972-73 and 1984-85, affecting much of Northern, Southern, Eastern and Sahelian Africa (Gommes and Petrassi 1996). Countries most regularly affected include Botswana, Burkina Faso, Chad, Ethiopia, Kenya, Mauritania and Mozambique (FAO 2001), where the impacts of famine are exacerbated by inadequate transport facilities to receive and distribute food and medical aid (Ehrlich and Ehrlich 1990). There are some indications that droughts are becoming more prolonged and their impacts more severe (DMC 2000, FAO 2000).

The risk of damage from heavy rain is greater in drier areas than in those that usually receive higher rainfall because there is less vegetation cover to absorb the water and stabilize soils. Expansion of informal settlements into the flood zone is putting many more people at risk of flooding, as illustrated in South Africa's Alexandra Township, Johannesburg, during the floods of 2000 when approximately 3 000 families living in shacks below the floodline were subjected to flooding and outbreaks of cholera (Kim 2000, World Bank 2001a).

Disasters can have severe economic impacts which are difficult to calculate. The Western Indian Ocean islands typically experience ten cyclones a year, between November and May, which bring strong winds and heavy rainfall. This causes destruction of infrastructure, particularly in low-lying areas and where settlements have encroached into flood-prone areas. Huge costs are incurred due to destruction of income-generation activities, including tourism revenues, and rehabilitation and replacement of damaged infrastructure and crops.

Globally, Africa suffers the least damage from disasters in purely financial terms but the significance of such losses may actually be greater in terms of impact on economic development. Africa's people and economies are heavily dependent on rainfed

### Some of the worst disasters in Africa, 1972–2000

|      |         |            | number killed | number affected |
|------|---------|------------|---------------|-----------------|
| 1972 | famine  | Ethiopia   | 600 000       | no data         |
| 1973 | drought | Ethiopia   | 100 000       | no data         |
| 1974 | drought | Ethiopia   | 200 000       | no data         |
| 1980 | drought | Mozambique | no data       | 6 000 000       |
| 1982 | famine  | Ghana      | no data       | 12 500 000      |
| 1983 | drought | Ethiopia   | no data       | 7 000 000       |
| 1984 | drought | Ethiopia   | 300 000       | 7 750 000       |
| 1984 | drought | Sudan      | 150 000       | 8 400 000       |
| 1985 | drought | Mozambique | 100 000       | 2 466 000       |
| 1987 | drought | Ethiopia   | no data       | 7 000 000       |
| 1990 | drought | Ethiopia   | no data       | 6 500 000       |
| 1991 | drought | Ethiopia   | no data       | 6 160 000       |
| 1991 | drought | Sudan      | no data       | 8 600 000       |
| 1993 | drought | Malawi     | no data       | 7 000 000       |
| 1993 | famine  | Ethiopia   | no data       | 6 700 000       |
| 1999 | famine  | Ethiopia   | no data       | 7 767 594       |
| 2000 | drought | Ethiopia   | no data       | 10 500 000      |

Source: CRED-OFDA 2002

agriculture, and are therefore vulnerable to rainfall fluctuations. It is usually the poor who suffer most from flood or drought-induced crop failure, because they often cultivate areas that are climatically marginal for crop production and they cannot accumulate reserves for times of hardship.

Both droughts and floods can result in malnutrition and famine, and the associated food imports and dependency on food aid can affect the economic growth potential of affected countries. In Kenya, low reservoir levels resulting from drought and siltation linked to deforestation led to reductions in hydropower generation, necessitating water and power rationing which devastated the country's economy in 1999 and 2000. Losses from power rationing alone were estimated at US$2 million per day, and the cost of unmet electricity demand was estimated at US$400-630 million, equal to 3.8-6.5 per cent of GDP (World Bank 2000). In Mozambique, the costs of floods in 2000 were estimated at US$273 million in physical damage, US$247 million in lost production, US$48 million in lost exports and US$31 million in increased imports (Mozambique National News Agency 2000).

## Human-caused disasters

Although climatic variability is a natural phenomenon, the increasing frequency and severity of extreme events can be in part attributed to human activities such as deforestation and inappropriate management of land and water resources. For example, clearing of tropical forests in Central and Western Africa has altered the local climate and rainfall patterns, and increased the risk of drought. Clearing of vegetation may also increase run-off and soil erosion. Damming of rivers and draining of wetlands reduces the environment's natural ability to absorb excess water, enhancing the impacts of floods. For example, countries in Southern Africa experienced devastating floods in 1999 and 2000 which affected more than 150 000 families (Mpofu 2000). Degradation of wetlands such as the Kafue wetlands in Zambia, damming of rivers, deforestation and overgrazing lowered the environment's ability to absorb excess water and magnified the impact of the floods (Chenje 2000, UNDHA 1994).

Over the past three decades, millions of Africans have sought refuge from natural and human-made disasters with both environmental and socio-economic

### Environmental impacts of refugees in Africa

Environmental rehabilitation of refugee camps in Africa alone could cost as much as US$150 million a year. Visible evidence of environmental degradation is most obvious in long-standing asylum countries such as Kenya and Sudan. Land surrounding the refugee camps has been stripped clean of trees and vegetation. In such situations, refugees may have to walk up to 12 km in search of water and firewood.

In the early 1990s, an estimated 20 000 ha of woodlands were cut each year in Malawi to provide firewood and timber for the various camps hosting Mozambican refugees, while in 1994, at the height of the refugee crisis near the Virunga National Park in the Democratic Republic of Congo (formerly Zaire), refugees were removing some 800 tonnes of timber and grass each day from the park — an amount far in excess of a possible sustainable yield. Despite efforts to restrict the impact on the park, almost 113 km$^2$ have been affected, of which more than 71 km$^2$ have been completely deforested. At another site in South Kivu, almost 38 km$^2$ of forest were lost within three weeks of the arrival of refugees. In December 1996, more than 600 000 refugees from Burundi and Rwanda were housed in the Kagera region in northwest Tanzania. More than 1 200 tonnes of firewood were consumed each day — a total of 570 km$^2$ of forest were affected, of which 167 km$^2$ were severely deforested.

*Source: UNHCR 2001a*

impacts. At the end of 2000, there were 3.6 million refugees in Africa, 56 per cent of whom were under 18 years of age (UNHCR 2001b). Often refugees are settled in fragile ecosystems where they exert considerable pressure on the natural resources, as they have no other means of survival (see box). Refugee populations also sometimes experience further conflicts with neighbouring communities, through competition for resources.

## Disaster responses

There have been no concerted regional efforts to manage disasters, and disaster responses in Africa have tended to focus on national and sub-regional levels. Efforts have also concentrated on responses rather than mitigation through improved environmental management and agricultural practices.

The unpredictable nature of extreme events, and the weak economic performance of most African countries, makes preparation for, and relief from, disasters all the more difficult. There have however been some successes in preventing famine resulting from drought, such as the Famine Early Warning System (FEWS) project, the implementation of a new efficient seed distribution system in Niger and promotion of more drought-resistant crop varieties.

In Northern Africa, efforts to respond to economic hardship during droughts include financing employment-generating projects to keep farmers from abandoning lands where productivity is declining, while in Eastern Africa afforestation and reforestation projects are being implemented to lessen the impact of future environmental changes, particularly climate change. In Southern Africa, the SADC Regional Early Warning Unit, the Regional Remote Sensing Project, the Drought Monitoring Centre and the FEWS Project advise governments on drought preparedness (see Chapter 3). A drought fund is also in place to mitigate the effects of poor rainfall (UNDHA 1994).

In some areas, including parts of West Africa, long-term measures such as urban planning regulations which prohibit developments along watercourses have been promulgated although resource constraints often prevent them from being strictly enforced. Additional responses include the development and implementation of early warning or forecasting mechanisms such as ENSO forecasting, which has been implemented in Southern Africa and the Western Indian Ocean area. While this has the potential to alert relief organizations and evacuate communities ahead of time, it has been limited by poor communications services (Dilley 1997). For example, only 152 of every 1 000 people in Africa had radios by 1997 (World Bank 2000b).

With global warming, the incidence of drought is likely to increase in many parts of Africa. The frequency and intensity of cyclones and floods in some areas are also likely to increase, adding to the stresses on water and food security, and possibly contributing to outbreaks of disease (IPCC 2001). For example, Seychelles is currently outside the cyclone zone but sea temperature rise could cause an increase in cyclone intensity and expansion of the cyclone zone to include the islands (UNEP 1999).

## References: Chapter 2, disasters, Africa

Chenje, M. (ed., 2000). *State of the Environment Zambezi Basin 2000*. Maseru, Lusaka and Harare, SADC, IUCN, ZRA and SARDC

Coe, M. and Foley, J. (2001). Human and Natural Impacts on the Water Resources of the Lake Chad Basin. *Journal of Geophysical Research* 27 February 2001, Vol. 106, No. D4

CRED-OFDA (2002). *EM-DAT: The OFDA/CRED International Disaster Database*. Centre for Research on the Epidemiology of Disasters http://www.cred.be/emdat [Geo-2-330]

Dilley, M. (1997). Warning and intervention: what kind of information does the response community need from the early warning community? *Internet Journal of African Studies, Vol. 2*. University of Bradford http://www.brad.ac.uk/research/ijas/ijasno2/dilley.html [Geo-2-336]

DMC (2000). *Ten-Day Bulletin*. DEKAD 19 Report (1-10 July, 2000). Nairobi, Drought Monitoring Centre

Ehrlich, P. and Ehrlich, A. (1990). *The Population Explosion*. London, Arrow Books

FAO (2000). *ACC Inter-Agency Task Force on the UN Response to Long Term Food Security, Agricultural Development and Related Aspects in the Horn of Africa*. Rome, Food and Agriculture Organization

FAO (2001). *17 Countries are Facing Exceptional Food Emergencies in Sub-Saharan Africa – FAO Concerned About Deteriorating Food Situation in Sudan, Somalia and Zimbabwe*. Press Release 01/48. Rome, Food and Agriculture Organization

Findlay, A.M. (1996). *Population and Environment in Arid Regions*. Policy and Research Paper No. 10, Paris, International Union for the Scientific Study of Population

Gommes, R. and Petrassi, F. (1996). *Rainfall Variability and Drought in Sub-Saharan Africa since 1960*. FAO Agrometeorology Working Paper No 9. Rome, Food and Agriculture Organization

IPCC (2001). *IPCC Third Assessment Report — Climate Change 2001. Working Group II: Impacts, Adaptation and Vulnerability*. Geneva, World Meteorological Organization and United Nations Environment Programme

Kim, S. (2000). *Southern Africa Swamped by Rains*. Disaster News Network http://www.disasternews.net/disasters/2-14-00_africa-swamped.shtml [Geo-2-337]

Mozambique National News Agency (2000). Government reports on flood damage and reconstruction. *AIM Reports,* Issue No. 194, 6 November 2000. Mozambique National News Agency http://www.poptel.org.uk/mozambique-news/newsletter/aim194.html#story1 [Geo-2-338]

Mpofu, B. (2000). *Assessment of Seed Requirements in Southern African Countries Ravaged by Floods and Drought 1999/2000*. SADC Food Security Programme http://www.sadc-fanr.org.zw/sssd/mozcalrep.htm [Geo-2-339]

UNDHA (1994). *First African Sub-Regional Workshop on Natural Disaster Reduction*, Gaborone, 28 November to 2 December 1994. Gaborone, United Nations Department of Humanitarian Affairs

UNEP (1999). *Western Indian Ocean Environment Outlook*. Nairobi, United Nations Environment Programme

UNHCR (2001a). *Refugees and the Environment — Caring for the Future*. Geneva, UNHCR – The UN Refugee Agency

UNHCR (2001b). *Refugee Children in Africa; Trends and Patterns in the Refugee Population in Africa Below the Age of 18 Years, 2000*. Geneva, UNHCR – The UN Refugee Agency

World Bank (2000). *World Bank Board Approves $72 million for Kenya*. World Bank News Release No: 2001/105/AFR. World Bank http://wbln0018.worldbank.org/news/pressrelease.nsf [Geo-2-340]

World Bank (2001a). *Upgrading Urban Communities, Version 2001. Spotlight on Alexandra, South Africa*. Massachusetts Institute of Technology http://web.mit.edu/urbanupgrading/upgrading/case-examples/overview-africa/alexandra-township.html [Geo-2-341]

World Bank (2001b). *World Development Indicators 2001*. Washington DC, World Bank http://www.worldbank.org/data/wdi2001/pdfs/tab3_8.pdf [Geo-2-024]

## Disasters: Asia and the Pacific

About 75 per cent of the world's major natural catastrophes between 1970 and 1997 occurred in the Asia and the Pacific region, mostly in poverty-ridden developing countries (UNESCAP and ADB 2000). There has been a general upward trend in the number of natural disasters due to hydrometeorological events (such as cyclones and flooding) in the region, while geophysical disasters such as volcanic eruptions, earthquakes and tsunamis have remained fairly steady (see figure).

### Natural disasters

Vulnerability to disasters is closely linked with population density and economic resources. The impact of natural disasters in the region is severe, with more than 1.4 million people killed, almost 4 000 million affected and US$438 million in damage over the past three decades (see table). During 1991-2000 alone, the total number of deaths caused by natural disasters in the region exceeded 550 000 or 83 per cent of the global total (IFRC 2001), the majority of them in Asian countries with low or medium levels of human development.

The highest number of deaths occurred in South Asia (the sub-region with the highest population density and the lowest per capita income) and the lowest number in Australia and New Zealand, the sub-region with the lowest population density and a high per capita income (UNPD 2001, World Bank 2001).

China experienced more than 300 natural disasters and recorded more than 311 000 deaths during 1971-2000; India with more than 300 disasters suffered more than 120 000 deaths; the Philippines, with nearly 300 events, lost about 34 000 people; Indonesia experienced about 200 disasters with more than 15 000 lives lost; and Bangladesh experienced 181 events and more than 250 000 people killed.

Some areas are more exposed to natural hazards because of location (on the coast, near a volcano or geological fault). Cyclones occur most frequently over the Northwest Pacific, over the southern end of the Bay of Bengal, east of India and south of Bangladesh (UNESCAP and ADB 1995, Ali 1999, Huang 1999, Kelly and Adger 2000). Bangladesh, China and India are the most flood-prone countries of the region (Mirza and Eriksen 1996, Ji and others 1993). Hilly and mountainous areas (China, India, Nepal, Philippines and

Thailand) are most prone to landslides, which are aggravated by deforestation and cultivation that destabilizes slopes. Countries along or adjacent to seismic zones (Afghanistan, China, India, Iran, Nepal, Philippines and the Pacific Islands) are more vulnerable to seismic events, while countries along the Pacific Rim are at risk from volcanic eruptions, particularly Indonesia, Japan and the Philippines (UNESCAP and ADB 1995). The El Niño phenomenon has significant impacts over large areas in the region, the most affected being Indonesia (Glantz 1999, Salafsky 1994, 1998).

### Other disasters

Environmental degradation and change are becoming increasingly important in relation to both the occurrence and impact of natural disasters. Deforestation, for example, is now frequently linked to severe flood events and landslides. Overexploitation of

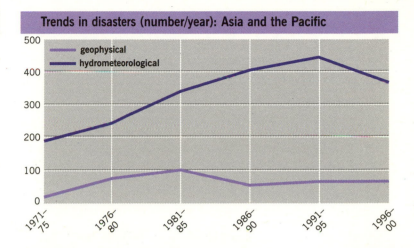

**Trends in disasters (number/year): Asia and the Pacific**

Disasters caused by water and weather (hydrometeorological disasters) have become more frequent while the number of geophysical disasters remains fairly constant

Source: CRED-OFDA 2002

### Impact of natural disasters in Asia and the Pacific, 1972–2000

| | number killed (thousands) | number affected (thousands) | damage (US$1 000) |
|---|---|---|---|
| South Asia | 761 | 2 164 034 | 60 881 |
| Southeast Asia | 73 | 284 074 | 33 570 |
| Northwest Pacific and East Asia | 606 | 1 447 643 | 317 174 |
| Central Asia | 3 | 4 895 | 986 |
| Australia and New Zealand | 1 | 15 761 | 21 900 |
| South Pacific | 4 | 4 061 | 3 139 |
| **total** | **1 447** | **3 920 467** | **437 649** |

Note: Central Asia figures are for 1992/93–2000
Source: CRED-OFDA 2002

## Selected natural disasters: Asia and the Pacific

- July 1976: an earthquake in China took 242 000 lives
- April 1991: a cyclone in Bangladesh accompanied by a storm surge caused 138 866 deaths
- February 1990 and December 1991: cyclones in Samoa caused losses of US$450 million, about four times the country's GDP
- January 1995: an earthquake in Kobe, Japan, became one of the costliest natural disasters in history — 5 502 people were killed and more than 1 800 000 affected, with damage estimated at US$131.5 billion
- October 1999: the Super Cyclone in the eastern state of Orissa in India caused more than 10 000 deaths, while 15 million people were rendered homeless, left without food, shelter or water and their livestock population devastated — the cyclone damaged 1.8 million ha of agricultural land and uprooted more than 90 million trees
- January 2001: an earthquake of magnitude 7.7 on the Richter scale rocked the state of Gujarat in India, causing more than 20 000 deaths and 167 000 injuries — economic losses estimated at US$2.1 billion

*Sources: ADPC 2001, CRED-OFDA 2002, DoAC India 2002*

located in coastal or lowland areas. For the small island developing states, climate change and extreme weather events may also have dramatic impacts on terrestrial biodiversity, subsistence cropping and forest food sources (IPCC 1998).

Rapid population growth, urbanization and weak land-use planning are some of the reasons why poor people move to fragile and high risk areas which are more exposed to natural hazards. Moreover, the rapid growth of industries in urban areas has induced rural–urban migration. This has sometimes led to more people being exposed to technological hazards such as the disaster in Bhopal, India, in 1984, in which escaping methyl isocyanate from an industrial plant killed more than 3 000 and affected more than 200 000 others (Robins 1990).

## Disaster responses

Asian countries are at different stages of institutional development with respect to disaster reduction. Some, such as Japan, have a long-established system of disaster management. Stimulated by the International Decade for Natural Disaster Reduction (IDNDR), other countries (such as Viet Nam, see box page 281) have either strengthened existing frameworks or are formulating new ones (UNESCAP and ADB 1995).

Despite some recent achievements, significant

water resources has already resulted in sub-regional environmental disasters such as the drying up of the Aral Sea in Central Asia (see box below and feature on page 296).

Most of the countries in the Northwest Pacific and East Asia sub-region and the Pacific Island countries will be particularly vulnerable to climate change and associated sea-level rise because so many human settlements and so much industrial infrastructure are

## The Aral Sea: a human-induced environmental and humanitarian disaster

The destruction of the Aral Sea is now a well-known example of unsustainable development. Atlases used to describe the sea as the world's fourth largest lake, with an area of 66 000 km$^2$ and a volume of more than 1 000 km$^3$. Its waters supplied local fisheries with annual catches of 40 000 tonnes, while the deltas of its tributaries hosted dozens of smaller lakes and biologically rich marshes and wetlands covering 550 000 ha.

In the 1960s, planners in the former Soviet Union assigned Central Asia the role of supplier of raw cotton. Irrigation was imperative, and the Aral Sea and its tributaries seemed a limitless source of water. Irrigated land was expanded from about 4.5 million ha in 1960 to almost 7 million ha in 1980. The local population also grew rapidly, from 14 million to about 27 million in the same period, while total water withdrawal almost doubled to an annual 120 km$^3$, more than 90 per cent of it for agriculture.

The result was the collapse of the prevailing

water balance in the basin. Waterlogging and salinization eventually affected about 40 per cent of irrigated land. Overuse of pesticides and fertilizer polluted surface water and groundwater, and the delta ecosystems simply perished: by 1990, more than 95 per cent of the marshes and wetlands had given way to sand deserts, and more than 50 delta lakes, covering 60 000 ha, had dried up.

The surface of the Aral Sea shrank by one-half and its volume by three-quarters. The mineral content of the water has increased fourfold, preventing the survival of most of the sea's fish and wildlife. Commercial fishing ended in 1982. Former seashore villages and towns are now 70 km from the present shoreline.

Communities face appalling health problems. In Karakalpakstan, Uzbekistan, drinking water is saline and polluted, with a high content of metals that causes a range of diseases. Over the past 15 years, there has been a 3 000 per cent increase in chronic bronchitis and in kidney and liver

diseases, especially cancer, while arthritic diseases have increased 6 000 per cent. The infant mortality rate is one of the world's highest.

Five newly independent Central Asian states have now established a joint commission for water coordination. Several international organizations and bilateral agencies are providing assistance, and an International Fund for the Aral Sea and the Interstate Council for the Aral Sea Problem have been set up to coordinate initiatives.

The Central Asian republics have decided to focus on demand management, aiming to reduce water withdrawal by raising irrigation efficiency. The primary objective is to satisfy crop water requirements. Total water withdrawal in the basin has now stabilized at 110-120 km$^3$/year but environmental degradation continues.

*Source: FAO 1998*

measures and actions still remain to be taken at the regional and national levels to reduce risks and losses due to disasters, namely:

- the impact of environmental degradation needs to be examined — raising awareness about the dangers of environmental degradation among the governments and people is of utmost importance;
- deforestation should be stopped;
- mitigation and preparedness measures already undertaken must be strengthened;
- actions are needed to reduce poverty levels with a view to maintaining the resource base and protecting biodiversity; and
- rural development is a prerequisite for reducing the migration of people to cities and coastal areas.

## Being prepared: Viet Nam's disaster reduction programme

Viet Nam has a long tradition of disaster mitigation. When the United Nations General Assembly designated the 1990s as the International Decade for Natural Disaster Reduction, Viet Nam responded by organizing a National Committee and strengthening the role its Central Committee for Flood and Storm Control (CCFSC) plays in disaster mitigation. The CCFSC has developed programmes, plans and measures for disaster reduction in coordination with other relevant organizations, directed the implementation of disaster mitigation activities and coordinated actions with relevant international organizations.

In the late 1990s, Viet Nam experienced a number of extreme events, including Typhoon Linda (1997) in the southern coastal area. Although the human and economic losses were tragic, agencies at all levels strengthened their search and rescue capacities, resulting in tens of thousands of evacuations. More than 5 000 people were saved by these efforts. Once the typhoon abated, the government provided assistance to the local fishing communities. As a result of this and other disasters, the government took policy decisions for each part of the country, including improving flood resistance and protecting populated areas, by strengthening the system of dykes and flood diversion structures in northern Viet Nam, policies to prevent and mitigate flood damage in central Viet Nam, and the Mekong River Delta policy which is designed to prepare measures for living with floods and minimizing their damage.

In recognition of these achievements, the United Nations awarded Viet Nam the Certificate of Distinction for Disaster Reduction on 11 October 2000, the International Day for Disaster Reduction.

*Source: UNEP 2001*

## References: Chapter 2, disasters, Asia and the Pacific

Ali, A. (1999). Climate Change Impacts and Adaptation Assessment in Bangladesh. *Climate Research,* special 6, 12 (2/3), 109–16

ADPC (2001). *Asian Disaster Management News,* Vol. 7, No. 1, January-March 2001. Bangkok, Asian Disaster Preparedness Centre, Asian Institute of Technology

CRED-OFDA (2002). *EM-DAT: The OFDA/CRED International Disaster Database.* Centre for Research on the Epidemiology of Disasters http://www.cred.be/emdat [Geo-2-330]

DoAC India (2002). Super Cyclone Orissa. Natural Disaster Management, Department of Agriculture and Cooperation, India http://ndmindia.nic.in/cycloneorissa/ [Geo-2-343]

FAO (1998). Time to save the Aral Sea? *Agriculture 21,* 1998 http://www.fao.org/WAICENT/FAOINFO/AGRICULT/ magazine/9809/spot2.htm (26/09/2001) [Geo-2-342]

Glantz, M. H. (1999). *Currents of Change: EL Nino's Impact on Climate and Society.* Cambridge, Cambridge University Press

Huang, Z.G. (1999). *Sea Level Changes in Guangdong and its Impacts.* Guangzhou, China, Guangdong Science and Technology Press (in Chinese)

IFRC (2001). *World Disaster Report 2000.* Geneva, International Federation of Red Cross and Red Crescent Societies

IPCC (1998). *The Regional Impacts of Climate Change: An Assessment of Vulnerability.* Cambridge, Cambridge University Press

Ji, Z.X., Jiang, Z.X and Zhu, J.W. (1993). Impacts of Sea Level Rise on Coastal Erosion in the Changjiang Delta Northern Jiangsu Coastal Plain. *Acta Geographica Sinica,* 48 (6), 516–26 (in Chinese with English Abstract)

Kelly, P.M. and Adger, W.N. (2000). Theory and Practice in Assessing Vulnerability to Climate Change and Facilitating Adaptation. *Climate Change,* 47, 325-52

Mirza, M.Q. and Ericksen, N.J. (1996). Impact of Water Control Projects on Fisheries Resources in Bangladesh. *Environmental Management,* 20(4), 527–39

Robins, J. (1990). *The World's Greatest Disasters.* London, Hamlyn

Salafsky, N. (1994). Drought in the Rainforest: Effects of the 1991 El Niño Southern Event on a Rural Economy in West Kailimantan, Indonesia. *Climate Change,* 27, 373–96

Salafsky, N. (1998). Drought in the Rainforest, Part II: an Update Based on the 1994 ENSO Event. *Climate Change,* 39, 601–3

UNEP (2001). Disasters. *Our Planet* http://www.ourplanet.com/imgversn/113/ngo.html [Geo-2-344]

UNESCAP and ADB (1995). *State of the Environment in Asia and the Pacific 1995.* United Nations Economic and Social Commission for Asia and the Pacific and the Asian Development Bank, United Nations, New York

UNESCAP and ADB (2000). *State of the Environment in Asia and Pacific 2000.* Economic and Social Commission for Asia and the Pacific and Asian Development Bank. New York, United Nations http://www.unescap.org/enrd/environ/soe.htm [Geo-2-266]

World Bank (2001). *World Development Indicators 2001.* Washington DC, World Bank http://www.worldbank.org/data/wdi2001/pdfs/tab3_ 8.pdf [Geo-2-024]

## Disasters: Europe

Disasters resulting from natural and human-caused hazards occur throughout Europe, often leading to significant environmental damage, economic loss, human injuries and premature mortality. The overall consequences depend on both the magnitude of the event and on factors such as population density, disaster prevention, preparedness and response measures and emergency planning. Europe generally suffers less from disasters than many developing countries, due to a higher level of 'coping capacity' in terms of government ability to prepare and respond to disasters.

### Natural disasters

In Europe, the most common natural disasters are storms and floods, although earthquakes do occur in some countries. Storms and floods are also the most costly in terms of economic and insured losses. The windstorms Lothar and Martin that occurred in December 1999 caused an estimated €5 billion damage to crops, forests and infrastructure while the cost of flood damage between 1991 and 1995 has been estimated at €99 billion. One of the worst years ever in terms of flood damage was 2000, accounting for

Lothar, the first of two severe storms that passed over Western Europe on 26–27 December 1999, caused severe damage. This image shows the storm passing over Europe at 12.00 UTC on 26 December, with the northern African coast outlined below

Source: copyright EUMETSAT 2002

### The Rhine Action Plan on Flood Defence

In January 1998, the 12th Conference of Rhine Ministers adopted an Action Plan on Flood Defence to be implemented over 20 years. The most important aims of the plan are to reduce damage by up to 10 per cent by the year 2005 and by up to 25 per cent by 2020. Extreme flood levels downstream of the regulated Upper Rhine are to be reduced by up to 30 cm by 2005 and by up to 70 cm by 2020. These ambitious targets are likely to be reached only through an integrated managerial approach at local, national, regional and international levels.

Over the past two centuries, the Rhine has lost more than 85 per cent of its natural floodplains to buildings and agriculture. There were severe floods in 1993 and 1995. The assets that could be affected in areas at flood risk may amount to €1 500 billion. Countermeasures, such as the preservation and expansion of floodplains, and improved water storage in the entire catchment area, must aim at the ecological improvement of the Rhine, its valley and catchment area.

Source: ICPR 2001

almost one-quarter of the total US$10.6 billion insured costs (Swiss Re 2001). In recent years, many European countries have experienced abnormally high precipitation intensity and duration, especially in winter months, which has led to floods in the Czech Republic, France, Germany, Hungary, Italy, Portugal, Switzerland, Ukraine and the United Kingdom. Between 1971 and 1996, 163 major floods occurred in Europe. The main factors that induce or intensify floods and their impacts include climate change, land sealing, changes in the catchment and floodplain land use, population growth, urbanization and increasing settlement, roads and railways and sometimes hydraulic engineering measures (EEA 2001a).

Forest fires and droughts are a problem in the southern countries along the rim of the Mediterranean (Croatia, France, Greece, Italy, Slovenia and Spain) and fires are also common in the Siberian region of the Russian Federation where economic recession has caused a severe decline in the response capacity of local authorities and forest fire teams. Each year, hundreds of thousand of hectares of taiga forest are lost due to fires. Around 80 per cent of forest fires are a result of people's ignorance of fire safety rules.

The average annual number of natural disasters appears to be increasing and since the late 1980s there has also been an increase in the impacts of these disasters and their related economic losses — at least in the European Union (EEA 1999). For example, at the French–German border, the floodwaters of the Rhine rose more than 7m above flood level about once every 20 years between 1900 and 1977. Since 1977, that level has been reached on average once every other year (UWIN 1996). Actions and measures are taken at both national and regional level to reduce the impacts of natural disasters (see box left), though there is no targeted policy. Integrated land-use planning can, to some extent, prevent impacts on humans. Emergency response plans have been produced throughout the European Union to react to various natural disasters, but these appear to be ad hoc, generally not tested, and are considered unlikely to work well in practice (EEA 1999).

## Major human-caused disasters

Human-caused disasters cause more human fatalities and economic losses than natural disasters in Europe. Despite overall higher technological and safety levels in Europe, the number of industrial accidents in the European Union continues to rise (EC undated). In 1997, there were 37 major industrial accidents — the highest annual number since records began in 1985 (EEA 1999). In contrast to accidents in fixed installations, major oil spills from marine transport and offshore installation accidents have shown a downward trend (ITOPF 2000) although the total number of oil spills appears to be increasing (EEA 2001b).

It is likely that the overall risk from nuclear accidents increased in the 1970s as more plants were commissioned but declined in the 1990s as older plants were taken out of service and the building of new ones either slowed or was completely abandoned due to public pressure. However, quantifying the risk from accidental releases of radionuclides is not possible due to lack of sufficiently detailed, comparable information. A widespread campaign on increasing the safety of new and already functioning civil nuclear reactors, especially in CEE countries, was catalysed by the 1986 nuclear accident at Chernobyl in the former Soviet Union. Significant resources have been allocated to increasing nuclear safety at nuclear processing plants (for example, €838 million was spent by the European Commission between 1991 and 1998 (EC 2001)). However, a complicating factor is the increasing deterioration of the older nuclear power plants in the Russian

Federation and Lithuania built to a similar design to the Chernobyl reactor.

Analyses of major industrial accidents indicate that component failure and operator error are the two most common immediate causes but the dominant underlying causes identified were poor safety and environmental management (Drogaris 1993, Rasmussen 1996). The age of process plants is a further factor as the probability of 'wear-out' failure increases with age (M&M Protection Consultants 1997). Lack of expenditure on safety and environmental management, and operating plants past their design life, are often a result of pressure from

Helicopter sprays water on one of the forest fires that periodically plague southern European countries such as Croatia, France, Greece, Italy, Slovenia and Spain; fires are also common in the Siberian region of the Russian Federation

*Source: UNEP, Rougier, Topham Picturepoint*

### Baia Mare: analysis of a mining accident

At 22:00 on 30 January 2000, a dam wall failed at a mine tailings reclamation facility at Baia Mare in northwestern Romania, spilling 100 000 m³ of wastewater polluted with cyanide into the Tisa river and then the Danube, eventually entering the Black Sea, by which time it had become significantly diluted. The spill devastated large numbers of plant and wildlife species in the river systems.

The Baia Mare Task Force, set up to investigate, reported that faults in the design of the operating plant, including inadequate construction of the dams, contributed to the accident. The key problem was believed to be the ineffectiveness of the permitting and enforcement authorities. The permitting process was over-complex and the Task Force concluded that the original environmental impact assessment was flawed. Furthermore, no measures were established to deal with an emergency, and monitoring of the water level in the tailings pond where the dam broke was inadequate.

*Source: BMTF 2000*

shareholders wishing to increase profitability, although this may result in major losses in the long run. However, they also reveal gaps in regulation and monitoring. The mining accident at Baia Mare, Romania, in January 2000 served as a rather sobering reminder of the shortcomings in enforcement of environmental regulations in the countries of Eastern Europe (see box on page 283).

## Policy responses

For many technological disasters, holistic approaches are becoming more prevalent, with increasing attention to reducing the risk of long-term environmental impacts as well as reducing acute health and property damage from accidents (EEA 1999). The European Commission's directive on the control of major-accident disasters involving dangerous substances (often referred to as the 'Seveso II Directive'), now also incorporated into the legal systems of most CEE countries, is important in this respect. Its Major Accident Reporting System (MARS) database and the Seveso Plants Information Retrieval System database are practical tools helping countries make decisions related to risk management.

Information on the extent and location of technological hazards is generally improving. Emergency response plans can now be made for technological accidents but further efforts are still

necessary to reduce risks (EEA 1999).

Since pollution does not stop at political boundaries, one of the most important multilateral agreements in this respect is the 1992 Helsinki Convention on the Protection and Use of Transboundary Watercourses and International Lakes, which entered into force in 1996. This convention includes requirements to conduct environmental impact analyses (EIAs), to notify downstream states of accidents and it enforces the 'polluter pays' principle. The 1991 Convention on Environmental Impact Assessment in the Transboundary Context, which entered into force in 1997, requires parties to notify and consult each other on all major potentially dangerous ongoing projects (ECE 1991). An innovative approach is under consideration with respect to a proposed joint protocol on liability under the Helsinki Convention and the Convention on the Transboundary Effects of Industrial Accidents (REC 2000).

Most European countries are parties to these multilateral treaties, and international cooperation under their provisions helps governments improve national policies in respect of human-caused disaster prevention and mitigation.

### References: Chapter 2, disasters, Europe

BMTF (2000). *Report of the International Task Force for Assessing the Baia Mare Accident.* Brussels, European Commission

Drogaris, G. (1993). Learning from major accidents involving dangerous substances. *Safety Science,* 16, 89-113

EEA (1999). *Environment in the European Union at the Turn of the Century.* Environmental Assessment Report No. 2. Copenhagen, European Environment Agency

EEA (2001a). *Sustainable Water Use in Europe. Part 3: Extreme Hydrological Events: Floods and Droughts.* Environmental Issues Report No. 21. Copenhagen, European Environment Agency

EEA (2001b). *Environmental Signals 2001.* Environmental Assessment Report No. 8. Copenhagen, European Environment Agency

EC (undated). *Major Accident Reporting System of the European Commission.* MARS http://mahbsrv.jrc.it/mars/Default.html [Geo-2-3??]

EC (2001). *Nuclear Safety in Central Europe and the New Independent States.* Europa http://europa.eu.int/comm/external_relations/nuclear _safety/intro/ [Geo-2-347]

ECE (2001). *Convention on Environmental Impact Assessment in a Transboundary Context.* United Nations Economic Commission for Europe, Environment and Human Settlements Division. http://www.unece.org/env/eia/ [Geo-2-352]

EUMETSAT (2002). Winter Storm Lothar over Europe as seen in Meteosat Images http://www.eumetsat.de/en/area5/special/storm_26 121999.html

ICPR (2001). *Action Plan on Flood Defense.* The International Commission for the Protection of the Rhine. http://www.iksr.org/icpr/11uk.htm [Geo-2-348]

ITOPF (2000). *Historical Data.* International Tanker Owners Pollution Federation http://www.itopf.com/stats.html

M&M Protection Consultants (1997). *Large Property Damage Losses in the Hydrocarbon-Chemical Industries A Thirty-year Review.* AcuSafe http://www.acusafe.com/Incidents/Statistics/MarshP etrochemicalLosses0201.pdf [Geo-2-351]

Rasmussen, K. (1996). *The Experience with the Major Accident Reporting System from 1984 to 1993.* CEC, EUR 16341 EN

REC (2000). *Europe 'Agreeing': 2000 Report on the Status and Implementation of Multilateral Environmental Agreements in the European Region.* Szentendre, Hungary, Regional Environmental Centre for Central and Eastern Europe and United Nations Environment Programme

Swiss Re (2001). Property claims service. *The Economist,* 31 March 2001

UWIN (1996). *Worldwide Paper on River and Wetland Development.* Carbondale, Universities Water Information Network, Southern Illinois University

## Disasters: Latin America and the Caribbean

In Latin America and the Caribbean, the main natural hazards are droughts, hurricanes, cyclones, tropical storms, floods, tidal waves, avalanches, landslides and mudslides, earthquakes and volcanoes. Mining and oil spill accidents represent the main human-caused disasters in the region.

A total of 65 260 deaths due to natural disasters were reported in the region during the 1990s. The deaths were mainly a result of floods (54 per cent), epidemics (18.4 per cent), storms, cyclones and hurricanes (17.7 per cent), earthquakes (5.2 per cent) and landslides (3.2 per cent) (CRED-OFDA 2002). Considering that floods and landslides are often associated with storms and hurricanes, this means that three-quarters of total human losses due to natural disasters in the region have a hydrometeorological origin.

The number of deaths due to disasters declined markedly between 1972 and 1999, coinciding with the global trend. Total fatalities in the 1990s were less than one-third of those in the 1970s while the number of people injured fell by almost one-half (after rising by nearly 30 per cent in the 1980s) (CEPAL 1999). This trend can be explained by fewer severe earthquakes in densely populated or highly vulnerable areas and by the establishment of early warning systems and disaster-preparedness measures in some countries over the past 30 years (PAHO 1998). Economic losses caused by disasters increased by almost 230 per cent between the 1960s and the 1990s (CEPAL 1999), again reflecting a global trend.

### Hydrometeorological events

The best known hydrometeorological event is the El Niño phenomenon, the impacts of which can be severe. For example, after the El Niño of 1983, Peru's GDP fell by 12 per cent, mostly because of a reduction in agricultural output and fishery. The national economy took a decade to recover. Damage in the Andean Community countries (Bolivia, Colombia, Ecuador, Peru and Venezuela) due to the 1997/98 El Niño was estimated at more than US$7 500 million (CEPAL 1999).

Most countries in Central America and the Caribbean are within the hurricane belt, on both the Atlantic and Pacific coasts. Hurricane Mitch, which

### El Niño and epidemic diseases

Cyclical temperature and rainfall variations associated with El Niño are particularly important since they can favour the development and proliferation of vectors of epidemic diseases such as malaria, dengue fever, yellow fever and bubonic plague (WHO 1999). In South America, the most severe outbreaks of malaria generally occur a year after the beginning of an El Niño event, whether associated with an increase in rainfall (as in 1983 in Bolivia, Ecuador and Peru) or with a reduction in rainfall and run-off (as in Colombia and Venezuela).

A similar link has been suggested between the warming of superficial oceanic waters by El Niño, the proliferation of marine algae, and the appearance of cholera in South America in 1992. The impact of extremes in precipitation (both too much and too little) is also important in the transmission of water-borne diseases such as cholera, gastrointestinal infections and various types of diarrhoea. There were outbreaks of cholera in 1997–98 in Honduras, Nicaragua and Peru related to the increase in precipitation, associated with El Niño (WHO 1999, PAHO 1998).

struck the region in 1998, affecting mostly Honduras and Nicaragua, killed more than 17 000 people and left three million homeless with damage estimated at US$3 000 million. The hurricane also caused fatalities and serious environmental and economic damage in Costa Rica, Dominican Republic, El Salvador and Guatemala (CRED-OFDA 2002).

The 1999 floods on the northern coast of Venezuela also had a strong impact, with damage estimated at more than US$ 3 200 million or 3.3 per cent of the country's GDP (World Bank 2000). In the state of Vargas, the hardest-hit area, more than 230 000 jobs were lost. The state of Miranda was also badly hit: the El Guapo dam collapsed, causing water shortages and 60 per cent of crops were reported lost (MoPD Venezuela 2000). It is estimated that there were 30 000 deaths, 30 000 families left homeless and more than 81 000 dwellings destroyed (IFRC 2002).

### Ecological and social impacts of earthquakes in El Salvador

The series of earthquakes that shook El Salvador in early 2001 began with one of 7.6 on the Richter scale that was initially considered an isolated event. However, it was only part of a series that spanned weeks and demonstrated the complex social and ecological implications of such events. Besides the loss of life and infrastructure during the original series of earthquakes, there has been a long-lasting impact on people and ecosystems. For example, the artisanal fishery lost an essential part of its docking infrastructure as well as service infrastructure for processing fish and transporting it to the market on land. A total of 30 772 farms were damaged and farmers were forced to wait for three months for the rains because they did not have the funds to repair their damaged irrigation systems. The destruction of 20 per cent of the country's coffee processing plants severely affected the jobs and income of thousands of rural families in a country that was also affected by Hurricane Fifi in 1974, civil conflict between 1978 and 1992, the 1986 earthquake and Hurricane Mitch in 1998.

*Source: UNICEF 2001*

## Geological events

Seismic and tectonic activities are particularly intense along the Pacific Ocean coast and in the Caribbean basin due to pressures generated between oceanic and continental plates. Such activity creates a relatively high risk of earthquakes, tsunamis and volcanic eruptions which in some areas add to the already high risk of hurricanes and floods. Between 1972 and 1999, extreme geological events killed 65 503 people and affected 4.4 million others (CRED-OFDA 2002).

### Vulnerability to natural hazards of Caribbean countries

| | hurricanes | earthquakes | volcanoes | floods | drought |
|---|---|---|---|---|---|
| Antigua and Barbuda | high | high | low | high | high |
| Bahamas | high | low | low | medium | low |
| Barbados | high | high | low | high | low |
| Belize | high | high | low | high | low |
| Cuba | high | high | low | high | high |
| Dominica | high | high | high | high | high |
| Dominican Republic | high | high | low | high | medium |
| Granada | high | high | high | medium | low |
| Guyana | low | low | low | medium | high |
| Haiti | high | high | high | high | high |
| Jamaica | high | high | low | high | high |
| Saint Kitts and Nevis | high | high | high | medium | low |
| St Lucia | high | high | high | high | low |
| St Vincent and the Grenadines | high | high | high | medium | low |
| Surinam | low | low | low | medium | medium |
| Trinidad and Tobago | low | high | high | medium | low |

● = high vulnerability  ● = medium vulnerability  ● = low vulnerability

## Human-caused disasters

Certain disasters such as spills of hazardous chemicals and oil products have a technological origin. In the Orinoco River delta and neighbouring regions of Venezuela, for example, the use of cyanide and mercury for gold extraction has increased by 500 per cent over the past decade with the growth in the exploitation of the mineral. In the Caroni Basin alone,

3 000 kg of mercury have been dumped and a spill of 1.5 million litres of cyanide-polluted waste has been reported in the Omai and Esequibo rivers in neighbouring Guyana (Filártiga and Agüero Wagner 2001, AMIGRANSA 1997). The largest regional oil spill was an underwater oil blow-out of the Ixtoc well in Campeche Bay in 1979, the second largest in world records at more than 500 000 tonnes (Cutter Information Corp 2000).

## Policy responses

Many countries, especially those located on islands, are vulnerable to natural disasters (see table). The major concerns with regard to policy include the following (UNEP 1999):

- deficiencies in disaster prevention, including the lack of zoning of vulnerable areas during the development planning process;
- weak mitigation mechanisms;
- deficiencies and limited use of anti-seismic building measures, as well as inadequate administrative arrangements and human resources for enforcement;
- lack of insurance policies for low-income households; and
- inadequate support systems for affected communities.

Improving management is critical to disaster reduction, especially non-structural mitigation actions using natural mechanisms. For example, wetlands reduce floods, woodlands reduce landslides and mangroves lessen the effect of coastal storms and extreme tides. In general, good land use maintains healthy ecosystems, provides resources and facilitates non-structural mitigation action. This strategy is particularly attractive in countries where risk insurance and structural mitigation come at a high price.

Given the enormous economic, social and environmental burden of disasters, considerable attention has been paid during the past decade to disaster preparedness, assessment and mitigation. Many of the actions took place in the context of the International Decade for Natural Disaster Reduction (IDNDR). At the regional level, its mandate for promoting international cooperation in this field was supported by the Inter-American Conference on Natural Disaster Reduction held in Cartagena, in March 1994.

## Vulnerability to natural hazards: a geo-referenced index for Honduras

Pre-existing conditions in the environment, demography, social system and infrastructure are among the major factors of vulnerability. The Centro Internacional de Agricultura (CIAT)-UNEP-World Bank rural sustainability indicators have generated a geo-referenced index of vulnerability that combines geographic information from four maps.

The environmental vulnerability map highlights areas at risk from landslides and flooding using data on forests, rivers, topography, slopes, soil permeability and vegetation. The population vulnerability map displays the population density per county and the social vulnerability map adds data on incomes and poverty. The infrastructure vulnerability map adds data on electricity lines and roads.

These four maps are then combined (see map right) to show the 60 counties of highest priority for disaster prevention and rehabilitation (top 10 in red, next 15 in orange and the other 35 in yellow). The information provided by the maps answers major questions such as why are some counties more vulnerable than others, what can be done about it and where should interventions be focused?

Source: Segnestam, Winograd and Farrow 2000

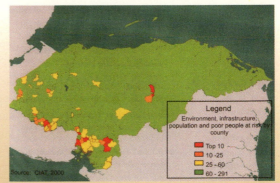

Legend
Environment, infrastructure, population and poor people at risk by county
Top 10
10 -25
25 - 60
60 - 291

Source: CIAT, 2000

Several countries in the region — such as Brazil, Costa Rica, Cuba, Chile, Colombia, Guatemala, Nicaragua and Panama — have created and strengthened national institutional frameworks in the area of disaster management. These include the Centre for Coordination of the Prevention of Natural Disasters in Central America, established in 1988, and the Caribbean Disaster Emergency Response Agency, established in 1991. Under the auspices of the Organization of American States, the Inter-American Convention to Facilitate Disaster Assistance was adopted in 1991 and entered into force in 1996 (PAHO 1998).

Experience has shown the positive effects of planning and building institutional capacities. A fundamental element is to strengthen and standardize data production methods at a regional level, not only to prevent inconsistencies during emergencies but also to assess losses. Also important are efforts to identify the vulnerability of the territories and populations when faced with natural and human-made hazards (see box). The prevailing disaster response is directed towards risk management. It has a growing component of local and community participation, and makes non-centralized use of non-governmental organizations and citizen groups. Within this framework, a new vision is emerging: the development process must reduce risk by lessening populations' and territories' social, economic and environmental vulnerability.

## References: Chapter 2, disasters, Latin America and the Caribbean

AMIGRANSA (1997). *Posición de AMIGRANSA ante el decreto 1.850 de explotación de los bosques de Imataca*. Press Release. Communications for a Sustainable Future, University of Colorado http://csf.colorado.edu/mail/elan/jul97/0068.html [Geo-2-353]

CEPAL (1999). *América Latina y el Caribe: El Impacto de los Desastres Naturales en el Desarrollo, 1972-1999*. Mexico City, Commisión Economica para America Latina y el Caribe, Naciones Unidas

CRED-OFDA (2002). *EM-DAT: The OFDA/CRED International Disaster Database*. Centre for Research on the Epidemiology of Disasters http://www.cred.be/emdat [Geo-2-330]

Cutter (2000). *Oil Spill Intelligence Report*. Cutter Information Corporation http://cutter.com/osir/biglist.htm [Geo-2-354]

Filártiga, J. and Agüero Wagner, L. (2001). Fiebre del oro y ecoapocalipsis en Venezuela. *Apocalipsis Geo-Ambiental. El Imperialismo Ecológico* http://www.quanta.net.py/userweb/apocalipsis/Venezuela/body_venezuela.html [Geo-2-355]

IFRC (2002). *Venezuela: Floods*. Situation Report No. 9. Geneva, International Federation of Red Cross and Red Crescent Societies

MoPD Venezuela (2000). *Venezuela Rises Above Destruction*. Caracas, Ministry of Planning and Development, Venezuela

PAHO (1998). *Health in the Americas. 1998 Edition*. Scientific Publication No. 569. Washington DC, Pan American Health Organization

Segnestam, L., Winograd, M. and Farrow, A. (2000). *Developing Indicators: Lessons Learned from Central America*. Washington DC, World Bank

UNEP (1999). *Caribbean Environment Outlook*. Mexico City, United Nations Environment Programme, Regional Office for Latin America and the Caribbean

UNICEF (2001). *El Salvador Earthquakes*. United Nations Children's Fund http://www.unicef.org/emerg/ElSalvador.htm [Geo-2-356]

WHO (1999). *El Niño and Health*. Geneva, World Health Organization

World Bank (2000). *In Wake of Floods, Bank Urges Venezuela to Protect Poor ....* Press release 7 March 2000 http://wbln0018.worldbank.org/external/lac/lac.nsf/ [Geo-2-357]

## Disasters: North America

Natural hazards such as earthquakes, volcanic eruptions, tornadoes, hurricanes, ice storms, droughts, dust storms and other extreme events threaten different parts of North America. Floods and forest fires are also priority concerns. North American governments have put in place many response mechanisms to prevent and alleviate the harm caused by such factors. Despite strong regulations governing the handling of hazardous material, occasionally serious accidents occur, prompting further preventive legislation.

### Floods and climate change

The disruption and intensification of the Earth's water cycle is believed to be one of the most fundamental effects of climate change (White House 2000). Changes may already be occurring in North America's hydrological conditions, as demonstrated by the increase in average annual precipitation over the past 30 years (see figure). In the United States, the average amount of moisture in the atmosphere increased by 5 per cent per decade between 1973 and 1993 (Trenberth 1999). Most of the increase has been due to heavier precipitation events resulting in floods and storms (O'Meara 1997, Easterling and others 2000).

During the 1960s and 1970s, more than 90 per cent of the natural disasters in the United States were the result of weather or climate extremes (Changnon and Easterling 2000). Flooding is natural and essential to the health of watersheds but floods can also be destructive and cause economic damage (see box right). In response to these events, the United States introduced the National Flood Insurance Act of 1968 and the 1974 Disaster Relief Act. Many of the separate and fragmented responsibilities of parallel state and local level disaster programmes were merged in 1979 under

### Major floods over the past 30 years

The 1993 Mississippi flood, which submerged 75 towns and killed 48 people, cost US$10–20 billion, surpassing all previous US floods in terms of economic losses, area, duration and amount of flooding (Dalgish 1998, USGCRP 2000). It was the result of record-breaking spring rains in the midwest, a larger than usual snow cover, and high soil moisture content — but levees and dykes also confined the river to its channel, helping increase the flood crest (Dalgish 1998). In 1996, Canada experienced its most destructive and costly flood in the Saguenay River valley in Quebec. Nearly 126 mm of rain fell in 48 hours, resulting in 10 deaths and about US$750 million in damages (EC 1998b, Francis and Hengeveld 1998, EC 2001). In 1997, the Red River, which flows north from the United States into Canada, experienced its worst flooding in 150 years, incurring costs of almost US$5 billion (IJC 2000).

Floods can have significant environmental consequences. The Mississippi flood, for example, damaged much of the midwest's fertile farmland and altered the natural ecosystems of the region's rivers and their floodplains (Dalgish 1998). Human modifications over the past century led to the loss of some 85 per cent of the river basin's wetlands, and changes in riparian and in-stream habitat. Wetlands and temporary lakes act as storage areas for excess water and their loss increases the vulnerability of the watershed to flooding (Searchinger and Tripp 1993).

the Federal Emergency Management Agency (FEMA 1999). In 1975, Canada introduced the Flood Damage Reduction Program (FDRP) and, in 1988, it established Emergency Preparedness Canada (EPC) (EC 2000). These programmes provided better flood mitigation, preparation, response and recovery measures.

Evidence shows that deaths and damage from floods have increased sharply since the early 1970s (USGRP 2000). More people and their settlements are exposed to floods because of population increase and concentration, and increasing affluence (Easterling and others 2000). A tendency to settle in flood-prone areas is also influenced by a perception that risk has been lowered by protective structures such as dams, dykes and diversions, and because of the availability of disaster relief (Brun and others 1997, Bruce and others 1999).

Structures that prevent rivers from flooding often provoke extremely damaging floods when water eventually overflows (see box above). In the 1990s, the United States, which is subject to more frequent and severe weather events than Canada, began to encourage non-structural approaches to flood prevention such as resettlement projects and wetland

In Canada (as in the United States), annual precipitation (running mean, solid line) has recently been above the 1951–80 mean

Source: EC 1998a

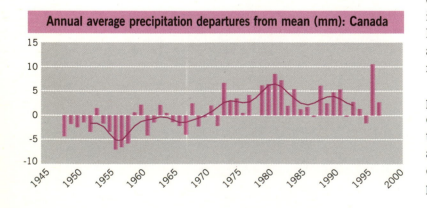

### Annual average precipitation departures from mean (mm): Canada

restoration. In Canada, settlement in flood-prone areas has been discouraged through mapping and the designation of more than 320 flood risk areas (EC 1998b). Canada established the Office of Critical Infrastructure and Emergency Preparedness (OCIPEP) in 2001 to develop and implement a more comprehensive approach to disaster prevention (OCIPEP 2001).

According to some climate change models, the magnitude, frequency and cost of extreme hydrological events in some regions of North America are forecast to increase (USGCRP 2000). Projected effects of climate change include changes in the El Niño. An uncommonly strong El Niño in 1997–98 is believed to account for heavy floods in Florida, California, some midwest states and parts of New England (Trenberth 1999). Where rainstorms intensify and flooding increases, there is greater potential for damage to low-lying settlements and dock and port facilities as well as for problems with water distribution and sewage systems that can have health implications (EC 1999a).

The International Joint Commission assists both governments in managing their shared waters. In a report on the 1997 Red River flooding, it cautioned that, given impending increased flooding due to climate change, a comprehensive, binational strategy should be developed and implemented (IJC 2000).

## Forest fires

Forest fires are a natural part of North America's landscape and play an important role in maintaining and regenerating some types of forests (NIFC 2000). Wild fires ignited by lightning are useful for clearing out old and dead trees which are then quickly replaced by robust new trees (CCFM 2000). Such fires open spaces for new seedlings, help increase diversity, clear debris and increase the availability of nutrients (Jardine 1994).

Since the 1970s, the annual area burned by forest fires has grown (see figure). The increase has been due to a number of factors: fuel build-up from past fire protection programmes; changes in policy related to prescribed burning; and increased public access to forests. Climate change has also been implicated. The relative importance of these factors is controversial.

The United States has long had an aggressive policy of fire suppression and, by the 1970s, fires were kept to about 2 million ha a year in the lower 48 states compared to the 16 million ha burned every year in

the 1930s (Booth 2000, CEQ 2000, H. John Heinz III Center 2001).

As a result, species normally eliminated by fire became dominant. Dead trees accumulated during periods of drought, creating excessive fuel loads. Fire suppression prevented natural low-intensity fires from burning this accumulated fuel. The result was increasingly large and disastrous fires (CEQ 2000).

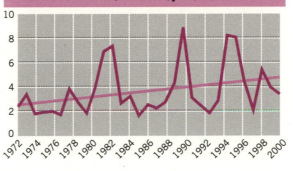

**Forest area burnt (million ha/year): North America**

Since forest authorities decided to let more natural fires burn themselves out, the area of forest burnt each year has been increasing

Source: CCFM 2000, CIFCC 2001 and NIFC 2000

The importance of periodic natural fires began to be recognized in the 1970s. US policies of suppressing all fires before they reached 4 ha in size by 10 am the next day ceased in the late 1970s (Gorte 1996). Decisions were taken not to interfere with fires in wilderness areas or national parks unless people or neighbouring land was threatened (COTF 2000, Turner 2001). In addition, prescribed burning and 'let burn' policies to reduce built-up fuels and protect settlements and businesses were introduced. Such fires are either purposefully lit or are lightning fires that are allowed to burn. Annually, more than 2 million ha are treated by prescribed fire in the United States (Mutch 1997).

These policies have not been without controversy, however. In 1988, parts of Yellowstone — the largest National Park in the United States — were allowed to burn after being struck by lightning. The fires spread quickly because of severe summer drought and high winds. Eventually a decision was made to suppress the fires. At the cost of US$120 million, this was the costliest fire-fighting event in US history (NPS 2000).

The challenge of managing wildfires has been exacerbated by population increases close to fire-prone areas. It is estimated that in the 1990s wildfires damaged six times as many homes as in the previous decade (Morrison and others 2000). Wildfires also create smoke hazards and some highways, airports and recreation areas periodically have to close because of reduced visibility. Smoke also constitutes a health hazard, due to the toxic chemicals it contains.

Changes in climate that may bring drier conditions and more severe storms may also play a role in changing fire patterns. In 1989, for example, record fires burned in western Canada and the areas east of James Bay. They were caused by unusual weather conditions and an unprecedented heat wave in the Arctic (Jardine 1994, Flannigan and others 2000). The severity of Canada's 1995 fire season, which burned 6.6 million ha of forestland, was also due in part to extremely dry conditions (EC 1999b).

In the future, North America's annual fire severity rating may well increase due to climate change, which is predicted to increase the number of lightning strikes and the intensity and frequency of windstorms (Jardine 1994). Research into the links between climate and forest change is being intensified.

## References: Chapter 2, disasters, North America

Booth, W. (2000). 'Natural' Forestry Plan Fights Fires With Fire. *Washington Post*, 24 Sep. 2000

Bruce, J.P., Burton, I. and Egener, I.D.M. (1999). *Disaster Mitigation and Preparedness in a Changing Climate*. Ottawa, Minister of Public Works and Government Services

Brun, S.E., Etkin, D., Law, D.G., Wallace, L., and White, R. (1997). *Coping with Natural Hazards in Canada*
http://www.utoronto.ca/env/nh/pt2ch2-3-2.htm [Geo-2-358]

CCFM (2000). *National Forestry Database Program*. Canadian Council of Forest Ministers
http://nfdp.ccfm.org/ [Geo-2-389]

CEQ (2000). Managing the Impact of Wildfires on Communities and the Environment. A Report to the President In Response to the Wildfires of 2000. Council on Environmental Quality
http://clinton4.nara.gov/CEQ/firereport.pdf

Changnon, S.A. and Easterling, D.R. (2000). US Policies Pertaining to Weather and Climate Extremes. *Science* 289, 5487, 2053-5

CIFFC (2001). Canadian Interagency Forest Fire Centre. Hectares by Year
http://www.ciffc.ca/graphs/hectares.html [Geo-2-359]

COTF (2000). *Exploring the Environment: Yellowstone Fires*. Wheeling Jesuit University/NASA Classroom of the Future
http://www.cotf.edu/ete/modules/yellowstone/YFfires1.html [Geo-2-360]

Dalgish, A. (1998). *The Mississippi Flooding of 1993*.
http://www.owlnet.rice.edu/~micastio/ann3.html

Easterling, D.R., Meehl, G.A., Parmesan, C., Changnon, S.A., Karl, T.R. and Mearns, L.O. (2000). Climate Extremes: Observations, Modelling, and Impacts. *Science* 289, 5487, 2068-74

EC (1998a). *Climate Trends and Variations Bulletin for Canada: Annual 1997 Temperature and Precipitation in Historical Perspective*. Environment Canada, Atmospheric Environment Service
http://www.msc-smc.ec.gc.ca/ccrm/bulletin/annual 97/ [Geo-2-361]

EC (1998b). *Canada and Freshwater: Experience and Practices*. Ottawa, Environment Canada

EC (1999a). *The Canada Country Study (CCS), Volume VIII, National Cross-Cutting Issues Volume*. Adaptation and Impacts Research Group
http://www.ec.gc.ca/climate/ccs/execsum8.htm [Geo-2-362]

EC (1999b). *Sustaining Canada's Forests: Timber Harvesting, National Environmental Indicator Series, SOE Bulletin No. 99-4*. Ottawa, Environment Canada

EC (2000). Environment Canada. Floods
http://www.ec.gc.ca/water/en/manage/floodgen/ e_intro.htm [Geo-2-363]

EC (2001). Environment Canada. Tracking Key Environmental Issues
http://www.ec.gc.ca/tkei/main_e.cfm [Geo-2-364]

FEMA (1999). About FEMA: History of the Federal Emergency Management Agency
http://www.fema.gov/about/history.htm [Geo-2-365]

Flannigan, M.D., Stocks, B.J., and Wotton, B.M. (2000). Climate Change and Forest Fires. *The Science of the Total Environment*, 262, 221-9

Francis, D. and Hengeveld, H. (1998). *Extreme Weather and Climate Change*. Downsview, Ontario, Ministry of the Environment
http://www.msc-smc.ec.gc.ca/saib/climate/ Climatechange/ccd_9801_e.pdf [Geo-2-366]

Gorte, R.W. (1996). *Congressional Research Service Report for Congress: Forest Fires and Forest Health*. The Committee for the National Institute for the Environment
http://cnie.org/NLE/CRSreports/Forests/for-23.cfm [Geo-2-367]

H. John Heinz III Center (2001). *Designing a Report on the State of the Nation's Ecosystem: Selected Measurements for Croplands, Forests, and Coasts and Oceans*. The H. John Heinz III Center for Science, Economics and the Environment
http://www.us-ecosystems.org/forests/index.html [Geo-2-368]

IJC (2000). *International Joint Commission Cautions that Efforts Must Remain Focused on Protecting Against Flood Damages*. International Joint Commission
http://www.ijc.org/news/redrelease3e.html [Geo-2-369]

Jardine, K. (1994). *The Carbon Bomb: Climate Change and the Fate of the Northern Boreal Forests*. Greenpeace International
http://www.subtleenergies.com/ormus/boreal.htm [Geo-2-370]

Morrison, P.H., Karl, J.W., Swope, L., Harma, K., Allen, T., Becwar, P. and Sabold, B. (2000). *Assessment of Summer 2000 Wildfires*. Pacific Biodiversity Institute
http://www.pacificbio.org/pubs/wildfire2000.pdf [Geo-2-371]

Mutch, R.W. (1997). *Use Of Fire As A Management Tool On The National Forests: Statement of Robert W. Mutch Before the Committee on Resources, United States House of Representatives Oversight Hearing*. Committee on Resources, US House of Representatives
http://resourcescommittee.house.gov/105cong/fullc omm/sep30.97/mutch.htm [Geo-2-372]

NIFC (2000). National Interagency Fire Center
http://www.nifc.gov/ [Geo-2-373]

NPS (2000). *Wildland Fire*. The National Park Service, Yellowstone National Park
http://www.nps.gov/yell/nature/fire/wildfire.htm [Geo-2-374]

O'Meara, M. (1997). The Risks of Disrupting Climate. *World Watch* 10, 6, 10-24

OCIPEP (2001). The Office of Critical Infrastructure Protection and Emergency Preparedness
http://www.epc-pcc.gc.ca/whoweare/index_e.html [Geo-2-375]

Searchinger, T.D. and Tripp, J.T.B. (1993). *Planning for Floods: Another Look at Rising Waters*. Environmental Defense Fund
http://www.edf.org/pubs/EDF-Letter/1993/Nov/ m_floodplan.html

Trenberth, K.E. (1999). The Extreme Weather Events of 1997 and 1998. *Consequences: Nature and Implications of Environmental Change* 5 (1)
http://www.gcrio.org/consequences/vol5no1/extreme .html [Geo-2-376]

Turner, C. (2001). *Fighting Fires: Blazing a Trail*. CBC News
http://cbc.ca/news/indepth/fightingfires/blazing.html [Geo-2-377]

USGCRP (2000). Climate Change Impacts on the United States: The Potential Consequences of Climate Variability and Change. US Global Change Research Program
http://sedac.ciesin.org/NationalAssessment/ [Geo-2-378]

White House (2000). Vulnerabilities and Potential Consequences. White House Initiative on Global Climate Change
http://clinton4.nara.gov/Initiatives/Climate/vulnerabil ities.html

## Disasters: West Asia

West Asia is arid and vulnerable to drought, with rainfall scanty and variable (ACSAD 1997). Nearly 80 per cent of the region is classified as semi-desert or desert (AOAD 1995). Drought is the most important natural disaster in the region.

### Drought

Rainfall appears to be declining in some countries bordering the Mediterranean Sea. Over the past 100 years, precipitation has decreased by more than 5 per cent over much of the land bordering the Mediterranean with a few exceptions such as Libya and Tunisia (IPCC 1996). The region suffered droughts during the 1930s, 1960s and the 1990s. In the winters of 1991–92 and 1992–93, snowfall was rare in many areas of the eastern Mediterranean (WMO and UNEP 1994). Cycles of drought have become intense and more frequent. The 1998–99 drought affected many countries and Syria was the worst hit, suffering its worst drought in 25 years (FAO 1999).

The most direct effects of the drought were crop failures and a decline in cereal and livestock production. In Iraq, for example, cereal production declined by 20 per cent compared to the previous year and by 40 per cent compared to the average production for the previous five years (FAO 1999). A report by a FAO/WFP mission to Syria stated that a large proportion of the nomadic herders were facing 'financial ruin', with 4 700 households seriously vulnerable to food shortages and in urgent need of food assistance. Cereal production was also seriously affected. Barley harvest was estimated to be only 380 000 tonnes — less than half the 1998 total and down 72 per cent from the previous five-year average. Local needs had to be satisfied through imports. Reduction in wheat production was less severe (28 per cent below average) because 40 per cent of Syria's wheat fields are irrigated. Jordan was also adversely affected by the drought, which reduced the country's wheat and barley production in 1999 by 88 per cent (WFP 2001).

Drought results in economic, social and environmental problems. Economic hardships during drought intensify and can lead to social conflict between land users, especially in the Mashriq countries and in Yemen where an agricultural economy prevails. Drought is also a major limiting factor to the region's economic development, affecting the development of agricultural and water schemes, and ultimately food production.

Forage and fodder become scarce in rangelands during droughts. In addition, the decline in cereal

The 1998–99 drought in the Mashriq countries had severe effects on the sheep population and their owners — many herders were forced to sell their flocks at cheap prices for want of grazing

Source: UNEP, Topham Picturepoint

A few of the 600 oil wells deliberately ignited during the second Gulf War in January 1999

*Source: UNEP, Sandro Pintras, Topham Picturepoint*

production and the limited availability of crop residues worsen the impact of drought on the sheep population and consequently on human well-being. Loss of sheep and the high price of supplementary feed led to a significant drop in farmers' incomes and many families were forced to sell off their animals and other assets at low prices (FAO 1999).

Land degradation, mostly in the form of desertification, is one of the region's most serious problems. Although desertification is often attributed to poor land use practices, drought deepens the effect and extends the area prone to desertification to encompass areas normally not at risk. Decreases in plant cover due to drought may also increase erosion and lead to a nearly irreversible loss of productive potential and subsequently desertification (Le Houérou 1993, Parton and others 1993).

Nations have responded to drought by improving national efforts to combat desertification and joining international ones with the same aim such as the United Nations Convention to Combat Desertification. Under the auspices of this international treaty, national action programmes have been developed and a sub-regional action programme to combat desertification and drought was adopted in 2000 (UNCCD 2001).

At the national level, actions and measures include modification of agricultural and water policies and giving priority to drought-affected areas.

## Human-induced disasters

Human-induced disasters are mostly associated with the oil industry. Intensive oil extraction in the region results in frequent oil discharges into the Gulf. It is estimated that about 10 per cent of the oil discharged in the region enters the marine environment (Al-Harmi 1998). Accidental oil spills also occur, with three such accidents being among the world's 20 largest: 300 million litres from the Nowruz Platform on 26 January 1991, 144 million litres from the tanker *Sea Star* on 19 December 1972 and 118 million litres from storage tanks in Kuwait on 20 August 1981 (Oil Spill Intelligence Report).

However, the biggest oil spill took place in January-February 1991, during the 1990-91 Gulf War, when 9 500 million litres of oil were deliberately released in the desert. An estimated 1 500 million litres of oil were released into Gulf waters and more than 600 Kuwaiti oil wells were set on fire (Bennett 1995). This human-made disaster had enormous impacts on the environment and human health. The long-term environmental effects of the Gulf War may persist for decades (UNEP 1991). Besides land and marine pollution, huge quantities of pollutants such as sulphur dioxide, nitrogen oxides, carbon monoxide and particulate matter were emitted by the burning oil wells. The high particulate matter levels have been associated with an allergic response in people. Hospital studies indicate that about 18 per cent of Kuwait's civilian population suffer from some respiratory complaint, primarily asthma, compared to roughly 6 per cent in the United States (US DoD 2000).

## Armed conflict

Along with natural disasters, the region has been plagued with wars. Since the beginning of the 20th century, the region has witnessed the 1948 Arab–Israeli war, the 1967 Six-Day war, the 1973 October war and the Israeli invasion of Southern Lebanon in 1982. In the 1980s and 1990s, the first and second Gulf wars caused major environmental problems. Environmental pollution was a major impact. Fires were set deliberately in forests, and water resources were polluted and/or destroyed. Artillery fire destroyed land resources. Marine resources were polluted as well as the atmosphere from oil well fires and soils were contaminated by oil spills during the second Gulf War.

Wars create refugees. In the aftermath of the 1948

## Kuwait Bay: a soup for disaster

Increases in nutrient concentrations in the Gulf have often been concentrated in the Kuwait Bay and the area around the outfall of the Shatt-Al-Arab river, and they have been cited as the cause of a number of eutrophication incidents. A major red tide and an associated fish kill occurred in 1999. The main conclusion of that incident was that unless pollution levels were reduced drastically, eutrophication conditions would worsen, causing more fish kills.

The 1999 event was one of a series. In 1986, tonnes of fish as well as other marine animals, including 527 dolphins, 7 dugongs, 58 turtles and more than 10 000 cuttle fish, had been found dead along the shores of the Gulf. During 1990 and 1991, 137 sea turtles were found dead along the Omani coast. In 1993, a fish kill was observed two months after the sinking of a Russian merchant vessel carrying chemicals. Similar phenomena were reported along the coasts of Bahrain, Iran, Kuwait, Oman, Qatar, Saudi Arabia and United Arab Emirates between 1993 and 1998.

Kuwait Bay has experienced a series of changes over the years, including the release of both treated and untreated sewage and oils and untreated wastes from sources connected directly to the storm water network. Two commercial ports and several marinas, three power stations, a commercial fish farm in the middle of the bay, and an artificial river in Iraq into which sewage and agriculture run-off from the newly drained marshes are released, exert pressure on the bay.

Another source of nutrients is wind-blown soil carried by the predominant northwesterly winds, which has increased over the past few years due to the shrinking marshlands in Iraq. The linkage between the marshes and the Gulf through the Shatt Al-Arab and its tributaries has allowed fish to migrate. In August-September 2001, more than 3 000 tonnes of fish, predominantly mullet, died. The pathogen identified, *Streptococcus iniae*, could have originated from sewage or contaminated fish-feed. The same species was reported in Bahrain in 1999 when there was massive mortality in rabbitfish populations. The combined effects of elimination of the Iraqi marshes as a natural wastewater treatment system and the continued input of organic matter from anthropogenic activities coupled with arid conditions have created a recipe for disaster, transforming the Gulf into a soup ready to provide a perfect media for bacterial and algal blooms.

*Source: Cynthia and others 2001*

Arab–Israeli war, more than 750 000 Palestinians were left landless and homeless. A second wave of approximately 350 000 Palestinians and more than 150 000 Syrians became refugees at the end of the Six-Day War. Towns and villages in Palestine and Golan Heights were depopulated and destroyed. Today, there are about 3.8 million refugees in 59 camps registered with the United Nations Relief and Works Agency (UNRWA 2002). Palestinian refugees are scattered in a number of countries, including Jordan, Lebanon and Syria. Most live in poor conditions, putting additional stress on already limited natural resources.

## References: Chapter 2, disasters, West Asia

ACSAD (1997). *Water Resources and their Utilization in the Arab World.* 2nd Water Resources Seminar, March 8–10, Kuwait

Al-Harmi, L. (1998). *Sources of Oil Pollution in Kuwait and Their Inputs in the Marine Environment.* EES-125 Final Report. Kuwait, Kuwait Institute for Scientific Research

AOAD (1995). *Study on Deterioration of Rangelands and Proposed Development Projects* (in Arabic). Khartoum, Arab Organizaton for Agricultural Development

Bennett, M. (1995). *The Gulf War.* Database for Use in Schools http://www.soton.ac.uk/~engenvir/environment/water/oil.gulf.war.html [Geo-1-002]

Cynthia, H.A., Gilbert, P.M., Al-Sarawi, M.A., Faraj, M., Behbehani, M. and Husain, M. (2001). First record of a fish-killing *Gymnodinium* sp. bloom in Kuwait Bay, Arabian Sea: chronology and potential causes. *Marine Ecology Progress Series* 214, 15-23.

FAO (1999). Special Report: Drought Causes Extensive Crop Damage in the Near East Raising Concerns for Food Supply Difficulties in Some Parts

http://www.fao.org/WAICENT/faoinfo/economic/giews/english/alertes/1999/SRNEA997.htm [Geo-2-379]

IPPC (1996). *Climate Change 1995: The Science of Climate Change.* Contribution of Working Group I to the Second Assessment Report of the Intergovernmental Panel on Climate Change. Cambridge University Press, Cambridge, United Kingdom, and New York, United States

Le Houérou, A. N. (1993). Vegetation and land-use in the Mediterranean Basin by the year 2050: a prospective study. In Jeftic, L., Milliman, J.D. and Sestini, G. (eds.). *Climatic Change and the Mediterranean.* London, Edward Arnold

Oil Spill Intelligence Report (2002). Oil spills involving more than 10 million gallons http://cutter.com/osir/biglist.htm [Geo-2-380]

Parton, W.J., Scurlock, J.M.O., Ojima, D.S., Gilmanov, T.G., Scholes, R.J., Schimel, D.S., Kirchner, T., Menaut, J.-C., Seastedt, T., Moya, E.G., Kamnalrut, A. and Kinyamario, J.I. (1993). Observations and modeling of biomass and soils organic matter dynamics for the grassland biome worldwide. *Global Geochemical Cycles* 7, 4, 785-805

UNCCD (2001). *Sub-Regional Action Programme (SRAP) to Combat Desertification and Drought in West Asia* http://www.unccd.int/actionprogrammes/asia/subregional/westasia/westasia.php [Geo-2-381]

UNEP (1991). *A Rapid Assessment of the Impacts of the Iraq-Kuwait Conflict on Terrestrial Ecosystems: Part II - the State of Kuwait.* Manama, Bahrain, UNEP Regional Office for West Asia

UNRWA (2002). United Nations Relief and Works Agency for Palestine Refugees in the Near East http://www.un.org/unrwa/about/index.html [Geo-2-383]

US DoD (2000). *Oil Well Fires Environmental Exposure Report.* The Department of Defense. http://www.gulflink.osd.mil/owf_ii/ [Geo-2-382]

WFP (2001). *Estimated Food Needs and Shortfalls for WFP Operations and Projects.* Rome, World Food Programme

WMO and UNEP (1994). *The Global Climate System Review. Climate System Monitoring June 1991 — November 1993.* Geneva, World Meteorological Organization

## Disasters: the Polar Regions

### Natural disasters

Impacts of natural hazards, combined with extreme polar climatic conditions (low temperatures, short summers, extensive snow and ice cover in winter), and vulnerable ecosystems and infrastructure can easily result in disasters in the Arctic. For example, during the five-year period 1996–2001, there were two catastrophic floods in the Lena River that exceeded all previous records. In the winter of 2001, temperatures hit a record low, some rivers froze solid, and therefore took longer to thaw, and blocks of ice clogged the natural flow. In addition, in that year, the snowfall was particularly severe. The water levels in the central part of the Lena exceeded the normal average by 9 metres or more. Economic losses and environmental devastation were severe (Kriner 2001a, b). Because climate change is likely to increase precipitation in the catchment areas of Arctic rivers (IPCC 2001a), there may be a corresponding increase in the frequency and magnitude of floods.

The temperature increase observed over the Arctic land masses in recent years results in permafrost thawing in many areas. In the developed areas of the Arctic, efforts will be needed to reduce the impacts of thawing on buildings and transport infrastructure (IPCC 2001b). The permafrost zone covers 58 per cent of the Russian Federation. The zone border may move 300–400 km northwards by 2100 (Interagency Commission 1998).

Another natural disaster affecting the Arctic ecosystem is pest invasion, which can devastate a forested area and affect the related economic activities. Pest outbreaks are a major problem in the forest-tundra zone. The spruce bark beetle (*Dendroctonus rufipennis*) has caused serious destruction and forest death in the spruce forests of Alaska. In Scandinavia, autumn moths (*Epirrita autumnata*) cause massive defoliation of birch forests at about 10-year intervals. These forests do not recover for up to centuries because of the slow recovery rate of vegetation in the Arctic (CAFF 2001).

### Human-caused disasters

With the exception of Finland, all the countries bordering the Arctic area have oil terminals, or major transportation routes of oil or hazardous materials in their Arctic areas. Other human activities include the exploitation of petroleum and mineral resources by all countries except Finland and Sweden. Iceland has a hazardous materials waste site, and the Russian Federation has several nuclear sites and radioactive waste sites in its Arctic area. An environmental risk survey of human activities in the Arctic, carried out under the auspices of the Arctic Council, concluded that the greatest threat from a release of a pollutant requiring emergency response is the transportation and storage of oil. Nuclear sites, although assessed as less of a threat overall, could affect much larger areas (EPPR 1997).

Pipeline ruptures and leakages, such as in the Usinsk area of Russia in 1994 when 116 million litres of crude oil were spilled (Oil Spill Intelligence Report 2002), and the *Exxon Valdez* tanker accident in Alaska in 1989 with almost 50 million litres of crude oil spilled (NOAA 2001), are examples of catastrophic environmental impacts in the region. Many smaller accidents, such as uncontrolled oil gushers and the accidental discharge of contaminated mud during drilling, also result in local environmental pollution (AMAP 1997).

Both past and current activities involving radioactive materials in the Arctic create a high potential risk of accidents, although there has been no large-scale radioactive pollution yet. For example, accidents such as the sinking of the Soviet nuclear submarine *Komsomolets* in 1989 and the Russian nuclear submarine *Kursk* in 2000, and the crash of a US aircraft with nuclear weapons aboard near Thule in Greenland in 1968, did not result in the release of radioactive substances to the environment.

The Soviet Union dumped high, intermediate and low level radioactive waste in the Kara and Barents Seas between 1959 and 1991 (see map opposite), including six nuclear submarine reactors and a shielding assembly from an icebreaker reactor containing spent fuel (AMAP 1997). Since then, the research and data collected have indicated that no significant amounts of radioactive materials have migrated from the dumping, and only very local samples show elevated radionuclide levels. The major risks may be over the long term as the containers corrode.

Radioactive contamination from European reprocessing plants in the 1970s and atmospheric weapons testing in the 1960s have contributed to current low-level Arctic contamination (AMAP 1997,

OTA 1995). There is limited data on how much or where radioactive materials have been dumped in the Arctic, and any of these sites may be 'a disaster waiting to happen' (AMAP 1997).

Governments, businesses and international organizations are all taking action to increase disaster preparedness in the region. Intergovernmental cooperation is carried out on both a bilateral and a multilateral basis, especially via the Arctic Council. Two of the Arctic Council's programmes — Emergency Prevention, Preparedness and Response (EPPR), and Protection of the Arctic Marine Environment (PAME) — have produced important information and guidelines on environmental risks in the Arctic. For example, EPPR developed the Arctic Offshore Oil and Gas Guidelines aimed at regulatory agencies in 1997. A guideline on the transfer of petroleum products from ship to shore and ship to ship has been produced by PAME (Arctic Council 2001). The IUCN and the Oil and Gas Producers Association have prepared guidelines for environmental protection in the Arctic and sub-Arctic (IUCN and E&P Forum 1993).

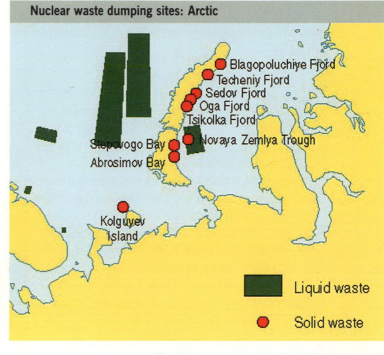

**Nuclear waste dumping sites: Arctic**

Blagopoluchiye Fjord
Techeniy Fjord
Sedov Fjord
Oga Fjord
Tsikolka Fjord
Stepovogo Bay
Abrosimov Bay
Novaya Zemlya Trough
Kolguyev Island

■ Liquid waste

● Solid waste

Map shows dumping sites for solid and liquid radioactive wastes in Arctic areas of the Russian Federation

*Source: AMAP 1997*

## References: Chapter 2, disasters, the Polar Regions

AMAP (1997). *Arctic Pollution Issues: a State of the Arctic Environment Report*. Oslo, Arctic Monitoring and Assessment Programme

Arctic Council (2001). Arctic Council Activities http://www.arctic-council.org/ac_projects.asp [Geo-2-384]

CAFF (2001). *Arctic Flora and Fauna: Status and Conservation*. Helsinki, Arctic Council Programme for the Conservation of Arctic Flora and Fauna

EPPR (1997). *Environmental Risk Analysis of Arctic Activities. Risk Analysis Report No. 2*. The Emergency Prevention Preparedness and Response Working Group of the Arctic Council http://eppr.arctic-council.org/risk/riskcover.html [Geo-2-385]

Interagency Commission (1998). *The Second National Communication to the UNFCCC*. Moscow, Interagency Commission of the Russian Federation on Climate Change Problems

IPCC (2001a). *Climate Change 2001: The Scientific Basis. Contribution of Working Group I to the Third Assessment Report of the Intergovernmental Panel on Climate Change*. Cambridge, United Kingdom, and New York, United States, Cambridge University Press

IPCC (2001b). *Climate Change 2001: Impacts, Adaptation and Vulnerability. Contribution of Working Group II to the Third Assessment Report of the Intergovernmental Panel on Climate Change*. Cambridge, United Kingdom, and New York, United States, Cambridge University Press

IUCN with E&P Forum (1993). *Oil and Gas Exploitation in Arctic and Subarctic Onshore Regions*. Gland, Switzerland, and Cambridge, United Kingdom, World Conservation Union with the Oil Industry Exploration and Production Forum

Kriner, S. (2001a). Winter Chills Bring Spring Floods to Siberia. American Red Cross, 17 May 2001 http://www.redcross.org/news/in/flood/010517siberia.html [Geo-2-386]

Kriner, S. (2001b). *Flood Disaster Averted Again in Siberian City*. American Red Cross, 23 May 2001 http://www.redcross.org/news/in/flood/010523siberia.html [Geo-2-387]

NOAA (2001). *The Exxon Valdez Oil Spill*. Office of Response and Restoration, National Ocean Service, National Oceanic and Atmospheric Administration http://response.restoration.noaa.gov/spotlight/spotlight.html [Geo-2-388]

Oil Spill Intelligence Report (2002). Oil spills involving more than 10 million gallons http://cutter.com/osir/biglist.htm [Geo-2-380]

OTA (1995). *Nuclear Wastes in the Arctic: An Analysis of Arctic and Other Regional Impacts from Soviet Nuclear Contamination*. Washington DC, US Office of Technology Assessment

# OUR CHANGING ENVIRONMENT: the Aral Sea, Central Asia

The destruction of the Aral Sea ecosystem has been sudden and severe. Beginning in the 1960s, agricultural demands deprived this large Central Asian salt lake of enough water to sustain itself, and it has shrunk rapidly. Uzbekistan, Kazakhstan, and other Central Asian states used this water to grow cotton and other export crops, in the face of widespread environmental consequences, including fisheries loss, water and soil contamination, and dangerous levels of polluted airborne sediments.

The Aral Sea is one of the greatest environmental catastrophes ever recorded. Humans have made use of the waters of the Aral basin for thousands of years, borrowing from its two major rivers: the Amu Darya, which flows into the Aral Sea from the south; and the Syr Darya, which reaches the sea at its north end. The Kara Kum Canal opened in 1956, diverting large amounts of water from the Amu Darya into the desert of Turkmenistan, and millions of hectares of land came under irrigation after 1960. While the sea had been receiving about 50 km$^3$ of water per year in 1965, by the early 1980s this had fallen to zero. As the Aral shrank, its salinity increased, and by the early 1980s commercially useful fish had been eliminated, shutting down an industry that had employed 60 000.

The declining sea level lowered the water table in the region, destroying many oases near its shores. Over-irrigation caused salt build-up in many agricultural areas. By the beginning of the 1990s, the surface area of the Aral had shrunk by nearly half, and its volume was down by 75 per cent. Winds picked up sediments laced with salts and pesticides, with devastating health consequences for surrounding regions (see also box on page 280).

Photo above shows an abandoned fishing boat in what was once the Aral Sea. Satellite images below show how the sea shrank between 1973 and 1999

Landsat data: USGS/EROS Data Center
Compilation: UNEP GRID Sioux Falls
Photo: UNEP, Topham Picturepoint

1973

1986

1999

# Conclusions

The preceding sections of this chapter show that there has been immense change in both human and environmental conditions over the past 30 years. In an unprecedented period of population increase, the environment has been heavily drawn upon to meet a multiplicity of human needs. In many areas, the state of the environment is much more fragile and degraded than it was in 1972. The result is that the world can now be categorized by four major divides:

- **The Environmental Divide** — characterized by a stable or improved environment in some regions, for example Europe and North America, and a degraded environment in the other regions, mostly the developing countries;
- **The Policy Divide** — characterized by two distinct dimensions involving policy development and implementation with some regions having strength in both and others still struggling in both areas;
- **The Vulnerability Gap** — which is widening within society, between countries and across regions with the disadvantaged more at risk to environmental change and disasters; and
- **The Lifestyle Divide** — partly a result of growing poverty and of affluence. One side of the lifestyle divide is characterized by excesses of consumption by the minority one-fifth of the world population, which is responsible for close to 90 per cent of total personal consumption; the other side by extreme poverty where 1.2 billion live on less than US$1 per day.

The four gaps are a serious threat to sustainable development. The following paragraphs highlight some of the environmental challenges facing humanity today and some of the successes that have been achieved in the past three decades.

## Environmental achievements

The policies articulated in documents such as the Stockholm *Declaration and Programme of Action*, the *World Conservation Strategy*, *Our Common Future*, the *Rio Declaration* and *Agenda 21*, have driven the environmental agenda in the period 1972-2002. Binding legal regimes — some from before 1972 — now form the body of international environmental law, providing the appropriate muscle necessary to encourage compliance. Along with the policies and legal framework, the past three decades have also seen a proliferation of environmental institutions across public and private sectors, and civil society in general. Ministries or departments of environment are now common in all regions. Sustainable development and environmental standards have become part of the *lingua franca* of major corporations, with many now making annual environmental reporting part of the corporate agenda. Civil society has come of age, recording many successes at different levels — from community to the international level. Some of the successes that have been achieved since 1972 include the following:

- Addressing stratospheric ozone depletion is a notable victory for global environmental governance. However, it needs continuing vigilance.
- Concern over levels of common air pollutants has resulted in encouraging reductions in many countries, achieved through specific policy measures, including emissions and air quality standards, as well as technology-based regulations and different market-based instruments.
- More holistic approaches to land management, such as integrated plant nutrition systems and integrated pest management, have been introduced with positive results for the health of agricultural ecosystems in some regions.
- Freshwater policies have begun to move away from a riparian rights focus and towards exploring efficiency improvements and river basin management. Integrated water resources management is now widely accepted as a strategic policy initiative.
- A new theoretical understanding of the benefits of ecosystem services has emerged but, in practice, information and policy instruments to protect these have been lacking or sporadic.
- There has been a recent evolution from 'end-of-

pipe' approaches to goals for sustainability and a modest shift to a more integrated approach to environmental policies and management, focusing on the sustainability of ecosystems and watersheds, for example, rather than on sustaining yields.

- It is now recognized that poverty reduction, economic development and environmental stability should be mutual goals. This breaks with the old thinking prevalent in the 1970s and 1980s which regarded environmental protection and economic development as conflicting aims.
- Prosperity and an informed and active civil society have been key drivers of policies to address various environmental problems that became apparent early in the 30-year period in developed nations. Ambient air quality and point-source water pollution have been addressed satisfactorily in many areas; recycling has become more common; wastewater treatment has improved; pulp-and-paper industry effluents have declined and hazardous waste threats have been reduced. Protected areas have been increasingly set aside for conservation and recreation.
- Successes in the developing world have been mixed: there has been a growing democratization and participation process positively underpinning environment-development in some regions, with a growing civil society awareness of the debate.
- A natural 'cluster' of biodiversity policies is emerging, of which the CBD is the core regime, but which also includes a host of other treaties and initiatives such as CITES, CMS and the Ramsar Convention.
- Technological change has helped to relieve some environmental pressures: lower material intensity in production; a shift from materials and energy supply to the provision of services; a modest boost in renewable technology; and a significant clean-up in some regions in previously 'dirty' industries.
- In recent years, risk reduction has been placed higher on political agendas, and response mechanisms and early warning systems have been strengthened.

An overall observation is that many of the policies mentioned in this chapter have either no clearly defined and specific performance criteria or the criteria are not readily related to environmental performance. This is true of, for example, economic policies related to taxation, trade and investment. Although some of them have significant links to environmental issues (in some cases, they are key drivers of environmental change), their built-in evaluation criteria are usually limited to economic performance. This has made their evaluation particularly challenging from an environmental and sustainable development perspective.

## Environmental challenges

Despite these achievements, a growing world population — to more than 6 000 million people (and still climbing) — is exacerbating the demand on resources and services, and increasing the generation of wastes to meet many of these demands. Overall, policy measures have not been adequate to counteract the pressures imposed by increasing poverty and uncontrolled consumption. Preceding Chapter 2 sections show indisputable evidence of continuing and widespread environmental degradation.

- Recent human impacts on the atmosphere have been enormous, with anthropogenic emissions a prime cause of environmental problems. Emissions of almost all greenhouse gases continue to rise.
- Ground-level ozone, smog and fine particulates have emerged as significant health risks, triggering or exacerbating respiratory and cardiac problems, especially in vulnerable people such as children, the elderly and asthmatics, in developed and developing nations alike.
- Overexploitation of many of the surface water resources and great aquifers upon which irrigated agriculture and domestic supplies depend has resulted in more and more countries facing water stress or scarcity. About 1 200 million people still lack access to clean drinking water and some 2 400 million to sanitation services. The consequences include the deaths of 3–5 million people annually from water-related diseases.
- The Earth's biological diversity is under increasing threat. The extinction rate of species is believed to be accelerating. Habitat destruction and/or modification are the main causes of biodiversity loss but invasive species are the second most important pressure.
- There has been a sharp global trend towards

increasingly intense exploitation and depletion of wild fish stocks. Numerous fisheries have collapsed and others are threatened with overexploitation.

- Land degradation continues to worsen, particularly in developing countries where the poor are forced onto marginal lands with fragile ecosystems and in areas where land is increasingly exploited to meet food and agricultural needs without adequate economic and political support to adopt appropriate agricultural practices.
- Many remaining forest ecosystems have been degraded and fragmented. Since 1972, extensive forest monocultures have been established in the developing world but these do not replace the ecological complexity of natural forests.
- Crop and livestock production has contributed to the large increase in reactive nitrogen in the global biosphere, contributing to the acidification and eutrophication of ecosystems.
- With almost half of the world's population living in less-developed countries, urban areas and mega-cities, infrastructure and municipal services are inadequate to accommodate millions of the urban poor. Urban air pollution and deteriorating water quality are having major health, economic and social impacts.
- An increase in the frequency and intensity of natural disasters over the past 30 years has put more people at greater risk, with the greatest burden falling on the poorest communities.

## Regional challenges

At the regional level, the major environmental issues include climate change, land and soil degradation, forest degradation and deforestation, freshwater stress and scarcity as well as quality/pollution, degradation and pollution of coastal and marine areas, loss of habitats and species, growth of unplanned settlements and mounting solid waste, and increasing droughts and floods. Many of the regions face similar environmental challenges, though the magnitude and extent of the problems varies.

### Africa

In Africa, the key environmental issues include land degradation, deforestation, habitat degradation, water stress and scarcity, coastal area erosion and degradation, floods and droughts, and armed conflict. These and other problems have contributed to environmental change that exacerbated under-development, poverty and food insecurity in the region. They have also limited the effectiveness of various response measures such as the Lagos Plan of Action and other environmental policies, which have been adopted by the region over the past 30 years. Tackling the region's environmental problems is now not just an option but is critical to achieving sustainable development, without which poverty will continue to worsen, contributing to even more overexploitation of the environment.

### Asia and the Pacific

The world's largest region in terms of land area and also human population has an eclectic portfolio of environmental challenges, reflecting the diversity of its sub-regions. Some of the key environmental issues facing the region include land and forest degradation, habitat loss, water scarcity and pollution, greenhouse gas emissions and climate change, waste management, and natural disasters such as floods, droughts and earthquakes. What emerges from the assessment in previous sections is that some parts of the region are under severe stress, placing livelihood options for millions of people at risk. Other parts of the region, for example Japan, New Zealand and Australia, are sufficiently developed to cope with inevitable environmental changes caused by both human activities and natural phenomena.

### Europe

In Europe, many of the key environmental issues are similar to those common in Africa, and Asia and the Pacific. These include forest degradation, water quantity and quality, coastal erosion and greenhouse gas emissions. Other, more specific issues analysed include soil degradation, sealing and contamination, and genetically modified organisms. Europe is generally one of the regions that is better placed to deal with its environmental challenges because of its economic development — and there are well established legal and institutional frameworks at both national and regional levels. Despite its advantages, however, the region cannot tackle global environmental issues alone and should continue to play a key role, particularly in the area of climate change.

## Latin America and the Caribbean

The region faces many of the same environmental problems as Africa, and Asia and the Pacific. Additional issues include land tenure, overexploitation of fisheries and disasters, including hurricanes, earthquakes and spills of hazardous substances. Such problems will continue to exert heavy tolls on human life and the environment, setting back any efforts towards sustainable development. The risk is that millions of people in the region will continue to be marginalized, undermining efforts to improve socio-economic conditions and effectively manage the environment for current and future generations. Without more effective policy responses, the current trend of worsening environmental conditions is likely to continue, contributing to increased human vulnerability to environmental change.

## North America

North America, the engine of globalization, has key environmental issues that include pesticide use, management of old growth forests, bio-invasion and quality of the Great Lakes. Despite its well developed institutional and legal framework, and successful enforcement of environmental laws, the region will continue to face a number of challenges, including the effective management of the commons. Its leadership role in international environmental management is important and this should be guided by the now widely accepted principle of common but differentiated responsibilities. The participation of governments, NGOs and civil society at national, regional and international levels is critical to progress in meeting *Agenda 21* and Millennium Declaration goals and others set by subsequent fora such as the World Summit on Sustainable Development. Many regions will continue to look to North America for assistance in terms of capacity building and development aid.

## West Asia

Policy conflicts, for example those related to water management, and food production and security, have been shown to undermine efforts to achieve sustainable development. Greater synergy is critical and strategic policy development and implementation should include different stakeholders to avoid overlaps and competition which undermine effectiveness. The region has identified integrated water resources management as one of the key policy initiatives needed to improve management of its limited water resources. Countries in the region will also continue to grapple with the problems of drought and desertification, both of which place heavy limitations on environment and development.

## Polar Regions

Some of the diagnosed environmental impacts on the polar regions are also clear symptoms of the excesses of human activity across the globe. The ozone-depleting substances used by humankind have manifested themselves in these regions with the discovery of the ozone hole some two decades ago. Greenhouse gas emissions are another example of how 'local' environmental problems may end up being global. The polar regions will continue to suffer the impacts of problems generated elsewhere. However, continued cooperation across various fronts at both t the regional and global levels should help address some of the existing problems and pinpoint emerging ones.

UNEP, Chaiwat Chittirapap, Topham Picturepoint

# *Chapter*

# 3

# Human Vulnerability to Environmental Change

Rosita Pedro was born in a tree, high above the raging, muddy waters of the Limpopo River in full flood. Rosita was born vulnerable, how much more precarious a start to life could anybody have? The reason for Rosita's plight, and that of her mother Sofia, was a mixture of natural phenomena and human impacts. The floods that devastated Mozambique in March 2000 were a natural occurrence but their severity was exacerbated by poor land management, serious erosion of wetlands and overgrazing of grasslands in the upper watersheds of the Limpopo river in Botswana, South Africa and Zimbabwe. Wetlands absorb excess water like a sponge and release it slowly into a watershed or river system, so their shrinking removes that safety valve. Grasslands damaged by overgrazing and burning had become compacted and hardened, allowing water to flow off into rivers instead of seeping into the soil. In addition, meteorologists attributed the torrential rains to exceptionally warm surface temperatures in the Indian Ocean and Mozambique Channel, possibly associated with global warming. In the resulting disaster, several hundred people were killed and thousands displaced and impoverished (Guardian 2000, Stoddard 2000).

## Understanding vulnerability

Vulnerability represents the interface between exposure to the physical threats to human well-being and the capacity of people and communities to cope with those threats. Threats may arise from a combination of social and physical processes. Human vulnerability thus integrates many environmental concerns. Since everyone is vulnerable to environmental threats, in some way, the issue cuts across rich and poor, urban and rural, North and South, and may undermine the entire sustainable development process in developing countries. Reducing vulnerability requires identifying points of intervention in the causal chain between the emergence of a hazard and the human consequences (Clark and others 1998).

Many natural phenomena pose threats, including extreme events such as floods, drought, fire, storms, tsunami, landslides, volcanic eruptions, earthquakes and insect swarms. Human activities have added to the list, with threats from explosions, chemical and radioactive contamination, and other technological incidents. The risk lies in the probability of exposure to any of these events, which can occur with varying severity at different geographical scales, suddenly and unexpectedly or gradually and predictably, and to the degree of exposure. With an increasing and more widely distributed global population, however, natural disasters are resulting in increasing damage, loss of life and displacement of populations. In addition, human-induced changes to the environment have reduced its capacity to absorb the impacts of change and to deliver the goods and services to satisfy human needs.

The analysis of environmental impacts in Chapter 2 revealed many examples of where individuals, communities and even countries are vulnerable to threats from their physical environment. Environmental change and social vulnerability to it is nothing new. More than 9 000 years ago, the Sumerians of Mesopotamia started irrigating land to meet increased demand for food from a growing population but their civilization eventually collapsed partly because of the waterlogging and salinization that resulted. The Mayan civilization collapsed around 900 B.C. mainly as a result of soil erosion, loss of agro-ecosystem viability and silting of rivers. The Dust Bowl phenomenon of the American prairies in the 20th century resulted from massive soil erosion, and led to communities being uprooted and widespread poverty. During the three days of London's 'Great Smog' of 1952, some 4 000 people died as a result of a lethal combination of air laden with particulates and $SO_2$ from the widespread burning of coal and a temperature inversion caused by anticyclonic conditions over the city (Met Office 2002).

Some people live in places of inherent risk to humans — areas, for example, that are too hot, too dry or too prone to natural hazards. Others such as Rosita Pedro are at risk because an existing threat has become more severe or extensive through time. Places or conditions which were once safe have been so altered that they no longer safeguard human health and well-being adequately. Many of the children under the age of five who die every year from diarrhoeal disease contract it from drinking contaminated water (see Chapter 2, 'Freshwater').

Most environments are in a constant state of flux because of natural causes and human modifications for food production, settlements, infrastructure, or to produce and trade goods. Most intentional changes are designed to harness the environment for human benefit. Domestication of land for intensive food production is one example; harnessing river resources to provide fresh water, energy and transport is another. Such changes may also unintentionally alter the quality or quantity of environmental resources and be difficult to cope with.

Analysing old and new threats to human security shows that human vulnerability to environmental conditions has social, economic and ecological dimensions. The most conspicuous and widely reported manifestation of this vulnerability is when people are affected suddenly and violently by natural hazards such as the eruption of Mount Nyiragongo resulting in the devastation of the town of Goma in the Democratic Republic of Congo (see box). These events turn into disasters when local communities are not able to cope with their impacts. The environmental factors that contribute to human vulnerability, however, are both varied and variable, and are not limited to disaster events; they span the whole sustainable development spectrum.

## Vulnerable groups

Although everyone is vulnerable to environmental impacts of some kind, the ability of people and societies to adapt to and cope with change is very varied. Developing countries, particularly the least developed, have less capacity to adapt to change and are more vulnerable to environmental threats and global change, just as they are more vulnerable to

other stresses. This condition is most extreme among the poorest people (IPCC 2001) and disadvantaged groups such as women and children.

The coping capacity of human society is a combination of all the natural and social characteristics and resources available in a particular location that are used to reduce the impacts of hazards (IATFDR 2001). These include factors such as wealth, technology, education, information, skills, infrastructure, access to resources and management capabilities. Between two and three times as many disaster events were reported in the United States in 1999 as in India or Bangladesh but there were 14 times and 34 times more deaths in India and in Bangladesh, respectively, than in the United States (UNEP 2000). The critical factor behind these statistics lies in the advantages enjoyed by US citizens in terms of levels of coping capacity (see also Chapter 2, 'Disasters'). There is, therefore, no direct correlation between the occurrence of extreme events and their level of human impact.

In many instances, coping capacity that was adequate in the past has not kept pace with environmental change. This can happen when traditional options are reduced or eliminated (the settlement of nomads, the introduction of regulations restricting resource use that was previously free), or when new threats emerge for which no coping mechanism exists, resources are lacking, and technology and skills are not available.

Some groups are more exposed than others to particular environmental risks: urban populations are exposed to high levels of contaminant and particulate pollution in the air, slum dwellers often lack the minimum protective infrastructure, employees may be exposed to particular hazards in the work place, and the uninformed may simply not know about the threats that surround them. A wide range of social and economic factors have direct and indirect bearing on human vulnerability to environmental change, including poverty and inequality, and the availability of natural resources. No standard framework exists for identifying all these factors.

Poverty is generally recognized as one of the most important causes of vulnerability to environmental threats, on the basis that the poor tend to have much lower coping capacities, and thus they bear a disproportionate burden of the impact of disasters, conflict, drought, desertification and pollution. But

## Culture and climate change

The culture of the indigenous peoples of the Mackenzie basin in northwest Canada is threatened by climate change. Over the past 35 years, temperatures have increased rapidly by about 1°C a decade, with significant results such as melting permafrost, increasing numbers of landslips and forest fires, and decreasing groundwater levels. More frequent forest fires will reduce traditionally important terrestrial, aquatic and bird species. Because of a decrease in water availability, muskrats have already disappeared from the Peace Athabasca delta. Changes such as these in the ecosystem and resource base jeopardize the sustainability of traditional lifestyles that are dependent on wildlife harvested by hunting, fishing and trapping as a prime source of food, income and traditional clothing.

*Sources: Cohen and others 1997*

poverty is not the only reason. The very young and the old, women and children are often identified as especially vulnerable groups. Refugees, migrants and other displaced groups lack both the physical resources and social structure necessary to respond to threats although paradoxically they may initially benefit from the high visibility of their plight. The urban poor, on the other hand, usually live in obscurity, and in times of disaster their numbers can swell enormously. The mosaics of vulnerability seem so complex as to cast doubt on attempts to describe patterns and estimate trends at the global or even the regional scale. General or gradual economic decline can affect vulnerable groups disproportionately, creating severe but largely hidden hardships (Downing and Bakker 2000).

The cultural dimension is important. Indigenous communities with unique lifestyles intimately adapted to local climate, vegetation and wildlife may be particularly threatened by environmental change (see box above). Traditionally, many indigenous communities developed highly specific coping mechanisms to deal with their environments and periodic extreme events. Such coping mechanisms included adaptive behaviour such as regular seasonal migration or exceptional relocation in times of flooding or drought, and changes in practices such as planting and gathering specific food crops; for example, fruits and foods that are not usually eaten during times of good harvests may be relied upon in times of crop failure. With the breakdown of social patterns, and reduction of options to continue following indigenous lifestyles, such coping mechanisms are also giving way or disappearing.

Poor and indigenous communities are considered to be more vulnerable to climate-related events such as storms, floods and droughts because of inadequacies in social support services and systems such as water management infrastructure (IPCC 2001). They are also more affected by pests and diseases — especially vector-borne, respiratory and other infectious diseases (Woodward and others 1998, Braaf 1999). In addition, since many poor inhabit isolated rural environments or the margins of large towns and cities, they are more exposed to social problems associated with economic insecurity, inadequate water supplies and lower health standards.

## Vulnerable places

Human exposure to environmental threats is not evenly distributed. Some locations, such as high latitudes (see box below), floodplains, river banks, small islands and coastal areas, may pose more risk than others. Human uses or modifications of the environment such as deforestation, increasing paved areas covered by buildings and roads, and river canalization have created impacts that often affect areas a long way from the source of the environmental change, such as far downstream.

Individual choices have an enormous bearing on where people live and work, with the result that human vulnerability is closely related to population density and distribution. Floodplains, low-lying coastal areas and volcanic areas have always been favoured for settlement because of their soil fertility or the availability of flat land. As populations increase and there is more competition for land and resources, areas of higher potential risk are increasingly being

## The hazards of living in high latitudes

People living in high latitudes are particularly vulnerable to malignant melanoma (skin cancer). The prevalence of this condition has increased dramatically in the 20th century and has been attributed to increased ultraviolet (UV) radiation resulting from ozone depletion, caused mainly by industrialized countries. Changes in behaviour, such as increasingly outdoor lifestyles and sunbathing, are contributory factors. In the year 2000, 78.5 per cent of melanoma cases, and 73 per cent of melanoma-related deaths reported worldwide, were in developed countries (Ferlay and others 2001). In the United States, there has been a 1 800 per cent rise in reported cases of malignant melanoma since 1930. One in five Americans develops skin cancer, and one American dies of it every hour (US EPA 1998).

settled, such as mountains, steep slopes and locations near sources of pollution. Such settlers are vulnerable to the associated single or combined hazards such as landslides, flooding, volcanic eruptions and toxic chemicals. Again, the poorest strata of society are often the most vulnerable because they have fewer options in where to live.

For various reasons, even the more affluent often choose to live or work in areas prone to environmental threats or hazards. Those living along the earthquake-prone San Andreas fault in California are a prime example, as are those who settle in hurricane belts, on sand spits, on eroding coastlines or in towns where water supplies are inadequate to meet demand. Clearly, the benefits of the location (employment, job security, leisure facilities) are perceived to outweigh the known risks. Measures to mitigate the risks may be sought in the form of insurance or purchasing a scarce commodity such as water but these options are not always appropriate, available or affordable to all members of the community.

In 2002, more than 1 billion urban dwellers, mostly in Africa, Asia and Latin America, live in slums or as squatters UNCHS 2001). Of the projected 1 billion new urban dwellers by 2010, most will probably be absorbed by cities in developing countries that already face multiple problems such as shortages of adequate housing, infrastructure, potable water supplies, adequate sanitation and transportation systems as well as environmental pollution. The urban poor, unable to

afford alternatives, are frequently forced to live in areas with the worst urban services and most unhealthy environmental conditions, exposed to multiple hazards and increased risk, their vulnerability enhanced by overcrowding.

Some communities have become more vulnerable because the scarcity of critical resources such as land, fresh water and forests is contributing to conflicts. These environmental scarcities do not usually cause wars among countries but they can generate severe

## Floods caused by glacial lake outbursts

Glacial lake outburst floods (GLOFs) are catastrophic discharges of water resulting primarily from melting glaciers.

Global warming over the past half century has led to an accelerated retreat of the glaciers and enlargement of several glacial lakes in the Hindu Kush and Tibetan Himalayas. In Bhutan, for example, some glaciers are retreating at a rate of 20-30 metres a year. Many glacial lakes are dammed by unstable moraines. Occasionally these dams burst and release large amounts of stored water, causing serious flooding downstream and along the river channel. The water contains substantial debris and causes serious damage — often at great distances from the outburst source; in Pakistan, damage has occurred 1 300 km from the outburst source. Such flash floods are a common problem in countries such as Bhutan, China (Tibet), India, Nepal and Pakistan.

In Nepal, records indicate that GLOFs occur once every three to ten years. Over the past few decades at least 12 GLOFs have caused major damage to infrastructure. For example, Dig Tsho glacial lake in Bhutan burst on 4 August 1985, causing significant loss of life and destroying the nearly completed Namche hydropower plant, as well as 14 bridges.

*Sources: WECS 1987, Watanabe and Rothacher 1996*

## Africa's Lake Victoria basin: multiple dimensions of vulnerability

An estimated 30 million people depend on Lake Victoria, a lake whose natural resources are under increasing stress. The population on the shore has grown fast over the past century with corresponding increases in the demand for fish and agricultural products. Following the introduction of gill nets by European settlers at the beginning of the 20th century, populations of indigenous fish species declined. Many were specially adapted to eat algae, decaying plant material, and snails that host the larvae of Schistosomes that cause bilharzia in humans. The lake started to eutrophicate and people became more vulnerable to disease.

As fish catches declined, non-native species were introduced, so causing further stress to indigenous fish. The greatest impact resulted from the introduction of nile perch (*Lates niloticus*) in

the 1960s, as the basis of commercial freshwater fisheries. This had repercussions on the local fishing economy and distribution of wealth. Local people who previously met most of their protein requirements from the lake began to suffer from malnutrition and protein deficiency. Although 20 000 tonnes of fish are exported annually to European and Asian markets, local people can afford only fish heads and bones from which the flesh has been removed.

Wetlands around the lake have been converted to grow rice, cotton and sugarcane, and their function as natural filters for silt and nutrients has been lost. Run-off now carries soil and excess nutrients from the cultivated areas straight into the lake. The resulting algal growth clouds the surface water and reduces oxygen availability, seriously affecting the habitat of endemic fish species, which

prefer clear waters, while their predator, the nile perch, thrives in such murky waters. This further aggravates food insecurity in lakeside communities.

Increased nutrients, much in the form of sewage, have stimulated the growth of the water hyacinth (*Eichornia crassipes*), one of the world's most invasive plants. This has seriously affected water transport and paralysed many local fisheries. By the end of 1997, the 70 per cent decline in economic activity reported at Kisumu port was attributable to water hyacinth choking the port and fish landings. The dense cover of water hyacinth also stimulated secondary weed growth, and provided habitats for snails and mosquitoes — this in an area where the incidence of bilharzia and malaria is already among the highest in the world.

*Source: Fuggle 2001*

social stresses within countries or across borders, helping to stimulate sub-national insurgencies, ethnic clashes and urban unrest. Such civil violence affects developing societies particularly because they are generally more dependent on environmental resources and less able to buffer themselves from the social crisis that environmental scarcities cause (Homer-Dixon 1999).

## Environmental change

Two basic functions performed by the environment are the 'source' or production function that supports the livelihood of millions who depend upon environmental resources, and the 'sink' or pollution absorption and cleansing function essential for human health and well-being. Not only are these two functions closely connected in a cycle of production and renewal but they are being increasingly impaired and degraded by human impacts.

### Watershed management and flooding

Poor land-use management can have profound effects on people. By 1986, deforestation in the upper reaches of the Yangtze basin in China had reduced forest cover from 22 per cent of total area in 1957 to only 10 per cent. As a result, soil erosion from the upper reaches and siltation in the middle and lower reaches had become intense. In 1998, the most severe flood in Chinese history hit the Yangtze valley, affecting 223 million people and causing more than US$36 billion in economic losses (Shougong 1999).

In July 1997, vast areas of southern Poland, the eastern Czech Republic and western Slovakia experienced one of the most disastrous floods in history when the Oder, Elbe, Vistula and Morava Rivers overflowed. In Poland alone, flooding affected one-quarter of the land area, including nearly 1 400 towns and villages, destroyed 50 000 homes and caused 162 000 people to be evacuated. Total damage was estimated at US$4 billion. The severity of the floods was attributed to the destruction of forest and wetlands, engineering works on the main rivers and tributaries, and the removal of water-retaining vegetation which made riverine areas more susceptible to flooding. Floods have become an increasingly regular occurrence for more than a decade (EEA 2001).

Degradation of natural resources such as land, fresh and marine waters, forests and biodiversity threatens the livelihood of many people but especially the poor. For example, water tables are falling fast under the North China plain. In 1997, almost 100 000 wells were abandoned apparently because they ran dry as the water table fell, but 221 900 new wells were drilled. The drilling of so many wells reflects a desperate quest for water (Brown 2001).

The 'sink' function of the environment operates through such processes as nutrient recycling,

decomposition, and the natural purification and filtering of air and water. When these functions are impaired, health can be jeopardized by contaminated household water, sanitation problems, indoor air pollution, urban air pollution and agrochemical pollution.

## How people are affected

Environmental change may have impacts on health, habitat and infrastructure, economy, society and culture, increasing vulnerability. The sections below discuss three of these areas: health, food security and economic effects.

## Health

Human health is increasingly determined by environmental conditions (Rapport and others 1999, McMichael 2001). According to a report from the World Health Organization (WHO 1997), for example:

- Deteriorating environmental conditions are a major contributory factor to poor health and poor quality of life. Mismanagement of natural resources, excessive waste production and associated environmental conditions that affect health pose major challenges to sustainable development.
- Impoverished populations living in rural and peri-urban areas are at greatest risk from degraded environmental conditions. The cumulative effects of inadequate and hazardous shelter, overcrowding, lack of water supply and sanitation, unsafe food, air and water pollution, and high accident rates, have serious effects on the health of these vulnerable groups.
- Poor environmental quality is directly responsible for some 25 per cent of all preventable ill health, with diarrhoeal diseases and acute respiratory infections heading the list.
- Two-thirds of all preventable ill health due to environmental conditions occurs among children.
- Air pollution is a major contributor to a number of diseases, and to a lowering of the quality of life in general.

There are regional differences in the way human health is vulnerable to environmental degradation. Communities in many parts of Central and South America, Central Africa and Asia are highly vulnerable to water-borne and vector-borne diseases. Air pollution threatens large urban areas and mega-cities, most of which are in developing countries. People in developed countries are more vulnerable to exposure to toxic chemicals and technological accidents but there are notable exceptions such as arsenic contamination in south Asia (see box).

Overall, it is estimated that 25-33 per cent of the global burden of disease is attributable to environmental factors (Smith, Corvalán and Kjellström 1999). Recent estimates suggest that environment-related premature death and illness account for 18 per cent of the total burden of disease in the developing world (Murray and Lopez 1996). This comprises contributions from water supply and sanitation (7 per cent), indoor air pollution (4 per cent), vector-borne diseases (3 per cent), urban air pollution (2 per cent) and agro-industrial waste (1 per cent). In sub-Saharan Africa the figure is even higher at 26.5 per cent, mainly related to water supply and sanitation (10 per cent) and vector-borne diseases (9 per cent).

Globally, 7 per cent of all deaths and diseases are due to inadequate water, sanitation and hygiene (UNDP, UNEP, World Bank and WRI 1998). Approximately 5 per cent are attributable to air pollution (Holdren and Smith 2000). Every year, environmental hazards kill 3 million children under the age of five (WHO 2002). Current estimates suggest that 40-60 per cent of those deaths are due to acute respiratory infection resulting from environmental factors, particularly particle emissions from solid fuel use (Smith, Corvalán and Kjellström 1999). In the United States, a 10 $\mu g/m^3$ increase in fine particle air

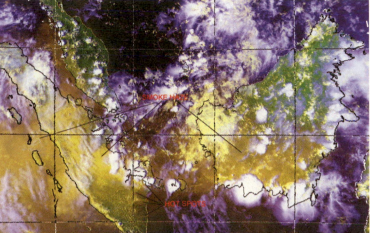

pollution results in a 4 per cent increase in general morbidity, a 6 per cent increase in cardio-pulmonary mortality and an 8 per cent increase in lung cancer mortality (Arden-Pope and others 2002).

In the short term, disease due to environmental change is likely to have more impact on developing countries than on developed ones. This is partly because developed countries have devoted considerable effort to reducing the health threat from dirty water, poor sanitation and using solid fuels in open fires inside homes. The same is not true for most developing countries. As a result, exposures to particulates for non-smokers are often an order of magnitude lower in developed countries than in developing ones. In Helsinki, for example, the particulates in the air come mainly from indoor dust, cleaning products, traffic and long-range transport (Koistinen and others 2002). In developing countries, the use of solid fuel as a primary energy supply dominates the exposure of non-smokers to particle pollution, especially among women and children in rural and slum environments. In the past decade, smoke haze from forest fires has also become an important source of respiratory disease (see image above). Furthermore, most developing countries still lack the resources to deal effectively with public health crises and are situated in regions where many water-borne and vector-borne diseases are acute.

Microbiological contamination of the sea by sewage pollution has precipitated a health crisis of massive proportions globally. Bathing in polluted seas is estimated to cause some 250 million cases of gastroenteritis and upper respiratory disease every year, with an estimated annual cost worldwide of about

Satellite image shows extensive smoke haze over Indonesia and neighbouring areas on 20 October 1997. Hot spots are probable areas of forest fires. Smoke haze had severe effects on the health of people over a wide area of Southeast Asia

*Source: Meteorological Service of Singapore 2002*

## Arsenic contamination in Bangladesh

In Bangladesh, naturally occurring arsenic in underground sediment leaches into the groundwater. More than 25 per cent of the 4 million tube wells that are the main source of drinking water contain dangerous levels of arsenic. Nearly 75 million people are vulnerable to arsenic poisoning which can cause skin cancer, kidney and liver failure, respiratory problems and death. About 24 million people have already been exposed to arsenic poisoning. Agricultural production is affected by arsenic-contaminated water in a 500-km swath of rice paddies and banana groves between the Ganges River and the Indian border.

*Sources: Karim 2000, BICN 2001a and 2001b, and UN Wire 2001*

US$1.6 billion. Some of these people will be disabled over the longer-term, suggesting that the global impacts of marine pollution are comparable to those of diphtheria and leprosy (see also page 181). Eating sewage-contaminated shellfish causes an estimated 2.5 million cases of infectious hepatitis a year, of whom some 25 000 die and another 25 000 suffer long-term disability resulting from liver damage. The annual global burden on human health is estimated to equal some 3.2 million DALYs — comparable to the worldwide impact of all upper respiratory infections and intestinal worm diseases — and to cost world society some US$10 billion annually (GESAMP 2001).

## Food security

There is only a fine line between harnessing environmental resources to provide goods and services to meet people's needs, and misusing, damaging or overexploiting those resources to the point where people's lives, health or well-being are put at risk and they become vulnerable.

Food security means being able to obtain a nutritionally adequate, culturally acceptable diet at all times through local non-emergency sources. This requires both adequate food production or imports, and economic access to food at the household level, at all times, to ensure a healthy active life (Vyas 2000). This idea goes well beyond the traditional concept of hunger: it embraces a systematic view of the causes of hunger and poor nutrition within a community

### Food security: is the green revolution losing momentum?

From independence until the mid-1970s, India faced problems of food scarcity. The green revolution that began in the mid-1960s combined new seed and fertilizer technology, substantial increases in irrigated land, infrastructure development and rural extension to all regions. The result was an unprecedented increase in the yield of major cereals such as wheat and rice, decreased production costs and a consequent fall in prices that enabled poor people to buy wheat and rice. The production of foodgrains increased from 50.8 million tonnes in 1950-51 to 199.3 million tonnes in 1996-97. By the mid-1970s, India was self-sufficient in food grains.

Despite the impressive results of the 1980s, recent trends in aggregate production growth have been a matter for serious concern. Foodgrain production grew by 3.43 per cent on average during the period 1991-92 to 1996-97 but the foodgrain production target of 210 million tonnes was not met. In 1996-97, the production of rice stood at 81.3 million tonnes, about 9 per cent less than the targeted 88 million. These figures must be viewed against a significant jump in the use of fertilizer and pesticides. The consumption of fertilizers (NPK) that had been stagnant at around 12 million tonnes between 1990-91 and 1993-94, increased to reach the level of 14.3 million tonnes in 1996-97.

*Source : Planning Commission of India 2001*

(Umrani and Shah 1999), recognizing both physical and economic vulnerability.

Projections of production increases suggest that the global availability of food should be adequate in

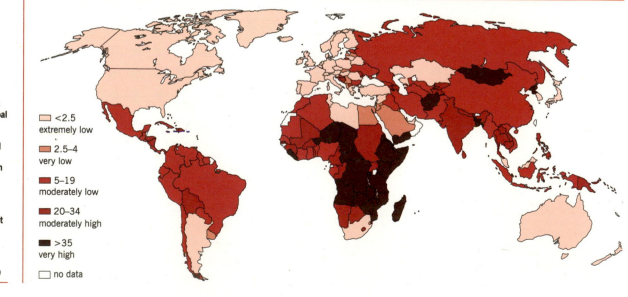

**Undernourishment by country (% of population undernourished)**

□ <2.5 extremely low

■ 2.5–4 very low

■ 5–19 moderately low

■ 20–34 moderately high

■ >35 very high

□ no data

Vulnerability to hunger is reflected in this map of the global state of undernourishment. Undernourished people are unable to obtain the food they need from production or imports, either because it is not available or because they cannot afford it

*Source: FAO 2000*

coming decades. Aggregate statistics, however, are often misleading, and can hide the real situation on the ground. For example, per capita food production in Africa has declined slightly over the past 30 years and decreased significantly in the former Soviet Union since 1990 (UNDP, UNEP, World Bank and WRI 1998).

Agricultural growth as a consequence of the Green Revolution has also had an adverse impact on the environment in terms of nutrient mining, increase in soil salinity, waterlogging, depletion of underground water and the release of nitrogen into watercourses (see box on page 308).

## Economic losses

Human vulnerability to environmental change has an important economic dimension. Human well-being is inextricably linked to ecosystems through the goods and services that ecosystems provide. This includes both marketed goods and services, such as food or forest products, and non-marketed ones such as water flow regulation, so that any reduction or degradation in supply leads to a loss of human welfare (see box below). In Japan, for example, the damage to agricultural crops caused by tropospheric ozone amounts to an estimated US$166.5 million yearly in the Kanto region alone (ECES 2001).

The economic dimensions of vulnerability to environmental change often focus on the impact of natural disasters or other extreme events. While total losses may be highest in developed countries, with their expensive infrastructure, the impact on the economies of developing regions may be greater. For example, the 1991-92 drought that hit most of Southern Africa resulted in a decline of 62 per cent in the Zimbabwe Stock Market (Benson and Clay 1994).

### The cost of resource degradation in India

Economic development has been the watchword in India's march into the 21st century, but a conservative estimate of environmental damage put the figure at more than US$10 billion a year, or 4.5 per cent of GDP, in 1992. A breakdown of the estimated costs shows that urban air pollution costs India US$1.3 billion a year; and water degradation has associated health costs of US$5.7 billion a year, nearly three-fifths of total environmental costs. Land degradation causes productivity losses of around US$2.4 billion and deforestation leads to annual losses of US$214 million.

*Source: Suchak 2002*

'It is not so much that humanity is trying to sustain the natural world, but rather that humanity is trying to sustain itself. The precariousness of nature is our peril, our fragility.' — *Amartya Sen, Nobel Laureate Economist*

The potential economic losses of non-marketed ecosystem goods and services and the impact on human vulnerability are likely to be even higher than for marketed goods and services. Equally, little attention is paid to the high economic cost of more gradual environmental degradation and loss of natural resource potential.

## Responding to human vulnerability

The cumulative evidence for increasing human vulnerability to environmental change calls for a significant policy response and action on several fronts. Social responses have frequently focused on 'downstream' measures, designed to mitigate the hardships and cushion the impacts of environmental change or natural disaster after the event, rather than on interventions intended to modify basic driving forces ahead of a potential crisis. The onset of conditions that give rise to threats and vulnerability can often be gradual or inconspicuous. Donors are often ready to offer relief once a high-profile disaster such as a famine or flood has occurred but they are less likely to finance precautionary measures. 'Upstream' intervention is generally highly cost-effective and should be given greater priority.

Levels and trends of vulnerability for different groups need to be assessed regularly as a basis for designing specific measures for vulnerability reduction and evaluating their impact. Governments need to assess and map national threats due to environmental change, particularly those that may be growing, and to institute early warning, mitigation and response measures to reduce the human and economic costs of disasters that are in part avoidable. Vulnerability should be recognized as a key indicator of the seriousness of environmental problems such as global warming (Adger and others 2001). It should be a focus for developing policies that seek to help people avoid, cope with or adapt to adverse effects of environmental change. Prior action to mitigate threats and to boost people's capacity to cope with or prepare for change makes more sense than remedial efforts after the event. The following sections discuss some possible approaches.

## Reducing vulnerability

There is a large and widening vulnerability gap between well-off people, with better all-round coping capacity, who are becoming gradually less vulnerable, and the poor who grow increasingly so. It is vital to the sustainable development effort that this gap is addressed, as well as vulnerability itself. For the most significant improvements, priority should go to policies that reduce the vulnerability of the poor as part of general strategies for poverty reduction. This is in keeping with the general priority being given to poverty reduction as essential to sustainable development.

Increasing human vulnerability is only now achieving wide recognition, so that few existing policies specifically address this issue. However, a number of studies, programmes and projects are currently addressing aspects of human vulnerability and these have already yielded valuable lessons for future policy action. Two types of policy response are possible: reducing the threat through prevention and preparedness initiatives, and improving the coping capacity of vulnerable groups to enable them to deal with the threat.

### Reducing exposure to threats

Exposure to threats can be minimized by reducing the risk — in other words the probability that damage will occur. In theory, exposure can always be avoided by moving people out of hazardous situations but this is not always feasible in practice. Currently, the prediction of threats is an imperfect science. People will not evacuate their homes and businesses unless absolutely necessary, and a few false alarms will quickly discourage any further response.

Human exposure can be reduced by reinforcing infrastructure — for example, by upgrading building codes, improving flood control, planting trees for soil stabilization or avalanche control, and providing safe havens or shelters. Many of these measures require significant long-term investments.

Better environmental management, improved policies to protect ecosystems and environmental restoration can be effective and practical ways to reduce vulnerability. In the long term, every effort to achieve sustainability in natural resource use, to reduce waste generation and pollution, and to bring society back into balance with the local environment and global systems should reduce human vulnerability. One of the main goals of integrated environmental planning should be the integration of vulnerability assessment and reduction.

Many natural systems evolved in response to specific major environmental threats and have a built-in capacity to absorb them. Vegetation stabilizes stream banks, slows run-off and prevents erosion. Beaches absorb wave energy and protect coastlines. Environmental threats may well increase with the destruction of such natural defences. Their restoration is the best response to the problem because it is usually less expensive and more permanent than artificial defensive construction which sometimes simply moves the threat elsewhere. Many flood control works have aggravated problems elsewhere on river systems and are now being systematically reversed.

### Reinforcing coping capacity

Improving the coping capacity of groups at greatest risk can do much to reduce the damage caused by extreme events or environmental degradation. The ability to cope with threats includes the ability to absorb impacts by guarding against or adapting to them. It also includes provisions made in advance to pay for potential damage, for instance by mobilizing insurance repayments, savings or contingency reserves.

**Attempts to conserve water upstream may simply shift the problem downstream — restoration of natural defences is often the best way to decrease overall vulnerability**

*Source: UNEP, John L. Perret, Topham Picturepoint*

People can draw on both tangible and hidden assets for coping with change, assets that can help to reduce the probability and magnitude of harm (Chambers 1997). They can be helped to identify and mobilize whatever assets they have in time of need and these may be decisive factors in damage prevention. They include economic assets, social and political assets, ecological assets, infrastructure assets and personal assets. Strategies that take account of the existing assets of vulnerable groups and their likely needs may also cushion the damaging impacts of unavoidable events or catastrophes. Restitution of lost or damaged assets through rapid response to sudden or extreme events in the form of rescue, relief and rehabilitation (for instance, provision of clean water, health care, shelter and food) may be all that is required to reduce hardship to manageable levels.

Institutional arrangements — including the preparedness of public, private and social services — are an important aspect of coping (Adger and others 2001). Institutional preparedness can be a decisive factor in reducing vulnerability. For example, the flooding of the River Oder in 1997 caused less damage on the German side than it did in Poland (GACGC 2000) because the Germans were better prepared. People in vulnerable areas should make institutional arrangements to respond to potential crises. This requires foresight but often can be done at little or no cost. The UNEP Awareness and Preparedness for Emergencies at Local Level programme (APELL) is a good example of institutional preparation to cope with potential environmental threats (UNEP 2002).

## Adapting to threat

Where a threat cannot be reduced or eliminated, adapting to it can be an effective response. Adaptation refers both to physical adjustments or technical measures (such as constructing a higher sea wall) and changing behaviour, economic activities and social organization to be more compatible with existing or emerging conditions or threats. The latter requires adaptive capacity, including the ability to develop new options and to deliver them to vulnerable populations.

Some environmental changes, such as expected climate change from global warming, have such long lead times that some degree of environmental change is inevitable even if measures to control the situation are implemented rapidly. Some adaptation measures may then be essential. Efforts to predict the probable

---

### Breakdown of traditional coping mechanisms: Kenyan pastoralists

Pastoralists' coping strategies for drought include migration to available water and pastures, setting aside dry grazing pastures and splitting herds to minimize risks. In the past, there were fewer pastoralists and they had large herds to survive droughts. During extreme droughts, animals would graze unused swamps, forests and areas remote from water. These ancient drought responses, however, are often no longer available to pastoralists, either because land has been sold or because of barriers erected by farmers, ranchers, industry and city residents. Other traditional drought responses, such as raiding neighbouring cattle and killing wildlife for meat, may be both illegal and no longer appropriate.

In 2000, Kenya experienced its worst drought for 40 years. Its effects were severe because of the:

- breakdown of traditional coping methods;
- increasing population pressure due to development of land formerly used as dry season grazing;
- land tenure system which restricts access to essential resources;
- extension of the drought to areas usually not affected;
- poor security, especially in arid and semi-arid land areas, that restricts animal and human movement;
- inadequate preparedness due to lack of access to or ignoring of weather forecasts;
- scepticism about traditional early warning systems and weather forecasts; and
- lack of an effective marketing infrastructure for livestock.

*Source: UNEP and Government of Kenya 2000*

---

impacts of climate change should help to determine the adaptive actions that are necessary and the speed with which they should be implemented.

Various investments in adaptive capacity have been made following advances in early warning. Several countries have tried to change patterns of agricultural practice so that crops more suited to periodic changes in growing conditions can be grown in years affected by climate fluctuations associated with El Niño and La Niña events (see box above). The risk of crop failure is thus reduced.

## Early warning

One of the most effective responses to human vulnerability to environmental change is to strengthen mechanisms for early warning. Many actions can be taken to protect life and property if warning is received in time. While some threats are inherently unpredictable, many of those arising from threats from environmental degradation and mismanagement, and from human activities, can now be anticipated with some precision. Early warning capacities are increasing steadily with technological advances in environmental observing, assessment and

develop over time such as famine and drought.

The term early warning is often taken to mean 'prediction' when in fact the occurrence of many threatening events is essentially unpredictable. Early warning simply means that an event is imminent and the time to escape from it or take action against it is now. Early warning information can be produced in the context of a broader vulnerability assessment process, which includes the production and communication of forecast information and the incorporation of that information in user decisions.

To be effective, an early warning system must be able to stimulate a timely response before an event takes place. It must identify who are the users of early warning information and what is the most efficient way to reach them with credible information to enhance their powers of decision-making. It must then translate relevant data into early warning indicators that decision-makers can easily interpret and use.

communications. Examples are the cyclone early warning systems that have been established in India and Mauritius.

Conventionally, early warning means an urgent indication of an impending hazard (ISDR Secretariat 2001). There is a need for both sudden onset warnings, for imminent disaster threats such as tropical storms and floods, and slow onset warnings for disseminating information about disasters that may

Ultimately, the single most important factor that will lead governments to incorporate the use of early warning systems and information in decision-making is the political will to invest in response systems, both nationally and internationally (Buchanan-Smith 2001). One example of an operational early warning system which has generated such a response is the Famine Early Warning System Network for Africa (see box).

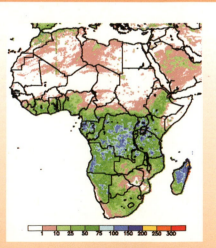

## Assessing and measuring vulnerability

Vulnerability assessment measures the seriousness of potential threats on the basis of known hazards and the level of vulnerability of societies and individuals. It can be used to translate early warning information into preventive action (IDNDR 1999) and is a necessary element in early warning and emergency preparedness. Ideally, the results should be incorporated directly into the long-term planning of institutions and governments, and should foster institutional responsiveness to increasing vulnerability, and action for disaster preparedness and mitigation. Vulnerability assessments are widely applied and used in the fields of climate change and natural disaster management, where they provide the basis for effective warning systems.

Assessments of vulnerability can be made for both people and the environmental systems that provide goods and services. They should identify the location of vulnerable populations, the threats to their well-being and the extent of their vulnerability; the risks to the environmental capacity to provide goods and services; and the preventive steps that can be taken to improve environmental conditions and reduce the negative impacts of human action on the environment. This information is then assembled into a knowledge base that is accessible, scientifically reliable and easy

to use, which can help policy-makers and planners seeking to formulate adequate responses (see box below).

Calculation of coping capacity would be a valuable tool for understanding how and why burdens of environmental degradation are unevenly distributed around the globe, and why the potential impact of different threats may be more or less catastrophic depending upon a group's ability to cope. In the case of diseases such as cholera, governments of high-income countries would be likely to respond to the risk of an outbreak with costly prevention and early warning programmes such as a cholera-monitoring network. Yet this response would not be affordable in many other parts of the world.

When calculating vulnerability, geographical scale is important. A single national figure may hide many significant variations. Although an assessment for high-income countries would show low overall vulnerability, there may be sub-populations that are highly vulnerable. For instance, one country may be less vulnerable to outbreaks of vector-borne disease triggered by climate change than another, because of the medical system's capacity to respond, but those without medical insurance may still be particularly vulnerable. Furthermore, societies that are well equipped to cope with present vulnerability may lack

### Environmental vulnerability of small island developing states

The South Pacific Applied Geosciences Commission (SOPAC) is developing an index of the vulnerability of the environment to both human and natural hazards. SOPAC identifies three aspects of environmental vulnerability: level of risks (or pressures) on the environment; resilience of the environment to pressures, or intrinsic vulnerability; and the level of degradation of ecosystems, or extrinsic resilience. A total of 47 indicators are used: 26 indicators of risk, 7 indicators of resilience and 14 indicators of environmental degradation. The indicators are also classified by category; meteorological, geological, biological,

anthropogenic and intrinsic country characteristics. Data were collected for five countries (Fiji, Samoa, Tuvalu, Vanuatu and Australia) for initial testing. The environmental vulnerability of small island developing states arises from an interplay of factors such as remoteness, geographical dispersion, vulnerability to natural disasters, ecological fragility, a high degree of economic openness and small internal markets, and limited natural resources.

The objective of the project is to promote the use of environmental vulnerability considerations in national development planning and thereby encourage sustainable development. The

Environmental Vulnerability Index (EVI) provides a relatively quick and inexpensive way of characterizing the vulnerability of natural systems at the level of a region, state, province or island.

The figure below shows the scores obtained by Fiji for each of the 47 indicators in the EVI. Areas of vulnerability can be easily identified, information that could lead to better management and possibly better vulnerability scores in the future. A score of 1 is the least vulnerable, 7 the most vulnerable.

*Sources: SOPAC 1999 and 2000, Kaly and Craig 2000, Pratt and others 2001*

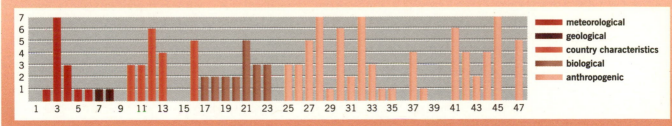

the experience or technology to respond to emerging threats.

## Conclusions

Levels of risk and associated human vulnerability change over time. In a resilient society, with appropriate interventions, recovery and mitigation can bring vulnerability back to a previous (baseline) level or reduce it to a lower level, but too fast a rate of change may exceed the capacity of the society to adapt. The long-term nature of environmental change may mean that potential future vulnerability is equally as important as present vulnerability. The capacity to adapt may be more important in determining human vulnerability in the long run than the ability to cope with present critical situations.

The degree and extent of vulnerability appears to be increasing because of a combination of such factors as the increasing impact of humans on the environment, reductions in the efficient functioning of ecosystems, the reduced ability of the environment to provide goods and services, growing and more spatially concentrated populations, and increasing human settlement in high risk areas. As human impact on the environment increases, so people's options decrease. Human vulnerability to environmental change thus increases, despite many instances of adequate coping capacity.

Assessments contribute to better-informed decisions on preparedness, mitigation, relief and rehabilitation activities but there is a lag between the time it takes to make such assessments and the optimal response time. There is a growing gap between rapid rates of environmental degradation and the slow pace of social response. This gap threatens to drain the environment of assets and options for future generations and to increase the costs of substitutes for missing resources (Kasperson and others 1999). High priority should therefore be given to rapid assessments of vulnerability and the design of initial protective responses, such as early warning systems, while longer-term remedial measures are put in place. Environmental restoration, with its potential to reduce vulnerability, will thus become an increasingly important component of sustainable development.

The complexity of the change process makes assessing and measuring human vulnerability to long-term or future environmental change highly speculative and it is hard to determine the kinds of investment that would most effectively deal with the threats in question. A better understanding of the interplay of the social and physical factors that determine human vulnerability needs to be developed to increase the ability to mitigate potentially harmful impacts that arise from environmental change. Cause-and-effect linkages need to be investigated. Systems modelling approaches and sensitivity analysis may help to determine the nature and timing of the most cost-effective measures to anticipate threats where uncertainty and complex relationships are important.

Delaying a response to an environmental threat often stems from uncertainty, or a lack of knowledge. Improving the assessment process can help resolve this although, even when the risks are known, action may not follow. Nevertheless, regional studies suggest that the breakdown in response is more attributable to narrow government policies aimed solely at economic growth, coupled with a lack of political will, government willingness to tolerate damage in marginal areas and among vulnerable peoples, and widespread political corruption than to public apathy or lack of awareness (Kasperson and others 1999). These are all issues to be tackled.

In the recent past, responses to human vulnerability have progressed from single measures to address a single issue (such as controlling floods by building dykes) to the development of a mix of measures serving different purposes (multipurpose dam projects, warning systems, insurance, land use zoning, integrated river basin management). Today, issues are being visualized in the even broader context of sustainable development (Mitchell 2000). To support these new kinds of policy making, approaches need to be even further integrated to improve the chances of capturing all aspects of human vulnerability.

In an increasing number of areas, environmental damage may be irreversible, or restoration and the reduction in threat may require such a long time that accommodation must accompany any remedial measures. Enabling people to adapt to such situations, especially where change may accelerate in the future, should accompany short-term disaster prevention and management measures. Adaptation is vital where the impacts to which people are vulnerable appear inevitable.

## A framework for assessing risk

In 1987, the World Commission on Environment and Development called for the:

- identification of critical threats to the survival, security or well-being of all or of a majority of people, globally and regionally;
- assessment of the causes and likely human, economic and ecological consequences of those threats, with regular and public reporting of the findings;
- provision of authoritative advice on what must be done to avoid, reduce, or adapt to these threats; and
- provision of an additional source of advice to governments and intergovernmental organizations on policies and programmes to address these threats.

Since the report of the Commission was published, IPCC has set up a vulnerability task group, and the System for Analysis, Research and Training (START) and the Project on Critical Environmental Zones were initiated. These studies demonstrated that the coping capacity of countries differs considerably. IPCC claims that vulnerability and coping capacity are inversely related and socially differentiated.

*Sources: WCED 1987, IPCC 1996*

Stakeholder participation is important in responding to human vulnerability, both to ensure a 'reality check' on coping capacity and to boost prospects of success by involving as many stakeholders as possible in implementing coping mechanisms (IFRC 1999). Stakeholders should review and strengthen their capabilities in the areas of preparedness and mitigation to increase coping capacities, and become involved in post-event examination of new initiatives that might reduce losses in the future. Communities with effective mitigation strategies could look into ways to help other populations at risk from similar threats. In all cases, assessments of community conditions should provide decision-makers with all the relevant information they need to make strategic decisions to counter vulnerability.

This consideration of human vulnerability has demonstrated that the continuing loss of environmental defences and accelerating global change are increasing threats to human well-being and are putting sustainable development at risk. The evidence suggests that many areas of the world are on trajectories that will lead them into crisis and that little time is left for creating effective responses if deteriorating situations are to be stabilized (Kasperson and others 1999). People are less and less the helpless victims of 'acts of God' and more and more the victims of 'acts of man'. But an increasing understanding of environmental processes and a growing capacity for early warning should help to identify threats and risks and react appropriately. There are now also better means of preventing and reducing harm to people and damage to economies and communities. An increased investment now in sound environmental management, community preparedness and vulnerability reduction will result in important savings in the future.

## References: Chapter 3, Human Vulnerability to Environmental Change

Adger, N., Kelly, M. and Bentham, G. (2001). *New Indicators of Vulnerability and Adaptive Capacity*. Paper presented at the International Workshop on Vulnerability and Global Environmental Change, Lila Nyagatan. Stockholm, 17-19 May 2001

Arden Pope III, C., Burnett, T.R., Thun, M.J., Calle, E.E., Krewski, D., Ito, K. and Thurston, G.D. (2002). Lung cancer, cardiopulmonary mortality, and long-term exposure to fine particulate air pollution. *Journal of the American Medical Association* 287, 9, 1132–41

Benson, C. and Clay, E. (1994). *The Impact of Drought on Sub-Saharan African Economies: A Preliminary Examination*. Working Paper 77. London, Overseas Development Institute

BICN (2001a). Over 20m people exposed to arsenic poisoning. *News From Bangladesh (NFB)* 22 May 2001. Bangladesh International Community News http://bicn.com/acic/resources/infobank/nfb/2001-05-22-nv4n574.htm [Geo-3-001]

BICN (2001b). Arsenic hits 24m in Bangladesh: WB. *News From Bangladesh (NFB)* 25 March 2001. Bangladesh International Community News http://bicn.com/acic/resources/infobank/nfb/2001-03-25-nv4n520.htm [Geo-3-002]

Braaf, R.R. (1999). Improving impact assessment methods: climate change and the health of indigenous Australians. *Global Environmental Change* 9, 95-104

Brown, L. R. (2001) *Eco-economy*. New York, W.W. Norton

Buchanan-Smith, M. (2001). Role of Early Warning Systems in Decision Making Processes. In Wilhite, D.A., Sivakumar, M.V.K. and Wood, D.A. (eds.), *Early Warning Systems for Drought Preparedness and Drought Management*. Geneva, World Meteorological Organization http://drought.unl.edu/ndmc/center/ch2_Buchanan-Smith.pdf [Geo-3-003]

Chambers, R. (1997). *Whose Reality Counts?* London, Intermediate Technology Development Group

Clark, E.G., Moser, C.S., Ratick, J.S., Kirstin, D., Meyer, B.W., Srinivas, E., Weigen, J., Kasperson, X.J., Kasperson, E.R. and Schwarz, E.H. (1998). Assessing the vulnerability of coastal communities to extreme storms: the case of Revere, MA, USA. *Mitigation and Adaptation Strategies for Global Change* 3, 59-82

CNA Peru (2001). *GEO Peru 2000*. Lima, Conseio Nacional del Ambiente, Peru

Cohen, S.J., Barret, R., Irlbacher, S., Kertland, P., Mortch, L., Pinter, L. and Zdan, T. (1997). Executive summary. In Cohen, S.J. (ed.), *The Mackenzie Basin Impact Study (MBIS) Final Report*. Ottawa, Environment Canada

CSE (1999). *State of India's Environment, The Citizen's Fifth Report. Part 1: National Overview*. New Delhi, Centre for Science and Environment

Downing, T. and Bakker, K. (2000). *Drought Discourse and Vulnerability*. In Wilhite, D. (ed.), *Drought: a global assessment, Vol. 2*. London, Routledge

ECES (2001). *Documenting the Collapse of a Dying Planet. Air Pollution*. Earth Crash Earth Spirit http://www.eces.org/ec/pollution/air.shtml [Geo-3-004]

EEA (2001). *Sustainable Water Use in Europe. Part 3: Extreme Hydrological Events: Floods and Droughts*. Environmental Issues Report No. 21. Copenhagen, European Environment Agency

ETE (2000). *Living with the Virunga Volcanoes*. Classroom of the Future www.cotf.edu/ete/modules/mgorilla/ mgvolcanoes.html

FAO (2000). *Crops and Drops*. Rome, Food and Agriculture Organization http://www.fao.org/landandwater/aglw/oldocsw. asp [Geo-3-005]

Ferlay, J., Bray, F., Pisani, P. and Parkin, D.M. (2001). *GLOBOCAN 2000: Cancer Incidence, Mortality and Prevalence Worldwide, Version 1.0*. IARC Cancer Base No. 5. Lyon, IARC Press

FEWS (2002). *Home Page* Famine Early Warning System Network http://www.fews.net/about/index.cfm [Geo-3-006]

Fuggle, R.F. (2001). *Lake Victoria: a case study of complex interrelationships*. Nairobi, United Nations Environment Programme

GACGC (2000). World in Transition: *strategies for managing global environmental risks*. German Advisory Council on Global Change, Annual Report 1998. Berlin, Springer-Verlag

GESAMP (2001). *Protecting the Oceans from Land-Based Activities. Land-based Sources and Activities Affecting the Quality and Uses of the Marine, Coastal and Associated Freshwater Environment*. GESAMP Reports and Studies No. 71. Nairobi, United Nations Environment Programme http://gesamp.imo.org/no71/index.htm [Geo-3-22]

*Guardian* (2000). Baby born in a tree – mother and child saved by helicopter crew, *The Guardian*, 3 March 2000

Holdren, J.P. and Smith, K.R. (2001). Energy, the environment and health. In Goldemberg, J. (ed.), *World Energy Assessment: Energy and the Challenge of Sustainability*. New York, United Nations Development Programme

Homer-Dixon, T.F. (1999). *Environment, Scarcity and Violence*. Princeton, Princeton University Press

IATFDR (2001). *Updated and Expanded Terminology of Disaster Reduction: First Draft Compilation*. Doc. # TF3/5, Inter-Agency Task Force on Disaster Reduction, Third Meeting of the Task Force, Geneva, 3-4 May 2001

IDNDR (1999). *Early Warning Programme Action Plan for the Future (1998–1999)*. Geneva, International Decade for Natural Disaster Reduction Secretariat

IFRC (1999). *Vulnerability and Capacity Assessment: An International Federation Guide*. Geneva, International Federation of Red Cross and Red Crescent Societies

IOC (1998). GOOS and El Niño forecasting. In IOC (ed.), *Intergovernmental Oceanographic Commission Annual Report 1998*. Paris, Intergovernmental Oceanographic Commission

IPCC (1996). *Climate Change 1995: Impacts, Adaptations and Mitigation of Climate Change: Scientific-Technical Analysis*. Contribution of Working Group II to the Second Assessment Report of the Intergovernmental Panel on Climate Change. Cambridge and New York, Cambridge University Press

IPCC (2001). *IPCC Third Assessment Report — Climate Change 2001. Working Group I: The Scientific Basis. Summary for Policy Makers*. Geneva, World Meteorological Organization and United Nations Environment Programme

ISDR Secretariat (2001). *Early Warning Issues: A Discussion Paper*. Paper presented at the Third Meeting of the Task Force, Geneva, 3-4 May 2001

Kaly, U. and Craig, P. (2000). Environmental Vulnerability Index: Development and provisional indices and profiles for Fiji, Samoa, Tuvalu and Vanatua. SOPAC Technical Report 306 http://www.sopac.org.fj/Projects/Evi/Files/EVI%20R eport%20Phase%20II.pdf [Geo-3-008]

Karim, R.N. (2001). *Arsenic the Silent Killer*. Bangladesh Centre for Advanced Studies http://www.bcas.net/arsenic/articles/2001/arsenic-May.htm [Geo-3-009]

Kasperson, R., Kasperson, J., and Turner II, B.L. (1999). Risk and Criticality: trajectories of regional environmental degradation. *Ambio* 28, 6, 562-568

Koistinen, K.J., Edwards, R.D., Mathys, P., Ruuskanen, J., Kuenzli, N., and Jantunen, M.J. (2002). Sources of PM2.5 In Personal Exposures and Residential Indoor, Outdoor and Workplace Microenvironments In EXPOLIS-Helsinki, Finland. *Scandinavian Journal of Work, Environment & Health* 28, Supplement 3, Multidisciplinary Research on Urban Air Particles in Finland (SYTTY programme)

McMichael, A.J. (2001). *Human Frontiers, Environments and Disease: Past Patterns, Uncertain Futures*. Cambridge, Cambridge University Press

Met Office (2002). The Great Smog of 1952 http://www.met-office.gov.uk/education/historic/smog.html [Geo-3-010]

Meteorological Service of Singapore (2002). Monitoring of Smoke Haze and Forest Fires in Southeast Asia http://www.gov.sg/metsin/hazed.html [Geo-3-011]

Mitchell, J.K. (2000). Urban metabolism and disaster vulnerability in an era. In Schellnhuber H-J. and Wenzel, V. (eds.), *Earth System Analysis: Integrating Science for Sustainability*. Berlin, Springer-Verlag

Murray, C.J.L. and Lopez, A.D. (1996). *The Global Burden of Disease*, Cambridge MA, Harvard University Press

NOAA (2002). NOAA Climate Prediction Center. Famine Early Warning System Network http://www.cpc.noaa.gov/products/fews/10day_pre cip.html [Geo-3-012]

NOAA/PMEL/TAO (1998). *Impacts of El Niño and Benefits of El Niño Prediction*. Seattle, NOAA/PMEL/TOA Project Office

Planning Commission of India (2001). *Mid Term Review, Ninth Five Year Plan (1997-2002)*. New Delhi ,Government of India

Pratt, C., Koshy, R., Kaly, U., Pal, R. and Sale-Mario, E. (2001). Environmental Vulnerability Index (EVI) Project; Progress Towards a Global EVI. South Pacific Applied Geoscience Commission, Progress Report 405 http://www.sopac.org.fj/Projects/Evi/archive.html# [Geo-3-013]

Rapport, D.J., Christensen, N., Karr, J.R. and Patil, G.P. (1999). The centrality of ecosystem health in achieving sustainability in the 21st century. In Hayne, D.M. (ed.), *Concepts and New Approaches to Environmental Management*. Transactions of the Royal Society of Canada, Series VI, v. IX, 3-40. Toronto, University of Toronto Press

Shougong, Z. (1999). Catastrophic Flood Disaster in 1998 and the Post Factum Ecological and Environmental Reconstruction in China. Paper presented at Natural Disasters and Policy Response in Asia: Implications for Food Security, Harvard University Asia Center, April 30-May 1 1999

Smith, K.R., Corvalán, C.F. and Kiellström, T. (1999). How much global ill health is attributable to environmental factors? *Journal of Epidemiology* 10, 5, 573–84 http://www.who.int/environmental_information/Dis burden/Articles/smith.pdf [Geo-3-020]

SOPAC (1999). Environmental Vulnerability Index (EVI) to summarize national environmental vulnerability profiles. Final Report. South Pacific Applied Geoscience Commission http://www.sopac.org.fj/Projects/Evi/archive.html# documents [Geo-3-014]

Stoddard, E. (2000). Mozambique floods worsened by wetlands loss. *Reuters*, 14 March 2000

Suchak, Y.K. (2002). *Development and Environment Issues with Special Reference to Gandhian Perspective*. Gahndian Institution, Bombay Sarvodaya Mandal http://www.mkgandhi-sarvodaya.org/kavita_ suchak.htm [Geo-3-015]

Umrani, A.P. and Ali Shah, S. (1999). *Food Security and Environment. Special Report.* Sustainable Livestock and Agriculture Production Bimonthly-Newsletter May & June 1999 of Progressive Agriculturist & Pastoralist Association. Pakistan, Shahnaz.Palijo http://csf.colorado.edu/bioregional/apr99/0064. html [Geo-3-016]

UN WIRE (2001). *Arsenic: Contaminated Water in Asia Puts Millions At Risk. UN Wire*, 10 May 2001. United Nations Foundation http://www.unfoundation.org/unwire/util/display_st ories.asp?objid=14683 [Geo-3-017]

UNCHS (2001). *State of the World's Cities 2001*. Nairobi, United Nations Centre for Human Settlements (Habitat)

UNDP, UNEP, World Bank and WRI (1998). *World Resources 1998-1999.* Washington DC, World Resources Institute

UNDP, UNEP, World Bank and WRI (2000). *World Resources 2000-2001.* Washington DC, World Resources Institute

UNEP (2000). *Assessing Human Vulnerability due to Environmental Change: Concepts, Issues, Methods and Case Studies.* UNEP/DEWA/TR, Nairobi, Kenya

UNEP (2002). APELL — Awareness and Preparedness for Emergencies at a Local Level http://www.uneptie.org/pc/apell/ [Geo-3-018]

UNEP and Government of Kenya (2000). *Devastating Drought in Kenya: Environmental Impacts and Responses.* Nairobi, United Nations Environment Programme

USAID (2002). *Democratic Republic of the Congo-Volcano.* Fact Sheet 12 (FY 2002). Washington DC, United States Agency for International Development

US EPA (1998). *Stay Healthy in the Sun.* Washington DC, United States Environmental Protection Agency http://www.epa.gov/ozone/uvindex/stayheal.html [Geo-3-019]

Vyas, V.S. (2000). *Presidential Address*, 3rd Annual Conference of Asian Society of Agricultural Economics, Jaipur, India, 18-20 October 2000

Watanabe, T. and Rothacher, D. (1996). The 1994 Lugge Tsho glacial lake outburst flood, Bhutan Himalayas. *Mountain Research and Development* 16, 1, 77–81

WCED (1987). *Our Common Future*. New York, Oxford University Press

WECS (1987). *Study of Glacier Lake Outburst Floods in the Nepal Himalayas*. Phase I, Interim Report, May 1997, WECS Report No.4/1/200587/1/1, Seq. No. 251. Kathmandu, Water and Energy Commission Secretariat

WHO (1997). *Health and Environment: Five Years after the Earth Summit*. Geneva, World Health Organization

WHO (2002). Environmental Hazards Kill at least 3 Million Children aged under 5 Every Year. http://www.who.int/inf/en/pr-2002-12.html [Geo-3-021]

Woodward, A., Hales, S. and Weinstein, P. (1998). Climate change and human health in the Asia Pacific: who will be most vulnerable? *Climate Research* 11, 1, 31-39

*Chapter*

# 4

# Outlook
# 2002–32

The record of the past three decades shows how tricky it can be to foresee the future course of events on such a time scale. Enormous social, economic and political changes have shaped and transformed present-day realities over that period, not least the oil crises of the 1970s, the end of China's isolation and the collapse of the Soviet system, that were not — and perhaps could not have been — predicted.

Some aspects of modern life might have been foreseen in general terms, by extending such long-term trends as reduction in trade barriers, continual technological innovation and the growing role of the service sector. Following the 1972 Stockholm Conference, the emergence of a worldwide environmental movement might have been anticipated and hoped for. But few, if any, recognized the major regional and global issues such as acidification, stratospheric ozone depletion and climate change, which have driven much of the action in recent years.

Moving into the future means travelling into uncharted waters. Some of the way ahead is clear but there is much that cannot be mapped out, even with advanced technologies. As before, there will be

'The record of the past three decades shows how tricky it can be to foresee the future course of events on such a time scale.'

challenges that can be prepared for but others that will seem to materialize from out of the blue.

How shall we proceed as a society? By placing faith in further globalization and liberalization, trusting primarily in the market economy to solve wider social and environmental concerns? Or by putting policy first, whereby coordinated action to solve social and environmental problems balances the drive for economic development? If and when troubles arise, will everyone work together to address these threats, or will groups that are better off focus on self-protection, creating fortress conditions that increasingly exclude the 'have-nots'? Or could a more visionary state of affairs emerge, where radical shifts in the way people interact with one another and with the world around them stimulate and support sustainable policy measures?

There is no knowing which of these — or other — possible futures will actually unfold over the next 30 years. Much of what will happen has already been set in motion by policy decisions and actions that have already been taken. Uncontrolled forces, both human and natural, will contribute to the course of events. But informed decision-making also has a real and vital role to play in the process of shaping the future.

Scenario analysis can make a difference to this process. By exploring an array of possible future scenarios, today's decision-makers can get a clearer picture of what tomorrow might bring in terms of human well-being and environmental security and what the impact of their decisions is likely to be. And they can determine more accurately what it would take — and what they can do — to create a more desirable future.

Scenarios are descriptions of journeys to possible futures. They reflect different assumptions about how current trends will unfold, how critical uncertainties will play out and what new factors will come into play. Since it emerged as a formal methodology in the middle of the past century, scenario analysis has evolved swiftly as a tool for anticipating the future. It is now generally accepted that scenarios do not predict. Rather, they paint pictures of possible futures and explore the differing outcomes that might result if basic assumptions are changed. Hence the relevant question that scenarios can answer is not what will happen but what might happen and how people could act to encourage or counteract particular events and trends. As a way of exploring the unknown, scenario analysis can result in surprising and innovative insights.

The scenarios developed for *GEO-3* have an environmental focus but recognize that the environment cannot be discussed without also considering what may be happening in the social and economic spheres. The scenarios therefore span eventualities in many overlapping areas, including population, economics, technology and governance. Moreover, though many issues are of global concern, some take on special relevance or sharper focus when viewed at a regional or smaller scale. To take account of this effect — and so that each can enrich the others — this chapter presents both global and regional perspectives. In addition, the role of policy choices in shaping the future is highlighted in the scenarios wherever possible, although this influence can be hard to judge because other policies and independent developments may cloud the effects of any single policy.

Drawing on the experience and work of other scenario initiatives, including those of the Global Scenario Group (Raskin and Kemp-Benedict 2002), a set of four scenarios has been developed for *GEO-3*.

The *Markets First* scenario envisages a world in which market-driven developments converge on the values and expectations that prevail in industrialized countries;

In a *Policy First* world, strong actions are undertaken by governments in an attempt to reach specific social and environmental goals;

The *Security First* scenario assumes a world of great disparities, where inequality and conflict prevail, brought about by socio-economic and environmental stresses; and

*Sustainability First* pictures a world in which a new development paradigm emerges in response to the challenge of sustainability, supported by new, more equitable values and institutions.

For each of these scenarios, an overall narrative — 'A tale of four futures' — describes the future in the next 30 years in a predominantly qualitative manner, providing both regional and global perspectives.

The stories of the four scenarios are followed by a more detailed examination of their environmental implications, drawing on quantitative data derived from a number of analytical tools — and with a regional focus intended to highlight particular concerns in the different regions. A brief comparison of qualitative and quantitative approaches is provided in the box. For more details of the *GEO-3* scenario analysis, see the technical annex to this chapter (page 398).

---

### Narratives or numbers?

Scenarios can be told in many ways. The two most common methods used in scenario analysis have been descriptive, written narratives (qualitative scenarios) and tables and figures incorporating numerical data, often generated by sophisticated computer models (quantitative scenarios). Both approaches have strengths and weaknesses and their relative worth has been much debated.

- Qualitative scenarios can explore relationships and trends for which few or no numerical data are available, including shocks and discontinuities. They can more easily incorporate human motivations, values and behaviour and create images that capture the imagination of those for whom they are intended.
- Quantitative scenarios can provide greater rigour, precision and consistency. Their assumptions are explicit and their conclusions can be traced back to the assumptions. The effects of changes in assumptions can be easily checked, pointing to important uncertainties. They can provide order-of-magnitude estimates of past, present and future trends in, for example, population growth, economic growth or resource use.

In *GEO-3*, qualitative narratives take centre stage with the quantitative tools playing a supporting role.

---

The chapter concludes with 'Lessons from the future', a discussion of important lessons arising from the scenario analysis for future environmentally relevant policy development. Before embarking on the journey through these four possible futures, however, it is useful to know the key assumptions made in constructing them and how these act as driving forces behind the scenarios. These assumptions are therefore outlined in the next section.

# Driving forces

Earlier chapters of this report have reviewed present conditions and trends in a number of socio-economic factors that are driving environmental change. How these factors evolve will shape global and regional development and the state of the environment far into the future. Trends may continue as they have in the past or change speed and direction — perhaps even going into reverse. Trends may lead to convergence or divergence between circumstances in different regions of the world. Trends in one region or responses to one driving force may oppose others that originate elsewhere, or they may run up against absolute physical limits.

The scenarios explored in the pages that follow are based on certain assumptions about how these driving forces will evolve and interact with developing situations, potential future shocks and human choices. This section briefly describes the assumptions made about driving forces underlying the scenarios and, in particular, how these assumptions differ from scenario to scenario. For descriptions of the scenarios see pages 329, 334, 339 and 344 in the next section.

The seven driving forces under consideration are demography, economic development, human development, science and technology, governance, culture and environment. The environment is included as a driving force because it is more than a passive receptacle for change. Just as the assumptions about human and societal behaviour shape the scenarios, so do the assumptions about pressures exerted by the environment.

Developments arising from each of the driving forces will not unfold in isolation from one another. Issues will interweave and chains of cause and effect are likely to be hard to trace back to individual sources. Finally, any number of possible future trends could be constructed from the available array of variables. Narrowing down this range to a small yet richly contrasting set of futures that are consistent, plausible, recognizable and challenging, depends on starting out with an intelligent set of assumptions.

## Demography

Population size, rate of change, distribution, age structure and migration are all critical aspects of demography. Population size to a great extent governs demand for natural resources and material flows. Population growth enlarges the challenge of improving living standards and providing essential social services, including housing, transport, sanitation, health, education, jobs and security. It can also make it harder to deal with poverty.

Rapid population growth can lead to political and social conflict between ethnic, religious, social and language groups. Increases in the numbers of people living in towns and cities are particularly important because urbanization means big changes in lifestyle, consumption patterns, infrastructure development and waste flows. Population structure — the relative proportions of children, persons of working age and elderly people within a population — has important repercussions for future population growth as well as for matching the provision of education, healthcare, incomes and pensions, to predicted needs. Finally, internal and international migration, whether voluntary or forced, can sometimes ease and sometimes worsen the pressures that other demographic factors and other forces place on society and the environment.

Because so many of the people who will have children over the next 30 years have already been born, much can already be said about population over that period. All of the scenarios assume continued growth in global population, tailing off at the end of the period as more countries pass through the demographic transition. Nearly all the growth occurs in developing countries, with North America the only developed region with noticeable growth. Slightly lower population levels are foreseen in *Policy First* and *Sustainability First*, reflecting the idea that policy actions and behavioural changes speed up the transition to slower growth. In *Security First*, lack of effective policy as well as much slower economic and social development, combine to slow down the transition. This leads to significantly higher population levels in this outlook, regardless of devastating demographic trends or events such as the HIV/AIDS pandemic in Africa that might be expected to have the contrary effect.

Urbanization increases or remains stable in almost all regions in all the scenarios, with the greatest increase in those regions currently least urbanized — Africa and much of Asia and the Pacific. In all regions, much of the development occurs in large coastal cities, a shift with serious implications for the coastal environment.

Apart from the Antarctic sub-region, which has no permanent resident population, current and future population structure differs markedly from region to region. North America, Europe and Japan have

---

'North America, Europe and Japan have significantly larger shares of elderly people in all scenarios.'

---

significantly larger shares of elderly people, a pattern that persists and increases in all scenarios. This trend is less marked in *Security First*, where advances in medical science (and hence in life expectancy) make less headway in all regions. Other areas, particularly Africa, West Asia, Latin America and the Caribbean and South Asia, are dominated by youth. Their share of the population in these regions — but not their absolute population size — gradually decreases over the next 30 years in all scenarios.

In terms of migration patterns, *Markets First* and especially *Security First* are likely to have more conflicts and inequality, provoking more and more movements of refugees and economic migrants. Whereas more openness is assumed under *Markets First*, barriers to migration are expected in *Security First*. *Policy First* and *Sustainability First* also assume more open migration, especially for refugees and displaced communities. At the same time, more equitable sharing of resources for economic development and international assistance reduce the need for migration.

## Economic development

Economic development encompasses many factors, including production, finance and the distribution of resources both between regions and across sectors of society. Although the pattern varies conspicuously, there has been a general trend towards more service-based economies. Product, financial and even labour markets are becoming increasingly integrated and interconnected in a worldwide economy with global commodity chains and financial markets. Similar trends are appearing at a regional level in several parts of the globe. These processes have been spurred on by advances in information technology, international pacts designed to remove trade barriers or liberalize investment flows and the progressive deregulation of national economies. The same advances have also allowed wealth produced by national and transnational mergers to become concentrated in fewer and fewer hands. There has

---

**'For many nations the problem of inequality is made worse by debt burdens that seriously constrain growth.'**

---

also been an increase in inequality in terms of income and resource use across — and often within — nations. For many nations the problem of inequality is made worse by debt burdens that seriously constrain growth. As transnational enterprises respond to global business opportunities, the traditional prerogatives of the nation-state and the capacity for macro-economic intervention by the state are challenged anew.

In *Markets First*, it is assumed that most of the trends noted above persist, if not accelerate. Economic development outweighs social and environmental concerns in most international discussions. Resistance continues but no radical changes in policy result. Recognition that maintenance of environmental and social conditions is important for ensuring economic development slows economic growth down over time, but not very noticeably.

In *Security First*, trends towards global integration continue for some parts of the economy, yet come to a halt or even go into reverse for others. Over time, more and more activity takes place in the grey or underground economy.

Integration trends persist in *Policy First* and *Sustainability First* but they are tempered by the introduction of new policies and institutions to tackle social and environmental concerns. This reflects improved understanding of the crucial roles of human, social and natural capital in determining economic health. Changes in attitudes and behaviour in *Sustainability First* affect these trends more than in the other scenarios as the whole notion of economic development becomes increasingly subsumed in the broader concept of human development.

The effect of these changes on per capita income varies strongly across regions and scenarios. Average income growth in all regions is lowest in *Security First* but also very unevenly distributed due to the greater inequality within regions. In the other scenarios, average growth at the global level is similar but there are key differences between and within regions. In *Policy First*, the more equable distribution of growth makes average incomes of the wealthy grow slightly slower than in *Markets First*, whereas incomes rise more rapidly among the poor. The most dramatic increases in income growth are seen in Africa, but also in parts of Latin America and the Caribbean, Asia and the Pacific, and West Asia. The convergence in per capita incomes is even greater in *Sustainability First*, especially as wealthier persons shift their emphasis away from market-oriented production and consumption. However, large differences remain at the end of the 30-year period.

## Human development

Health, education, security, identity and freedom are aspects of human development that are all clearly related to economic development, yet go well beyond it. Dramatic differences in access to these important human needs are a feature of the contemporary global scene. Impoverishment and inequity are critical problems for the poorer countries but conspicuous pockets exist even in the richest countries. As the world grows more interconnected, these forces affect everyone directly or indirectly, through immigration pressure, geopolitical instability, environmental degradation and constraints on global economic opportunity.

The United Nations, World Bank, International Labour Organization (ILO) and International Monetary Fund (IMF) recently set out specific international development goals for poverty reduction, universal primary education, gender equality, infant and child mortality, maternal mortality, reproductive health and the environment. Achieving these goals depends on: 'Stronger voices for the poor, economic stability and growth that favours the poor, basic social services for all, open markets for trade and technology, and enough development resources, used well' (IMF and others 2000).

Among obstacles to achieving these goals are: 'weak governance; bad policies; human rights abuses; conflicts; natural disasters, and other external shocks. The spread of HIV/AIDS. The failure to address inequities in income, education and access to health care, and the inequalities between men and women. But there is more. Limits on developing country access to global markets, the burden of debt, the decline in development aid and, sometimes, inconsistencies in donor policies also hinder faster progress' (IMF and others 2000).

*Policy First* and *Sustainability First* place emphasis on meeting basic needs and providing the resources to meet them, even where this may hinder short-term economic growth. In *Sustainability First*, relatively more of the provision of basic needs comes from groups outside the public sector, both businesses and nongovernmental organizations.

In *Markets First*, these issues are not addressed to the same extent, as it is taken for granted that economic development naturally leads to social improvement. In addition, more of the facilities that have traditionally been provided as public services are privatized. These trends are even more pronounced in *Security First*, accompanied by greater inequality in terms of access. Where new funds, whether public or private, are invested in development, physical security increasingly takes precedence over social welfare.

## Science and technology

Science and technology continue to transform the structure of production, the nature of work and the use of leisure time. Continuing advances in computer and information technology are at the forefront of the current wave of hi-tech innovation. Biotechnology galvanizes agricultural practices, pharmaceuticals

development and disease prevention, though it raises a host of ethical and environmental issues. Advances in miniaturized technologies transform medical practices, materials science, computer performance and much more.

The importance of science and technology extends beyond the acquisition of knowledge and how it is used. Continuing concerns over the distribution of the benefits and costs of technological development provoke much national and international debate. Such concerns include technology transfer, intellectual property rights, appropriate technologies, trade-offs between privacy and security, and the potential for information-poor countries to find themselves on the

**'In Markets First, it is assumed that the rapid technological advances of recent years continue, but are increasingly driven by profit motives.'**

wrong side of a 'digital divide'. The ultimate resolution of these matters influences the future development of science and technology, as well as their impacts upon society and the environment.

In *Markets First*, it is assumed that the rapid technological advances of recent years continue, but are increasingly driven by profit motives. Over time this may actually slow down development as basic research is given less priority. Technology transfer, intellectual property rights and other issues are tackled, but mainly to the advantage of those with greater power in the marketplace. Environmental benefits largely come about as side effects of efforts to improve the efficiency of resource use. These patterns are even more pronounced in *Security First*, where — in addition — the diversion of more and more public funding into security provision, coupled with social, economic and environmental crises, means slower progress all round.

Rapid advances in science and technology are also assumed in the *Policy First* and *Sustainability First* scenarios, but these are driven by different factors. Direct investment by governments, subsidies and regulation — for example, pollution taxes — play a dominant role in *Policy First*. In *Sustainability First*, these levers are overshadowed by changing preferences of both consumers and producers. In both scenarios, greater caution on the part of governments and society at large may slow technological development in some areas, but it also helps to head off serious side effects. Greater efforts are also made to share the benefits of science and technology.

## Governance

Governance refers to actions, processes, traditions and institutions by which authority is exercised. It is most often associated with governmental bodies at the national level and with regional or global institutions such as the United Nations, but this need not always be the case. Private institutions, such as corporations and non-governmental organizations, also play an important role in governance. In all cases, developments that affect participation, accountability, transparency, corruption and civil strife have an important influence on the shape of the future.

Although the forms and effectiveness of governance differ markedly around the world, various tendencies can be identified. One tendency is towards greater individual autonomy and the devolution of authority. This shift is expressed at the personal level in terms of a growing emphasis on individual 'rights' — human rights, women's rights and the like. It is also noticeable in the devolution of governmental authority to smaller and more local units and in separatist movements. The private sector, too, has moved towards 'flatter' corporate structures and decentralized decision-making. A second and somewhat opposite tendency is towards forms of greater regional integration and global governance through such mechanisms as international trade and environmental agreements. Another tendency is towards greater integration and the growth of networks within and across private and public

---

**'In Policy First, continual movement towards greater coordination is assumed ... in pursuit of a broader agenda.'**

---

institutions. This is seen, in part, in the rise of global public policy networks and the emergence of civil society as an important voice in decision-making in many regions.

In *Markets First*, present trends are assumed to continue but with heavier emphasis on ensuring the smooth functioning of markets. Efforts are focused on the development of international institutions which encourage free markets for resources, finance and products. In *Policy First*, greater coordination is assumed, particularly at the level of international governance. This includes the development of new institutions and more cooperation between the public and private sectors. Significantly, these changes are driven from the top, by governments, corporations or large non-governmental organizations (NGOs).

In *Sustainability First*, the shifts in governance are assumed to be driven much more from the bottom up. Reflecting the changing values and making use of the trends towards greater participation in general, individuals and grass-roots organizations become more and more involved in setting the agenda, a lead that larger organizations then follow. Governments continue to govern but do so in a fashion that involves more power sharing.

As with much else in the *Security First* scenario, assumed trends regarding governance differ over time and across groups more than in the other scenarios. Corruption, ineffective governance and reactions against both, contribute to breakdown in parts of society. As societies regroup, governance among the 'haves' is assumed to become more centralized and autocratic; but largely effective. International co-ordination also bolsters the relative stability of these groups. Among the 'have-nots', the nature and effectiveness of governance is mixed.

## Culture

Culture includes the set of values and institutions that enables a society to develop and maintain its identity. Cultural signatures differ around the globe and reflect, for instance, conflicting ideas about the worth of economics as an integrating system of values or about the importance of technology and technological change as springboards for human progress. They also hinge on differing concepts of justice and fairness, and on differing beliefs about the relationship between people and the natural and spiritual world.

Recent history, particularly where racism, colonialism and genocide have occurred, cannot be overlooked. Much has been said about the expansion of Western culture to the detriment of others, about reactions to this spread and about possible clashes of civilizations as a result. It is clear that many individuals aspire to Western lifestyles, while others see Western values permeating societies and associate them with selfish individualism and excessive consumption. This spread is both a cause and an effect of economic globalization, aided by the far-reaching penetration of information technologies and electronic media. At the same time, there have been clear signs of nationalist and religious reaction against it, sometimes resulting in terrorist activities and in open warfare within or between nations.

Among the four scenarios, *Sustainability First* assumes the largest shift from current trends in terms of culture. The ascendance of the values of solidarity, reciprocity, sufficiency and stewardship is at the heart of this scenario. To the extent that these core values are not violated, tolerance is also a key aspect of culture in this scenario. In *Markets First*, little change in current trends is assumed. As befits the basic notion of a market, the trend towards individualism accelerates, as does a trend towards homogenization of culture. At the same time, so do passive and active resistance by particular groups and regions. In *Security First*, these and other trends lead to clashes that undermine many elements of society. *Policy First* assumes a middle path between *Markets First* and *Sustainability First*; efforts to encourage some of the trends of the latter compete with tendencies to follow the trends of the former.

## Environment

Though the focus of this section is on the importance of socio-economic change in triggering environmental impacts, it is clear that environmental change is a potent driving force in its own right. Countries and regions must contend not only with unequal environmental endowments, but also with acute environmental problems. Human impacts on the environment have aroused growing anxiety. Atmosphere, land and water resources have been spoiled. Persistent organic pollutants and toxic substances have accumulated in living organisms.

'Among the four scenarios, Sustainability First assumes the largest shift from current trends in terms of culture.'

Species have been lost and ecosystems degraded. In addition, social and ecological systems are vulnerable to natural and human-influenced hazards and catastrophes.

The way natural systems react to these pressures (the rate, for instance, at which climate patterns change as a result of higher concentrations of greenhouse gases, or the response of coastal ecosystems to pollution), can have a big impact on social, economic and other natural systems. The realization that individual states cannot shield themselves from environmental change is already changing the basis of geopolitics and global governance.

The scenarios presented here do not differ greatly in their assumptions about the environment as a driving force. Most significantly, it is assumed that natural systems are in a more fragile condition in *Security First* than in the other scenarios. This implies that ecosystem collapses and curbs on the capacity of certain natural systems to provide goods and services are more likely, even when facing the same pressures. In *Policy First* and especially in *Sustainability First*, the values of stewardship and caring for the environment play a greater role in guiding science, technology and governance, as well as in shaping economic and social development.

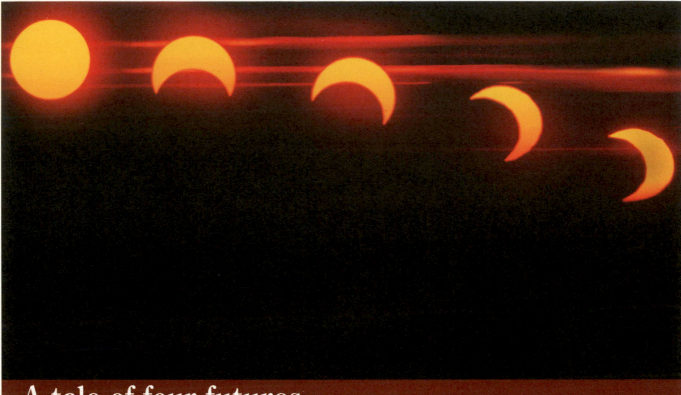

UNEP, V Bugaldon, Still Pictures

# A tale of four futures

The turn of the 21st century was an opportunity to reflect on the past and speculate about the future. This milestone not only heralded the beginning of a new millennium but also marked more than 50 years of several key global institutions, not least the United Nations and World Bank.

Events at regional level also provide much food for thought. The countries of the European Union (EU) face the possibility of membership nearly doubling in one or two decades, spurred on by the end of the Cold War and the collapse of the eastern bloc. In Africa, the relatively peaceful end of apartheid in South Africa and the transition from military to civilian rule in Nigeria have changed the political climate. These turnabouts

**'When sizing up prospects for the future, some find grounds for optimism but others are more apprehensive.'**

in the continent's two most populous countries open the door for new debate on how to solve Africa's persistent problems, including civil wars, poverty, inequality and the AIDS pandemic. Political changes in

Asia and the Pacific, notably in Indonesia and the Philippines, and the repercussions of the economic crisis in the late 1990s are stimulating fresh dialogue about the future of the region. In Latin America and the Caribbean, a period of relative stability has prompted increased willingness to address important issues inherited from the past. As they find themselves in the centre of some of the most publicized geopolitical events, the people of West Asia eye their future warily. Meanwhile, the recent economic slowdown and terrorist attacks have led many North Americans to reassess their actions at home and abroad to a degree not seen in decades.

At this time, the world is marked by tumultuous change. A global system seems to be taking shape as economic interdependence increases. Information technology accelerates the spread of ideas and the human transformation of nature becomes evident on a planetary scale. As economies grow, the rich get richer and many of the poor manage to escape from poverty. But huge disparities persist as vast wealth coexists with abject poverty and each extreme generates its own characteristic environmental pressures.

When sizing up prospects for the future, some find grounds for optimism but others are more apprehensive. In spite of potentially powerful anti-globalization forces, the optimists foresee the formation of a true global market and relish the opportunities for greater efficiency and connectedness. The pursuit of individual wealth on a global economic playing field made level by universal governance mechanisms to reduce market barriers can, they believe, open the way to a new age of affluence for all. If developing country institutions can be adapted to benefit from the new technologies and the emerging borderless economy, and if appropriate forms of global governance can be created, the rising tide of global prosperity will lift everyone to new heights of well-being.

Sceptics, looking at the same phenomena, see riskier times ahead. They point to wealth and power accumulating in just a few hands, especially those of transnational corporations. They see unequal expansion of modern production methods around the world, two-track development and stubbornly one-sided and manipulative approaches to global negotiations. The pessimists fear the result will be erosion of trust between the North and the South and between populations within both, ending up in a chronic inability to forge credible, legitimate and enforceable agreements on sustainable development. How, they wonder, can unbridled pursuit of economic growth be kept within environmental limits? Will market-driven global development, far from engendering a sense of participation in a common global society, tend instead to continue to split humanity into privileged and excluded, North and South, modernist and traditionalist factions? If the accelerated transition to a global economy fails to give institutions time to adapt, will community cohesion and democratic participation be sacrificed to it?

Many feel apprehensive, too, about the prospect that their children will inherit an impoverished and fragile world that is ecologically, socially and economically depleted. More fundamentally, some object to the encouragement of traits and lifestyles founded on individualism and greed, which they see emerging from this global consumer culture.

## Markets First

Most of the world adopts the values and expectations prevailing in today's industrialized countries. The wealth of nations and the optimal play of market forces dominate social and political agendas. Trust is placed in further globalization and liberalization to enhance corporate wealth, create new enterprises and livelihoods, and so help people and communities to afford to insure against — or pay to fix — social and environmental problems. Ethical investors, together with citizen and consumer groups, try to exercise growing corrective influence but are undermined by economic imperatives. The powers of state officials, planners and lawmakers to regulate society, economy and the environment continue to be overwhelmed by expanding demands.

Several important initiatives pave the way for the major developments in the new century. The Doha round of negotiations within the World Trade Organization (WTO) — including its newest member, China — provides the legal basis for an expanded global trading system. Significantly, it has written into it a recognition that this system must take into account important social and environmental concerns, in addition to the core economic goals. A multilateral agreement on investment liberalizes investment regimes first in Organization for Economic Cooperation and Development (OECD) countries, with expectations that this will follow shortly throughout the world. The coalition against terrorism paves the way for new approaches to international security.

Meanwhile, efforts continue to salvage the climate negotiations, to build upon multilateral

**'Factors combine to make the shift to a liberalized, market-oriented society almost universal.'**

environmental agreements in other areas and to address important social issues. Much of this effort initially hinges on international activities, particularly the World Summit on Sustainable Development (WSSD) and follow-up activities, which galvanize a renewed commitment to action.

This commitment revolves around a mixture of old and new initiatives designed to gain a better understanding of the issues that cause concern and to tackle them more effectively. Goals and targets related to basic needs (food security, access to clean water, sanitation, literacy and life expectancy) and environmental conditions (urban air quality, availability of fresh water, resource use, waste disposal and habitat/species preservation) are reiterated. A commitment is also made to strengthen international institutions of governance.

## The best laid plans …

Businesses and NGOs play an important role. The industry lobby argues for clear and economically efficient rules and regulations. It also points to the value of voluntary standards and programmes, such as the Global Compact and Global Reporting Initiative

---

**'Privatization spreads, social safety nets are reduced and reliance is placed on market-based approaches.'**

---

negotiated with the United Nations. The NGOs, along with some business groups, stress issues of equity and fairness for current and future generations, as well as respect for other species.

Over the next decade there is a clear divergence in the follow-through on these various sets of activities. Barriers to trade and movements of capital gradually vanish, as protectionism becomes a thing of the past. New instruments promote market openness and global competition. Virtually all national governments advance a package of policy adjustments, including modernization of financial systems and investment in education to create a workforce that is competitive in the emerging global market. Privatization spreads, social safety nets are reduced and reliance is placed on market-based approaches.

There is still distrust of what is viewed as a typically Western mode of development, growing at times into outright hostility. Gradually, however, the shift to a liberalized, market-oriented society becomes almost universal. New technologies, particularly in the form of digital information and communication technologies (ICTs) continue to increase connectivity between different parts of the world. This is reinforced by the presence of multinational corporations, or at the very least their products, in many parts of the world.

Businesses benefit from liberalization and globalization, and increasingly operate across national borders. At an institutional level, international bodies maintain an important role in guiding economic and related policy in many countries, particularly those that are still burdened by high debt loads. At a personal level, more young people from around the world take the opportunity to travel and study in other countries. Taken together, these factors seem to imply that an air of inevitability surrounds the ongoing processes of globalization. How they play out, however, differs from region to region.

In Europe, a major focus is on the continuing project of broadening and deepening the EU. The extension of the EU to the east continues with a number of countries being added in waves of accession. Economic interdependence between nations continues to grow, along with widespread adoption of the Euro and harmonization of financial systems. Political union proceeds more slowly, however, as countries prove less willing to forgo their sovereignty in other areas. For example, although most nations are intent on cutting back social safety nets, there are differences over how far and how fast these cuts should be applied. Taxation is also a point of contention. Nevertheless, there is a general shift in governance away from the nation state, to higher as well as to lower levels. By the end of the second decade of the century, various regional bodies, some of which override national borders, play as large a role as some nation states.

Even as it struggles to deal with persistent conflicts and the AIDS pandemic, Africa pushes ahead with economic modernization and greater integration into the global economy. Shifts away from official development assistance towards foreign direct investment give multinational corporations more influence. At the same time, the influence of international organizations is maintained as efforts continue to restructure and pay off foreign debts. These efforts strongly shape the portfolio of economic investments, which continues to emphasize the production of exports. Regional cooperation, in the form of free trade zones and power pools, works to better integrate the continent. Similarly, transboundary collaboration is expanded in an attempt to deal in some areas with water conflicts, in others to pursue cross-border conservation and development initiatives.

Continuing dependence on oil throughout the world still provides a strong economic base for much of West Asia, the development of alternative energy sources and efficiency improvements having failed to make more than minimal advances. The strategic importance of the region increases as the world's remaining oil supplies become even more concentrated here and in nearby Central Asia and is a major reason why countries in other regions want to ensure stability in West Asia. Along with local traditions, oil dependence keeps the globalization process from proceeding as quickly in certain areas of society here by comparison with some other regions. Some countries in West Asia continue to grapple with foreign debt. The repayment process keeps moving forward, however, thanks to flexible conditions for debt restructuring. An Arab Free Trade Agreement is eventually reached.

In the Western Hemisphere, Latin America and the Caribbean become ever more economically integrated with North America. This development is spurred on by the assistance provided by the United States to Mexico in the 1990s and to Argentina and other nations in the 2000s, boosted by the interests of large corporations. It is also seen as a way to address, in part, the joint problems of an ageing and shrinking workforce in the United States and immigration from the south. Moves towards integration culminate in a Free Trade Area for the Americas (FTAA) in the middle of the second decade of the century. In the process, existing trade agreements like North America Free Trade Agreement (NAFTA), Commom Market of the South (MERCOSUR) and Caribbean Community (CARICOM), get absorbed under the FTAA umbrella. A number of nations go further, adopting the US dollar as a national currency.

In the Asia and the Pacific region, the recovery from the economic downturn of the late 1990s and from the decade-long recession in Japan, sees many countries return to the patterns of growth and degree of integration into the world economy they had previously experienced. To this are added the continued economic reforms in China and India, the two most populous nations in the world. With its accession into the WTO, China becomes a major world importer and exporter, eventually growing to rival the United States as the world's largest economy. The advances in technology coming out of Asia and the Pacific, the impact on corporations that set up facilities

here and the increased exposure of its cultures all enlarge the role this region plays on the global stage.

## ... gradually go astray

While systems of governance and longer term planning remain poorly developed, the regional shifts described above modify relationships between regions and the concerted management of common resources. These resources are increasingly incorporated into the global economic system but authorities in charge of their management persist in putting economic potential first. In polar regions multinationals negotiate agreements, either with nations or, in the

> 'China becomes a major world importer and exporter, eventually growing to rival the United States as the world's largest economy.'

case of the Arctic, directly with indigenous populations. More areas and more resources (such as freshwater) are laid open to commercial exploitation.

Developments in international security look still less promising. The United States falls back on a more unilateralist stance, involving only a limited number of partners. This encourages other nations and regions to continue development of their military forces. Thus opportunities for broad-based international cooperation are not pursued. Acts of terrorism are followed by periods of retaliation involving short-lived coalitions. This keeps the level of the problem fairly low in the short term, but does little to address the root causes of discontent in the long term.

Influenced by large national and multinational corporations based inside their borders, many countries adopt a fairly narrow approach to global negotiations, in which the paramount concern is the protection of their respective national interests rather than shared or common resources. Efforts to ratify a treaty to address climate issues drag on without fruition and are set aside part way through the first decade. There is more success in other arenas, such as dealing with selected persistent organic pollutants, but even here the scope of the agreements is limited and difficulties with enforcement mechanisms lead to disappointing results.

Actions continue to address social and environmental issues, but are mainly taken at local level. Europe drafts regional conventions which deal primarily with transboundary pollutants and the burdensome environmental legacy of the former Soviet Bloc. Similar efforts arise in other regions, though not always resulting in formal conventions and even then many of the signed conventions are not effectively implemented. There are attempts to cross-link these instruments to trade and other economic agreements. When conflicts arise, however, it is the economic imperative that usually takes precedence. Most notably, the agreement on Trade-Related Aspects of Intellectual Property Rights (TRIPS) of the WTO tends to override competing pacts reflected in the Convention on Biological Diversity (CBD) and other multilateral environmental agreements. In Europe, the policy change that arguably has the greatest impact on the environment, the reform of the Common Agricultural Policy at the end of the first decade of the century, is pursued for primarily economic reasons.

The United Nations, other international bodies, NGOs and some businesses persist in their efforts to make advances on the goals set out in *Agenda 21*, at the WSSD and in other high-profile arenas. Nevertheless, without full commitment from its member nations and without fundamental reform, the United Nations continues to struggle to play the role many expect of it. It makes slow progress in

---

**'Most advances in social and environmental arenas are by-products of efforts to improve economic development.'**

---

international coordination on environmental and social issues. It scores moderate successes in peacekeeping and disaster relief efforts, which are called on more and more frequently as the years pass. However, the organization finds itself operating in a primarily reactive, as distinct from a proactive, mode. NGOs also find their efforts hindered by more powerful forces, including the steady ascendancy of individualistic over altruistic values in civil society and public life. When NGOs urge others to work for the common good, their appeals tend to be met with complacent apathy. NGOs that prosper tend to be those that adopt a more market-oriented approach or form partnerships directly with businesses, industry or both.

Overall, most advances in social and environmental arenas are by-products of efforts to improve economic development.

## Constraints are lifted ...

Throughout the world, cuts in subsidies to agriculture and the opening of trade in agricultural products modify the environmental impacts of agriculture. The use of debt-for-nature swaps and the outright purchase of debt for the right to exploit genetic resources contribute to the preservation of some natural areas, especially within tropical regions, while at the same time easing the debt burdens of these countries. Similar actions are taken to preserve natural or cultural heritage sites that also happen to be key tourist attractions.

Somewhat less directly, certain advances in technology and structural changes in economies produce environmental and social benefits, through improvements in efficiency. In transportation, the development and spread of more efficient and cleaner fuel burning vehicles, beginning with hybrid and moving towards fuel celled vehicles (with methanol as the carrier of hydrogen) curbs the increase in fossil fuel use. The growth in transportation is also tempered by continued progress in ICTs. More people now work from home.

Energy efficiency continues to improve as deregulation proceeds, opening up markets in micro-power developments. Micro-power becomes increasingly important in rural areas of the poorer regions, where the high cost of extending electricity grids has restricted the power supply network. Improvements in irrigation techniques and advances in desalination improve water use efficiency, particularly in West Asia and arid parts of other regions. Agriculture further benefits from progress in biotechnology, which increases yields and helps to reduce the pressure on ecosystem resources in many regions. Biotechnology also has positive effects in the areas of wastewater treatment. Advances in nano-technology improve materials use efficiency.

## ... but not for all

These developments, along with improvements in medical science and healthcare, enhance the lives of many. At the same time, these trends create new or intensify existing social and environmental concerns. Advances in biotechnology and genetic engineering, both in combating disease vectors and creating hardier crops, open up areas of Africa and other regions to intensive exploitation by large-scale commercial agriculture and ranching. This jeopardizes both natural and agro-biodiversity and it leads to far worse land degradation than before, destroying harvests and livelihoods and driving even more people into poverty.

Improvements in information technology help draw attention to the vast differences between how different people live, often causing great frustration among the less well off. In the polar regions, resource exploitation speeds up as a result of technological advances and easier access due to climatic changes, putting ecosystems in those regions at greater risk. More use is made of hydropower resources in the Arctic, as well as in Asia and the Pacific, Latin America, parts of Europe, and Africa. Water is also transported over increasing distances to drier regions to cater to soaring demand. This trend is highlighted by the initiation of large-scale projects in the 2010s to move water from the Great Lakes and the Pacific Northwest to the arid regions in the southwest of North America. These steps are followed by similar efforts in Europe and parts of the Asia and the Pacific region.

At the heart of all these market-led concerns is a seemingly never-ending obligation on society to muster enough technological and structural progress to catch up with the skyrocketing demand for goods and services. Meanwhile, environmental conditions are constantly shifting. The effects of climate change are becoming clearer, particularly in the polar regions, in poorer countries and along the world's coastlines. Plans are already being made to evacuate some small island states. Other environmental changes, including imbalances in the nitrogen cycle and the continued dispersion of persistent organic pollutants, are also having their impacts, evidenced by the 'red tides' that hit the Mediterranean in the 2010s and the Indian Ocean in the 2020s.

Prolonged (though decelerating) population growth in Africa, West Asia and parts of Asia and the Pacific and increasing urbanization in almost all regions, aggravate problems such as biodiversity loss, water stress and the frequent breakdown of basic services. These are reflected, in turn, in persistent regional conflicts and migration pressures. As a consequence, the economic advances that have characterized the past few decades begin to slow noticeably. More and more effort is needed simply to maintain the achievements realized so far. Social and environmental goals, which are still in the minds of many even though other concerns have relegated them to the back seat, seem to be moving further beyond reach every year.

---

**'The economic advances that have characterized the past few decades begin to slow noticeably. More and more effort is needed simply to maintain the achievements realized so far.'**

---

## What lies ahead?

By 2032, many of the same questions that were being posed at the turn of the century remain unanswered. The world has achieved much in terms of modernization and economic growth, presenting new opportunities for millions of people. Yet fundamental questions are still being raised about the sustainability and desirability of this pattern of development. Environmental standards continue to fall and pressures on resources remain severe, raising again the spectres of economic uncertainty and conflict. Social stresses threaten socio-economic sustainability as persistent poverty and growing inequality, exacerbated by environmental degradation, undermine social cohesion, spur migration and weaken international security.

Opinions differ as to where the world is heading. Depending on which indicators the observer chooses to focus upon, arguments can be made for either side. Many argue that the cases of breakdown already seen in some social, environmental and ecological systems portend even more fundamental and widespread collapses in the future. These same groups express particular concern that efforts have not been made to develop the institutions that will be needed to handle these predicaments. Others point out that we have been able to handle most of the crises we have faced and that there is no reason to assume we will not do likewise in the future.

Most people stick to their daily routines, leaving the big questions to others. *Plus ça change, plus c'est la même chose*; the more things change, the more they stay the same.

## Policy First

Decisive initiatives are taken by governments in an attempt to reach specific social and environmental goals. A coordinated pro-environment and anti-poverty drive balances the momentum for economic development at any cost. Environmental and social costs and gains are factored into policy measures, regulatory frameworks and planning processes. All these are reinforced by fiscal levers or incentives such as carbon taxes and tax breaks. International 'soft law' treaties and binding instruments affecting environment and development are integrated into unified blueprints and their status in law is upgraded, though fresh provision is made for open consultation processes to allow for regional and local variants.

In the early years of the century, there are signs of a great desire and demand for coordinated leadership from the local to the global level, not only among governments, but also in industry and among NGOs and other citizens' groups. The terrorist attacks on the United States and the subsequent retaliation lend immediacy to the calls for policy reform to come to terms with economic, social and environmental concerns that many see as the root causes of these actions.

### Renewing commitments

The award of the 2001 Nobel Prize for Peace to the Secretary General of the United Nations and to the family of organizations that he leads, highlights the renewed interest shown in systems of international and regional governance. To begin with, much of this interest is expressed at and around international

**'A common characteristic of these initiatives is a highly structured approach, complete with the establishment of formal institutions and the setting of very specific targets.'**

activities, including the WSSD, meetings of the G7/G8 and the negotiations of the WTO and multilateral environmental agreements. Protests and demonstrations, coupled with less adversarial side events and more open consultations involving officials, NGOs and the broader public, help to galvanize renewed commitment to action by formal institutions.

This commitment is translated into initiatives to better understand and deal with issues of current concern. A common characteristic of these initiatives is a highly structured approach, complete with the establishment of formal institutions and the setting of very specific targets. Efforts to improve knowledge of the issues build upon existing activities, including the Intergovernmental Panel on Climate Change, Millennium Ecosystem Assessment and Global International Water Assessment. To these are added an Arctic Climate Impact Assessment and a global assessment of the nitrogen cycle.

Target-setting draws on the efforts of international conferences in the 1990s. These were outlined in *A Better World for All* (IMF and others 2000). Following this precedent, global environmental and social priorities are expressed in terms of measures that target basic needs such as reducing extreme poverty, cutting infant and child mortality, improving reproductive health, promoting gender equity, upgrading environmental conditions and achieving universal primary education. Quantifiable indicators are agreed to help track progress towards each of these goals.

The environmental targets fall into two broad categories. Climate stabilization, improving eco-efficiency and reducing toxic wastes require a focus on industrial activities and the demands of modern lifestyles. Halting deforestation and land degradation, maintaining biodiversity, sustaining fisheries and improving access to clean water and sanitation, require issues of poverty and growing populations to be addressed as well. The targets agreed for developing countries reflect a general acceptance that the process of development and industrialization must continue in these regions. Thus, although per capita materials use and releases of pollutants will grow, they should not exceed the levels recorded in the OECD regions and will gradually converge to similar values.

### Customizing the blueprint

Although the ultimate goals are similar, the particular circumstances of each region — political, economic, cultural and environmental — dictate different emphases in each region. In Africa, a premium is placed on food security, governance, economic diversification, population growth and urbanization, universal primary and secondary education, poverty, health (particularly in relation to HIV/AIDS), deforestation and land degradation.

Deforestation, inequity, poverty, urbanization, freshwater resources and regional air pollution head the reform agenda in Asia and the Pacific. In Europe, the accent is on energy, governance (especially in relation to EU enlargement), agriculture, transport and the preservation of natural areas. Governance, healthcare, universal primary and secondary education, deforestation, poverty and inequity, and urbanization are highlighted in Latin America and the Caribbean.

Discussions in North America focus on energy use, perverse subsidies, trade regimes and water availability in the arid west. The principal concerns in West Asia are water availability, food security, diversifying the economy, healthcare and universal primary and secondary education. In the polar regions, the focus is on governance in relation to international activities in the Antarctic, rights of indigenous peoples in the Arctic and resource exploitation in both.

## Collaborative frameworks

The strengthening of governance institutions at all levels is critical to achieving agreed goals. At the global level, these include the United Nations organizations and Bretton Woods institutions, which implement new or step up ongoing reform efforts. Fresh impetus also boosts existing multilateral environmental agreements, while existing protocols, such as those on climate and biosafety, are ratified.

Complementing this drive are efforts at regional level to increase intra- and inter-regional cooperation mechanisms and make them more efficient. These efforts are stimulated by a series of regional meetings, drawing together nation states and regional and sub-regional entities. The most conspicuous of these is held in Africa by the newly formed African Union, which results in the Africa Millennium Charter for Sustainable Development.

Of course, the efforts at both regional and global levels require action at the national level. Furthermore, intentions expressed at the higher levels need to be translated into meaningful goals and actions to be implemented at national and sub-national levels. This requires nations to place greater faith in — and assign more authority to — ministries focusing on social and environmental policies.

It is understood that significant changes in social and economic systems will be needed to achieve the targets that have been set and that these changes will take time. Action is required at many different levels. Certain areas stand out in which nations must cooperate with one another and with global

institutions. Among them are global environmental issues such as stratospheric ozone depletion, climate change, biodiversity loss and the long-range transport of persistent organic pollutants. Perhaps more important because they lie at the root of these environmental concerns are economic issues like trade and foreign debt. Technology development and transfer (particularly in the areas of ICTs, biotechnology and

---

**'It is understood that significant changes in social and economic systems will be needed to achieve the targets that have been set, and that these changes will take time.'**

---

energy use) and the maintenance of intellectual property rights are also on the joint agenda. Other issues that demand attention are migration, security and sharing common resources from, for example, the oceans, the polar regions and space.

## Trade and industry take a lead

Not all activity is limited to the governmental sphere. Business groups, such as the International Chamber of Commerce (ICC), World Business Council on Sustainable Development (WBCSD) and the International Standards Organization (ISO), work to enhance the positive role in policy making played by industry. NGOs continue to build partnerships, between themselves and with business groups and government organizations.

In trade, the opening up of international markets continues, with much of the action occurring at the regional level. New entities, such as the Arab Free Trade Association in West Asia, are formed, while existing unions survive and grow. A Free Trade Area of the South is initiated by an agreement between MERCOSUR and South Africa.

The role of the World Trade Organization continues to evolve. The Doha round of negotiations works to balance free trade with social and environmental considerations. It plays a special part in opening up agricultural markets by means of the Agreement on Agriculture (AoA) and in managing the exploitation of resources in the Arctic and Antarctic, including total prohibition of trade in certain resources. It also seeks to tackle the broader issues of trade in biological and genetic resources, working in close coordination with the parties to the CBD and associated protocols.

## Dealing with debt and conflict

In terms of foreign debt, many developing countries feel they need and deserve special help to pursue sustainability. Key lenders, including the World Bank and the IMF, work together with borrowers to restructure and — in some cases — eliminate existing debts. Options such as debt for nature or debt for poverty alleviation swaps are explored as options to manage international debts in ways that help achieve sustainability goals. Development aid is increasingly seen as a matter of national and international security,

---

'Efforts at international and regional levels help provide economic and political support for policy changes needed at national and sub-national levels.'

---

prompting nations to increase contributions progressively to target levels set — but rarely achieved — in the previous century.

Increasingly, regional and international bodies adopt a more direct role in resolving conflicts within and between nations. One of the lessons learned from periodic terrorist activities and the responses to them is that greater cooperation between nations, even where it may involve sacrificing some elements of sovereignty, can bring definite benefits in terms of national security.

Efforts at international and regional levels help provide economic and political support for policy changes needed at national and sub-national levels. Comprehensive environmental and social policy frameworks are established. Where necessary, international actions such as insisting on treaty compliance and limiting aid and capital flows, help to put pressure on governments that are slow to introduce reforms. More often, however, nations are proactive in taking action internally.

## Tax breaks and other instruments

A vital step in many countries is to restructure tax systems and subsidy programmes in order to bring them more in line with social and environmental goals. Such reforms also enable governments to acquire some of the huge amounts needed to finance the changes in public sector systems needed to achieve set targets.

In other cases, more stringent and direct

regulations are introduced, including restrictions or outright bans on particular activities, such as logging in national parks, the use of particular chemicals and even driving in urban areas. These efforts can also be very costly, at least in the short term.

Although hampered at times by the actions of governments and NGOs, businesses play a positive role in many areas. As a sequel to the 14000 series of standards on environmental management systems, the ISO introduces a series of standards related to the social and ethical dimensions of business. These actions build upon and complement joint efforts by governments and business, such as the Global Compact for Business and the Global Reporting Initiative. Businesses take an increasingly active role in the consultation processes associated with many policy initiatives, a form of intervention that does much to stimulate technology development and transfer.

Action by NGOs and consumer groups includes the use of consumer boycotts and media campaigns to push less progressive businesses to act. They lobby for new labelling and reporting requirements to ensure that business practice is more transparent and accountable. Several of these groups are explicitly included in later rounds of the WTO negotiations. At the same time, these pressure groups also act as watchdogs on governments, ensuring that leaders act responsibly. Stricter limits are placed on how government officials behave, allowing most who overstep reasonable bounds to be voted out of office.

## Challenges remain

Most people support these efforts and exhibit trust in and patience with their leaders. Tension exists, though, as most citizens mistakenly assume that the changes can be made in ways that do not fundamentally alter their lifestyles in terms of convenience, mobility and similar comforts. In addition, some people resent the higher direct and hidden costs that they are being forced to pay to effect these changes. Others are impatient with the time it takes to make the dramatic changes they see as necessary. Frustrations also arise as the evolution of social, economic and natural systems does not always progress on the same schedule as the institutional changes that are being implemented.

Potential conflicts of interest arise in achieving desired goals. One example is the effort to meet increasing demands for food from populations that are growing in both size and affluence, without impairing biological diversity or soil fertility. This dilemma stimulates calls for a new global Green Revolution, although the social and environmental drawbacks of the first are still evident. Questions are raised about the risks of biotechnology, including genetic engineering, on which any such drive will have to rely. The environmental, medical, social, economic and ethical issues surrounding these technologies raise the temperature of public debate to heights not seen since the era of the nuclear debate.

## Biotechnology watchdog

Early efforts to address specific issues arising from biotechnology and gene transfer, such as the Cartagena Protocol on Biosafety, had set the stage for a regulatory regime for biotechnology development and use, to ensure that 'the planet's biological diversity (including human systems) will be able to coexist with this powerful technology' (UNEP 2000). Such efforts lead to the founding of a new international regulatory body in the early 2010s, patterned on the International Atomic Energy Agency but with greater authority.

Despite these challenges the signs of positive change strengthen the resolve to ensure that the agreed targets will be met. The initial responses of the institutions increase their legitimacy and stature. Events such as the 75th anniversary of the United Nations and World Bank and the 50th anniversary of UNEP present occasions to celebrate the progress that is being made, but also to acknowledge the challenges that remain and to reassert the need for continuing action.

The demands of continued population and economic growth still outweigh many incremental advances in sustainable production. Regional conflicts, often over contested resources, persist in several parts of the world, directly causing social and environmental damage, as well as diverting scarce resources from other priorities. And tropical storms, droughts, floods, wildfires, earthquakes, chemical spills and other industrial accidents remind society that natural and technological systems do not always behave according to plan.

It takes time for many to accept the idea of global public policy for the pursuit of sustainable development. Furthermore, the path pursued has meant adopting a highly technocratic approach and has not engendered a widespread shift in basic attitudes and behaviour. This makes certain policy actions either unfeasible or less effective than had been assumed.

## Reviewing progress

As the world looks back after three decades, there are mixed feelings. Much has been accomplished, but much remains to be done. Although not all the long-range targets have yet been achieved, the world is on a fair trajectory to meet them. It is clear, though, that there are significant differences in progress on the different goals and in different regions.

There has been broad success in reducing extreme poverty, achieving universal primary education, improving gender equity, reducing infant and child mortality and improving reproductive health. International debt relief has contributed to the funding required to meet these targets in many developing countries. Areas of concern remain, including much of Africa, where 10 per cent of the population go hungry in most sub-regions. But even this represents reductions of two-thirds to three-quarters over the 30-year period. Similarly, the more technology-dependent

**'Growing (although stabilizing) populations and improving lifestyles continue to intensify demands for water, food, forest resources and space.'**

environmental targets — increases in materials use efficiency and reductions in the releases of toxic materials — have proved to be achievable.

A key role has been played by the private sector, which has accepted major responsibility and ploughed more profits back into research and development and into global and regional business coalitions. These new groupings have actively supported technology transfer to developing countries. The effect of private sector initiatives is further reflected in the achievement of such goals as improving urban air quality and providing access to safe water.

For the goals related to water stress, land degradation, deforestation and marine overfishing, significant though costly advances have been made, but considerable risks remain. Growing (although stabilizing) populations and improving lifestyles continue to intensify demands for water, food, forest resources and space. Changes in climate have contributed to these concerns. Whilst the percentage of the population living in areas of high and severe water stress remains stable, the total number of persons potentially affected has risen.

Crises have been prevented through expensive infrastructural developments and pricing policies, which place a greater financial burden on end users. The amount of land at risk from water-induced soil degradation has risen significantly due to agricultural expansion into marginal lands and climate changes. But the rate at which degradation is actually taking place has fallen substantially over the period as farmers have implemented more stringent land conservation measures in response to changing tax

'The actions required to keep the world on track to meet the long-term goals have not always been popular and have often been expensive.'

and subsidy structures. By 2032 there is almost no net advance of degradation.

There has been success in halting deforestation. Total forest area has even increased in most regions, in part because the area under plantations has expanded. However, the level of exploitation of forests has continued to increase. Similarly, growth in aquaculture and better management of fishery systems (including stricter controls on marine fish catches) have prevented further decline in most fish stocks, but overall exploitation has not fallen significantly.

Finally, the scale and nature of the efforts needed to address climate change and biodiversity decline have proved to be enormous. Emissions of carbon dioxide and other greenhouse gases per unit of economic activity have fallen significantly throughout the world and absolute levels have fallen in the wealthier regions. More rapid economic development and continued population growth in other regions have resulted in higher absolute emissions, even

though per capita emissions in these regions remain relatively low. The net result is a continuing rise in global emissions.

Atmospheric concentrations of $CO_2$ continue to climb, indicating that much more stringent measures will be required in the future to bring them back down to the target levels. Global temperatures have risen by nearly 0.75°C since the turn of the century and continue to increase, although models indicate that, as reductions already negotiated take effect, this rate of increase has reached a plateau and will begin to decline in a few decades. The regional manifestations of climate change and the infrastructure development that has taken place to meet growing human needs and to achieve the other goals have placed many human and natural systems at increased risk.

In summary, the forces driving the world in unsustainable directions, while not necessarily defeated, appear to be on the way to being tamed. Not all the alarming trends have been reversed, though even in the worst cases 'things are getting worse at a slower rate' (Meadows 2000). The actions that have been required to keep the world on track to meet the long-term goals have not always been popular and have often been expensive. Halting deforestation, land degradation and marine overfishing has required drastic measures, at times including total bans on human activity in some areas.

Efforts to reduce emissions of greenhouse gases have required fairly high levels of taxation on most energy sources and certain industrial chemicals, as well as expensive shifts in agricultural practices. There is a question as to how much more can be accomplished with similar policies, even given fresh technological advances. There is also a question mark over how long businesses and the general public will carry on accepting such policies. Without fundamental changes in human behaviour and demands, the achievement of sustainability could well mean an ever more managed, bureaucratic, technocratic and ultimately dehumanized world.

## Security First

This scenario assumes a world of striking disparities where inequality and conflict prevail. Socio-economic and environmental stresses give rise to waves of protest and counteraction. As such troubles become increasingly prevalent, the more powerful and wealthy groups focus on self-protection, creating enclaves akin to the present day 'gated communities'. Such islands of advantage provide a degree of enhanced security and economic benefits for dependent communities in their immediate surroundings but they exclude the disadvantaged mass of outsiders. Welfare and regulatory services fall into disuse but market forces continue to operate outside the walls.

In the early years of the century, a world view that puts market principles and security concerns to the fore, dominates global development. This is reflected at international level in the half-hearted mood of debates at the WSSD and similar meetings. Negotiations on climate change and other multilateral environmental agreements drag on with minimal progress.

Where there are advances at international level, these tend to be in areas with a more economic focus, such as international trade and foreign investment. Even in this arena, promising initiatives like the Global Compact for Business, the Global Reporting Initiative and the Doha round of trade negotiations under the WTO, are slow to deliver on their promises to create the basis for more equitable and sustainable economic globalization.

In the aftermath of the terrorist attacks on the United States and the initial armed response in Afghanistan, the emphasis is on providing security by more traditional means, such as military power and control of arms and financial flows. Little attention is paid to the social and environmental issues that many argue provide the motivation for terrorist activity.

### The market's call: the need for security

The momentum for sustainable development, so promising in the 1990s, gradually fizzles out, for a wide range of reasons. The voices that urge the world to build upon this momentum and achieve agreed goals go unheeded as the belief spreads that free markets alone can come up with flexible enough checks and balances to deal with issues of social justice and global environmental care. This complacency also reflects competing concerns, such as recurring fiscal crises and downturns in national economies, cycles of terrorist

activity and retaliation and the continuation of armed conflicts in several parts of the world. Hence the first decade of the new century is in many ways a period of muddling through.

In Africa, the decade is characterized by prolonged civil conflicts affecting many nations and often drawing in neighbouring countries. In these cases little progress is made in introducing greater transparency and accountability into governments. At the same time, the AIDS pandemic continues, curtailing economic advances even in those countries that enjoy political stability.

Conflicts also continue to simmer in parts of West Asia, at times boiling over into periods of intense violence. Disputes over water, oil and other resources are intensified by, and contribute to, these conflicts. Instability in the price of oil, due to fluctuating demand and the inability to control supply in the region and elsewhere, slows economic growth in the region.

Economic problems remain significant in many parts of the Asia and the Pacific region. Downturns reminiscent of the crash that occurred in the late 1990s periodically resurface and impact upon a broader range of countries. Here, also, internal and external conflicts continue to command attention and divert valuable resources.

In Latin America and the Caribbean, problems posed by the continuing growth of mega-cities plague many countries while internal conflicts, often related to the drug trade, persist. At the same time, pushed

---

**'A world view that puts market principles and security concerns to the fore, dominates global development.'**

---

by the countries of North America and multinational corporations, the primary focus of many politicians is on the continued expansion of free trade in the region, rather than on social and environmental concerns.

Security is a consuming preoccupation in North America, giving rise to concern not only over the threat of direct physical attacks but also over dependence on foreign suppliers for strategic resources. The latter fear increases the pressure to exploit resources within the region, including parts of the Arctic. Arctic resources are made more accessible as ice-free periods in the north are extended by the warming of the climate. Access is also eased by a wave of privatization in the region, extending to the control of natural resources.

Similar bursts of resource exploitation are also occurring in the Arctic parts of the Russian Federation and the Nordic countries. Much of the effort of European policy-makers is focused on dealing with expansion of the EU. A few more countries are admitted into the Union, but persistent tensions related to taxes, subsidies, immigration, freedom of

---

**'In all regions and at the global level, large, non-state entities increasingly influence and drive the political agenda. These include multinational corporations, but also crime syndicates.'**

---

movement and other issues, slow this process. Disagreements also linger on between a central core of countries that wishes to move towards much greater integration and others that prefer a looser union. Meanwhile, countries in Eastern Europe generally make little economic progress and suffer further tensions and internal conflicts.

In all these regions and at the global level, large, non-state entities increasingly influence and drive the political agenda. These include multinational corporations, but also crime syndicates. The level of corruption within governments is generally understood to be increasing, although given little improvement in transparency and accountability, this is not easy to verify.

The start of the second decade of the new century sees the world functioning in a more *laissez faire* manner than before. Businesses wield enormous power but maintain a focus on enhancing shareholder value, believing it is the job of governments to address environmental and social issues. They, however, expend resources to build up private police forces to protect their assets in areas with strategic resources, especially in countries where protection is considered unreliable.

### Veering towards breakdown

Government efforts to tackle environmental and social problems are generally late in coming and ineffective in scope. Furthermore, governments use much of their power to protect the economic interests of national and corporate enterprises to which they are increasingly tied. NGOs and other groups in civil society find themselves focusing more and more on short-term crises, rather than working to influence long-term development patterns.

This trend is epitomized by the collapse of the Antarctic Treaty system, a result of pressure from non-claimant states and non-state actors, coupled with the failure of claimant states to reach agreement on resource exploitation and environmental protection. There is a rush to exploit the region's mineral and marine living assets, including freshwater in the form of ice. This free-for-all does not mean equal access for all groups, as the more powerful states and large corporations still exert dominance. Exploitation of resources by these groups also speeds up in the Arctic. There, the impacts have an important social element as native peoples gain little benefit. Although many people move north to take part in the expanded economic activity, most income flows out of the region.

As the decade proceeds, the effects of the erosion of institutions at the international and national levels become more apparent. If the first decade was a period of muddling through, this is one of stumbling and serious falls. Conflicts in various parts of the world never coalesce to form what might be called a Third World War. They do, however, escalate in particular regions and at particular times to destabilize nations. Of even more concern to some is the sporadic use of chemical, biological and other non-conventional weapons. The sheer numbers of refugees also creates severe problems in neighbouring (mainly non-combatant) states. The ability of international institutions such as the United Nations High Commission for Refugees to cope with these events has been compromised by reductions in support, leaving them overwhelmed.

These conflicts, along with enduring economic weaknesses and environmental deterioration, affect regions further afield, as migration pressures increase throughout the world. These pressures stem not only from factors within regions forcing migration, but also from tantalizing images broadcast by the media that lure them elsewhere. The response of the receiving countries is mixed, with some more open to new immigrants than others. Over time, however, even the countries and regions with relatively open borders begin clamping down as they focus on problems at home.

Some of these problems spring from recurrent economic malaise. In North America, Europe and parts of Asia and the Pacific, part of the problem is the declining size of workforces. Allowing highly educated and skilled workers from other regions to immigrate eases this shortage somewhat. Unfortunately the deterioration of educational opportunities in many regions has reduced the availability of such workers. From the perspective of their home regions, the departure of even a small number of skilled migrant workers represents a significant loss of indigenous capacity. The repercussions affect economic and political stability, further widening the gap between have and have-not nations.

Environmental changes and events also have widespread effects, in wealthy and poorer regions alike. The impacts of climate change and variability become more apparent. The gradual rise in sea level is punctuated by severe storms that cause heavy damage to coastal (and even some inland) areas. In Europe, North America and the wealthier parts of Asia and the Pacific, the financial losses are staggering, even if there are no dramatic losses of life. Re-financing on a huge scale, not only to recover the losses where possible, but also to prepare for future events, diverts important resources from other parts of the economy.

In other regions, particularly Latin America and the Caribbean, and the poorer parts of Asia and the Pacific, the loss of life is significant and the financial losses seriously damage economies. After the immediate clean-up, there is little funding left to make ravaged areas less vulnerable in the future. Elsewhere, droughts are adding to water stress, already on the increase because of runaway growth in water demand. This shortfall cripples agriculture in many parts of West Asia and Africa, where it directly menaces the very survival of many people and increases regional tensions, and also in North America, where it tips the balance in favour of pursuing risky, large-scale water transfer projects.

Many sectors bear the mark of developments in the areas of biotechnology and genetic engineering. Difficulties in mastering these new technologies are made worse by a drop in public funding for research and development. Finance for these purposes is now concentrated in the hands of private firms that are biased in favour of those applications that will yield the highest profits. Minimal social and environmental safeguards characterize the early phases of biotechnology development.

Significant advances are achieved in medicine, agriculture and environmental clean-up technologies,

but detrimental side effects also arise. These include accidental releases, illicit use by terrorist groups, epidemics among human and animal populations and negative impacts on various plant species. Attacks on biotechnology trials by eco-terrorists and pro-nature activists further complicate matters. Ultimately, a clampdown on research and application trials is imposed by governments and key firms involved in these fields.

The net result is a slowdown in advances in those areas with potentially the highest impacts for the broadest section of society, such as the production of food crops. In combination with the deterioration of arable land in many areas, food stocks fall perpetually short in some regions. Cutbacks in foreign assistance have left relief agencies unable to handle many of the resulting crises. In general, conventional forms of development aid decline and poverty rises.

Little action is taken to alleviate the debt burden of poorer nations. The global economy remains stratified and fails to embrace the billions who are economically and politically marginalized. This split is deepened by institutions of international trade that focus on freeing up markets in developing countries,

*'The global economy remains stratified and fails to embrace the billions who are economically and politically marginalized ... traditional livelihoods and communities also erode.'*

without also doing so in industrialized regions. The flow of new technology and training from the industrialized countries also declines.

Not only are the poor excluded from the new economy, but also traditional livelihoods and communities erode as global markets penetrate peripheral regions, seeking cheap labour and control of resources. In poorer countries especially, economies increasingly come under the control of transnational corporations. In parts of Latin America and the Caribbean, Asia and the Pacific, and Africa, this takeover is very clearly seen in the commercial exploitation of biological resources with little compensation for the majority of the people in these regions.

The drawdown of fiscal resources of the state treasury in poor countries leads to disintegration of social and civic services. In particular, systems of education, especially higher education, collapse. This deepens the divide between the rich and the poor and exacerbates absolute poverty. Furthermore, as a result of cutbacks in public provision of education, much of the alternative schooling that is available is laden with prejudicial seeds of intolerance and violence.

As conditions worsen in many places the excluded grow increasingly restive. Many seek their fortunes in exploding mega-cities. The pace of urbanization puts extra strain on already overextended infrastructures, leading to more problems with air pollution and lack of access to clean water and sanitation. Limited economic opportunities in cities foster the growth of organized crime. In an atmosphere of despair, illegal drugs find ready markets. Many of the poor try to migrate to rich countries and rising numbers of them resort to illegal entry. The stream of people on the move grows into a river of the desperate flowing (both within and across national boundaries) towards the wealthy areas. Affluent groups respond with growing xenophobia and oppressive policing of borders. Social polarization spreads and extremists and terrorist groups find ready recruits.

In this atmosphere of rising social, environmental and economic tension, violence is endemic. Poor countries begin to fragment as civil order collapses and various forms of criminal anarchy fill the vacuum. War and environmental degradation lead to massive movements of refugees in some regions. Environmental changes and overloaded infrastructures also favour another kind of migrant; new and resurgent infectious diseases and the vectors that carry them.

## Divided world

Alarmed by migration, terrorism and disease, members of the affluent minority fear that they too will be engulfed. Even some of the more prosperous nations feel the sting as infrastructure decays,

---

'Many of the poor try to migrate to rich countries and rising numbers of them resort to illegal entry. Affluent groups respond with growing xenophobia and oppressive policing of borders.'

---

technology fails and institutions collapse. As OECD economies falter and their populations age, social programmes introduced in the 20th century but neglected year after year, begin to unravel.

These and other factors lead to a dramatic swing in approaches to governance. Having stood by, sometimes willingly, and seen their powers eroded, governments strive to reassert their authority. To stem the collapse, the forces of order react with sufficient cohesion and force to impose an authoritarian order throughout much of the world. In many regions these shifts appear merely as a continuation of normal practice or a return to the not-so-distant past. In others, though, sacrificing long cherished ideals (such as democracy, transparency and participation in governance) for greater security is no easy trade-off. A growing sense of lifeboat ethics — an acceptance that only by letting some drown can the others remain afloat — allows the governments and citizens of these countries to make certain consensual choices. Other decisions are eventually made without popular consent and are accepted without question.

This process takes time to develop, but a pattern gradually emerges. In rich nations, the wealthiest people flourish in protected enclaves and the general public receives some assurance from the increased level of security. Strongholds also persist in the poorer nations, protecting the remaining elites and strategic resources. In some regions, control is unstable; the power base shifts as one faction or ethnic group overpowers another.

The strongholds are 'islands of prosperity in an ocean of poverty and despair' (Hammond 1998), descendants of the walled cities of earlier eras and the gated communities of more recent times. Sometimes the walls are physical; at other times they are more metaphorical. Nevertheless, these bubbles of wealth are not isolated. They are connected in a global network with shared economic, environmental and security interests. Through this network, globalization continues, albeit in a distorted form.

Within the walls, life proceeds with some semblance of order. Technological advances continue to be made. Health and educational services continue to be provided, consumption patterns do not shift dramatically and environmental conditions hold steady. Businesses assist in the provision of some socially important programmes, especially those directly related to their interests, for example, education to address skill shortages and provision of basic needs to workers. Still, there is always a recognition that security is of paramount importance.

It is pursued by various authoritarian policies and institutions, whose methods include surveillance and the profiling and harassment of particular dissident groups.

Outside the walls, the majority is trapped in poverty. The provision of basic needs — water, health services, sanitation, food, shelter and energy — is piecemeal or often non-existent. Many people are denied basic freedoms. By comparison with the cohesive societies within the walls, this world is increasingly chaotic and disconnected. Technological progress continues to be made in these communities, at times by theft or leakage from within the walls, but also by indigenous enterprises. Such breakthroughs tend to be small-scale, however, and the lack of harmonization and capacity building prevents dramatic advances that might prompt large improvements. The inability to achieve economies of scale further hinders progress and growth.

The interplay between life inside and outside the enclaves goes well beyond merely policing the borders between the two. The bubbles of prosperity depend heavily on a constant flow of resources from areas not fully under their control. Where the elite are able to exert control, there is strict management of source areas for products of commercial value and those that serve a more basic life support function. These well-protected areas, both on land and in the oceans, provide a haven for many other species, but do little to improve the lot of people who are excluded. Where areas are simply mined and abandoned, those on the outside are expected to deal with the aftermath.

The elite also rely upon the broader world to absorb the excesses of their lifestyles. Wastes produced within the strongholds are transported into outlying areas. The pressures that such wastes place on unprotected natural systems add to the problems of people struggling to survive. These problems include overuse and fouling of water sources above and below ground, the effects of uncontrolled use of dirty fossil fuels, contamination from untreated solid wastes, continued deforestation to provide fuelwood and the degradation of marginal areas used for agriculture.

Trade also crosses the boundaries between the two worlds. Those inside the walls have not lost their taste for products that must come from outside, including illegal drugs and those derived from rare species. Both money and military supplies find their way outside in return, where they trigger not just external chaos and lawlessness but also periodic

---

**'The forces of order react with sufficient cohesion and force to impose an authoritarian order throughout much of the world.'**

---

terrorist attacks against the fortresses.

In this atmosphere, both the informal and legitimate small enterprises flourish by serving local needs. Charities and other welfare providers in civil society try to assist where governments and businesses fall short in the provision of basic needs, which happens in many cases, but the task proves far from simple and their efforts far from effective.

## What lies ahead?

By 2032, an air of uneasy stability has begun to settle on this divided world. It is unclear, though, how long this truce can last. The forces for further breakdown are ever present. At the same time, dreams of a better way still beckon. Whereas many of the fears of the pessimists have come true, fresh opportunities for positive change have not ceased to appear. Outside the walls, small islands of calm exist and work is under way there to build links with others and with progressive elements within the fortresses, offering hope that someday, like the phoenix rising from its ashes, a better world for all might yet emerge.

**Sustainability First**

A new environment and development paradigm emerges in response to the challenge of sustainability, supported by new, more equitable values and institutions. A more visionary state of affairs prevails, where radical shifts in the way people interact with one another and with the world around them stimulate and support sustainable policy measures and accountable corporate behaviour. There is much fuller collaboration between governments, citizens and other stakeholder groups in decision-making on issues of close common concern. A consensus is reached on what needs to be done to satisfy basic needs and realize personal goals without beggaring others or spoiling the outlook for posterity.

In the early years of the century, there is evidence of a compelling desire and demand among people everywhere for action to address the social, economic and environmental concerns affecting many regions of the world. The terrorist attacks on the United States and subsequent retaliation lend immediacy to calls to address economic, social and environmental concerns that are seen as the root causes of such extreme actions. A reinvigorated NGO community becomes a key channel through which citizens everywhere express their demands. The Internet amplifies what has become a global dialogue, or more accurately a multitude of dialogues, on the need for action.

## An age of reflection ...
Some of these exchanges take place in formal government arenas. Others, partly prompted by pressures from shareholders, employees and customers, are happening in industry, both within and among firms. Similarly, NGOs (including many that have a multinational presence) are reflecting upon their roles and missions.

*'There is evidence of a compelling desire and demand among people everywhere for action to address the social, economic and environmental concerns affecting many regions of the world.'*

There are also fresh attempts to collaborate across the governmental, industrial and NGO sectors. In total, however, these efforts pale by comparison with the myriad dialogues between individuals and small groups of interested citizens within and across regions.

Much of this desire for remedial action is expressed in and around the lobbies of international activities, including the WSSD and other United Nations conferences, meetings of the G7/G8 group of nations, at the negotiations of the WTO and multilateral environmental agreements, and at meetings on specific social and environmental issues, such as climate change and HIV/AIDS.

At times, the formal events are overshadowed by parallel gatherings. For the most part, the mood of these gatherings is peaceable, akin to that of the Global Forum linked to the 1992 Earth Summit. Less in evidence are the anti-globalization protests seen at the meetings of the WTO in Seattle in 1999 and the G8 in Genoa in 2001. Their goal is to highlight the advances that are being made and to shape the agenda of the governmental meetings. There is greater emphasis on presenting the positive aspects of a societal transformation rather than the negative consequences of inaction. Over time, increasing numbers of representatives from industry and governments participate in these encounters, making them more successful in achieving this goal.

## ... and a time for action
Much of what is happening goes beyond mere dialogue. Rather than waiting for political leaders to take the initiative, many individuals and groups have begun to act on their own. They note the contrasting outcomes of the 1992 Earth Summit on an informal and local scale, such as the spread of Local Agenda 21 initiatives and those pitched at the more formal and international level, such as the United Nations Framework Convention on Climate Change. They draw inspiration from past and present efforts of local grass-roots movements like the Green Belt movement in Kenya and the Chipko Andalan movement in India. They also recall successful interventions at international level, such as the campaign to end the production and use of landmines.

The business community is another source of inspiration, principally for its success in developing social investment funds and establishing social stock indices. Firms that address environmental issues ahead of regulation, exemplified by companies in the Climate Neutral Network, serve as role models. Also held up as role models are partnerships between governments and other groups, such as Ecotourism Namibia and Community-Based Fisheries Management in Phang-Nga Bay, Thailand.

The more that individuals and groups apply themselves to practical initiatives, the more hope grows that significant changes are possible. The media assist by making these efforts more visible. Progressive elements in government and business communities realize that this is the most promising channel for reform. They also recognize that efforts like these are needed to get to the sources of dissatisfaction that lie at the root of terrorist activities. This realization leads to the creation of alliances amongst individuals from various stakeholder groups in support of key initiatives.

The result is a mixture of old and new initiatives. Some initiatives are highly coordinated and involve large numbers of people. Others are pursued by small groups with wide ranging, but loosely knit connections at local, regional and global levels. Whereas some are formal and embedded in national and international law, many take a voluntary approach, such as the Global Reporting Initiative, Global Compact Initiative and financial initiatives set up by the United Nations and businesses.

Efforts continue to incorporate the results of scientific research and analysis more thoroughly into the policy making process. The Millennium Ecosystem Assessment, the Global International Water Assessment and new studies on the nitrogen cycle and persistent organic pollutants (POPs) complement the ongoing investigation of climate change by the Intergovernmental Panel on Climate Change. The POPs assessment is in part a response to compelling new evidence of the long-range transport of these pollutants and the effects of their presence on animal life in the polar regions. Much like the discovery of the ozone hole over Antarctica in the 1980s, these revelations stimulate intense effort to measure and counter the risk.

These new assessments differ fundamentally from past efforts. Firstly, they are designed to include more expertise from developing regions, and to build capacity in these regions. Secondly, the contributions of social scientists are given equal weight to those of the physical and natural scientists. Thirdly, wherever possible, the many regional and local studies that comprise large parts of these assessments recruit local and lay communities as partners in the research. This stems from the desire of these groups to have a voice in the development and understanding of the issues and in how to address particular concerns.

The knowledge that these individuals and groups (particularly indigenous groups) possess has been accorded increasing recognition. The participatory approach also acknowledges that scope for action extends beyond official government channels and depends upon involvement of local communities.

Setting goals and targets and designing activities to achieve them, builds upon ongoing efforts, but also

---

**'Some initiatives are highly coordinated and involve large numbers of people. Others are pursued by small groups ... some are formal ... many take a voluntary approach.'**

---

reflects progress in striking a balance between formal and informal institutions. Social and environmental goals are re-affirmed, among them reducing food insecurity and infant mortality, increasing life expectancy and literacy, stabilizing climate, halting deforestation and reversing declines in fisheries.

Rather than laying down specific numbers, quotas and timetables, however, more attention is paid to increasing accountability and transparency by instituting monitoring systems and placing responsibility on governments, industries, NGOs and others to disclose information in relation to agreed goals. The underlying principle is that the widespread availability of good information and appropriate checks and balances will encourage progress towards these goals, either directly or by way of pressure from an increasingly vocal citizenry. The goal of policy, in this scenario, is to support the efforts of individuals and groups, in government as well as in civil society, within the non-profit sector as well in the marketplace, to pursue sustainable development.

This evolving approach calls for a reappraisal of existing multilateral agreements. The list includes environmentally oriented agreements such as the United Nations Convention on the Law of the Sea and the Basel Convention on the Control of Transboundary Movements of Hazardous Wastes and their Disposal. It also features more socially oriented conventions such as those on the Elimination of All Forms of Discrimination Against Women and on the Rights of the Child.

The process of revision provides momentum, too, for the continuing reassessment of international institutions of governance, with a view to transforming them into more effective organizations. The United Nations, major financial institutions such as the World Bank, regional development banks and the IMF and the WTO are all included. Transparency and accountability are key aspects of this course of action. Similar processes are ongoing in business, voluntary and other sectors.

At regional level, new and old organizations become increasingly active. The Federation of Caribbean Nations grows out of the former CARICOM. In Europe, the growth of the EU proceeds with considerable deference paid to maintaining and improving relationships with the Russian Federation. Africa sees the further evolution of the African Ministerial Conference on the Environment (AMCEN). Most regions also explore greater integration of policies related to trade, migration, the management of water resources and similar transboundary issues. In this way, the regional efforts become part of a semi-formal web of global public policy networks.

## A great swing

The journey that these processes set in motion is a long one. It takes many years and does not proceed without constant pressure and action from many sectors of society. A profound set of changes, which were only hinted at in the early years of the century, gradually unfolds, quietly most of the time, not so quietly at others. People everywhere begin to embrace the idea of a 'new sustainability paradigm' that promises to transcend conventional values and lifestyles. This new paradigm combines a powerful personal and philosophical dimension with concern over economic growth, technological potential and political eventualities.

Among more affluent people and groups, disenchantment with consumerism sparks off a quest for more fulfilling and ethical ways of living

**'A profound set of changes gradually unfolds, quietly most of the time, not so quietly at others. People everywhere begin to embrace the idea of a 'new sustainability paradigm.'**

that can restore a sense of meaning and purpose to their existence. The values of simplicity, cooperation and community begin to displace those of

consumerism, competition and individualism. More time is spent on study, art, hobbies and engaging in the wider community.

The success of the Truth and Reconciliation Commissions in South Africa, East Timor and elsewhere stimulate similar exercises in other places, including less strictly political settings, such as within the tobacco and chemicals industries. The positive results of the peacemaking process in Northern Ireland and Bosnia enhance efforts in other regions. Dialogues between the world's major religions, directly stimulated by the terrorist activities against the United States and subsequent retaliation, further help to create the foundation for greater understanding and cooperation.

In some regions, the mood of society is a mixture of battle fatigue and disgust with current leaders. Small-scale but locally significant environmental disasters also have an effect on this mood. These factors combine to make more people willing to explore and question fundamental beliefs.

Citizens and consumers, where possible with their votes and wallets and otherwise with their feet and their voices, make it clear that progressive businesses and governments will be rewarded while others will be rejected. At some point, a critical mass is reached, whereby activities that have until now appeared isolated and of little consequence, begin to spread and affect broader regions.

In developing regions and amongst indigenous communities everywhere, a new generation of thinkers, leaders and activists emerges to join and shape the global dialogue. Many regions draw on the dual legacy of nature-conscious traditional societies and ideas of visionary thinkers seeking better paths for development. Cultural renaissance evolves in many regions, rooted in respect for tradition and an appreciation of local human and natural resources. Young people from all regions and cultures play a key role in promoting these values. The increased opportunity to meet and learn from others of their generation, both virtually and in person, fuels a rediscovery of idealism as they join together in the project of forging a global community.

What is new in the current discussion is the willingness of people to reflect upon the positive and negative aspects of their own actions and legacies as well as those of other cultures. Many of these debates are launched within the developing world, engaging an ever-expanding circle of stakeholders.

The notion that the prevailing market oriented wisdom is both insufficient and undesirable garners more and more support. This switch is most significant in North America and Western Europe, as well as among many of the affluent in other regions, who have been seen as the key purveyors and beneficiaries of this approach to development. At the same time, it is recognized that the increasing openness and participation in governance have played a key role in the advances that have improved life for many people in many parts of the world.

This change of heart gives rise to more measured discussions about the seemingly inexorable spread of globalization in all of its forms. The realization grows that, even if it were possible, it would not be desirable to stem this tide completely. Around the world, from Latin America to Africa to West Asia, the re-examination of history leads to new approaches for dealing with the changes happening in and outside their regions. Inevitably, this re-think is influenced in part by the return of many former emigrants, for brief periods or permanently, who have gained experience and understanding of how cultures can learn from each other without losing their own identity.

## A redefinition of roles ...

With the growth in global public policy networks, governments, particularly at the national level, often find themselves trying to keep up with what is happening in other sectors and at other levels. In a sense, the leaders have become followers, although they continue to have significant roles. They remain responsible for setting and implementing overall national policy and negotiating and ratifying international treaties. Nation states remain the key players in the areas of national and international security. The public sector retains a pivotal regulatory role, as awareness dawns that *laissez faire* policies often promoted in the name of economic development do nothing to correct flaws in market practices. It also holds a brief to amend existing policies (notably subsidies for natural resource extraction) that encourage such imperfections.

Demand for more participation, transparency and accountability on all sides drives a number of policy shifts. A move away from reliance on exported raw materials towards producing more value added locally is highlighted in Latin America, Eastern Europe,

Africa and parts of North America. Expansion of micro-credit and similar schemes is particularly important in the developing world, enabling small-scale producers and manufacturers to purchase the inputs needed to increase the scale and productivity of their operations. Another pattern that emerges worldwide is a shift in the nature of taxes and subsidies towards promoting more sustainable habits of resource use.

New opportunities arise from looking at problems on a larger scale, with a view to recognizing limits and identifying solutions. One example is the opportunity

---

**'The values of simplicity, cooperation and community begin to displace those of consumerism, competition and individualism.'**

---

to couple the issues of ageing and shrinking workforces in Europe and parts of Asia and the Pacific, with continued population growth and migration pressures in other regions. Another involves drawing more conscious links between the issue of water stress and the trading of 'virtual' water in the form of agricultural products. This linkage is accorded high priority within susceptible regions, such as West Asia as part of the Arab Free Trade Association, but it also occurs in region-to-region discussions.

## ... and a redirection of actions

Actions are taken in many regions to preserve major biodiversity hotspots. In Europe and North America, major efforts are made to establish large-scale networks of protected areas and green corridors. Some of the most significant activities hinge on the management of common resources. Ocean fisheries receive greater attention. For this and other reasons, the high Arctic regions and the continent of Antarctica are increasingly recognized as part of a common global heritage. A fundamental revision of the Antarctic legal regime sets an example for similar action in the Arctic, where indigenous groups play a significant role, individually and through the Arctic Council. It becomes widely accepted that the polar regions have to be maintained as places apart, with special rules regarding human activity.

Cooperation on these and other issues also prompts moves to address the tensions at the root of many ongoing conflicts. Sometimes these conflicts and their impact on other regions catalyse the formation of broad coalitions. The changing nature of security threats, as evidenced in the early part of the century and the pressures from businesses and other groups with strong cross-national connections, push nations towards increasingly multilateral efforts on many issues. At other times, the resolution and avoidance of conflicts are the results of networks and policies that have been established for other purposes. For example, as borders become more open and responsibility shifts from the nation state both downward to more local levels and upward to more multinational levels, many disputes in countries and in border areas in several regions, calm down or fade away entirely.

Underlying many of these shifts are policies to boost transparency and accountability. These policies include more and better certification and labelling requirements, often building upon efforts started by industry. The Forest Stewardship Council, Global Forest Watch and Marine Stewardship Council spawn similar efforts focusing on other resources. These

---

**'What is new in the current discussion is the willingness of people to reflect upon the positive and negative aspects of their own actions and legacies as well as those of other cultures.'**

---

efforts in turn influence other areas of policy, such as trade, foreign debt and the enforcement of multilateral environmental treaties. In the developing world, a major investment programme is undertaken to strengthen capacities of governments, businesses (especially small and medium enterprises), NGOs and local communities to develop, access and use information. These changes are reflected in increased monitoring and communication. As much as any other business sector, the commercial media has shifted away from a pure emphasis on profit towards establishing a broader role in society.

There are also fundamental shifts in terms of how the data used to track development are measured, analysed and presented. Aggregate figures that hide discrepancies between, for example, genders and social groups, or between urban and rural areas, give way to more disaggregated data collection and reporting. The changes are highlighted by the continuing evolution of the United Nations System of National Accounts,

especially the shift away from Gross Domestic Product as the major indicator of development. Environmental, economic and social indicators track real progress at all scales — business, national, regional and global — giving the public a more informed basis for seeking change. New technologies also play a big role, both as catalysts for, and in response to, many of these changes.

Developments in information and communication technologies enable groups to connect to and learn from each other, by sharing success stories, but also by exposing behaviour, whether legal or illegal, existing or planned, that gives cause for disquiet. These technologies also become more instrumental in coordinating social, political and economic activities. They are the natural medium for a new consciousness, providing a sense of immediacy and unity to a diverse and pluralistic movement.

New technologies play an instrumental role in progress towards goals already set. Among such advances are improvements in energy and water use efficiency, desalination and medical technologies and treatment. These breakthroughs are closely linked to general developments in the areas of nano-technology and biotechnology. Governments, businesses and other private organizations stimulate much of the technological development, not only by direct investment in research and development, but also by offering worthwhile prizes for new developments.

In the areas of biotechnology and genetic engineering, there is strong awareness of potential issues related to biosafety, bioterrorism and moral concerns. Biotechnology also becomes increasingly linked to biodiversity research within regions. Concerns over genetic engineering continue to run high, but they are eased somewhat as developments in this area take on a more regional profile, both in terms of who is undertaking and benefiting from the research and the raw materials used in the processes. Carefully controlled studies in many regions, including Asia and the Pacific, West Asia, Latin America and the Caribbean and Africa, highlight the use of endemic resources.

Small and large businesses, in partnership with NGOs, provide valuable support in setting standards and guidelines, technology transfer and mentoring programmes. They also take greater responsibility for the whole life cycle of projects and products. This includes not only activities related to normal practice, but also those related to infrastructure development, recovery of post-consumption wastes, capacity building and preparing employees and communities for periods of transition, such as when projects end or operations shift to another locality.

## No turning back?

These widespread changes unfold at different rates in different regions. By the year 2032, some shifts are already well on the way to a new, more stable level of functional completion, while others are only beginning to take off. Although there have been setbacks, these have not been major or widespread. The reason for this smooth passage lies in the nature of the process which, while somewhat chaotic and unplanned at times has been driven from the grass roots up with strong support at higher levels. The degree of participation between governments and society, and the ongoing evolution of basic beliefs have been instrumental in allowing governments to pursue policies that would not otherwise have been possible. Examples are the establishment of land and marine sanctuaries and major shifts in the constructive use of tax breaks and penalties.

Furthermore, as businesses, NGOs and governments, working together or apart, achieve notable success, they push for action to encourage others to follow. The evidence of these accrued benefits helps governments in taking action, as they make it very difficult for those who are opposed to

**'New technologies play a big role, both as catalysts for, and in response to, many of these changes.'**

them to argue against the feasibility of meeting new targets. And as formal actions are taken, they act as a ratchet, keeping the advances from slipping back.

The interlinked sets of changes that have occurred during the first three decades of the new millennium are clearly part of a broad societal transformation. Although no one would argue that sustainability has been achieved, there is a clear sense that the world is moving in the right direction and there is no turning back.

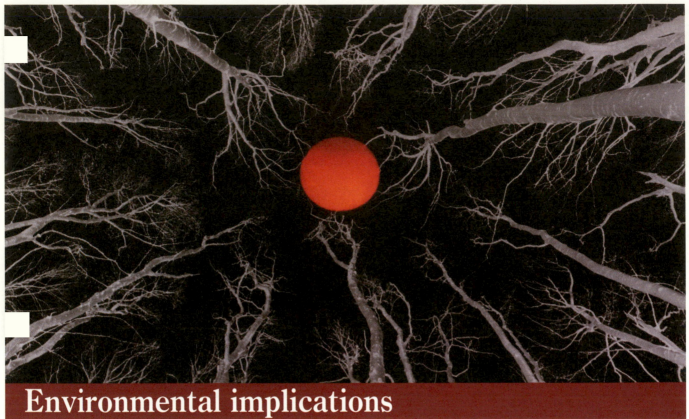

# Environmental implications

The foregoing section of this chapter presented stories of four possible futures. Elements of each can be observed in today's world, as can the trends and drivers that could push the world in the direction of one or another of them. Which scenario — or which mixture of scenarios — prevails in reality is a matter partly of contingency and partly of choice.

This section illustrates what the four scenarios can tell us about the consequences of policy and management for the environment over the next three decades. The pressures exerted on the environment, the changes in its state and the impacts on people differ from one scenario to the next. When interpreting the results it should be remembered that not all natural and human systems operate on the same time scale: both feature fast, medium and slow processes. Hence some of the effects of our actions emerge only slowly and much of what will happen in the next 30 years has already been determined. Decisions made over the next 30 years will have significant impacts and implications that reach far beyond this period.

Quantitative material is included to help illustrate the trends that would be expected under each scenario. The quantitative results presented here as charts and diagrams have been derived, in consultation with regional experts, using a range of analytical tools. The results underline the magnitude of the challenges we face in developing environmentally relevant policies for the future. The emphasis is on general trends and the proportional differences under different scenarios, rather than on the precise levels of impacts. More details of the analytical tools used and the variables presented are provided in the technical annex to this chapter.

Certain environmental implications only make sense when viewed at the global scale. It is important to remember, however, that the origins of these global effects are often local, national or regional. The initial global perspective of environmental implications presented below also provides a backdrop for the more detailed examination of the environmental outlook that follows for each region. A box in each regional section outlines a fictitious, but plausible, region-specific 'event' and examines how the event might play out under the four scenarios. Also summarized is the impact that different policy approaches have on the possible outcomes of the event.

**Key to charts**

Markets First

Policy First

Security First

Sustainability First

## Implications: Global

### Climate trends

Climate change is one of the most pressing and complex global environmental issues to come to the fore in the past 30 years. The absence of effective policies to reduce emissions of carbon dioxide ($CO_2$) and other greenhouse gases in the *Markets First* and *Security First* scenarios, as well as slow transfer of technology under the latter, leads to significant increases in $CO_2$ emissions over the next 30 years (see chart, right). The effects of the economic troubles in a *Security First* world push down per capita energy consumption and lead to the slower emission growth seen at the end of this period. The policy actions taken under a *Policy First* scenario, notably carbon taxes and investments in non-fossil-fuel energy sources, effectively curb growth in global emissions. Actual reductions would start around the year 2030. The dramatic behavioural shifts implied under *Sustainability First*, in conjunction with significantly improved production and conversion efficiencies, result in a very rapid levelling off of emissions followed by a decline by the middle of the 2020s.

Because of time lags in the climate system, these changes in emission patterns will have a delayed effect on the atmospheric concentrations of $CO_2$ and even more so on the actual changes in climate. Even by the year 2050, some 20 to 25 years after the start of the decline in emissions in the *Policy First* and *Sustainability First* scenarios, the atmospheric concentrations are only beginning to level off in *Sustainability First* and have yet to do so in *Policy First* (see chart). Carbon dioxide trajectories in *Markets First* and *Security First* continue to climb rapidly, reflecting the weak policies and lack of behavioural changes in these scenarios.

The rate at which climate is changing is indicated by the rate of change in average global temperature (see chart, overleaf). The relatively long delay in the response of the climate system shows up in the relatively small differences between the scenarios in their early stages. This figure also reflects the complexity of this issue. There are strong links between climate change and other environmental issues, specifically local and regional air pollution. Reduction in emissions of sulphur dioxide ($SO_2$), for example, leads to temperature increases which can temporarily more than offset the effects of reducing

$CO_2$ emissions. The higher rates of temperature change in the *Policy First* and *Sustainability First* scenarios between now and 2032 reflect the successful implementation of $SO_2$ reduction policies in these scenarios. In the longer term, however, the dynamics in a world resembling *Markets First* or *Security First* imply much faster and greater overall temperature rises, whilst the rate of temperature increase slows down in *Sustainability First*.

Delays in the response of the climate system are also apparent in other ways. For instance, by 2032, there is very little difference between the scenarios in terms of sea level rise. The total increase since the beginning of the century is approximately 10 cm, yet this level and rate of rise has serious implications for

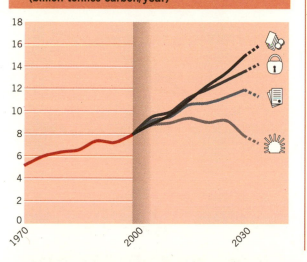

**Carbon dioxide emissions from all sources (billion tonnes carbon/year)**

Carbon dioxide is emitted above all from the use of fossil fuels. For all four scenarios, it is assumed that stabilization of primary energy use is first reached at the end of the 21st century.

Source: IMAGE 2.2 (see technical annex)

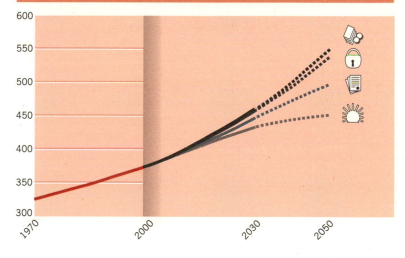

**Atmospheric concentrations of carbon dioxide (parts per million by volume)**

The build-up of greenhouse gases follows trends in emissions but the stock has a long life span once in the atmosphere. Only the *Sustainability First* scenario is on a trajectory to stabilize at 450 ppm (parts per million) carbon dioxide equivalent.

Source: IMAGE 2.2 (see technical annex)

Temperature change up to the 2030s can no longer be avoided. In all scenarios its rate far exceeds 0.10°C per ten years — the level above which damage to ecosystems is likely.

Source: IMAGE 2.2 (see technical annex)

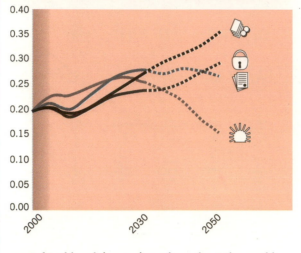

**Global temperature change (°C per ten years)**

coastal and low-lying regions throughout the world, implying that adaptation measures are important to consider along with attempts to reduce emissions.

## Ecosystems under pressure

Biodiversity preservation represents another major environmental challenge at the global level. Without strenuous policy action, humans continue to develop more of the planet, reducing and fragmenting natural ecosystems. The built-up area increases in nearly all regions and scenarios, the only exceptions being North America and Europe where the area declines slightly in *Sustainability First* (see chart opposite).

Lack of effective controls, including realistic price hurdles to urban land expansion, is most evident in the *Security First* scenario. The percentage of built-up land may seem small, but the infrastructure network (roads, power lines, airports, harbours and dams) that supports these sites affects much larger areas and also sees dramatic expansion over the next 30 years (see chart opposite and maps on page 354). The introduction of such infrastructure can lead to uncontrolled resource exploitation often linked to hunting and poaching, deforestation, land and water degradation, growing of illegal crops, tourism and land conflicts. In both *Markets First* and *Security First*, these resource-driven processes accelerate, with rapid losses of remaining wilderness areas and severe impacts on biodiversity and indigenous peoples. A *Policy First* world continues to protect additional areas and introduce mitigation measures. It does so, however, at rates far below that of development, as in the previous century. Even under *Sustainability First*

conditions, increasing impacts from infrastructure — the modern world's central nervous system — as well as continued growth in human consumption of fuels, minerals and goods and services from natural resources, cannot be completely avoided. However, levels may stabilize across the 30-year period.

Together with the growing impacts of climate change, these developments severely deplete biodiversity in most regions in all scenarios (see maps on page 355). One particularly troublesome result related to climate change is that significant areas are at risk because the natural vegetation cannot adapt to the rates of change in temperature and precipitation.

Some change for the worse appears unavoidable in almost any scenario that can be considered for the next 30 years. Nevertheless, reductions in the emission of greenhouse gases, coupled with bold conservation initiatives, including the following, can have a significant limiting effect on the impacts:

- a sharp reduction in further expansion of infrastructure into remaining wilderness areas;
- curbs on further fragmentation of already impacted areas;
- implementation of mitigation measures to reduce impacts on biodiversity from existing networks;
- introduction of potentially costly restoration measures; and
- demarcation of wide buffer areas around nature reserves.

Pressures also increase on coastal ecosystems in most regions and scenarios. In addition to pressures from the direct exploitation of resources in these areas, there are also impacts from coastal infrastructure and land-based sources of pollution (see chart on page 355). These pressures are especially large in Asia and the Pacific, where they stem from various sources, dominated by agricultural activity. West Asia also faces rising pressures under *Security First* and *Markets First* conditions, but generally sound water management practices in the region have a very positive effect, especially in *Sustainability First*.

In Europe the Mediterranean coast comes under special pressure through a combination of urban growth with inadequate waste water treatment facilities, tourism and intensively farmed croplands

## Extent of built-up areas (% of total land area)

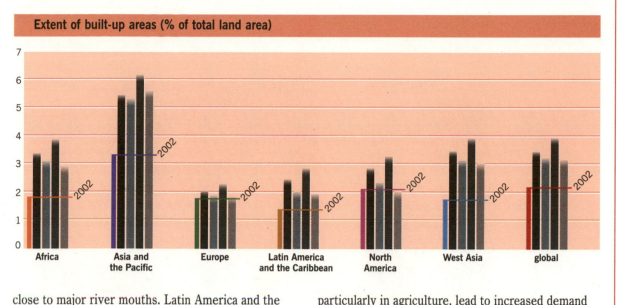

Regions: Africa; Asia and the Pacific; Europe; Latin America and the Caribbean; North America; West Asia; global

Population growth and urbanization are drivers of expanding land use for human settlements. Asia and the Pacific, Africa and West Asia see big increases to 2032, irrespective of scenario.

Source: PoleStar (see technical annex)

close to major river mouths. Latin America and the Caribbean currently features minor pressure from land-based sources of pollution along much of its coastline, compared to other regions, but this rises sharply over the coming years. North America and Africa also start from a relatively low base, but certain areas, such as the mouths of large river systems like the Mississippi and the Nile are of key concern.

## Pressure on people

The scenarios carry important implications for the provision of basic human needs that are related to broader environmental impacts. In the longer term, global climate change can have a strong impact on the local availability of freshwater. Meanwhile, growing populations and increased economic activity,

particularly in agriculture, lead to increased demand for freshwater in most scenarios.

Permutations of these pressures determine those areas and populations that face the greatest challenges in meeting needs. Outside North America and Europe, these challenges increase in all scenarios, along with a trend toward more extreme water stress (see charts on page 356). Differences in policy actions, such as reforms in the pricing of water and shifts in subsidies, and technological improvements can have a strong effect on the size of these challenges. The ability to meet these challenges reflects broader social and economic policies.

Under the *Markets First* and *Security First* scenarios, the number of people living in areas with severe water stress increases in both absolute and

### Key to charts

**Markets First**

**Policy First**

**Security First**

**Sustainability First**

## Land area impacted by infrastructure (% of total land area)

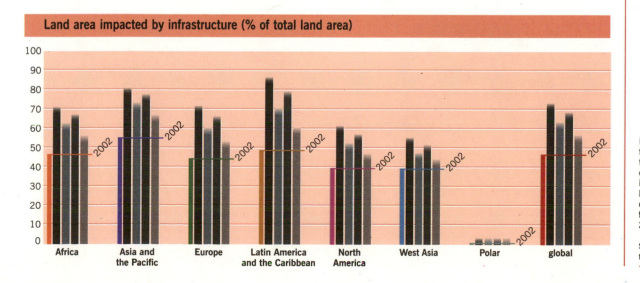

Regions: Africa; Asia and the Pacific; Europe; Latin America and the Caribbean; North America; West Asia; Polar; global

Human demands for resources and transportation continue to impact on biodiversity and ecosystem function up to 2032.

Source: GLOBIO (see technical annex)

## Ecosystems impacted by infrastructure expansion 2002

- ■ high impact
- ■ medium – high impact
- ■ low – medium impact
- □ semi-deserts and deserts
- ■ wetlands
- ■ forests
- ■ grassland/savannah
- ■ croplands
- ■ water

### Markets First 2032

### Policy First 2032

### Security First 2032

### Sustainability First 2032

Human resource demand continues to take an ever-greater toll on biodiversity. Land-use induced impacts are most often associated with existing infrastructure. In a *Markets First* scenario, biodiversity comes under threat in nearly 72 per cent of the land area by 2032. The situation is particularly critical in Southeast Asia, the Congo Basin and also parts of the Amazon. The pattern is however evident across all continents and terrestrial ecosystems with the exception of tropical and polar deserts. As much as 48 per cent is directly converted to agricultural land, plantations and built-up areas, compared to 22 per cent today, suggesting widespread depletion of biodiversity. Even the *Sustainability First* scenario suggests continued biodiversity loss across nearly 56 per cent of the land area by 2032.

Source: GLOBIO (see technical annex)

## Change in selected pressures on natural ecosystems 2002–32

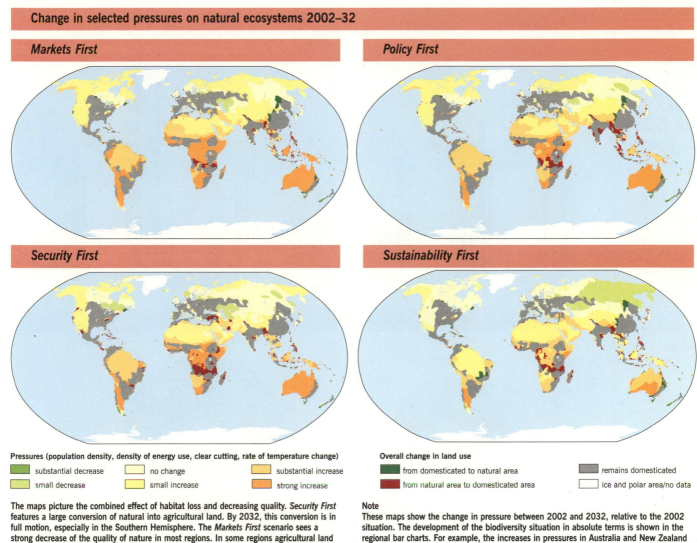

### Markets First

### Policy First

### Security First

### Sustainability First

**Pressures (population density, density of energy use, clear cutting, rate of temperature change)**

- ▮ substantial decrease
- ▮ small decrease
- ▮ no change
- ▮ small increase
- ▮ substantial increase
- ▮ strong increase

**Overall change in land use**

- ▮ from domesticated to natural area
- ▮ from natural area to domesticated area
- ▮ remains domesticated
- ☐ ice and polar area/no data

The maps picture the combined effect of habitat loss and decreasing quality. *Security First* features a large conversion of natural into agricultural land. By 2032, this conversion is in full motion, especially in the Southern Hemisphere. The *Markets First* scenario sees a strong decrease of the quality of nature in most regions. In some regions agricultural land is taken out of production and presumed to be reconverted into natural area. However, in biodiversity terms this reconverted land is of low quality during the first decades or longer. *Policy First* and *Sustainability First* show roughly comparable results in the scenario period. But their trends by 2032 are different, with *Sustainability First* moving towards a sharp decrease in pressures.

**Note**

These maps show the change in pressure between 2002 and 2032, relative to the 2002 situation. The development of the biodiversity situation in absolute terms is shown in the regional bar charts. For example, the increases in pressures in Australia and New Zealand are large in relative terms because the pressures in 2002 are small. The reverse applies to West Asia.

Source: IMAGE 2.2 (see technical annex)

## Potential increase in nitrogen loading on coastal ecosystems

| | North America | Latin America and the Caribbean | Africa | Europe and Central Asia (without Turkey) | West Asia (with Iran and Turkey) | Asia and the Pacific (without Iran) |
|---|---|---|---|---|---|---|
| *Markets First* | ●● | ●●● | ●● | ●● | ●●● | ●●● |
| *Policy First* | ● | ●●● | ●● | ● | ● | ●●● |
| *Security First* | ● | ●● | ● | ● | ●● | ●● |
| *Sustainability First* | ● | ● | ● | ● | ● | ●● |

**Expected increase by 2032**  ● small  ●● large  ●●● very large

Nitrogen loading can be taken as a proxy for a wider range of land-based pollution on coastal ecosystems. Currently it is especially large in East Asia, and Western and Central Europe and along the Mediterranean coast of West Asia and Northern Africa.

Source: IMAGE 2.2 (see technical annex)

## Key to charts

*Markets First*

*Policy First*

*Security First*

*Sustainability First*

When more than 40 per cent of the renewable water resources of a river basin are being withdrawn for human use the river basin is considered to be under severe water stress.

Source: WaterGAP 2.1 (see technical annex)

All the pie charts show total global impacts. The top left pie shows the current situation, the relative size of the others reflects the magnitude of impacts by 2032 under the four scenarios.

Source: WaterGAP 2.1 (see technical annex)

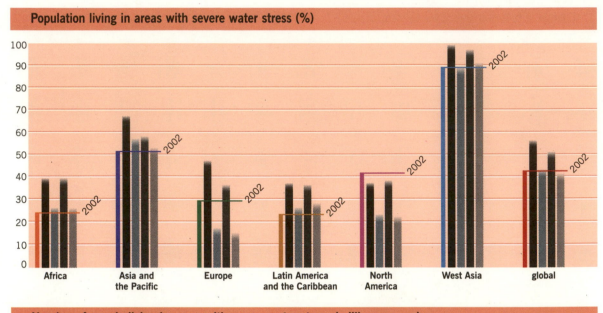

**Population living in areas with severe water stress (%)**

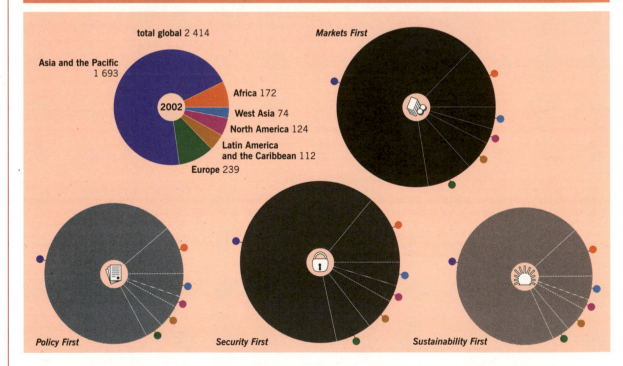

**Number of people living in areas with severe water stress (million persons)**

total global 2 414

Asia and the Pacific 1 693

2002

Africa 172

West Asia 74

North America 124

Latin America and the Caribbean 112

Europe 239

*Markets First*

*Policy First*

*Security First*

*Sustainability First*

relative terms in almost all parts of the world. These increases are partly due to continuing population growth in water-stressed areas and partly due to new areas experiencing severe water stress (namely large parts of Africa, North and Latin America and Europe). The situation is different under the *Policy First* and *Sustainability First* scenarios. In most regions the actual area under severe water stress remains more or less constant or even decreases, due to stable or

decreasing water withdrawals, particularly for irrigation. This results in little change in the overall proportion of people living in water-stressed areas by 2032. Nevertheless, the absolute number of people living in water-stressed regions increases significantly across the developing world.

Similarly, the size of demands for food and the ability to meet them in the different scenarios reflects a combination of shifts in supply and demand, which

All the pie charts show total global impacts. The top left pie shows the current situation, the relative size of the others reflects the magnitude of impacts by 2032 under the four scenarios.

Source: PoleStar (see technical annex)

## Population living with hunger (million persons)

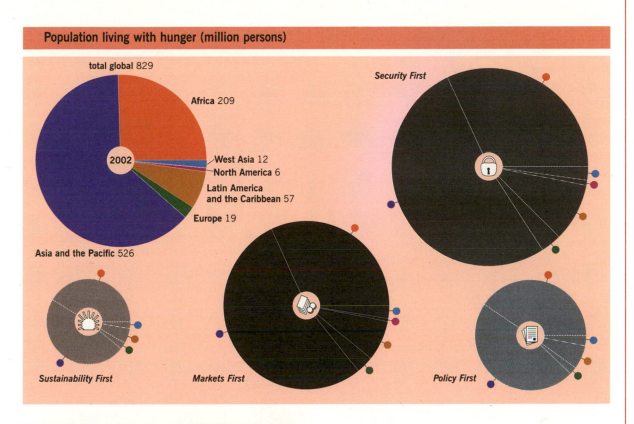

total global 829

2002

Africa 209

West Asia 12
North America 6
Latin America and the Caribbean 57
Europe 19

Asia and the Pacific 526

Security First

Sustainability First

Markets First

Policy First

## Population living with hunger (%)

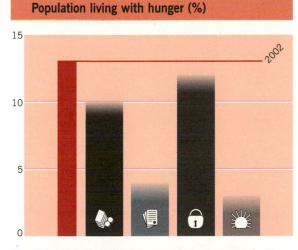

15

10

5

0

2002

A world of *Markets First*, although by no means equity-oriented, would reduce the percentage of the population living in poverty, and with it hunger. But in some regions, most notably in Africa, this does not counterbalance population growth. Committed action towards achieving social goals could bring hunger levels back into line with global targets in the Millennium Declaration.

Source: PoleStar (see technical annex)

can be influenced by social, environmental and economic policies. In a *Markets First* world, even with decreases in the percentage of the population facing hunger, the total number affected changes relatively little and even increases in some regions as populations grow (see charts). The targeting of hunger reduction as a key goal under the *Policy First* or *Sustainability First* scenarios, and the general emphasis on more balanced development between regions, helps to achieve dramatic reductions in both the percentages and the total numbers of people affected. The sharp increases in most regions in *Security First* points to the unsustainability of such a scenario in terms of social acceptability.

## Implications: Africa

Poverty is endemic in many areas of Africa and a rapidly growing population continues to rely on natural resources and agriculture for much of its economic productivity and for the provision of basic human needs. These conditions leave the region highly vulnerable to adverse impacts of environmental change. Further insights are offered below into what the scenarios mean for land, forests, biodiversity, freshwater and coastal and marine resources, all crucial to the sustainability of Africa's economies and livelihoods. Also explored (see box, page 362) is the destiny under each scenario of an African Environmental Protection Commission, established under the recently formed African Union.

### Land hunger bites

Growing populations, economic development and changes in climate all contribute to increasing the risk of land degradation in much of Africa (see chart below). Stronger economic growth in the region under *Policy First* and *Sustainability First* conditions, implies that the risk of land degradation is higher than in *Markets First*. The sharper increase apparent in *Security First* reflects the greater area of land brought into agriculture under this scenario in order to meet the demands of the still rapidly increasing population. It also indicates relative inability to fall back on food imports and diminishing rates of return from improving agricultural practice.

The translation from risk to actual degradation may be mediated in a number of ways, however (see chart). Cropland has been extensively degraded in the past in Africa due to salinization, wind and water erosion. In the worlds of *Policy First* and *Sustainability First*, easier access to support services helps farmers to manage soils better, curtailing problems like compaction,

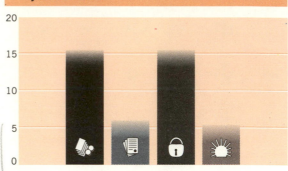

**Percentage of 2002 cropland severely degraded by 2032: Africa**

Bars represent the percentage of 2002 cropland that has become so degraded by 2032 that it is of little value for production.

Source: PoleStar (see technical annex)

erosion and salinization. Policies based on integrated land use management, including more stable land tenure systems, become commonplace in most parts of the region. Technological advances prompted by a combination of government incentives and private sector innovations, help improve productivity of degraded land. The slightly higher level of degradation in *Policy First* versus *Sustainability First* reflects slight differences in demand for food — particularly animal products. At the other end of the spectrum, in a *Security First* scenario, a combination of inequitable land distribution, poor farming methods, unfavourable land tenure systems and inefficient irrigation systems leads to declining productivity of grazing and agricultural lands. Better conditions are, however, maintained in the protected areas serving the elite. The concentration of large numbers of people in fragile areas beyond the control of the land-owning elite further contributes to the degradation of land and severe soil erosion. Similar problems arise in a *Markets First* situation as better quality agricultural land is taken over for commodity and cash crop production. The environment suffers as a result as soils are 'mined' and the use of fertilizers and pesticides becomes more extensive. Water resources and aquatic ecosystems are particularly damaged.

### Forests in flux

Much of the increased demand for food is met by conversion of forests to cropland. This is reflected in both loss of total forest area and increased exploitation of remaining forests (see chart opposite). Patterns of forest loss vary by sub-region. Very little natural forest remains in Northern Africa in any of the scenarios.

Africa is at high risk from water-induced soil erosion, except for Northern Africa where low rainfall keeps the risk extremely low. The area under risk grows considerably in all scenarios as a result of intensifying agriculture, combined with adverse consequences of climatic change.

Source: IMAGE 2.2 (see technical annex)

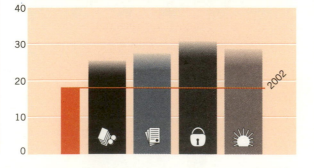

**Area with high risk of water-induced soil degradation: Africa (% of total land area)**

2002

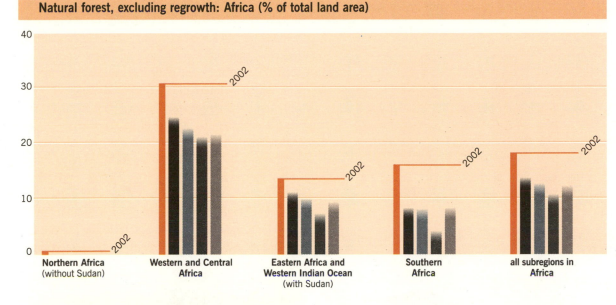

**Natural forest, excluding regrowth: Africa (% of total land area)**

Northern Africa (without Sudan)    Western and Central Africa    Eastern Africa and Western Indian Ocean (with Sudan)    Southern Africa    all subregions in Africa

Conspicuous deforestation can be expected in Africa, especially in a *Security First* scenario.

Source: IMAGE 2.2 (see technical annex)

**Land area impacted by infrastructure expansion: Africa (% of total land area)**

Source: GLOBIO (see technical annex)

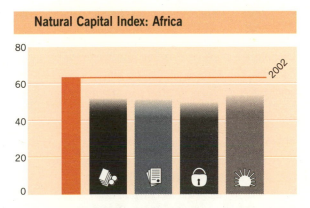

**Natural Capital Index: Africa**

An index of 100 is the situation when total land area is undomesticated and all pressures are below the minimum threshold (see technical annex). Reduction in the Natural Capital Index indicates habitat loss and increasing pressure on terrestrial and aquatic biodiversity. Pressures on biodiversity increase between 2002 and 2032 in all scenarios.

Source: IMAGE 2.2 (see technical annex)

**Key to charts**

*Markets First*

*Policy First*

*Security First*

*Sustainability First*

Elsewhere, the percentage losses are greatest in Southern Africa, but the total losses are higher in Western and Central Africa given their larger forest areas. The lack of political and market controls in a *Security First* scenario, results in the worst forest and woodland losses. Some areas are protected for the exclusive benefit of the elite, but elsewhere forest resources are overexploited for the export market. Poverty leads to overexploitation of the remaining natural forest resources for fuel, food, medicines and shelter. In a *Markets First* world, advances in agricultural efficiency and the efforts of governments and business to protect forests that serve as the backbone of an expanding forest products industry, actually keep the losses somewhat lower than in a *Policy First* world. In the latter scenario, however, benefits from the products of the forest are more broadly shared and the degree of exploitation is not as damaging. Similarly, community-based natural resources management, including reforestation programmes, help to limit the total losses in both *Policy First* and *Sustainability First* scenarios.

## Biodiversity besieged

Along with expanding infrastructure (see chart) and climate changes, land transformations leading to fragmentation and loss of habitats play a key role in determining the future of biodiversity. The combined pressures result in a lowering of Natural Capital Index in all scenarios (see chart). Strenuous efforts are made to control the degree of fragmentation in *Policy First* and *Sustainability First* even as the amount of land

When more than 40 per cent of the renewable water resources of a river basin are being withdrawn for human use the river basin is considered to be under severe water stress.

Source: WaterGAP 2.1 (see technical annex)

**Population living in areas with severe water stress: Africa (%)**

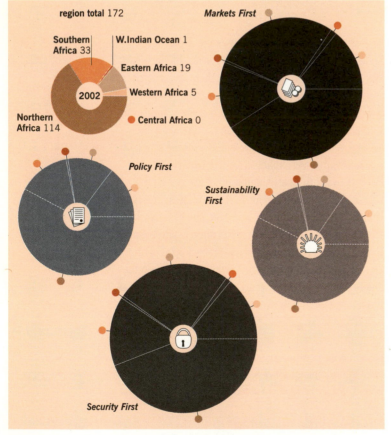

**Number of people living in areas with severe water stress: Africa (million persons)**

region total 172

Southern Africa 33    W. Indian Ocean 1

Eastern Africa 19

Western Africa 5

2002

Central Africa 0

Northern Africa 114

Markets First

Policy First

Sustainability First

Security First

All the pie charts show total region impacts. The top left pie shows the current situation, the relative size of the others reflects the magnitude of impacts by 2032 under the four scenarios.

Source: WaterGAP 2.1 (see technical annex)

converted grows to meet the demands of increasingly better-off populations. Even in these cases, biodiversity loss is unavoidable in the short term, particularly from the effects of climate change.

Although policy efforts are not quite so determined in a *Markets First* world, the protection of commercially valuable natural areas and improvements in agricultural technology provide some benefit. In a *Security First* scenario, regulatory and trade mechanisms such as the Convention on International Trade in Endangered Species of Wild Fauna and Flora (CITES) break down completely, resulting in more illegal trade in endangered species. This setback spurs further loss of biodiversity, both directly and indirectly. As populations of key species are driven to extremely low levels, the ecosystems become increasingly fragile and vulnerable to slight changes in climate and other factors. At the same time, more coercive efforts, including the use of public and private armies, do allow for the protection of strategic areas.

## Water and food: gains and strains

With a growing population and economy, the demand for water in the region is expected to grow in all scenarios. Policies regarding water pricing and technological advances may temper this in all scenarios other than *Security First*. Under the *Markets First* scenario, total water withdrawals are expected to nearly double in Africa, with particularly high increases in sub-Saharan Africa. The rise in water use linked to economic growth will outpace any savings on a per unit basis in both agriculture and industry. Similar increases are expected under *Security First* conditions, although conflicts between nations and the generally slow growth in the economy will slow the increased demand somewhat. Controls are largely absent outside of the wealthy enclaves, although pollution from these enclaves is likely to increasingly affect other areas. On both the *Markets First* and the *Security First* horizons, the African population living in areas under severe water stress increases to around 40 per cent (see charts). An especially steep rise in the number and percentage of people affected occurs in Eastern Africa, as rising water withdrawals in the Upper Nile river basin bring it into the severe water stress category under both scenarios.

Water withdrawals increase in most of sub-Saharan Africa under the *Policy First* and *Sustainability First* scenarios, yet by considerably less than in the other two scenarios — due to a combination of technology transfer and additional policies that encourage water savings. With such

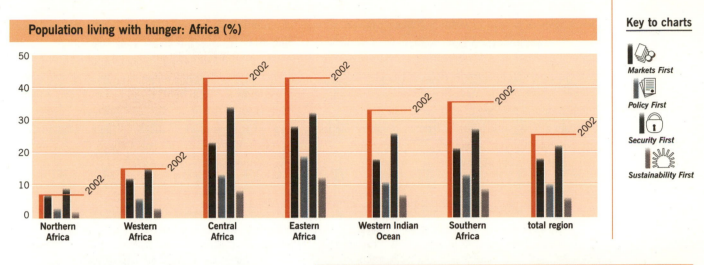

### Population living with hunger: Africa (%)

Average incomes rise in all sub-regions, contributing to a drop in the percentage of the population that is hungry. However, rapid population growth can lead to an increase in the hungry population, even as the percentage hungry declines.

Source: PoleStar (see technical annex)

**Key to charts**

Markets First

Policy First

Security First

Sustainability First

policies in place, even water withdrawals in Northern Africa are tempered, mainly by restructuring the irrigation sector. Efforts are made to enhance transboundary basin-wide management of water resources, and water quality issues receive particular attention by policy-makers, especially as these are linked to human health. Nevertheless, as population growth continues, the number of people living in areas with severe water stress still doubles in Africa under these two more reform-oriented scenarios.

The net result of all these effects is that the numbers of people living in areas experiencing severe water stress increase in all sub-regions in all scenarios, but most notably in *Markets First* and *Security First*. The percentage of people affected rises only slightly in *Policy First* and *Sustainability First* for the region as a whole, but varies within the region. Southern Africa, for example, sees a decline in these scenarios whereas Western Africa has a marked increase. Under *Markets First* and *Security First* there is an increase in all parts of the region except the Western Indian Ocean islands. In all scenarios, the most striking increases, in terms of percentages of the population affected, occur in Eastern Africa. Arid Northern Africa continues to have the highest percentage of the population impacted, whereas wet Central Africa and the Western Indian Ocean Islands have the fewest. Of course, the ability to cope with the stresses on freshwater supply will differ across the scenarios and sub-regions.

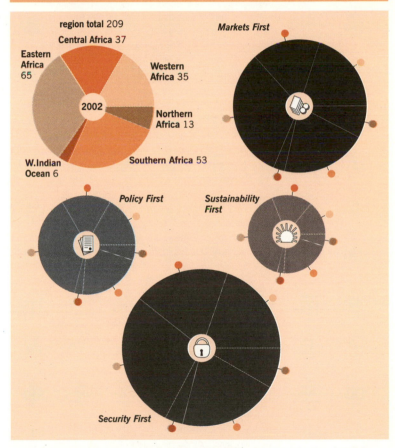

### Population living with hunger: Africa (million persons)

All the pie charts show total region impacts. The top left pie shows the current situation, the relative size of the others reflects the magnitude of impacts by 2032 under the four scenarios.

Source: PoleStar (see technical annex)

Trends in water and land, along with more broadly distributed economic growth and effective social and economic policies, are reflected in the incidence of hunger in the region (see charts). Although the percentage of people experiencing hunger falls in all scenarios, the reduction is more than offset by a rise in total population in *Markets First* and *Security First* over this period. In *Security First* the numbers of people at risk rise by more than 50 per cent. Rising inequality in both scenarios serves to negate any benefits of economic growth. Dramatic improvements are possible, though, as seen in *Policy First* and *Sustainability First*. A key here is the broader distribution of economic growth, both between Africa and other regions, but also within Africa itself.

Increased food aid and reduced conflict also have direct effects. The fundamental shifts in *Sustainability First* allow the total numbers to be cut by more than half. Despite the progress made, however, certain sub-regions remain problematic. Most notably, hunger levels in Eastern Africa remain above 10 per cent, even under *Sustainability First*.

## Imagine ... an Environmental Protection Commission for Africa

The African Union (AU) established by African countries in 2001 to replace the Organization of African Unity launches an African Environmental Protection Commission (AEPC) in the near future. The activities of the African Ministerial Conference on the Environment (AMCEN) are subsumed within the AEPC. The goal of this body is to be an environmental watchdog in the region with powers to monitor and sanction states violating regional and sub-regional environmental agreements and threatening sustainable development in the region.

This is the first time that African countries have a regional organization specifically dealing with environmental issues. Although it falls under the aegis of the AU, the AEPC charter guarantees its autonomy from political influence, though member states contribute directly to its budget. The mandate of the AEPC is to not only promote the adoption of new regional and sub-regional environmental agreements, but also monitor national-level implementation through sub-regional organizations. Strong links are established with the United Nations Environment Programme.

### In the case of ...

### Markets First

- Enforcement of conventions and protocols is compromised by the need to encourage foreign direct investment.
- Rising debt in the region fuels destructive natural resource exploitation in defiance of policy responses to Multilateral Environmental Agreements.
- Delayed impact of AEPC on sub-regional institutions hinders national enforcement of environmental measures.

### Policy First

- National governments commit themselves to strengthening AEPC by paying annual dues to the Commission.
- Governments endorse the establishment by AEPC of two standing committees of senior officials responsible for social and economic planning to boost sustainable development policy formulation and implementation.
- Regional, sub-regional and national institutions responsible for the environment are revamped to better respond to the AEPC mandate.

### Security First

- Budgetary constraints reduce AEPC to a token force funded by donors. National interests weaken AEPC initiatives, which are overruled by strict insistence on sovereignty claims.
- The role of AEPC remains peripheral at the global level as the environmental agenda continues to be set by rich countries that are reluctant to fund environmental programmes.
- Linkages with similar organizations in other regions are minimal as each region focuses on internal issues.

### Sustainability First

- National governments cede some of their authority to the AU and AEPC.
- Traditional environmental programmes are linked to innovative social and economic programmes addressing poverty in rural and urban areas in order to reduce overexploitation of resources.
- The AEPC introduces stringent measures to protect the region's intellectual property rights, thereby strengthening Africa's role in the global biotechnology trade.

### The lessons

Regional and global environmental institutions are only as strong as the commitments made to them by national governments. Without continued support, both financially and politically, their efforts are less effective and liable to lose out to conflicting interests. Nations may need to sacrifice some sovereignty in order to achieve broader environmental benefits.

## Implications: Asia and the Pacific

It is no easy matter to generalize about environmental implications of the scenarios for a region as large and varied as Asia and the Pacific. It contains the two most populated countries in the world, India and China, as well as oceanic island nations and the land-locked states of the former Asian republics of the Soviet Union. It includes some of the poorest nations of the world, some of the most dynamic economies of recent times and several industrially advanced OECD countries.

The future of the environment in the region depends on a number of currently unanswered questions. Can the region recover from the recession of the late 1990s, as all the scenarios apart from *Security First* presume? How are pressures of continued population and urban growth handled — in a relatively hands-off manner as in *Markets First* and *Security First*, or with more hands-on planning and consideration as in *Policy First* and *Sustainability First*? How does technological development fare, especially in relation to the provision of energy? Do abundant coal resources dominate energy production as in the worlds of *Markets First* and *Security First*? How do national, regional and international governance structures develop and regional and international trade regimes evolve?

The specific themes of land, forests, freshwater, urban issues and biodiversity are addressed in more detail and at the sub-regional level in the remainder of this section. The potential impacts of a dramatic decline in the availability of clean freshwater are explored in the box on page 369.

Growing populations, the spread of agriculture and climatic changes imply that the risk of land degradation increases in many parts of the region in all scenarios (see chart). Of particular concern are loss of soil fertility and soil erosion in mountainous areas, which increase downstream sedimentation. The oceanic sub-regions — the South Pacific and Australia and New Zealand — are the least threatened and South and Southeast Asia the most affected. The effect of more rapid climate change in the *Policy First* and *Sustainability First* scenarios implies somewhat higher risk than might be expected, but as the rate of change slows in the longer term compared with *Markets First* and *Security First* conditions, other effects predominate.

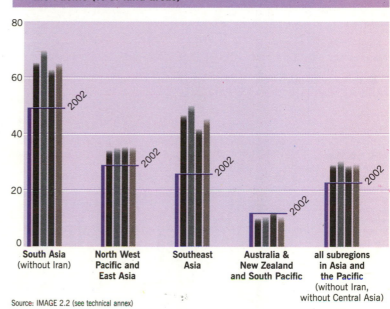

**Area with high risk of water-induced soil degradation: Asia and the Pacific (% of land areas)**

Source: IMAGE 2.2 (see technical annex)

Measures taken in *Policy First* and *Sustainability First* scenarios to improve agricultural practices limit the actual amount of degradation, at least on croplands (see chart). These policies include improvements in land tenure systems and regional cooperation in managing erosion, particularly on steep slopes. In addition, some degraded land is restored. Cropland damage is exacerbated in a *Security First* world, where there is greater reliance on uncontrolled use of chemical fertilizers and less regional and international cooperation. Such agriculture practices decline in the world of *Markets First*, but the sheer volume of economic growth and associated demand leads to degradation as great as in *Security First*.

### Key to charts

*Markets First*

*Policy First*

*Security First*

*Sustainability First*

**Percentage of 2002 cropland severely degraded by 2032: Asia and the Pacific**

Bars represent the percentage of 2002 cropland that has become so degraded by 2032 that it is of little value for production.

Source: PoleStar (see technical annex)

## Key to charts

**Markets First**

**Policy First**

**Security First**

**Sustainability First**

When more than 40 per cent of the renewable water resources of a river basin are being withdrawn for human use the river basin is considered to be under severe water stress. Nearly 1 700 million of the world's 2 400 million people in areas facing severe water stress live in Asia and numbers are highest in South Asia. Apart from wealthier countries in the region, demand for water rises significantly, with more and more people living in regions suffering from severe water stress.

Source: WaterGAP 2.1 (see technical annex)

All the pie charts show total region impacts. The top left pie shows the current situation, the relative size of the others reflects the magnitude of impacts by 2032 under the four scenarios.

Source: WaterGAP 2.1 (see technical annex)

## Population living in areas with severe water stress: Asia and the Pacific (%)

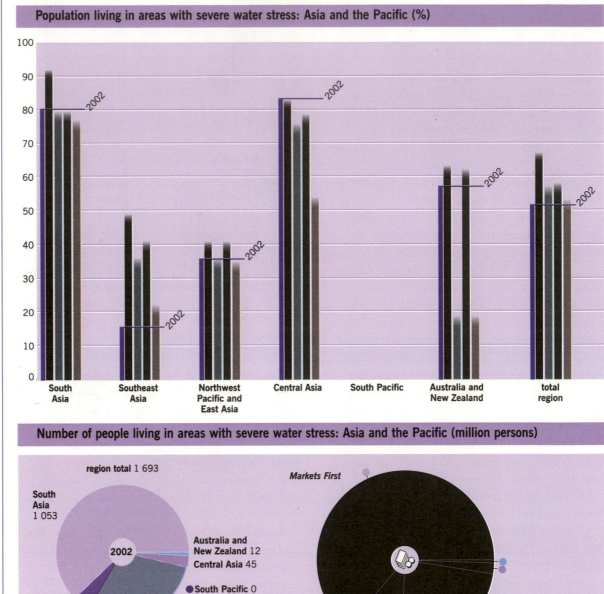

## Number of people living in areas with severe water stress: Asia and the Pacific (million persons)

## Deforestation and water stress

The risk of land degradation is linked to forest cover. A complex set of forces determines the future of forests in the region. Population growth, including urban expansion in all scenarios and economic improvements in all but a *Security First* situation, lead to mounting demand for agricultural land at the expense of forest area. Efforts to address the problems of mega-cities in the worlds of *Policy First* and *Sustainability First* also increase deforestation as settlement programmes encourage wider dispersal. In a *Security First* world there are added pressures as the poor are pushed onto ever more marginal lands.

These pressures are cushioned to some degree by advances in agricultural technology but the effects differ across scenarios. Advances may be most rapid in *Markets First*, but probably do not have environmental protection as their key goal. More importantly, economic forces such as rising prices for timber and non-timber forest products, which can encourage both deforestation and reforestation, are balanced against reductions in subsidies that have driven conversion of forest and woodlands to agriculture, and other economic instruments introduced to improve conservation. These all influence the area and condition of remaining forests. Market instruments play the biggest role in a world of *Markets First*. These are complemented in the worlds of *Policy First* and *Sustainability First* by government and local programmes to subsidize reforestation and encourage a shift to agroforestry, and by direct efforts to preserve biodiversity.

The net result is that the total area of forest in Asia and the Pacific declines over this period, but this effect differs significantly across sub-regions and scenarios. South and Southeast Asia suffer the most significant losses in total forest area. Whereas Northwest Pacific and East Asia experience a net increase in forest area due to plantations, the total area of undisturbed natural forest declines. In Australia and New Zealand and the South Pacific, the effect of replanting is such that more new forest is created than is used for logging or other production.

Water stress is presently one of the most contentious problems in Asia and the Pacific, leaving aside the small Pacific Island Countries (PICs), and it remains high on the agenda for the foreseeable future (see opposite). Growth in demand is especially high in a *Markets First* world, but also in *Policy First* and *Sustainability First*, where economic growth is similarly

robust. Water pricing and more efficient use of water in agriculture due to advances in biotechnology help to temper this growth. Under the *Markets First* scenario, water withdrawals increase in all sectors, especially when further expansion of irrigated area is assumed. These increases in water withdrawals lead to an expansion of areas with severe water stress in South and Southeast Asia in all scenarios and more people are affected throughout the region. In *Security First* overall growth in demand is moderated by slower economic growth in many sub-regions and no further expansion in irrigated areas, rather than any significant efforts to become more efficient.

Under the *Policy First* and *Sustainability First* scenarios, where effective policies and lifestyle changes combine with greater regional cooperation and technology transfer, water withdrawals remain at current levels or even decrease in most of the rest of Asia. However, with population growth continuing, the number of people living in areas under severe water stress continues to increase across Asia.

Urban areas, especially the growing mega-cities in South, Southeast and East Asia, face many trials in addition to water stress. They include land use pressures, air and water pollution and solid waste overload. All these challenges are related to rapidly growing populations, from both natural growth and rural–urban migration, and increasing economic activity. Trends in local and regional air pollution depend heavily on choices in energy production. If coal continues to dominate, as is likely in a *Security First* situation with reduced trade or in a world of *Markets First* where the cost is what counts, then local air pollution tends to worsen significantly.

The increase is most evident in *Security First*, where little effort is made to control sulphur emissions from stationary sources and nitrogen oxide emissions from stationary and mobile sources (see charts overleaf). The setting and enforcement of regulations prescribing cleaner fuels and fuel uses, cleaner technology and upgraded emission standards, all help to curb these trends in a *Policy First* world. In *Sustainability First*, major efforts towards decentralization with dispersed satellite cities relieve the pressures. This step, combined with better physical planning and management of urban systems, leads to more effective coordination of growth, distribution of clean industry, servicing, handling of pollution streams and housing design.

## Energy-related sulphur dioxide emissions: Asia and the Pacific (million tonnes sulphur)

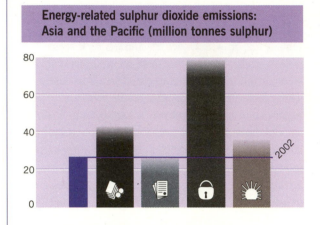

Sulphur dioxide emissions increase most rapidly in a *Security First* world because little money is invested to reduce emissions. In the other scenarios, especially in *Policy First* and *Sustainability First*, the increase of $SO_2$ emissions is less as steps are taken to avoid severe air pollution. In some sub-regions emissions drop below 2002 levels.

Source: AIM (see technical annex)

## Energy-related nitrogen oxide emissions: Asia and the Pacific (million tonnes nitrogen)

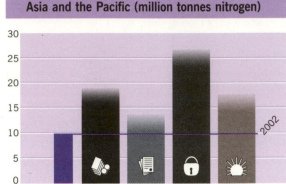

Nitrogen oxide emissions grow rapidly with the increase of motorization and rise even in a *Policy First* scenario. A very high increase is expected in South Asia in line with the large increase in motor traffic.

Source: AIM (see technical annex)

### Key to charts

**Markets First**

**Policy First**

**Security First**

**Sustainability First**

These policies help to buffer ill-effects in the *Policy First* and *Sustainability First* scenarios, but the higher levels of economic growth make environmental protection difficult. In all scenarios, the amount of built-over land grows significantly across the region (see chart below).

Similarly, $CO_2$ emissions and production of solid waste (see opposite) increase in most scenarios. Emission standards, which tend to be weak or lacking in a *Security First* situation, help to limit the growth in air pollutants in the other scenarios, especially in *Policy First*. Emissions of $CO_2$ increase more rapidly in *Markets*

*First* circumstances because of high economic growth. In *Policy First*, advanced technologies are introduced to reduce $CO_2$ emissions. Because a *Sustainability First* society shifts from conventional to sustainable lifestyles, $CO_2$ emissions are somewhat mitigated. On the other hand a *Security First* society holds on to technologies with low energy efficiency. $CO_2$ emissions increase most rapidly in this scenario everywhere except in Central Asia where low economic activities mitigate $CO_2$ emissions vis-à-vis *Markets First*. The effects of lifestyle changes are also evident in the lower levels of solid waste production in *Sustainability First*.

Built-up area expands as both population and built environment per head of population grow. The latter value is among the lowest in the world in Asia, but with rising incomes and expanding infrastructure, each person's footprint, as measured in built land, grows over the course of the scenarios.

Source: PoleStar (see technical annex)

## Extent of built-up areas: Asia and the Pacific (% of total land area)

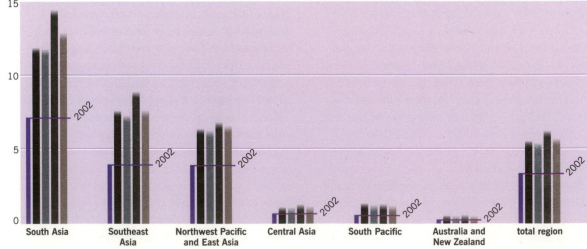

**Energy-related carbon dioxide emissions: Asia and the Pacific (million tonnes carbon)**

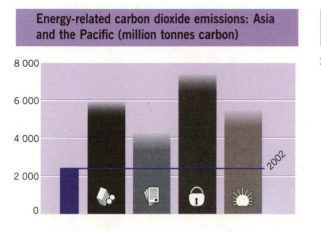

Trends under different scenarios are similar throughout the region and reflect both state of technology and lifestyles.

Source: AIM (see technical annex)

**Land area impacted by infrastructure expansion: Asia and the Pacific (% of total land area)**

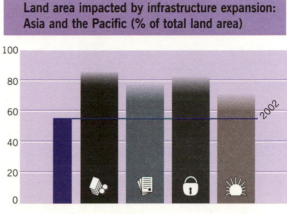

All sub-regions in Asia and the Pacific show a similar pattern between scenarios as infrastructure expands.

Source: GLOBIO (see technical annex)

**Municipal solid waste generation: Asia and the Pacific (index related to value of 1 for base year 1995)**

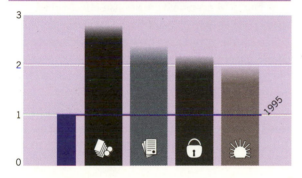

Total municipal waste is expected to increase more than 150 per cent by 2032 in South Asia, Southeast Asia and Central Asia in a *Markets First* scenario. Municipal waste generation is closely linked to income level and size of population.

Source: AIM (see technical annex)

## Bad news for biodiversity

Growing populations, expanding urban and declining forest areas and increasing economic activity put increased pressures on terrestrial and marine biodiversity. The growth in infrastructure alone to meet growing demands has a large and increasingly significant impact across the region in all scenarios (see chart). Better planning, coordination and enforcement of land use policies alleviates this somewhat in *Policy First* and *Sustainability First*. The lack of such policies in a *Security First* world, coupled with higher population growth, leads to impacts almost

as large as in *Markets First*, even with much slower economic growth.

At the same time as infrastructure is expanding, changing climate affects biodiversity, resulting in significant reductions in the quantity and quality of natural capital in some sub-regions over the next 30 years. As with other pressures, these differ significantly across the sub-regions, with the most significant pressures on biodiversity occurring in South and Southeast Asia under all scenarios (see overleaf).

Finally, increases in trade affect biodiversity, particularly in the worlds of *Markets First* and *Policy First*. Under *Security First* conditions, reductions in trade and greater control of the exploitation of particular areas may actually benefit biodiversity in these areas, whereas other areas suffer from lack of control.

Some of these pressures on biodiversity are countered in a *Policy First* world by regional cooperation to reduce illegal extraction and establish more protected areas. In a world of *Sustainability First*, advances in technology enable real-time identification and monitoring of biodiversity assets and sensitive ecosystems. Communities are better equipped with knowledge and understanding of the dynamics of environmental systems, tools for strategic assessment and planning. Over time this results in a greater representation of species, communities and genes within protected areas. Maintenance of endemic genetic stocks provides

An index of 100 is the situation when total land area is undomesticated and all pressures are below the minimum threshold (see technical annex). Reduction in the Natural Capital Index indicates habitat loss and increasing pressure on terrestrial and aquatic biodiversity. Pressures on biodiversity increase between 2002 and 2032 in all scenarios.

Source: IMAGE 2.2 (see technical annex)

Average incomes rise in all sub-regions, contributing to a drop in the percentage of the population that is hungry. However, rapid population growth can lead to an increase in the incidence of hunger, even as the percentage of people at risk declines.

Source: PoleStar (see technical annex)

All the pie charts show total region impacts. The top left pie shows the current situation, the relative size of the others reflects the magnitude of impacts by 2032 under the four scenarios.

Source: PoleStar (see technical annex)

## Key to charts

Markets First

Policy First

Security First

Sustainability First

## Natural Capital Index: Asia and the Pacific

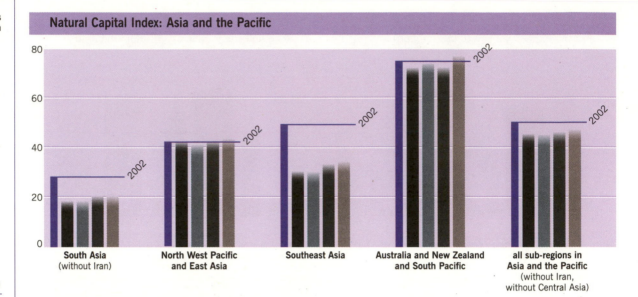

## Population living with hunger: Asia and the Pacific (%)

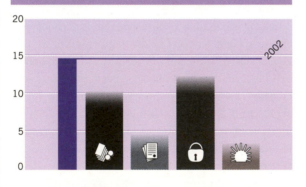

valuable source materials for biotechnology advances, captures benefits for local communities and reduces opportunities for invasive species to take over.

Relevant environmental trends, along with the distribution of economic growth and effectiveness of social policies, are reflected in the incidence of hunger in the region (see charts). The percentage of people experiencing hunger remains high in much of the region in *Markets First* and *Security First*. With growing populations, this implies only slight reductions in absolute numbers in the former and small increases in the latter. Dramatic improvements

## Population living with hunger: Asia and the Pacific (million persons)

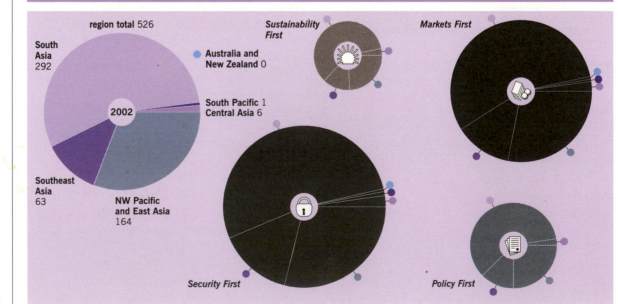

are possible, though, as seen in the *Policy First* and *Sustainability First* results where there are steep reductions in both the percentage and the total hungry. In the *Policy First* scenario this is achieved through a combination of relatively high growth and more equitable income distribution. In the *Sustainability First* scenario it comes about as greater equity both between and within countries is reflected in rapid economic growth and a narrowing of income distributions.

## Imagine ... widespread surface and groundwater contamination in Asia and the Pacific

Rapidly growing populations and economies escalate demand for food and living space, leading to greater intensification of agriculture. More irrigation and fertilizer use in rural areas, together with unimpeded growth of urban centres and mega-cities, mean more competition for water resources between geographic regions and economic sectors. This rivalry reaches crisis proportions around 2010, when the quality of surface and ground waters across the region begins to go into widespread, rapid and accelerating decline. The surface water changes are a reaction by aquatic ecosystems to the cumulative loading of nitrogen and other organic materials from inadequately treated agricultural and municipal solid waste. The impacts on groundwater arise from the run-off of chemical fertilizers and pesticides from agriculture as well as toxic materials from industry. The effect is enhanced by the more rapid extraction of groundwater resources, resulting in a further increase in the concentration of these pollutants in the remaining groundwater as well as increased rates of salt water intrusion in the region's extensive coastal areas.

**In the case of ...**

### Markets First
- Some agricultural production is affected and food prices rise significantly, stimulating increasing food trade within the region and imports from other regions.
- Private biotechnology companies compete to provide genetically engineered pollutant-eating bacteria.
- Private companies contract with urban governments to transport uncontaminated water from other regions, including freshwater in the form of icebergs from the Antarctic.

### Policy First
- Policies to move industry toward zero emissions production are accelerated.
- Public investment into genetic engineering in order to produce pollutant-eating bacteria increases.
- Water rationing is introduced and water saving devices distributed to urban populations, where treatment is unable to make up for water lost due to quality declines.
- Policies to integrate water resources management into development plans are promoted, with a focus on the integration of land and water related issues within a river basin or water catchment area.

### Security First
- Water resources are placed under public and private military control.
- There is a sharp increase in deaths related to water-borne diseases such as cholera.

### Sustainability First
- The move toward more organic and low-input sustainable agriculture receives a major boost as producers using these methods cope better with the disruptions and are seen as having a neutral impact on the problem.
- Urban areas that have already implemented advanced water-saving, waste reduction and waste treatment practices expand their campaign to accelerate the introduction of similar practices across the region.

**The lessons**

It can often take crisis situations to induce necessary changes that lead to more sustainable practices. In any case, coping with issues such as freshwater quantity and quality requires an integrated perspective that recognizes interactions between sectors and the potential for threshold effects in natural systems from cumulative pressures. Part of this shift involves encouraging diversity in agricultural and other economic systems so that when surprises and crises occur, a versatile repertoire enables new strategies to be formed.

## Implications: Europe

Over the next 30 years, Europe is dominated by the reintegration of Western, Central and Eastern Europe following the end of the Cold War. In both *Markets First* and *Policy First* worlds, expectations of a significant expansion of the European Union are borne out. This process may stall in a *Security First* scenario or take on a very different form in a world of *Sustainability First*. In all four scenarios, the relationships between those countries within the EU and those outside — notably the Russian Federation — are significant in determining, among other things, the state of the environment in this region. The differences in the evolution of such bodies as the European Environment Agency, which is likely to become much stronger in a world of *Policy First* or *Sustainability First*, also play a role.

Developments in Europe's relationships with other regions are also important. The contrast between greater openness to trade and migration in *Markets First* and *Policy First* worlds and a possible reversal of both in a *Security First* situation, imply significant impacts either way. Similarly, differences in the evolution of multilateral environmental agreements make a conspicuous mark.

Two critical areas of development are agricultural policy and the relationship between climate, energy and transport. They are explored here together with other issues, in the contexts of atmosphere, land, biodiversity, freshwater and coastal and marine areas. Finally, the implications under each scenario of a major food scare brought on by a combination of factors are explored in the box on page 373.

Europe's scope to address the issues of large-scale air pollution and greenhouse gas emissions depends heavily upon developments in the areas of energy use and transportation. Whereas extremely active policies to improve public transportation, for reasons of both pollution and congestion control, and to improve energy efficiency can be expected in *Policy First* and *Sustainability First* worlds, these advances are unlikely in *Security First* or even *Markets First* circumstances. In the *Markets First* case, some economic policies, such as road and carbon taxes, are likely and technological developments will continue to improve the energy use per unit of activity. Growth in volume of travel and economic activity in general is, however, expected to outweigh per unit improvements in response to these

policies. In a *Security First* situation, lack of economic development in Central and Eastern Europe restrains energy use in general.

### Emissions and land use — turning points

These changes in energy use, along with shifts in fuel use, are reflected in gaseous emissions, notably of carbon dioxide (see chart). There are some striking differences between scenarios and sub-regions. The growth in emissions is quite significant in all regions in *Markets First*, with transport contributing a major share. The economic difficulties in *Security First* for Eastern Europe result in approximately the same level of emissions as in *Policy First*, where more proactive policy action prompts improved energy use and a switch to non-carbon fuels. In a *Sustainability First* situation, strong policy actions and changes in lifestyles, including the willingness of more people to shift to public transport, achieve significant reductions, heralding a turning-point in the battle to reduce human-induced climate change.

Land use change in Europe is affected by decisions related to spatial planning of development and transportation policies. It is also driven by the evolution of agricultural policy, including changes in agricultural trade regimes and the reform of the Common Agricultural Policy. In the *Markets First* scenario, the built-up area grows over time in Western Europe (see opposite). Elsewhere, population decline leads to a stable or modest decrease in the total built-

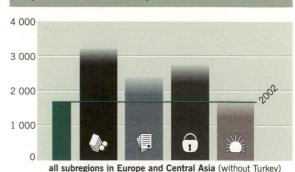

**Energy-related carbon dioxide emissions: Europe (million tonnes carbon)**

**all subregions in Europe and Central Asia** (without Turkey)

In three of the four scenarios, Europe's total carbon dioxide emissions increase, diminishing the chances of eventual climate control. The shorter term target of the Kyoto Protocol may be met in a *Policy First* world, but certainly not in a *Markets First* or a *Security First* scenario.

Source: IMAGE 2.2 (see technical annex)

up area in *Markets First* and throughout the region in *Policy First* and *Sustainability First*, where already compact settlement patterns combine with lower population growth to reduce the need for expansion of built-up areas. In *Security First*, rising populations and more sprawling settlements trigger sizeable growth of built-up areas in Western Europe but little increase in the rest of the region.

At the same time, continued development of roads, plantations and other human works will lead to the extension of infrastructure throughout the region and in all scenarios, with a general increase in levels of impact (see chart). Even so, careful policies — including restrictions on the siting of infrastructure — can help to lessen the effect of this expansion. This potential is most evident in Eastern Europe. In *Markets First* and *Security First*, rising pressures to develop resources and infrastructure reduce remaining biodiversity. Impacts include loss of reindeer and wolf populations and of many insects and plants adapted to farmed conditions. To restore lost habitat, particularly where lost agro-ecosystems and wetlands are concerned, would require *Sustainability First* conditions.

These pressures play a role in determining land-based biodiversity in the region. Europe must also contend with the effects of changing climate conditions, including those determined by greenhouse gas emissions that have already occurred. Overall, differences between the various scenarios by 2032 are small, owing to the delayed effect of climatic changes over foregoing decades. Furthermore, in the short term, the greater regional and global reductions in sulphur oxides and other pollutants seen in *Policy First* and *Sustainability First* actually result in faster climate change, increasing the pressure on ecosystems. However, present-day initiatives such as the EU's Natura 2000 take effect and pan-European networks of protected areas and green corridors are launched to protect biodiversity more effectively in *Sustainability First* and possibly in *Policy First*, too. Effective action to rehabilitate former agricultural land as additional habitats for wildlife also plays an important role. This is reflected in the somewhat better results for the Natural Capital Index (see chart overleaf) in *Sustainability First*.

Shifts in agriculture, along with improved technologies, management practices and shifts in crop choices reduce overall water demand in agriculture in

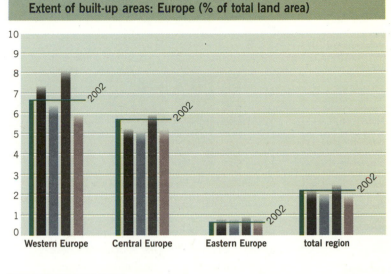

**Extent of built-up areas: Europe (% of total land area)**

Source: PoleStar (see technical annex)

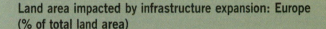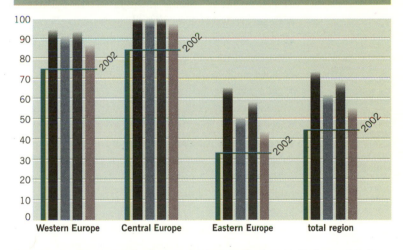

**Land area impacted by infrastructure expansion: Europe (% of total land area)**

Much of Central and Western Europe has been directly converted to farmland. The few remaining low-disturbance areas are limited to Scandinavia and protected areas, where tourism and recreational development is putting increasingly greater strain on mountain ecosystems. Restoration of former wetlands has begun, but still on a much smaller scale than the continued development of infrastructure.

Source: GLOBIO (see technical annex)

all scenarios other than *Security First*. Under the *Markets First* scenario, however, economic development still leads to sharp increases in overall water demand, especially in Eastern and Central Europe. With these increases comes expansion of areas in the severe water stress category. Overall demand in a *Security First* scenario is similar, with the greater population by comparison with *Markets First* somewhat offset by reduced economic activity.

**Key to charts**

Markets First

Policy First

Security First

Sustainability First

An index of 100 is the situation when total land area is undomesticated and all pressures are below the minimum threshold (see technical annex). Reduction in the Natural Capital Index indicates habitat loss and increasing pressure on terrestrial and aquatic biodiversity. As the pressure from agriculture stabilizes and starts to decrease, the general biodiversity situation in Europe over 30 years does not deviate much from the present.

Source: IMAGE 2.2 (see technical annex)

When more than 40 per cent of the renewable water resources of a river basin are being withdrawn for human use the river basin is considered to be under severe water stress. Water stress in Europe is as much about water quality as it is about water quantity, and due to high water withdrawals many of Europe's waters are severely over-used. However, in regions in which demand for industrial purposes dominates the water use sector, water can often be heavily re-used, mitigating the effects of severe water stress.

Source: WaterGAP 2.1 (see technical annex)

### Natural Capital Index: Europe

all subregions in Europe and Central Asia (without Turkey)

The situation is very different under the *Policy First* and *Sustainability First* scenarios, where structural changes lead to reductions in water withdrawals in all sectors across Europe. Through these continuing efforts to save water, some of the river basins that currently experience severe water stress, no longer do so under these scenarios. With this advance, the number of people who live in areas with severe water stress drops significantly. These changes are most dramatic in *Sustainability First*, where declines in meat consumption augment policies, such as water pricing, introduced in the other scenarios. Differences in the amount of wastewater that is purified and industrial recycling of water amplify the differences between the scenarios. These changes are reflected in the number of persons subject to water stress in the sub-regions across the different scenarios (see charts). Potential problems related to water stress in *Policy First* and *Sustainability First* are reduced by full implementation of the Water Framework Directive and agreements regarding regional seas. Meanwhile, these problems intensify in a *Security First* world,

### Population living in areas with severe water stress: Europe (%)

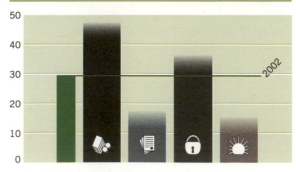

leading to conflict over water and contamination from uncontrolled industrial activity and the inability to deal with the legacies of former lax policies.

## Coastal concerns

Coastal and marine environments are also a key concern in Europe. In a world of *Markets First*, tourism exercises an ever-increasing pressure on coastal zones throughout the region, leading to an

### Number of people living in areas with severe water stress: Europe (million persons)

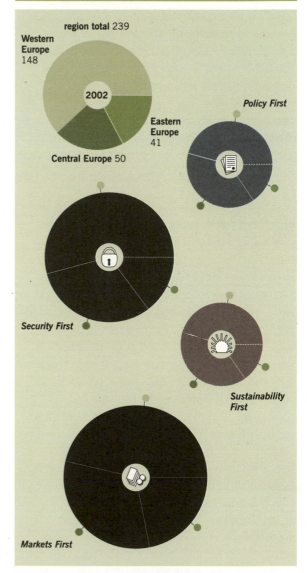

All the pie charts show total region impacts. The top left pie shows the current situation, the relative size of the others reflects the magnitude of impacts by 2032 under the four scenarios.

Source: WaterGAP 2.1 (see technical annex)

increase of local environmental problems such as salinization. In addition, second homes exercise a considerable footprint in some areas such as the Baltic. Specifically in Eastern Europe, coastal zones are increasingly left to local authorities to manage, with somewhat unpredictable outcomes.

Under *Policy First* conditions, governments acquire some coastal zones in Western Europe for full protection status. In Eastern Europe, basic legislation regarding coastal zone protection is put in place and zoning plans are revitalized. In a *Security First* situation, coastal zones in Western Europe see a continuation of industrial development, tourism development, airport construction and other infrastructure. In Central Europe, coastal zones remain by and large as they were in 2002.

In Eastern Europe, coastal zones may be re-militarized, restricting access, but also used for new port development. On balance, pressures remain at approximately the same level as in 2002. In *Sustainability First*, integrated coastal zone management schemes based on voluntary partnerships and participatory arrangements, significantly improve coastal environments.

**Key to charts**

Markets First

Policy First

Security First

Sustainability First

---

## Imagine ... a major food scare in Europe

A major food scare breaks out in Europe in the middle of the 2010s, reminiscent in some respects of the Spanish cooking oil disaster in the 1980s or the BSE crisis in the 1990s. But this crisis is on a much larger scale and so is its psychological impact. It erupts with simultaneous outbreaks of death and illness among young children in various parts of Western and Central Europe. With casualties growing, the cause remains elusive for at least a year. Speculation is widespread about a link with genetically modified organisms or biotransplants, but there is no conclusive evidence. Eventually, the cause is found to be a hitherto uncommon mycotoxin. It turns out that a fungus in many cereals, the emergence and spread of which appears related to the changing climate, produces this toxin. Unfortunately, the news does little to diminish the problem for a culture that relies on bread as a staple food.

**In the case of . . .**

### Markets First
- Consumer distrust rises in Western and Central Europe. This leads to agricultural demise in countries for which the EU is a key export market in the 2010s, such as Argentina, Ukraine, Romania, Latvia and Kenya.
- Stricter certification schemes are put in place, stimulated by initiatives by transnational corporations.

### Policy First
- There is European-wide coordination on issues such as sharing the burden of the costly recall of cereals and a rush programme to develop alternative bases for common children's food, many of which rely on the affected cereals. Heavy reliance is set on early warning systems and regulation of developments in biotechnology to avoid similar outbreaks in the future.
- There is a renewed global effort to address climate change.

### Security First
- Initial fears of a biological weapons attack cause several nations to place themselves on military alert.
- Xenophobic reactions to illegal immigrants increase as they are seen as potential carriers of exotic viruses.
- Trade disputes increase, stemming from fears of other possible outbreaks.

### Sustainability First
- Efficient support systems, notably at local level, help to minimize deaths and to optimize treatment of victims.
- Ongoing agricultural reforms, which are further accelerated in the aftermath, help reduce the spread of the fungus.

**The lessons**

The roots of many environmental crises can lie in the very complexity of human and natural systems and their interactions. Recognizing this and remaining alert to unexpected developments can help to reduce shocks and to respond to crises when they occur. Foresight, early warning and flexible response provisions can play key roles.

## Implications: Latin America and the Caribbean

The future of the environment in Latin America and the Caribbean is driven by many internal and external factors that differ across the four scenarios. At the heart of issues such as economic growth, social development and environmental health are the region's internal policies and its unbalanced relationship to its neighbours to the north. An increasingly integrated Western Hemisphere is envisioned in both *Markets First* and *Policy First* scenarios. Greater cooperation, but in a less formal setting is expected in *Sustainability First*. Developments in regional and international trade regimes have both positive and negative effects. The greatly increased trade posited in a world of *Markets First* opens the door to bigger exports of agricultural and forest products. While these may be beneficial economically, they also put increased pressure on resources. More care is taken to consider social and environmental impacts in both *Policy First* and *Sustainability First*.

Internally, evolving governance concerns and the issues of poverty, inequality and urbanization in large part determine environmental developments in the region. Major issues to be confronted by the region include deforestation, water shortages and land degradation. All these issues are explored here, focusing on the themes of land, forests, coastal and marine areas, biodiversity and urban areas. The box on page 379 explores the possible impacts in the region of a major world recession.

### Forests — a mixed fate

Land and forest degradation as well as forest fragmentation remain among the most relevant environmental issues in this region in all scenarios. The patterns of conversion of forests to pasture and agricultural land vary by scenario and sub-region. Just as important as the total forest area is the level of exploitation of the forests.

Significant loss of forest area occurs in a *Markets First* scenario. This scenario also sees much greater exploitation of existing forests. In a *Security First* world, the control over forest resources by transnational companies that create cartels in association with the national groups in power, promote the growth of some forest areas, but this is not enough to stop net deforestation. Private control of forests also leads to occasional violent resistance from forest dwellers and nearby settlers who need access to the forests to meet their daily needs.

More effective management remedies some of these problems in *Policy First*. In this scenario, policies to promote forest plantations are enacted and institutional strengthening creates better forest control, reducing illegal extraction of timber from native forests and promoting sound forest management practices for commercial production. However, deforestation remains a problem and pressures also arise on forests from the desire to be more self-sufficient in food production. Unsound deforestation stops almost completely in *Sustainability First*. Policies addressing the restoration of degraded forests through the natural regeneration of forest ecosystems are implemented as the value of forest services is internalized by world markets. Moreover, the use of alternative fuels to firewood is now more scientifically and economically feasible, while commercial use of forests under forest management certification regimes has turned out to be highly profitable.

Changes in land cover pose risks for land degradation (see chart opposite). In *Markets First* and *Security First* worlds, the agricultural frontier continues to expand into rainforest ecosystems. This expansion is driven by large commercial livestock farming and industrial cropping, along with influxes of immigrants attracted by these developments and by new infrastructure projects. Exacerbated by drought, many more desertification hotspots are evident by 2032. Land tenure reforms ameliorate these drivers in *Policy First* and *Sustainability First* but not in the other scenarios. However, enforcement of direct and indirect regulations does lead to improvements in controlling soil erosion, dramatically reducing the amount of cropland lost to degradation. In addition, some degraded land is restored, leading to markedly lower net rates than in *Markets First* or *Security First* (see opposite).

### Cities sprawl

Prominent among other land use changes is the continued growth of urban areas (see opposite). Built-up area per person continues to grow in the *Markets First* scenario, tending towards the sprawling settlement patterns of North America. Despite relatively compact settlement patterns in *Policy First* compared to *Markets First*, higher income growth is

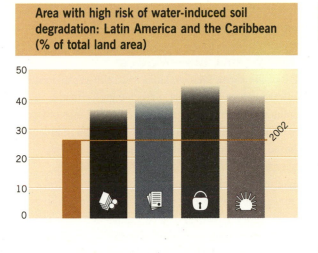

**Area with high risk of water-induced soil degradation: Latin America and the Caribbean (% of total land area)**

Source: IMAGE 2.2 (see technical annex)

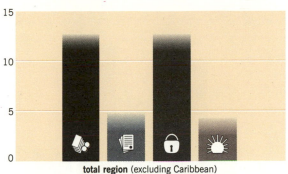

**Percentage of 2002 cropland severely degraded by 2032: Latin America and the Caribbean**

**total region** (excluding Caribbean)

Bars represent the percentage of cropland that has become so degraded by 2032 that it is of little value for production.

Source: PoleStar (see technical annex)

accompanied by a more rapid expansion in built-up land. As a result, the built-up area in *Policy First* is only slightly below *Markets First*. Unplanned expansion and rapid population growth lead to substantial growth in built-up area in *Security First*. In *Sustainability First*, as in *Policy First*, a tendency towards compact settlement patterns is offset by more rapid economic expansion. However, the offset is only partial and total built-up area grows least in this scenario.

Expansion of urban conditions raises problems of water quality, waste management, air pollution and general sprawl throughout much of Latin America. Economic driving forces continue to attract people to the cities, especially in *Markets First*. Without improved planning and organization, the environmental pressures on urban areas, especially in mega-cities, continue to grow as the rates of population growth outpace that of infrastructure development. This effect is stepped up in a *Security First* world, where the affluent increasingly withdraw into their enclaves, denying the poor access to safe drinking water, sanitation and health services. The quality and quantity of water and the disposal of solid waste are major worries in the small island countries and territories of the Caribbean. Unchecked air pollution has serious and costly health impacts, especially for urban populations (see chart overleaf).

In a world of *Policy First*, measures to curb urban migration and to improve public transportation systems and the collection, disposal and recycling of domestic

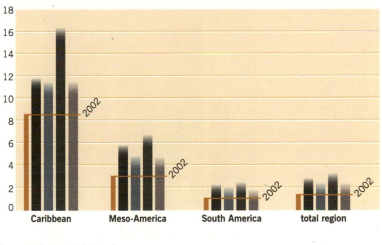

**Extent of built-up areas: Latin America and the Caribbean (% of total land area)**

Caribbean    Meso-America    South America    total region

Source: PoleStar (see technical annex)

and industrial wastes, diminish — but do not eliminate — the vulnerability of cities and their inhabitants to human-induced and natural disasters. More success is achieved in a world of *Sustainability First*. Air pollution declines due to effective regulation and targeted technological progress. The dissemination of sound knowledge and scientific advice, and the transfer of appropriate technology, further improve waste management. Waste generation declines in relative terms and its quality and composition allows for higher rates of reuse, recycling and use in energy production. Finally, more equitable distribution of income and

**Key to charts**

Markets First

Policy First

Security First

Sustainability First

Source: IMAGE 2.2
(see technical annex)

## Key to charts

*Markets First*

*Policy First*

*Security First*

*Sustainability First*

Increased industrial exploration for oil, gas and minerals accelerates road construction, which in places encourages encroachment into forests and subsequent conversion of land to plantations and farmland. Conversion of tropical rainforest to farmland and for ranching purposes constitutes one of the greatest threats to biodiversity.

Source: GLOBIO (see technical annex)

An index of 100 is the situation when total land area is undomesticated and all pressures are below the minimum threshold (see technical annex). Reduction in the Natural Capital Index indicates habitat loss and increasing pressure on terrestrial and aquatic biodiversity.

Source: IMAGE 2.2
(see technical annex)

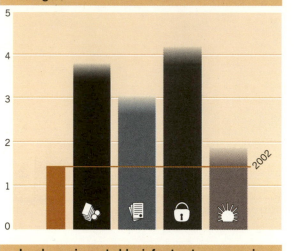

**Energy-related nitrogen oxide emissions: Latin America and the Caribbean (million tonnes nitrogen)**

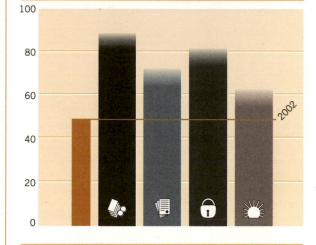

**Land area impacted by infrastructure expansion: Latin America and the Caribbean (% of total land area)**

**Natural Capital Index: Latin America and the Caribbean**

wealth between urban and rural areas has a moderating effect on rural-to-urban migration.

## Ecosystems and species at risk

All of the above factors, along with the expansion of infrastructure (see chart) and changing climate, influence biodiversity in the region. The loss of forest area leads to decreases in natural capital and in land-based biodiversity in all but a *Sustainability First* scenario (see chart). In *Policy First* conditions, improved monitoring and management of critical ecosystems in the protected areas help to conserve biodiversity. However, the continued demands and somewhat higher economic growth than in a *Markets First* situation work against these changes.

Better knowledge of — and keener concern for — ecological systems foster more effective stewardship of both marine and terrestrial biodiversity in *Sustainability First*. Innovative approaches help many previously threatened species to recover. From both the scientific and aesthetic perspectives, biodiversity has been given a high value, widening the number of species available for pharmaceutical and food purposes. New areas have also been incorporated into the national protected areas systems for the protection of biodiversity, as well as to provide environmental services and recreation. In both *Markets First* and *Security First* scenarios there is likely to be extreme degradation and even destruction or disappearance of unique ecosystems and some endangered species.

## Shadow over seas and coasts

In *Markets First*, the uncontrolled expansion of coastal settlements, proliferation of tourist resorts, uncontrolled discharge of wastes into oceans, expansion of aquaculture and lack of strong regulations and enforcement over fisheries all pose dangers for the marine and coastal environment, especially for small islands in the region. In *Policy First*, some pressure on fisheries is reduced by direct regulation efforts and the implementation of market-based instruments, but still the biomass of certain inshore species drops significantly. In a *Security First* situation, reduced economic activity may outweigh the lack of controls, sparing some areas from these effects. More integrated ecosystem management schemes, such as coastal and river basin management plans, including surveillance systems and the control

**Population living in areas with severe water stress: Latin America and the Caribbean (%)**

When more than 40 per cent of the renewable water resources of a river basin are being withdrawn for human use the river basin is considered to be under severe water stress.

Source: WaterGAP 2.1 (see technical annex)

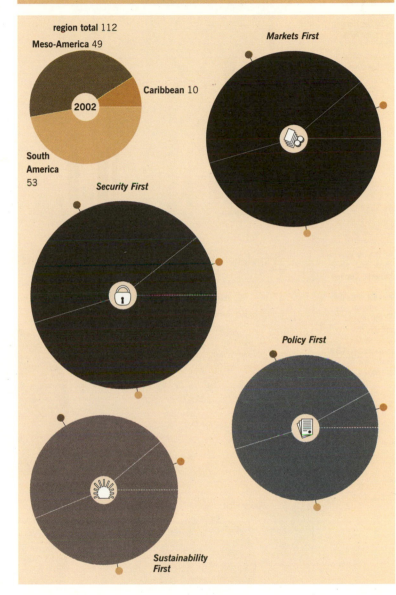

**Number of people living in areas with severe water stress: Latin America and the Caribbean (million persons)**

region total 112
Meso-America 49
Caribbean 10
2002
South America 53
Markets First
Security First
Policy First
Sustainability First

All the pie charts show total region impacts. The top left pie shows the current situation, the relative size of the others reflects the magnitude of impacts by 2032 under the four scenarios. In Latin America about a quarter of the total population — more than 100 million people — are estimated to live in water stressed areas, mostly in Mexico, Argentina and countries along the Western coastline of the continent.

Source: WaterGAP 2.1 (see technical annex)

of land-based sources of pollution that affect inland and marine waters, ease the situation in *Policy First* and still more so in *Sustainability First*.

## Food and water fears

The scenarios also have important implications for the provision of basic needs that are related to the broader environmental impacts. While global climate change affects the availability of freshwater, growing populations and increased economic activity, particularly in agriculture, lead to increased demand for freshwater in most scenarios. Similarly, more people live in areas experiencing water stress in all scenarios (see charts). Under the *Markets First* and *Security First* scenarios, the area affected by severe water stress increases in Meso-America and the Caribbean, while it remains constant in South America. Nevertheless when population growth is factored in, numbers of people living in areas with severe water stress increase by a factor of two to three. The number of people living in areas with severe water stress is also on the rise under the *Policy First* and *Sustainability First* scenarios, despite total water withdrawals staying roughly at current levels. In *Policy First* circumstances, reforms in the pricing of water and shifts in subsidies, and technological improvements have a positive effect on addressing demands.

Similarly, the size of, and ability to meet, demands

for food in the different scenarios reflects a combination of shifts in supply and demand, which can be influenced by social, environmental and economic policies. Average incomes rise in all regions, contributing to a drop in the percentage of the population that is hungry. In the *Markets First*

Rise in average incomes and improvement in equity are key factors in reducing hunger in *Policy First* and *Sustainability First* scenarios.

Source: PoleStar (see technical annex)

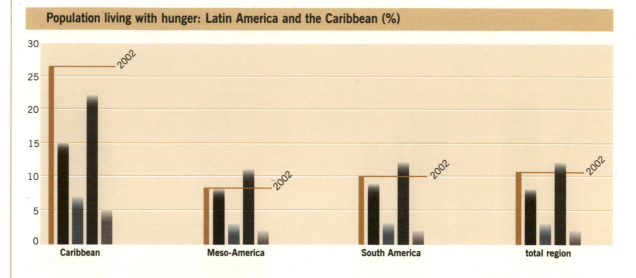

**Population living with hunger: Latin America and the Caribbean (%)**

All the pie charts show total region impacts. The top left pie shows the current situation, the relative size of the others reflects the magnitude of impacts by 2032 under the four scenarios.

Source: PoleStar (see technical annex)

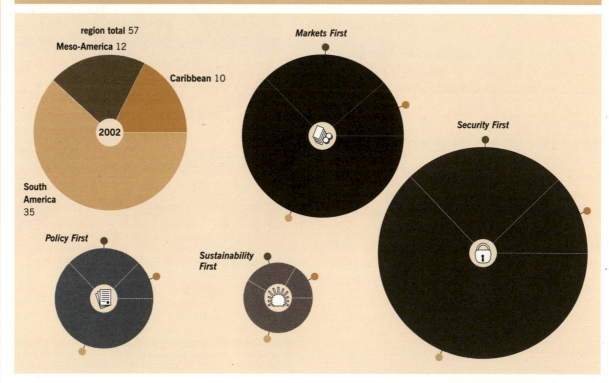

**Population living with hunger: Latin America and the Caribbean (million persons)**

region total 57
Meso-America 12
Caribbean 10
2002
South America 35
Markets First
Security First
Policy First
Sustainability First

**Key to charts**

Markets First

Policy First

Security First

Sustainability First

scenario, the relatively high inequality in Latin America today is moderated somewhat as regional patterns converge towards those of the industrialized regions. Nevertheless, the benefits of growth and narrowing income distribution are not enough to offset the growth in population and total numbers rise. In the *Policy First* scenario, a combination of relatively high growth and comparatively equitable income distributions leads to a sharp drop in the percentage

hungry, as well as in the total. In the *Security First* scenario, diverging income distributions lead to a worsening in both the percentage and the total who are hungry in the region as a whole. In the *Sustainability First* scenario, greater equity both between and within countries is reflected in rapid economic growth and narrowing income distributions, leading to a strong decline in both the percentage and the total who are hungry (see charts).

## Imagine ... effects on Latin America and the Caribbean of a profound world recession

A profound economic recession starts in the industrialized world and soon spreads around the world, destabilizing most of the leading developing economies. The flow of capital between the developed and developing countries changes direction as international investors move financial assets back home or to wealthier countries. Local capital is moved towards more attractive and safe destinations. Serious fiscal and trade deficits force governments to implement restrictive policies to reduce expenses and imports while encouraging more exports. Environmental budgets are among the first to be cut and exploitation of natural raw materials is intensified to boost export earnings, though with little effect on employment. Social expenditures are also cut drastically.

**In the case of ...**

### Markets First

- Public and private sector expenditures are cut and funds reallocated among sectors to favour exports. Overall production is significantly reduced. Treasury officials neglect issues that they regard as low priority, not least environmental and social programmes, and those relating to compliance with environmental law.
- Adverse social effects include increases in poverty and inequality and a rising flood of migrants.
- Virtually uncontrolled exploitation of natural resources runs to extremes. The Amazon Basin and other rainforest areas are ruthlessly exploited and invaded by migrants from depressed areas. New desertification hotspots appear and numbers of people in areas under water stress expand. Fishing and aquaculture thrive, heedless of environmental impacts.

### Policy First

- New policies boost production of exports and import substitutes and raise the region's competitiveness.
- International agreements on environment and labour standards among countries of the region are consolidated.
- Although the recession harms all sectors of the economy and sets back environmental and social progress — especially in least-developed countries — the region is well-placed to overcome the crisis.

### Security First

- Impacts of recession are most keenly felt in mega-cities. Unprecedented levels of unemployment prompt migration from relatively urbanized sectors of cities to the outskirts and to sites exposed to landslides, floods and other risks. People grow increasingly vulnerable to outbreaks of infectious diseases.
- Domestic and industrial solid waste overload becomes a major environmental hazard.
- In rural areas, poverty and loss of environmental quality create a vicious spiral. Land degradation intensifies and desertification hotspots increase.

### Sustainability First

- The events and aftermath of 11 September 2001, joined to the outcomes of the Johannesburg Summit, spark awareness of anti-poverty and pro-environment imperatives and governments commit themselves to change. By 2010, the world and the region are both firmly set on a path towards sustainability.

### The lessons

Pressure to produce exports is best directed onto activities that are founded on sustainable production practices. Impacts of recession on employment can be lessened, health problems can be minimized and the tide of economic and environmental migrants can be stemmed without resorting to destructive or exploitative practices. Even so, it may sometimes take negative impacts caused by overexploitation of natural resources to create the awareness that production systems relying on them for raw materials need to be improved along more sustainable lines.

## Implications: North America

The North American region is one of the world's least densely populated and consists of just two countries, both advanced industrial economies undergoing a transition to more information-based systems. Both have relatively long records of environmental management. For these reasons, more than perhaps any other region, the environmental impacts of the four scenarios on this region are reflected as much in its influence on inter-regional and global issues. A more internationally engaged North America, as in the worlds of *Policy First* and *Sustainability First*, has a strikingly positive effect on environmental impacts at a global level and in other regions. Similarly, a North America that is only engaged at an economic level, as in a world of *Markets First*, or with only selected groups in other regions, as in a *Security First* world, has big and often negative impacts.

Environmental impacts still occur within the region, however, and these vary between scenarios. This

To a large extent, policies to reduce emissions in *Policy First* and *Sustainability First* can harvest co-benefits with other policy imperatives.

Source: IMAGE 2.2
(see technical annex)

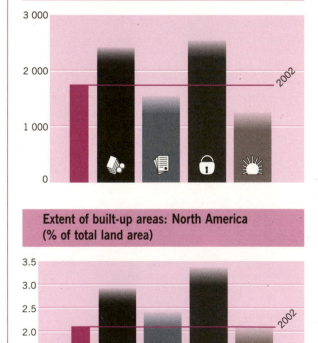

**Energy-related carbon dioxide emissions: North America (million tonnes carbon)**

Source: PoleStar
(see technical annex)

**Extent of built-up areas: North America (% of total land area)**

section takes a look at a number of these in the areas of the atmosphere, urban areas, water stress, land degradation, land-based biodiversity and coastal and marine areas. The specific issue of potential water stress in the mid-continent and its wider repercussions is explored in the box on page 383.

### Emissions pendulum

As a predominant emitter of greenhouse gases, North America plays a major role in determining the future climate of the planet. In *Markets First* the region's refusal to participate notably hampers international efforts to control emissions of these gases. The region remains the highest emitter on a per person basis and also among the highest in absolute terms (see chart). This happens despite overall improvements in energy efficiency stimulated by increasing fuel prices and general technological advance. Transportation-related emissions show the sharpest increase as motor fuel gains a greater share of total energy consumption, pushing up total emissions as it does so. The collapse of parts of the transport infrastructure and the growing restriction of ownership of fossil-fuel-powered vehicles to the elite in *Security First* are not enough to counteract the overall impacts of expanding population, resulting in even greater increases in emissions in this scenario.

In a world of *Policy First*, North America's success in implementing policies to reduce carbon emissions in an economically efficient manner leads to reductions in the region's contribution to global emissions. Nevertheless, emissions per person remain relatively high, at over twice the world average. Emissions from transport and other sources decline through a combination of increased fuel efficiency and greater use of public transport. Even more spectacular results are seen in a world of *Sustainability First* as greenhouse gas emissions plummet, a goal thought to be unrealistic just a few decades earlier. This transformation is due to technological advances, but more importantly to changes in lifestyle reflected in reductions in per person energy use to the point where it is only slightly higher than that in other developed countries.

One of the most visible impacts of reliance on the automobile is urban sprawl — low urban population densities with heavy reliance on personal transport. The dominance of the automobile culture is also a major factor in local air pollution. These issues continue to plague many cities in the region in both *Markets First* and *Security First*. In the *Markets First* scenario, the built-up area expands over time (see chart opposite), continuing an upward trend in the region, albeit more slowly than in the past. Combined with rising population, the built environment per person expands significantly.

In *Security First*, faster population increase and sprawling settlements lead to even greater growth in built-up areas. Here, the sprawling urban spaces that are the legacy of the 20th century are further burdened with a decaying infrastructure. Waste treatment declines steeply and water-borne diseases spread. Populations also rise in the *Policy First* scenario, but a tendency towards more compact settlements stabilizes the built-up area. In *Sustainability First*, the values of the scenario are reflected in much more compact settlements than in the past, or in the other scenarios. Combined with relatively smaller populations, the built-up area declines as the scenario unfolds.

A *Policy First* world sees the built-up environment creating less pressure on land resources and ecosystems (see chart). More effort is put into repairing ageing infrastructure, particularly in the inner cities. In Canada, large land areas continue to be set aside for indigenous people, with likely positive future outlook for many of the ecosystems involved. However, very extensive mining, hydropower, oil and gas development projects, along with forest road construction continue to reduce wilderness areas. In *Security First* and *Markets First*, exploration processes increase substantially, not least in Alaska, Yukon and Quebec, although these inroads are slightly smaller in the former scenario due to lower economic growth.

Going further in a world of *Sustainability First*, the great urban centres of North America begin a slow process of reorganization in response to the popular desire for greater proximity of home, work, commerce and leisure activity. For many, the 'towns within cities' that begin to emerge from the process by 2032 provide an attractive balance between access to a lively culture and the immediacy of a small community. Others opt for greater access to green spaces, leading to small towns dispersed around larger metropolitan centres, connected by advanced transport systems.

Continued advances in information technology expand the options for living and working arrangements and a diverse range of lifestyle choices emerges. A common feature of most of these lifestyles is that they are far less resource intensive, automobile-dependent and stressful than their 20th century antecedents.

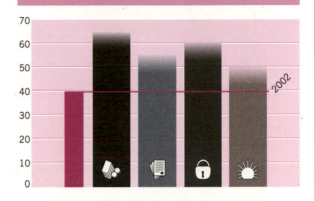

**Land area impacted by infrastructure expansion: North America (% of total land area)**

Source: GLOBIO
(see technical annex)

People enjoy a strong sense of affiliation with their local, national and global communities.

Climatic change and the introduction of exotic species pose additional threats to land-based biodiversity in the region. Although natural forest area remains relatively constant in the region in all scenarios, in some cases there is swift expansion of plantations, built areas and agricultural land, with associated infrastructure. This is particularly the case under the *Markets First* scenario with its strong economic growth. The diverse biota found in wetlands also continues to be threatened by conversion and degradation of these ecosystems.

Natural vegetation in much of the region, particularly in the north, is threatened by changes in climate. There are slightly greater impacts of climate change in *Policy First* and *Sustainability First* scenarios, reflecting the short-term effects of efforts to reduce other pollutants, especially sulphur dioxide, in addition to greenhouse gases. However, over the next 30 years the climate change situation is dominated by the momentum built up before 2002 and there is little overall difference in Natural Capital Index between the scenarios (see chart overleaf). The full effects of climate change will be apparent only after 2032.

Biodiversity in coastal and marine ecosystems also faces threats from infrastructure development, pollution and climate change. In the cases of *Sustainability First* and *Policy First*, the slower growth in infrastructure and significant changes in agricultural policy lead to important reductions in land-based sources of pollution. The effects of climatic changes lag somewhat behind those on land-based biodiversity, because of the slower changes in water temperature, but significant threshold effects

An index of 100 is the situation when total land area is undomesticated and all pressures are below the minimum threshold (see technical annex). Reduction in the Natural Capital Index indicates habitat loss and increasing pressure on terrestrial and aquatic biodiversity.

Source: IMAGE 2.2 (see technical annex)

**Key to charts**

Markets First

Policy First

Security First

Sustainability First

## Natural Capital Index: North America

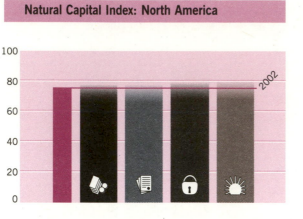

may play a role here. In fisheries, greater cooperation both within the region and with other regions in *Policy First* and *Sustainability First* contributes to the preservation and restoration of important fish stocks. Some of the pressure on marine resources is reduced by the expansion of aquaculture in these scenarios, as well as in *Markets First*. The potential for international conflicts over marine resources within the region and with other regions is high in *Security First*, with negative implications for the health of aquatic ecosystems.

### Water withdrawals ease

Certain areas of North America, particularly the southwest of the United States, are already subject to high levels of water stress. Without strong action to reduce water use, this is likely to grow with population increases and shifts in geographic distribution. Local policies, such as water pricing, can significantly affect demand. In addition, international policies related to agricultural trade can strongly affect crop type and therefore, irrigation requirements and water use. Advanced technologies, including biotechnologies to develop more water efficient crops and improve irrigation efficiency, can also have a striking effect. Total water withdrawals decrease under the *Policy First* and *Sustainability First* scenarios, where structural changes lead to reduced withdrawals in all sectors across North America.

## Population living in areas with severe water stress: North America (%)

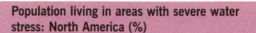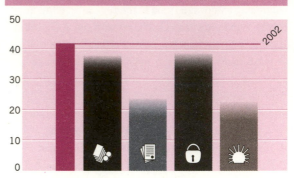

When more than 40 per cent of the renewable water resources of a river basin are being withdrawn for human use the river basin is considered to be under severe water stress. In many of the river basins of the western United States, home to over 100 million people, withdrawals currently exceed these limits.

Source: WaterGAP 2.1 (see technical annex)

## Number of people living in areas with severe water stress: North America (million persons)

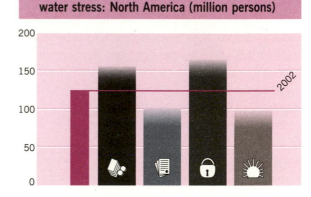

Source: WaterGAP 2.1 (see technical annex)

Under *Markets First* and *Security First* conditions, the number of people living in areas with severe water stress increases with population growth although there is a decline in percentage of population affected. Regulatory efforts in *Policy First* and *Sustainability First* lead to much more significant decreases in percentages as well as reductions in total numbers (see chart).

## Imagine ... increased water stress in mid-continental North America

A number of trends point to increased vulnerability of large areas of mid-continental North America to water stress. These include continued draw down of major aquifers and indications of chemical contamination. At the same time, climate models point to mid-continental drying and lowering of both lake and river levels. An extended hot, dry period starting midway through the 2010s exacerbates these trends. The demand for irrigation water increases at the same time as its availability declines. Transport on the Great Lakes and on major rivers such as the Mississippi, faces disruption.

### In the case of ...

#### Markets First

- Widespread introduction of water pricing and the removal of agricultural subsidies have already led to the reduction of agriculture in the region, somewhat reducing pressures on water demand.
- Deals are struck to explore transport of water from the Great Lakes or even more remote sources, to increase water levels in the Mississippi River system.
- Amounts of goods transported by road increase.
- Production loss drives more intensive farming elsewhere in the United States, such as California's Central Valley, fuelling water conflicts there. Higher water prices almost everywhere hit marginal businesses and the poor.
- The region increases imports from abroad to meet domestic shortfalls. This move boosts economies in some producer countries but also makes local and national food security problems worse in situations where land is taken out of the local food production system to meet export demands or quotas.

#### Policy First

- Research and legislative efforts are implemented to encourage the introduction of more efficient irrigation methods such as drip irrigation.
- Processes of reform are accelerated to introduce water pricing and begin to reduce agricultural subsidies.
- Initiatives are launched throughout the region to enhance rail transport.
- There is a new push for a strong international climate stabilization treaty.
- Energy efficiency, renewable energy and forest conservation programmes are promoted and speeded up.
- Bio-engineered cultivars that yield more 'crop per drop' are researched, developed and introduced faster.

#### Security First

- Competing interests in the United States and Canada contest plans for big-scale transfer of water from the Great Lakes.
- A powerful farm lobby continues to oppose reform in the system of agricultural supports and water subsidies.
- Knock-on effects of water diversions aggravate long-standing Mexico–United States rows over shared water resources.
- Falling food exports and rising prices for food commodities on the world market contribute to food shortages, heightening geopolitical tension and giving rise to violence in hotspot areas.

#### Sustainability First

- A shift to rain-fed crops and restoration of much of the region to its original tall grass prairie is accelerated.
- Efforts to enhance rail transport throughout the region are introduced.
- There is a more rapid shift away from meat-based diets, allowing more efficient land uses for human food rather than animal fodder.
- Consumer movements call for and galvanize more dispersed, sustainable and localized farming systems.
- There is a fundamental re-think of lifestyles, economic development and social policy, responding to an emerging awareness that intensive use of capital, water and chemicals by agri-business cannot be sustained, as well as to awareness of parallel problems in other economic sectors and environmental frameworks.

### The lessons

Many — if not all — economic systems depend heavily on natural systems but regrettably the latter are too often taken for granted or assumed to be unlimited or easily replaceable. Given the inherent variability and mutability of natural systems, policies should be designed to reduce excessive levels of dependence, especially in the presence of potential threshold effects whereby small changes can prompt catastrophic effects.

## Implications: West Asia

West Asia is characterized by relatively high population growth rates, heavy economic dependence on oil production, fairly severe water stress and pockets of conflict or unrest. Developments in all these respects, along with the promotion of technological advances in areas such as desalination and biotechnology, vary markedly between the four scenarios. As in other regions, these shifts are largely driven by trends and events in the areas of governance and culture, and in relations between nations within and outside the region. Possible outcomes in terms of environmental impacts are considered in more detail below for land, freshwater, biodiversity, urban areas and coastal and marine resources. The repercussions of an extended drought in the region are explored in the box on page 389.

### Vulnerable land

Pressures on West Asia's limited arable lands are driven by the ever-expanding food demands of a growing population and expansion of other land uses, including urbanization, industrial activities, infrastructure and tourism. In *Markets First* and *Security First* scenarios, transfer of arable land to these sectors continues in the absence of effective arable land protection policies. The built-up area expands (see chart) in step with growth in population. Built environment per person continues to grow in *Markets First*, with sprawling settlement patterns.

**Key to charts**

*Markets First*

*Policy First*

*Security First*

*Sustainability First*

Rapid population growth and unplanned expansion lead to even greater growth in built-up area in a *Security First* world. In *Sustainability First* and *Policy First*, more rapid economic expansion is partially offset by a tendency towards compact settlement patterns. Expansion of built-over land in *Sustainability First* is the smallest among all four scenarios.

The land that remains in agriculture is susceptible to water-induced soil degradation (see chart). In *Policy First*, implementation of a regional food demand management strategy results in more food being imported from other regions. This spares arable land from increased pressure for local food production. In

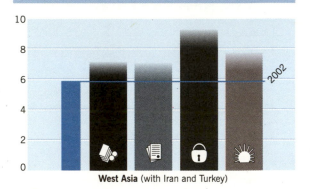

**Area with high risk of water-induced soil degradation: West Asia (% of total land area)**

West Asia (with Iran and Turkey)

Water-induced soil degradation continues to be a risk throughout the region.

Source: IMAGE 2.2 (see technical annex)

**Extent of built-up areas: West Asia (% of total land area)**

Arabian Peninsula    Mashriq    total region

Source: PoleStar (see technical annex)

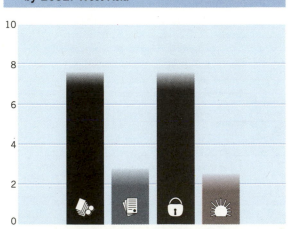

**Percentage of 2002 cropland severely degraded by 2032: West Asia**

Bars represent the percentage of cropland that has become so degraded by 2032 that it is of little value for production.

Source: PoleStar (see technical annex)

*Sustainability First*, there is slightly more land susceptible to soil degradation than in either the *Policy First* or *Markets First* scenarios because more arable land is kept in production. The greatest risk is in a *Security First* situation, where management is poorest and more marginal land is used.

## Coping with land and water problems

In all scenarios except *Security First*, some forms of land use planning and effective arable land protection policies are implemented to prevent actual degradation of the extremely scarce cultivable land in the region. As a result, the rate of land degradation and loss slows down and gradually stabilizes. In a *Markets First* scenario, the available cropland is managed more carefully than in the past, in the interest of protecting agricultural markets. However, population and economic growth more than counteract these efforts (see chart opposite). Land conservation in *Policy First* and *Sustainability First* leads to much slower cropland degradation. In addition, some degraded land is restored, leading to substantially lower net rates than in *Markets First* or *Security First*. In *Sustainability First* reductions in population growth and well-researched advances in biotechnology and genetic engineering further offset these pressures.

Water stress in West Asia continues to increase as water demands exceed available water resources, owing to population growth and expansion of different development sectors (see charts). In *Markets First* and *Security First*, deteriorating water quality and increasing competition between sectors, users or both, hampers food production and leads to conflicts (mainly between the domestic and agricultural sectors), increasing water-related health problems. Water withdrawals are slightly higher in *Security First*, due to more water-cooled thermal electricity production. Improved irrigation efficiency and minor shifts in irrigated areas (under *Markets First* only) lead to decreasing water withdrawals for irrigation. In total, water withdrawals increase slightly under both scenarios, leading to an increase in areas with severe water stress and affecting over 200 million people. Demand management and conservation policies are introduced gradually in *Markets First* as the degree of water scarcity rises in individual countries but there is no strategic water resources planning in a *Security First* world. In this scenario, water scarcity reaches its highest levels in the Arabian Peninsula, in terms of

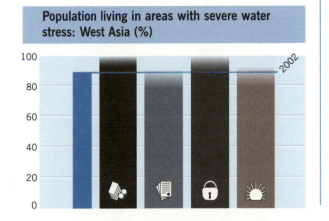

**Population living in areas with severe water stress: West Asia (%)**

When more than 40 per cent of the renewable water resources of a river basin are being withdrawn for human use the river basin is considered to be under severe water stress.

Source: WaterGAP 2.1 (see technical annex)

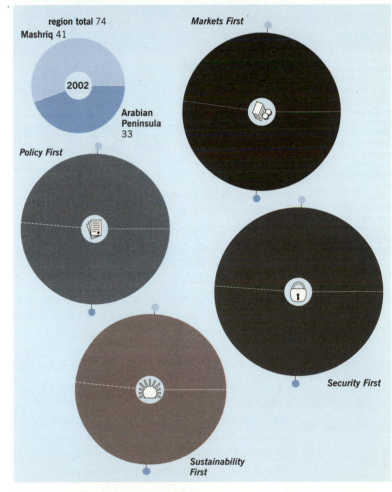

**Number of people living in areas with severe water stress: West Asia (million persons)**

region total 74
Mashriq 41
2002
Arabian Peninsula 33

Markets First

Policy First

Security First

Sustainability First

All the pie charts show total region impacts. The top left pie shows the current situation, the relative size of the others reflects the magnitude of impacts by 2032 under the four scenarios. West Asia is one of the most water stressed regions of the world, with over 80 per cent of its area under severe water stress and over 70 million people (or nearly 90 per cent of the region's total population) living in these areas. In both sub-regions, the irrigation sector dominates the total water withdrawals, both under current conditions as well as under all four scenarios.

Source: WaterGAP 2.1 (see technical annex)

Source: GLOBIO
(see technical annex)

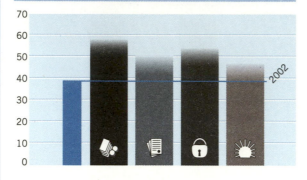

**Land area impacted by infrastructure expansion: West Asia (% of total land area)**

**Natural Capital Index: West Asia**

West Asia (with Iran and Turkey)

An index of 100 is the situation when total land area is undomesticated and all pressures are below the minimum threshold (see technical annex). Reduction in the Natural Capital Index indicates habitat loss and increasing pressure on terrestrial and aquatic biodiversity. Biodiversity is severely impacted between 2002 and 2032 in all scenarios, but especially under *Security First*.

Source: IMAGE 2.2
(see technical annex)

**Key to charts**

*Markets First*

*Policy First*

*Security First*

*Sustainability First*

the number of the population affected, and groundwater resources, the principal source of water in this sub-region, are depleted and deteriorate to the extent that they are no longer directly usable.

Under the *Policy First* and *Sustainability First* scenarios, reductions in irrigated areas in the region, combined with structural changes in the way water is used in industry, lead to reductions in total water withdrawals. Accordingly some river basins drop out of the severe water stress category. In *Policy First*, the area under water stress is stabilized by adopting strategic water resources management to increase water use efficiency and resource protection. A major policy shift, from 'supply augmentation' towards 'demand management and conservation' occurs. This shift is achieved through water pricing, awareness and education campaigns, enforcement of legislation and management of marginal water, as well as more efficient allocation of water resources among the competing economic sectors. In *Sustainability First*, the increase of freshwater made available by desalination technology, wide application of

biotechnology in the field of food production and decrease in population growth rate in the region, help to counteract the effects of additional demand related to higher economic growth. In both scenarios, however, water scarcity persists and affects growing numbers of people as water demand continues to exceed available water resources.

The impact of water stress in the different scenarios also depends on relations between individual countries in West Asia and on West Asia's relations with other regions. About 60 per cent of surface water resources originate from outside the region. In *Security First*, countries sharing river basins fail to sign conventions and agreements on sharing and management of water resources, including surface and groundwater, or on monitoring their quantity and quality. In *Markets First*, equitable sharing of surface water resources among such countries might eventually be reached, limiting conflicts and tension. This shift also helps overall development, increases agricultural production and reduces uncertainty in planning. Even so, construction of dams in upstream countries continues, curbing downstream flows, increasing tension in the region and impacting river and marine ecosystems downstream. This situation is exacerbated by cyclical droughts common to the region. In *Security First*, conflicts and tension increase within the region, as well as with countries outside the region, eventually leading to water wars. These concerns ease in *Policy First* and *Sustainability First* as countries negotiate agreements on the equitable sharing of surface water resources.

Such steps are taken further in *Sustainability First*. A total catchment management approach is widely adopted and conventions agreed on sharing and managing groundwater resources to safeguard both quantity and quality. There is also greater cooperation between countries on dam construction, including environmental impact assessments that look at potential impacts on downstream parts of the river and marine ecosystems.

## Natural capital leaks away

West Asia also faces increasing pressures on its biodiversity. Infrastructure expands in all scenarios (see chart), destroying and fragmenting the region's ecosystems. These pressures lead to steady decline in populations of wild species, a growing list of threatened species and an overall and continual loss of biodiversity. These trends are counteracted to some degree in *Policy First* and *Sustainability First* circumstances by implementing land use management plans to reduce human pressures on natural ecosystems. Other counter measures include legislation protecting biodiversity and endangered species as well as regulating the introduction of foreign and genetically modified organisms. Only slower economic growth in *Security First* keeps the expansion of infrastructure and its impacts below that of *Markets First*.

Other problems, particularly climate change, join with these pressures to diminish natural capital in the region in all scenarios. In *Policy First*, present efforts to enlarge protected areas continue and may reach international targets. In addition, regional cooperation and transboundary reserves are established between neighbouring countries. Public awareness is stimulated through botanical gardens and museums. These efforts go further in *Sustainability First* where there is greater local control of resources. The extent of protected areas reaches target levels, halting depletion of biological resources. Furthermore, the region witnesses an increase in cooperative regional research, investment and sustainable use of genetic and biological resources through the use of advanced technology. However, even here the efforts are not enough to fully counteract the effects of changing climate (see chart opposite).

The somewhat slower onset of climate change in *Markets First* means that the losses to natural capital are somewhat less than in *Policy First* and *Security First*. In *Security First*, the introduction of foreign and genetically modified species carries on unregulated, posing a major additional threat to indigenous species in the region. Moreover, efforts already under way become increasingly ineffective under declining economic and environmental conditions and food insecurity. Significantly, many indigenous biological resources in the region could be completely lost.

Differences in population growth, urban planning and zoning, rural area development and the situation of refugees all influence the level, type and impact of urbanization across the region. Rapid unplanned urbanization and high population concentrations caused by rapid population growth, rural to urban migration and the increase in refugee numbers are

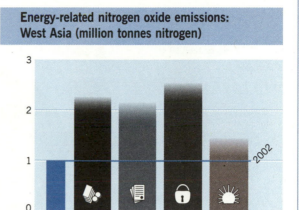

**Energy-related nitrogen oxide emissions: West Asia (million tonnes nitrogen)**

West Asia (with Iran and Turkey)

Source: IMAGE 2.2
(see technical annex)

factors in both *Markets First* and *Security First*. All have negative environmental and health consequences in terms of local air pollution (see chart), add to waste production and encourage encroachment on limited agricultural and recreational areas. Basic healthcare, sanitation and infrastructure facilities fail to cope.

More effective urban planning and zoning prevail in *Policy First* and *Sustainability First* scenarios. Rural to urban migration is reduced conspicuously by well-planned integrated development of rural areas. In *Sustainability First*, rural area development includes environmental considerations to minimize encroachment and loss of agricultural and recreational lands, stimulating some reverse migration. Finally, in the Mashriq, the environmental and health problems associated with refugee centres are solved as part of the resolution of conflicts in the region.

Associated with the differences in land use and freshwater management, as well as other developments, the scenarios also differ in their implications for coastal and marine areas. Under the *Policy First* and *Sustainability First* scenarios, member states in the Arabian Gulf ratify the Convention for the Prevention of Marine Pollution from Ships (MARPOL) 73/78 and other established protocols, establish waste oil reception facilities and declare the Regional Organization for the Protection of the Marine Environment (ROPME) Sea Area a Special Area, which reduces oil pollution significantly. The Global Programme of Action for the Protection of the Marine Environment from Land-Based Activities is strictly implemented, controlling and significantly reducing sewage releases into the sea.

All the pie charts show total region impacts. The top left pie shows the current situation, the relative size of the others reflects the magnitude of impacts by 2032 under the four scenarios. Average incomes rise in all regions, contributing to a drop in the percentage of the population that is hungry, but in *Markets First* and *Security First*, the benefits of growth are not enough to offset the growth in population and the total number of people affected by food shortages.

Source: PoleStar
(see technical annex)

## Population living with hunger: West Asia (million persons)

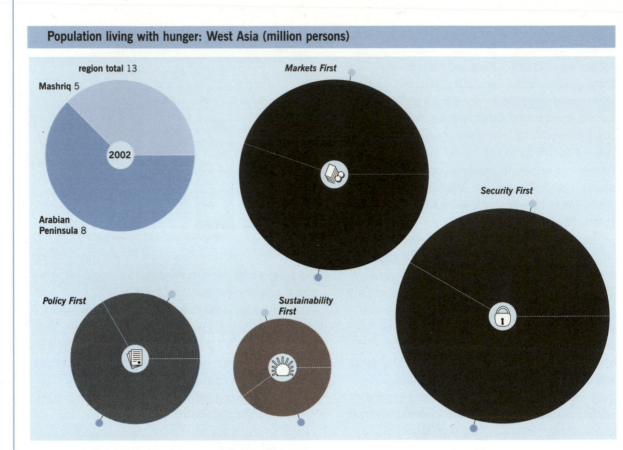

region total 13

Mashriq 5

Arabian Peninsula 8

2002

*Markets First*

*Security First*

*Policy First*

*Sustainability First*

Source: PoleStar
(see technical annex)

### Key to chart

*Markets First*

*Policy First*

*Security First*

*Sustainability First*

## Population living with hunger: West Asia (%)

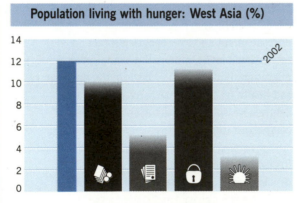

2002

These environmental trends, along with more broadly distributed economic growth and effective social policies, are reflected in the incidence of hunger in the region (see charts). In both *Markets First* and *Security First*, the levels of hunger are still near 10 per cent in 2032. In the *Markets First* scenario, relatively high inequality persists, limiting the improvements that can be achieved from economic growth. In the *Security First* scenario, divergent income distributions worsen the situation even more. Combined with the population growth, the numbers of persons experiencing hunger increase by half in *Markets First* and approximately double in *Security First*. In *Policy First* and *Sustainability First*, a combination of relatively high economic growth and comparatively equitable income distributions leads to a sharp drop in the percentage hungry, as well as in the total.

## Imagine ... a major seven-year drought in West Asia

An extended drought occurs, starting late in the first decade of the century. A significant drop in groundwater resources has affected major aquifers in the region since the mid-1990s. Growing scarcity of irrigation and clean drinking water in the Mashriq sub-region leads to more dependency on food imports in the Gulf Cooperation Council (GCC) countries and proliferation of hunger and poverty in Mashriq countries and Yemen. As approximately 60 per cent of surface water resources in the region originate from outside, the potential exists for disagreements to escalate between countries over shared and depleted water resources.

### In the case of ...

#### Markets First

- Water resources policies focusing almost exclusively on 'supply augmentation' prove unwise in this drought-prone region. There is some movement towards demand management but this is not implemented quickly enough to avert major water shortages.
- There is mass dependency on desalination facilities in GCC countries.
- Cash crops in irrigated areas are halved, resulting in major deficits in locally grown food.
- New, genetically engineered, more drought-tolerant crops are introduced.
- Water-related health problems proliferate.

#### Policy First

- Sweeping institutional reforms strengthen authorities in charge of water resources management.
- An existing policy focus on demand management, conservation and protection makes it relatively easy to introduce prompt additional measures that help eke out water supplies while drought conditions persist.
- Remedial instruments and programmes are introduced, including water pricing mechanisms, awareness and education campaigns, legislation to strengthen powers of enforcement, measures to boost the management of marginal waters, and codes to enable efficient water resources allocation among competing economic sectors.
- Economic integration and regional cooperation help modify agricultural policies in the Arabian Peninsula and reduce water consumption in the agricultural sector.
- Temporary agreements deal with the problems of shared water resources and help enhance regional stability.

#### Security First

- Competition and conflicts between sectors and users increase, leading to social unrest.
- There are widespread signs of increase in the rate of desertification and deterioration of biological resources combined with extinction of some species due to over-hunting and habitat destruction.
- Water-related health problems proliferate.
- Political instability and conflicts in the region mount, leading to open war over water resources, threatening regional and international stability.

#### Sustainability First

- Strategic regional water resource and river basin management planning reduce impacts of drought, in turn enhancing the efficiency of water use, resource protection and water resources augmentation.
- Major institutional reforms further consolidate the authority of water resources management bodies. Previous policy shifts in favour of 'demand management and conservation' ease the way for additional measures to eke out water supplies.
- More freshwater is made available by desalination technology in the GCC countries, increasingly using alternative and renewable energy sources, such as solar and wind power, to run desalination plants.
- There is widespread application of biotechnology to crop production, to boost drought resistance and yields.
- More equitable sharing of surface and groundwater resources is achieved as riparian countries sign and ratify treaties to that effect. This process is helped by the resolution of the Arab–Israeli conflict.

### The lessons

Developments not directly related to the environment, such as improvements in regional cooperation, can have a major impact on environmental issues. Similarly, the ways in which one environmental issue is tackled can have significant impacts on others, for instance the choice of renewable energy sources to power desalinization works reduces fossil-fuel burning. Experience and adoption of a mixed set of policy instruments allows greater flexibility to react swiftly in times of unexpected and increased environmental stress.

## Implications: the Polar Regions

Far more than in other regions, the environmental future of the polar regions is largely determined by global developments. The Arctic and Antarctic share various environmental concerns with other regions and with one another.

Despite shared concerns, the two sub-regions that make up the *GEO-3* Polar Region are very different in geographical circumstances, in their degree of isolation from major centres of population and human activity and in their legal status. In addition, unlike the Antarctic, the Arctic has a permanent human population, including indigenous peoples (see Chapter 2).

### Carving up the Arctic

The evolution of governance structures for the Arctic and Antarctic determines, to a large extent, the environmental futures of the region. In a *Markets First* scenario, the Arctic Council does not live up to its goals and has limited impact on policy decisions affecting the Arctic and its constituent states. In the early 21st century, land-claim agreements are reached with all indigenous groups, giving them varying degrees of ownership and rights to Arctic resources. Multinational entrepreneurs negotiate legally binding agreements with local populations and indigenous people's organizations for the rights to exploit the resources in exchange for cash and the promise of long-term local employment. However, much of this promised benefit does not play out and the local populations can do little to enforce the agreements.

In *Policy First*, the Council partially lives up to its goals and its advice has significant impact on policy decisions affecting the region. The Council's working groups and its observers successfully facilitate a vibrant environmental ethic and networks — especially among younger people — throughout the circumpolar world. Agreements reached between multinational entrepreneurs and local populations not only make provision for cash outlays and employment in exchange for exploration and production rights but also guarantee long-term management, part ownership and profit sharing rights. Where needed, the Council is effective in guaranteeing the latter are adhered to.

In *Security First*, a highly splintered, factional circumpolar world emerges, in which the United States, the Russian Federation, the Nordic states, and Canada compete to protect their respective northlands and their prized resources. Further splintering leaves power in the hands of an elite of commercial stakeholders. Some areas are subjected to ruthless exploitation and resource depletion. Local and indigenous peoples are increasingly marginalized. Unanimity of purpose is ruptured within communities of indigenous peoples, as key members of these communities and some of their organizations join forces with the multinational stakeholders. Although many people living in the Arctic gain a measure of economic independence, their existence becomes unstable.

In *Sustainability First*, the Arctic Council becomes a forceful advocate for the new thinking about sustainable livelihoods. Strong social and environmental support networks are established throughout the circumpolar world. An overall conservation and development plan for the region is agreed and partly implemented by Arctic states. It includes a system of protected areas to ensure the continuing survival and development of Arctic biodiversity and heritage. The Arctic peoples strengthen traditional alliances and modern international partnerships to serve the common good as well as specific interests.

### Southern legal regime

In a *Markets First* scenario, the Antarctic legal regime responds to some emerging issues yet increasingly runs up against entrenched stakeholder positions on points such as sovereignty and freedom of commercial access. There is a gradual addition of states, regional economic groupings and other international entities to the Antarctic Treaty System but most states continue to remain outside. Developing states are still (in effect) excluded from the system by lack of technology and funds. The Antarctic is increasingly penetrated by 'pirate' operators beyond the effective legal control of individual states or of international regimes. These operators are increasingly able to 'regime-pick' to sanction their particular activity.

In a *Policy First* situation, the Antarctic legal regime recognizes the need to adopt new agreements and harmonize regional legal and global approaches. This stimulates new membership and new forms of membership, including non-state entities. Administering regional agreements becomes more complex as membership grows and the increasing involvement of developing countries highlights the need to address equity issues such as burden-sharing and technology-sharing, in appropriate ways.

Under *Security First*, the Antarctic legal regime essentially collapses as a result of rivalry between claimant states seeking to secure their putative rights, and other advanced technology states and entities that do not recognize those rights. In practice a small number of very large corporations and powerful states operate Antarctica as a joint franchise. The wider international community contests the legitimacy of this deal, but is unable to challenge the new hegemony to any practical effect.

In *Sustainability First*, the Antarctic legal regime initially continues its gradual development. By the century's third decade, however, piecemeal changes are no longer seen as sufficient. With more fundamental shifts in international norms under way, it becomes possible to tackle some of the key issues, including the claims to sovereignty in Antarctica and policies of the high seas. As resolution of these issues becomes feasible, the possibility arises of a more fundamental revision of the Antarctic legal regime. Under a new legal structure, no property rights can be assigned to any part of the continent or its resources.

## Heating up

These differences, combined with the impacts on polar areas of activities and processes in other parts of the world, translate into a varied range of environmental implications under the four scenarios. Large increases in average polar temperatures are to be expected in all the scenarios, especially in the Arctic (see chart). *Policy First* and *Sustainability First* feature the highest increases up to 2032, reflecting the rapid abatement of emissions of sulphur oxides under these scenarios. Warming in Antarctica is less pronounced on account of the ocean currents in the area.

In *Security First*, both areas suffer from proliferation of illegal production of ozone depleting substances, which obliterates the gains made earlier, in the late 20th and early 21st centuries. Likewise, chemical pollutants originating from outside the region increase significantly in *Security First* due to weak regulation and in *Markets First*, where economic growth is higher. In *Policy First* and *Sustainability First*, efforts to phase out pollutants effectively terminate these problems.

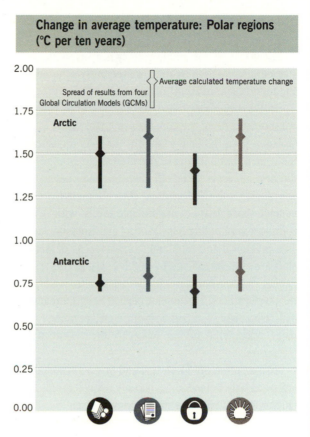

**Change in average temperature: Polar regions (°C per ten years)**

Spread of results from four Global Circulation Models (GCMs)

Average calculated temperature change

Arctic

Antarctic

Large increases in average polar temperature are to be expected for each of the scenarios, especially in the Arctic. The graph clearly shows that the change of temperature between 2002 and 2032 is far larger than the uncertainty.

Source: IMAGE 2.2 (see technical annex)

*Markets First*

*Policy First*

*Security First*

*Sustainability First*

## Safety-nets for fish stocks

A key area of concern in both regions is the health of fish and other marine stocks. The effects of a crash in Antarctic krill are examined in the box on page 393. There is a big increase in the number and sophistication of vessels employed, and harvesting increases massively in both the Antarctic and the Arctic in *Markets First*. The very rapid rate of industrial exploitation and abandonment of targeted fisheries means that management responses often lag behind events. Continued depletion of target populations leads to some population crashes and adverse impacts on associated species.

In *Policy First*, the Antarctic marine ecosystem is placed under ever-increasing pressure as fishing proves the hardest resource activity to manage. Stark choices between commercial and development imperatives on the one hand, and environmental and ethical considerations on the other, prove difficult to reconcile. Underwater setting of lines and other technological developments eliminate seabird by-catch, but other forms of by-catch are unaffected and target stocks continue to be exploited beyond sustainable limits. In the Arctic, provision is made for traditional local fisheries and for the engagement of local communities in international Arctic fisheries. Total collapse of any single fishery is averted using stringent harvesting quotas, limited entry schemes, and enforceable bilateral regimes.

In *Security First*, illegal, unregulated and unreported fishing activities cease under direct pressure from the powerful new interests regulating the region. Exploitation of marine living resources by the new interests takes off, however, and rises to very high levels. Self-interest sees attempts to manage this activity at sustainable levels, with approaches including fish-farming and biotechnology. The ecological and economic consequences of this shift are still unresolved by 2032. In the Arctic, fishing rights are unilaterally withdrawn from all but the Arctic states. However, overfishing has already exacted a heavy toll and desperate conservation measures may be too late to secure the resources for the future.

In *Sustainability First*, fish and marine mammals are rigorously defended against overexploitation. Quotas are reasonable and the resource base is healthy. Penalties for abuse are severe — and robustly enforced. One option being explored is to cap catches but set initial limits at a liberal level, then scale down from this level over a period of several decades. In the Antarctic, rights to fisheries are incrementally transferred from developed to developing world fleets. In the Arctic, local communities now manage most of the fisheries and potentially harmful practices such as trawling are outlawed in most areas.

## Wildlife rearguard

Infrastructure developments, often related to fishing and tourism in both the Arctic and the Antarctic, and to oil, gas and other mineral development in the Arctic, expand significantly in a *Markets First* world (see chart for the situation in the Arctic). In the Antarctic, this includes spontaneous private colonization by a limited number of economically and technology-rich individuals or entities. In the Arctic, habitats of wide-ranging species, such as the caribou, reindeer, grizzly bear and musk ox are severely fragmented and encroached upon. All Arctic wildlife is substantially affected either directly or indirectly from the disruption of the food chain, from habitat loss and from the insidious impacts of climate change. Excessive hunting further reduces some of the populations to biologically unsustainable levels.

In *Policy First*, these pressures are kept in check, although effects of decades of warming — on land and sea — are visible over large expanses. Responsible planning decisions have prevailed and wildlife habitat has remained relatively intact. In many cases this is due to the improved effectiveness of habitat management, particularly in protected areas which are now integrated into circumpolar and north–south networks. The numbers and size of protected areas have increased significantly, but many sites still have inadequate regulations on mineral, oil and gas exploration and extraction and hydropower generation. Hunting is sustainable in most parts of the Arctic and quotas are based on much improved scientific evidence.

*Security First* sees permanent residence in Antarctica becoming possible for personnel employed by industries active in the area and as a status symbol for the wealthy. Numbers of endemic wildlife in the Arctic plummet, the food chain is disrupted and genetic diversity is weakened due to habitat degradation and fragmentation. Opportunistic alien species able to survive in the warming climate have filled available niches. However, even they are having a hard time due to contamination by wastes and habitat destruction.

In *Sustainability First*, biodiversity hot spots and habitats are protected and large areas are set aside as national parks or nature reserves to help wildlife cope with climate change. Small, regulated subsistence hunts are still allowed in accordance with agreements negotiated with indigenous peoples. The public does not tolerate poaching. Residence in the Antarctic is denied for anything other than specifically agreed purposes, generally scientific research.

### Key to chart

**Markets First**

**Policy First**

**Security First**

**Sustainability First**

The Arctic holds the largest remaining undisturbed — but highly sensitive — wilderness in the world.

Source: GLOBIO
(see technical annex)

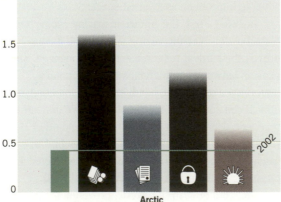

**Land area impacted by infrastructure expansion: Arctic (% of total land area)**

2.0

1.5

1.0

0.5

0

2002

Arctic

In the Arctic, the condition of the boreal forests differs markedly between scenarios. Large areas of forest in the region have come under stress from rapid climate change, leading to long-term shifts in temperature and precipitation, as well as to increasing incidence of fires. Continued and increasing levels of logging in *Markets First* and *Security First* further exacerbate these pressures. Most notably, in *Security First* muddy plains and clear-cut forested areas have replaced many of the once vast pristine landscapes.

## Imagine... a crash in circumpolar Antarctic krill stocks

Clear signs emerge that circumpolar Antarctic krill (*Euphausia superba*) stocks are crashing. The immediate cause is believed to be commercial over-harvesting, but the picture is complicated by simultaneous sea-ice changes and rises in ultraviolet radiation levels, both of which are believed to affect krill population dynamics. There is evidence of serious adverse impacts on breeding success of Antarctic birds, seals and cetaceans within a few seasons, leading to serious concerns over the viability of populations of higher predators. Indications of severe damage to stocks of other marine species — initially evident through declining stocks of fin-fish and squid — raise concern about the stability of the entire Antarctic marine ecosystem, and knock-on effects on other ecosystems in and around the sub-region. Dramatic falls in catches of krill and commercial fisheries stocks that prey on krill, result in widespread reduction in fishing activity and collapse of the fishing industry in some areas. The treaties, institutions and other international arrangements set up to conserve and manage the fishery are seen as having failed. Public concern runs high at the prospect of threats to charismatic wildlife species such as penguins, seals and whales.

### In the case of...
#### Markets First
- Some regulatory steps are taken, but market mechanisms are the prime response measures used — reducing krill demand by raising prices, and harvesting by raising costs.
- Harvesting switches to other species, including those that are not dependent upon krill themselves and may be competitors. Where these responses fail, the fishing industry abandons the area.
- It is widely presumed that krill stocks will in time recover, and that the adverse knock-on effects will turn out to be reversible.

#### Policy First
- Moratoria on krill harvesting are agreed to allow stock recovery.
- These steps are accompanied by reductions in fisheries activities across all target species.
- Major research effort is directed to understanding what has happened and underpinning policy responses.
- The regulatory regime for the marine environment is revised.

#### Security First
- Measures are taken to ban some operators from the region as a way to curb pressures on krill stocks.
- Market mechanisms are employed when they underpin the interests of key stakeholders in the region.
- In a bid for short-term 'use-it-or-lose-it' exploitation, harvesting switches to other species, including those expected to decline steeply as a result of krill stock collapse.
- Active management of the marine environment begins by seeding new krill stocks (including genetically modified types), enhancing nutrient levels and depressing predators or competitors.

#### Sustainability First
- There is an immediate closure of all krill fisheries pending recovery of stocks.
- Substantial reductions in other fisheries are introduced as a precautionary measure — although directed harvesting of particular predator populations is considered in some areas.
- A renewed effort is made to understand the functioning of the Antarctic marine environment.
- Negotiation begins for a new legal regime to manage the marine environment and regulate more limited harvesting when stocks have recovered.

### The lessons
Existing knowledge of many natural systems is limited, including the thresholds for resource exploitation, beyond which systems collapse. Such thresholds may be reached in a comparatively sudden way. It makes sense, therefore, to continue efforts to improve understanding, but also to take a precautionary approach where baseline data are lacking, where uncertainty is high and where irreversible impacts are possible. This course of action may avoid the need to take more drastic action in the event of a system crash.

UNEP, Pramkaew, Still Pictures

# Lessons from the future

As we step back into the world in which we live now, a number of important lessons arise from the foregoing scenarios that can help to provide general policy guidance.

## LESSON ONE
**Contrasting yet plausible stories can be told for how the world and its regions will develop in the next 30 years; each has fundamentally different implications for the environment.**

Earlier chapters of *GEO-3* have outlined important and very specific changes that emerged over the past 30 years, and there is no reason to believe that the next 30 will be any less dynamic. Using scenarios, it is possible to tell strongly contrasting but plausible stories about how the world and its regions might develop in the future. None of the stories requires exotic surprises to materialize and elements of each of the four scenarios can already be discerned in today's world. In appreciating the scenarios, it is important to realize that, in real life, they are not mutually exclusive. A given region may experience all four or a combination of several at once. And although the scenarios have been presented as fairly uniform across the world, it is clear that not all regions have experienced, are experiencing, or will experience the same developments.

Examining the environmental implications casts a spotlight on the differences across scenarios, regions and issues. These variations have been illustrated in the narratives, the quantitative material and the differing outcomes of particular events or trends.

*Sustainability First* implies the most positive environmental outlook of the four scenarios. *Markets First* and *Security First* conjure up much more pessimistic pictures, but for very different reasons. This contrast is reflected in the issues that come most conspicuously to the fore in each scenario. For example, water shortages are generally more of a problem in *Markets First*, reflecting increasing resource demand, whereas urban pollution and loss of biodiversity are more marked in *Security First*, reflecting a lack of effective environmental policies. *Policy First* falls somewhere in between — some of the environmental targets are met, through a mainly top-down approach, whereas it is unrealistic to make significant progress on others without a broader commitment to change.

---

## LESSON TWO
**There can be significant delays between human actions, including policy decisions, and associated impacts on the environment, specifically:**

- **much of the environmental change that will occur over the next 30 years has already been set in motion by past and current actions**
- **many of the effects of environmentally relevant policies put into place over the next 30 years will not be apparent until long afterwards.**

Social and economic systems can be notoriously slow to change. The basic infrastructure of modern society, including transportation and energy systems, cannot be refashioned rapidly without great expense. Financial and political systems, and basic behaviour patterns also tend to exhibit overpowering inertia. Furthermore, even when social systems change,

resulting in reduced pressures on the environment, time lags in natural systems can delay the ultimate response to these changes. Therefore, it is important to consider not only the state of the environment at the end of the time horizon for these scenarios, but also the trends.

This proviso is perhaps most clearly seen in the case of climate change impacts, which differ minimally between the scenarios in most regions over the next 30 years. This is because much of the climatic change expected to occur over the next 30 years is the result of actions that have already been taken. It is not surprising that the issues which stand out as the most difficult to tackle — halting land degradation, preserving biodiversity and ensuring access to freshwater — are all linked to climate change among other factors. The intractable nature of these impacts is also related to the fact that they are driven by fundamental human demands and are not easily amenable to technical fixes.

---

## LESSON THREE
**Achieving widely agreed environmental and social goals will require dramatic and coordinated action starting now and continuing for a number of years. Steps must include policies based on prevention and adaptation.**

The environmental implications of the various scenarios illustrate the legacy of the past decades and the level of effort that will be needed to reverse powerful trends. These challenges can only be met with robust and coordinated action at all levels of government and among many different sectors of society. The scenarios also demonstrate that it can take many years for important social and environmental indicators to diverge from one another. Given the likelihood that large numbers of people will continue to be vulnerable to environmental change, even where the scenarios point to eventual achievement of environmental goals, adaptation policies will be needed to complement mitigation policies. Among other reasons, these may be necessary to meet social goals, minimize the transient effects of environmental change, prevent irreversible losses, and maintain the enthusiasm for the necessary social and political will to achieve the long-term goals.

## LESSON FOUR
**Important linkages exist between different environmental issues and between environmental and broader social issues. It follows that:**

- **policy can be made more effective by looking for synergies or 'co-benefits'**
- **care must be taken to avoid conflicts between policies.**

The scenarios presented here demonstrate the importance of interlinkages between the environmental, social, economic and political spheres, both within and across regions. The complex interplay between human and natural systems calls for approaches that treat social, economic and environmental concerns in an integrated fashion.

Positive synergies between policies can be maximized. For example, well-designed policies can simultaneously address issues such as climate change, transport, and urban and regional air pollution. Thus, ambitious climate policies could serve as a cornerstone of modern, integrated environmental programmes in many situations.

In other cases, connections imply potential conflicts. The large-scale introduction of modern biofuels in certain regions as a substitute for fossil fuels, a feature of the *Policy First* scenario, could have adverse implications for biodiversity and agriculture in these areas. Similarly, the use of biotechnology and genetic engineering to improve agricultural productivity could, rather than reducing the demand for agricultural land, lead to a dramatic expansion if organisms are genetically modified to be able to thrive in areas currently unsuitable for widespread crop production or grazing. This outcome would have serious implications for biodiversity and land management.

There is a need to be aware of both the small and the large-scale effects of policies, particularly those related to the introduction of new technologies. On a small scale, stimulating better technology to deliver the same services with less resource use is clearly a robust policy that makes sense in almost any conceivable scenario. If scaled up, however, two possible drawbacks arise. First, the improved efficiency may induce an increased level of activity (such as additional travelling in improved motor vehicles), which outweighs the gains achieved by better technology (in this instance lower fuel consumption or lower pollution emissions per kilometre travelled). Second, new technologies that increase dependence, either on other countries or on the technology itself, can increase vulnerability of regions to disruptions in, or misuse of, these technologies.

### Reflections on the use of scenarios

For this Global Environment Outlook a scenario approach has been chosen that deliberately emphasizes the possibility of many different futures rather than the probability of any single one. None of the four scenarios that has been presented should be viewed as more or less likely than the others, or as a reference scenario from which the others represent variants. Recent experience and reflections upon issues such as insufficient information (ignorance), the complexity of human and natural systems (surprise), and the ability of humans to choose (volition), suggests that for longer range policy thinking it is not only disingenuous to presume we can know the most likely future, but that it is also detrimental to good policy making because it unnecessarily narrows our vision (Raskin and Kemp-Benedict 2002).

The process also revealed some of the challenges in such a scenario exercise. The choice to begin with global archetypes aided in the effort to create sets of nested global and regional scenarios that were consistent with each other. At the same time, this choice arguably limited the range of scenarios that might have arisen had the regional scenario teams been able to operate more independently. The efforts to combine narrative scenarios with quantitative information coming out of models and other analytical tools also drew attention to the need to use consistent assumptions in the two approaches. The quantitative underpinning certainly helped to stimulate the development of the narrative scenarios and provided both consistency checks and powerful means of depicting the differences between the four scenarios in the different regions. It remains apparent, though, that the existing quantitative tools are limited in their ability to capture the richness of narrative scenarios, particularly where these involve significant departures from the current situation.

## LESSON FIVE
**The establishment of strong institutions for environmental governance is a prerequisite for almost all other policies.**

A fundamental distinction between the four scenarios lies in the existence and effectiveness of strong institutions for environmental governance. The scenarios represent largely different political attitudes, citizen values and degrees of acceptance of (or action against) inequality. The political will and vision of governments and other authorities determine, above all else, whether environmentally sustainable development comes within reach worldwide. Where strong institutions for environmental governance are absent, as in *Security First*, or afforded a lower status than other institutions, as in *Markets First*, improvements in environmental conditions are less likely to occur. As the range of concerns traverses the local to the global, so must these institutions. Furthermore, as all sectors of society are, in some way, both responsible for and impacted by the status of natural and human systems, these institutions must reach across these sectors. Thus, not only formal governments, but also business, NGOs and other elements of civil society must play a role, individually and in partnership, in establishing and maintaining these institutions.

## LESSON SIX
**Ensuring timely access to accurate information is a robust policy, as it:**

- **allows for early warning of environmental problems**
- **can stimulate voluntary action by business and industry**
- **can support formal and informal market-based mechanisms that promote good environmental conduct.**

Ensuring and stimulating timely access to information is crucial not only for keeping abreast of the current state of environmental and social systems and trends in both, but also for coordinating action to address emerging or existing problems. Efforts are required to ensure that key public information remains accessible, and that more flows are established. A fundamental message, from *Policy First* and *Sustainability First* in particular, is that information can both encourage voluntary action and increase the effectiveness of other policies. The flow of accurate information can therefore actively support other policies. Conversely, as *Security First* most notably shows, when economic and political relations polarize, the control of information can be an important instrument of power.

## LESSON SEVEN
**Not all policy instruments are appropriate for all situations.**

It is clear that there are particular policy instruments that are more in accordance with different types of worlds. For example, market-based instruments such as capping and trading systems for curbing pollutants will find a niche in a world that resembles *Markets First*, whereas ambitious zoning and other spatial planning measures would not go down so well. Similarly, eco-labelling will be suited to a world that resembles *Sustainability First*, but forcibly restricting access to protected areas would be much less suitable. This same argument implies that the most appropriate choice of policy instruments can vary between different regions or at different times. Careful selection of specific and appropriate policy instruments is clearly very important.

The final lesson from the scenarios presented in this chapter may be one of perspective.

## LESSON EIGHT
**The achievement of environmental goals will require decisive action, will encounter unforeseen eventualities and will not happen overnight. Fortunately or unfortunately, much of the success or failure of this endeavour is in our hands.**

The four scenarios show that the future is not something that we should wait for passively. Rather, the choices we have made in the past, those we are currently making and those we will make in the future all strongly influence in which world we will live. There will be many branch points when stakeholders will have the opportunity to turn in one direction or another, whether towards *Markets First* or towards *Policy First*, *Security First*, *Sustainability First* or another, as yet unimagined, scenario. Being aware of threats, opportunities and the possible outcomes of different choices is a prerequisite to effective policy making.

## Technical annex

The quantitative results presented in this chapter were developed to illustrate the narrative scenarios and to provide an indication of their likely environmental implications. These results were derived using a range of analytical tools, in consultation with regional experts. They emphasize general trends and differences between scenarios, rather than precise levels of impact. This technical annex outlines the scenario development process followed for *GEO-3*, and presents summary descriptions of the analytical tools employed, and the indicators presented in the chapter. More extensive information, including more detailed data tables and figures, is presented in Raskin and Kemp-Benedict (2002) and in a separate technical report (RIVM and UNEP, in press).

### The scenario development process

Drawing from previous work of the Global Scenario Group (see Raskin and Kemp-Benedict 2002), four global storylines were designed by a core scenario team of global and regional experts. An initial quantification for a small set of indicators was prepared at the level of the GEO sub-regions. Teams in each of the seven major GEO regions then elaborated the storylines at regional level and provided input to the quantitative analyses, particularly with respect to key driving forces. The results of the regional efforts were used to refine the global narratives and to undertake the subsequent quantitative analyses associated with the scenario narratives. Further refinement of both the narratives and the quantitative analyses was achieved through an iterative process involving the core scenario team and the modelling groups. During the development process the work underwent two formal rounds of review and was scrutinized at a special workshop with a group of scenario experts from around the world.

### Quantitative analytical tools

**AIM** (Asian Pacific Integrated Model) is an integrated environment-economy model developed by the National Institute for Environmental Studies (NIES) and Kyoto University, Japan, to assess future scenarios of socio-economic development and environmental change in Asia and the Pacific as well as at global level. The set of AIM modules was developed primarily for assessing effects of climate change policies and climate change impacts, but it can also be applied to other environmental fields such as air pollution, water resources, land use change and ecosystem assessment. With externally derived socio-economic data as input, the model estimates future environmental conditions of 42 countries in Asia and the Pacific. The ecosystem module uses a latitude-longitude grid with a spatial resolution of 2.5 x 2.5 minutes to facilitate policy analyses. The model has been extensively reviewed and frequently used by the IPCC. More information about AIM is available at http://www-cger.nies.go.jp/ipcc/aim/

**GLOBIO** (Global methodology for mapping human impacts on the biosphere) is a simple transparent global model developed under the GLOBIO project, coordinated by the Norwegian Institute for Nature Research (NINA), UNEP-GRID-Arendal, UNEP-WCMC and UNEP/DEWA. It is used to visualize, at a scale of 1 x 1 km, the cumulative impacts on biodiversity and ecosystem function of growth in human resource demand and associated infrastructure development. The model provides a statistical risk assessment of probability of human impacts using buffer zones from infrastructure that vary with type of human activity and density of infrastructure, region, vegetation, climate and sensitivity of species and ecosystems. Satellite imagery is used to derive overviews of cumulative impacts of ongoing development. Future scenario situations are derived from data on existing infrastructure, historic growth rates of infrastructure, availability of petroleum and mineral reserves, vegetation cover, population density, distance to coast and projected development. More information on GLOBIO can be found at http://www.globio.info and in UNEP 2001.

**IMAGE 2.2** (Integrated Model to Assess the Global Environment) is a dynamic integrated assessment model for global change developed by the National Institute for Public Health and the Environment (RIVM), The Netherlands. IMAGE quantifies the consequences of different future developments for a broad range of environmental issues. Driving forces are modelled for 17 world regions, partly via the WorldScan general equilibrium model. Impacts are calculated over long time frames (typically 100 years), and with a high spatial resolution (0.5 x 0.5 degree latitude-longitude grid). Long historical series are used to calibrate the model and place future developments in perspective. The model has been extensively reviewed and frequently used by the IPCC. More information about IMAGE is available at http://www.rivm.nl/image/ and in Alcamo and others (1998) and IMAGE Team (2001a and 2001b).

**PoleStar** is a comprehensive and flexible software tool for sustainability studies developed by the Stockholm Environment Institute (SEI), Boston Centre, USA. Rather than being a rigid model, the software provides an adaptable accounting framework and modelling environment for mounting economic, resource and environmental information and for examining alternative development scenarios. PoleStar has been used in a number of international assessments, including quantification of the scenarios of the Global Scenario Group (GSG). Technical documentation on PoleStar and details of the GSG scenarios can be found online at http://www.seib.org/polestar and http://www.gsg.org

**WaterGAP 2.1** model (Water — Global Assessment and Prognosis) is the first global model that computes both water availability and water use on the river basin scale. WaterGAP, developed by the Center for Environmental Systems Research (CESR), University of Kassel, Germany, has two main components, a Global Hydrology Model and a Global Water Use Model. The Global Hydrology Model simulates the characteristic macro-scale behaviour of the terrestrial water cycle to estimate water availability. The Global Water Use Model consists of three main sub-models that compute water use for the domestic, industry and agriculture sectors. All computations cover the entire land surface of the globe on a 0.5 x 0.5 degree latitude-longitude grid. A global drainage direction map then allows the analysis of the water resources situation in all large drainage basins worldwide. For a more detailed description of the model see Alcamo and others (2000) and Center for Environmental Systems Research (2002).

**Note:** *Any discrepancies between the GEO-3 regions and sub-regions and the regions represented in data sets used to generate charts and other figures are noted with the individual graphics.*

### Variables

Variables charted or mapped in the Outlook section of *GEO-3* are (in alphabetical order) as follows.

**Area with high risk of water-induced soil degradation** indicates the land area that is at high risk from water erosion under a specific form of land use. The sensitivity to water erosion is computed from the soil and terrain characteristics, rainfall erosivity and land cover. In global terms, water erosion is the most serious form of land degradation and it is irreversible. Whether erosion actually occurs depends on implementation of soil conservation measures at farm and landscape levels.

Source: IMAGE 2.2; Hootsmans and others 2001. For definition of erosion risk see UNEP/ISRIC 1991

**Atmospheric concentrations of carbon dioxide** presents the global $CO_2$ concentration in the atmosphere as the net balance between $CO_2$ emissions from fossil fuel combustion, industrial production, deforestation and $CO_2$ uptake by mature and regrowing vegetation, and by the oceans.

Source: AIM for Asia and the Pacific; IMAGE 2.2 for other regions and global chart; De Vries and others 2001

**Carbon dioxide emissions** covers emissions from land use, industrial production and energy use. Emissions from industrial sources include the emissions from non-energy use of fossil fuels (mainly feedstocks) and industrial activities. Land-use sources of carbon dioxide include burning forest biomass (after deforestation) and fuelwood, and releases by waste processes after disposal of consumer goods such as paper, furniture and building materials.

Source: AIM for Asia and the Pacific; IMAGE 2.2 for other regions and global chart; De Vries and others 2001

**Change in average temperature, 2002–32.** Given the uncertainties in the regional distribution of temperature increase, this graph is based on results from four different Global Circulation Models (GCMs) in combination with IMAGE 2.2. For each of the GCMs, the spatially differentiated pattern of temperature change for a reference scenario (1 per cent per annum growth in equivalent greenhouse gas concentration from 1990 onwards) was taken, north of 66°N and south of 66°S latitude. This pattern was then scaled on the basis of global average temperature changes for each of the scenarios as calculated by IMAGE 2.2. Finally, the average temperature change for the Arctic and Antarctic was calculated. The GCMs used are HadCM2, ECHAM4, CSIRO Mk2 and CGCM1. The GCM results were taken from the IPCC Data Distribution Centre for Climate Change and Related Scenarios for Impacts Assessment (IPCC-DCC 1999).

Source: four GCMs and IMAGE 2.2

**Change in selected pressures on natural ecosystems 2002–32.** For the ecosystem quality component, see the explanation of the Natural Capital Index. Values for the cumulative pressures were derived as described under Natural Capital Index. The maps show the relative increase or decrease in pressure between 2002 and 2032. 'No change' means less than 10 per cent change in pressure over the scenario period; small increase or decrease means between 10 and 50 per cent change; substantial increase or decrease means 50 to 100 per cent change; strong increase means more than doubling of pressure. Areas which switch between natural and domesticated land uses are recorded separately.

Source: IMAGE 2.2

**Ecosystems impacted by infrastructure expansion** reflects the probability of human impact on biodiversity based on distances to different types of infrastructure, such as roads, dams and other utilities. Impact zones vary according to climate, vegetation and political region.

Source: GLOBIO

**Energy-related carbon dioxide emissions** are total $CO_2$ emissions from all energy uses.

Source: AIM for Asia and the Pacific; IMAGE 2.2 for other regions and global chart; De Vries and others 2001

**Energy-related nitrogen oxide emissions** are total $NO_x$ emissions from all energy uses.

Source: AIM for Asia and the Pacific; IMAGE 2.2

for other regions and global chart; De Vries and others 2001

**Energy-related sulphur dioxide emissions** are total $SO_2$ emissions from all energy uses.

Source: AIM for Asia and the Pacific; IMAGE 2.2 for other regions and global chart; De Vries and others 2001

**Extent of built-up areas** includes land cleared and altered for businesses, residences, roads, parking lots, parks, landfills, burial grounds and other similar uses. A combination of different sources was used to arrive at regional estimates for built-up land.

Source: Polestar

**Global temperature change** is the average increase of global temperature, expressed in degrees per ten years. The rate of temperature change is important since sensitive ecosystems may not be able to adapt at high rates. Research has shown that, at rates larger than 0.1 °C per ten years, extensive damage to ecosystems is probable (Vellinga and Swart 1991).

Source: IMAGE 2.2

**Land area impacted by infrastructure expansion.** See note under *Ecosystems impacted by infrastructure expansion*, above.

Source: GLOBIO

**Municipal solid waste generation** is an index of solid waste generation from household and commercial sources. Total solid waste generation in the Asia and Pacific region in the year 1995 has been allocated an index value of 1. Index values for 2032 under each scenario relate to the index for the base year.

Source: AIM

**Natural Capital Index** is a measure for terrestrial and aquatic biodiversity of natural ecosystems and agricultural land. The index is calculated as the product of habitat area times ecosystem quality, expressed as a percentage. The habitat area is taken as the percentage of remaining surface of natural ecosystems. Ecosystem quality is approximated from four pressure factors that are considered to have a major influence on biodiversity and for which global data are available. Based on literature, for each pressure factor a range is defined from no effect to complete deterioration of habitats if the maximum value is exceeded over a long time. Pressure factors are population density (min-max: 10–150 persons per km$^2$), primary energy use (min-max: 0.5–100 peta Joules per km$^2$), rate of temperature change (min-max: 0.2–2.0 °C in a 20 year period) and restoration time for exhausted agricultural land, livestock area and deforested zones in re-conversion towards natural, low-impacted ecosystems (min-max: 100–0 restoration time). The proxy for ecosystem quality is a reversed function of these pressures,

calculated as a percentage of the low-impacted baseline state. The higher the pressure, the lower the quality. Finally, the percentages for habitat area and quality are multiplied, resulting in a pressure-based Natural Capital Index. The calculations were carried out on a detailed latitude-longitude grid, before aggregation to sub-regions and regions.

Source: IMAGE 2.2; ten Brink 2000 and 2001, ten Brink and others 2000

**Natural forest, excluding regrowth** is the area of mature forests (excluding plantations) that has not been harvested using clear cutting since 1972.

Source: IMAGE 2.2

**Potential increase in nitrogen loading on coastal ecosystems.** At the sub-regional aggregation level employed in GEO, nitrogen loading can be taken as a proxy for a wider range of land-based pollution on the coastal ecosystems. The potential growth of the subregional nitrogen load under each of the scenarios has been estimated by rating the change in determinants such as sewage inputs and level of treatment, fertilizer use and airborne emissions, on a ten-point scale.

Source: IMAGE 2.2; van Drecht and others (in press)

**Percentage of 2002 cropland that is severely degraded by 2032** represents cropland so degraded that it is of little value for production. The degraded area is expressed as a percentage of land that was under crops in 2002.

Source: Polestar

**Population living in areas with severe water stress.** Water stress is measured by the 'withdrawal-to-availability' ratio (wta-ratio). This ratio captures how much of the average annual renewable water resources of a river basin are withdrawn for human purposes in the domestic, industry and agricultural sectors. In principle, the higher the ratio, the more intensively the water in a river is used; this reduces either water quantity or water quality or even both for downstream users. Commonly it is assumed that when the wta-ratio in a river basin exceeds 0.4, or 40 per cent, the river basin experiences severe water stress.

Source: WaterGAP 2.1

**Population living with hunger** refers to the incidence of chronic under-nutrition in developing and transitional regions (using 1995 data based on FAO estimates), the incidence of food insecurity in the United States and estimates for other countries based on income distribution. Hunger patterns are determined in the scenarios by changes in income, income distribution and population.

Source: PoleStar

## References: Chapter 4, Outlook 2002–32

Alcamo, J., Leemans, R. and Kreileman, E. (eds 1998). *Global change scenarios of the 21st century. Results from the IMAGE 2.1 Model*. Oxford, United Kingdom, Elsevier Science

Alcamo, J., Henrichs, T. and Rosch, T. (2000). *World Water in 2025. Global modelling and scenario analysis for the World Commission on Water for the 21st Century*. Kassel World Water Series 2. University of Kassel, Germany, Center for Environmental Systems Research

Center for Environmental Systems Research (2002). *Results from WaterGAP for the GEO-3 Scenarios*. Report A0201. University of Kassel, Germany, Center for Environmental Systems Research

De Vries, H.J.M., van Vuuren, D.P., den Elzen, M.G.J. and Janssen, M.A. (2001). *The Timer Image Energy Regional (TIMER) Model. Technical Documentation*. Bilthoven, The Netherlands, National Institute for Public Health and the Environment

Hammond, A. (1998). *Which World? Scenarios for the 21st Century*. Washington DC, Island Press

Hootsmans, R.M., Bouwman, A.F., Leemans, R. and Kreileman, G.J.J. (2001). *Modelling land degradation in IMAGE 2*. RIVM report 481508009. Bilthoven, The Netherlands, National Institute for Public Health and the Environment

IMAGE Team (2001a). *The IMAGE 2.2 implementation of the SRES scenarios. A comprehensive analysis of emissions, climate change and impacts in the 21st century*. RIVM CD-ROM publication 481508018. Bilthoven, the Netherlands, National Institute for Public Health and the Environment

IMAGE Team (2001b). *The IMAGE 2.2 implementation of the SRES scenarios: Climate change scenarios resulting from runs with several GCMs*. RIVM CD-ROM Publication 481508019. Bilthoven, the Netherlands, National Institute for Public Health and the Environment

IMF, OECD, United Nations and World Bank (2000). *A Better World for All: Progress Towards the International Development Goals*. Washington DC and Paris, IMF, OECD, United Nations and World Bank. See also http://www.paris21.org/betterworld [Geo-4-004]

IPCC-DDC (1999). Accessing Scenario Information. IPCC Data Distribution Centre for Climate Change and Related Scenarios for Impacts Assessment, CD-ROM, Version 1.0. Norwich, United Kingdom http://ipcc-ddc.cru.uea.ac.uk/cru_data/cru_index.html [Geo-4-001]

Meadows, D.H. (2000) Things are getting worse at a slower rate. *The Global Citizen*, 29 June 2000

Raskin, P.D. and Kemp-Benedict, E. (2002). *Global Environment Outlook Scenario Framework*. UNEP/DEWA Technical Report. Nairobi, United Nations Environment Programme

RIVM and UNEP (in press). *The GEO-3 Scenarios 2002-2032: Quantification and Analysis of Environmental Impacts*. UNEP/DEWA Technical Report. Nairobi, United Nations Environment Programme

ten Brink, B.J.E. (2000). *Biodiversity indicators for the OECD Environmental Outlook and Strategy*. RIVM feasibility study report 402001014. Bilthoven, The Netherlands, National Institute for Public Health and the Environment

ten Brink, B.J.E. (2001). *The state of agro-biodiversity in the Netherlands. Integrating habitat and species indicators*. Paper for the OECD workshop on agri-biodiversity indicators, 5-8 October 2001, Zurich, Switzerland

ten Brink, B.J.E., van Vliet, A.J.H., Heunks, C., Pearce, D.W. and Howarth, A. (2000). *Technical report on biodiversity in Europe: an integrated economic and environmental assessment*. Prepared by RIVM, EFTEC, NTUA and IIASA in association with TME and TNO. RIVM Report 481505019. Bilthoven, The Netherlands, National Institute for Public Health and the Environment

UNEP (2000). *Global Treaty Adopted on Genetically Modified Organisms*. Press release issued in Nairobi and Montreal, 31 January 2000 http://www.unep.org/Documents/Default.asp?DocumentID=98&ArticleID=1531 [Geo-4-002]

UNEP (2001). Nellemann, C., Kullerud, L., Vistnes, I., Forbes, B.C., Foresman, T., Husby, E., Kofinas, G.P., Kaltenborn, B.P., Rouaud, J., Magomedova, M., Bobiwash, R., Lambrechts, C., Shei, P.J., Tveitdal, S., Grøn, O. and Larsen, T.S. *GLOBIO. Global methodology for mapping human impacts on the biosphere*. UNEP/DEWA/TR.01-3 http://www.globio.info/ [Geo-4-003]

UNEP/ISRIC (1991). *World Map of the Status of Human-Induced Soil Degradation (GLASOD). An Explanatory Note*, second revised edition (edited by Oldeman, L.R., Hakkeling, R.T. and Sombroek, W.G.). UNEP, Nairobi, Kenya, and ISRIC, Wageningen, Netherlands

van Drecht, G., Bouwman, A.F., Knoop, J.M., Meinardi, C.R. and Beusen, A.H.W. (in press). Global pollution of surface waters from point and nonpoint sources of nitrogen. Submitted to *The Scientific World*

Vellinga, P. and Swart, R. (1991) The greenhouse marathon: a proposal for a global strategy. *Climatic Change* 18, vii-xii

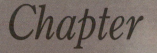

Chapter

# 5

# Options for Action

The year 2002 is the beginning of the fourth decade since the international community laid the foundation in 1972 for collective global action to mitigate adverse impacts on the environment. It finds one of the three pillars of sustainable development — the environment — seriously listing because of the distortions placed on it by the actions of a human population that now numbers more than 6 000 million. The importance of the environment is often underplayed even though its value to human survival and development is incalculable. The collapse of the environmental pillar is a serious possibility if action — from local to global — is not taken as a matter of urgency to address human impacts, which have left:

- increased pollutants in the atmosphere;
- vast areas of land resources degraded;
- depleted and degraded forests;
- biodiversity under threat;
- increasingly inadequate freshwater resources of deteriorating quality; and
- seriously depleted marine resources.

The environment is under siege. Unless both short- and long-term changes are instigated, sustainable development will remain a chimera — possibly only in the haze on a distant horizon. There is need for a balanced approach towards sustainable development. All three pillars — social, economic and environmental — are mutually supportive and all three are essential. Neglecting any one, and this is all too frequently the case with the environmental pillar, is not only shortsighted but leads to a policy dead end. The disintegration of the environmental pillar will lead to the inevitable collapse of the other, more charismatic pillars of sustainable development to which policy makers everywhere pay particular attention.

## The future is now

The world is now split into the haves and the have-nots by four major divisions, all of which continue to widen. These divisions became evident in the *GEO-3* assessment and were addressed in the conclusions to Chapter 2. They are:

- the environmental divide;
- the policy divide;
- the vulnerability gap; and
- the lifestyle divide.

These four divisions are a serious threat to sustainable development. The environmental assessment in the preceding chapters shows that, despite increased awareness of the environment, efforts to stem deterioration have met with mixed results. There are notable successes and spectacular failures. Over the past three decades, massive investments of human and financial resources have been used to exploit the environment. On the other hand, research has opened up new frontiers in terms of humanity's understanding of the complex web of ecological processes.

Policies have been introduced to address many of the key issues. Targets have been set and met in some areas, such as the phase out of ozone-depleting substances, but success has been limited in others, for example the adoption of more stringent targets to reduce anthropogenic greenhouse gas emissions under the Kyoto Protocol. Many other initiatives critical to closing the lifestyle divide and the success of sustainable development have been identified. These include:

- *Alleviating poverty.* The international community has set a target of halving by 2015 the proportion of the world population (currently 22 per cent) which survives on less than US$1 a day. The day-to-day lives of the majority of the poor are much more closely linked to the state of the environment than is the case for the better off — a healthy, productive environment is one of the few stepping stones out of poverty. As long as millions of the world's population remain poor, and the environment stays on the periphery of mainstream policy making, sustainable development will be an unachievable ideal.
- *Reducing the excessive consumption of the more affluent.* As long as the richest 20 per cent of the world population continues to account for 86 per cent of total personal consumption expenditure, it is unlikely that sustainable development will ever be achieved. The resulting pockets of wealth in a sea of poverty heighten tensions and overexploit resources.

- *Improving governance* has become a major issue, not only at the institutional and national levels, but also at the global level where disparities between North and South often fuel conflict and intransigence in negotiating policies for effective environmental management.
- *Providing adequate funding* for environmental programmes is a major factor. Inadequate resources have been blamed for the unsatisfactory implementation of *Agenda 21*, and inaction may ultimately undermine this blueprint for a sustainable future.
- *Eliminating debt*, particularly for the Highly Indebted Poor Countries, is also an important factor in a world in which debtor nations often use more foreign currency to repay debts than they earn. Indebtedness frequently leads to the overexploitation of the environment. As long as this situation is perpetuated, many of the debtor nations are unlikely to ever achieve sustainable development.

Many complex processes — social, economic and environmental — are at play in terms of greater impacts on people as a result of environmental change. Human vulnerability has been highlighted in Chapter 3, which emphasizes that everyone is at risk in one way or another to environmental change. The main difference is in coping capacity and ability to recover, and this difference means that the poor are generally more vulnerable. This vulnerability gap is undermining sustainable development. Human vulnerability to environmental change encompasses the quality of the environment, threats to that environment and the differing coping strategies of individuals and communities in any location, country or region. Closing the vulnerability gap would have a huge impact on the well-being and security of millions.

Reducing and eliminating poverty are inextricably linked with sound environmental management, which includes such issues as property and usage rights, the provision of basic services to protect the environmental asset base, adequate infrastructure, and funding for development and environment activities. One way forward here would be for donors to give direct support to community-based initiatives, especially those channelled towards sustainable development activities, through funding channels

accessible to low-income, disadvantaged and vulnerable groups.

Changes in consumption levels are needed by the more affluent individuals and nations of the world. Prosperity is closely linked to the ability to address environmental problems but it is also one of the forces behind excessive consumption, which is the cause of other problems with far-reaching impacts. Economic and political concerns have stalled attempts to change consumption patterns through new policies or instruments. A realization that changing consumption patterns does not have to curtail or prejudice quality of life, and can in fact do the opposite, must be brought home to the people concerned. There is sufficient evidence that this is the case but no coordinated effort to get the message across has yet been undertaken. Changing mindsets needs to go hand in hand with increased acceptance of responsibility for environmental and social impacts, and the creation of consumer ethics.

The provision of financial resources is insufficient in the absence of adequate capacity. Targeted capacity building and, more importantly, capacity mobilization and retention to minimize the brain drain are needed for more effective environmental governance and public participation. It is particularly important to ensure that capacity development is a shared experience rather than top-down or North-to-South instruction. With enhanced capacity, developing regions may be better able to cope with environmental change and disasters, which have increased their vulnerability.

The following are some of the additional environment-related challenges policy makers at all levels face over the coming decades:

- Large numbers of people, especially in developing countries, in both rural and urban areas, still lack access to clean water and adequate sanitation, good outdoor and indoor air quality, cleaner energy and waste management. This continues to lead to the degradation of the natural assets base, ill health and vulnerability to environmental threats.
- Unresolved conflicts remain over the ownership and management of common property resources (such as water, air, land, forests and oceans).
- Highly complex environmental issues which are not yet adequately addressed include the increasing prevalence of persistent toxic

substances, unsafe handling, disposal and dispersal of chemical and hazardous wastes, non-point pollution sources, management of transboundary river systems and shared water bodies, and excessive nitrogen loading.

- Climate change will cause inevitable damage in the medium and long term (low-lying islands and coastal areas, arid and semi-arid ecosystems, increased scale and intensity of environmental disasters). Developing countries, particularly Small Island Developing states, are the least able to adapt to events caused by climate change but are the most likely to be affected by them.
- The global environmental impact (ecological footprint) of the developed world and prosperous communities elsewhere is larger than that of the poor in the developing world but future economic development and population growth in the latter are likely to dramatically increase environmental impacts.

## Role of information

Information is the foundation of sustainable development and is fundamental to successful planning and decision making. If decisions are made without sound data and information, they will be little better than best guesses and are likely to be wrong. Economic and social data are widely available and are relatively reliable and well understood. The situation with environmental data and information is somewhat different. High quality, comprehensive and timely information on the environment remains a scarce resource, and finding the 'right' information can pose problems: data are more difficult and expensive to obtain. It is also difficult to find indicators that capture and reflect the complexity of the environment and human vulnerability to environmental change. Environmental data acquisition remains a basic need in all countries.

Despite the problems, scientific consensus based on best available data and knowledge, although sometimes partial and limited, has proved a powerful tool for bringing environmental issues to international attention, and prompting action. There have been great improvements in environmental research and monitoring but it is important that these efforts are maintained and improved to ensure a flow of timely and reliable information. A sub-set of that information

needs to underpin early warning in relation to disasters and emerging issues, and to the factors underlying human vulnerability to environmental change.

The provision of information will benefit from:

- Structured and nested monitoring and observing systems including global satellites for collection of timely and reliable data on environmental components, using harmonized units of measurement and terms.
- An effective, globally acceptable environmental information system supported by a harmonized set of data, indicators and indices and closely integrated with socio-economic information systems to provide basic information for decision making.
- Maximizing the use of the Internet as a cheap and effective means of information exchange worldwide.
- Identifying indicators and indices to capture the sustainability of environmental trends as well as trends in human vulnerability to environmental change.
- Tools to create a knowledge base accessible to environmental policy and decision makers.
- Presentation of complex data and information in an easily understandable form to decision makers.

## Changing policies and strengthening implementation

The following policy options, based on UNEP experience, the *GEO-3* assessment, and wide consultation with experts and stakeholders, provide a current perspective on initiatives needed now to set a sustainable course for the next 30 years and beyond. Action is needed at many levels. The suggestions for action that follow may be applicable to multiple or specific levels; they are intended as a check-list from which to make appropriate selections. The overriding need in policy development is to adopt a balanced approach towards sustainable development, giving adequate weight and strength to all three pillars; from the environmental perspective, this means mainstreaming the environment, bringing it in from the margins to the heart of development. How can this be achieved?

## Rethinking institutions

Many environmental institutions were originally set up under different conditions and to perform different functions from those they are expected to exercise today. They now need to adapt to new roles and partnerships, especially in view of the development of multiple, nested levels of action from the global to the local, and the spread of responsibilities to civil society. Many institutions are constrained by a lack of human capacity and funding, despite increased environmental challenges, and this limits their effectiveness. These are clearly issues that need to be addressed if institutions are to fulfil their present obligations and confront emerging environmental issues.

### What to aim for

- Reform, streamline and strengthen existing environmental institutions. Reforms should be directed towards creating flexibility, adaptability and adequate capacity.
- Reinforce the linkages between global and local levels, and ensure that implementation and capacity are passed on to local authorities wherever possible.
- Rationalize the range of environmentally related mandates among the many international organizations and conventions that result in overlap, duplication, poor assignment of responsibilities and difficulties in information sharing.
- Promote synergies between public institutions, think tanks and the private sector to facilitate the exchange of ideas, capacity and skills

## Strengthening the policy cycle

The most successful environmental management approaches are based on policies that incorporate a range of tried and tested principles. Policy development processes for the environment need tightening to become more rigorous, systematic and integrated, turning out policies tailored for specific localities and situations. This implies a clearer understanding of the environmental implications of decision-making processes, better information on the quality of environmental management, the prioritization of issues, the setting of goals, targets and time frames, and the development of tools for monitoring progress and evaluating results.

Environmental policy development is a dynamic, iterative process encompassing assessment of the problems and options, target setting and policy formulation, followed by implementation, monitoring, review, evaluation, regular reassessment and adjustment. Without the complete cycle, it is not possible to determine if policies are having their intended effect or to make informed adjustments. Effective environmental policies form part of mainstream politics and should be incorporated into all political sectors and levels of government, especially into economic decision making. Effective national plans and sustainability strategies bring together governments, civil society and the private sector; they incorporate diverse initiatives such as 'green' and 'brown' agendas and country-specific best practices. Achieving this implies shifting the focus of policy from

# Suggestions for Action

## Improving policy performance monitoring

At the international level:

- Support the Global Reporting Initiative (GRI) and encourage more countries to join
- Support international efforts to improve compliance with MEAs and strengthen capacities to build effective national compliance regimes
- Strengthen regular dialogue between the international community and civil society through an open forum to discuss relevant environmental policy issues, share ideas and propose recommendations

Within civil society:

- Strengthen the existing monitoring of political will and performance, continue to raise awareness of environmental concerns and act as a 'watchdog' over the private sector, governments and international organizations
- Encourage individual responsibility and provide the missing link between people and policy development
- Support private sector initiatives on environmental performance standards and reporting, such as voluntary disclosure on progress in stemming pollution, protecting environmental assets and promoting sustainable development

environmental protection to the broader concept of sustainable resource management.

## Providing an international policy framework

The fragmentation, duplication and overlap among international Multilateral Environmental Agreements (MEAs) reflects their piecemeal origin in response to each new problem. There are more meetings and reporting requirements than many governments can cope with or afford. Compliance rates are at best patchy. In the long term, a different approach aimed at building a coherent body of international environmental legislation is needed; meanwhile, short-term initiatives may help the system function more effectively.

## Suggestions for Action

### Strengthening international environmental legislation and compliance

- Increase information exchange to foster coordination between related agreements
- Hold joint meetings of the conferences of the Parties or the scientific advisory bodies of related MEAs, such as those for climate change and ozone
- Establish joint financial systems to cover various MEA provisions and integrate regional secretariats with a view to bringing related MEA secretariats under a uniform system
- Revitalize regional and global MEA mechanisms that have been beneficial in the past but have been sidelined
- Encourage NGOs, action groups, and regional and international organizations to promote conventions among their constituencies and leverage them effectively into policy
- Mandate UNEP to strengthen coordination of MEAs
- Establish a system of national reporting on international conventions to facilitate their close linkage to national policies and programmes
- Formulate transparent monitoring rules, procedures and regimes for the review and revision of commitments, conflict mediation and the provision of scientific, technical and economic advice upon request
- Assign shared but differentiated responsibilities and obligations under environmental agreements, whereby richer states are given greater responsibilities for action than poorer states
- Allow international and regional institutions to handle environmental disputes and encourage them to enforce sanctions against non-compliant parties to strengthen the effectiveness of international agreements
- Establish transparent and doable non-compliance procedures under existing MEAs

## Using trade to the benefit of sustainable development

Western trade barriers restrict the ability of developing countries to grow economically and finance sustainable development expenditure. Global trade patterns and increasing globalization can threaten the environment but they can also provide mechanisms and incentives for sustainable development. The open market brings new opportunities for flows of capital, technology and labour to benefit developing countries. The danger of trade liberalization, however, is that environmental policies can be undermined and pollution havens created unless adequate checks and balances are in place.

Some form of sustainable trade is therefore needed. Sustainable trade is defined as an international exchange of goods and services that yields positive social, economic and environmental benefits, and reflects the core criteria of sustainable development. If trade, environment and development are to be brought together successfully, three critical needs must be addressed:

- the need for transparency;
- the need for equity and fairness — especially so that countries or stakeholders historically excluded from trade opportunities really benefit; and
- the need to ensure that social and environmental benefits provide lasting value for developing countries in terms of the capacity for innovation in the future.

## Suggestions for Action

### Changing trade patterns to benefit the environment

- Conduct research on issues such as the:
  - impacts of trade liberalization on environmental and human well-being
  - effects of environmentally and socially sustainable trade on communities and environments
- Build on the valuable lessons of prior experience such as those acquired since 1994 by the North American Commission for Environmental Cooperation which implements the environmental accord to NAFTA
- Strengthen the sustainable development emphasis of trade policies
- Prepare guidelines for export credit agencies

## Harnessing technology for the environment

Promising new technologies can help to secure basic goods and services, especially for the poor in developing countries, but they remain largely the province of commercial interests in developed countries. Environmental technologies in water and energy (wind and solar power, fuel cells), recycling, biotechnology and ecological farming all offer great potential. Ways must be found to capitalize on these innovations, transfer the technologies to the needy at affordable cost and include them in the development of technologies. Developing countries must become 'partners in the process' of technology rather than 'partners in the products' of technology.

In spite of the enormous potential for environmental and social gains from new technology, there are certain risks that need to be managed. Methodologies and capacity to evaluate these risks, to establish 'rules of conduct' and to facilitate appropriate transfer provide the challenge. The precautionary approach, polluter and user pays principles, full information dissemination and disclosure of risks, technology impact assessment, and the cost benefit analyses of adopting the technology must all be taken into account.

There are a number of ways forward:

- the creation of incentives using trade-related intellectual property rights (TRIPs);
- technology transfer to developing countries and poorer communities on preferential terms; and
- investment in alternative, relevant and more environmentally sound technologies, combining traditional and indigenous wisdom with cutting-edge science.

## Making policy instruments and packages work for the environment

The backbone of national policy for the environment is legislation but other options are available. The most effective and appropriate policy packages incorporate a range of different policy tools and instruments.

### *Valuing environmental goods and services*

When environmental goods and services are costed, rather than considered as free, there is an appreciation of the immense value of the environmental assets that underpin human well-being and security. This value is proportionally greater for the livelihoods, survival ability and resilience of the poorest and most marginalized communities. Valuing the environment is one way of raising the profile of the environment in the national policy arena. There have been numerous attempts to develop methods to assign a monetary value to environmental goods and services and the environmental impacts of economic activity. Such methods need further development and validation.

### Technology transfer: lessons from the Montreal Protocol

Technology transfer has been successfully carried out through the Multilateral Fund of the Montreal Protocol. Analysis of case studies has demonstrated that:

- Technology transfer is a collaborative effort: active cooperation, partnership and synergy between all stakeholders are required
- The process cannot take place in isolation and requires a supportive environment with actions taken by government and industry, through a proper balance of incentives and disincentives
- Technology transfer needs to be consistent with national programmes
- Project planning should be comprehensive and geared to local conditions, requirements and capabilities of the receiving enterprises
- Market forces play a crucial role in affecting or facilitating the technology transfer process
- New technology should complement indigenous technologies where possible
- Training is essential
- Public awareness leads to public support
- Presentation of clear political guidelines is required

## Suggestions for Action

### Valuing the environment

- Refine and improve methods of calculating the economic value of environmental goods and services, and the environmental impacts of economic activity
- Evaluate environmental costs and benefits in all sectors of the economy to incorporate environmental accounting as standard practice in local or national accounting and at company level
- Support and encourage those involved in education and economics courses to incorporate tools and methods for environmental accounting into all curricula
- Consider environmental costs and benefits in policy development

## Making the market work for sustainable development

A plethora of instruments exists that can make the market work for sustainable development, including tradable permit schemes, removing market barriers and environmentally damaging government subsidies, subsidizing the start-up of environmentally sound businesses, creating markets for environmental services, encouraging disclosure policies and recycling tax revenues. In the right context, market instruments can often be more effective than command-and-control measures. Furthermore, their flexibility encourages private sector innovation in ways that binding policies do not. The market is not very effective, however, in dealing with the long time horizons and uncertainty that characterize some environmental problems.

## Suggestions for Action

### Making the market work for sustainable development

- Promote tailored policies that combine market instruments with traditional command-and-control measures, such as internalizing environmental costs, introducing environmental taxes and removing perverse subsidies
- Build partnerships between government, industry and others to shape the markets for environmental goods and services, using tools such as legislation, incentives, market mechanisms and other methods of influencing market and consumer behaviour
- Analyse and reform market imbalances and imperfections, including decreasing the subsidies that allow prices to be held artificially below the costs of production and use for resources such as as fuel, pesticides, water and electricity
- Develop more and better incentives to capitalize on 'win-win' situations, whereby both the economy and the environment benefit, such as:
  - increasing community benefits from environmental markets (e.g. fair trade)
  - introducing a public disclosure policy to reveal those most responsible for pollution — such as the publicly available pollutant release and transfer registries through which industries report emissions to air, water and land
- Promote the growing catalytic, cooperative role of governments (rather than the regulatory one) and encourage better national coordination between international trade decisions and environmental policy
- Bring 'green' goods and services to the market
- Take active measures to stimulate sustainable consumption and production practices
- Provide incentives for eco-efficient (cleaner) production and innovation

## Voluntary initiatives

More attention should be paid to harnessing the potential of both voluntary action by individuals and formal voluntary initiatives in business. Voluntary initiatives are increasingly recognized by the private sector as a way of contributing to the environmental agenda and being seen to be 'green'. At the individual level, voluntary action is the foundation for many forms of environmentally responsible behaviour.

## Suggestions for Action

### Further voluntary action

- Encourage the further adoption of voluntary initiatives such as:
  - commitments by companies to achieve additional environmental targets
  - codes of conduct for sectoral industry associations regarding environmental responsibility
  - environmental performance targets agreed between government and a company or sector
  - legally binding covenants
- Support NGO-led voluntary initiatives such as:
  - environmental clean-up and recycling campaigns
  - tree planting
  - restoration of degraded areas

## Policy performance monitoring

Governments are often good at adopting declarations and action plans but not at implementing them. The lack of political will, implementation, enforcement and compliance requires urgent action. Open processes of performance monitoring are often absent and the responsibilities for it at each level of governance unclear. NGOs play an essential role in independent review at national level, drawing attention to policy failures and poor performance. While specific criticisms may irritate those who are targeted, the existence of such public review provides a strong motivation for good performance. Its constructive role in the overall transparency and efficiency of the system should be acknowledged.

## Shifting and sharing roles and responsibilities

The creative interaction of individuals and small units often provides efficient solutions to managing complicated and variable situations. Local responsiveness and adaptability are important. This approach can be applied at a variety of scales and has important implications for environmental management, suggesting the need to distribute roles and responsibilities in new ways.

The transfer of certain responsibilities through subsidiarity and decentralization is emerging as an effective way to ensure more timely policy development and implementation. Responsibility for many aspects of environmental and social health and safety lies at the local or municipal level, where action is crucial for poverty reduction, improving local environments and providing early warning on issues with current or potential national and international prominence. The effectiveness of devolving power to this level depends on the nature of participatory management systems of environmental governance, identifying all stakeholders and ensuring that they are 'at the policy table'. Particularly in developing countries, providing for more meaningful participation in environment and resource use decision-making, and giving all stakeholders the confidence that they can make a difference, will decrease mutual suspicion and enable major groups to participate in managing the shared environment on an equal footing.

### Local action

The way that Local *Agenda 21* principles have been successfully embraced in both the developing and the industrialized world is a powerful encouragement for decentralization. However, decentralization to the municipal level has not always increased policy effectiveness, particularly in low and middle-income countries. This is because:

- local democracy is often lacking;
- responsibilities among different authorities overlap;
- power and control over resources are often retained by higher levels of government, including the ability to raise revenues; and
- local technical and institutional capacity is weak and affected by inefficient local governance.

Local measures are especially important to support the fight against poverty. As the scenarios in Chapter 4 have shown, the more desirable outcomes have involved rather than ignored individuals and local communities, which must be enabled to participate fully in decision-making affecting access to and management of common environmental assets and services. For this to happen, strong democratic local institutions are essential.

# Suggestions for Action

## Participatory management

- Develop strategic partnerships between governments, communities, the private sector and NGOs, particularly for advisory, implementation and funding activities, with clearly defined responsibilities assigned to the members
- Provide encouragement and opportunities to industry and the private sector to contribute further to developing and implementing sustainable development programmes
- Give civil society a more central role in environmental management by removing systemic barriers to participation, especially by women, indigenous peoples and youth, and give due attention to indigenous knowledge and coping strategies
- Improve institutional mechanisms for participation for stakeholders from civil society and the private sector
- Provide institutional legitimacy to community-based resource management practices by making communities part of the national legal and regulatory framework
- Give people a clear stake in the environment through legal and regulatory measures that define and recognize individual or community property and tenure rights
- Assign common but differentiated responsibilities to all involved

## Ways to strengthen local action

- Integrate Local *Agenda 21s* into urban politics and policies while respecting their consultative and participatory nature
- Create awareness and ownership over the local environment (whether rural or urban) and its links to the global environment among the general public
- Create opportunities for public involvement in decision-making on local environmental issues, and support community rights to own and care for the land their members inhabit and the resources they use

## Regional action

Regional levels of environmental policy development are also important, requiring the strengthening of regional bodies, initiatives, institutes and alliances. Strengthening regional level roles creates capacity for successful policy at an appropriate scale for many environmental processes and threats. In the inter-linked chain from local to global levels, regional blocks are becoming more important, new ones are being formed and stalled initiatives are being given new life. Increased attention is needed to develop regional level environmental policy, with a clear definition of responsibilities among local, national, regional and global institutions.

## Global action

There is a growing range of global stakeholders including intergovernmental organizations, multinational corporations and international NGOs. Environmental NGOs are increasingly involved in international environmental governance, including the implementation of activities under the Global Environment Facility, the World Bank and regional development banks. This experience should be drawn on more extensively both in multi-stakeholder dialogues during international negotiations and in the implementation of international programmes.

# Acronyms and Abbreviations

| | |
|---|---|
| ABC | Asian Brown Cloud |
| AEPC | African Environmental Protection Commission |
| AEPS | Arctic Environmental Protection Strategy |
| AEWA | African-Eurasian Waterbird Agreement |
| AIDS | acquired immunodeficiency syndrome |
| ALGAS | Asia Least Cost Greenhouse Gas Abatement Strategies |
| AMCEN | African Ministerial Conference on the Environment |
| AMU | Arab Maghreb Union |
| ANWR | Arctic National Wildlife Refuge |
| AoA | Agreement on Agriculture |
| AOC | Areas of Concern |
| APELL | Awareness and Preparedness for Emergencies at Local Level |
| AQIS | Australian Quarantine and Inspection Service |
| ASEAN | Association of Southeast Asian Nations |
| AU | African Union |
| BOD | biological oxygen demand |
| BSE | bovine spongiform encephalopathy |
| CAB | Centre for Agriculture and Biosciences |
| CAMP | Coastal Area Management Project |
| CAP | Common Agricultural Policy |
| CARICOM | Caribbean Community |
| CBC | community-based conservation |
| CBD | Convention on Biological Diversity |
| CBO | community-based organization |
| CCAB-AP | Central American Council for Forests and Protected Areas |
| CCAMLR | Commission on the Conservation of Antarctic Marine Living Resources |
| CCD | Convention to Combat Desertification |
| CCFSC | Central Committee for Flood and Storm Control |
| CD-ROM | Compact disk–read only memory |
| CEC | Commission for Environmental Cooperation |
| CEE | Central and Eastern Europe |
| CEIT | Countries with Economies in Transition |
| CEP | Committee for Environmental Protection |
| CERES | Coalition for Environmentally Responsible Economics |
| CFC | Chlorofluorocarbon |
| CGIAR | Consultative Group on International Agricultural Research |
| $CH_4$ | methane |
| CIAT | International Centre for Tropical Agriculture |
| CILSS | Permanent Interstate Committee for Drought Control in the Sahel |
| CITES | Convention on International Trade in Endangered Species of Wild Fauna and Flora |
| CLRTAP | Convention on Long-Range Transboundary Air Pollution |
| cm | centimetre |

| | |
|---|---|
| CMS | Convention on the Conservation of Migratory Species of Wild Animals |
| CNC | Chinese National Committee |
| CNG | compressed natural gas |
| CO | carbon monoxide |
| $CO_2$ | carbon dioxide |
| COP | Conference of the Parties |
| CPACC | Caribbean Planning for the Adaptation of Global Climate Change |
| CPF | collaborative partnerships on forests |
| CRAMRA | Convention on the Regulation of Antarctic Mineral Resource Activities |
| CRP | Conservation Reserve Program (United States) |
| CSD | Commission on Sustainable Development |
| CTBT | Comprehensive Nuclear Test Ban Treaty |
| CZIMP | Coastal Zone Integrated Management Plan |
| DALY | disability adjusted life year |
| DDT | dichlorodiphenyltrichloroethane |
| DPSIR | driving force-pressure-state-impact-response |
| EANET | Acid Deposition Monitoring Network |
| EBRD | European Bank for Reconstruction and Development |
| EC | European Community |
| ECOWAS | Economic Community of West African States |
| EEZ | Exclusive Economic Zone |
| EfE | Environment for Europe |
| EIA | environmental impact assessment |
| EMEP | Monitoring and Evaluation of the Long-Range Transmission of Air Pollutants in Europe |
| EMS | Environmental Management System |
| ENSO | El Niño Southern Oscillation |
| EPC | Emergency Preparedness Canada |
| EPCRA | Emergency Planning and Community Right-to-Know Act |
| EPPR | Emergency Prevention, Preparedness and Response |
| ESA | Endangered Species Act (United States) |
| ESDP | European Spatial Development Perspective |
| ESP | electrostatic precipitator |
| EU | European Union |
| EVI | Environmental Vulnerability Index |
| FAO | Food and Agriculture Organization of the United Nations |
| FDI | foreign direct investment |
| FDRP | Flood Damage Reduction Program |
| FEMA | Federal Emergency Management Agency |
| FEWS | Famine Early Warning System |
| FEWS NET | Famine Early Warning System Network |
| FMCN | Mexican Fund for Nature Conservation |
| FSC | Forest Stewardship Council |
| FSU | former Soviet Union |
| FTAA | Free Trade Area for the Americas |

| | | | | |
|---|---|---|---|---|
| G7 | Group of Seven: Canada, France, Germany, Italy, Japan, United Kingdom, United States | | IRWR | internal renewable water resources |
| G8 | Group of Eight: Canada, France, Germany, Italy, Japan, Russian Federation, United Kingdom, United States | | ISDR | International Strategy for Disaster Reduction |
| | | | ISO | International Organization for Standardization |
| GATT | General Agreement on Tariffs and Trade | | IT | information technology |
| GAW | Global Atmosphere Watch | | ITTO | International Tropical Timber Organization |
| GBIF | Global Biodiversity Information Facility | | IUCN | World Conservation Union |
| GCC | Gulf Cooperation Council | | IWC | International Whaling Commission |
| GCOS | Global Climate Observing System | | IWRM | integrated water resources management |
| GCRMN | Global Coral Reef Monitoring Network | | IYM | International Year of Mountains |
| GDP | gross domestic product | | km | kilometre |
| GEF | Global Environment Facility | | LADA | Land Degradation Assessment of Drylands |
| GEMS | Global Environment Monitoring System | | LCBP | Lake Champlain Basin Program (United States) |
| GEO | Global Environment Outlook | | LMO | living modified organism |
| GISP | Global Invasive Species Programme | | LPG | low-propane gas |
| GIWA | Global International Waters Assessment | | LRT | light rapid transit |
| GLASOD | Global Assessment of Soil Degradation | | LUCAS | European Land Use/Land Cover Statistical Survey |
| GLOF | glacial flood outburst lake | | MA | Millennium Ecosystem Assessment |
| GLWQA | Great Lakes Waters Quality Agreement | | MAP | Mediterranean Action Plan |
| GM | genetically modified | | MARPOL | International Convention for the Prevention of Pollution from Ships |
| GMO | genetically modified organism | | | |
| GNP | gross national product | | MARS | Major Accident Reporting System |
| GRI | Global Reporting Initiative | | MCPFE | Ministerial Conference on the Protection of Forests in Europe |
| GRID | Global Resource Information Database | | | |
| GSP | gross state product | | MEA | multilateral environmental agreement |
| HABs | harmful algal blooms | | MEMAC | Marine Emergency Mutual Aid Centre |
| HCFC | hydrochloroflourocarbon | | MERCOSUR | Mercado Común del Sur |
| HDI | Human Development Index | | MRT | mass rapid transit |
| HELCOM | Helsinki Commission | | $N_2O$ | nitrous oxide |
| HFC | hydrofluorocarbon | | NAACO | National Ambient Air Quality Objectives (Canada) |
| HIPC | Heavily Indebted Poor Country | | NAACS | National Ambient Air Quality Standards (United States) |
| HIV | human immunodeficiency virus | | | |
| IABIN | Inter-American Biodiversity Information Network | | NABIN | North American Biodiversity Information Network |
| ICC | International Chamber of Commerce | | NAFTA | North American Free Trade Agreement |
| ICLEI | International Council for Local Environmental Initiatives | | NARSTO | North American Research Strategy for Tropospheric Ozone |
| ICM | Integrated Coastal Management | | | |
| ICRAN | International Coral Reef Action Network | | NAWMP | North American Waterfowl Management Plan |
| ICRI | International Coral Reef Initiative | | NCAR | National Center for Atmospheric Research |
| ICT | information and communication technology | | NEAP | National Environmental Action Plan |
| IDNDR | International Decade for Natural Disaster Reduction | | NECD | EU Directive on National Emission Ceilings for Certain Atmospheric Pollutants |
| IFAD | International Fund for Agricultural Development | | | |
| IFF | Intergovernmental Forum on Forests | | NEPA | National Environmental Protection Agency |
| IJC | International Joint Commission | | NEPM | National Environmental Protection Measure |
| ILO | International Labour Organization | | NGO | non-governmental organization |
| IMF | International Monetary Fund | | $NH_3$ | ammonia |
| IMO | International Maritime Organization | | NIS | Newly Independent States |
| INBO | International Network of Basin Organizations | | NO | nitrogen oxide |
| INDOEX | Indian Ocean Experiment | | $NO_2$ | nitrogen dioxide |
| IPCC | Intergovernmental Panel on Climate Change | | $NO_x$ | nitrous oxides |
| IPF | Intergovernmental Panel on Forests | | NPK | nitrogen, potassium and phosphorus (fertilizer) |
| IPM | integrated pest management | | NSSD | National Strategy for Sustainable Development |
| IPR | intellectual property rights | | $O_3$ | ozone |
| | | | OAU | Organization for African Unity |
| | | | ODA | official development assistance |
| | | | ODS | ozone-depleting substance |

| | |
|---|---|
| OECD | Organization for Economic Cooperation and Development |
| OCIPEP | Office of Critical Infrastructure and Emergency Preparedness |
| OSPAR | Convention for the Protection of the Marine Environment of the North-East Atlantic |
| PACD | Plan of Action to Combat Desertification |
| PAME | Protection of the Arctic Marine Environment |
| PCB | polychlorinated biphenyls |
| PCP | Permanent Cover Program (Canada) |
| PEBLDS | Pan-European Biological and Landscape Diversity Strategy |
| PEEN | Pan-European Ecological Network |
| PEFC | Pan-European Forest Certification |
| PERSGA | Protection of the Environment of the Red Sea and Gulf of Aden |
| PFRA | Prairie Farm Rehabilitation Administration (Canada) |
| PICs | Pacific Island Countries |
| PM2.5 | particulate matter with a diameter of 2.5 microns or less |
| POPs | persistent organic pollutants |
| PRRC | Pasig River Rehabilitation Commission (Philippines) |
| PSR | pressure-state-response |
| RAP | remedial action plan |
| REMPEC | Regional Marine Pollution Emergency Response Centre for the Mediterranean Sea |
| ROPME | Regional Organization for the Protection of the Marine Environment |
| SACEP | South Asia Cooperative Environment Programme |
| SADC | Southern African Development Community |
| SANAA | National Autonomous Water and Sewage Authority (Honduras) |
| SAP | structural adjustment programme |
| SARA | Species At Risk Act (Canada) |
| SCOPE | Scientific Committee on Problems of the Environment |
| SEA | strategic environmental assessment |
| SEI | Stockholm Environment Institute |
| SIDS | Small Island Developing State or States |
| SO$_2$ | sulphur dioxide |
| SOE | state of the environment |
| SOPAC | South Pacific Applied Geosciences Commission |
| SPIRS | Seveso Plants Information Retrieval System |
| SPM | suspended particulate matter |
| SPRD | Strategic Planning and Research Department (Singapore) |
| START | System for Analysis, Research and Training |
| TAI | Technology Achievement Index |
| TAO | tropical atmospheric ocean |
| TCA | Treaty for Amazonian Cooperation |
| TCDD | 2,3,7,8-tetrachlorodibenzo-p-dioxin |
| TEA | Transportation Equity Act |
| TEK | traditional ecological knowledge |
| TEN | Trans-European Network |
| TFAP | Tropical Forestry Action Plan |
| TRAFFIC | Trade Records Analysis for Flora and Fauna in International Commerce |
| TRI | Toxics Release Inventory |
| TRIPs | Trade-Related Aspects of International Property Rights |
| UEBD | Executive Unit for Settlements in Development (Honduras) |
| UK | United Kingdom |
| UN | United Nations |
| UNCED | United Nations Conference on Environment and Development |
| UNCHS | United Nations Commission on Human Settlements |
| UNCLOS | United Nations Convention on the Law of the Sea |
| UNCOD | United Nations Conference on Desertification |
| UNCTAD | United Nations Conference on Trade and Development |
| UNDP | United Nations Development Programme |
| UNECE | United Nations Economic Commission for Europe |
| UNEP | United Nations Environment Programme |
| UNEP-WCMC | United Nations Environment Programme-World Conservation Monitoring Centre |
| UNESCAP | United Nations Economic and Social Commission for Asia and the Pacific |
| UNESCO | United Nations Educational, Scientific and Cultural Organization |
| UNF | United Nations Foundation |
| UNFCCC | United Nations Framework Convention on Climate Change |
| UNFF | United Nations Forum on Forests |
| UNHCR | United Nations High Commission for Refugees |
| UNICEF | United Nations Children's Fund |
| UNOCHA | United Nations Office for the Coordination of Humanitarian Affairs |
| UNSO | United Nations Sudano-Sahelian Office (now UNDP Office to Combat Desertification) |
| US | United States |
| US EPA | United States Environmental Protection Agency |
| USAID | United States Agency for International Development |
| USFWS | United States Fish and Wildlife Service |
| USGS | United States Geological Survey |
| UV | ultraviolet |
| VOC | volatile organic compound |
| WBCSD | World Business Council for Sustainable Development |
| WCED | World Commission on Environment and Development |
| WCP | World Climate Programme |
| WCS | World Conservation Strategy |
| WFP | World Food Programme |
| WHO | World Health Organization |
| WHYCOS | World Hydrological Cycle Observing System |
| WIPO | World Intellectual Property Organization |
| WMO | World Meteorological Organization |
| WSSCC | Water Supply and Sanitation Collaborative Council |
| WSSD | World Summit on Sustainable Development |
| WTO | World Trade Organization |
| WWC | World Water Council |
| WWF | World Wide Fund for Nature |
| ZACPLAN | Zambezi River System Action Plan |
| ZAMCOM | Zambezi Basin Commission |

# Collaborating Centres

Arab Centre for the Studies of Arid Zones & Drylands
(ACSAD)
P.O. Box 2440, Damascus, Syria
Tel: +963 11 574 3039/3087
Fax: +963 11 574 3063
E-mail: acsad@net.sy and majdjama@scs-net.org
http://www.acsad.org

Arabian Gulf University (AGU)
P.O. Box 26671, Manama, Bahrain
Tel:     +973 239 602 or +973 965 3553
Fax:     +973 272 555/274 028
E-mail: nabeel@mail.agu.edu.bh
http://www.agu.edu.bh

Asian Institute of Technology (AIT)
P.O. Box 4, Klong Luang, Pathumthani 12120,
Thailand
Tel: +662 524 5406
Fax: +662 524 5439 or 516 2126
E-mail: ram@ait.ac.th
http://www.ait.ac.th

Association pour le Développement de l'Information
Environnementale (ADIE)
B.P. 4080 Libreville, Gabon
Tel: +241 763040, 763019, 763032
Fax: +241 774261
E-mail: jpvandeweghe@adie-plgie.org

Bangladesh Centre for Advanced Studies (BCAS)
House 23, Road 10A Dhammondi R/A
Dhaka 1209, Bangladesh
Tel: +880-2 8113977
Fax: +880-2-8111-344
E-mail: bcas@bdonline.com
http://www.bcas.net

Brazilian Institute of the Environment and Natural
Renewable Resources (IBAMA)
SAIN Av. L4 Norte
Ed. Sede do IBAMA, Bloco C, 1° andar
CEP: 70 800 200, Brasilia DF, Brazil
Tel: +55 61 316 1284/316 1282
Fax: +55 61 225 0564
E-mail: jcamara@sede.ibama.gov.br
http://www.ibama.gov.br

Central European University (CEU)
Nador u.9, Budapest H-1051, Hungary
Tel: +36 1 327 3021
Fax: +36 1 327 3031
E-mail: envsci@ceu.hu
http://www.ceu.hu/departs/envsci

Centre for Environment and Development for the Arab
Region & Europe (CEDARE)
2 El Hegaz St., Heliopolis
P.O. Box 1057 Heliopolis Bahary, Cairo, Egypt
Tel: +202 451 3921/2/3/4
Fax: +202 451 3918
E-mail: ahrehim@cedare.org.eg
http://www.cedare.org.eg

Commission for Environmental Cooperation of the
North American Agreement on Environmental
Cooperation (CEC of NAAEC)
393, rue St-Jacques Quest, Suite 200
Montréal, Québec, Canada, H2Y 1N9
Tel: +1 514 350 4330
Fax: +1 514 350 4314
E-mail: gblock@ccemtl.org

Earth Council
Apartado 2323-1002, San José, Costa Rica
Tel: +506 256 1611
Fax: +506 255 2197
E-mail: rleger@ecouncil.ac.cr

European Environment Agency (EEA)
Kongens Nytorv 6, DK-1050 Copenhagen, Denmark
Tel: +45 3336 7101
Fax: +45 3336 7128
E-mail: david.stanners@eea.eu.int
http://www.eea.eu.int

GRID Christchurch
Centre for Antarctic Studies and Research
University of Canterbury
Private Bag 4800
Christchurch, New Zealand
Tel: +643 364 2136
Fax: +643 364 2197
E-mail: m.finnemore@anta.canterbury.ac.nz

Indian Ocean Commission (IOC)
Q4 Avenue Sir Guy Forget
P.O. Box 7 Quatre Bornes, Mauritius
Tel: +230 425 9564/1652
Fax: +230 425 2709
E-mail: Rajmohabeer@coi.intnet.mu
http://www.coi-info.org

International Centre for Integrative Studies (ICIS)
P.O. Box 616, 6200 MD Maastricht, The Netherlands
Tel: +31 43 3882691
Fax: +31 43 3884916
E-mail: icis@icis.unimaas.nl
http://www.icis.unimaas.nl

International Global Change Institute (IGCI)
University of Waikato
Private Bag 3105, New Zealand
Tel: +64 7 858 5647
Fax: +64 7 858 5689
E-mail: n.ericksen@waikato.ac.nz
http://www.waikato.ac.nz/igci/

International Institute for Sustainable Development (IISD)
161 Portage Avenue East, 6th Floor
Winnipeg, Manitoba, Canada R3B 0Y4
Tel: +1 204 958 7715
Fax: +1 204 958 7710
E-mail: lpinter@iisd.ca
http://www.iisd.ca

Island Resources Foundation
6292 Estate Nazareth, # 100
St Thomas, VI 00802-1104
US Virgin Islands
Tel: +1 340 775 6225
Fax: +1 340 779 2022
E-mail: etowle@irf.org
http://www.irf.org

Moscow State University (MSU)
119899 Moscow, Russian Federation
Tel:     +7 095 939 3962
Fax:     +7 095 932 8836
E-mail: nick@dronin.geogr.msu.su

Musokotwane Environment Resource Centre for Southern Africa (IMERCSA), Southern African Research and Documentation Centre (SARDC)
15 Downie Ave, Belgravia
P.O. Box 5690, Harare, Zimbabwe
Tel: +263-4-791141
Fax: +263-4-791271
E-mail: cmafuta@sardc.net

National Environmental Management Authority (NEMA)
P.O. Box 22255, Kampala, Uganda
Tel: +256 41 251064/5/8
Fax: +256 41 232680/257521
E-mail: csebukeera@nemaug.org

National Institute for Environmental Studies (NIES)
16-2 Onogawa, Tsukuba, 305-0053, Japan
Tel: +81-298-50-2598
Fax: +81-298-58-2645
E-mail: toshiaki@nies.go.jp
http://www.nies.go.jp

National Institute for Public Health and the Environment (RIVM)
P.O. Box 1, 3720 BA Bilthoven, The Netherlands
Tel: +31 30 274 3112
Fax: +31 30 274 4435
E-mail: jan.bakkes@rivm.nl

Network for Environment and Sustainable Development in Africa (NESDA)
24 BP 95 Guichet Annexe BAD
Abidjan, Côte d'Ivoire
Tel: +225 20 20 54 19/18
Fax: +225 20 20 59 22
E-mail: abamba@nesda.org
http://www.nesda.org

Regional Environmental Center for Central and Eastern Europe (REC)
Ady Endre ut 9 11, 2000 Szentendre, Hungary
Tel: +36 26 504 040
Fax: +36 26 311 294
E-mail: mmckinley@rec.org
http://www.rec.org

RING Alliance of Policy Research Organizations
c/o International Institute for Environment and Development (IIED)
3 Endsleigh Street
London WC1H 0DD, United Kingdom
Tel: +44 20 7388 2117
Fax: +44 20 7388 2826
http://www.iied.org/index.html

Scientific Committee on Problems of the Environment (SCOPE)
51 Boulevard de Montmorency
75016 Paris, France
Tel: +33 1 45 25 04 98
Fax: +33 1 42 88 14 66
E-mail: secretariat@icsu-scope.org
http://www.icsu-scope.org

Scientific Information Centre (SIC)
15 Bitarap Turkmeninstan Str.,
744000 Ashkhabad, Turkmenistan
Tel: +99312 390586
Fax: +99312 353716
E-mail: nfp-tm@online.tm

South Pacific Regional Environmental Programme (SPREP)
P.O. Box 240, Apia, Samoa
Tel: +685 21 929
Fax: +685 20 231
E-mail: MattM@sprep.org.ws

State Environmental Protection Administration (SEPA)
No. 115 Xizhimen Nei Nanxiaojie
Beijing 100035, P.R. China
Tel: +86 10 6615 1933
Fax: +86 10 6615 1762
E-mail: yuers@svr1-pek.unep.net

 SEI

Stockholm Environment Institute (SEI)
11 Arlington Street
Boston, MA 02116-3411, United States
Tel: +1 617 266 8090
Fax: +1 617 266 8303
E-mail: praskin@tellus.org

Tata Energy Research Institute (TERI)
Darbari Seth Block, Habitat Place, Lodhi Road
New Delhi 110 003, India
Tel: +91 11 468 2100 and 468 2111
Fax: +91 11 468 2144 and 468 2145
E-mail: meetam@teri.res.in

สถาบันสิ่งแวดล้อมไทย
Thailand Environment Institute

Thailand Environment Institute (TEI)
210 Sukhumvit 64
Bangchak Refinery Building 4, 2nd floor
Prakhanong, Bangkok 10260, Thailand
Tel: +66 2 331 0047/331 0060
Fax: +66 2 332 4873
E-mail: somrudee@tei.or.th
http://www.tei.th

University of Chile
Diagonal Paraguay 265, Torre 15, Floor 13
Santiago, Chile
Tel: +562 678 2272/2308
Fax: +562 678 2581
E-mail: osunkel@uchile.cl
http://www.capp.uchile.cl

University of Costa Rica
San José, Costa Rica
Tel: +506 207 4854/4855
Fax: +506 207 3329
E-mail: egutierr@cariari.ucr.ac.cr
http://www.odd.ucr.ac.cr

University of West Indies, Centre for Environment and Development (UWICED)
3 Gibraltar Camp Road
Mona, Kingston 7, Jamaica
Tel: +1 876 977 1659/5530/5545
Fax: +1 876 977 1658
E-mail: abinger@uwimona.edu.jm
http://www.isis.uwimona.edu.jm

World Conservation Union (IUCN)
Rue Mauverney 28, CH-1196 Gland, Switzerland
Tel: +41 22 999 02 71
Fax: +41 22 999 00 25
E-mail: nmm@hq.iucn.org

World Resources Institute (WRI)
10 G Street, NE
Washington, DC 20002, United States
Tel: +1 202 729 7771
Fax: +1 202 729 7775
E-mail: robinw@wri.org

# Contributors

Those listed below have contributed to *GEO-3* in a variety of ways, as authors, reviewers, participants in GEO consultations and survey respondents.

## Africa

Ahmed Mohamed Ali Abdelrehim, Centre for Environment and Development for the Arab Region and Europe, Egypt; Hamidkhan Abddullakhan, Indian Ocean Commission, Mauritius; Sherif Abdou, Centre for Environment and Development for the Arab Region and Europe, Egypt; Mohamed A. Abdrabo, Institute of Graduate Studies and Research, Alexandria University, Egypt; Emad Adly, Arab Network for Environment and Development, Egypt; Sam Aboah, Sambus Company Limited, Ghana; Wilna Accouche, Division de l'Environnement, Ministère de l'Environnement et du Transport, Seychelles; Nimbe O. Adedipe, Department of Crop Protection and Environmental Biology, University of Ibadan, Nigeria; P.B.K.L. Agyirey-Kwakye, Youth Club for Nature Conservation, Ghana; Maha Akrouk, Centre for Environment and Development for the Arab Region and Europe, Egypt; Fatma Al-Mallah, Technical Secretariat, Council of Arab Ministers Responsible for the Environment, League of Arab States, Egypt; Emile Amougou, Ministère de l'Environnement et des Forêts, Cameroon; Mike Anane, Ghana; Willy Andre, Division de l'Environnement, Ministère de l'Environnement et du Transport, Seychelles; Linda Arendse, Council for Scientific and Industrial Research-Environmentek, South Africa; Kader Asmal, Ministry of Education, South Africa; Franck Attere, World Wide Fund for Nature, Gabon; Rajen Awotar, Council for Development, Environmental Studies and Conservation, Mauritius; Bola Ayeni, Department of Geography, University of Ibadan, Nigeria; Abou Bamba, Network for Environment and Sustainable Development in Africa, Côte d'Ivoire; Patricia Baquero, Ministère de l'Aménagement du Territoire et de l'Habitat, Seychelles; Louis Guyto Barbe, Division de l'Environnement, Seychelles; André Bassolé, Environment Information Systems in Sub-Saharan Africa, Burkina Faso; H. Beekhee, c/o Indian Ocean Commission, Mauritius; Sitotaw Berhanu, Environment Protection Authority, Ethiopia; Wilfrid Bertile, Indian Ocean Commission, Mauritius; Foday Bojang, Organization of African Unity, Ethiopia; Thomas Chiramba, Southern African Development Community Water Sector Coordinating Unit, Lesotho; Francis Coeur de Lion, Geographical Information System Centre, c/o Indian Ocean Commission, Mauritius; Harvey Croze, Kenya; Berhe Debalkew, Inter-Governmental Authority on Development, Djibouti; Koulthoum Djamadar, Programme Investissement Public, Comoros; G. Domingue, Seychelles Fisheries Authority, Seychelles; Clement Dorm-Adzobu, Water Resources Commission, Ghana; Mohamed El-Anbaawy, Faculty of Science, Cairo University, Egypt; Ismail El-Bagouri, Centre for Environment and Development for the Arab Region and Europe, Egypt; Aly El-Beltagy, Shore Process Laboratory, National Institute of Oceanography and Fisheries, Egypt; Dina El-Naggar, Egyptian Environmental Affairs Agency, Ministry of Environment, Egypt; Mahmoud Khamis El-Sayed, University of Alexandria, Egypt; RoseEmma Mamaa Entsua-Mensah, Water Research Institute, Council for Scientific and Industrial Research, Ghana; Rachid Firadi, Departement de l'Environnement, L'Observatoire National de l'Environnement, Ministère de l'Aménagement du Territoire, de l'Urbanisme, de l'Habitat et de l'Environnement, Morocco; Peter G.H. Frost, Institute of Environmental Studies, University of Zimbabwe, Zimbabwe; Richard F. Fuggle, Environmental Evaluation Unit, University of Cape Town, South Africa; Frederick Gikandi, Ngomongo Environmental and Poverty Alleviation Initiative, Kenya; Chris Gordon, Centre for African Wetlands, University of Ghana, Ghana; Troy Govender, Eskom, South Africa; Betty Gowa, National Environment Management Authority, Uganda; Jacob Gyamfi-Aidoo, Environmental Information Systems-Africa, c/o Council for Scientific and Industrial Research-Environmentek, South Africa; Craig I. Haskins, Environmental Management Department, Cape Metropolitan Council Administration, South Africa; Ahmed Hegazy, Faculty of Science, Cairo University, Egypt; Mahmoud Hewehy, Ain Shams University, Egypt; Paddington Hodza, Remote Sensing Division, Environment and Remote Sensing Institute, Zimbabwe; M. Timm Hoffman,

Botany Department, Institute for Plant Conservation, University of Cape Town, South Africa; Hamadi Idaroussi, Ministère de la Production et de l'Environnement, Comoros; Joseph Ipalaka Yobwa, Programme Régional de Gestion de l'Information Environnementale, Democratic Republic of Congo; Danae Issaias, Kenya; Prem C. Jain, Physics Department, The University of Zambia, Zambia; Godfrey Kamukala, Health and Environment Concerns, Tanzania; Etienne Kayengeyenge, Ministère de l'Amenagement du Territoire et de l'Environnement, Burundi; Yemi Katerere, IUCN - The World Conservation Union, Zimbabwe; Consolata W. Kiragu, National Environment Secretariat, Kenya; Evans Kituyi, African Centre for Technology Studies, Kenya; Ebenezer Laing, Department of Botany, University of Ghana, Ghana; Elton Laisi, Centre for Development Research and Information in Southern Africa, Malawi; Tamuka Magadzire, Southern African Development Community Regional Remote Sensing Unit, Zimbabwe; Clever Mafuta, Southern African Research and Documentation Centre, Musokotwane Environment Resource Centre for Southern Africa, Zimbabwe; Betty C. Maina, Institute of Economic Affairs, Kenya; Denis Eddy Matatiken, Division de l'Environnement, Seychelles; Khohlooa, Likobo and Matholoana Herdsboys, Lesotho; Mantso Matsoso, Herdsboys Organization, Lesotho; Simon K. Mbarire, National Environment Secretariat, Kenya; Denzil Miller, Antarctic Resources, South Africa; Mildred Mkandla, EarthCare Africa Monitoring Institute, Kenya; Rajendranath Mohabeer, Indian Ocean Commission, Mauritius; Yaqoub Abdalla Mohamed, Higher Council for Environment and Natural Resources, Ministry of Environment and Physical Development, Sudan; Santaram Mooloo, Department of Environment, Ministry of Local Government and Environment, Mauritius; John Mugabe*, African Centre for Technology Studies, Kenya; Lucy Mulenkei, Indigenous Information Network, Kenya; Joselyne Mutegeki, Environmental Management Associate, Uganda; Fannie Mutepfa, ZERO-A Regional Environment Organization, Zimbabwe; Leonard Ntonga Mvondo, Ecosystèmes Forestiers d'Afrique Centrale, Cameroon; John Nevill, Division de l'Environnement, Ministère de l'environnement et du Transport, Seychelles; Protasius Nghileendele, Directorate of Environmental Affairs, Ministry of Environment and Tourism, Namibia; Deborah Manzolillo Nightingale, Environmental Management Advisors, Kenya; Petros Nyathi, Department of Research and Specialist Services, Zimbabwe; Charles Obol, Southern African Development Community-Environment and Land Management Sector Coordination Unit, Lesotho; Benson Owuor Ochieng, African Centre for Technology Studies, Kenya; Eric Odada, Pan-African Start Secretariat, Kenya National Academy of Sciences, University of Nairobi, Kenya; Ojijo Odhiambo, Resource Management and Policy Analysis Insitute, Kenya; David Okali, Nigeria Environmental Study Action Team, Nigeria; Mary Omosa, Institute for Development Studies, University of Nairobi, Kenya; Peter O. Ondiege, Keipet Consultants Ltd, Kenya; A. A. Oteng-Yeboah, Department of Botany, University of Ghana, Ghana; John O. Oucho, International Training Programme in Population and Sustainable Development, University of Botswana, Botswana; Mohamed Youssouf Oumouri, Directeur Général de l'Environnement Conseiller Technique, Ministère de l'Environnement, Comores; Rajesh Parboteeah, De Chazal du Mée, Mauritius; Rolph Payet, Ministère de l'Environnement et du Transport, Seychelles; Fatou Planchon, Centre de Suivi Ecologique, Sénégal; Danny Poiret, Division de l'Environnement, Ministère de la Santé, Seychelles; Deepnarain Prithipaul, Ministère de l'Environnement et du Développement Rural et Urbain, Mauritius; Faoud Abdou Rabi, Association pour le Développement de l'Information Environnementale, Comoros; Georges Rafomanana, Ministère de l'Environnement, Madagascar; Côme Ramakararo, Division de la Promotion Environnementale, Ministère de l'Environnement, Madagascar; A. Ramsewak, Ministère des Affaires Etrangéres et de la Coopération Regionale, Mauritius; Pierre Randah, Communauté Économique et Monétaire de l'Afrique Centrale, Central African Republic; Jean de Dieu Ratefinanahary, Division des Problèmes Environnementaux et des Affaires Culturelles - Service des Nations Unies et Institutions Spécialisées, Direction de la Coopération Multilatérale, Ministère des Affaires Etrangères, Madagascar; Herisoa Razafinjato, Système d'Information Environnemental, Office National pour l'Environnement, Madagascar; Dave Richardson, Institute for Plant Conservation, Botany Department, University of Cape Town, South Africa; John Laing Roberts, Ministry of Health, Mauritius;

Soonil Dutt Rughooputh, Faculté des Sciences, Université de Maurice, Mauritius; Osama Salem, Centre for Environment and Development for the Arab Region and Europe, Egypt; Pedro A. Sanchez, International Centre for Research on Agroforestry, Kenya; Robert J. Scholes, Council for Scientific and Industrial Research-Environmentek, South Africa; Craig Schwabe, Geographic Information System Centre, Human Sciences Research Council, South Africa; Charles Sebukeera, National Environment Management Authority, Uganda; Staff of Shoals of Capricorn, Seychelles; Didier Slachmuylder, Indian Ocean Commission, Mauritius; Soondaree Devi Soborun, Ministère des Infrastructures Publiques, du Transport Intérieur et de la Marine, Mauritius; Youba Sokona, Programme Energie, Environnement et Développement du Tiers-Monde, Sénégal; Nouri Soussi, Ministry for Environment and Land Management, Centre Urbain Nord, Tunisia; Thomas Fofung Tata, Cameroon; Marie Nkom Tamoifo, Association Jeunesse Verte du Cameroun, UNEP Youth Advisory Council, Cameroon; Jonathan Timberlake, Biodiversity Foundation for Africa, Zimbabwe; Mostafa Kamal Tolba, International Center for Environment and Development, Egypt; Frank Turyatunga, Environment Protection and Economic Development Project, Uganda; Michel Vieille, Division de l'Environnement, Ministère de l'Environnement et du Transport, Seychelles; Ahmed Wagdy, Centre for Environment and Development for the Arab Region and Europe, Egypt; David M. Walker, Space Physics Research Institute, South Africa; Dominic Walubengo, Forest Action Network, Kenya; Conmary Wesseh, Center for Democratic Empowerment, Cote d'Ivoire; Keith Wiseman, Environmental Management Department, Cape Metropolitan Council Administration, South Africa; E. Alaphia Wright, Faculty of Engineering, University of Zimbabwe, Zimbabwe; Hassan Musa Yousif, African Futures, Côte d'Ivoire.

## Asia and the Pacific

Evelyn Adolph, Department of Economic Affairs, National Government, Federated States of Micronesia; Anil Kumar Agarwal, Centre for Science and Environment, India; Makhtumkuli Akmuradov, Ministry of Nature Protection, Turkmenistan; Mozaharul Alam, Bangladesh Centre for Advanced Studies, Bangladesh; Mau Alipate, Department of Commerce, American Samoa; Beki Annaev, International Fund for Aral Sea, Turkmenistan; Iswandi Anas, Department of Soil Sciences, Faculty of Agriculture, Bogor Agricultural University, Indonesia; Samuel Antiko, Strategic Coordination, Department of Environment and Conservation, Papua New Guinea; Saparmamet Ashirov, Scientific Information Centre of Intergovernmental Sustainable Development Commission, Turkmenistan; Lydia Astanina, Ecological News Agency 'Greenwomen', Kazakhstan; Irina Atamuradova, Focal Point for Global Resource Information Database Arendal, Turkmenistan; Saeed Ather, Ministry of Environment, Local Government and Rural Development, Pakistan; Ellie Austin, Environment Assessment and Reporting, South Pacific Regional Environment Programme, Samoa; Agadzhan G. Babaev, Regional Research and Education Center to Combat Desertification, Turkmenistan; Dzuma B. Bairamov, National Institute of Statistics and Information under the Council of Ministers, Turkmenistan; Joe Baker, Commissioner for the Environment A.C.T., Australia; Shilpi Banerjee, Tata Energy Research Institute, India; Ernest Bani, Environment Unit, Department of Foreign Affairs, Government of Republic of Vanuatu, Vanuatu; Adletbek Bekeyev, Ministry of Natural Resources and Environment Protection, Kazakhstan; Tao Bie, State Environmental Protection Administration, China; Moses Biliki, Department of Forest, Environment and Conservation, Ministry of Forests, Environment and Conservation, Solomon Islands; Con Boekel, Environmental Information and Technology Strategies Branch, Department of Environment and Heritage, Australia; S. Boldbaatar, Ministry of Nature and Environment, Mongolia; Kodyr Boturov, Ministry of Nature Protection, Tajikistan; Djalil Buzrukov, Ministry of Nature Protection, Tajikistan; Genevieve Brighouse, American Samoa Coastal Management Program, Department of Commerce, American Samoa; Paul Broady, Department of Plant and Microbial Sciences, University of Canterbury, New Zealand; Budag A. Budagov, Institute of Geography, Azerbaijan Academy of Sciences, Azerbaijan; Anvar D. Buzurukov, Tajik Social and Ecological Union, Tajikistan; Xin Cao, Center for Environmental Science, Peking University, China; Ian Carruthers, Greenhouse Policy Group, Australian Greenhouse Office, Australia; Weerawat Chanthanakome, The Federation of Thai Industries, Thailand; Ralph Chapman, Strategy and Policy Group, New Zealand Ministry for the Environment, New Zealand; Ying Chen, Institute of World Economics and Politics, Chinese Academy of Social Sciences, China; Joanne Chew, International Relations Department, Ministry of the Environment, Republic of Singapore; Twinkle Chopra, Centre for

Environment Education, India; Atiqul Islam Chowdhury, Ministry of Environment and Forest, Bangladesh; Tagaloa Cooper, Department of Community Affairs, Niue; Pham Ngoc Dang, Center for Environmental Engineering of Towns and Industrial Areas, Hanoi University of Civil Engineering, Vietnam; Aditi Dass, Energy Program, Asian Institute of Technology, Thailand; Surojit Dass*, Urbanization and Environment Programme, Thailand Environment Institute, Thailand; Neil de Wet, International Global Change Institute, University of Waikato, New Zealand; Kiran Desai, Center for Environment Education, Nehru Foundation for Development, India; Yujie Ding, State Environmental Protection Administration, China; Viengsavanh Douangsavanh, Department of Environment. Science, Technology and Environment Agency, Lao People's Democratic Republic; Amanmurad Durdyev, Center of Ecological Monitoring, Turkmenistan; Elrid Egorov, National Institute of Desert, Flora and Fauna of Ministry of Nature Protection, Turkmenistan; Mehboob Elahi, South Asia Cooperative Environment Programme, Sri Lanka; Neil Ericksen, International Global Change Institute, University of Waikato, New Zealand; Paltamet Esenov, National Institute of Desert, Flora and Fauna of Ministry of Nature Protection, Turkmenistan; Muhammad Eusuf, Bangladesh Centre for Advanced Studies, Bangladesh; S. Faizi, India; Grahame Fraser, Department of Physics and Astronomy, University of Canterbury, New Zealand; Mitsuo Fukuchi, Antarctic Biology and Conservation Group, Scientific Committee on Antarctic Research, National Institute of Polar Research, Japan; Vladimir Glazovskiy, Ministry of Nature Protection, Turkmenistan; Harsh K. Gupta, Department of Ocean Development, Government of India, India; Sujata Gupta*, Tata Energy Research Institute, India; A. Sh. Habibullaev, State Committee for Nature Protection, Uzbekistan; Jacquelyn Harman, International Global Change Institute, University of Waikato, New Zealand; Barry T. Hart, Water Studies Centre, Monash University, Australia; John Hay, International Global Change Institute, University of Waikato, New Zealand; Xiaoxia He, Center for Environmental Science, Peking University, China; Alan D. Hemmings, Environmental Consultant, Polar Regions, New Zealand; Barry L. Henricksen, Australia; Srikantha Herath, Water Resources Engineering, International Center for Disaster-Mitigation Engineering, Japan; Thosapala Hewage, Ministry of Forestry and Environment, Sri Lanka; Katsunori Hirokane, National Institute for Environmental Studies, Environment Agency of Japan, Japan; Wakako Hironaka, House of Councillors, The National Diet of Japan, Japan; Kasemsri Homchean, Mabtaput Industrial Estate, Industrial Estate Authority of Thailand, Thailand; Naw Wah Wah Htoo, United Nations Environment Programme Regional Resource Centre for Asia and the Pacific, Thailand; Than Htoo, National Commission for Environmental Affairs, Ministry of Foreign Affairs, Myanmar; Xiulian Hu, Center for Energy, Environment and Climate Change Research, Energy Research Institute, State Development Planning Commission of China, China; Xuan Hu, Center for Environmental Science, Peking University, China; Michael Huber, Global Coastal Strategies, Australia; Akmukhamet Ibragimov, Ecological Fund, Turkmenistan; Toshiaki Ichinose, Center for Global Environmental Research, National Institute for Environmental Studies, Environment Agency of Japan, Japan; Sovannora Ieng, Ministry of Environment, Cambodia; Bogdan Ivakhov, Scientific Information Centre of Intergovernmental Sustainable Development Commission, Turkmenistan; Mylvakanam Iyngararasan, United Nations Environment Programme Regional Resource Centre for Asia and the Pacific, Thailand; Porntip Jaisin, Office of Environmental Policy and Planning, Ministry of Science, Technology and Environment, Thailand; Kejun Jiang, Center for Energy, Environment and Climate Change, Energy Research Institute, State Development Planning Commission of China, China; Ananda Raj Joshi, South Asia Cooperative Environment Programme, Sri Lanka; Shailendra K. Joshi, International Cooperation, Ministry of Environment and Forests, India; Inkar Kadyrzhanova, United Nations Environment Programme Regional Resource Centre for Asia and the Pacific, Thailand; David Kaimowitz, Center for International Forestry Research, Indonesia; Mikiko Kainuma, National Institute for Environmental Studies, Environment Agency of Japan, Japan; Aditi Kapoor, Alternative Futures, India; Yasuko Kameyama, National Institute for Environmental Studies, Environment Agency of Japan, Japan; Dana A. Kartakusuma, State Ministry for Environment, Indonesia; Paul Kench, International Global Change Institute, University of Waikato, New Zealand; Jonathan L. Kennett, Department of National Planning and Monitoring, Papua New Guinea; Nanthiwa Kerdchuen, Pollution Control Department, Ministry of Science, Technology and Environment, Thailand; Nariman S. Kerimov, Department of Ecological Projects of State Committee on and Ecology Control of Natural Resources Management, Azerbaijan; Shaheen Rafi Khan, Sustainable Development Policy Institute, Pakistan; Ashok Khosla, Development Alternatives, India; Solos Khunkhrua,

Environmental Research and Training Center, Department of Environmental Quality Promotion, Ministry of Science, Technology and Environment, Thailand; Ian Kiernan, Clean Up the World, Australia; Jiro Kondo, The Science and Technology Foundation of Japan, Japan; Tord Kjellstrom, Environmental Health, Department of Community Health, The University of Auckland, New Zealand; Chaiyuth Klinsukont, Thailand Institute of Scientific and Technological Research, Thailand; Pradyumna Kumar Kotta, South Asia Co-operative Environment Programme, Sri Lanka; Rieko Kubota, Yokohama City University, Japan; Premila Kumar, Department of Environment, Fiji; M. A. Kumaradasa, Ministry of Forestry and Environment, Sri Lanka; Purushottam Kunwar, Ministry of Population and Environment, Nepal; K. Vijaya Lakshmi, Environment Systems Branch, Development Alternatives, India; Murari Lal, Centre for Atmospheric Sciences, Indian Institute of Technology, India; Lusitania Latu, Central Planning Department, Tonga; Maggie Lawton, Landcare Research New Zealand Limited, New Zealand; Valeriy Lelevkin, Scientific Information Centre of Intergovernmental Sustainable Development Commission, Kyrgyz Republic; Sione Tukia Lepa, Department of Environment, Tonga; Raman Letchumanan, The Association of South-East Asian Nations Secretariat, Indonesia; Ahohiva Levi, Department of Justice, Lands and Survey and Environmental Planning, Nieu; Loren Legarda Leviste, Senate of the Philippines, Philippines; Yaguang Li, Beijing Forestry University, China; Zhu Li, Energy Research Institute, China; Wenyan Liang, Beijing Forestry University, China; Ruth Liloqula, Ministry of National Planning and Human Resources, Solomon Islands; Khin Thida Linn, Asian Institute of Technology, Thailand; Faumuina Sailimalo P. Liu, Division of Environment and Conservation, Department of Lands, Surveys and Environment, Samoa; Shengji Luan, Center for Environmental Science, Peking University, China; Harvey F. Ludwig, Seatec International Consulting Engineers, Thailand; H. N. Luptpullaev, Department of International Cooperation, Programs of the State Committee for Nature Protection, Uzbekistan; Laavasa Malua, Division of Environment and Conservation, Department of Lands, Surveys and Environment, Samoa; Nabat Mamedova, Scientific Center on Sustainable Development and Health Protection, Turkmenistan; Irina Mamieva, Scientific Information Centre of Intergovernmental Sustainable Development Commission, Turkmenistan; Parvin Maroufi, Public Relations and International Affairs, Department of the Environment, The Islamic Republic of Iran; Toshihiko Masui, Global Environment Division, National Institute for Environmental Studies, Japan; Vikrom Mathur, Stockholm Environment Institute, c/o Asian Institute of Technology, Thailand; Kan-ichiro Matsumura, Institute of Industrial Science, University of Tokyo, National Institute for Environmental Studies, Japan; Matt McGlone, Landcare Research, New Zealand; Matthew McIntyre, Environmental Management and Planning Division, South Pacific Regional Environment Programme, Samoa; Meeta Mehra, Tata Energy Research Institute, India; Anton D. Meister, Department of Applied and International Economics, Massey University, New Zealand; Gerald Miles, Environmental Management and Planning Division, South Pacific Regional Environment Programme, Samoa; R. C. Mishra, Doordarshan Bhavan, India; A. P. Mitra, National Physical Laboratory, India; Srinivas Mudrakarta, Vikram Sarabhai Centre for Development Interaction, Nehru Foundation for Development, India; Chary Muradov, National Institute of Desert, Flora and Fauna of Ministry of Nature Protection, Turkmenistan; Mei Ng, Friends of the Earth, Hong Kong; Somrudee Nicro, Urbanization and Environment Programme, Thailand Environment Institute, Thailand; Elena Nosova, Scientific Information Centre of Intgovernmental Sustainable Development Commission, Turkmenistan; Makoto Numata, Chiba University, Natural History Museum and Institute, Japan; Alty Orazov, Nature Protection Society, Turkmenistan; R. K. Pachauri, Tata Energy Research Institute, India; Thongchai Panswad, Thailand Environment Institute, Thailand; Kruti Parekh, Kruti Eco Foundation, India; Jung Hee Park, Korea Woman Environment Movement Center, Republic of Korea; Matthew Paterson, Antarctic policy Unit, New Zealand Ministry of Foreign Affairs and Trade, New Zealand; Nishanti Perera, South Asia Co-operative Environment Programme, Sri Lanka; Dean Peterson, Antarctica New Zealand - The New Zealand Antarctic Institute, New Zealand; Ken Piddington, New Zealand; Urbano Pilar, Department of Environment and Natural Resources, Philippines; Sharon Potoi-Aiafi, Ministry of Foreign Affairs, Samoa; Mary Power, Conservation and Natural Resources Division, South Pacific Regional Environment Programme, Samoa; Bidya Banmali Pradhan, International Centre for Integrated Mountain Development, Nepal; Bandana Kayasta Pradhan, International Centre for Integrated Mountain Development, Nepal; Pramod Pradhan, International Centre for Integrated Mountain Development, Nepal; Cristelle Pratt, South Pacific Applied Geoscience Commission, Fiji; Lin Qiang, Heilongjiang

Environmental Protection Bureau, China; John Quinn, National Institute of Water and Atmospheric Research, New Zealand; Albert Rafikov, Scientific Information Centre of Intergovernmental Sustainable Development Commission, Uzbekistan; Meena Raghunathan, Centre for Environment Education, Nehru Foundation for Development, India; Atiq Rahman; Bangladesh Centre for Advanced Studies, Bangladesh; R. Rajamani, India; Purna Chandra Lall Rajbhandari, United Nations Environment Programme Regional Resource Centre for Asia and the Pacific, Thailand; Karma L. Rapten, National Environment Commission, Bhutan; Michelle Rogan-Finnemore, Gateway Antarctica, Centre for Antarctic Studies and Research, Univeristy of Canterbury, New Zealand; Tatyana Saakova, Scientific Information Centre of Intergovernmental Sustainable Development Commission, Turkmenistan; Vladislav Sadomskiy, Scientific Information Centre of Intergovernmental Sustainable Development Commission, Kazakhstan; Sopaporn Saeung, Youth Environment Envoy Club, Thailand; Naimatulla M. Safarov, Research Laboratory for Nature Protection of Hydrometeorological Service, Tajikistan; Ken Sakou*, Center for Global Environmental Research, National Institute for Environmental Studies, Environment Agency of Japan, Japan; Sergey Samoylov, Department Economy and Management of Nature Resoures Use of the State Committee for Nature Protection, Uzbekistan; Usman Saparov, Executive Committee of International Fund for Aral Sea, Turkmenistan; Kartikeya Sarabhai, Centre for Environment Education, Nehru Foundation for Development, India; Setijati Didin Sastrapradja, Yayasan Keanekaragaman Hayati, Indonesia Biodiversity Foundation, Indonesia; Cedric Schuster, World Wide Fund for Nature, South Pacific Programme, Fiji; Nailia G. Shadieva, International Relations and Programmes, Department of State Committee for Nature Protection of the Republic of Uzbekistan, Uzbekistan; Jianzhong Shen, Department of Rural and Social Development, Ministry of Science and Technology, China; Chiranjeevi L. Shrestha, Nepal; Rabin Shrestha, Asian Institute of Technology, Thailand; Ram Manohar Shrestha, Asian Institute of Technology, Thailand; Mohamed Sinclair, Malaysia; J. S. Singh, Banaras Hindu University, India; Chakkrabhong Singharachai, Young Environment Envoy Club, Thailand; Prapassit Siribhodi, Environmental Research and Training Center, Department of Environmental Quality Promotion, Ministry of Science, Technology and Environment, Thailand; John F. Smith, International Global Change Institute, University of Waikato, New Zealand; Wanchai Sophonsakulrat, Asian Institute of Technology, Thailand; Ogultach Soyunova, Scientific Information Centre of Intergovernmental Sustainable Development Commission, Turkmenistan; Tunnie Srisakulchairak, Asian Institute of Technology, Thailand; Bryan Storey, Gateway Antarctica, Centre for Antarctic Studies and Research, University of Canterbury, New Zealand; Kesrat Sukasam, Bureau of Economic and Functional Cooperation, The Association of South-East Asian Nations, Indonesia; Muktarbek Sulaimanov, International Relations Department, Ministry of Nature Protection, Kyrgyz Republic; Canaganayagan Suriyakumaran, Sri Lanka; M. S. Swaminathan, M. S. Swaminathan Research Foundation, India; Monthip Sriratana Tabucanon, Environmental Research and Training Centre, Department of Environmental Quality Promotion, Ministry of Science, Technology and Environment, Thailand; Bakhar Tashlieva, Scientific Information Centre of Intergovernmental Sustainable Development Commission, Turkmenistan; Ngaina Teiwaki, Ministry of Finance and Economic Planning, Kiribati; Tania Temata, Environment Service, Cook Islands; Lameko Tesimale, Division of Environment and Conservation, Department of Lands, Surveys and Environment, Samoa; Sina To'a, South Pacific Regional Environment Programme, Samoa; Robinson Toka, Ministry of Lands and Natural Resources, Vanuatu; Hiroyasu Tokuda, Institute of Advanced Studies, The United Nations University, Japan; Tsuneyuki Ueki, System Planning Office, Integrated Solution Business Promotion Center, Environmental Engineering Group, Ebara Corporation, Japan; Galy Umarov, Scientific Information Centre of Intergovernmental Sustainable Development Commission, Kazakhstan; Kelera Vakaloloma, Ministry of National Planning, Fiji; Orazmamed Vasov, Supreme Council on Science and Technology, Turkmenistan; Caroline Vieux, Conservation and Natural Resources Division, South Pacific Regional Environment Programme, Samoa; Nathaniel Von Einsiedel, Urban Management Programme, Asian Institute of Technololgy, Thailand; Hui Wang, School of Public Health, Peking University, China; Pucai Wang, The Institute of Atmospheric Physics, Chinese Academy of Sciences, China; Zhijia Wang, State Environmental Protection Administration, China; Richard Warrick, International Global Change Institute, University of Waikato, New Zealand; Clive Wilkinson, Global Coral Reef Monitoring Network, c/o Australian Institute of Marine Science, Australia; Felicity Wong, Antarctic Policy Unit, New Zealand Ministry of Foreign Affairs and Trade, New Zealand; Guang Xia, State Environmental Protection Administration, China; Lijiang

Xia, China Agricultural University, China; Zhuyu Xu, Seoul National University, South Korea; Artyk Yazkuliev, National Institute of Desert, Flora and Fauna, Ministry of Nature Protection, Turkmenistan; Wenhu Ye, Center for Environmental Science, Peking University, China; Xia Yingxian, Division for International Organizations, Department of International Cooperation, State Environmental Protection Administration, China; Di Yu, Dalian Environment Protection Agency, Dalian Municipal Government, China; Ruisheng Yue, Division for International Organizations, Department of International Cooperation, State Environmental Protection Administration, China; Xiaofang Yue, Center for Environmental Science, Peking University, China; Hj Mohd Zakaria Bin Hj Sarudin, Ministry of Development, Brunei Darussalam; Mengheng Zhang, State Environmental Protection Administration, China; Xiangshu Zhang, People University of China, China; Xiaohong Zhao, School of Public Health, Peking University, China; Yisheng Zheng, Institute of Quantitative and Technical Economics, Chinese Academy of Social Sciences, China; Zhuang Zhuo, State Environmental Protection Administration, China.

## Europe

Joan Albaigés, Departament de Química Ambiental, Centre d'Investigació i Desenvolupament-Consell Superior d'Investigacions Científiques a Catalunya, Spain; Georgios T. Amanatidis, European Commission, Belgium; Michel Amand, Ministère de la Région Wallonne, Belgium; Chris Anastasi, British Energy plc, United Kingdom; Marina Archinova, Faculty of Geography, Moscow State University, Russian Federation; Günther Bachmann, The National Council on Sustainable Development, German Council for Sustainable Development, Germany; Philip Bagnoli, Environment Directorate, Organization for Economic Co-operation and Development, France; Jan Bakkes, National Institute of Public Health and the Environment, The Netherlands; Snorri Baldursson, Conservation of Arctic Flora and Fauna International Secretariat, Iceland; Anna Ballance, Global Resource Information Database, Arendal, Norway; Marek Baranowski, Global Resource Information Database, Warsaw, Poland; Steve Bass, International Institute for Environment and Development, United Kingdom; Michel Batisse, Plan Bleu pour l'Environnement et le Développement en Mediterranée, France; Didier Biau, Direction Régional de l'Environnement, France; Tom Bigg, International Institute for Environment and Development, United Kingdom; Joshua Bishop, International Institute for Environment and Development, United Kingdom; Winfried E. H. Blum, International Union of Soil Sciences, Austria; Edgars Bojars, Latvian Environment Agency, Latvia; Peter Bosch, European Environment Agency, Denmark; Philippe Bourdeau, Université Libre de Bruxelles, Belgium; Melih Boydak, Faculty of Forestry, University of Istanbul, Turkey; Pal Bozo, Global Resource Information Database, Budapest, Hungary; Valerie Brachya, Ministry of Environment, Israel; Lawson Brigham, Scott Polar Research Institute, University of Cambridge, United Kingdom; Bernd Brouns, Wuppertal Institute for Climate, Environment and Energy, Germany; Philip Bubb, United Nations Environment Programme World Conservation Monitoring Centre, United Kingdom; Rudolf Bruno, Global Precipitation Climatology Centre, Germany; Berhnard Burdick, Climate Policy Division, Wuppertal Institute for Climate, Environment and Energy, Germany; Wolfgang E. Burhenne, International Council of Environmental Law, Germany; Davide Calamari, Environmental Research Group, Department of Structural and Functional Biology, University of Insubria, Austria; Robert Chambers, The Institute of Development Studies, University of Sussex, United Kingdom; Nis Christensen, Danish Environmental Protection Agency, Danish Ministry of Environment and Energy, Denmark; Leif E. Christoffersen, Global Resource Information Database, Arendal, Norway; Petru Cocirta, National Institute of Ecology, Republic of Moldova; William M. Connolley, British Antarctic Survey, United Kingdom; Tatiana Constantinova, Institute of Geography of Moldova, Republic of Moldova; Peter Convey, British Antarctic Survey, United Kingdom; Neil Cox*, United Nations Environment Programme World Conservation Monitoring Centre, United Kingdom; Paul Crutzen, Max-Planck Institute for Chemistry, Germany; Paul Csagoly, The Regional Environmental Centre for Central and Eastern Europe, Hungary; Barry Dalal-Clayton, International Institute for Environment and Development, United Kingdom; Karine S. Danielyan, The Association for Sustainable Human Development, Armenia; Ged Davis, Global Business Environment, Shell International Ltd., Shell Centre, United Kingdom; Vivian Davies, International Institute for Environment and Development, United Kingdom;

Andrea DeBono, Global Resource Information Database, Geneva, Switzerland; Dick de Bruijn, Ministry of Housing, Spatial Planning and the Environment, The Netherlands; Anatoly Debinsky, Science Department of the Council of Ministers of the Ukraine Republic, Ukraine; Valeriy Demyanenko, Environmental Department, Engineering and Technology Institute, Ukraine; Nikolai Denisov, Global Resource Information Database, Arendal, Norway; Carlos de Prada, COPE, Spain; Juliette de Villers, Département Observatoire des Données de l'Environnement, Division Information et Actions de proximité, Belgium; Bert J.M. de Vries, National Institute of Public Health and the Environment, The Netherlands; Anne-France Didier, Direction Régional de l'Environnement, France; Kliment Dilianov, Ministry of Environment and Water, Bulgaria; Nikolai M. Dronin, Faculty of Geography, Moscow State University, Russian Federation; John Fanshawe, BirdLife International, United Kingdom; Phillip Fox, United Nations Environment Programme World Conservation Monitoring Centre, United Kingdom; Gerardo Fragoso, United Nations Environment Programme World Conservation Monitoring Centre, United Kingdom; Claude Füssler, World Business Council for Sustainable Development, Switzerland; Alexander V. Fyodorov, Russian Ecological Federal Information Agency, Russian Federation; Aart Gaasbeek, Shell International B.V., The Netherlands; Nadezhda Gaponenko, Analytical Center on Science and Industrial Policy, Russian Academy of Sciences, Russian Federation; Rosalie Gardiner, Stakeholder Forum for our Common Future, United Kingdom; Bachtang Sh. Geladze, Department of Hydrology, Institute of Geography, Georgian Academy of Sciences, Georgia; Anna-Rita Gentile, European Environment Agency, Denmark; Herbert Girardet, Sustainable London Trust, United Kingdom; Gregory Giuliani, Global Resource Information Database, Geneva, Switzerland; Pietro Giuliani, Ente Per le Nuove Tecnologie, l'Energia e l'Ambiente - Antartide, Italy; Inga O. Gorlenko, Department of Social-Geographic Researches, Institute of Geography, Ukrainian Academy of Sciences, Ukraine; Genady N. Golubev, Faculty of Geography, Moscow State University, Russian Federation; Elena I. Golubeva, Faculty of Geography, Moscow State University, Russian Federation; Mikhail Gorbachev, Greencross International, Switzerland; Andrew Goudie, School of Geography and the Environment, University of Oxford, United Kingdom; Nikita F. Glazovsky, Institute of Geography, Russian Academy of Sciences, Russian Federation; Edmund Green, United Nations Environment Programme World Conservation Monitoring Centre, United Kingdom; Brian Groombridge, United Nations Environment Programme World Conservation Monitoring Centre, United Kingdom; Arnulf Gruebler, Transitions to New Technologies, International Institute for Applied Systems Analysis, Austria; Donat-Peter Häder, Institut für Botanik und Pharmazeutische Biologie, Friedrich-Alexander Universität, Germany; Leif A. Halonen, Saami Council, Norwegian Section, Norway; Neil Harris, European Ozone Research Coordinating Unit, United Kingdom; Mark Harvey, Television Trust for the Environment International, United Kingdom; Oliver W. Heal, United Kingdom; Melanie Heath, BirdLife International, United Kingdom; Peter Herkenrath, BirdLife International, United Kingdom; Olav Hesjedal, Norwegian University Network for Life Long Learning, Norway; Jan-Petter Huberth-Hansen, Conservation of Arctic Flora and Fauna International Secretariat, Directorate for Nature Management, Norway; David R. Humphreys, Faculty of Social Sciences, The Open University, United Kingdom; Tsvetan Ivanov, National Association of UN Youth Clubs, Bulgaria; Yuri Izrael, Institute of Global Climate and Ecology, Russian Federation; Klaus Jacob, Forschungstelle Freie Universitat, Germany; Bengt-Owe Jansson, Department of Systems Ecology, Stockholm University, Sweden; Martin Jenkins, United Nations Environment Programme World Conservation Monitoring Centre, United Kingdom; Zurab Jintcharadze, Global Resource Information Database, Tbilisi, Georgia; Kathrine Johnsen, Global Resource Information Database, Arendal, Norway; André Jol, European Environment Agency, Denmark; Valerie Kapos United Nations Environment Programme World Conservation Monitoring Centre, United Kingdom; Stephane Kluser, Global Resource Information Database, Geneva, Switzerland; Manana Kurtabadze, Global Resource Information Database, Tbilisi, Georgia; Bruno Kestemont, Institut National de Statistique Environnement, Belgium; Vitaly Kimstach, Arctic Monitoring and Assessment Programme, Norway; John C. King, British Antarctic Survey, United Kingdom; Margarita Korkhmazyan, Department of International Cooperation, Ministry of Nature Protection of Republic of Armenia, Armenia; Stepan B. Kotchanovsky, Department of Economic Research Institute, Belarus; Peter Kouwenhoven, Resource Analysis, The Netherlands; Alexsei Kouraev, Museum of Sciences of the Earth, Moscow State University, Russian Federation; Isabella Koziell, International Institute for Environment and Development, United Kingdom; Anita Küntizer, European Environment Agency, Denmark; Roland Kupers, Shell International Limited, Shell Centre, United Kingdom; Michael Kyriamarios, Management Unit of the North Sea Mathematical Models, Belgium; Thomas Langrock, Wuppertal Institute for Climate, Environment and Energy, Germany; Thor S. Larsen, Global Resource Information Database, Arendal, Norway; Norman Lee, Environmental Impact Assessment Centre, School of Planning, University of Manchester, United Kingdom; Christian Leger, Direction Régional de l'Environnement, France; Jeremy Legget, Solar Century, United Kingdom; Erich Lippert, Ministry of the Environment, Czech Republic; Elena Lobanova, Global Resouce Information Database, Moscow, Russian Federation; Vladimir F. Loginov, Institute of Problems of Natural Resources Use and Ecology, National Academy of Sciences, Belarus; Anneliese Looss, Federal Environmental Agency, Germany; Kim S. Losev, Faculty of Geography, Moscow State University, Russian Federation; Franco Lovisolo, Triciclo Centre, Italy; Svetlana M. Malkhazova, Faculty of Geography, Moscow State University, Russian Federation; Thierry Marechal, International Association of Public Transport, Belgium; Julia Marton-Lefévre, Leadership for Environment and Development International, United Kingdom; Yuri Mazourov, Russian Heritage Institute, Russian Federation; Douglas McCallum, McCallum Consultancy, United Kingdom; Gordon McGranahan, International Institute for Environment and Development, United Kingdom; Alasdair D. McIntyre, Department of Zoology, University of Aberdeen, United Kingdom; Doug McKay, Shell International Limited, Shell Centre, United Kingdom; Mary McKinley, The Regional Environmental Center for Central and Eastern Europe, Hungary; Anthony J. McMichael, Department of Epidemiology and Population Health, London School of Hygiene and Tropical Medicine, United Kingdom; Nancy MacPherson, IUCN – The World Conservation Union, Switzerland; Gérard Mégie, Centre National de la Recherche Scientifique, France; Andrus Meiner, Estonian Environment Information Centre, Estonia; Jacek Mizak, Ministry of the Environment, Poland; Ruben Mnatsakanian, Central European University, Hungary; Arild Moe, The Fridtjof Nansen Institute, Norway; Kjell Are Moe, Alpha Environment Company, Norway; Alex Moiseev, IUCN - The World Conservation Union, Switzerland; Fran Monks, Global Business Environment, Shell International Limited, Shell Centre, United Kingdom; Lars Mortensen, Environment Directorate, Organization for Economic Co-operation and Development, France; Helen Mountford, Environment Directorate, Organization for Economic Co-operation and Development, France; Hemmo Muntingh, International Fund for Animal Welfare, Belgium; Bazha E. Naidze, Department of Economical Geography, Institute of Geography, Georgian Academy of Sciences, Georgia; Christian Nellemann, Division for Man-Environment Studies, Norwegian Institute of Nature Research, Norway; Adrian Newton, United Nations Environment Programme World Conservation Monitoring Centre, United Kingdom; Michail E. Nikiforov, Institute of Zoology, Byelorussian Academy of Sciences, Belarus; Birgit Njåstad, Polar Environmental Centre, Norwegian Polar Institute, Norway; Ola Nordbeck, Global Resource Information Database, Geneva, Switzerland; Zygfryd Nowak, Gliwice Polish Cleaner Production Center, Silesian Technical University, Poland; Markku Nurmi, Ministry of the Environment, Finland; Vyacheslav I. Oleschenko, Juridical Department, Administration of the President of Ukraine, Ukraine; Johannes B. Opschoor, Institute of Social Studies, The Netherlands; Willy Østereng, The Fridtjof Nansen Institute, Norway; Hermann E. Ott, Wuppertal Institute for Climate, Environment and Energy, Germany; Jiahua Pan, National Institute of Public Health and the Environment, The Netherlands; Hassan Partow, Global Resource Information Database, Geneva, Switzerland; Ian Payne, Marine Resources Assessment Group, United Kingdom; Lloyd Peck, British Antarctic Survey, United Kingdom; Pascal Peduzzi, Global Resource Information Database, Geneva, Switzerland; Ivone Perera-Martins, European Environment Agency, Denmark; Nicolas Perritaz, European Environment Agency, Denmark; Jonathan C. Pershing, Energy and Environment Division, International Energy Agency, France; Beat Peter, Global Resource Information Database, Arendal, Norway; Ulla Pinborg, European Environment Agency, Denmark; Kornelija Pintaric, Ministry of Environment, Croatia; Véronique Plocq Fichelet, Scientific Committee on Problems of the Environment, France; Elena Popovici, Ministry of Waters and Environmental Protection, Romania; Yiannakis D. Potamitis, Environmental Committee of Limassol, Cyprus; José Potting, National Institute of Public Health and the Environment, The Netherlands; Martin Price, Centre for Mountain Studies, Perth College, UHI Millennium Institute, United Kingdom; Hanna Rådberg, Swedish Ecodemics, Sweden; Oscar Ravera, National Research Council, Instituto Italiano di Idrobiologia,

Italy; Lars-Otto Reiersen, Arctic Monitoring and Assessment Programme, Norway; Teresa Ribeiro, European Environment Agency, Denmark; Henning Rodhe, Department of Meteorology, Stockholm University, Sweden; Odd Rogne, International Arctic Science Committee, Norway; Dale S. Rothman, International Centre for Integrative Studies, Maastricht University, The Netherlands; Jan Rotmans, International Centre for Integrative Studies, Maastricht University, The Netherlands; Leonid G. Rudenko, Institute of Geography, Ukrainian National Academy of Sciences, Ukraine; Kenneth Ruffing, Environment Directorate, Organization for Economic Co-operation and Development, France; Wolfgang Sachs, Wuppertal Institute for Climate, Environment and Energy, Germany; Elisabeth Samec, Danube-Carpathian Programme, World Wide Fund for Nature International, Austria; Peter H. Sand, International Environmental Law, University of Munich, Germany; Mirjam Schomaker, France; Stefan Schwarzer, Global Resource Information Database, Geneva, Switzerland; Hans Martin Seip, Centre for International Climate and Environmental Research University, Norway; Richard Sigman, Environment, Health and Safety Division, Organization for Economic Co-operation and Development, France; Otto Simonett, Global Resource Information Database, Arendal, Norway; Otto Spaargaren, International Soil Reference and Information Centre, The Netherlands; David Stanners, European Environment Agency, Denmark; Alison Stattersfield, BirdLife International, United Kingdom; Chris Steenmans, European Environment Agency, Denmark; Carolyn Stephens, Environmental Epidemiology Unit, Department of Public Health and Policy, London School of Hygiene and Tropical Medicine, United Kingdom; Eliahu Stern, Ministry of Environment, Israel; Volker Straub, Aventis, France; Jakob Ström, Ministry of the Environment, Sweden; Helen Sullivan, Shell International Limited, Shell Centre, United Kingdom; Zurab K. Tatashidze, Institute of Geography, Georgian Academy of Sciences, Georgia; Jean Thie, IUCN – The World Conservation Union, Switzerland; Marechal Thierry, International Association of Public Transport, Belgium; Hans Willi Thoenes, Scientific Council on Soil Protection of the German Federal Environmental, Germany; Hazell Thompson, BirdLife International, United Kingdom; Niels Thyssen, European Environment Agency, Denmark; Hardin Tibbs, Synthesys Strategic Consulting Ltd, United Kingdom; Rita Tijunaite, Ministry of Environment, Lithuania; Ferenc Toth, Potsdam Institute for Climate Impact Research, Germany; Camilla Toulmin, International Institute for Environment and Development, United Kingdom; Emil D. Tsereteli, Institute of Geography of Georgian Academy of Sciences, Georgia; Svein Tveitdal, Global Resource Information Database, Arendal, Norway; Ronan Uhel, European Environment Agency, Denmark; Dirk-Willem van Gulik, WebWeaving Consultancy, Italy; Tom A. Veldkamp, Laboratory of Soil Science and Geology, Wageningen University, The Netherlands; Kimberley Villar, International Institute for Environment and Development, United Kingdom; Axel Volkery, Environmental Policy Research Unit, Free University of Berlin, Germany; Friedrich Mumm von Mallinckrodt, Germany; Margot Wallström, European Commission, Belgium; Jonathan Walter, International Federation of Red Cross and Red Crescent Societies, Switzerland; Phil Watts, Shell International Limited, Shell Centre, United Kingdom; David Wege, BirdLife International, United Kingdom; Jacob Werksman, Foundation for International Environmental Law and Development, School of Oriental and African Studies, University of London, United Kingdom; Angela Wilkinson, Global Business Environment, Shell International Limited, Shell Centre, United Kingdom; Paul Wilkinson, Department of Epidemiology and Population Health, London School of Hygiene and Tropical Medicine, United Kingdom; Simon Wilson, Arctic Monitoring and Assessment Programme, The Netherlands; Angelika Wirtz, Munich Reinsurance Company, Germany; Alexey V. Yablokov, Centre for Russian Environmental Policy, Russian Federation; Olga Zharskaya, Ministry for Environment, Belarus; Christoph Zöckler, United Nations Environment Programme World Conservation Monitoring Centre, United Kingdom.

## Latin America and the Caribbean

Bebe Arcifa Khan Ajodha, Ministry of Education and Environmental Management Authority, Rudranath Capildeo Learning Resource Centre, Trinidad and Tobago; Manuel Alepuz, Centro de Ingeniería y Manejo Ambiental de Bahías y Costas, Cuba; Luiz Amore, Water Resources Secretariat, Ministry of the Environment, Brazil; Angela Andrade, Ministry of Environment, Colombia; Carlos Barboza, Dirección de Planificación, Ministério de Ambiente y Energía, Costa Rica; Jesús Beltrán, Centro de Ingeniería y Manejo Ambiental de Bahías y Costas, Cuba; Al Binger, Centre for Environment and Development, University of West Indies, Jamaica; Nicola Borregaard, Centro de Investigatión y Planificatión del Medio Ambiente, Chile; Hazel Brenes Umaña, Observatorio del Desarrollo, Universidad de Costa Rica, Costa Rica; Francisco Brzovic Parilo, Centro de Análisis de Políticas Públicas, Universidad de Chile, Chile; Jorge Cabrera Medaglia, Instituto Nacional de Biodiversidad, Costa Rica; João Batista Drummond Câmara, Instituto Brasileiro do Meio Ambiente e dos Recursos Naturais Renováveis, Brazil; Jose Casal, Centro de Ingeniería y Manejo Ambiental de Bahías y Costas, Cuba; Brian Cooper, Ministry of Agriculture, Government of Antigua-Barbuda, Antigua and Barbuda; Christopher Corbin, Ministry of Planning, Development, Environment and Housing, St. Lucia; Angela Cropper, Iwokrama International Centre for Rainforest Conservation and Development, Trinidad and Tobago; Roberto De La Cruz, Autoridad Nacional del Ambiente, Panamá; Exequiel Ezcurra, National Institute of Ecology, Secretary of Environment and Natural Resources, Mexico; Álvaro Fernández González, Observatorio del Desarrollo, Universidad de Costa Rica, Costa Rica; Argelia Fernández, Ministerio de Ciencia, Tecnología y Medio Ambiente, Cuba; Cornelius Fevrier, Caribbean Community Secretariat, Guyana; Pascal O. Girot, Universidad de Costa Rica, Costa Rica; Nicolo Gligo, Programa de Desarrollo Sustentable, Centro de Análisis de Políticas Públicas, Universidad de Chile, Chile; Lourdes González, Unidad de Planeamiento y Evaluación de la Gestión, Secretaría de Recursos Naturales y Ambiente, Honduras; David Gorriti Miranda, Sistema Nacional de Información para el Desarrollo Sostenible, Ministerio de Desarrollo Sostenible y Planificación, Bolivia; Eduardo Gudynas, Centro Latino Americano de Ecología Social, Uruguay; Edgar E. Gutiérrez-Espeleta, Observatorio del Desarrollo, Universidad de Costa Rica, Costa Rica; Cathal Healy-Singh, Caribbean Regional Environmental Programme, Caribbean Conservation Association, Barbados; Daniel David Hoggarth, SCALES Inc., Barbados; Luis Carlos Jemio, Corporación Andina de Fomento Economista de País, Bolivia; Jorge Arturo Jiménez, Organization for Tropical Studies, Costa Rica; Yolanda Kakabadse, Fundacion Futuro Latino Americano, Ecuador; Ian King, Regional Project Implementation Unit, Caribbean Planning for Adaptation to Global Climate Change, Barbados; Carlos Augusto Klink, Universidade de Brasília, Brazil; Nelson Koutaka Miyake, STCP Engenharia de Projetos Ltda., Brazil; Sharon Laurent, Caribbean Industrial Research Institute, Trinidad and Tobago; Ronald Léger, Earth Council, Costa Rica; Daniel López López, Centro de Investigación en Geografía y Geomática, Mexico; Magna Luduvice, Ministério do Meio Ambiente, Brazil; Maria Inês Miranda de Andrade, Instituto Brasileiro do Meio Ambiente e dos Recursos Naturais Renováveis, Brazil; Luis E. Molinas B., Secretaría del Ambiente, Paraguay; Julián Monge Nájera, Universidad de Costa Rica, Costa Rica; Oscar de Morais Cordeiro Neto, Universidade de Brasília, Brazil; C. Roberto Morales, Ministério de Ambiente y Recursos Naturales, Guatemala; Cedric Nelom, National Institute for Environment and Development, Suriname National Institute for Environment, Suriname; Rochelle Newbold, The Bahamas Environment, Science, and Technology Commission, Bahamas; Manuel Angel Núñez Soto, Government of the State of Hidalgo, Palacio de Gobierno, Pachua, Hidalgo, Mexico; Maria Onestini, Centro de Estudios Ambientales, Argentina; Álida Ortiz Sotomayor, Puerto Rico; Ramón Pichs Madruga, Centro de Investigaciones de la Economía Mundial, Cuba; Bruce Potter, Island Resources Foundation, US Virgin Islands; Alejandro Quiroz Soriano, Comisión para el Uso y la Conservación de la Biodiversidad en México, Mexico; Oscar M. Ramírez-Flores, Centro de Investigacion en Biodiversidad y Ambiente, Mexico; Marc Rammelaere, National Environment Planning Agency, Jamaica; Angela de L. Rebello Wagener, Pontificia Universidade Católica do Rio de Janeiro, Brazil; Carmen Reyes, Centro de Investigación en Geografía y Geomática, Mexico; María Luisa Robleto Aguilar, Comisión Nacional del Medio Ambiente, Chile; Yosu Rodríguez Aldabe, Secretaría de Medio Ambiente y Recursos Naturales, Mexico; Marisabel Romaggi Chiesa, Centro de Análisis de Políticas Públicas, Universidad de Chile, Chile; Juan José Romero, Proyecto Gestión Integrada de los Recursos Hídricos y Desarrollo Sostenible de la Cuenca del Río San Juan, Ministério del Ambiente y Recursos Naturales, Nicaragua; Herbert Otto R. Shubart, Secretaría de Coordinación de la Amazonia, Ministério del Medio Ambiente, Brazil; Rosa Virginia Salas Aguilar, Consejo Nacional del Ambiente, Perú; Sonia Ivett Sánchez, Ministério de Medio Ambiente y Recursos Naturales, El Salvador; Eugenio Sanhueza, Laboratorio de Quimica Atmosferica, Centro de Quimica, Instituto Venezolano de Investigaciones Cientificas, Venezuela; Lorena San Román, Earth Council, Costa Rica; Fernando R. Santibáñez, Centro de Agricultura y Medio Ambiente, Universidad de Chile, Chile; Enrique José Schaljo, Secretaría de Desarrollo Sustentable y Política Ambiental, Ministério de Desarrollo Social y Medio Ambiente, Argentina; Ricardo Schustermann, International Institute for Environment and Development-América Latina, Argentina; Joth Singh, Caribbean Conservation Association, Barbados; Osvaldo Sunkel, Centro de Análisis de Politicas Públicas, Universidad de Chile, Chile; Izabella Teixeira, Programa de Qualidade Ambiental, Ministério do Meio Ambiente, Secretaria de Qualidade Ambiental nos Assentamentos Humanos, Brazil; Peter Toledo, Museu Paraense Emilio Goeldi, Paraná, Brazil; Ivan Tomaselli, STCP Engenharia de Projetos Ltda., Brazil; Soffa Torey, Casa de la Paz, Chile; Francisco Javier Velazco, Ministerio del Ambiente, Venezuela; María del Carmen Vera Díaz, Instituto de Pesquisa Ambiental da Amazonia, Ministério do Meio Ambiente, Brazil; Sebastián Wesselman, Tropical Agricultural Research and Higher Education Centre, Costa Rica; José Ximenes De Mesquita, Instituto Brasileiro do Meio Ambiente e dos Recursos Naturais Renováveis, Brazil.

## North America

Sarah Albertini, Bureau of Transportation Statistics, United States Department of Transportation, United States; Paul Allen, Environment Canada, Canada; Stephen O. Andersen, Atmospheric Pollution Prevention Division, United States Environmental Protection Agency, United States; Geoffrey Anderson, Office of Policy Economics and Innovation, United States Environmental Protection Agency, United States; Ray C. Anderson, Interface Inc., United States; Bruce Angle, Meteorological Service, Environment Canada, Canada; Assaf Anyamba, Biospheric Sciences Branch, National Aeronautics and Space Administration Goddard Space Flight Center, United States; Gérald Aubry, Canadian Environmental Assessment Agency, Environment Canada, Canada; Richard D. Ballhorn, International Environmental Affairs Bureau, Canadian Foreign Affairs, Canada; Tariq Banuri, Stockholm Environment Institute, Boston, United States; Sabrina Barker, International Policy and Cooperation Branch, Environment Canada, Canada; Jane Barr*, Commission for Environmental Cooperation, Canada; David Bassett, United States Department of Energy, United States; Steve Bernow, Tellus Institute, United States; David Berry, Department of the Interior, Council on Environmental Quality, United States; Leonard Berry, Florida Center for Environmental Studies, Florida Atlantic University, United States; John Michael Bewers, Bedford Institute of Oceanography, Canada; Roger L. Blair, National Health and Environmental Effects Research Laboratory, United States Environmental Protection Agency, United States; Greg Block, Commission for Environmental Cooperation, Canada; Harvey Bootsma, Great Lakes Water Institute, University of Wisconsin, United States; Ian Bowles, Council on Environmental Quality, United States; Thomas J. Brennan, Bureau of International Organizations Affairs, United States Department of State, United States; Keith W. Brickley, Department of Fisheries and Oceans, Canada; Terry Bronson, American Public Transportation Policy Project, United States; Lillith Brook, Canada; Thomas M. Brooks, Center for Applied Biodiversity Science, Conservation International, United States; Ronald J. Brown, Canada Center for Remote Sensing, Canada; Ian Burton, Canada; Eric Bush, Centers for Epidemiology and Animal Health, United States; Laurence Campbell, United States Department of Commerce, United States; Danielle Cantin, Boreal and Temperate Forests Programme, IUCN - The World Conservation Union, Canada; Arcadie M. Capcelea, The World Bank, United States; Franklin G. Cardy, The World Bank, United States; Jeff Carmichael, Sustainable Development Research Institute, University of British Columbia, Canada; Chantal-Line Carpentier, North American Commission for Environmental Cooperation, Canada; Jennifer Castleden, International Institute for Sustainable Development, Canada; Julie Charbonneau, Environment Canada, Canada; Alain Chung, Pollution Data Branch, Environment Canada, Canada; William Clark, The John F. Kennedy School of Government at Harvard, United States; Cynthia Cluck, National Mapping Division, United States Geological Survey, United States; Richard Connor, World Water Council, Canada; Ted Cooke, Fisheries and Oceans Canada, Canada; Tom Cooney, United States Department of State, United States; Robert Costanza, Center for Environmental Science and Biology, University of Maryland, United States; Philippe Crabbé, Institute for Research on Environment and Economy, University of Ottawa, Canada; Rudy D'Alessandro, United States Department of the Interior, United States; Edward C. De Fabo, Medical Centre, School of Medicine, The George Washington University, United States; Patricia V. Dickerson, Bureau of Census, United States; Robert A. Duce, Department of Oceanography and Atmospheric Sciences, Texas A&M

University, United States; Jennifer Duggan, International Institute for Sustainable Development, Canada; Linda Dunn, Industry Canada-Trade Team, Canada; Paul R. Epstein, Center for Health and the Global Environment, Harvard Medical School, United States; Mark Ernste, Global Resource Information Database, Sioux Falls, United States; Hari Eswaran, United States Department of Agriculture, The Natural Resources Conservation Service, United States; Dan Fantozzi, Bureau of Oceans and International Environmental and Scientific Affairs, United States Department of State, United States; Camilla Feibelman, Sierra Student Coalition, United States; Lowell Feld, Energy Information Administration, United States Department of Energy, United States; Angus Ferguson, Environment Canada, Canada; Karen Fisher, Department of Fisheries and Oceans, Canada; Eugene Fosnight, Global Resource Information Database, Sioux Falls, United States; Amy Fraenkel, Senate Committee on Commerce, Science and Transportation, United States; Karen Freedman, Energy Information Administration, United States Department of Energy, United States; Peter Frenzen, Mount St. Helens National Volcanic Monument, United States; David Frost, Geography Department, Concordia University, Canada; Tom Furmanczyk, Environment Canada, Canada; Jacques Gagnon, Natural Resources Canada, Canada; Michelle Garland, Surface Transportation Policy Project, United States; Kim Giese, Global Resource Information Database, Sioux Falls, United States; Mark Gillis, Natural Resources Canada, Canada; Andy Gilman, Office of Sustainable Development, Health Canada, Canada; Dagny Gingrich, Biodiversity Convention Office, Environment Canada, Canada; Jerome Glenn, American Council for the United Nations University, United States; Peter H. Gleick, Environment and Security, Pacific Institute for Studies in Development, United States; Theodore Gordon, American Council for the United Nations University, United States; Stephen Gray, Landscape Management, Natural Resources Canada, Canada; Michael Grillot, United States Department of Energy, United States; Pablo Gutman, United States; Brian Haddon, National Forestry Database Programme, Natural Resources Canada Statistics, Canada; Andrew Hamilton, Resource Futures International, Canada; Allen Hammond, World Resources Institute, United States; Arthur J. Hanson, International Institute for Sustainable Development, Canada; Peter Hardi, International Institute for Sustainable Development, Canada; Asit Hazra, Environment Canada, Canada; Alan D. Hecht, Office of International Activities, United States Environmental Protection Agency, United States; David Henry, Canadian Heritage, Environment Canada, Canada; John Herity, Environment Canada, Canada; George Herrfuth, United States Department of State, United States; Christine T. Hogan, International Affairs Directorate, Environment Canada, Canada; Nazmul Hossain, Global Resource Information Database, Sioux Falls, United States; Mark Hovorka, Environment Canada, Canada; Tom Iavari, Natural Resources Conservation Service, United States; Gary Ironside, Environment Canada, Canada; Heather James, Pacific Operations, Fisheries and Oceans, Canada; Sachidamand Jha, Department of Biology, University of Massachusetts-Boston, United States; Yvan Jobin, Foreign Affairs and International Trade, Canada; Ian Johnson, The World Bank, United States; Calestous Juma, The John F. Kennedy School of Government at Harvard, United States; Margaret Kain, Forest Service, United States Department of Agriculture, United States; Shashi Kant, Faculty of Forestry, University of Toronto, Canada; John Karau, Fisheries and Oceans Canada, Canada; Robert Kates, United States; Sivan Kartha, Stockholm Environment Institute, Boston, United States; Eric Kemp-Benedict, Stockholm Environment Institute, Boston, United States; Margaret Kenny, Environment Canada, Canada; Ann Kerr, Environment Canada, Canada; Mara Kerry, Canadian Nature Federation, Canada; Frederick W. Kutz, United States Environmental Protection Agency, United States; Jim LaBau, Forest Service, United States Department of Agriculture, United States; Keith Laughlin*, Council on Environmental Quality, United States; Jay Lawimore, National Oceanic and Atmospheric Agency, United States; Douglas J. Lawrence, Natural Resources Conservation Service, United States Department of Agriculture United States; Rick Lee, University of Victoria, Canada; Annick LeHenaff, Environment Canada, Canada; Perry Lindstrom, United States Department of Energy, United States; Amory Lovins, Rocky Mountain Institute, United States; H. Gyde Lund, Forest Information Services, United States; Mary Ann Lyle, Federal Emergency Management Agency, United States; Late Elisabeth Mann Borgese, International Ocean Institute, Dalhousie University, Canada; Alex Manson, Environment Canada, Canada; Ian Marshall, Environment Canada, Canada; Tim Marta, Agriculture and Agri-Food Canada, Canada; Gordon McBean, University of Western Ontario, Canada; Jessica McCann, Community Transportation Association of America, United States; Beverly D. McIntyre, Office of Global Change, United States Department of State,

United States; Elizabeth McLanahan, National Oceanic and Atmospheric Agency, United States; Mary Lou McQuaide, Solid Waste Association of North America, United States; Terry McRae, Agriculture and Agri-Food Canada, Canada; Richard Meganck, Unit for Sustainable Development and Environment, Organization of American States, United States; Valdis E. Mezainis, International Programs, United States Forest Service, United States; Craig Miller, Environment Canada, Canada; Paul Miller, North American Commission for Environmental Cooperation, Canada; Rebecca Milo, Environment Canada, Canada; Mario J. Molina, Massachusetts Institute of Technology, United States; Charles E. Morrison, East-West Center, United States; Gloria Mundo, United States Census Bureau, United States; Ted Munn, Institute for Environmental Studies, University of Toronto, Canada; Pumulo Muyatwa, International Institute for Sustainable Development, Canada; Tony Myers, Health Canada, Canada; Adil Najam, Department of International Relations, Center for Energy and Environmental Studies, Boston University, United States; Brenda O'Conner, Environment Canada, Canada; Edward Ohanion, Office of Water, United States Environmental Protection Agency, United States; Robin O'Malley, The H. John Heinz III Center for Science, Economics and the Environment, United States; Jim Osborne, Environment Canada, Canada; Gail Osherenko, Dartmouth College, United States; Christine Padoch, The New York Botanical Garden, United States; Jeanne Pagnan, Twin Dolphins Consultants, Canada; Dennis Peacock, United States National Science Foundation, United States; Phil Perkins, Yellowstone National Park, United States; Erica Phipps, North American Commission for Environmental Cooperation, Canada; László Pintér, International Institute for Sustainable Development, Canada; Cindy Pollack-Shea, Florida Sustainable Communities Center, United States; Sharon Powers, National Agricultural Statistics Service, United States; Don Pryor, National Oceanic and Atmospheric Agency, United States; Thomas Pyle, Office of Polar Programs, United States National Science Foundation, United States; David J. Rapport, The University of Western Ontario, Canada; Paul Raskin, Stockholm Environment Institute, Boston, United States; Walter Rast, Great Lakes Water Quality Board, International Joint Commission, Canada; David Redford, United States Environmental Protection Agency, United States; Dieter Riedel, Health Canada, Canada; Elliot Riordan, The World Bank, United States; Richard Robarts, Environment Canada, Canada; Brian Roberts, Indian and Northern Affairs, Canada; John B. Robinson, Sustainable Development Research Institute, University of British Columbia, Canada; Guy Rochon, Environment Canada, Canada; Jane M. Rohling, United States Department of Agriculture, United States; David Roodman, World Watch Institute, United States; Carol Rosen, World Resources Institute, United States; Denyse Rousseau, Foreign Affairs and International Trade, Canada; Clay Rubec, Environment Canada, Canada; David Runnalls, International Institute for Sustainable Development, Canada; Daniel Meredith Schwartz, University of Toronto, Canada; Kathleen Sullivan Sealey, Department of Biology, University of Miami, United States; Stephen Seidel, United States Environmental Protection Agency, United States; Parvina A. Shamsieva-Cohen*, Global Resource Information Database, Sioux Falls, United States; Victor Shantora, Commission for Environmental Cooperation, United States; Hua Shi, Global Resource Information Database, Sioux Falls, United States; Cameron Siles, Environment Canada, Canada; Karn Deo Singh, Center for International Development, University of Harvard, United States; Brad Smith, Forest Service, United States Department of Agriculture, United States; Bryan Smith, Environment Canada, Canada; Jane Smith, Global Resource Information Database, Sioux Falls, United States; Sharon Lee Smith, Environment Canada, Canada; Susan Solomon, National Ocean and Atmospheric Administration, United States; Jim Steele, Commercial Services, Environment Canada, Canada; Janet Stephenson, Natural Resources Canada, Canada; John W. B. Stewart, University of Saskatchewan, Canada; Anita Street, Office of Planning, Analysis and Accountability, United States Environmental Protection Agency, United States; Nick Sundt, United States Global Change Research Program, United States; David Sutherland, National Ocean and Atmospheric Administration, United States; James Tansey, University of British Columbia, Canada; Charles Tarnocai, Agriculture and Agri-Food, Canada Research Branch, Canada; Jeffrey A. Thornton, International Environmental Management Services Ltd., United States; Kelly Torck, Environment Canada, Canada; John R. Townshend, University of Maryland, United States; Suzanne Tremblay, Statistics Canada, Statistical Reference Centre, Canada; Jacques Trencia, Canadian Forest Service-Science Branch, Natural Resources Canada, Canada; Daniel Tunstall, World Resources Institute, United States; David G. Victor, Science and Technology Council on Foreign Relations, United States; Jean-Louis Wallace, Environmental Relations Division, Foreign Affairs and International Trade,

Canada; Frank Wania, University of Toronto at Scarborough Canada; R. Douglas Wells, Forestry Transportation Operations Branch, Transportation and Works Department, Canada; Thomas E. Werkema, Atofina Chemicals Inc., United States; Denis White, United States Environmental Protection Agency, United States; Gilbert F. White, University of Colorado, United States; Robin White, World Resources Institute, United States; Keith Wiebe, United States Department of Agriculture, United States; Tara Wilkinson, Commission for Environmental Cooperation, Canada; Heather Wood, Environment Canada, Canada; Oran R. Young, Dartmouth College, United States; John Zacharias, Urban Studies Programme, Department of Geography, Concordia University, Canada.

## West Asia

Jameel Abdulla Abbas, University of Bahrain, Bahrain; Essa Abdellatif, The Zayed International Prize for the Environment, United Arab Emirates; Mohammad S. Abido, School of Graduate Studies, Arabian Gulf University, Bahrain; Ziad Hamzah Abu-Ghararah, Meteorology and Environment Protection Administration, Saudi Arabia; Anwar S. Abdu, Arabian Gulf University, Bahrain; Farouk Adli*, Ministry of State of Environment Affairs, Syria; Emad Adly, Arab Network for Environment and Development, Egypt; Yasser Abdulrahhim Ahmed, Gulf Petroleum Industries Company, Bahrain; Mohammed Suleiman Al-Abry, Ministry of Regional Municipalities Environment and Water Resources, Oman; Fahmi H. A. Al-Ali, Secretariat of the Gulf Cooperation Council, Saudi Arabia; Mohamed Al-Araimi, Ministry of Regional Municipalities and Environment, Oman; Nedhal Al Ashqar, Lebanon; Abdul Rahman A. Al-Awadi, Regional Organization for the Protection of the Marine Environment, Kuwait; Basma Al-Baharna, Arabian Gulf University, Bahrain; Anwar S. Shaikh Al-Deen, School of Graduate Studies, Arabian Gulf University, Bahrain; Salem Al-Dhaheri, Federal Environmental Agency, United Arab Emirates; Abdullah Al-Droubi, Arab Centre for the Studies of Arid Zones and Drylands, Syria; Dawoud Mohammad Al-Eisawi, School of Graduate Studies, Arabian Gulf University, Bahrain; Hussein Alawi Al-Gunied, Environmental Protection Council, Yemen; Yousef Ebrahim Al Hamar, Supreme Council for the Environment and Natural Reserves, Qatar; Abdulaziz Al-Jalal, Secretariat of the Gulf Cooperation Council, Saudi Arabia; A. M. Al-Janahi, Marine Emergency Mutual Aid Centre, Bahrain; Sabah Saleh Al-Jenaid, School of Graduate Studies, Arabian Gulf University, Bahrain; Ozaina Al-Jundi, Ministry of State for Environmental Affairs, Syria; Saiyed F. Al Khouli, Meteorology and Environment Protection Administration, Saudi Arabia; Zahwa M. S. Al Kuwari, Environmental Affairs, Ministry of State for Municipalities Affairs and Environmental Affairs, Bahrain; Wajdi Suliman Moh'd Al-Mahalah, Environmental Affairs, Ministry of State for Municipalities Affairs and Environmental Affairs, Bahrain; Abdul Mohsin Al-Mahmood, Environmental Affairs, Ministry of State for Municipalities Affairs and Environmental Affairs, Bahrain; Naheda Al-Majed, Regional Organization for the Protection of the Marine Environment, Kuwait; Majed Al Mansouri, Environmental Research and Wildlife Development Agency, United Arab Emirates; Meshal A. Al-Meshan, Kuwait Environment Protection Society, Kuwait; Khawla Al-Obeiden, Environment Public Authority, Kuwait; Fozi Mahmood Al-Okor, Environmental Affairs, Ministry of State for Municipalities Affairs and Environmental Affairs, Bahrain; Mohammed F. Al-Rashed, Kuwait Institute for Scientific Research, Kuwait; Naim Abdel Nabi Al Sa'ud, General Corporation for the Environment Protection, Jordan; Mostafa Al-Sayed, Gulf Petroleum Industries Company, Bahrain; Jasim Mohammed Al-Shammari, Zayed International Prize for the Environment, United Arab Emirates; Abdulrahman Al-Sharhan, Faculty of Science, United Arab Emirates University, United Arab Emirates; Mohaned S. Al-Sheriadeh, Environmental Research, University of Bahrain, Bahrain; Hayel Mansoor Turki Al-Zabin, General Corporation for the Environmental Protection, Oman; Waleed K. Al-Zubari, School of Graduate Studies, Arabian Gulf University, Bahrain; Mohamed Nabil Alaa El-Din, School of Graduate Studies, Arabian Gulf University, Bahrain; Mohamed Ait Belaid, School of Graduate Studies, Arabian Gulf University, Bahrain; Murad Jabay Bino, Inter Islamic Network on Water Resources Development Management, Jordan; Talat A. Diab, School of Graduate Studies, Arabian Gulf University, Bahrain; Alia El Husseini, IUCN National Committee, Lebanon; Late Osama El-Khouly, Technology Management Graduate Programme, Arabian Gulf University, Bahrain; Najat Ennich, Arab Planning Institute, Kuwait; Khalid M. Fakhro, Environmental Affairs, Ministry of State for Municipalities Affairs and Environmental Affairs, Bahrain; Ali Mohammed Fakhro, Bahrain Centre for Studies and

Research, Bahrain; Mohammed Fawzi, Regional Organization for the Conservation of the Marine Environment of the Red Sea and Gulf of Aden, Saudi Arabia; Abdelgawad Gilani, Arab Centre for the Studies of Arid Zones and Dry Lands, Syria; Ahmed Hamed Abu Hilal, University of Bahrain, Bahrain; Asma Ali Aba Hussain, School of Graduate Studies, Arabian Gulf University, Bahrain; Ahmed Kasara, Ministry of State of Environment Affairs, Syria; Adel M. Khalifa, United Arab Emirates; Hratch M. Kouyoumjian, National Council for Scientific Research, Lebanon; Ibrahim Loari, Arabian Gulf University, Bahrain; Mohammed H. Malack, King Fahad University of Petroleum and Minerals, Saudi Arabia; Desiree Chawki Milette, Association of Children's SOS, Lebanon; Saeed Abdulla Mohamed, School of Graduate Studies, Arabian Gulf University, Bahrain; Abdullah Omar Nasseef, King Abdulaziz University, Saudi Arabia; Shambhu Prasad, Gulf Organization for Industrial Consulting, Qatar; Nuri Rohuma, Arab Centre for the Studies of Arid Zones and Drylands, Syria; Yousef Abu Safieh, Ministry of Environmental Affairs, Palestinian National Authority, Occupied Palestinian Territories; Mahboob Hassan Saleh, Federal Environment Agency, United Arab Emirates; Nizar Ibrahim Tawfiq, Meteorology and Environmental Protection Administration, Saudi Arabia; Tayseir M. Toman, Ministry of Environmental Affairs, Occupied Palestinian Territories.

## United Nations Environment Programme

Hussein Abaza; Adel Farid Abdel-Kader; Mahmood Y. Abdulraheem; Yinka Adebayo; Ellik Adler; Johannes Akiwumi; Paul Akiwumi; Jacqueline Aloisi de Larderel; Abdu Gassim Al-Assiri; Abdul Elah Al Wadaee; Basel Al Yousfi; Alex Alusa; Subramonia Ananthakrishnan; Nirmal Andrews; Issam J. Azouri*; Marco Barbieri (Secretariat of the Convention on Migratory Species); Françoise Belmont; Hassane Bendahmane*; Nancy Bennett; Robert Bisset; Cristina Boelcke; Tore Brevik; Amedeo Buonajuti; Lucien Chabason (Coordinating Unit for the Mediterranean Action Plan); Manab Chakraborty*; Gerard Cunningham; Mark Collins (United Nations Environment Programme World Conservation Monitoring Centre); Nelson Andrade Colmenares (Regional Coordinating Unit for Caribbean Environment Programme); Arthur Lyon Dahl; Ahmed Djoghlaf; Halifa Drammeh; David Duthie; Omar E. El-Arini (Secretariat of the Multilateral Fund for the Implementation of the Montreal Protocol); Eduardo Ganem (Secretariat of the Multilateral Fund for the Implementation of the Montreal Protocol); Hiremagalur N. B. Gopalan; Michael Graber (Secretariat of the Vienna Convention and the Montreal Protocol); Steve Halls; Mariko Hara; Melanie Hatchinson; Rob Hepworth; Alexander Heydendael (Secretariat of the Convention on Biological Diversity); Tim Higham; Ivonne Higuero; John Hilborn; Arab Hoballah (Coordinating Unit for the Mediterranean Action Plan); Andrei Iatsenia; Jorge Illueca; Beth Ingraham; Steve Jackson; Olivier Jalbert (Secretariat of the Convention on Biological Diversity); Maaike Jansen; Tim Johnson (United Nations Environment Programme World Conservation Monitoring Centre); Shafqat Kakakhel; James Kamara; Donald Kaniaru; Bakary Kante; Rungano Karimanzira; Levis Kavagi; Jamshed Kazi; Elizabeth Khaka; Jesper Kofoed; Christian Lambrechts; Jean-Pierre Le Danff (Secretariat of the Convention on Biological Diversity); Bert Lenten (Secretariat of the African-Eurasian Waterbird Agreement); Dennis Lisbjerg; Jens Mackensen; William Mansfield; Isabel Martínez Villardel; Elizabeth Migongo-Bake; Beverly Miller; Parastu Mirabzadeh (Secretariat of the Convention on Biological Diversity); Strike Mkandla; Patrick L. M'may; Sylvie Motard; Jo Mulongoy (Secretariat of the Convention on Biological Diversity); Takehiro Nakamura; Nick Nuttall; Charles O. Okidi; Naomi Poulton; Daniel Puig; Anisur Rahman; Rossana Silva Repetto; Nelson Sabogal (Secretariat of the Vienna Convention and the Montreal Protocol); Frits Schlingemann; Ines Schusdziarra*; Staff of the Secretariat of the Convention on International Trade of Endangered Species; Megumi Seki; Ravi Sharma; Rajendra Shende; Marcos Silva (Secretariat of the Convention on Biological Diversity); David Smith; James Sniffen; Ricardo Sánchez Sosa; Cheikh O. Sow; Luc St Pierre (United Nations Environment Programme Regional Coordinating Unit for Caribbean Environment Programme); Heikki Toivonen (Secretariat of the Convention on Biological Diversity); Klaus Töpfer; Beatriz Torres (Secretariat of the Convention on Migratory Species); Sekou Toure; Veerle Vanderweerd; Brennan Van Dyke; Omar Vidal; Marjo Vierros (Secretariat of the Convention on Biological Diversity); John Whitelaw; Willem Wijnstekers (Secretariat of the Convention on International Trade of Endangered Species); Laura E. Williamson; James B. Willis; Hamdallah Zedan (Secretariat of the Convention on Biological Diversity).

## Other United Nations bodies

Iyad Abomoghli, United Nations Development Programme; Zafar Adeel, The United Nations University; Mohamed Al-Sharif, United Nations Development Programme; J. Bartram, World Health Organization; Nefise Bazoglu, United Nations Human Settlements Programme; Mike Bonell, Secretariat of International Hydrological Programme, United Nations Educational, Scientific and Cultural Organization; R. Bos, World Health Organization; Peter Bridgewater, United Nations Educational, Scientific and Cultural Organization; Jacob Burke, Food and Agriculture Organization; He Changchui, Food and Agriculture Organization; Patricia Charlebois, Joint United Nations Environment Programme and Office for the Coordination of Humanitarian Affairs; Ralph Chipman, United Nations Department of Economic and Social Affairs; Linda Collette, Food and Agriculture Organization; Carlos Corvalan, World Health Organization; John Crayston, International Civil Aviation Organization; Zoltan Csizer, United Nations Industrial Development Organization; Andriy Demydenko, United Nations Development Programme; Jocelyn Fenard, United Nations Institute for Training and Research; Gilberto C. Gallopín, Division of Environment and Human Settlements, Economic Commission for Latin America and the Caribbean, Chile; Peter T. Gilruth, United Nations Development Programme; Rene Gommes, Food and Agriculture Organization; John Alan Haines, International Programme on Chemical Safety, World Health Organization; John Harding, United Nations Secretariat for the International Decade for Natural Disaster Reduction; Elena Ivannikova, United Nations Development Programme; Terry Jeggle, United Nations Secretariat for the International Decade for Natural Disaster Reduction; Mohammad Aslam Khan, United Nations Economic and Social Commission for Asia Pacific; Hosny K. Khordagui, United Nations Economic and Social Commission for West Asia; Mikhael Kokine, Environment and Human Settlements Division, United Nations Economic Commission for Europe; Parviz Koohafkan, Food and Agriculture Organization; Leslie Lipper, Food and Agriculture Organization; Joseph Maseland, United Nations Human Settlements Programme; Bettina Menne, World Health Organization; Tim Meredith, World Health Organization; Robert Missotten; United Nations Educational, Scientific and Cultural Organization; Jay Moor, United Nations Human Settlements Programme; Freddy Nachtergaele, Food and Agriculture Organization; Verity Nyagah, United Nations Somalia Office; Hisashi Ogawa, World Health Organization Western Pacific Regional Office; Henrik Oksfeldt Enevoldsen, Intergovernmental Oceanographic Commission of United Nations Educational, Scientific and Cultural Organization; Elina Palm, United Nations Secretariat for the International Decade for Natural Disaster Reduction; A. Pruess, World Health Organization; M. Repacholi, World Health Organization; Mukul Sanwal, United Nations Framework Convention on Climate Change Secretariat; Zharas Takenov, Sustainable Development Policy, United Nations Development Programme; Hiroyasu Tokuda, Institute of Advanced Studies, The United Nations University, Japan; Etsuko Tsunozaki, United Nations Secretariat for the International Decade for Natural Disaster Reduction; Kwadwo Tutu, Economic Commission for Africa of the United Nations; Sheila Mwanundu, International Fund for Agricultural Development; Yasmin Von Schirnding, World Health Organization; Joke Waller-Hunter, United Nations Framework Convention on Climate Change; Edmund Wolfe, United Nations Somalia Office; Staff of World Meteorological Organization.

Note: * since moved or retired.

# Index